SUBJECT AND STRUCTURE

An Anthology for Writers

FIFTH EDITION

SUBJECT AND STRUCTURE

An Anthology for Writers

JOHN M. WASSON
Washington State University

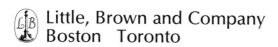 Little, Brown and Company
Boston   Toronto

PREFACE

This fifth edition retains the dual focus of earlier editions of *Subject and Structure:* in each section, every selection is on the same general subject and illustrates the same rhetorical technique. The student is thus provided with several examples of the kind of thing he himself will be asked to write. This arrangement should stimulate comparison of structure and technique — as well as content — during class discussion.

The first selection in each of the nine sections is a purposely short essay approximating the length of a student theme and clearly illustrating the rhetorical technique under consideration. In general, the selections are then arranged in increasing order of difficulty, with short stories and poems placed last.

The introductions to the sections discuss the philosophy, importance, and utility of each rhetorical technique. They also offer general principles to guide the student in his theme writing and to warn him against pitfalls common to each writing problem.

The questions for discussion in this edition have been divided into two categories: "Subject" and "Structure." By this means, the student is encouraged to see that organization, sentence construction, perhaps even word choice depend upon both the subject and the author's choice of rhetorical technique. Most "Structure" questions are aimed at solutions to specific writing problems and often refer back to the general principles outlined in the introduction to each section. If the book is to be used effectively, these questions should consume at least as much class discussion time as those dealing with subject matter.

The author and the publisher are eager to receive from students and teachers alike suggestions and evaluations of this book's effectiveness. Only through such communication can we hope to arrive at a truly satisfactory text. To this end we have included at the back of the book an evaluation form which users are urged to complete and return to Little, Brown.

CONTENTS

1

TURNING POINTS   1
Example

Seeing   5
Annie Dillard
A nature writer discusses the importance of learning how to see the little things
instead of looking always for riches or the spectacular.

The First Major Turning Point   10
Malcolm X
In a passage from his autobiography, Brother Malcolm describes his early
recognition that he would be accepted in white society only if he "stays in
his place."

Salvation   13
Langston Hughes
Hughes gives a humorous account of a twelve-year-old boy's "salvation" at
an old-fashioned revival meeting with serious consequences.

My Sixth Christmas   16
Floyd Dell
A young boy recognizes on Christmas Eve why his parents had kept mysteri-
ously silent about the coming holiday.

Hymns in a Man's Life   20
D. H. Lawrence
The famous novelist wonders why the church hymns of his childhood stick
in his memory better than his favorite poems.

Death in the Woods   26
Sherwood Anderson

It took Anderson years to understand fully a childhood experience he describes
in this fictionalized, first-person account.

Acquainted with the Night   37
Robert Frost

The poet admired for his down-to-earth wisdom here admits to the difficulty of
knowing who he is.

The Abortion   39
Anne Sexton

This poem is an intense expression of personal anguish at having to sacrifice
the life of a child.

2

THE WORLD AROUND US   41

Description

Miss Abbott   46
Willie Morris

Morris describes a fundamentalist Mississippi school teacher from an intimidated boy's point of view.

The Mosquito   50
Sally Carrighar

A famous nature writer shares her insight into the struggles for survival of
a mosquito at Teton Marsh.

The Turtle   56
John Steinbeck

A description of a turtle crossing the road from *The Grapes of Wrath* becomes
an allegory of nature's life cycle.

The Way to Rainy Mountain   59
N. Scott Momaday

A pilgrimage to his grandmother's grave stimulates a description of her American Indian heritage.

Knoxville: Summer 1915   65
   James Agee
   The writer recalls sights and sounds of a summer evening in his youth.

Powerhouse   70
   Eudora Welty
   Welty has written a bizarre story of a jazz pianist — the outer world of his
   music and the inner world of his imagination.

Mr. Flood's Party   81
   Edwin Arlington Robinson
   This poem is a portrait of a lonely old man with nothing but whiskey and the
   moon for company.

3

AMERICA'S ENTERTAINMENT   85

   Comparison and Contrast

A Large Number of Persons   90
   Paul Gallico
   Gallico distinguishes between the kinds of people who attend various sporting
   events.

The American Nature of Football   95
   John L. Finlay
   A Canadian compares America's national game, football, with the world's
   favorite game, soccer, and finds soccer much more "suited to the electronic
   age."

Football Red and Baseball Green   99
   Murray Ross
   A sociologist sees baseball as the embodiment of a peaceful, pastoral myth
   and football as reflective of a more violent, heroic myth.

On Sex and Violence in the Movies   109
   Peter Bogdanovitch
   The film critic and director finds modern explicit sex and violence less effective
   than the implied sex and violence in the days of rigid film censorship.

Films, Television, and Tennis   113
Richard E. Peck

A television scriptwriter outlines the differences between films for movie theaters and those for television, and assesses the influence of the new medium on the older one.

Rock on the Rocks; or, Bubblegum Anybody?   121
Irving Horowitz

Horowitz shows that the rise and fall of rock music is strikingly similar to the earlier rise and fall of jazz.

A Patriotic Short   128
F. Scott Fitzgerald

This is one of the Pat Hobby stories, contrasting the Hollywood scriptwriter's early days with the evil times into which he has fallen.

To an Athlete Dying Young   133
A. E. Housman

Through his consolation to a dead athlete the poet questions the value of striving for fame in physical exploits.

4

THE COMPUTER-CARD CULTURE   137
Process

The Art of the Memorandum   140
Joseph Porter Clerk, Jr.

A Washington bureaucrat explains how one must learn to use the system to get anything done — in triplicate.

The Peter Principle   144
Raymond Hull

Dr. Peter's collaborator explains the famous principle: "In a hierarchy each employee tends to rise to his level of incompetence — every post tends to be occupied by an employee incompetent to execute its duties."

Parkinson's Law   150
C. Northcote Parkinson

Professor Parkinson explains his "law" accounting for the inevitable growth of bureaucracies, which, because of their very size, are able to accomplish less.

Bigness in Business: Petrie's Law 157
Robert Townsend

The author of *Up the Organization* explains the only way to prosper in the modern business world: "Fire the vice-presidents, the secretaries, and half the staff; then pay the rest to Try Harder."

Upward Failure 162
William Zinsser

The remarkable story of how Harley Waller moves through failure after failure to become president of a corporation and, finally, secretary of defense.

Computers Don't Argue 171
Gordon R. Dickson

The science fiction writer explains what happens when an innocent citizen tries to argue with a book club computer about his bill.

The Unknown Citizen 186
W. H. Auden

The poem represents an inscription on the tomb of the perfectly programmed citizen — known only by his ID number.

5

WORK IN AN ALIENATED SOCIETY 189
Cause and Effect

The Protest of Young Factory Workers 192
Herbert J. Gans

Gans analyzes why factory workers are dissatisfied, and why their protest activities are a greater threat to the establishment than those of students or civil rights groups.

Communes and the Work Crisis 196
Lewis M. Andrews

The author of *Requiem for Democracy* explains why the most capable young people tend to be dropouts from the work force, and suggests work communes as a possible solution to the problem.

The Ecology of Unemployment 203
Edward Goldsmith

It is assumed that the cure for unemployment is economic growth. The editor of *The Ecologist* argues that such growth paradoxically must lead to increased unemployment and should be abandoned as a goal of public policy.

Work in an Alienated Society   211
Erich Fromm

A psychologist analyzes what happens to a man when his work becomes meaningless in an automated society.

Counterparts   217
James Joyce

Joyce portrays the rage and frustration of a strong man forced to do boring copy work and to take orders from a pipsqueak boss.

Bloodstains   226
Joyce Carol Oates

In a fictional illustration of Fromm's thesis, a wealthy doctor tries to understand what has gone wrong with his life.

Bronzeville Woman in a Red Hat   239
Gwendolyn Brooks

This poem is about a white woman's reactions to her first black maid.

6

LANGUAGE AND STYLE   243
Definition

The Language of Soul   247
Claude Brown

The author of *Manchild in the Promised Land* discusses the roots, characteristic features, and future of the black American language.

The Language of Nowspeak   253
Valerie Carnes

Carnes describes the sources of the language of the youth movement.

An Ethic of Clarity   271
Donald Hall

The poet defines the ideal modern prose style, a style which is above all clear and honest.

Style and Good Style 277
Monroe Beardsley

A philosophy professor argues the relation between style and meaning: "faults of style must be faults of logic," and good style is that which best communicates to the reader what the writer intended.

Gobbledygook 292
Stuart Chase

Chase illustrates bureaucratic, legal, and academic jargon.

Contexts 301
S. I. Hayakawa

The process of definition and the necessity for defining a word in its context are studied.

At the Fringe of Language 311
C. S. Lewis

"Emotional" language is defined, as well as its differences from "language."

Sonnet 76, "Why Is My Verse So Barren of New Pride?" 320
William Shakespeare

Shakespeare tries to define and defend his own style.

7

FREEDOM AND RESPONSIBILITY 323

Argument

Power 326
John Cogley

"All power to no one" is Cogley's answer to the revolutionary demand for "all power to the people."

The Limits of Law and Order 329
Robert M. Hutchins

Hutchins argues that the government's get-tough policy has not reduced crime in the streets and that we need, instead, penal and judicial reforms, as well as "decriminalization" — particularly in the areas of gambling and drug use.

Letter from Delano   334

César Chavez

The leader of Mexican-American migrant workers defends the right to "militant nonviolence as our means for social revolution and to achieve justice for our people."

Letter to the Fourth Congress of Soviet Writers   338

Aleksandr Solzhenitsyn

The Russian writer pleads for an end to rigid censorship and for help to writers who are attacked or jailed unfairly.

On the Duty of Civil Disobedience   344

Henry David Thoreau

Thoreau wrote the classic American defense of nonviolent protest against laws that cannot be reconciled to one's conscience.

The Declaration of Independence   359

Thomas Jefferson

The people have the right to alter or abolish any government that fails to guarantee the rights to life, liberty, and the pursuit of happiness.

The Declaration of Independence   364

Stan Freberg

This is a humorous view of Jefferson as he might be seen today by those who feel that all critics of government are subversive.

The Bear   369

William Faulkner

A lesson in this fiction is that freedom cannot be hidden and conserved: if it is to be free, it must expose itself to attack.

8

A MATTER OF FAITH   383

Persuasion

from The Apology of Socrates   386

Plato

Socrates gives a farewell speech to the Athenians about his right to believe, and teach, the truth.

The Way of Life 390
Laotzu
The ancient Chinese sage speaks on the way to the good life: set people free "from private greeds and wanton needs."

A Letter to Street Christians 395
Two Brothers from Berkeley
In an adaptation of 1 Thessalonians in the language of Jesus freaks, converts are exhorted to keep the faith and spread the word.

The Essence of OM 399
The Upanishads
"The highest symbol," which has been so badly misused by do-it-yourself theologians in recent years, is explained.

A Free Man's Worship 402
Bertrand Russell
Lord Russell propounds a religion of man in an alien, inhuman, and hostile universe in which man is doomed to destruction.

The Efficacy of Prayer 410
C. S. Lewis
A conventional Christian gives a modern interpretation of prayer.

Packed Dirt, Churchgoing, a Dying Cat, a Traded Car 416
John Updike
The author concludes that "We in America need ceremonies."

Dover Beach 435
Matthew Arnold
The poet decides that in a world lacking joy and certitude and peace his only faith can be in his loved one: "let us be true to one another."

9

LESSONS FOR THE FUTURE 437

Evaluation

Looking Back 442
Joyce Maynard
A college sophomore evaluates the attitudes and plans of her own generation.

A Very Easy Death   445

Simone de Beauvoir

The French author shares her insight into the loneliness and humiliation of
the dying and into the effect of death on the living.

The Power of the Presidency   449

Tom Wicker

A Washington newspaperman explains the growth of presidential power and
suggests some ways of limiting it in the future.

I Want a Wife   463

Judy Syfers

A housewife assesses the overwhelming demands made upon her by a husband.

The Weak Are the Second Sex   466

Elizabeth Janeway

A leader of the women's movement evaluates the male objections to it that
have arisen over the past ten years.

The Suicide of the Sexes   476

George Gilder

Gilder sees the women's movement as working hand in hand with the Playboy
philosophy, and argues for separation of the sexes as essential to orderly society.

The Door   481

E. B. White

How does one find meaning in a programmed society, in which values are
constantly being changed? The disoriented subject of this short story is given
a prefrontal lobotomy.

The Other Side of the Hedge   486

E. M. Forster

This parable suggests that the goal in the race for progress is the same place
we started from long ago.

SUBJECT AND STRUCTURE
An Anthology for Writers

1

TURNING POINTS

Example

Among the first lessons a writer must learn is that personal opinions and generalizations usually need illustrations drawn from firsthand observation if the reader is to understand them clearly and be convinced of their validity. Although one example cannot prove an opinion's worth, it will at least make clear what the writer means and will indicate that supporting evidence is available. Because of its versatility, the personal example is one of the writer's basic tools: it may be, and usually is, employed as secondary support for every other method of developing ideas described in this book.

Almost certainly the earliest attempts at written communication were in the form of pictures, at first single pictures and then a related series of pictures which told a story, perhaps of a warrior's success in battle or of a narrow escape from some wild animal. From such crude beginnings, written languages were developed, based at first on stylized abbreviations of the earlier picture writing. But as early as the Sumerian culture of 3000 B.C., man had discovered that he needed phonetic characters to express concepts which could not be "pictured." The subsequent history of written languages shows a clear trend toward developing simpler, more flexible alphabets capable of expressing relationships between ideas in words which refer to no "pictures" at all — "God is love," "Truth is Beauty," and so on.

Until comparatively recently, however, man was so accustomed to thinking in pictures that he instinctively avoided such totally abstract statements whenever possible. He preferred to express the abstract

1

thought in "pictorial" language. When the author of Ecclesiastes wrote "all is vanity," he added "and chasing after wind." When Shakespeare wanted his character Macbeth to complain that life is meaningless, he avoided the unimpressive abstract statement in favor of the now famous lines:

> Life's but a walking shadow, a poor player
> That struts and frets his hour upon the stage,
> And then is heard no more: it is a tale
> Told by an idiot, full of sound and fury,
> Signifying nothing.

The ability to express generalizations in abstract language is certainly an important advance: scientific laws, for instance, can only be expressed with difficulty and at great length in pictorial language. But we must recognize that there are certain weaknesses in abstract language and that we are not justified in dismissing the pictorial techniques of the older writers without good reason.

At its best, a generalization in abstract language forces the reader to supply a concrete illustration from his own experience. The writer thus loses an important means of control, for the reader's illustration may vary widely from what the author has in mind. To avoid this, when the writer of a physics textbook, for instance, states in general terms Boyle's law of gases he is careful either to give specific illustrations of the law's application or to give instructions for a controlled experiment whereby the reader can see for himself the operation of Boyle's law.

At its worst, highly abstract language may leave the reader with only the vaguest notion of its meaning and without a ready example to clarify it. Suppose you were to read, instead of Shakespeare's clear statement, "Life's but a walking shadow . . . ," something as atrocious as this:

> In the opinion of the author of the present
> investigation, it is a not unjustifiable assumption
> that the normal experiences of human existence
> seem to indicate that it may be without a demonstrable
> teleological basis.

There are two related methods of avoiding this sort of vagueness: (1) the use of specific, concrete language, including figures of speech where appropriate (a figure of speech should always be used to *clarify*, not to *decorate* the writing); and (2) the use of examples. You should not, of course, try to fill your writing with imagery of the florid, "limpid pools in the moonlight" variety. And you need not pile up superfluous examples. But you should remember to support and clarify your generalizations with illustrative evidence.

Example   3

When asked to write opinion papers, college students often feel handicapped by a lack of adequate knowledge. They may even disregard as unimportant their best source of material, personal experience and observation. The best writers in every age have used their personal experiences as examples of general principles, partly because they can relate these experiences vividly and partly because firsthand reports are usually more reliable than borrowed ones. Many fiction writers — nearly all of the best novelists, in fact — have kept notebooks in which they jotted down for future use firsthand observations of places, events, and people. A wealth of such material is available to anyone who will use his eyes and his memory, even to an "inexperienced" college student. If you think back carefully, you may find that your experience includes acquaintance with such apparently remote subjects as communism (a room and toys "communally" owned by you and a brother or sister) and totalitarianism (a father, perhaps, whose "word was law" in the home).

Even though your personal experiences may not seem to be of tremendous significance, there are several good reasons why you should draw on them for illustrative evidence. (1) Accurate personal observation makes writing more *vivid*. When you give a vague hypothetical example or none at all, the reader gets no mental picture from the writing; and what he can "see" clearly he understands better. If you are writing about the need for minimum speed laws on freeways, describe in graphic detail the time you nearly smashed into the back end of a slow-moving vehicle in the midst of sixty-mile-per-hour traffic.

(2) Such writing is not only clearer, but it is more *interesting*. You must know from experience how dull a textbook can be when the writer fails to give concrete examples. You may "read" several pages and suddenly realize you haven't any notion of what you have read. And you probably remember as a child that you avoided checking out library books which contained no pictures. While an adult can usually maintain interest without pictures, he at least wants "word-pictures."

(3) Personal examples make writing more *convincing*. A hypothetical example beginning, "Someone might be driving along the highway sometime when . . ." would hardly carry the authoritative force of "I had pushed my '59 Ford up to seventy on the long straight stretch of Highway 101 just south of San Jose when. . .". A reader might, at worst, argue that your example isn't typical, but he would still be convinced that it did actually happen. And if the example does not seem too unlikely, the reader will probably be reminded of supporting evidence from his own experience.

(4) Finally, writing containing accounts of firsthand experiences is necessarily more *personal:* that is, it establishes a bond of intimacy between you and your reader. The reader, feeling that you are taking him into your confidence and that you sincerely want to communicate with

him, will be much more willing to give you a fair chance to make your point. Nothing will alienate a reader more quickly than the suspicion that you do not really care whether or not he understands and agrees with you. An impersonal approach is a great producer of that suspicion.

In relating personal examples, be sure to include enough concrete facts to create a clear picture for your reader. Use actual names of people, places, and things when possible, and select verbs that convey a sense of action. "The coffee burned my tongue" is much more vivid than "The coffee was hot" and is just as easy to write if you employ verbs which carry part of the meaning of the sentence instead of being mere *links*. Try to re-create your experience in such a way that the reader can relive it vicariously. As you read the selections in this section, notice how the writers have accomplished this sense of vicarious experience through the use of concrete detail and active verbs. Note, for instance, how Brother Malcolm, in "The First Major Turning Point," gives names of actual people, quotes his teacher as nearly as he can remember, and even recalls such apparently unimportant details as the particular jobs his classmates were interested in — details which, precisely because there would be no sense reporting them unless they were true, give the account its impact of immediacy.

One word of caution: be sure to avoid trite expressions in relating a personal experience. In striving for vividness, you may be tempted to use such "tried and true" phrases as those in this passage from a student theme.

I was so excited I could hardly wait for the trip to start. But the day finally came. We arose bright-eyed and bushy-tailed, ate a hurried breakfast, and were on our way.

Such worn-out phrases destroy the very bond of intimacy you are trying to establish between you and your reader. The reader feels that you are not interested enough in what you are saying to think up your own expressions. Furthermore, he loses interest because he feels that he has "read all this before." Trite language, in short, destroys the sense of uniqueness your writing should convey. The reader is not just concerned with the nature of your experience; he is interested in your personal view of it and your reaction to it. For it is precisely your point of view that makes your experience unique and therefore worth reading: remember that no two people experience events in precisely the same way. Even two people in the same automobile accident will "see" it differently because of differences in past experience, intelligence, and emotional nature. Do not sell yourself short; your experience does count, and it will be worth reading if you write it so that it will be "seen" in the way that you saw it.

Seeing

Annie Dillard

Annie Dillard grew up in Pittsburgh, attended Hollins College, and since 1965 has lived in the Roanoke Valley of Virginia. She is a contributing editor to Harper's Magazine *and a columnist for* The Wilderness Society. *Her first book of poems,* Tickets for a Prayer Wheel *(1973), was published at the University of Missouri. The following passage is from her first book of nature writing,* Pilgrim at Tinker Creek *(1974). Most of the book is a description of what she sees at her farm on Tinker Creek; here she discusses the problem of learning how to "see."*

When I was six or seven years old, growing up in Pittsburgh, I used to take   1
a precious penny of my own and hide it for someone else to find. It was a curious compulsion; sadly, I've never been seized by it since. For some reason I always "hid" the penny along the same stretch of sidewalk up the street. I would cradle it at the roots of a sycamore, say, or in a hole left by a chipped-off piece of sidewalk. Then I would take a piece of chalk, and, starting at either end of the block, draw huge arrows leading up to the penny from both directions. After I learned to write I labeled the arrows: SURPRISE AHEAD or MONEY THIS WAY. I was greatly excited, during all this arrow-drawing, at the thought of the first lucky passer-by who would receive in this way, regardless of merit, a free gift from the universe. But I never lurked about. I would go straight home and not give the matter another thought, until, some months later, I would be gripped again by the impulse to hide another penny.

It is still the first week in January, and I've got great plans. I've been thinking   2
about seeing. There are lots of things to see, unwrapped gifts and free surprises. The world is fairly studded and strewn with pennies cast broadside from a generous hand. But — and this is the point — who gets excited by a mere penny? If you follow one arrow, if you crouch motionless on a bank to watch a tremulous ripple thrill on the water and are rewarded by the sight of a muskrat kit paddling from its den, will you count that sight a chip of copper only, and go your rueful way? It is dire poverty indeed when a man is so

malnourished and fatigued that he won't stoop to pick up a penny. But if you cultivate a healthy poverty and simplicity, so that finding a penny will literally make your day, then, since the world is in fact planted in pennies, you have with your poverty bought a lifetime of days. It is that simple. What you see is what you get.

I used to be able to see flying insects in the air. I'd look ahead and see,   3 not the row of hemlocks across the road, but the air in front of it. My eyes would focus along that column of air, picking out flying insects. But I lost interest, I guess, for I dropped the habit. Now I can see birds. Probably some people can look at the grass at their feet and discover all the crawling creatures. I would like to know grasses and sedges — and care. Then my least journey into the world would be a field trip, a series of happy recognitions. Thoreau, in an expansive mood, exulted, "What a rich book might be made about buds, including, perhaps, sprouts!" It would be nice to think so. I cherish mental images I have of three perfectly happy people. One collects stones. Another — an Englishman, say — watches clouds. The third lives on a coast and collects drops of seawater which he examines microscopically and mounts. But I don't see what the specialist sees, and so I cut myself off, not only from the total picture, but from the various forms of happiness.

Unfortunately, nature is very much a now-you-see-it, now-you-don't   4 affair. A fish flashes, then dissolves in the water before my eyes like so much salt. Deer apparently ascend bodily into heaven; the brightest oriole fades into leaves. These disappearances stun me into stillness and concentration; they say of nature that it conceals with a grand nonchalance, and they say of vision that it is a deliberate gift, the revelation of a dancer who for my eyes only flings away her seven veils. For nature does reveal as well as conceal: now-you-don't-see-it, now-you-do. For a week last September migrating red-winged blackbirds were feeding heavily down by the creek at the back of the house. One day I went out to investigate the racket; I walked up to a tree, an Osage orange, and a hundred birds flew away. They simply materialized out of the tree. I saw a tree, then a whisk of color, then a tree again. I walked closer and another hundred blackbirds took flight. Not a branch, not a twig budged: the birds were apparently weightless as well as invisible. Or, it was as if the leaves of the Osage orange had been freed from a spell in the form of red-winged blackbirds; they flew from the tree, caught my eye in the sky, and vanished. When I looked again at the tree the leaves had reassembled as if nothing had happened. Finally I walked directly to the trunk of the tree and a final hundred, the real diehards, appeared, spread, and vanished. How could so many hide in the tree without my seeing them? The Osage orange, unruffled, looked just as it had looked from the house, when three hundred red-winged blackbirds cried from its crown. I looked downstream where they flew, and they were gone. Searching, I couldn't spot one. I wandered downstream to force them to play their hand, but they'd crossed the creek and scattered. One show to a customer. These appearances catch at my throat; they are the free gifts, the bright coppers at the roots of trees.

It's all a matter of keeping my eyes open. Nature is like one of those line drawings of a tree that are puzzles for children: Can you find hidden in the leaves a duck, a house, a boy, a bucket, a zebra, and a boot? Specialists can find the most incredibly well-hidden things. A book I read when I was young recommended an easy way to find caterpillars to rear: you simply find some fresh caterpillar droppings, look up, and there's your caterpillar. More recently an author advised me to set my mind at ease about those piles of cut stems on the ground in grassy fields. Field mice make them; they cut the grass down by degrees to reach the seeds at the head. It seems that when the grass is tightly packed, as in a field of ripe grain, the blade won't topple at a single cut through the stem; instead, the cut stem simply drops vertically, held in the crush of grain. The mouse severs the bottom again and again, the stem keeps dropping an inch at a time, and finally the head is low enough for the mouse to reach the seeds. Meanwhile, the mouse is positively littering the field with its little piles of cut stems into which, presumably, the author of the book is constantly stumbling.

If I can't see these minutiae, I still try to keep my eyes open. I'm always on the lookout for antlion traps in sandy soil, monarch pupae near milkweed, skipper larvae in locust leaves. These things are utterly common, and I've not seen one. I bang on hollow trees near water, but so far no flying squirrels have appeared. In flat country I watch every sunset in hopes of seeing the green ray. The green ray is a seldom-seen streak of light that rises from the sun like a spurting fountain at the moment of sunset; it throbs into the sky for two seconds and disappears. One more reason to keep my eyes open. A photography professor at the University of Florida just happened to see a bird die in midflight; it jerked, died, dropped, and smashed on the ground. I squint at the wind because I read Stewart Edward White: "I have always maintained that if you looked closely enough you could *see* the wind — the dim, hardly-made-out, fine débris fleeing high in the air." White was an excellent observer, and devoted an entire chapter of *The Mountains* to the subject of seeing deer: "As soon as you can forget the naturally obvious and construct an artificial obvious, then you too will see deer."

But the artificial obvious is hard to see. My eyes account for less than one percent of the weight of my head; I'm bony and dense; I see what I expect. I once spent a full three minutes looking at a bullfrog that was so unexpectedly large I couldn't see it even though a dozen enthusiastic campers were shouting directions. Finally I asked, "What color am I looking for?" and a fellow said, "Green." When at last I picked out the frog, I saw what painters are up against: the thing wasn't green at all, but the color of wet hickory bark.

The lover can see, and the knowledgeable. I visited an aunt and uncle at a quarter-horse ranch in Cody, Wyoming. I couldn't do much of anything useful, but I could, I thought, draw. So, as we all sat around the kitchen table after supper, I produced a sheet of paper and drew a horse. "That's one lame horse," my aunt volunteered. The rest of the family joined in: "Only place to saddle that one is his neck"; "Looks like we better shoot the poor thing, on account of those terrible growths." Meekly, I slid the pencil and paper down the table. Everyone in that family, including my three young cousins, could draw a horse. Beautifully. When the paper came back it looked as though five shining, real quarter horses had been corraled by mistake with a papier-mâché moose; the real horses seemed to gaze at the monster with a steady, puzzled air. I stay away from horses now, but I can do a creditable goldfish. The point is that I just don't know what the lover knows; I just can't see the artificial obvious that those in the know construct. The herpetologist asks the native, "Are there snakes in that ravine?" "Nosir." And the herpetologist comes home with, yessir, three bags full. Are there butterflies on that mountain? Are the bluets in bloom, are there arrowheads here, or fossil shells in the shale?

Peeping through my keyhole I see within the range of only about thirty   9 percent of the light that comes from the sun; the rest is infrared and some little ultraviolet, perfectly apparent to many animals, but invisible to me. A nightmare network of ganglia, charged and firing without my knowledge, cuts and splices what I do see, editing it for my brain. Donald E. Carr points out that the sense impressions of one-celled animals are *not* edited for the brain: "This is philosophically interesting in a rather mournful way, since it means that only the simplest animals perceive the universe as it is."

A fog that won't burn away drifts and flows across my field of vision.   10 When you see fog move against a backdrop of deep pines, you don't see the fog itself, but streaks of clearness floating across the air in dark shreds. So I see only tatters of clearness through a pervading obscurity. I can't distinguish the fog from the overcast sky; I can't be sure if the light is direct or reflected. Everywhere darkness and the presence of the unseen appalls. We estimate now that only one atom dances alone in every cubic meter of intergalactic space. I blink and squint. What planet or power yanks Halley's Comet out of orbit? We haven't seen that force yet; it's a question of distance, density, and the pallor of reflected light. We rock, cradled in the swaddling band of darkness. Even the simple darkness of night whispers suggestions to the mind. . . .

SUBJECT QUESTIONS

1. Annie Dillard complains that she fails to see most of what goes on around her. What evidence is there that she does in fact notice more than the average person might? Why does she complain, then, about her limitations?

2. The examples Ms. Dillard cites are natural phenomena that one might go a lifetime without noticing. Is there any value in even bothering to see them? Examine her argument toward the end of paragraph 2.
3. Because Ms. Dillard does "see" better than most of us, do you think there is an element of false modesty in her attitude here? What purpose is served by her lumping herself with the rest of us? Consider the point of her story about drawing pictures of horses in Wyoming (paragraph 8).
4. Would you say that her chief aim is to make us interested in what she sees, in the "problem of seeing" itself, or in improving our own vision?

STRUCTURE QUESTIONS

1. The opening anecdote about hiding pennies for others to find seems at first to have little to do with the subject of appreciating nature; how does Ms. Dillard relate it to her subject? Is use of the anecdote an effective way to open the essay?
2. The examples of phenomena to be seen by a careful observer are not very startling. Should she have included some more spectacular occurrences — tornadoes, or volcanic eruptions, perhaps? Would the point of the essay have been altered had she selected more thrilling examples?
3. By what techniques does Ms. Dillard make her personal experience an example to others? (Remember that no two people will see life in quite the same ways.)
4. Does her frequent citing of previous nature writers give this informal essay too much the look of a research paper? What does she achieve by these references to Thoreau, Donald Carr, the expert on caterpillars, and others?
5. Consider the ways in which Ms. Dillard makes her descriptions of ordinary events vivid without destroying (with exotic, overly poetic language) the very common quality she wants to emphasize. Does she balance the work load among verbs, adjectives, and nouns, or does she depend too heavily on one part of speech?
6. Although the tone of this essay is generally informal, Ms. Dillard often uses uncommon words where ordinary ones might do — "malnourished and fatigued" instead of "hungry and tired," for instance. Examine a few of these choices, and decide whether or not they confuse the tone of the essay, and whether their specific purpose justifies their inclusion.

The First Major
Turning Point

Malcolm X

*Malcolm X, born Malcolm Little in Omaha, Nebraska in 1925, was assassi-
nated in Harlem on February 21, 1965. The ultimate influence in this powerful civil rights leader's turbulent career is still difficult to assess, partly because his own views changed from black militancy to black nationalism to
a deep sense of the brotherhood of man. It can be said with assurance
that more than any other leader he gave the black man a sense of his
manhood, and that, as Wyatt Tee Walker says, "Malcolm had the 'book'
on white America and he read it loud and clear for all to hear." The Autobiography of Malcolm X (1964), whatever one thinks of its author, is probably the most sensitive book yet written by an Afro-American. The following
extract is about his experience in junior high school at Mason, Michigan
early in 1941.*

I kept close to the top of the class, though. The topmost scholastic standing, 1
I remember, kept shifting between me, a girl named Audrey Slaugh, and a
boy named Jimmy Cotton.

It went on that way, as I became increasingly restless and disturbed 2
through the first semester. And then one day, just about when those of us
who had passed were about to move up to 8-A, from which we would enter
high school the next year, something happened which was to become the first
major turning point of my life.

Somehow, I happened to be alone in the classroom with Mr. Ostrowski, 3
my English teacher. He was a tall, rather reddish white man and he had a
thick mustache. I had gotten some of my best marks under him, and he had
always made me feel that he liked me. He was, as I have mentioned, a natu-
ral-born "advisor," about what you ought to read, to do, or think — about
any and everything. We used to make unkind jokes about him: why was he
teaching in Mason instead of somewhere else, getting for himself some of the
"success in life" that he kept telling us how to get?

I know that he probably meant well in what he happened to advise 4
me that day. I doubt that he meant any harm. It was just in his nature as

an American white man. I was one of his top students, one of the school's top students — but all he could see for me was the kind of future "in your place" that all white people see for black people.

He told me, "Malcolm, you ought to be thinking about a career. Have   5
you been giving it thought?"

The truth is, I hadn't. I never have figured out why I told him, "Well,   6
yes, sir, I've been thinking I'd like to be a lawyer." Lansing certainly had
no Negro lawyers — or doctors either — in those days, to hold up an image
I might have aspired to. All I really knew for certain was that a lawyer didn't
wash dishes, as I was doing.

Mr. Ostrowski looked surprised, I remember, and leaned back in his   7
chair and clasped his hands behind his head. He kind of half-smiled and said,
"Malcolm, one of life's first needs is for us to be realistic. Don't misunderstand
me, now. We all here like you, you know that. But you've got to be realistic
about being a nigger. A lawyer — that's no realistic goal for a nigger. You
need to think about something you *can* be. You're good with your hands —
making things. Everybody admires your carpentry shop work. Why don't you
plan on carpentry? People like you as a person — you'd get all kinds of work."

The more I thought afterwards about what he said, the more uneasy   8
it made me. It just kept treading around in my mind.

What made it really begin to disturb me was Mr. Ostrowski's advice   9
to others in my class — all of them white. Most of them had told him they
were planning to become farmers, like their parents — to one day take over
their family farms. But those who wanted to strike out on their own, to try
something new, he had encouraged. Some, mostly girls, wanted to be teachers.
A few wanted other professions, such as one boy who wanted to become a
county agent; another, a veterinarian; and one girl wanted to be a nurse. They
all reported that Mr. Ostrowski had encouraged whatever they had wanted.
Yet nearly none of them had earned marks equal to mine.

It was a surprising thing that I had never thought of it that way before,   10
but I realized that whatever I wasn't, I *was* smarter than nearly all of those
white kids. But apparently I was still not intelligent enough, in their eyes,
to become whatever I wanted to be.

It was then that I began to change — inside.   11

SUBJECT QUESTIONS

1. Do you think Mr. Ostrowski's advice to Malcolm arises from (perhaps
   unrecognized) prejudice, or from an honest desire to be "realistic"?
   What does Malcolm think?
2. Malcolm relates this incident with calm objectivity. Since it is to be a
   "major turning point," should he have jazzed it up a bit?

3. What is Malcolm's attitude toward Mr. Ostrowski after twenty-four years? Does this attitude seem characteristic of a man who had become an impassioned denouncer of white racism? What clues do you have that the attitude is genuine?
4. Does the account make clear why Malcolm should have been so disturbed by Mr. Ostrowski's advice — considering that Malcolm had no intention of being a lawyer, anyway? (Note that Malcolm was more upset by the advice than by being called "nigger." Clearly he was already aware of his "difference" from the other students in the class.)

STRUCTURE QUESTIONS

1. Since Mr. Ostrowski is referred to a number of times, it is clearly more convenient to call him by his name than to keep repeating "my English teacher." But the same reasoning does not explain Malcolm's inclusion of the names Audrey Slaugh and Jimmy Cotton, who are not referred to again. What effect does Malcolm achieve by naming them, an effect which would be lost if he simply wrote "two other students"?
2. Point out some of the descriptive details which have nothing to do with the aim of the story but which help reconstruct the scene in the reader's mind. (Note that Malcolm does not clutter the account with such details — just enough for verisimilitude.)
3. Malcolm might have achieved more marked contrast between the advice he received and that of the whites had he included some with less realistic ambitions than nurse, schoolteacher, or extension agent. Why do you suppose he doesn't? (Even if he had invented a couple of ambitions — brain surgeon, ambassador, president — no reader would be greatly surprised by such responses from eighth graders.)
4. This account describes, of course, a purely personal experience; does Malcolm give any indication that he thinks of it as an example of a much more widespread problem? Using this essay as an example, consider the problem of making a personal experience seem both unique and something which "speaks" to the readers.

Salvation

Langston Hughes

Langston Hughes (1902–1967) was a poet, jazz expert, and columnist for
The New York Post. At the age of twenty, he quit college for several years
and worked as a common seaman, whence the title of his autobiography,
The Big Sea (1940), from which the following episode is taken.

I was saved from sin when I was going on thirteen. But not really saved. It   1
happened like this. There was a big revival at my Auntie Reed's church. Every
night for weeks there had been much preaching, singing, praying, and shouting, and some very hardened sinners had been brought to Christ, and the
membership of the church had grown by leaps and bounds. Then just before
the revival ended, they held a special meeting for children, "to bring the young
lambs to the fold." My aunt spoke of it for days ahead. That night I was
escorted to the front row and placed on the mourners' bench with all the
other young sinners, who had not yet been brought to Jesus.

My aunt told me that when you were saved you saw a light, and some-   2
thing happened to you inside! And Jesus came into your life! And God was
with you from then on! She said you could see and hear and feel Jesus in
your soul. I believed her. I had heard a great many old people say the same
thing and it seemed to me they ought to know. So I sat there calmly in the
hot, crowded church, waiting for Jesus to come to me.

The preacher preached a wonderful rhythmical sermon, all moans and   3
shouts and lonely cries and dire pictures of hell, and then he sang a song about
the ninety and nine safe in the fold, but one little lamb was left out in the
cold. Then he said: "Won't you come? Won't you come to Jesus? Young lambs,
won't you come?" And he held out his arms to all us young sinners there
on the mourners' bench. And the little girls cried. And some of them jumped
up and went to Jesus right away. But most of us just sat there.

A great many old people came and knelt around us and prayed, old   4
women with jet-black faces and braided hair, old men with work-gnarled
hands. And the church sang a song about the lower lights are burning, some
poor sinners to be saved. And the whole building rocked with prayer and
song.

Still I kept waiting to *see* Jesus.   5

Finally all the young people had gone to the altar and were saved, but   6
one boy and me. He was a rounder's son named Westley. Westley and I were
surrounded by sisters and deacons praying. It was very hot in the church,
and getting late now. Finally Westley said to me in a whisper: "God damn!
I'm tired o' sitting here. Let's get up and be saved." So he got up and was
saved.

Then I was left all alone on the mourners' bench. My aunt came and   7
knelt at my knees and cried, while prayers and songs swirled all around me
in the little church. The whole congregation prayed for me alone, in a mighty
wail of moans and voices. And I kept waiting serenely for Jesus, waiting,
waiting — but he didn't come. I wanted to see him, but nothing happened
to me. Nothing! I wanted something to happen to me, but nothing happened.

I heard the songs and the minister saying: "Why don't you come? My   8
dear child, why don't you come to Jesus? Jesus is waiting for you. He wants
you. Why don't you come? Sister Reed, what is this child's name?"

"Langston," my aunt sobbed.   9

"Langston, why don't you come? Why don't you come and be saved?   10
Oh, Lamb of God! Why don't you come?"

Now it was really getting late. I began to be ashamed of myself, holding   11
everything up so long. I began to wonder what God thought about Westley,
who certainly hadn't seen Jesus either, but who was now sitting proudly on
the platform, swinging his knickerbockered legs and grinning down at me,
surrounded by deacons and old women on their knees praying. God had not
struck Westley dead for taking his name in vain or for lying in the temple.
So I decided that maybe to save further trouble, I'd better lie, too, and say
that Jesus had come, and get up and be saved.

So I got up.   12

Suddenly the whole room broke into a sea of shouting, as they saw me   13
rise. Waves of rejoicing swept the place. Women leaped in the air. My aunt
threw her arms around me. The minister took me by the hand and led me
to the platform.

When things quieted down, in a hushed silence, punctuated by a few   14
ecstatic "Amens," all the new young lambs were blessed in the name of God.
Then joyous singing filled the room.

That night, for the last time in my life but one — for I was a big boy   15
twelve years old — I cried. I cried, in bed alone, and couldn't stop. I buried
my head under the quilts, but my aunt heard me. She woke up and told my
uncle I was crying because the Holy Ghost had come into my life, and because
I had seen Jesus. But I was really crying because I couldn't bear to tell her
that I had lied, that I had deceived everybody in the church, and I hadn't
seen Jesus, and that now I didn't believe there was a Jesus any more, since
he didn't come to help me.

SUBJECT QUESTIONS

1. Do you think that Hughes is concentrating more on giving an honest self-analysis or on entertaining the reader with the humorous account itself? What saves the story from being funny but pointless?
2. Does Langston's pretense at salvation seem to be a typical trick for a boy that age? Is it at least believable? How would you have reacted at age twelve to pressures like those exerted on Hughes?
3. Hughes implies in his last paragraph that this apparently harmless event had an important and lasting effect on him. Does this seem psychologically valid? Can you recall any small events from your childhood which have had lasting effects?
4. Do you think that, in addition to the analysis of himself, Hughes intends some social criticism? Of religion? Of "saving" children at too early an age?

STRUCTURE QUESTIONS

1. Examine Hughes's employment of concrete detail. Point out details which are especially effective in making the essay vivid, authentic, and interesting.
2. What special devices does Hughes employ to achieve realism? Were you able to picture yourself in his place?
3. How does Hughes convey the impression that the story is told from the point of view of a young boy? Analyze the sentence structure in the second and third paragraphs, for instance.

My Sixth Christmas
Floyd Dell

Floyd Dell (1887–1969) was born in Barry, Illinois. Although he was a prolific writer, his radical politics and pacifism fifty years before such beliefs were fashionable have caused him to be virtually obliterated from biographies and histories of politics and literature. During World War I, he was editor of a radical journal, The Masses *(1914–17). When the paper, with Dell as defendant, was accused of violating the Espionage Act, Dell promptly started another radical journal,* The Liberator *(1918–24). During the twenties and early thirties, Dell published ten novels, six books of nonfiction, numerous plays, and his autobiography,* Homecoming *(1933) — from which the following passage is taken.*

That fall, before it was discovered that the soles of both my shoes were worn clear through, I still went to Sunday school. And one time the Sunday-school superintendent made a speech to all the classes. He said that these were hard times, and that many poor children weren't getting enough to eat. It was the first that I had heard about it. He asked everybody to bring some food for the poor children next Sunday. I felt very sorry for the poor children.

Also, little envelopes were distributed to all the classes. Each little boy and girl was to bring money for the poor, next Sunday. The pretty Sunday-school teacher explained that we were to write our names, or have our parents write them, up in the left-hand corner of the little envelopes. . . . I told my mother all about it when I came home. And my mother gave me, the next Sunday, a small bag of potatoes to carry to Sunday school. I supposed the poor children's mothers would make potato soup out of them. . . . Potato soup was good. My father, who was quite a joker, would always say, as if he were surprised, "Ah! I see we have some nourishing potato soup today!" It was so good that we had it every day. My father was at home all day long and every day, now; and I liked that, even if he was grumpy as he sat reading Grant's "Memoirs." I had my parents all to myself, too; the others were away. My oldest brother was in Quincy, and memory does not reveal where the others were: perhaps with relatives in the country.

Taking my small bag of potatoes to Sunday school, I looked around for the poor children; I was disappointed not to see them. I had heard about poor children in stories. But I was told just to put my contribution with the others on the big table in the side room.

I had brought with me the little yellow envelope, with some money 4
in it for the poor children. My mother had put the money in it and sealed
it up. She wouldn't tell me how much money she had put in it, but it felt
like several dimes. Only she wouldn't let me write my name on the envelope.
I had learned to write my name, and I was proud of being able to do it. But
my mother said firmly, no, I must not write my name on the envelope; she
didn't tell me why. On the way to Sunday school I had pressed the envelope
against the coins until I could tell what they were; they weren't dimes but
pennies.

When I handed in my envelope, my Sunday-school teacher noticed that 5
my name wasn't on it, and she gave me a pencil; I could write my own name,
she said. So I did. But I was confused because my mother had said not to;
and when I came home, I confessed what I had done. She looked distressed.
"I told you not to!" she said. But she didn't explain why. . . .

I didn't go back to school that fall. My mother said it was because I 6
was sick. I did have a cold the week that school opened; I had been playing
in the gutters and had got my feet wet, because there were holes in my shoes.
My father cut insoles out of cardboard, and I wore those in my shoes. As
long as I had to stay in the house anyway, they were all right.

I stayed cooped up in the house, without any companionship. We didn't 7
take a Sunday paper any more, but the Barry *Adage* came every week in
the mails; and though I did not read small print, I could see the Santa Clauses
and holly wreaths in the advertisements.

There was a calendar in the kitchen. The red days were Sundays and 8
holidays; and that red 25 was Christmas. (It was on a Monday, and the two
red figures would come right together in 1893; but this represents research
in the World Almanac, not memory.) I knew when Sunday was, because I
could look out of the window and see the neighbor's children, all dressed up,
going to Sunday school. I knew just when Christmas was going to be.

But there was something queer! My father and mother didn't say a word 9
about Christmas. And once, when I spoke of it, there was a strange, embarrassed silence; so I didn't say anything more about it. But I wondered, and
was troubled. Why didn't they say anything about it? Was what I had said
I wanted (memory refuses to supply that detail) too expensive?

I wasn't arrogant and talkative now. I was silent and frightened. What 10
was the matter? Why didn't my father and mother say anything about
Christmas? As the day approached, my chest grew tighter with anxiety.

Now it was the day before Christmas. I couldn't be mistaken. But not 11
a word about it from my father and mother. I waited in painful bewilderment
all day. I had supper with them, and was allowed to sit up for an hour. I
was waiting for them to say something. "It's time for you to go to bed," my
mother said gently. I had to say something.

"This is Christmas Eve, isn't it?" I asked, as if I didn't know. 12

My father and mother looked at one another. Then my mother looked 13 away. Her face was pale and stony. My father cleared his throat, and his face took on a joking look. He pretended he hadn't known it was Christmas Eve, because he hadn't been reading the papers. He said he would go downtown and find out.

My mother got up and walked out of the room. I didn't want my father to have to keep on being funny about it, so I got up and went to bed. I went by myself without having a light. I undressed in the dark and crawled into bed. 14

I was numb. As if I had been hit by something. It was hard to breathe. I ached all through. I was stunned — with finding out the truth. 15

My body knew before my mind quite did. In a minute, when I could think, my mind would know. And as the pain in my body ebbed, the pain in my mind began. I knew. I couldn't put it into words yet. But I knew why I had taken only a little bag of potatoes to Sunday school that fall. I knew why there had been only pennies in my little yellow envelope. I knew why I hadn't gone to school that fall — why I hadn't any new shoes — why we had been living on potato soup all winter. All these things, and others, many others, fitted themselves together in my mind, and meant something. 16

Then the words came into my mind and I whispered them into the darkness: 17

"We're poor!" 18

That was it. I was one of those poor children I had been sorry for, when I heard about them in Sunday school. My mother hadn't told me. My father was out of work, and we hadn't any money. That was why there wasn't going to be any Christmas at our house. 19

Then I remembered something that made me squirm with shame — a boast. (Memory will not yield this up. Had I said to some Nice little boy, "I'm going to be President of the United States"? Or to a Nice little girl: "I'll marry you when I grow up."? It was some boast as horribly shameful to remember.) 20

"We're poor." There in bed in the dark, I whispered it over and over to myself. I was making myself get used to it. (Or — just torturing myself, as one presses the tongue against a sore tooth? No, memory says not like that — but to keep myself from ever being such a fool again: suffering now, to keep this awful thing from ever happening again. Memory is clear on that; it was more like pulling the tooth, to get it over with — never mind the pain, this will be the end!) 21

It wasn't so bad, now that I knew. I just hadn't known! I had thought all sorts of foolish things: that I was going to Ann Arbor — going to be a lawyer — going to make speeches in the Square, going to be President. Now I knew better. 22

I had wanted (something) for Christmas. I didn't want it, now. I didn't want anything. 23

I lay there in the dark, feeling the cold emotion of renunciation. (The 24 tendrils of desire unfold their clasp on the outer world of objects, withdraw, shrivel up. Wishes shrivel up, turn black, die. It is like that.)

It hurt. But nothing would ever hurt again. I would never let myself 25 want anything again.

I lay there stretched out straight and stiff in the dark, my fists clenched 26 hard upon Nothing. . . .

In the morning it had been like a nightmare that is not clearly remembered — 27 that one wishes to forget. Though I hadn't hung up any stocking, there was one hanging at the foot of my bed. A bag of popcorn, and a lead pencil, for me. They had done the best they could, now they realized that I knew about Christmas. But they needn't have thought they had to. I didn't want anything.

SUBJECT QUESTIONS

1. At what point in the story does the reader become aware that the Dell family is poor? Why does it take the child so much longer to make this discovery?
2. Given Floyd's new attitude at the end, how might he have felt had his family received some of the Sunday school's gifts for poor children? How does his mother feel about letting people know the family is poor? Why?
3. In some ways Christmas Eve was the worst possible time for Floyd to make his discovery; in what respects might it be the right time?
4. The worst part of the discovery for the boy is the shame over his boast; shouldn't the prospect of hunger and hardship be more of a worry? Which is normally more important to a person, the preservation of his life or of his self-respect?

STRUCTURE QUESTIONS

1. Which details in this passage mark it as uniquely Dell's experience? Which details make it a typical example of the experiences of almost all poor children in America?
2. How does Dell separate the immediate experience of the child from his mature comments on that experience? The device is somewhat mechanical; does it work all right? Would there have been a better way to achieve the same separation? What do the "grown-ups's" comments add to the story?
3. Contrast the way feelings are communicated in paragraphs 4 and 10; which way is more effective? How could Dell have improved the weaker paragraph?
4. Since the reader finds out almost at once the point of Floyd's much later discovery, how does the author maintain interest (or suspense) until he can come to the boy's crucial reaction to this discovery?

Hymns in a Man's Life

D. H. Lawrence

D. H. Lawrence (1885-1930) is probably best known to college students as the author of Lady Chatterley's Lover, *though he wrote a number of other novels and some of the finest poems and short stories of this century. Being the son of a coal miner and having received a provincial, rigorous, and very traditional education, Lawrence became convinced that civilization's dying conventions and traditions were stifling modern man. His solution was a return to a more primitive and instinctual existence — including more natural and spontaneous sexual relationships. Somewhat ironically, his attempt to liberate women from passive and convention-bound sex roles has brought Lawrence under recent attack by writers of the women's liberation movement, who see him as regarding women merely as sex objects. Lawrence's perception and appreciation of nature and the minutiae of life may have been heightened by the tuberculosis that afflicted him and of which he died at forty-five. The essay that follows is typical of this appreciation as well as of Lawrence's romanticism.*

Nothing is more difficult than to determine what a child takes in, and does   1
not take in, of its environment and its teaching. This fact is brought home
to me by the hymns which I learned as a child, and never forgot. They mean
to me almost more than the finest poetry, and they have for me a more
permanent value, somehow or other.

It is almost shameful to confess that the poems which have meant most   2
to me, like Wordsworth's *Ode to Immortality* and Keats's *Odes*, and pieces
of *Macbeth* and *As You Like It* or *Midsummer Night's Dream*, and Goethe's
lyrics, such as "Uber allen Gipfeln ist Ruh," and Verlaine's "Ayant poussé
la porte qui chancelle" — all these lovely poems which after all give the
ultimate shape to one's life; all these lovely poems woven deep into a man's
consciousness, are still not woven so deep in me as the rather banal Nonconformist hymns that penetrated through and through my childhood.

> Each gentle dove
> And sighing bough
> That makes the eve
> So fair to me
> Has something far   5

From *Phoenix II: Uncollected, Unpublished, and Other Prose Works* by D. H. Lawrence, edited by Warren Roberts and Harry T. Moore. All rights reserved. Reprinted by permission of The Viking Press, Inc., and Lawrence Pollinger Ltd. for the Estate of Mrs. Frieda Lawrence.

Diviner now
To draw me back
To Galilee.
O Galilee, sweet Galilee,
Where Jesus loved so much to be,   10
O Galilee, sweet Galilee,
Come sing thy songs again to me!

To me the word Galilee has a wonderful sound. The Lake of Galilee! I   3
don't want to know where it is. I never want to go to Palestine. Galilee is
one of those lovely, glamorous worlds, not places, that exist in the golden
haze of a child's half-formed imagination. And in my man's imagination it
is just the same. It has been left untouched. With regard to the hymns which
had such a profound influence on my childish consciousness, there has been
no crystallizing out, no dwindling into actuality, no hardening into the commonplace. They are the same to my man's experience as they were to me
nearly forty years ago.

The moon, perhaps, has shrunken a little. One has been forced to learn   4
about orbits, eclipses, relative distances, dead worlds, craters of the moon,
and so on. The crescent at evening still startles the soul with its delicate
flashing. But the mind works automatically and says: "Ah, she is in her first
quarter. She is all there, in spite of the fact that we see only the slim blade.
The earth's shadow is over her." And, willy-nilly, the intrusion of the mental
processes dims the brilliance, the magic of the first apperception.

It is the same with all things. The sheer delight of a child's apperception   5
is based on *wonder;* and deny it as we may, knowledge and wonder counteract
one another. So that as knowledge increases wonder decreases. We say again:
Familiarity breeds contempt. So that as we grow older, and become more
familiar with phenomena, we become more contemptuous of them. But that
is only partly true. It has taken some races of men thousands of years to become
contemptuous of the moon, and to the Hindu the cow is still wondrous. It
is not familiarity that breeds contempt: it is the assumption of knowledge.
Anybody who looks at the moon and says, "I know all about that poor orb,"
is, of course, bored by the moon.

Now the great and fatal fruit of our civilization, which is a civilization   6
based on knowledge, and hostile to experience, is boredom. All our wonderful
education and learning is producing a grand sum-total of boredom. Modern
people are inwardly thoroughly bored. Do as they may, they are bored.

They are bored because they experience nothing. And they experience   7
nothing because the wonder has gone out of them. And when the wonder
has gone out of a man he is dead. He is henceforth only an insect.

When all comes to all, the most precious element in life is wonder. Love   8
is a great emotion, and power is power. But both love and power are based
on wonder. Love without wonder is a sensational affair, and power without

wonder is mere force and compulsion. The one universal element in consciousness which is fundamental to life is the element of wonder. You cannot
help feeling it in a bean as it starts to grow and pulls itself out of its jacket.
You cannot help feeling it in the glisten of the nucleus of the amoeba. You
recognize it, willy-nilly, in an ant busily tugging at a straw; in a rook, as it
walks the frosty grass.

They all have their own obstinate will. But also they all live with a   9
sense of wonder. Plant consciousness, insect consciousness, fish consciousness,
animal consciousness, all are related by one permanent element, which we
may call the religious element inherent in all life, even in a flea: the sense
of wonder. That is our sixth sense. And it is the *natural* religious sense.

Somebody says that mystery is nothing, because mystery is something   10
you don't know, and what you don't know is nothing to you. But there is
more than one way of knowing.

Even the real scientist works in the sense of wonder. The pity is, when   11
he comes out of his laboratory he puts aside his wonder along with his apparatus and tries to make it all perfectly didactic. Science in its true condition
of wonder is as religious as any religion. But didactic science is as dead and
boring as dogmatic religion. Both are wonderless and productive of boredom,
endless boredom.

Now we come back to the hymns. They live and glisten in the depths   12
of the man's consciousness in undimmed wonder, because they have not been
subjected to any criticism or analysis. By the time I was sixteen I had criticized
and got over the Christian dogma.

It was quite easy for me; my immediate forebears had already done it   13
for me. Salvation, heaven, Virgin birth, miracles, even the Christian dogmas
of right and wrong — one soon got them adjusted. I never could really worry
about them. Heaven is one of the instinctive dreams. Right and wrong is
something you can't dogmatize about; it's not so easy. As for my soul, I simply
don't and never did understand how I could "save" it. One can save one's
pennies. But how can one save one's soul? One can only *live* one's soul. The
business is to live, really alive. And this needs wonder.

So that the miracle of the loaves and fishes is just as good to me now   14
as when I was a child. I don't care whether it is historically a fact or not.
What does it matter? It is part of the genuine wonder. The same with all
the religious teaching I had as a child, *apart* from the didacticism and sentimentalism. I am eternally grateful for the wonder with which it filled my
childhood.

> Sun of my soul, thou Saviour dear,
>   It is not night if Thou be near —

That was the last hymn at the board school. It did not mean to me any   15
Christian dogma or any salvation. Just the words, "Sun of my soul, thou

Saviour dear," penetrated me with wonder and the mystery of twilight. At another time the last hymn was:

> Fair waved the golden corn
> In Canaan's pleasant land —

And again I loved "Canaan's pleasant land," the wonder of "Canaan," which could never be localized.

I think it was good to be brought up a Protestant: and among Protestants, a Nonconformist, and among Nonconformists, a Congregationalist. Which sounds pharisaic. But I should have missed bitterly a direct knowledge of the Bible, and a direct relation to Galilee and Canaan, Moab and Kedron, those places that never existed on earth. And in the Church of England one would hardly have escaped those snobbish hierarchies of class, which spoil so much for a child. And the Primitive Methodists, when I was a boy, were always having "revivals" and being "saved," and I always had a horror of being saved. 16

So, altogether, I am grateful to my "Congregational" upbringing. The Congregationalists are the oldest Nonconformists, descendants of the Oliver Cromwell Independents. They still had the Puritan tradition of no ritual. But they avoided the personal emotionalism which one found among the Methodists when I was a boy. 17

I liked our chapel, which was tall and full of light, and yet still; and colour-washed pale green and blue, with a bit of lotus pattern. And over the organ-loft, "O worship the Lord in the beauty of holiness," in big letters. 18

That was a favourite hymn too: 19

> O worship the Lord, in the beauty of holiness,
>   Bow down before Him, His glory proclaim;
> With gold of obedience and incense of lowliness
>   Kneel and adore Him, the Lord is His name.

I don't know what the "beauty of holiness" is, exactly. It easily becomes cant, or nonsense, but if you don't think about it — and why should you? — it has a magic. The same with the whole verse. It is rather bad, really, "gold of obedience" and "incense of lowliness." But in me, to the music, it still produces a sense of splendour. 20

I am always glad we had the Bristol hymn-book, not Moody and Sankey. And I am glad our Scotch minister on the whole avoided sentimental messes such as "Lead, Kindly Light," or even "Abide With Me." He had a healthy preference for healthy hymns. 21

> At even, ere the sun was set,
>   The sick, O Lord, around Thee lay,
> Oh, in what divers pains they met!
>   Oh, in what joy they went away!

And often we had "Fight the good fight with all thy might." 22

In Sunday School I am eternally grateful to old Mr. Remington, with   23
his round white beard and his ferocity. He made us sing! And he loved the
martial hymns:

> Sound the battle-cry,
> See the foe is nigh.
> Raise the standard high
> For the Lord.

The ghastly sentimentalism that came like a leprosy over religion had   24
not yet got hold of our colliery village. I remember when I was in Class II
in the Sunday School, when I was about seven, a woman teacher trying to
harrow us about the Crucifixion. And she kept saying: "And aren't you sorry
for Jesus? Aren't you sorry?" And most of the children wept. I believe I shed
a crocodile tear or two, but very vivid is my memory of saying to myself:
"I don't *really* care a bit." And I could never go back on it. I never *cared*
about the Crucifixion, one way or another. Yet the *wonder* of it penetrated
very deep in me.

Thirty-six years ago men, even Sunday School teachers, still believed   25
in the fight for life and the fun of it. "Hold the fort, for I am coming." It
was far, far, from any militarism or gun-fighting. But it was the battle-cry
of a stout soul, and a fine thing too.

> Stand up, stand up for Jesus,
> Ye soldiers of the Lord.

Here is the clue to the ordinary Englishman — in the Nonconformist   26
hymns.

SUBJECT QUESTIONS

1. Lawrence argues that knowledge kills the sense of wonder. Annie Dillard maintained that "I don't see what the specialist sees, and so I cut myself off, not only from the total picture, but from the various forms of happiness." With which of these conflicting views do you agree? Does Lawrence's discussion of the scientist in paragraph 11 help resolve the conflict?
2. Does Lawrence successfully explain how his knowledge – and rejection – of religion failed to dull his sense of wonder at the hymns he sang as a child?
3. Lawrence says at the beginning that he does not know why the "banal" hymns of his childhood are more precious to him than the great poetry of Wordsworth, Keats, and Shakespeare; does this essay itself suggest an answer?
4. Would you agree that the product of education is boredom? In what sense is knowledge "hostile to experience"?

5. Toward the end of the essay, does Lawrence make clear how the wonder of the Crucifixion could affect him deeply without his caring about it? Does the preceding discussion of hymns help to clarify this problem?

STRUCTURE QUESTIONS

1. Lawrence begins and ends with a discussion of hymns from his childhood; but the thrust of his essay is in the section (paragraphs 4–11) on wonder being destroyed by knowledge. How does he make the transition from one part to the next? Is one transition better than the other?
2. Does Lawrence succeed in making his personal experience an example of his thesis? The thesis is stated in general terms; is there any attempt to universalize the personal experience which illustrates it?
3. What does Lawrence accomplish by quoting so many passages from the hymns? Is he simply proving that he still remembers them?
4. Because religion is no longer meaningful to Lawrence, why does he select hymns as his example? (If he were still a Christian, would the choice be more, or less, effective?)
5. By examining a typical passage (paragraph 3, for instance), consider how Lawrence is able to use so many simple sentences without letting the writing degenerate into "primer prose." Does he tend to use short sentences for simplicity, or for emphasis? Are the long sentences hard to follow amidst all the short ones?
6. Ending with a generalization which the essay has not proved is not usually the best practice. Is there any thematic justification for Lawrence's final sentence?

Death in the Woods

Sherwood Anderson

Sherwood Anderson (1876–1941) began his literary career as a journalist and newspaper editor, but he is known today as one of America's finest short story writers. His best-known work is Winesburg, Ohio *(1920), a collection of Freudian stories about the inhabitants of a small town. "Death in the Woods," typical of Anderson's abiding interest in everyday, unimportant people, was written in 1926.*

She was an old woman and lived on a farm near the town in which I lived. 1
All country and small-town people have seen such old women, but no one knows much about them. Such an old woman comes into town driving an old worn-out horse or she comes afoot carrying a basket. She may own a few hens and have eggs to sell. She brings them in a basket and takes them to a grocer. There she trades them in. She gets some salt pork and some beans. Then she gets a pound or two of sugar and some flour.

Afterwards she goes to the butcher's and asks for some dog-meat. She 2
may spend ten or fifteen cents, but when she does she asks for something. Formerly the butchers gave liver to any one who wanted to carry it away. In our family we were always having it. Once one of my brothers got a whole cow's liver at the slaughter-house near the fairgrounds in our town. We had it until we were sick of it. It never cost a cent. I have hated the thought of it ever since.

The old farm woman got some liver and a soup-bone. She never visited 3
with any one, and as soon as she got what she wanted she lit out for home. It made quite a load for such an old body. No one gave her a lift. People drive right down a road and never notice an old woman like that.

There was such an old woman who used to come into town past our 4
house one Summer and Fall when I was a young boy and was sick with what was called inflammatory rheumatism. She went home later carrying a heavy pack on her back. Two or three large gaunt-looking dogs followed at her heels.

The old woman was nothing special. She was one of the nameless ones 5
that hardly any one knows, but she got into my thoughts. I have just suddenly now, after all these years, remembered her and what happened. It is a story. Her name was Grimes, and she lived with her husband and son in a small unpainted house on the bank of a small creek four miles from town.

The husband and son were a tough lot. Although the son was but 6
twenty-one, he had already served a term in jail. It was whispered about that
the woman's husband stole horses and ran them off to some other county.
Now and then, when a horse turned up missing, the man had also disappeared.
No one ever caught him. Once, when I was loafing at Tom Whitehead's
livery-barn, the man came there and sat on the bench in front. Two or three
other men were there, but no one spoke to him. He sat for a few minutes
and then got up and went away. When he was leaving he turned around and
stared at the men. There was a look of defiance in his eyes. "Well, I have
tried to be friendly. You don't want to talk to me. It has been so wherever
I have gone in this town. If, some day, one of your fine horses turns up missing,
well, then what?" He did not say anything actually: "I'd like to bust one of
you on the jaw," was about what his eyes said. I remember how the look
in his eyes made me shiver.

The old man belonged to a family that had had money once. His name 7
was Jake Grimes. It all comes back clearly now. His father, John Grimes, had
owned a sawmill when the country was new, and had made money. Then
he got to drinking and running after women. When he died there wasn't much
left.

Jake blew in the rest. Pretty soon there wasn't any more lumber to cut 8
and his land was nearly all gone.

He got his wife off a German farmer, for whom he went to work one 9
June day in the wheat harvest. She was a young thing then and scared to
death. You see, the farmer was up to something with the girl — she was, I
think, a bound girl and his wife had her suspicions. She took it out on the
girl when the man wasn't around. Then, when the wife had to go off to town
for supplies, the farmer got after her. She told young Jake that nothing really
ever happened, but he didn't know whether to believe it or not.

He got her pretty easy himself, the first time he was out with her. He 10
wouldn't have married her if the German farmer hadn't tried to tell him where
to get off. He got her to go riding with him in his buggy one night when
he was threshing on the place, and then he came for her the next Sunday
night.

She managed to get out of the house without her employer's seeing, 11
but when she was getting into the buggy he showed up. It was almost dark,
and he just popped up suddenly at the horse's head. He grabbed the horse
by the bridle and Jake got out his buggy-whip.

They had it out all right! The German was a tough one. Maybe he didn't 12
care whether his wife knew or not. Jake hit him over the face and shoulders
with the buggy-whip, but the horse got to acting up and he had to get out.

Then the two men went for it. The girl didn't see it. The horse started 13
to run away and went nearly a mile down the road before the girl got him
stopped. Then she managed to tie him to a tree beside the road. (I wonder
how I know all this. It must have stuck in my mind from small-town tales

when I was a boy.) Jake found her there after he got through with the German. She was huddled up in the buggy seat, crying, scared to death. She told Jake a lot of stuff, how the German had tried to get her, how he chased her once into the barn, how another time, when they happened to be alone in the house together, he tore her dress open clear down the front. The German, she said, might have got her that time if he hadn't heard his old woman drive in at the gate. She had been off to town for supplies. Well, she would be putting the horse in the barn. The German managed to sneak off to the fields without his wife seeing. He told the girl he would kill her if she told. What could she do? She told a lie about ripping her dress in the barn when she was feeding the stock. I remember now that she was a bound girl and did not know where her father and mother were. Maybe she did not have any father. You know what I mean.

Such bound children were often enough cruelly treated. They were 14
children who had no parents, slaves really. There were very few orphan homes then. They were legally bound into some home. It was a matter of pure luck how it came out.

II

She married Jake and had a son and daughter, but the daughter died. 15

Then she settled down to feed stock. That was her job. At the German's 16
place she had cooked the food for the German and his wife. The wife was a strong woman with big hips and worked most of the time in the fields with her husband. She fed them and fed the cows in the barn, fed the pigs, the horses and the chickens. Every moment of every day, as a young girl, was spent feeding something.

Then she married Jake Grimes and he had to be fed. She was a slight 17
thing, and when she had been married for three or four years, and after the two children were born, her slender shoulders became stooped.

Jake always had a lot of big dogs around the house, that stood near the 18
unused sawmill near the creek. He was always trading horses when he wasn't stealing something and had a lot of poor bony ones about. Also he kept three or four pigs and a cow. They were all pastured in the few acres left of the Grimes place and Jake did little enough work.

He went into debt for a threshing outfit and ran it for several years, 19
but it did not pay. People did not trust him. They were afraid he would steal the grain at night. He had to go a long way off to get work and it cost too much to get there. In the Winter he hunted and cut a little firewood, to be sold in some nearby town. When the son grew up he was just like the father. They got drunk together. If there wasn't anything to eat in the house when they came home the old man gave his old woman a cut over the head. She had a few chickens of her own and had to kill one of them in a hurry. When

they were all killed she wouldn't have any eggs to sell when she went to town, and then what would she do?

She had to scheme all her life about getting things fed, getting the pigs fed so they would grow fat and could be butchered in the Fall. When they were butchered her husband took most of the meat off to town and sold it. If he did not do it first the boy did. They fought sometimes and when they fought the old woman stood aside trembling.

She had got the habit of silence anyway — that was fixed. Sometimes, when she began to look old — she wasn't forty yet — and when the husband and son were both off, trading horses or drinking or hunting or stealing, she went around the house and the barnyard muttering to herself.

How was she going to get everything fed? — that was her problem. The dogs had to be fed. There wasn't enough hay in the barn for the horses and the cow. If she didn't feed the chickens how could they lay eggs? Without eggs to sell how could she get things in town, things she had to have to keep the life of the farm going? Thank heaven, she did not have to feed her husband — in a certain way. That hadn't lasted long after their marriage and after the babies came. Where he went on his long trips she did not know. Sometimes he was gone from home for weeks, and after the boy grew up they went off together.

They left everything at home for her to manage and she had no money. She knew no one. No one ever talked to her in town. When it was Winter she had to gather sticks of wood for her fire, had to try to keep the stock fed with very little grain.

The stock in the barn cried to her hungrily, the dogs followed her about. In the Winter the hens laid few enough eggs. They huddled in the corners of the barn and she kept watching them. If a hen lays an egg in the barn in the Winter and you do not find it, it freezes and breaks.

One day in Winter the old woman went off to town with a few eggs and the dogs followed her. She did not get started until nearly three o'clock and the snow was heavy. She hadn't been feeling very well for several days and so she went muttering along, scantily clad, her shoulders stooped. She had an old grain bag in which she carried her eggs, tucked away down in the bottom. There weren't many of them, but in Winter the price of eggs is up. She would get a little meat in exchange for the eggs, some salt pork, a little sugar, and some coffee perhaps. It might be the butcher would give her a piece of liver.

When she had got to town and was trading in her eggs the dogs lay by the door outside. She did pretty well, got the things she needed, more than she had hoped. Then she went to the butcher and he gave her some liver and some dog-meat.

It was the first time any one had spoken to her in a friendly way for a long time. The butcher was alone in his shop when she came in and was annoyed by the thought of such a sick-looking old woman out on such a day. It was bitter cold and the snow, that had let up during the afternoon, was falling again. The butcher said something about her husband and her son, swore at them, and the old woman stared at him, a look of mild surprise in her eyes as he talked. He said that if either the husband or the son were going to get any of the liver or the heavy bones with scraps of meat hanging to them that he had put into the grain bag, he'd see him starve first.

Starve, eh? Well, things had to be fed. Men had to be fed, and the horses that weren't any good but maybe could be traded off, and the poor thin cow that hadn't given any milk for three months.

Horses, cows, pigs, dogs, men.

III

The old woman had to get back before darkness came if she could. The dogs followed at her heels, sniffing at the heavy grain bag she had fastened on her back. When she got to the edge of town she stopped by a fence and tied the bag on her back with a piece of rope she had carried in her dress-pocket for just that purpose. That was an easier way to carry it. Her arms ached. It was hard when she had to crawl over fences and once she fell over and landed in the snow. The dogs went frisking about. She had to struggle to get to her feet again, but she made it. The point of climbing over the fences was that there was a short cut over a hill and through a woods. She might have gone around by the road, but it was a mile farther that way. She was afraid she couldn't make it. And then, besides, the stock had to be fed. There was a little hay left and a little corn. Perhaps her husband and son would bring some home when they came. They had driven off in the only buggy the Grimes family had, a rickety thing, a rickety horse hitched to the buggy, two other rickety horses led by halters. They were going to trade horses, get a little money if they could. They might come home drunk. It would be well to have something in the house when they came back.

The son had an affair on with a woman at the county seat, fifteen miles away. She was a rough enough woman, a tough one. Once, in the Summer, the son had brought her to the house. Both she and the son had been drinking. Jake Grimes was away and the son and his woman ordered the old woman about like a servant. She didn't mind much; she was used to it. Whatever happened she never said anything. That was her way of getting along. She had managed that way when she was a young girl at the German's and ever since she had married Jake. That time her son brought his woman to the house they stayed all night, sleeping together just as though they were married. It hadn't shocked the old woman, not much. She had got past being shocked early in life.

With the pack on her back she went painfully along across an open field, wading in the deep snow, and got into the woods.

There was a path, but it was hard to follow. Just beyond the top of the hill, where the woods was thickest, there was a small clearing. Had some one once thought of building a house there? The clearing was as large as a building lot in town, large enough for a house and a garden. The path ran along the side of the clearing, and when she got there the old woman sat down to rest at the foot of a tree.

It was a foolish thing to do. When she got herself placed, the pack against the tree's trunk, it was nice, but what about getting up again? She worried about that for a moment and then quietly closed her eyes.

She must have slept for a time. When you are about so cold you can't get any colder. The afternoon grew a little warmer and the snow came thicker than ever. Then after a time the weather cleared. The moon even came out.

There were four Grimes dogs that had followed Mrs. Grimes into town, all tall gaunt fellows. Such men as Jake Grimes and his son always keep just such dogs. They kick and abuse them, but they stay. The Grimes dogs, in order to keep from starving, had to do a lot of foraging for themselves, and they had been at it while the old woman slept with her back to the tree at the side of the clearing. They had been chasing rabbits in the woods and in adjoining fields and in their ranging had picked up three other farm dogs.

After a time all the dogs came back to the clearing. They were excited about something. Such nights, cold and clear and with a moon, do things to dogs. It may be that some old instinct, come down from the time when they were wolves and ranged the woods in packs on Winter nights, comes back into them.

The dogs in the clearing, before the old woman, had caught two or three rabbits and their immediate hunger had been satisfied. They began to play, running in circles in the clearing. Round and round they ran, each dog's nose at the tail of the next dog. In the clearing, under the snow-laden trees and under the wintry moon they made a strange picture, running thus silently, in a circle their running had beaten in the soft snow. The dogs made no sound. They ran around and around in the circle.

It may have been that the old woman saw them doing that before she died. She may have awakened once or twice and looked at the strange sight with dim old eyes.

She wouldn't be very cold now, just drowsy. Life hangs on a long time. Perhaps the old woman was out of her head. She may have dreamed of her girlhood, at the German's, and before that, when she was a child and before her mother lit out and left her.

Her dreams couldn't have been very pleasant. Not many pleasant things had happened to her. Now and then one of the Grimes dogs left the running circle and came to stand before her. The dog thrust his face close to her face. His red tongue was hanging out.

The running of the dogs may have been a kind of death ceremony. It 42
may have been that the primitive instinct of the wolf, having been aroused
in the dogs by the night and the running, made them somehow afraid.

"Now we are no longer wolves. We are dogs, the servants of men. Keep 43
alive, man! When man dies we become wolves again."

When one of the dogs came to where the old woman sat with her back 44
against the tree and thrust his nose close to her face he seemed satisfied and
went back to run with the pack. All the Grimes dogs did it at some time
during the evening, before she died. I knew all about it afterward, when I
grew to be a man, because once in a woods in Illinois, on another Winter
night, I saw a pack of dogs act just like that. The dogs were waiting for me
to die as they had waited for the old woman that night when I was a child,
but when it happened to me I was a young man and had no intention whatever
of dying.

The old woman died softly and quietly. When she was dead and when 45
one of the Grimes dogs had come to her and had found her dead all the dogs
stopped running.

They gathered about her. 46

Well, she was dead now. She had fed the Grimes dogs when she was 47
alive, what about now?

There was the pack on her back, the grain bag containing the piece 48
of salt pork, the liver the butcher had given her, the dog-meat, the soup bones.
The butcher in town, having been suddenly overcome with a feeling of pity,
had loaded her grain bag heavily. It had been a big haul for the old woman.

It was a big haul for the dogs now. 49

IV

One of the Grimes dogs sprang suddenly out from among the others and began 50
worrying the pack on the old woman's back. Had the dogs really been wolves
that one would have been the leader of the pack. What he did, all the others
did.

All of them sank their teeth into the grain bag the old woman had 51
fastened with ropes to her back.

They dragged the old woman's body out into the open clearing. The 52
worn-out dress was quickly torn from her shoulders. When she was found,
a day or two later, the dress had been torn from her body clear to the hips,
but the dogs had not touched her body. They had got the meat out of the
grain bag, that was all. Her body was frozen stiff when it was found, and
the shoulders were so narrow and the body so slight that in death it looked
like the body of some charming young girl.

Such things happened in towns of the Middle West, on farms near town, 53
when I was a boy. A hunter out after rabbits found the old woman's body

and did not touch it. Something, the beaten round path in the little snow-covered clearing, the silence of the place, the place where the dogs had worried the body trying to pull the grain bag away or tear it open — something startled the man and he hurried off to town.

I was in Main street with one of my brothers who was town newsboy   54
and who was taking the afternoon papers to the stores. It was almost night.

The hunter came into a grocery and told his story. Then he went to   55
a hardware-shop and into a drugstore. Men began to gather on the sidewalks.
Then they started out along the road to the place in the woods.

My brother should have gone on about his business of distributing papers   56
but he didn't. Every one was going to the woods. The undertaker went and
the town marshal. Several men got on a dray and rode out to where the path
left the road and went into the woods, but the horses weren't very sharply
shod and slid about on the slippery roads. They made no better time than
those of us who walked.

The town marshal was a large man whose leg had been injured in the   57
Civil War. He carried a heavy cane and limped rapidly along the road. My
brother and I followed at his heels, and as we went other men and boys joined
the crowd.

It had grown dark by the time we got to where the old woman had   58
left the road but the moon had come out. The marshal was thinking there
might have been a murder. He kept asking the hunter questions. The hunter
went along with his gun across his shoulders, a dog following at his heels.
It isn't often a rabbit hunter has a chance to be so conspicuous. He was taking
full advantage of it, leading the procession with the town marshal. "I didn't
see any wounds. She was a beautiful young girl. Her face was buried in the
snow. No, I didn't know her." As a matter of fact, the hunter had not looked
closely at the body. He had been frightened. She might have been murdered
and some one might spring out from behind a tree and murder him. In a woods,
in the late afternoon, when the trees are all bare and there is white snow
on the ground, when all is silent, something creepy steals over the mind and
body. If something strange or uncanny has happened in the neighborhood
all you think about is getting away from there as fast as you can.

The crowd of men and boys had got to where the old woman had crossed   59
the field and went, following the marshal and the hunter, up the slight incline
and into the woods.

My brother and I were silent. He had his bundle of papers in a bag   60
slung across his shoulder. When he got back to town he would have to go
on distributing his papers before he went home to supper. If I went along,
as he had no doubt already determined I should, we would both be late. Either
mother or our older sister would have to warm our supper.

Well, we would have something to tell. A boy did not get such a chance   61
very often. It was lucky we just happened to go into the grocery when the

hunter came in. The hunter was a country fellow. Neither of us had ever seen him before.

Now the crowd of men and boys had got to the clearing. Darkness comes quickly on such Winter nights, but the full moon made everything clear. My brother and I stood near the tree, beneath which the old woman had died.   62

She did not look old, lying there in that light, frozen and still. One of the men turned her over in the snow and I saw everything. My body trembled with some strange mystical feeling and so did my brother's. It might have been the cold.   63

Neither of us had even seen a woman's body before. It may have been the snow, clinging to the frozen flesh, that made it look so white and lovely, so like marble. No woman had come with the party from town; but one of the men, he was the town blacksmith, took off his overcoat and spread it over her. Then he gathered her into his arms and started off to town, all the others following silently. At that time no one knew who she was.   64

V

I had seen everything, had seen the oval in the snow, like a miniature race-track, where the dogs had run, had seen how the men were mystified, had seen the white bare young-looking shoulders, had heard the whispered comments of the men.   65

The men were simply mystified. They took the body to the undertaker's, and when the blacksmith, the hunter, the marshal and several others had got inside they closed the door. If father had been there perhaps he could have got in, but we boys couldn't.   66

I went with my brother to distribute the rest of his papers and when we got home it was my brother who told the story.   67

I kept silent and went to bed early. It may have been I was not satisfied with the way he told it.   68

Later, in the town, I must have heard other fragments of the old woman's story. She was recognized the next day and there was an investigation.   69

The husband and son were found somewhere and brought to town and there was an attempt to connect them with the woman's death, but it did not work. They had perfect enough alibis.   70

However, the town was against them. They had to get out. Where they went I never heard.   71

I remember only the picture there in the forest, the men standing about, the naked girlish-looking figure, face down in the snow, the tracks made by the running dogs and the clear cold Winter sky above. White fragments of clouds were drifting across the sky. They went racing across the little open space among the trees.   72

The scene in the forest had become for me, without my knowing it,   73 the foundation for the real story I am now trying to tell. The fragments, you see, had to be picked up slowly, long afterwards.

Things happened. When I was a young man I worked on the farm of 74 a German. The hired-girl was afraid of her employer. The farmer's wife hated her.

I saw things at that place. Once later, I had a half-uncanny, mystical 75 adventure with dogs in an Illinois forest on a clear, moon-lit Winter night. When I was a schoolboy, and on a Summer day, I went with a boy friend out along a creek some miles from town and came to the house where the old woman had lived. No one had lived in the house since her death. The doors were broken from the hinges; the window lights were all broken. As the boy and I stood in the road outside, two dogs, just roving farm dogs no doubt, came running around the corner of the house. The dogs were tall, gaunt fellows and came down to the fence and glared through at us, standing in the road.

The whole thing, the story of the old woman's death, was to me as I 76 grew older like music heard from far off. The notes had to be picked up slowly one at a time. Something had to be understood.

The woman who died was one destined to feed animal life. Anyway, 77 that is all she ever did. She was feeding animal life before she was born, as a child, as a young woman working on the farm of the German, after she married, when she grew old and when she died. She fed animal life in cows, in chickens, in pigs, in horses, in dogs, in men. Her daughter had died in childhood and with her one son she had no articulate relations. On the night when she died she was hurrying homeward, bearing on her body food for animal life.

She died in the clearing in the woods and even after her death continued 78 feeding animal life.

You see it is likely that, when my brother told the story, that night when 79 we got home and my mother and sister sat listening, I did not think he got the point. He was too young and so was I. A thing so complete has its own beauty.

I shall not try to emphasize the point. I am only explaining why I was 80 dissatisfied then and have been ever since. I speak of that only that you may understand why I have been impelled to try to tell the simple story over again.

SUBJECT QUESTIONS

1. Why is the story-teller so careful to explain how he came by his facts and pieced the story together? (This is a short story; is "documentation" necessary?)
2. If we take a common definition of "the main character" as the one who

undergoes a change in mental attitude as a result of some important event in his life, who is the main character in this story?

3. The boy seems to find a kind of beauty in the story of Mrs. Grimes; what kind of beauty?

4. Mrs. Grimes's dress is torn twice in the story; is there any relation between those two events?

5. What do the dogs have to do with the story? Why does Anderson devote so much time to them?

6. Is there any significance to the fact that the hunter failed to recognize Mrs. Grimes, thinking her a beautiful young girl instead?

7. What does the story tell you about the moral attitudes of the townspeople?

8. What does it tell you about Anderson's view of art?

STRUCTURE QUESTIONS

1. Would you say that this story has unity, or that it contains too much irrelevant detail? (Your answer may depend on who you decide is the main character.)

2. Did you find the concrete detail (the whole calf's liver, for example) interesting or annoying? Was it convincing (that is, did you sometimes think of this as autobiography rather than fiction)?

3. What devices other than concrete detail does Anderson employ to give a sense of realism to his story? Which part seems least realistic? Might Anderson have a reason for making certain parts less realistic than others?

4. Does Anderson seem to have overemphasized the importance of such an event as the death of Mrs. Grimes on the life of a boy? (That is, the description of events may be true to life at the same time the impression made on the boy is untrue to experience.)

5. Comment on the organization of the story: would it have been more, or less, effective had Anderson told it straight through without skipping back and forth in time?

Acquainted with the Night

Robert Frost

Robert Frost (1874–1963) was one of America's most successful poets, winner of countless awards and honors, and often considered the unofficial poet laureate. He was the honored poet at President Kennedy's inauguration in 1961.

I have been one acquainted with the night.
I have walked out in rain — and back in rain.
I have outwalked the furthest city light.

I have looked down the saddest city lane.
I have passed by the watchman on his beat   5
And dropped my eyes, unwilling to explain.

I have stood still and stopped the sound of feet
When far away an interrupted cry
Came over houses from another street,

But not to call me back or say good-by;   10
And further still at an unearthly height
One luminary clock against the sky

Proclaimed the time was neither wrong nor right.
I have been one acquainted with the night.

SUBJECT QUESTIONS

1. The statement "I have been one acquainted with the night" is in the nature of a confession rather than a statement of fact or a boast. To what failing or weakness is the poet admitting?
2. Do you think Frost is using "night" with a symbolic meaning? If so, is it an appropriate symbol?
3. The poet seems to be looking — and listening — for something. Can you tell what? Should Frost have been more specific?

4. For what is the time "neither wrong nor right"? Is it possible that Frost himself doesn't know?

STRUCTURE QUESTIONS

1. The form of this poem is that used by Shelley in "Ode to the West Wind": a sonnet in "terza rima" with a concluding couplet. Analyze the rhyme scheme and meter. Does the tighter structure give the poem any advantages over free verse?
2. Is it possible that Frost has been too concrete in his choice of words? Might his meaning be clearer if he gave an abstract statement of it? Why would he avoid doing so? Would you say that it is possible to express ideas in concrete language that cannot be put into abstract language?
3. What is the pervading mood of this poem? How does Frost create the mood?
4. Far more than does a prose writer, the poet suggests meanings through images and accumulated connotations; thus, his approach is much more subjective. But he must still try to see and interpret accurately. Does Frost try to be honest with his reader? with himself?
5. The personal lyric is the most concentrated and powerful form of written expression. It is also the most difficult to write. If you have never tried your hand at one, you will find the experience enlightening — and perhaps a bit humiliating. Why is honesty so difficult to achieve in the short lyric?

The Abortion

Anne Sexton

Anne Sexton's first book of poems, To Bedlam and Part Way Back, *was published in 1960. In the years that followed she completed a number of other volumes, one of which,* Live or Die (1966), *won a Pulitzer Prize. She married and lived in Weston, Massachusetts before her death in 1974.*

Somebody who should have been born
is gone.

Just as the earth puckered its mouth,
each bud puffing out from its knot,
I changed my shoes, and then drove south.   5

Up past the Blue Mountains, where
Pennsylvania humps on endlessly,
wearing, like a crayoned cat, its green hair,

its roads sunken in like a gray washboard;
where, in truth, the ground cracks evilly,   10
a dark socket from which the coal has poured,

Somebody who should have been born
is gone.

the grass as bristly and stout as chives,
and me wondering when the ground would break,   15
and me wondering how anything fragile survives;

up in Pennsylvania, I met a little man,
not Rumpelstiltskin, at all, at all . . .
he took the fullness that love began.

Returning north, even the sky grew thin   20
like a high window looking nowhere.
The road was as flat as a sheet of tin.

Somebody who should have been born
is gone.

Yes, woman, such logic will lead   25
to loss without death. Or say what you meant,
you coward . . . this baby that I bleed.

SUBJECT QUESTIONS

1. Whether the experience related here was real or imaginary, the poet has
   used it as an example of a fairly common occurrence. Does she depend
   on the reader's knowledge of such experiences, or does the poem itself
   imply more universal extension?
2. Judging by this one poem only, what side would you expect Ms. Sexton
   to take in a debate over birth control legislation?
3. If the man she met was not at all like Rumpelstiltskin, why does she
   bother to drag in a fairy tale character? In what ways might Rumpelstiltskin be contrasted with the lover? (The phrase "at all, at all" seems to
   imply that more than one point of contrast is intended.) What about
   the one point of comparison, that both men were "little"?
4. Do you find the nature description distracting from the "story"? Why do
   you suppose it is included?

STRUCTURE QUESTIONS

1. The refrain line, though a familiar device in folk ballads of lamentable
   love affairs, usually occurs after a stanza or series of stanzas; what does
   the poet accomplish by putting her refrain first? Would the last refrain
   be more effective at the end of the poem?
2. Consider the images in the nature description ("the earth puckered its
   mouth," "like a crayoned cat," etc.) How does each relate to the
   meaning of the poem?
3. What effect does the imagery have on the tone or mood of the poem?
   Does the attitude toward nature remain constant?
4. Until the final stanza the poet has carefully controlled — perhaps even
   disguised — her feelings; but the last two lines are shockingly blunt.
   Does this sudden switch give added impact, or spoil the poem's integrity?
   On looking back, can you say that the bitterness was in the poem from
   the beginning?

2

THE WORLD
AROUND US

Description

In some ways description is an extension of the use of personal example discussed in the preceding section. It is an extension from the writer's self to the places and people he has observed. If written properly, description conveys the same sense of immediacy, vividness, and interest. And it makes the same demand that the writer keep his eyes and ears open to the world around him. There are differences too, of course. For one thing, the personal experience is usually presented in a narrative framework rather than a purely descriptive one. For another, description has numerous uses other than to provide a concrete illustration of a general principle.

Except in very short pieces, description is seldom found isolated from some other method of developing ideas. Yet it is an essential tool for virtually every kind of writer; a botanist can get along without it no better than a novelist can. For description is normally a means to an end rather than an end in itself — and the possible uses to which it can be put are infinite. The writer of a Boy Scout manual may carefully describe poison ivy so that his readers will be able to avoid it. A public relations man may want to describe a tract of New Mexico scabland in such a way that his readers will want to purchase an acre of it. A playwright describes his protagonist so that an actor will have a better idea of how to play that role. A novelist may describe the setting for action to give a sense of realism to his fiction — or he may use the description to create a mood

41

of cheerfulness or desolation or foreboding. Compare Juliet's description of night as she awaits her new husband:

> Gallop apace, you fiery-footed steeds,
> Towards Phoebus' lodging: such a waggoner
> As Phaethon would whip you to the west,
> And bring in cloudy night immediately.
> Spread thy close curtain, love-performing night,
> That runaways' eyes may wink, and Romeo
> Leap to these arms, untalk'd of and unseen.
> Lovers can see to do their amorous rites
> By their own beauties; or, if love be blind,
> It best agrees with night. Come, civil night,
> Thou sober-suited matron, all in black,
> And learn me how to lose a winning match,
> Play'd for a pair of stainless maidenhoods:
> Hood my unmann'd blood, bating in my cheeks,
> With thy black mantle; till strange love, grown bold,
> Think true love acted simple modesty.
> Come, night; come, Romeo; come, thou day in night;
> For thou wilt lie upon the wings of night
> Whiter than new snow on a raven's back.
> Come, gentle night, come, loving, black-brow'd night,
> Give me my Romeo; and, when he shall die,
> Take him and cut him out in little stars,
> And he will make the face of heaven so fine
> That all the world will be in love with night
> And pay no worship to the garish sun.

with Macbeth's description as he prepares to murder Duncan:

> Now o'er the one half-world
> Nature seems dead, and wicked dreams abuse
> The curtain'd sleep; witchcraft celebrates
> Pale Hecate's offerings, and wither'd murder,
> Alarum'd by his sentinel, the wolf,
> Whose howl's his watch, thus with his stealthy pace,
> With Tarquin's ravishing strides, towards his design
> Moves like a ghost.

Regardless of the writer's purpose, what he is after in description is the "essential nature" of the thing described — the special characteristics of poison ivy which will allow one to distinguish it from other forest plants. The problem is that a thing may have many "essences," and the writer must decide which one best fits his purposes. What is the "essential nature" of a harmless drop of water, for instance? Much depends on the context in which it occurs. Obviously there is a considerable difference between a glistening drop of dew on a rose petal at sunrise and the first drop of rain spattering in the dust at second base during a World Series game. And the writer's attitude toward what he describes is also important: the baseball fan may be dismayed by that drop of rain and see it as an agent of evil; but if the pitcher is in a jam, that lovely mud-producing raindrop may to him seem sent from heaven.

The writer of description, then, must keep in mind both the occasion for which he is writing and the attitude toward his subject which he wants to re-create in the reader. In college writing, the nature of an assignment will frequently suggest the proper approach. (If the biology professor wants you to describe a drop of water as seen under a microscope, it is best to describe as accurately and objectively as possible, leaving your feelings out of it.) But when you are on your own, remember that, important as *accuracy of detail* is, just as crucial is proper *selection of detail*. You cannot describe everything about your subject, nor should you wish to. For many details, perhaps even obvious ones, may be irrelevant to the dominant impression you wish to convey. If you were describing Albert Einstein, his height and weight would probably not be mentioned. On the other hand, a description of Abraham Lincoln might very well employ vivid physical details — the long loose frame, the huge floppy hands, the intense eyes — as outward manifestations of his inner personality. Surely the fact that Lincoln wore formal clothing uncomfortably is revealing of the man. Or what was the significance of Einstein's wild long hair? Was he setting a fashion trend for hippies, was he so modest that careful grooming seemed affectatious, was he so busy that haircuts were a waste of time? The details you select and the way in which you describe them should imply answers to such questions and thus convey a coherent impression of the subject.

The suggestions made in the introduction to the preceding section on proper word choice for personal example apply as well to description; you should review those pages before attempting to write a description. But a few other suggestions need to be added here. Be sure to evaluate the relevance of descriptive details before you include them. Abraham Lincoln may have had a prominent mole on his cheek, but how does that information contribute to the impression you wish to convey? Will a description of poison ivy's root system be useful in avoiding the itch? If not, leave it out.

One danger in writing description is the temptation to control the reader's attitude by using strings of interpretive adjectives — adjectives which really tell how you feel rather than what the subject looked like. "He was quite impressive" or "It was a really beautiful day" tell us little. Was it warm and sunny, or was there a fresh snowfall? Was it still snowing, or had the sun come out? Such details are what the reader needs to know.

Not only are readers quite capable of inferring the effect you want —
provided you supply the right details — but their impression will be much
deeper if you let them draw the conclusion themselves. Cantankerous
creatures that they are, readers have a natural resistance to being *told* how
to feel, but a pliant willingness to feel anything you want them to if you
simply provide the relevant details:

> For all the history of grief,
> An empty doorway and a maple leaf.

Let us go back to that harmless drop of water one more time. Suppose
you had written for the biology professor an objective account of what
you had seen under the microscope; but then you wanted to convey to
a friend your repulsion at the sight of so many "animals" in your drinking
water. If you wrote something like this:

It was just ghastly; I can't tell you how ill the sight of that horrible water drop
made me,

you would neither be telling him what you saw nor making him feel what
you felt. He would only understand that *you* felt revulsion. But if you left
out the "ghastly" and the "horrible," you could describe with vivid details
which would re-create your feeling. A beginning of this sort might do:

Although it was a drop of ordinary tap water — drinking water — under the microscope it came alive. Great green eels squirmed and slithered through it. Purple
creatures like tadpoles, all head and tail, thrashed and churned blindly, colliding
with other more sluggish monsters. A few blobs without tails for propulsion
bobbed in the wake, expanding and contracting like lungs. . . .

Finally, you should remember that to describe what you have experienced, all the senses should be appealed to which were involved in your
original experience, not just the sense of sight which inexperienced writers
rely on almost exclusively. For the qualities perceived by sight, such as
color, shape, size, and movement, are probably not the only "essential"
characteristics of a person or a landscape. It might be possible, in fact,
to write a vivid description — say of a wharf on a pitch black night —
without once appealing to the sense of sight. Sounds would be important:
the water lapping, unseen gulls screeching, the rubbing of a boat against
the dock. And the sense of touch: the night breeze, the chill moisture
in the air, the spongy give of old boards underfoot. Perhaps even taste
and smell: the odor of fish, the slight salt taste on the lips. For most
descriptions, probably you will rely mainly on the sense of sight, but do
not neglect the others; they can bring to life a "photographic" description.
    The best way to organize materials for description depends both
on what is being described and the impression of it you wish to convey.
In describing a person, you might want to go from a photographic im-

pression — physical features, clothing — to characterizing movements, to deeds and statements which reveal the inner person. In describing a scene, you might move like a movie camera from left to right, or from a long-range view to a closeup, or from the outside (of a building, for instance) to the inside. Or your purpose might better be served by proceeding from a broad view — snow-capped mountains and sparkling streams — to sharper details — hot dog wrappers, broken beer bottles, and the rusted car fender on the sand bar. But whatever method of organization you decide on, stick with it. The rapid alternation of long shot and zoom, or flashes of the past stuck into the present, may be all right for experimental movies, but they are difficult to handle in written description.

Miss Abbott

Willie Morris

Willie Morris was born in Yazoo City, Mississippi, in 1934. He has been editor of the Texas Observer *and from 1967 to 1971 was editor-in-chief of* Harper's Magazine. *His first book,* North Toward Home, *won the Houghton Mifflin Library Fellowship in 1967. The following sketch is taken from that autobiographical account.*

Terror lurked for me in that school. The name *Miss Abbott* brings back long 1
dreary afternoons, weary recitations, secret rage, and wounded bafflement over my own unexpected failure. She was my fourth-grade teacher; I was nine, and for the first time my grades were erratic and my conduct report questionable. My own mother, who had pushed me onward as the nicest and brightest boy in the county, predicted I would never work out, and began blaming the social effects of Radical Reconstruction, always an ominous sign.

Miss Abbott had a pink nose and came from a small town in South 2
Mississippi. She pronounced words like "night," "bright" and "sight" with the "i's" prolonged and nasal, a sure sign of hill-country origins. The only book she read through and through, she told us, was the Bible, and you lived to believe her, and to rue the day she got hold of that book. I myself had my own private relationship with God, which embraced the good old hymns and quiet mumbled prayers and holy vengeance when it was really deserved, and in that town and at that age you took God so much for granted that you knew he was keeping a separate ledger on you simply as a matter of course. But Miss Abbott's religion was Christianity by fear and by rote — so tenacious it got you by the extremities and never let go; it was a thing of interminable monologues, crazed soliloquies; she wanted you to believe she herself was in radio contact with the Deity, and had hung the moon for Him on day number six. When she talked about the time she had been saved, a moist glint began creeping into her eyes, which invariably meant the sermon was on its way. She learned to play a little plastic flute, the kind you could get in Woolworth's for a quarter, and she would play us rousing hymns and Christian marches, heedless of the saliva trickling down that instrument onto the floor. After the music she would preach us on sin and redemption, there being more of the former than the latter, or what the Old Testament said

about niggers or Japs, or why we would all end up in hell if God caught us in a backfire. She would not drink Coca-Colas, she said, because of their alcoholic content. Sometimes she would lapse into a sweet, unexpected silence, and gaze out the nearest window for endless minutes. Her features would be bathed in gentle peace. Then I knew Miss Abbott was praying to herself.

Twice a day, in the morning when the class convened, and in the afternoon after lunch, she would call on each of us to pray. We would all begin by blessing our soldiers and then ripping into the Germans and the Japs. Once Bo, from Graball Hill, began his prayer by saying, "Dear Lord, thank you for the bombs that ain't fallin' on us," and then stopped. "What's wrong?" the teacher asked, and Bo said, "I just can't think of nuthin' else to say." The worst tortures were the Bible verses. Two hours each morning she had us recite the verses she had assigned us to learn by heart; when we forgot a verse, she would rap our palm with a twelve-inch ruler. Then out would come that flute again, and if she caught you drowsing, while she piped away on "Onward Christian Soldiers," or scratching at your weary tail, she would go to her "conduct book," and with a slight little flourish, write down a "5."

I made the mistake of correcting her one day, during one of the rare intervals in which we were doing schoolwork. The capital of Missouri, she said, was St. Louis. I held up my hand.

"What is it, Willie?"

"Miss Abbott, the capital of Missouri is Jefferson City."

"No, it's St. Louis."

"I bet it's Jefferson City," and then immediately regretted it, because of the scriptural attitude on gambling.

"Kay King," she snapped, "look in the book and show him it's St. Louis."

The little girl looked in the book and turned red. "Well," she said, "it says here Jefferson City," but obsequiously, like everyone in that ill-fated class, she added, "But Miss Abbott ought to — "

"We'll see," Miss Abbott snapped, and changed the subject. Later, during "silent study," I caught her glowering at me. Why couldn't those people in Missouri have settled on St. Louis?

At noon recess that spring, while the teacher sat on the grass with a group of fawning little girls around her, fetching things for her and scratching her back when it itched, giving her little compliments and practicing their Bible verses, holding her hand and looking for four-leaf clovers to put behind her red ears, we were playing softball nearby. Honest Ed Upton hoisted a lazy foul that went high into the air behind third base; from shortstop I watched its slow descent with interest, with an almost fanatic regard, as it drifted earthward and smacked Miss Abbott on the head. She sprawled on the ground, with a moo like a milk cow's — out cold. *Oh joy of joys!* The other teachers picked her up and carried her away in a car. In our room later, supervised by the principal, all the little girls cried — silent little bawls — and even Honest Ed Upton shed tears. The boys scratched their heads and fiddled with pencils; such was the tyranny in that room, they dared not look into one another's eyes. Except Bo — he caught a glance of mine and puckered his lips, and before long a penciled note came over from him — "i wich the old bich got hit with a hardbal insted." I prayed that she would die.

But back she returned, risen on the third day, and on a Friday afternoon, 13 when she had stepped out of the room, I made a spitball and threw it two rows over at Kay King. *"William!"* The sound of Miss Abbott's voice sent terror to my soul. Each afternoon during that incomparable spring I had to "stay in" — two hours a day for six weeks, working long division. Miss Abbott would sit at her desk, reading the Bible or *Reader's Digest*, while the shadows got longer and the sound of boys' voices wafted in through the open window. And when that year ended, with the C on my report card in math, I had crossed, swum, waded the Sea of Galilee, and joyously entered the city limits of old Jerusalem.

SUBJECT QUESTIONS

1. Morris provides only two minor details about Miss Abbott's physical appearance. Since these hardly give a photographic impression of Miss Abbott (we do not even know if she is thin or plump, rawboned or petite), what justification is there for their inclusion?

2. Which aspect of Miss Abbott seems to be the "essential" one? Are the details conveying this impression more vivid, more numerous, or both?

3. Can you judge by the essay any lasting effects a teacher like Miss Abbott would have on her students? Consider Morris's implied attitude toward religion and mathematics, for instance. Does there seem to be a difference between the effects on the boys and on the girls in the class?

4. What does the argument over the capital of Missouri reveal about Miss Abbott? Does this impression fit with the description of her brand of religion in paragraph 2?

5. Does Morris give enough information for the reader to form a coherent (if incomplete) impression of Miss Abbott? Did you feel that certain other information should have been included?

STRUCTURE QUESTIONS

1. Which descriptive details about Miss Abbott do you recall most vividly? Is your recollection due more to their concreteness or to something unusual about them?

2. The opening paragraph contains a considerable number of "interpretive" adjectives — *dreary, weary,* and *ominous* being the most obvious. Do

you find these objectionable in the context? How frequently does Morris resort to such words in the remainder of the essay?

3. Clearly, Morris has tried to be selective as well as accurate in his use of detail. Do the details chosen seem adequate and appropriate to his purpose?

4. Note that some of the most telling details in this description seem at first glance matter-of-fact and almost irrelevant — for instance, "reading the Bible or *Reader's Digest,*" or "heedless of the saliva trickling down that instrument onto the floor." Discuss the qualities that make a descriptive detail effective.

5. What principle of organization directs the order in which descriptive details and characterizing incidents are included?

The Mosquito
Sally Carrighar

Sally Carrighar achieved instant fame with the publication of her first book,
One Day on Beetle Rock *(1944). In 1946, she published* One Day at Teton
Marsh, *like her first book a series of descriptions of one day in the lives
of the fauna of a small locality. In the 1950's, Mrs. Carrighar lived in Alaska,
where she published* Icebound Summer, *which topped the bestseller lists.
Her most recent book is* Wild Heritage. *With the recent interest in matters
ecological, Mrs. Carrighar's books are once again being widely read, and
all are now available in paperback. A native of Cleveland now living in a
small town in New Jersey, Mrs. Carrighar received from her father an early
love of nature. She combines this love with detailed scientific knowledge
and imaginative insight into the constant struggle for survival in the wilderness. She has twice received Guggenheim Fellowships to pursue her investigations. The following passage on the mosquito is taken from* One Day
at Teton Marsh.

In the two days since her latest molt, the Mosquito had wanted desperately   1
to be ignored. Her life had reached some kind of climax. She had molted four
times during the few weeks since she cut her way out of her eggshell. The
first three molts she had emerged in about the same shape, only larger — a
small gray larva torso, very lively, with a hairy body, a black head, and a
tail from which a breathing tube branched off. She still felt like the same
Mosquito after the fourth molt, for she had the same nerves, but she was a
different form now, heavy at the top, with a flattened abdomen curled under.
Odd new structures, packed around her like an inner coat, had begun to grow.
It seemed that her skin would burst at once, it felt so full.

In other ways her life had changed. Until two days ago the satisfactory   2
thing had been to eat. Sometimes she hung at the surface, caught on the film
by the tip of her breathing tube. She was upside-down but whirling the brushes
on her face to send a stream of tinier animals and plants into her mouth. The
motion of the brushes was so vigorous that it moved her over the top of the
cove. At other times she fed on the pond floor, still with her tail-end up as
she bit off specks of the ooze or brushed them in. In either place she had
been an energetic little body, seldom resting.

Food meant nothing to her in her present stage. This was a time to be   3
quietly secret: strange for one who had been so active, yet she did as her
new needs were directing.

Leaning passively against the floating twig, she could look about. The   4
eyes she had had as a larva could distinguish only light and movement. The
new, more complex eyes she was developing may have shown her shapes — and
redness. See the brilliant tongue of the garter snake that hangs so close above
her from the willow. See the spinning bloodworm. See — oh, *see* — the scarlet
on the throat of the trout. If he sees *her*, she never will escape to the air
above.

The Mosquito waited, giving her energy to the transformation taking   5
place inside her. But during the afternoon her peace came suddenly to an
end. Ripples swelled across the cove. And now she sinks in a swirling vortex
as a webbed foot pushes down above her.

The pelican was wading through her cove. The silt he stirred up clogged   6
the gills of some of the underwater creatures, killing them. The Mosquito pupa
flipped about, erratically darting, as she tried to find a refuge.

Her final surging washed her in among the willow stalks. The snake was   7
gone. And no breeze entered the close-grown willow. The water of the miniature lagoon was just what water should be — quiet wetness in which to lie
and grow. Shadows stained it to a darkness the Mosquito matched; no enemy
discovered her. But if she felt that she could stay, she was mistaken.

Her bounding had strained her fragile envelope of pupal skin. No sooner   8
was the water leveled than the skin split down her back. Ready or not, she
must begin her life in the air.

Her abdomen stretched back along the surface, and her head and chest   9
came out of the split, for the first time into the world above the pond. She
took a great breath, filling the air-tubes meshed through her insect body. It
swelled her out, and her skin more widely opened. Legs flexible as hairs
unwound from around her shoulders. The first pair pulled themselves free,
stiffening at once. Their folds unbent.

With a look of slow, experimental wonder the Mosquito laid one foot   10
on the water. She put the other down. A middle pair of legs came out and
lowered, and a hind pair. On her sides had been two flattened sacs, and from
them now she pulled out — wings! Up from their veins and edges when they
dried would stand exquisite iridescent fringes. From beneath her chest a beak
swung forward; and her abdomen slid from its outworn sheath. She found
a slippery stand on the surface, rested on her feet, and waited. She was a
real Mosquito now, though very pale and still too soft.

If the pelican had come plunging back, she would have drowned. The   11
least breeze, even ripples caused by a jumping trout, would have tipped her
over. She seemed too delicate for a world so hazardous and rough. But none
of the violent things that could have happened did.

One by one she held her feet in the air to dry. When they had hardened,   12
she dared to take a few steps on the film. She reached a willow stem and
lifted a foot against it. The foot stuck; she had claws! She climbed the stalk
a short way, stopping with her claws caught into the bark. Never in the water
had she felt a thing so solid. Her body had touched the plants and the pond
floor, but she had had no way to grip them.

She stayed on the stem until her tissues stiffened and her color changed   13
to brown. But her eyes were nearly blinded by the shine here. As the sun
went down, the pond became more glaring. The floating bur-reeds held the
dazzle on their flat wet blades, and the water-lily pads were discs of light.

Hungry dragonflies were hawking up and down the shore. Their wings   14
were brittle-bright and rattled as they beat. Instinct may have warned the
Mosquito of new dangers in the dry-land world; she may have felt uneasy
at the dragons' clatter. Or possibly her own wings simply opened and began
to whir when they were firm.

Their fanning swung her off the stalk. She did not move across the air,   15
as the dragons did, but up and down as she had bounded from the bottom
to the top of the pond. Gradually she flitted up through the willow, higher
with each wavering vibration. But she found no film above the air to which
she could attach herself and float, as she had clung to the water's film.

She fluttered down, away from the shore and over a water-meadow.   16
The sunshine drained away, and she flew in the dusk more confidently. Ahead
was a cluster of gleaming waxen drops, snowberries, obviously juicy. Some
new impulse made her stop.

She alighted on a berry and pointed her beak to its skin. The beak had   17
an outer sheath, which was elastic. She pushed it up and down. Within the
sheath were four long blades with saw-toothed points, and a slim tongue.
Several times she straightened the sheath and pulled it back along the blades.
Those inside tools could fit together to form a tube. She thrust them into the
berry. They were still too soft to do much cutting, but the berry skin was
tender. They worked in far enough to let her pump out juice. It did not go
to her stomach but to sacs behind her throat. She would keep her stomach
empty till her hardened beak could pierce some firmer substance, from which
it would drain a different, richer nourishment — what?

A chill was striking through the air, a threat to small things like mosqui-   18
toes. She lifted from the berry, hovered till she found a sheltered nook beneath
the drooping head of a thistle. Moonlight spread across the meadow, silvering
the night, creating a world congenial to an insect nearly as unsubstantial. Bats
would be skimming prey, but dragonflies and insect-eating birds would not
be out. This was a mosquito's time — but not her weather.

Perhaps she was the last mosquito to emerge from the pond this season.   19
There never were many at this marsh. Fish were too numerous; they caught
the young before they left the water. Most of those who did escape the fish

had come out earlier. The Mosquito had seen no others in her brief time in the air.

In the morning, sunlight quickly warmed the meadow. She stayed in the thistle then because of the brightness and the breeze. Around her she sensed a multitude of new strange things. The Leopard Frog was sunning himself beside a stone. He had a look of life. She was not one of those mosquitoes who would like a frog's blood, but he evidently had possibilities that no stone had. The Varying Hare was nosing over a clover patch. At a sound the tall ears rose, high as the thistle-head. The ears would be a tubelike shelter, and had some other meaning, not yet understood.

Even nearer than the Frog or Hare were creatures more important to the young Mosquito. In the grass below the thistle lay a dried fur foot; for half the summer it had lain there. On this autumn day six male mosquitoes huddled under it. They did not know of her, nor she of them. Instinct would send them out to seek each other only in the dusk. These days the temperature went down with the sun, however, and they could not risk the cold.

But sometimes nature's great events bring benefits to the smallest creatures. The recent winds had been forerunners of the equinoctial storm. That vast disturbance reached the marsh soon after noon. Ahead of it dense layers of clouds rolled over the sky, so darkening the valley that any mosquito might mistake the twilight of the storm for the twilight of the day. And yet the noon warmth lingered on the quickly shadowed earth.

The male mosquitoes were deceived. They left their nook and flew above the willow. Moved by a last unlikely hope, they formed themselves into a little swarm. Six only, not a hundred or more, they whirled and swung together on the chance that female eyes would find them, and females hear the whine of their song. But how could so few send a call throughout the marsh?

One female heard it. She left the thistle, like a bit of the down herself, and with her airy, tossing flight rose through the twig-ends to the top of the tree.

She alighted on the highest leaf. The males have sensed her presence. Frenzied, they will drive their wings to their utmost speed. Their summons has become a twang. They have gathered in a closer living cloud, that sways above the tree. How can the female not be stirred by such a desperate dance?

She rose from the leaf, hung over it; then darted to the swarm. The six males closed around her. The boldest clutched her, and the pair fell, lightly tumbling, to the ground. In the grass below the tree they clung together, holding a long embrace for creatures so fine-spun and slight. They separated, the male with his destiny completed, the female with hers just begun.

In a drastic climate like that of Jackson Hole, instinct must be answered with a quick obedience; the time may be so short, the opportunities so few.

Swiftly the young Mosquito gave herself to a new obsession. She must find a certain kind of nourishment, needed to mature her eggs. Male mosquitoes live on the juice of plants, and so could she, but her eggs would develop best on a different sort of food.

All the scents around her suddenly became engrossing. To smell them, her antennae swung in one direction and another. They found the odor of the Frog's skin, of the snail shells left by a muskrat; found the clammy fragrance of the daisies, and many others, but not yet the one that will attract her.   29

Then — a wave of moose scent from the pond! The Mosquito flew out toward it, finally to the bay where two grown moose and a calf were resting in the shallows. The large bull was asleep. His fleshy nose, his muffle, stretched along the top of the pond.   30

The Mosquito came down on it. At once her beak began to work. She inserted the stylets in the short fur, to the flesh. With the blades held firmly in the sheath-end, she was sawing. Soon the blades were through the skin. On in they cut. The Mosquito lined her mouth-parts into a tube and started a pumping in her throat. A steady flow of the Moose's rich blood drained into her stomach.   31

Her saliva entered the Moose's tissues. Possibly it kept the blood from clotting; whatever its use, however, it stung the Moose's nerves. He tossed his head and dropped it into the water. The Mosquito could have drowned. But, startled by the movement, she withdrew her beak in time. She fluttered off as the muffle plunged below the surface.   32

She hovered before the bull Moose, waiting to take another drink of blood. If the marsh had been a world planned for mosquitoes, she might have spent the afternoon on the muffle. But the marsh was a home for many creatures — also for this dragonfly who sweeps out from the shore.   33

The Mosquito had no chance to dodge. The other did not give her time. Flying with her legs held forward, basketlike, the dragonfly surrounded the Mosquito with them. The pond, now quiet, mirrored that embrace, the quick uptilting of the dragon's body, brilliant blue and, as she flew away with her captured prey, the leveling of her shiny wings.   34

SUBJECT QUESTIONS

1. Does Mrs. Carrighar destroy credibility by "humanizing" the mosquito, or does the "human interest" increase the reader's interest? How would *you* make a mosquito interesting?
2. Does the physical description allow you to form a clear picture of how a mosquito is put together? How much do you learn about mosquitoes from this description?
3. Do you find the physical description or the description of the mosquito's life cycle more interesting? On which does Carrighar devote more attention?

STRUCTURE QUESTIONS

1. Why do you think the author has chosen to cast her description in the form of a chronological narrative? What advantages does this form give her?
2. Mrs. Carrighar has chosen to end the mosquito's life before it could complete its cycle by laying eggs. Should this sudden ending have been made more dramatic, more "tragic"? What is implied by the quick and matter-of-fact tone of this ending?
3. Certainly a mosquito may react strongly to outside stimuli; whether it has anything like "human emotions," however, may be doubted. How often, if at all, does Carrighar resort to interpretive words that imply human emotion? If you find any such words, do they damage the description?
4. At one point (paragraph 25), the verbs suddenly shift from past to present tense. What effect is achieved by this shift?
5. Once the mosquito has emerged into the air, Carrighar wants to provide the reader with a description of this new environment, but she needs to limit that description to what the mosquito itself can sense. Does she keep within this limitation? Does the limitation provide the reader with an adequate picture?
6. Locate the points at which the author departs from the "mosquito's-eye view." Do these breaks in point of view damage the essay? Do they seem necessary? (That is, are there things the reader needs to know that the mosquito could not know?)

The Turtle

John Steinbeck

John Steinbeck (1902–1968) attended Stanford for one year, in 1919, then dropped out and became a reporter. His first novel, Cup of Gold, *was published in 1929. During World War II, Steinbeck was an overseas war correspondent. He won the Pulitzer Prize (1940), the Nobel Prize for Litera-ture (1962), and the President's Freedom Medal (1964). Among his many best-sellers were* Tortilla Flat *(1935),* Of Mice and Men *(1937),* Cannery Row *(1945), and* East of Eden *(1952). The description of the turtle that follows is from an early chapter of his most famous novel,* The Grapes of Wrath *(1939). Steinbeck uses the painful progress of the turtle as an allegory of the struggle for survival, which is the theme of the novel.*

The concrete highway was edged with a mat of tangled, broken, dry grass, and the grass heads were heavy with oat beards to catch on a dog's coat, and foxtails to tangle in a horse's fetlocks, and clover burrs to fasten in sheep's wool; sleeping life waiting to be spread and dispersed, every seed armed with an appliance of dispersal, twisting darts and parachutes for the wind, little spears and balls of tiny thorns, and all waiting for animals and for the wind, for a man's trouser cuff or the hem of a woman's skirt, all passive but armed with appliances of activity, still, but each possessed of the anlage of movement. 1

The sun lay on the grass and warmed it, and in the shade under the grass the insects moved, ants and ant lions to set traps for them, grasshoppers to jump into the air and flick their yellow wings for a second, sow bugs like little armadillos, plodding restlessly on many tender feet. And over the grass at the roadside a land turtle crawled, turning aside for nothing, dragging his high-domed shell over the grass. His hard legs and yellow-nailed feet threshed slowly through the grass, not really walking, but boosting and dragging his shell along. The barley beards slid off his shell, and the clover burrs fell on him and rolled to the ground. His horny beak was partly open, and his fierce, humorous eyes, under brows like fingernails, stared straight ahead. He came over the grass leaving a beaten trail behind him, and the hill, which was the highway embankment, reared up ahead of him. For a moment he stopped, his head held high. He blinked and looked up and down. At last he started 2 to climb the embankment. Front clawed feet reached forward but did not touch. The hind feet kicked his shell along, and it scraped on the grass, and on the gravel. As the embankment grew steeper and steeper, the more frantic were the efforts of the land turtle. Pushing hind legs strained and slipped, boosting the shell along, and the horny head protruded as far as the neck could stretch. Little by little the shell slid up the embankment until at last a parapet cut straight across its line of march, the shoulder of the road, a concrete wall four inches high. As though they worked independently the hind legs pushed the shell against the wall. The head upraised and peered over the wall to the broad smooth plain of cement. Now the hands, braced on top of the wall, strained and lifted, and the shell came slowly up and rested its front end on the wall. For a moment the turtle rested. A red ant ran into the shell, into the soft skin inside the shell, and suddenly head and legs snapped in, and the armored tail clamped in sideways. The red ant was crushed between body and legs. And one head of wild oats was clamped into the shell by a front leg. For a long moment the turtle lay still, and then the neck crept out and the old humorous frowning eyes looked about and the legs and tail came out. The back legs went to work, straining like elephant legs, and the shell tipped to an angle so that the front legs could not reach the level cement plain. But higher and higher the hind legs boosted it, until at last the center of balance was reached, the front tipped down, the front legs scratched at the pavement, and it was up. But the head of wild oats was held by its stem around the front legs.

Now the going was easy, and all the legs worked, and the shell boosted   3
along, waggling from side to side. A sedan driven by a forty-year-old woman approached. She saw the turtle and swung to the right, off the highway, the wheels screamed and a cloud of dust boiled up. Two wheels lifted for a moment and then settled. The car skidded back onto the road, and went on, but more slowly. The turtle had jerked into its shell, but now it hurried on, for the highway was burning hot.

And now a light truck approached, and as it came near the driver saw   4
the turtle and swerved to hit it. His front wheel struck the edge of the shell, flipped the turtle like a tiddly-wink, spun it like a coin, and rolled it off the highway. The truck went back to its course along the right side. Lying on its back, the turtle was tight in its shell for a long time. But at last its legs waved in the air, reaching for something to pull it over. Its front foot caught a piece of quartz and little by little the shell pulled over and flopped upright. The wild oat head fell out and three of the spearhead seeds stuck in the ground. And as the turtle crawled on down the embankment, its shell dragged dirt over the seeds. The turtle entered a dust road and jerked itself along, drawing a wavy shallow trench in the dust with its shell. The old humorous eyes looked ahead, and the horny beak opened a little. His yellow toe nails slipped a fraction in the dust.

SUBJECT QUESTIONS

1. What justifications can you see for Steinbeck's including this description in *The Grapes of Wrath*, a novel not about turtles but about the migration of the Joad family from the dust bowl of Oklahoma to California and of their struggle for existence?
2. Are there significant points of comparison between Sally Carrighar's mosquito and Steinbeck's turtle?
3. Do you think Steinbeck is ultimately more interested in the turtle or in the wild oat seeds? What difference does your decision make to an interpretation of the passage?
4. Steinbeck has added to his nature description two very different kinds of motorists. Are these drivers atypical, or do they represent a significant proportion of all drivers? Why has Steinbeck bothered to include them?
5. Would you say that Steinbeck's attitude toward the natural processes he describes is basically optimistic, pessimistic, or simply mechanistic?

STRUCTURE QUESTIONS

1. Clearly Steinbeck has not tried to "psychoanalyze" the turtle. Would you say that the descriptive passages are also from the point of view of a detached observer, or does Steinbeck try to see what the turtle might see? (Consider, for instance, the passage in the middle of paragraph 2 describing the turtle's getting up onto the highway.)
2. Most writers of description overuse linking verbs and depend for descriptive force on their adjectives. ("The study desk was old and wobbly; its surface was uneven from the carved initials of two generations of students.") Steinbeck's first paragraph also uses two linking verbs, "was" and "were"; how many do you find thereafter? Consider how Steinbeck uses verbs to get action and drama into a virtually static scene.
3. Near the end of paragraph 2, Steinbeck shifts from active to passive voice in three sentences: "The red ant was crushed between body and legs. And one head of wild oats was clamped into the shell by a front leg. . . . But the head of wild oats was held by its stem around the front legs." Turn the sentences into active voice to see why Steinbeck made this shift.
4. Like all descriptions, Steinbeck's must be selective. Do his descriptive details create a consistent impression, an "essence" he wants to convey?
5. Which details best convey a sense of authenticity? Do they seem to be gratuitous details, or integral to the description? (Consider the age of the woman driver, for instance.)
6. One phrase is repeated like a refrain in the passage — reference to the old turtle's "humorous eyes." The phrase is ambiguous: the eyes might be funny to look at, the turtle might have a sense of humor, or in the archaic sense of "humour," his eyes could be dripping matter. Why do you think Steinbeck uses, and repeats, the phrase?

The Way to Rainy Mountain

N. Scott Momaday

N. Scott Momaday (born in 1934) is professor of comparative literature at the University of California, Berkeley, a poet, and winner of the 1969 Pulitzer Prize for his novel House Made of Dawn. He has also published books on American poetry and on Indian folktales. "The Way to Rainy Mountain" is interesting as description because Momaday attempts to characterize his grandmother by concentrating on her background and environment rather than on her physical characteristics.

A single knoll rises out of the plain in Oklahoma, north and west of the Wichita   1
range. For my people, the Kiowas, it is an old landmark, and they gave it the name Rainy Mountain. The hardest weather in the world is there. Winter brings blizzards, hot tornadic winds arise in the spring, and in summer the prairie is an anvil's edge. The grass turns brittle and brown, and it cracks beneath your feet. There are green belts along the rivers and creeks, linear groves of hickory and pecan, willow and witch hazel. At a distance in July or August the steaming foliage seems almost to writhe in fire. Great green and yellow grasshoppers are everywhere in the tall grass, popping up like corn to sting the flesh, and tortoises crawl about on the red earth, going nowhere in the plenty of time. Loneliness is an aspect of the land. All things in the plain are isolate; there is no confusion of objects in the eye, but *one* hill or *one* tree or *one* man. To look upon that landscape in the early morning, with the sun at your back, is to lose the sense of proportion. Your imagination comes to life, and this, you think, is where Creation was begun.

I returned to Rainy Mountain in July. My grandmother had died in the spring,   2
and I wanted to be at her grave. She had lived to be very old and at last infirm. Her only living daughter was with her when she died, and I was told that in death her face was that of a child.

I like to think of her as a child. When she was born, the Kiowas were   3
living the last great moment of their history. For more than a hundred years they had controlled the open range from the Smoky Hill River to the Red, from the headwaters of the Canadian to the fork of the Arkansas and Cimarron. In alliance with the Comanches, they had ruled the whole of the Southern

Reprinted by permission of the author from *The Reporter* (January 26, 1967), pp. 41–43.

Plains. War was their sacred business, and they were the finest horsemen the world has ever known. But warfare for the Kiowas was pre-eminently a matter of disposition rather than of survival, and they never understood the grim, unrelenting advance of the U.S. Cavalry. When at last, divided and ill provisioned, they were driven onto the Staked Plains in the cold of autumn, they fell into panic. In Palo Duro Canyon they abandoned their crucial stores to pillage and had nothing then but their lives. In order to save themselves, they surrendered to the soldiers at Fort Sill and were imprisoned in the old stone corral that now stands as a military museum. My grandmother was spared the humiliation of those high gray walls by eight or ten years, but she must have known from birth the affliction of defeat, the dark brooding of old warriors.

Her name was Aho, and she belonged to the last culture to evolve in   4
North America. Her forebears came down from the high country in western Montana nearly three centuries ago. They were a mountain people, a mysterious tribe of hunters whose language has never been classified in any major group. In the late seventeenth century they began a long migration to the south and east. It was a journey toward the dawn, and it led to a golden age. Along the way the Kiowas were befriended by the Crows, who gave them the culture and religion of the Plains. They acquired horses, and their ancient nomadic spirit was suddenly free of the ground. They acquired Tai-me, the sacred sun-dance doll, from that moment the object and symbol of their worship, and so shared in the divinity of the sun. Not least, they acquired the sense of destiny, therefore courage and pride. When they entered upon the Southern Plains they had been transformed. No longer were they slaves to the simple necessity of survival; they were a lordly and dangerous society of fighters and thieves, hunters and priests of the sun. According to their origin myth, they entered the world through a hollow log. From one point of view, their migration was the fruit of an old prophecy, for indeed they emerged from a sunless world.

Though my grandmother lived out her long life in the shadow of Rainy   5
Mountain, the immense landscape of the continental interior lay like memory in her blood. She could tell of the Crows, whom she had never seen, and of the Black Hills, where she had never been. I wanted to see in reality what she had seen more perfectly in the mind's eye, and drove fifteen hundred miles to begin my pilgrimage.

A dark mist lay over the Black Hills, and the land was like iron. At   6
the top of a ridge I caught sight of Devil's Tower upthrust against the gray sky as if in the birth of time the core of the earth had broken through its crust and the motion of the world was begun. There are things in nature that engender an awful quiet in the heart of man; Devil's Tower is one of them.

Two centuries ago, because of their need to explain it, the Kiowas made a legend at the base of the rock. My grandmother said:

"Eight children were there at play, seven sisters and their brother. Sud-   7 denly the boy was struck dumb; he trembled and began to run upon his hands and feet. His fingers became claws, and his body was covered with fur. There was a bear where the boy had been. The sisters were terrified; they ran, and the bear after them. They came to the stump of a great tree, and the tree spoke to them. It bade them climb upon it, and as they did so, it began to rise into the air. The bear came to kill them, but they were just beyond its reach. It reared against the tree and scored the bark all around with its claws. The seven sisters were borne into the sky, and they became the stars of the Big Dipper." From that moment, and so long as the legend lives, the Kiowas have kinsmen in the night sky. Whatever they were in the mountains, they could be no more. However tenuous their well-being, however much they had suffered and would suffer again, they had found a way out of the wilderness.

My grandmother had a reverence for the sun, a holy regard that now   8 is all but gone out of mankind. There was a wariness in her, and an ancient awe. She was a Christian in her later years, but she had come a long way about, and she never forgot her birthright. As a child she had been to the sun dances; she had taken part in that annual rite, and by it she had learned the restoration of her people in the presence of Tai-me. She was about seven when the last Kiowa sun dance was held in 1887 on the Washita River above Rainy Mountain Creek. The buffalo were gone. In order to consummate the ancient sacrifice — to impale the head of a buffalo bull upon the Tai-me tree — a delegation of old men journeyed into Texas, there to beg and barter for an animal from the Goodnight herd. She was ten when the Kiowas came together for the last time as a living sun-dance culture. They could find no buffalo; they had to hang an old hide from the sacred tree. Before the dance could begin, a company of soldiers rode out from Fort Sill under orders to disperse the tribe. Forbidden without cause the essential act of their faith, having seen the wild herds slaughtered and left to rot upon the ground, the Kiowas backed away forever from the tree. That was July 20, 1890, at the great bend of the Washita. My grandmother was there. Without bitterness, and for as long as she lived, she bore a vision of deicide.

Now that I can have her only in memory, I see my grandmother in the several   9 postures that were peculiar to her: standing at the wood stove on a winter morning and turning meat in a great iron skillet; sitting at the south window, bent above her beadwork, and afterwards, when her vision failed, looking down for a long time into the fold of her hands; going out upon a cane, very slowly as she did when the weight of age came upon her; praying. I remember her most often at prayer. She made long, rambling prayers out of suffering and hope, having seen many things. I was never sure that I had the right to hear, so exclusive were they of all mere custom and company. The last time I saw her she prayed standing by the side of her bed at night, naked to the waist, the light of a kerosene lamp moving upon her dark skin. Her long black hair, always drawn and braided in the day, lay upon her shoulders and against her breasts like a shawl. I do not speak Kiowa, and I never understood her prayers, but there was something inherently sad in the sound, some merest hesitation upon the syllables of sorrow. She began in a high and descending pitch, exhausting her breath to silence; then again and again — and always the same intensity of effort, of something that is, and is not, like urgency in the human voice. Transported so in the dancing light among the shadows of her room, she seemed beyond the reach of time. But that was illusion; I think I knew then that I should not see her again.

Houses are like sentinels in the plain, old keepers of the weather watch.   10 There, in a very little while, wood takes on the appearance of great age. All colors wear soon away in the wind and rain, and then the wood is burned gray and the grain appears and the nails turn red with rust. The window panes are black and opaque; you imagine there is nothing within, and indeed there are many ghosts, bones given up to the land. They stand here and there against the sky, and you approach them for a longer time than you expect. They belong in the distance; it is their domain.

Once there was a lot of sound in my grandmother's house, a lot of coming   11 and going, feasting and talk. The summers there were full of excitement and reunion. The Kiowas are a summer people; they abide the cold and keep to themselves, but when the season turns and the land becomes warm and vital they cannot hold still; an old love of going returns upon them. The aged visitors who came to my grandmother's house when I was a child were made of lean and leather, and they bore themselves upright. They wore great black hats and bright ample shirts that shook in the wind. They rubbed fat upon their hair and wound their braids with strips of colored cloth. Some of them painted their faces and carried the scars of old and cherished enmities. They were an old council of warlords, come to remind and be reminded of who they were. Their wives and daughters served them well. The women might indulge themselves; gossip was at once the mark and compensation of their servitude. They made loud and elaborate talk among themselves, full of jest and gesture, fright and false alarm. They went abroad in fringed and flowered shawls, bright beadwork and German silver. They were at home in the kitchen, and they prepared meals that were banquets.

There were frequent prayer meetings, and nocturnal feasts. When I was   12 a child I played with my cousins outside, where the lamplight fell upon the ground and the singing of the old people rose up around us and carried away into the darkness. There were a lot of good things to eat, a lot of laughter and surprise. And afterwards, when the quiet returned, I lay down with my grandmother and could hear the frogs away by the river and feel the motion of the air.

Now there is a funeral silence in the rooms, the endless wake of some 13 final word. The walls have closed in upon my grandmother's house. When I returned to it in mourning, I saw for the first time in my life how small it was. It was late at night, and there was a white moon, nearly full. I sat for a long time on the stone steps by the kitchen door. From there I could see out across the land; I could see the long row of trees by the creek, the low light upon the rolling plains, and the stars of the Big Dipper. Once I looked at the moon and caught sight of a strange thing. A cricket had perched upon the handrail, only a few inches away. My line of vision was such that the creature filled the moon like a fossil. It had gone there, I thought, to live and die, for there, of all places, was its small definition made whole and eternal. A warm wind rose up and purled like the longing within me.

The next morning, I awoke at dawn and went out on the dirt road to 14 Rainy Mountain. It was already hot, and the grasshoppers began to fill the air. Still, it was early in the morning, and birds sang out of the shadows. The long yellow grass on the mountain shone in the bright light, and a scissortail hied above the land. There, where it ought to be, at the end of a long and legendary way, was my grandmother's grave. She had at last succeeded to that holy ground. Here and there on the dark stones were ancestral names. Looking back once, I saw the mountain and came away.

SUBJECT QUESTIONS

1. The brief history of the Kiowa people is interesting in itself; does it also contribute to a better understanding of Momaday's grandmother?
2. What purpose is served by the contrasting descriptions of the Kiowas' former territories in the misty Black Hills country and the sun-baked plains to which they migrated?
3. How clear a picture do you get of Aho? From what is given, do you see anything physically unusual about her? Is Momaday using her as a "symbol"?
4. What is the "essential characteristic" of Aho that Momaday wants to convey?
5. Does the loud and talkative aspect of Aho in the company of other women seem out of character with the other aspects of her character?
6. Why is the essay called "The Way to Rainy Mountain"? Would "My Grandmother Aho" be more appropriate?

STRUCTURE QUESTIONS

1. What principle of organization controls the order in which materials are presented? Does anything seem to be extraneous? (Consider, for instance, the legend about Devil's Tower and the paragraph on houses as "sentinels in the plain.")

2. Examine one of the more vivid descriptive passages — that of the family reunion, for instance. Would you say that the verbs, the adjectives, or the nouns do most of the work in creating a sense of vividness? Is your answer what you would have expected?

3. Particularly in the passages relating Kiowa history, Momaday employs interpretive adjectives fairly heavily, rather than letting the description indicate whether the Indians were lordly, terrified, or humiliated. Do you see any reason for this use, or would you judge it a flaw in the writing?

4. The reasons for the descriptive details about the Kiowas and about Aho in particular are apparent. But at least half of the details in this article are devoted to the landscape. Can you relate this heavy use of nature description to Momaday's purpose in writing the article?

Knoxville: Summer 1915

James Agee

James Agee (1910–1955), whose brilliant and promising career was cut short by a heart attack at the age of forty-five, was primarily a poet and writer of screenplays. (His African Queen *has become a film classic.) Although his novel,* A Death in the Family, *was not quite finished at his death, it has been called "a near-perfect work of art," and was awarded the Pulitzer Prize in 1958. The editors of the manuscript added the separate piece, "Knoxville: Summer 1915," as a prologue to the novel.*

We are talking now of summer evenings in Knoxville, Tennessee in the time   1
that I lived there so successfully disguised to myself as a child. It was a little
bit mixed sort of block, fairly solidly lower middle class, with one or two
juts apiece on either side of that. The houses corresponded: middle-sized
gracefully fretted wood houses built in the late nineties and early nineteen
hundreds, with small front and side and more spacious back yards, and trees
in the yards, and porches. These were softwooded trees, poplars, tulip trees,
cottonwoods. There were fences around one or two of the houses, but mainly
the yards ran into each other with only now and then a low hedge that wasn't
doing very well. There were few good friends among the grown people, and
they were not poor enough for the other sort of intimate acquaintance, but
everyone nodded and spoke, and even might talk short times, trivially, and
at the two extremes of the general or the particular, and ordinarily nextdoor
neighbors talked quite a bit when they happened to run into each other, and
never paid calls. The men were mostly small businessmen, one or two very
modestly executives, one or two worked with their hands, most of them cleri-
cal, and most of them between thirty and forty-five.

But it is of these evenings, I speak.   2

Supper was at six and was over by half past. There was still daylight,   3
shining softly and with a tarnish, like the lining of a shell; and the carbon
lamps lifted at the corners were on in the light, and the locusts were started,
and the fire flies were out, and a few frogs were flopping in the dewy grass,
by the time the fathers and the children came out. The children ran out first
hell bent and yelling those names by which they were known; then the fathers
sank out leisurely in crossed suspenders, their collars removed and their necks

looking tall and shy. The mothers stayed back in the kitchen washing and drying, putting things away, recrossing their traceless footsteps like the lifetime journeys of bees, measuring out the dry cocoa for breakfast. When they came out they had taken off their aprons and their skirts were dampened and they sat in rockers on their porches quietly.

It is not of the games children played in the evening that I want to speak now, it is of a contemporaneous atmosphere that has little to do with them: that of the fathers of families, each in his space of lawn, his shirt fishlike pale in the unnatural light and his face nearly anonymous, hosing their lawns. The hoses were attached at spigots that stood out of the brick foundations of the houses. The nozzles were variously set but usually so there was a long sweet stream of spray, the nozzle wet in the hand, the water trickling the right forearm and the peeled-back cuff, and the water whishing out a long loose and low-curved cone, and so gentle a sound. First an insane noise of violence in the nozzle, then the still irregular sound of adjustment, then the smoothing into steadiness and a pitch as accurately tuned to the size and style of stream as any violin. So many qualities of sound out of one hose: so many choral differences out of those several hoses that were in earshot. Out of any one hose, the almost dead silence of the release, and the short still arch of the separate big drops, silent as a held breath, and the only noise the flattering noise on leaves and the slapped grass at the fall of each big drop. That, and the intense hiss with the intense stream; that, and that same intensity not growing less but growing more quiet and delicate with the turn of the nozzle, up to that extreme tender whisper when the water was just a wide bell of film. Chiefly, though, the hoses were set much alike, in a compromise between distance and tenderness of spray (and quite surely a sense of art behind this compromise, and a quiet deep joy, too real to recognize itself), and the sounds therefore were pitched much alike; pointed by the snorting start of a new hose; decorated by some man playful with the nozzle; left empty, like God by the sparrow's fall, when any single one of them desists: and all, though near alike, of various pitch; and in this unison. These sweet pale streamings in the light lift out their pallors and their voices all together, mothers hushing their children, the hushing unnaturally prolonged, the men gentle and silent and each snail-like withdrawn into the quietude of what he singly is doing, the urination of huge children stood loosely military against an invisible wall, and gentle happy and peaceful, tasting the mean goodness of their living like the last of their suppers in their mouths; while the locusts carry on this noise of hoses on their much higher and sharper key. The noise of the locust is dry, and it seems not to be rasped or vibrated but urged from him as if through a small orifice by breath that can never give out. Also there is never one locust but an illusion of at least a thousand. The noise of each locust is pitched in some classic locust range out of which none of them varies more than two full tones: and yet you seem to hear each locust discrete from all the rest, and there is a long, slow pulse in their noise, like the scarcely defined arch of a long and high set bridge. They are all around in every tree, so that the noise seems to come from nowhere and everywhere at once, from the whole shell heaven, shivering in your flesh and teasing your eardrums, the boldest of all the sounds of night. And yet it is habitual to summer nights, and is of the great order of noises, like the noises of the sea and of the blood her precocious grandchild, which you realize you are hearing only when you catch yourself listening. Meantime from low in the dark, just outside the swaying horizons of the hoses, conveying always grass in the damp of dew and its strong green-black smear of smell, the regular yet spaced noises of the crickets, each a sweet cold silver noise threenoted, like the slipping each time of three matched links of a small chain.

But the men by now, one by one, have silenced their hoses and drained   5
and coiled them. Now only two, and now only one, is left, and you see only ghostlike shirt with the sleeve garters, and sober mystery of his mild face like the lifted face of large cattle enquiring of your presence in a pitchdark pool of meadow; and now he too is gone; and it has become that time of evening when people sit on their porches, rocking gently and talking gently and watching the street and the standing up into their sphere of possession of the trees, of birds hung havens, hangars. People go by; things go by. A horse, drawing a buggy, breaking his hollow iron music on the asphalt; a loud auto; a quiet auto; people in pairs, not in a hurry, scuffling, switching their weight of aestival body, talking casually, the taste hovering over them of vanilla, strawberry, pasteboard and starched milk, the image upon them of lovers and horsemen, squared with clowns in hueless amber. A street car raising its iron moan; stopping, belling and starting; stertorous; rousing and raising again its iron increasing moan and swimming its gold windows and straw seats on past and past and past, the bleak spark crackling and cursing above it like a small malignant spirit set to dog its tracks; the iron whine rises on rising speed; still risen, faints; halts; the faint stinging bell; rises again, still fainter; fainting, lifting, lifts, faints forgone: forgotten. Now is the night one blue dew.

> Now is the night one blue dew, my father has drained, he has coiled the hose.
> Low on the length of lawns, a frailing of fire who breathes.
> Content, silver, like peeps of light, each cricket makes his comment over and over in the drowned grass.   5
> A cold toad thumpily flounders.
> Within the edges of damp shadows of side yards are hovering children nearly sick with joy of fear, who watch the unguarding of a telephone pole.
> Around white carbon corner lamps bugs of all sizes are lifted elliptic, solar   10 systems. Big hardshells bruise themselves, assailant: he is fallen on his back, legs squiggling.

Parents on porches: rock and rock: From damp strings morning glories:
hang their ancient faces.
The dry and exalted noise of the locusts from all the air at once enchants   15
my eardrums.

On the rough wet grass of the back yard my father and mother have   6
spread quilts. We all lie there, my mother, my father, my uncle, my aunt,
and I too am lying there. First we were sitting up, then one of us lay down,
and then we all lay down, on our stomachs, or on our sides, or on our backs,
and they have kept on talking. They are not talking much, and the talk is
quiet, of nothing in particular, of nothing at all in particular, of nothing at
all. The stars are wide and alive, they seem each like a smile of great sweetness,
and they seem very near. All my people are larger bodies than mine, quiet,
with voices gentle and meaningless like the voices of sleeping birds. One is
an artist, he is living at home. One is a musician, she is living at home. One
is my mother who is good to me. One is my father who is good to me. By
some chance, here they are, all on this earth; and who shall ever tell the sorrow
of being on this earth, lying, on quilts, on the grass, in a summer evening,
among the sounds of the night. May God bless my people, my uncle, my aunt,
my mother, my good father, oh, remember them kindly in their time of
trouble; and in the hour of their taking away.

After a little I am taken in and put to bed. Sleep, soft smiling, draws   7
me unto her: and those receive me, who quietly treat me, as one familiar
and well beloved in that home: but will not, oh, will not, not now, not ever;
but will not ever tell me who I am.

SUBJECT QUESTIONS

1. The first paragraph attempts to characterize Agee's neighborhood as
   "fairly solidly lower middle class." Examine the details Agee uses to make
   this characterization. Are they the right ones?
2. What point is Agee trying to make through this mass of detail? How
   successfully does the author relate himself to his environment?
3. The closely detailed description of water from the hose nozzles, although
   remarkably vivid and realistic, seems to be inserted for its own sake,
   or perhaps only because Agee remembered it. What does it contribute
   either to atmosphere or total meaning?
4. The boy's environment seems peaceful enough, and he assures us that
   he is loved and well treated. Yet at the end he mentions "the sorrow
   of being on this earth" and complains that no one will tell him who he
   is. Does Agee contradict himself here? Is he creating a deliberate paradox?
5. Do you think the last sentence means that Agee's parents *refuse* to tell
   him who he is, or that they *cannot* tell him? Does it make any difference?

STRUCTURE QUESTIONS

1. Some of Agee's sentences are beautifully and correctly constructed; others are in the more turbulent stream-of-consciousness technique, frequently "incorrect" grammatically. Should Agee have mixed two styles in this way? Does one style seem to be more effective than the other? Does the author's point of view shift when the style shifts?
2. Do you see any excuse for the sudden outburst of poetry in the midst of the description? What function does the poem serve?
3. Why does Agee insert into his poem the singularly unpoetic line "A cold toad thumpily flounders"?
4. Agee tries to tie the essay together by returning in the last sentence to the thought expressed in the first sentence — that the author is "disguised" to himself. Is the unity thus achieved artificial, or does the rest of the essay contribute to this theme?
5. What is the dominant impression or "mood" created by the descriptive details? Does Agee ever tell the reader directly what this mood is?
6. After the first paragraph, Agee reinforces his description with numerous similes. Do these in any way alter the effect of the description?

Powerhouse

Eudora Welty

Eudora Welty (born in 1909) was born and still lives in Jackson, Mississippi. As a novelist and short story writer, she has won numerous awards and honors, especially for her novel, The Ponder Heart *(1955). Among her collections of short stories are* A Curtain of Green *(1941),* The Wide Net *(1943), and* The Golden Apples *(1949). Her most recent book is* Losing Battles *(1970). A regionalist, Miss Welty combines homely details of life in Mississippi with strange fantasies and dreamlike occurrences. Katherine Anne Porter said that she exhibits "the waking faculty of daylight reason recollecting and recording the crazy logic of the dream." "Powerhouse" is a good example of that faculty; it also shows Miss Welty's fine ability to establish character through carefully selected descriptive details.*

Powerhouse is playing! 1

He's here on tour from the city — "Powerhouse and His Keyboard" — 2
"Powerhouse and His Tasmanians" — think of the things he calls himself! There's no one in the world like him. You can't tell what he is. "Nigger man"? — he looks more Asiatic, monkey, Jewish, Babylonian, Peruvian, fanatic, devil. He has pale gray eyes, heavy lids, maybe horny like a lizard's, but big glowing eyes when they're open. He has African feet of the greatest size, stomping, both together, on each side of the pedals. He's not coal black — beverage colored — looks like a preacher when his mouth is shut, but then it opens — vast and obscene. And his mouth is going every minute: like a monkey's when it looks for something. Improvising, coming on a light and childish melody — *smooch* — he loves it with his mouth.

Is it possible that he could be this! When you have him there performing 3
for you, that's what you feel. You know people on a stage — and people of a darker race — so likely to be marvelous, frightening.

This is a white dance. Powerhouse is not a show-off like the Harlem 4
boys, not drunk, not crazy — he's in a trance; he's a person of joy, a fanatic. He listens as much as he performs, a look of hideous, powerful rapture on his face. Big arched eyebrows that never stop traveling, like a Jew's — wandering-Jew eyebrows. When he plays he beats down piano and seat and wears them away. He is in motion every moment — what could be more obscene? There he is with his great head, fat stomach, and little round piston legs, and long yellow-sectioned strong big fingers, at rest about the size of bananas.

Of course you know how he sounds — you've heard him on records — but still you need to see him. He's going all the time, like skating around the skating rink or rowing a boat. It makes everybody crowd around, here in this shadowless steel-trussed hall with the rose-like posters of Nelson Eddy and the testimonial for the mind-reading horse in handwriting magnified five hundred times. Then all quietly he lays his finger on a key with the promise and serenity of a sibyl touching the book.

Powerhouse is so monstrous he sends everybody into oblivion. When any group, any performers, come to town, don't people always come out and hover near, leaning inward about them, to learn what it is? What is it? Listen. Remember how it was with the acrobats. Watch them carefully, hear the least word, especially what they say to one another, in another language — don't let them escape you; it's the only time for hallucination, the last time. They can't stay. They'll be somewhere else this time tomorrow.

Powerhouse has as much as possible done by signals. Everybody, laughing as if to hide a weakness, will sooner or later hand him up a written request. Powerhouse reads each one, studying with a secret face: that is the face which looks like a mask — anybody's; there is a moment when he makes a decision. Then a light slides under his eyelids, and he says, "92!" or some combination of figures — never a name. Before a number the band is all frantic, misbehaving, pushing, like children in a schoolroom, and he is the teacher getting silence. His hands over the keys, he says sternly, "You-all ready? You-all ready to do some serious walking?" — waits — then, STAMP. Quiet. STAMP, for the second time. This is absolute. Then a set of rhythmic kicks against the floor to communicate the tempo. Then, O Lord! say the distended eyes from beyond the boundary of the trumpets, Hello and good-bye, and they are all down the first note like a waterfall.

This note marks the end of any known discipline. Powerhouse seems to abandon them all — he himself seems lost — down in the song, yelling up like somebody in a whirlpool — not guiding them — hailing them only. But he knows, really. He cries out, but he must know exactly. "Mercy! . . . What I say! . . . Yeah!" And then drifting, listening — "Where that skin beater?" — wanting drums, and starting up and pouring it out in the greatest delight and brutality. On the sweet pieces such a leer for everybody! He looks down so benevolently upon all our faces and whispers the lyrics to us. And if you could hear him at this moment on "Marie, the Dawn is Breaking"! He's going up the keyboard with a few fingers in some very derogatory triplet-routine, he gets higher and higher, and then he looks over the end of the piano, as if over a cliff. But not in a show-off way — the song makes him do it.

He loves the way they all play, too — all those next to him. The far section of the band is all studious, wearing glasses, every one — they don't count. Only those playing around Powerhouse are the real ones. He has a bass fiddler from Vicksburg, black as pitch, named Valentine, who plays with his eyes shut and talking to himself, very young: Powerhouse has to keep encouraging him. "Go on, go on, give it up, bring it on out there!" When you heard him like that on records, did you know he was really pleading?

He calls Valentine out to take a solo.   9

"What you going to play?" Powerhouse looks out kindly from behind   10
the piano; he opens his mouth and shows his tongue, listening.

Valentine looks down, drawing against his instrument, and says without   11
a lip movement, " 'Honeysuckle Rose.' "

He has a clarinet player named Little Brother, and loves to listen to   12
anything he does. He'll smile and say, "Beautiful!" Little Brother takes a step forward when he plays and stands at the very front, with the whites of his eyes like fishes swimming. Once when he played a low note, Powerhouse muttered in dirty praise, "He went clear downstairs to get that one!"

After a long time, he holds up the number of fingers to tell the band   13
how many choruses still to go — usually five. He keeps his directions down to signals.

It's a bad night outside. It's a white dance, and nobody dances, except   14
a few straggling jitterbugs and two elderly couples. Everybody just stands around the band and watches Powerhouse. Sometimes they steal glances at one another, as if to say, Of course, you know how it is with *them* — Negroes — band leaders — they would play the same way, giving all they've got, for an audience of one.... When somebody, no matter who, gives everything, it makes people feel ashamed for him.

Late at night they play the one waltz they will ever consent to play — by   15
request, "Pagan Love Song." Powerhouse's head rolls and sinks like a weight between his waving shoulders. He groans, and his fingers drag into the keys heavily, holding on to the notes, retrieving. It is a sad song.

"You know what happened to me?" says Powerhouse.   16

Valentine hums a response, dreaming at the bass.   17

"I got a telegram my wife is dead," says Powerhouse, with wandering   18
fingers.

"Uh-huh?"   19

His mouth gathers and forms a barbarous O while his fingers walk up   20
straight, unwillingly, three octaves.

"Gypsy? Why how come her to die, didn't you just phone her up in   21
the night last night long distance?"

"Telegram say — here the words: Your wife is dead." He puts 4/4 over   22
the 3/4.

"Not but four words?" This is the drummer, an unpopular boy named   23
Scoot, a disbelieving maniac.

Powerhouse is shaking his vast cheeks. "What the hell was she trying   24
to do? What was she up to?"

"What name has it got signed, if you got a telegram?" Scoot is spitting   25
away with those wire brushes.

Little Brother, the clarinet player, who cannot now speak, glares and   26
tilts back.

"Uranus Knockwood is the name signed." Powerhouse lifts his eyes open.   27
"Ever heard of him?" A bubble shoots out on his lip like a plate on a counter.

Valentine is beating slowly on with his palm and scratching the strings   28
with his long blue nails. He is fond of a waltz, Powerhouse interrupts him.

"I don't know him. Don't know who he is." Valentine shakes his head   29
with the closed eyes.

"Say it again."   30

"Uranus Knockwood."   31

"That ain't Lenox Avenue."   32

"It ain't Broadway."   33

"Ain't ever seen it wrote out in any print, even for horse racing."   34

"Hell, that's on a star, boy, ain't it?" Crash of the cymbals.   35

"What the hell was she up to?" Powerhouse shudders. "Tell me, tell   36
me, tell me." He makes triplets, and begins a new chorus. He holds three
fingers up.

"You say you got a telegram." This is Valentine, patient and sleepy,   37
beginning again.

Powerhouse is elaborate. "Yas, the time I go out, go way downstairs   38
along a long cor-ri-dor to where they puts us: coming back along the cor-ri-
dor: steps out and hands me a telegram: Your wife is dead."

"Gypsy?" The drummer like a spider over his drums.   39

"Aaaaaaaaa!" shouts Powerhouse, flinging out both powerful arms for   40
three whole beats to flex his muscles, then kneading a dough of bass notes.
His eyes glitter. He plays the piano like a drum sometimes — why not?

"Gypsy? Such a dancer?"   41

"Why you don't hear it straight from your agent? Why it ain't come   42
from headquarters? What you been doing, getting telegrams in the *corridor*,
signed nobody?"

They all laugh. End of that chorus.   43

"What time is it?" Powerhouse calls. "What the hell place is this? Where   44
is my watch and chain?"

"I hang it on you," whimpers Valentine. "It still there."   45

There it rides on Powerhouse's great stomach, down where he can never   46
see it.

"Sure did hear some clock striking twelve while ago. Must be *midnight*."   47

"It going to be intermission," Powerhouse declares, lifting up his finger   48
with the signet ring.

He draws the chorus to an end. He pulls a big Northern hotel towel   49
out of the deep pocket in his vast, special-cut tux pants and pushes his forehead
into it.

"If she went and killed herself!" he says with a hidden face. "If she up   50
and jumped out that window!" He gets to his feet, turning vaguely, wearing
the towel on his head.

"Ha, ha!"   51

"Sheik, sheik!"   52

"She wouldn't do that." Little Brother sets down his clarinet like a   53
precious vase, and speaks. He still looks like an East Indian queen, implacable,
divine, and full of snakes. "You ain't going to expect people doing what they
says over long distance."

"Come on!" roars Powerhouse. He is already at the back door, he has   54
pulled it wide open, and with a wild, gathered-up face is smelling the terrible
night.

Powerhouse, Valentine, Scoot and Little Brother step outside into the   55
drenching rain.

"Well, they emptying buckets," says Powerhouse in a mollified voice.   56
On the street he holds his hands out and turns up the blanched palms like
sieves.

A hundred dark, ragged, silent, delighted Negroes have come around   57
from under the eaves of the hall, and follow wherever they go.

"Watch out Little Brother don't shrink," says Powerhouse. "You just   58
the right size now, clarinet don't suck you in. You got a dry throat, Little
Brother, you in the desert?" He reaches into the pocket and pulls out a paper
of mints. "Now hold 'em in your mouth — don't chew 'em. I don't carry around
nothing without limit."

"Go in that joint and have beer," says Scoot, who walks ahead.   59

"Beer? Beer? You know what beer is? What do they say is beer? What's   60
beer? Where I been?"

"Down yonder where it say World Café — that do?" They are in Negro-   61
town now.

Valentine patters over and holds open a screen door warped like a sea   62
shell, bitter in the wet, and they walk in, stained darker with the rain and
leaving footprints. Inside, sheltered dry smells stand like screens around a table
covered with a red-checkered cloth, in the center of which flies hang onto
an obelisk-shaped ketchup bottle. The midnight walls are checkered again
with admonishing "Not Responsible" signs and black-figured, smoky calen-
dars. It is a waiting, silent, limp room. There is a burned-out-looking nickelodeon and right beside it a long-necked wall instrument labeled "Business
Phone, Don't Keep Talking." Circled phone numbers are written up everywhere. There is a worn-out peacock feather hanging by a thread to an old,
thin, pink, exposed light bulb, where it slowly turns around and around, whoever breathes.

A waitress watches.   63

"Come here, living statue, and get all this big order of beer we fixing   64
to give."

"Never seen you before anywhere." The waitress moves and comes   65
forward and slowly shows little gold leaves and tendrils over her teeth. She
shoves up her shoulders and breasts. "How I going to know who you might
be? Robbers? Coming in out of the black of night right at midnight, setting
down so big at my table?"

"Boogers," says Powerhouse, his eyes opening lazily as in a cave.   66

The girl screams delicately with pleasure. O Lord, she likes talk and   67
scares.

"Where you going to find enough beer to put out on this here table?"   68

She runs to the kitchen with bent elbows and sliding steps.   69

"Here's a million nickels," says Powerhouse, pulling his hand out of his   70
pocket and sprinkling coins out, all but the last one, which he makes vanish
like a magician.

Valentine and Scoot take the money over to the nickelodeon, which   71
looks as battered as a slot machine, and read all the names of the records
out loud.

"Whose 'Tuxedo Junction'?" asks Powerhouse.   72

"You know whose."   73

"Nickelodeon, I request you please to play 'Empty Bed Blues' and let   74
Bessie Smith sing."

Silence: they hold it like a measure.   75

"Bring me all those nickels on back here," says Powerhouse. "Look at   76
that! What you tell me the name of this place?"

"White dance, week night, raining, Alligator, Mississippi, long ways   77
from home."

"Uh-huh."   78

"Sent for You Yesterday and Here You Come Today" plays.   79

The waitress, setting the tray of beer down on a back table, comes up   80
taut and apprehensive as a hen. "Says in the kitchen, back there putting their
eyes to little hole peeping out, that you is Mr. Powerhouse. . . . They knows
from a picture they seen."

"They seeing right tonight, that is him," says Little Brother.   81

"You him?"   82

"That is him in the flesh," says Scoot.   83

"Does you wish to touch him?" asks Valentine. "Because he don't bite."   84

"You passing through?"   85

"Now you got everything right."   86

She waits like a drop, hands languishing together in front.   87

"Little-Bit, ain't you going to bring the beer?"   88

She brings it, and goes behind the cash register and smiles, turning   89
different ways. The little fillet of gold in her mouth is gleaming.

"The Mississippi River's here," she says once.   90

Now all the watching Negroes press in gently and bright-eyed through   91
the door, as many as can get in. One is a little boy in a straw sombrero which
has been coated with aluminum paint all over.

Powerhouse, Valentine, Scoot and Little Brother drink beer, and their   92
eyelids come together like curtains. The wall and the rain and the humble
beautiful waitress waiting on them and the other Negroes watching enclose
them.

"Listen!" whispers Powerhouse, looking into the ketchup bottle and   93
slowly spreading his performer's hands over the damp, wrinkling cloth with
the red squares. "Listen how it is. My wife gets missing me. Gypsy. She goes
to the window. She looks out and sees you know what. Street. Sign saying
Hotel. People walking. Somebody looks up. Old man. She looks down, out
the window. Well? ... *Sssst! Plooey!* What she do? Jump out and bust her
brains all over the world."

He opens his eyes.   94

"That's it," agrees Valentine. "You gets a telegram."   95

"Sure she misses you," Little Brother adds.   96

"No, it's night time." How softly he tells them! "Sure. It's the night   97
time. She say, What do I hear? Footsteps walking up the hall? That him?
Footsteps go on off. It's not me. I'm in Alligator, Mississippi, she's crazy.
Shaking all over. Listens till her ears and all grow out like old music-box horns
but still she can't hear a thing. She says, All right! I'll jump out the window
then. Got on her nightgown. I know that nightgown, and her thinking there.
Says, Ho hum, all right, and jumps out the window. Is she mad at me! Is
she crazy! She don't leave *nothing* behind her!"

"Ya! Ha!"   98

"Brains and insides everywhere, Lord, Lord."   99

All the watching Negroes stir in their delight, and to their higher delight   100
he says affectionately, "Listen! Rats in here."

"That must be the way, boss."   101

"Only, naw, Powerhouse, that ain't true. That sound too *bad.*"   102

"Does? I even know who finds her," cries Powerhouse. "That no-good   103
pussyfooted crooning creeper, that creeper that follow around after me, coming up like weeds behind me, following around after me everything I do and
messing around on the trail I leave. Bets my numbers, sings my songs, gets
close to my agent like a Betsybug; when I going out he just coming in. I
got him now! I got my eye on him."

"Know who he is?"   104

"Why, it's that old Uranus Knockwood!"   105

"Ya! Ha!"   106

"Yeah, and he coming now, he going to find Gypsy. There he is, coming   107
around that corner, and Gypsy kadoodling down, oh-oh, watch out! *Sssst!*

Plooey! See, there she is in her little old nightgown, and her insides and brains all scattered round."

A sigh fills the room. 108

"Hush about her brains. Hush about her insides." 109

"Ya! Ha! You talking about her brains and insides — old Uranus Knock- 110
wood," says Powerhouse, "look down and say Jesus! He say, Look here what
I'm walking round in!"

They all burst into halloos of laughter. Powerhouse's face looks like a 111
big hot iron stove.

"Why, he picks her up and carries her off!" he says. 112

"Ya! Ha!" 113

"Carries her *back* around the corner...." 114

"Oh, Powerhouse!" 115

"You know him." 116

"Uranus Knockwood!" 117

"Yeahhh!" 118

"He take our wives when we gone!" 119

"He come in when we goes out!" 120

"Uh-huh!" 121

"He go out when we comes in!" 122

"Yeahhh!" 123

"He standing behind the door!" 124

"Old Uranus Knockwood." 125

"You know him." 126

"Middle-size man." 127

"Wears a hat." 128

"That's him." 129

Everybody in the room moans with pleasure. The little boy in the fine 130
silver hat opens a paper and divides out a jelly roll among his followers.

And out of the breathless ring somebody moves forward like a slave, 131
leading a great logy Negro with bursting eyes, and says, "This here is Sugar-
Stick Thompson, that dove down to the bottom of July Creek and pulled up
all those drownded white people fall out of a boat. Last summer, pulled up
fourteen."

"Hello," says Powerhouse, turning and looking around at them all with 132
his great daring face until they nearly suffocate.

Sugar-Stick, their instrument, cannot speak; he can only look back at 133
the others.

"Can't even swim. Done it by holding his breath," says the fellow with 134
the hero.

Powerhouse looks at him seekingly. 135

"I his half brother," the fellow puts in. 136

They step back. 137

"Gypsy say," Powerhouse rumbles gently again, looking at *them*,   138
" 'What is the use? I'm gonna jump out so far — so far. . . .' *Sssssst — !"*

"Don't, boss, don't do it again," says Little Brother.   139

"It's awful," says the waitress. "I hates that Mr. Knockwoods. All that   140
the truth?"

"Want to see the telegram I got from him?" Powerhouse's hand goes   141
to the vast pocket.

"Now wait, now wait, boss." They all watch him.   142

"It must be the real truth," says the waitress, sucking in her lower lip,   143
her luminous eyes turning sadly, seeking the windows.

"No, babe, it ain't the truth." His eyebrows fly up, and he begins to   144
whisper to her out of his vast oven mouth. His hand stays in his pocket. "Truth
is something worse, I ain't said what, yet. It's something hasn't come to me,
but I ain't saying it won't. And when it does, then want me to tell you?"
He sniffs all at once, his eyes come open and turn up, almost too far. He
is dreamily smiling.

"Don't, boss, don't, Powerhouse!"   145

"Oh!" the waitress screams.   146

"Go on git out of here!" bellows Powerhouse, taking his hand out of   147
his pocket and clapping after her red dress.

The ring of watchers breaks and falls away.   148

"*Look* at that! Intermission is up," says Powerhouse.   149

He folds money under a glass, and after they go out, Valentine leans   150
back in and drops a nickel in the nickelodeon behind them, and it lights up
and begins to play "The Goona Goo." The feather dangles still.

"Take a telegram!" Powerhouse shouts suddenly up into the rain over the   151
street. "Take a answer. Now what was that name?"

They get a little tired.   152

"Uranus Knockwood."   153

"You ought to know."   154

"Yas? Spell it to me."   155

They spell it all the ways it could be spelled. It puts them in a wonderful   156
humor.

"Here's the answer. I got it right here. 'What in the hell you talking   157
about? Don't make any difference: I gotcha.' Name signed: Powerhouse."

"That going to reach him, Powerhouse?" Valentine speaks in a maternal   158
voice.

"Yas, yas."   159

All hushing, following him up the dark street at a distance, like old   160
rained-on black ghosts, the Negroes are afraid they will die laughing.

Powerhouse throws back his vast head into the steaming rain, and a look   161
of hopeful desire seems to blow somehow like a vapor from his own dilated
nostrils over his face and bring a mist to his eyes.

"Reach him and come out the other side."   162

"That's it, Powerhouse, that's it. You got him now."   163

Powerhouse lets out a long sigh.   164

"But ain't you going back there to call up Gypsy long distance, the way   165
you did last night in that other place? I seen a telephone. . . . Just to see if
she there at home?"

There is a measure of silence. That is one crazy drummer that's going   166
to get his neck broken some day.

"No," growls Powerhouse. "No! How many thousand times tonight I   167
got to say No?"

He holds up his arm in the rain.   168

"You sure-enough unroll your voice some night, it about reach up yonder   169
to her," says Little Brother, dismayed.

They go on up the street, shaking the rain off and on them like birds.   170

Back in the dance hall, they play "San" (99). The jitterbugs start up like   171
windmills stationed over the floor, and in their orbits — one circle, another,
a long stretch and a zigzag — dance the elderly couples with old smoothness,
undisturbed and stately.

When Powerhouse first came back from intermission, no doubt full of   172
beer, they said, he got the band tuned up again in his own way. He didn't
strike the piano keys for pitch — he simply opened his mouth and gave falsetto
howls — in A, D and so on — they tuned by him. Then he took hold of the
piano, as if he saw it for the first time in his life, and tested it for strength,
hit it down in the bass, played an octave with his elbow, lifted the top, looked
inside, and leaned against it with all his might. He sat down and played it
for a few minutes with outrageous force and got it under his power — a bass
deep and coarse as a sea net — then produced something glimmering and
fragile, and smiled. And who could ever remember any of the things he says?
They are just inspired remarks that roll out of his mouth like smoke.

They've requested "Somebody Loves Me," and he's already down twelve   173
or fourteen choruses, piling them up nobody knows how, and it will be a
wonder if he ever gets through. Now and then he calls and shouts, " 'Somebody
loves me! Somebody loves me, I wonder who!' " His mouth gets to be nothing
but a volcano. "I wonder who!"

"Maybe . . ." He uses all his right hand on a trill.   174

"Maybe . . ." He pulls back his spread fingers, and looks out upon the   175
place where he is. A vast, impersonal and yet furious grimace transfigures
his wet face.

". . . Maybe it's you!"   176

SUBJECT QUESTIONS

1. Why do you suppose Miss Welty chose such an unlikely sounding name as Alligator, Mississippi, as the setting for this story?
2. Why doesn't Powerhouse tell his band about the telegram until halfway through the concert? Does anyone else ever see the telegram?
3. Do you think Powerhouse really believes his wife is dead? Are there any clues that he is more shaken than he acts? Why doesn't he telephone home to find out the truth, as his drummer suggests?
4. Does Powerhouse know who Uranus Knockwood is? Do the other band members?
5. Note that Powerhouse treats his band members almost as children; does his mother-hen quality seem in character with the rest of his artistic temperament? What kind of a man *is* Powerhouse?

STRUCTURE QUESTIONS

1. Does Miss Welty capture an "essential nature" of Powerhouse? Does she emphasize more than one aspect of the man's personality?
2. Is there a correlation between the organization of the story and the points of view from which it is told? Do you find the shift in point of view distracting?
3. The opening paragraphs contain numerous concrete descriptive details; they also contain several interpretive words ("obscene," "hideous," "monstrous"). Do these adjectives seem appropriate to the description? What do they tell you about the anonymous describer?
4. Are the descriptive details selected to convey a consistent, unified view of Powerhouse, or do they strike you as random observations?
5. Do you find in the description appeals to senses other than sight? Are there places in the story where the author could have used such appeals more effectively?

Mr. Flood's Party

Edwin Arlington Robinson

Edwin Arlington Robinson (1869–1935) was born in Maine. He dropped out of Harvard after two years to become a poet. In 1905, Theodore Roosevelt rescued him from poverty by appointing him to a post in the Customs House in New York. From then on, his prestige as a poet rose rapidly, and he won Pulitzer Prizes in 1922, 1925, and 1928. Although much of his talent was spent on long narrative poems, these are seldom read today. His fame rests on a series of brilliant verse characterizations of typical New Englanders and embittered people whom life had passed by — people like Richard Cory and Miniver Cheevy. Robinson's lasting influence has been most obvious recently in the songs of Simon and Garfunkel. "Mr. Flood's Party" is one of the most touching of his verse characterizations.

Old Eben Flood, climbing alone one night
Over the hill between the town below
And the forsaken upland hermitage
That held as much as he should ever know
On earth again of home, paused warily.   5
The road was his with not a native near;
And Eben, having leisure, said aloud,
For no man else in Tilbury Town to hear:

"Well, Mr. Flood, we have the harvest moon
Again, and we may not have many more;   10
The bird is on the wing, the poet says,
And you and I have said it here before.
Drink to the bird." He raised up to the light
The jug that he had gone so far to fill,
And answered huskily: "Well, Mr. Flood,   15
Since you propose it, I believe I will."

Alone, as if enduring to the end
A valiant armor of scarred hopes outworn,

He stood there in the middle of the road
Like Roland's ghost winding a silent horn.   20
Below him, in the town among the trees,
Where friends of other days had honored him,
A phantom salutation of the dead
Rang thinly till old Eben's eyes were dim.

Then, as a mother lays her sleeping child   25
Down tenderly, fearing it may awake,
He set the jug down slowly at his feet
With trembling care, knowing that most things break;
And only when assured that on firm earth
It stood, as the uncertain lives of men   30
Assuredly did not, he paced away,
And with his hand extended paused again:

"Well, Mr. Flood, we have not met like this
In a long time; and many a change has come
To both of us, I fear, since last it was   35
We had a drop together. Welcome home!"
Convivially returning with himself,
Again he raised the jug up to the light;
And with an acquiescent quaver said:
"Well, Mr. Flood, if you insist, I might.   40

"Only a very little, Mr. Flood —
For auld lang syne. No more, sir; that will do."
So, for the time, apparently it did,
And Eben evidently thought so too;
For soon amid the silver loneliness   45
Of night he lifted up his voice and sang,
Secure, with only two moons listening,
Until the whole harmonious landscape rang —

"For auld lang syne." The weary throat gave out;
The last word wavered, and the song was done.   50
He raised again the jug regretfully
And shook his head, and was again alone.
There was not much that was ahead of him,
And there was nothing in the town below —
Where strangers would have shut the many doors   55
That many friends had opened long ago.

SUBJECT QUESTIONS

1. Eben Flood's "excuse" for talking to himself is that he is drunk; what is his "reason" for doing so?
2. There is some physical description of the setting, but none of Eben Flood himself; how is it that Robinson is able to characterize him?
3. What is the "essence" of Mr. Flood that Robinson wants to convey?
4. When Flood sings his song there are "only two moons listening." There was one moon at the beginning of the poem; what has happened?
5. What indication do you have that this is not the first of Eben Flood's "parties"?

STRUCTURE QUESTIONS

1. Robinson several times resorts to explanation rather than letting the description convey the meaning — as in the final four lines. Do these interpretations strengthen or weaken the poem? Are they needed?
2. What rhyme scheme does the poem employ? Is it appropriate to the tone and subject? (Suppose Robinson had made all the lines rhyme; would the effect have been different?)
3. In lines 17–32, Robinson uses similes of a medieval knight in armor and of a mother with her child. Are they appropriate to the context? What effect is achieved by juxtaposing such unlike comparisons?
4. What does the moonlit setting do for the poem? Would a cloudy day, or a sunrise, have done just as well? How would the selection of descriptive details have had to be changed in a daylight setting?
5. Examine the words which Eben Flood speaks to himself; to what extent is his conversation characterizing of him? (Note that he does not say anything especially profound.)

3

AMERICA'S ENTERTAINMENT

Comparison and Contrast

Comparison and contrast are perhaps the most natural of all methods of establishing or clarifying an attitude. They are the product of man's important ability to see relationships and differences where none would be apparent to other animals. All of us utilize this ability daily, sometimes in making important decisions, sometimes in situations so insignificant that we are not even aware of employing comparison and contrast. We use it in deciding whether to sleep late or get up in time for breakfast, whether to sign up for biology or chemistry. But this ability to see likenesses and differences is the basis of what may be man's most significant capacity, evaluation. Before one can say, "Professor X is a better teacher than Professor Z," he must, of course, recognize that important differences exist between the two men or between their methods of presenting material.

Frequently in writing expository prose, a student finds it necessary to employ the methods of comparison and contrast in order to clarify either his subject or his attitude toward it. If he were writing a paper on socialism, for instance, he would almost surely want to point out the similarities and differences between socialism and communism. He would probably also want to compare and contrast two or more existing types of socialism — English, French, and Mexican, perhaps. Although writing comparison and contrast is not as difficult as some other writing assignments, it does require meticulous care, and the student should remember a few basic rules.

In the first place, the writer must *establish a clear basis for comparison*. Particularly in dealing with broad concepts or with groups of people, he may have to choose from a number of possible bases for comparison, and it would not do for him to confuse those bases or switch from one to another without warning. Suppose he wishes to compare socialism and communism; to consider and cover all possible bases for comparison would require a large volume. If he is writing a short paper he will probably have to limit his investigation to only one area – the extent of arbitrary political control by the government in power, perhaps, or the similarities and differences in economic theory and practice, the use of secret police and other methods of coercion to prevent internal resistance, or the degree of control over communications media. Once he has selected his basis of comparison, the writer should stick with it, developing it fully and clearly through both sides of the comparison. It would hardly be cricket, for instance, to discuss communism's totalitarian political system and then switch to socialism's economic system.

If the topic on which the student is writing is sufficiently limited there is, of course, no reason that he can't utilize several bases of comparison in the same essay – as long as he treats each one separately and fully before going on to the next. In a paper on the adequacy of preparation for college given by public high schools and private preparatory schools, the writer would probably consider outside reading assignments, research paper writing, and intellectual stimulation from fellow students as well as actual classroom preparation. But there would be no point in dragging in other comparisons which might occur to the writer – social life, or athletic programs, for instance.

A second rule is that the writer must *observe accurately*. Quite often minute details will be the most important, particularly since they are the ones an average observer is likely to miss. A good writer will never dismiss distinctions without examining them or be so careless as to claim, for instance, that "communism and fascism are really just two names for the same thing." Both terms may imply totalitarian governments and police states, but there must be some reason for the mutual hatred between fascist and communist. A closer examination would reveal such vital differences as the attitudes toward class structure and toward racial integration.

Obviously, then, the writer must also have an *adequate knowledge* of his subject. A passing acquaintance, half-hearted guesswork, or simply a vivid imagination will not do: the really important similarities and differences between two types of skin rash will only be apparent to a person trained in dermatology. The student who tries to write comparison and contrast without familiarizing himself with his subject is merely wasting the reader's time as well as his own. If he has an interest in the subject but not full knowledge of it, he can make good use of the college library.

The preceding three rules, though applicable to all comparison, are virtually useless without a fourth. Far more frequently than chance would justify, composition teachers are disappointed by students who hand in "comparison" papers somewhat like the one on which the following summary is based:

> As I look out my window I cannot help noticing the staunch old oak tree which stands so majestically beside the dormitory.... In many ways, it seems to me that this oak tree is very like my religion....
>
> In the first place, the oak has its roots deep in a firm foundation, from which it receives material sustenance. The roots of my religion, too, are deep....
>
> Secondly, the oak has a mighty trunk which is not shaken by the winds of chance. In the same way, my faith is unshakable....
>
> And finally, the branches of the tree reach up to heaven, whence comes eternal light. The aim of my religion, similarly, is to reach up to heaven....

Such a "comparison" may give a connotative indication of the firmness of the writer's faith and perhaps an appreciation of his ingenuity. But it does not give the reader any specific information about trees, about the exact nature of the writer's religious beliefs, or about any real relationship between the two. It is, in short, not true comparison at all, but analogy.

Comparison shows likenesses between things in the same class, whereas analogy points out a similarity between things in different classes. "The cloud from an atomic blast is shaped like a mushroom" is an analogy, because atomic clouds and mushrooms have little in common except shape. Analogy usually compares the unfamiliar with the familiar, not to establish relationships but to clarify the less familiar. Comparison, on the other hand, seeks both to clarify and to demonstrate relations. In other words, something is said about both objects or ideas being compared, and the points of comparison, though generally more subtle than those in analogy, are at the same time more significant. "Jeffersonian democracy was similar to modern liberal Republicanism" is the beginning of a comparison, for the two concepts are in the same general class. Clearly such a comparison, to be worthwhile, must be developed much more carefully than a simple analogy. And something must be said about both Jeffersonian Democrats and liberal Republicans if the comparison is to be meaningful. Would they have the same views on states' rights, or on civil liberties, for instance? It is not enough to say merely that both are "mildly conservative" by modern standards.

In comparing two concepts the writer should remember to look for significant points of comparison that are not commonly recognized. To dwell on the obvious would be a waste of time for reader and writer alike. On the other hand, the writer should not strain for comparison where there is only a remote and unimportant similarity, if any. Comparison should never be merely an exercise in ingenuity.

Most of the rules for comparison also apply to its opposite, contrast: the things or ideas must be in the same class, the differences developed at length should be significant but not boringly obvious, and the writer should never search for differences for their own sake, regardless of whether or not they are worth mentioning. It is possible, however, to develop fully only one side of a contrast if the writer can assume that his reader is already familiar with the other side.

Because contrast is only useful if the concepts being contrasted have many aspects in common or are frequently confused, comparison and contrast are usually employed in the same essay. If a student were to write a paper on "My High School and College Math Classes," he would want to point out both similarities and differences. He would not dwell on such obvious distinctions as "College courses are harder than the ones I had in high school," but would concentrate on similarities in methods of explaining abstract laws, perhaps, or differences in methods of integrating algebra and trigonometry.

Combining comparison and contrast is likely to be a matter of intellectual honesty. A writer who devotes a paper to proving that "Democracy and communism are in *all* respects unalterably opposed" or that "Democrats and Republicans really have identical beliefs" is either misguided or dishonest. Democracy and communism are not "unalterably opposed" on such issues as the liberation of African colonies from European domination or foreign aid for underdeveloped countries; and Democrats and Republicans hardly agree *en masse* on excess profits taxes or federal power projects.

The student who intends to write a comparison and contrast paper must first limit his subject to something he can treat in depth and with some insight. The title "High School and College Compared" would probably be much too broad for a short paper: the writer would be tempted to dwell on obvious differences — "College is harder than high school," "Students at college are more serious," "Most college students live away from home for the first time." A more useful subject might be "Using the Library: High School and College" or "Classroom Discussion in High School and College." Remember that writing should never be a mere exercise: the writer should learn something, at least by clarifying his views, and the reader should gain insight into both the subject and the ways in which different people view the same subject.

Comparison and contrast may be employed both as the chief method of development and as the primary aim of an essay, or they may be used to furnish background information necessary for some further purpose. But in either case, certain basic principles are observed: the basis of the comparison is made clear, and distinctions and similarities pointed out are real and significant, neither blatantly obvious nor merely clever.

The writer will encounter some problems in organizing a comparison and contrast paper, for he must organize his materials in two ways at once — by the divisions of the subject matter and by the two concepts that he is comparing. Depending on the length of the paper and the complexity of the subject, he can select from three possible methods of organization: (1) present all the points about one side of the comparison, and then in the same order all the points about the other side; (2) alternate paragraphs about side A and side B according to subject divisions; or (3) alternate sentences about side A and side B within a paragraph. Suppose the writer were comparing and contrasting public high schools with private preparatory schools. If his paper were fairly short, so that the reader could keep the first half in mind while reading the second half, his outline might look something like this:

I. High Schools
   A. Classroom preparation
   B. Library assignments
   C. Research paper writing
   D. Intellectual environment
II. Private Schools
   A. Classroom preparation
   B. Library assignments
   C. Research paper writing
   D. Intellectual environment

If, on the other hand, the paper were to be rather long and the writer had a number of facts on each basis for comparison, he would probably do well to alternate paragraphs. His outline would then look like this:

I. Classroom Preparation
   A. High schools
   B. Private schools
II. Library Assignments
   A. High schools
   B. Private schools
III. Research Paper Writing
   A. High schools
   B. Private schools
IV. Intellectual Environment
   A. High schools
   B. Private schools

The third possibility, alternating sentences about high school and preparatory school within a paragraph on classroom preparation, etc., though sometimes employed, is generally satisfactory only for very brief and relatively simple papers or when time is a factor — as in essay examinations or in-class themes. But regardless of which method the writer chooses, he should employ it consistently throughout the paper. Careful planning always pays in better grades and time saved; the writer who "waits for an inspiration" will waste hours and perhaps never get his inspiration.

A Large Number
of Persons

Paul Gallico

Born in New York in 1897, Paul Gallico began his writing career as a movie critic. In 1924, he became a sports reporter and columnist, probably the most widely read of his time. Renouncing this career with his book Farewell to Sport *(1938), Gallico turned to writing fiction. His short stories were widely published, as well as several novels. He is probably best-known today as the author of* The Snow Goose *(1941); it was made into a successful film that is frequently rerun on television. The following essay was first published in* Vanity Fair *in 1931.*

> *Crowd: A large number of persons congregated or collected into a close body without order; a great number of persons; especially, the great body of people; the populace; the masses; the multitude. . . .*
>
> — Webster's New International Dictionary

The fight crowd is a beast that lurks in the darkness behind the fringe of white light shed over the first six rows by the incandescents atop the ring, and is not to be trusted with pop bottles or other hardware. The tennis crowd is the pansy of all the great sports mobs and is always preening and shushing itself. The golf crowd is the most unwieldy and most sympathetic, and is the only horde given to mass production of that absurd noise written generally as "tsk tsk tsk tsk," and made between tongue and teeth with head-waggings to denote extreme commiseration. The baseball crowd is the most hysterical, the football crowd the best-natured and the polo crowd the most aristocratic. Racing crowds are the most restless, wrestling crowds the most tolerant, and soccer crowds the most easily incitable to riot and disorder. Every sports crowd takes on the characteristics of the individuals who compose it. Each has its particular note of hysteria, its own little cruelties, mannerisms, and bad mannerisms, its own code of sportsmanship and its own method of expressing its emotions.

For instance, people who go to horse races want to win money. People who follow golf matches are bad golfers. People who go to tennis matches are pleased with rhythm and beauty. People who go to baseball games are all grandstand experts and thoroughly familiar with the game. People who attend the polo matches are either somebody or trying to be. The spectators at big college football games are the most wholesome people in the world, but they know nothing about the game and care less.

People who go to prize fights are sadistic.   3

When two prominent pugilists are scheduled to pummel one another   4 in public on a summer's evening, men and women file into the stadium in the guise of human beings, and thereafter become a part of a gray thing that squats in the dark until, at the conclusion of the blood-letting, they may be seen leaving the arena in the same guise they wore when they entered.

The only time I ever knew a fight crowd to do the proper thing was   5 the night that Jack Sharkey fought Max Schmeling for the heavyweight championship of the world, at the Yankee Stadium, and came running down the aisles and into the ring with an American flag draped around his shoulders. There were eighty thousand people sitting in the darkness waiting to acclaim the American champion. Shocked by the display of inexcusable vulgarity on the part of the fighter's handlers, they loosed upon him instead a sirocco of boos and jeers that all but swept him from the platform.

But, as a rule, the mob that gathers to see men fight is unjust, vindictive,   6 swept by intense, unreasoning hatreds, vain of its swift recognition of what it believes to be sportsmanship. It is quick to greet the purely phony move of the boxer who extends his gloves to his rival, who has slipped or been pushed to the floor, and to reward this stimulating but still baloney *beau geste* with a pattering of hands which indicates the following: "You are a good sport. We recognize that you are a good sport, and we know a sporting gesture when we see one. Therefore we are all good sports, too. Hurrah for us!"

The same crowd doesn't see the same boxer stick his thumb in his oppo-   7 nent's eye or try to cut him with the laces of his glove, butt him or dig him a low one when the referee isn't in a position to see. It roots consistently for the smaller man, and never for a moment considers the desperate psychological dilemma of the larger of the two. It howls with glee at a good finisher making his kill. The Roman hordes were more civilized. Their gladiators asked them whether the *coup de grâce* should be administered or not. The *pièce de résistance* at the modern prize fight is the spectacle of a man clubbing a helpless and vanquished opponent into complete insensibility. The referee who stops a bout to save a slugged and punchdrunken man from the final ignominy is hissed by the assembled sportsmen. The crowd in Cleveland was apathetic and voiceless until Schmeling suddenly battered Stribling to the floor and swayed forward, tigerlike, to finish his work of destruction, as somehow the stricken boy arose. Then the spectators were up out of their seats, swaying towards the ring, the white-crested wave again rolled out of their throats, and as I stood up and dictated the finish of the battle, I could see their hot, angry eyes reflecting the ring-lights and their inhuman, distorted, cry-torn mouths.

The golf gallery is the Punchinello of the great sports mob, the clown   8
crowd, an uncontrollable, galloping, galumphing horde, that wanders hysteri-
cally over manicured pasture acreage of an afternoon, clucking to itself, trying
to keep quiet, making funny noises, sweating, thundering over hills ten thousand strong, and gathering, mousey-still, around a little hole in the ground
to see a man push a little ball into the bottom of it with a crooked iron stick.
If the ball goes in they raise a great shout and clap their hands and sometimes
slap one another on the back, crying "Oh, boy!" and "Beautiful, beautiful,
magnificent!" And when the white pellet just sneaks past the rim of the orifice
or twists out of it, or goes up and looks in and sticks on the edge, a great
mass murmur of pity runs through the group and they sound their "Oh's"
like a Greek chorus greeting the arrival of a new set of catastrophes. Then
it is that they make their absurd clucking noises and shake their heads, some
in unison, some in anti-unison, like mechanical dolls all set off at once.

The golf gallery is closest of any to the game that is being played. Every   9
individual in the stampede is familiar with the implements used and the
problems that arise from tee to green. They are really vicarious players, and
the crass outsider who rattles a toy movie camera at one of the artists just
as he is about to apply a delicate brush of his poker against the side of the
quiescent ball, is given the hissing and glaring-at of his life. The Jones galleries
were something to see, up and away over the hills before the master had
completed the poem of his follow-through, running, crowding, tearing, galloping, hustling — men, women and children, in sunshine or in cloudburst,
their tongues hanging out, their faces red, their sports clothing dishevelled,
elbowing one another in the wild route over the lea to secure a momentary
vantage point from which to bear witness to the next miracle.

The tennis audiences were always my favorites, preening themselves,   10
bestowing refined approval in well-bred and well-repressed little outbursts,
beaming upon the contestants and on one another, glaring at someone rustling
a piece of paper, expressing righteous indignation at the unwelcome intrusion
of an ordinary spectator who vulgarly screams, "Come on, you Johnny, sock
it again!"

They are experts at registering shocked and delighted approval when   11
an erring player cries "Nuts," or "Damn," to let them know that they feel
he has been a muggins, but withal a virile and manly one. They, too, hum
with smug sympathy when a player pouts or makes a move at a missed ball,
pat-a-caking their hands to indicate recognition of the fine points of the game,
and rooting for the player with the most slickum on his hair.

Baseball and football crowds are happiest when they feel that they have   12
become a part of the game that is being played for them. The solidly packed
football stands begin to chant, "We want a touchdown," or "Hold that line!"
And when the touchdown is scored or the line holds, the crowd takes part
credit. In baseball, sections of the rooters set out deliberately to rattle a pitcher

with rhythmic or anti-rhythmic hand-clappings, whichever they think will annoy him the most, or by setting up a bedlam of sound, or by waving somewhat cloudy pocket-handkerchiefs at him. Most rooting, as a matter of fact, grows out of the individual spectator's desire to identify himself with the proceedings on the field, to shake himself free of the anonymity of the crowd and become an active participant in a sport for which nature happens not to have fitted him.

The loveliest girls in the world sit in the football crowds, their fresh faces framed in fur. The toughest babies in town seem to collect at the ball games, idle sisters sitting in pairs chewing gum, fanning themselves with their score cards and adding their harsh screams to the hullabaloo that accompanies a sharply hit ball or the race between ball and man for the base. The baseball crowd is cosmopolitan. It contains representatives from every walk in life and from every profession. It is the most expert gathering in the world, and the most appreciative of skill. The crowd of sixty thousand that sits in the Yankee Stadium on a Sunday afternoon in midsummer, and the World Series crowd of the same number that watches the inter-league play-off in the fall, are as different as black and white, although both are looking at the same game. World Series spectators aren't regular baseball fans. Most of them have never seen a game before. They are drawn by the ballyhoo, the publicity and the higher prices. They sit on their hands and refuse to warm up to the rising and falling tides of battle. The bleacher crowd gets a better view of the game than the snootier patrons in the stands and boxes. They see the game the way the players see it. 13

Horse-racing crowds are nervous, greedy, fortune-hunting, always milling and moving about, whispering, circulating, muttering until the wheeling ponies suddenly freeze them into a temporary immobility, feverish in its intensity, the same pregnant calm that falls upon the onlookers when the little pill is hippity-skipping on the whirling wheel, between *rouge et noir*. 14

SUBJECT QUESTIONS

1. To contrast different sports crowds, Gallico is forced to generalize about each kind of crowd. Allowing for exceptions, do his generalizations seem fair and accurate? (Consider his comparison of fight crowds to "Roman hordes.")
2. Gallico says his favorites are the tennis crowds; why do you think he spends less time on them than on several other kinds of crowds?
3. Would you agree that football fans are the least knowledgeable of sports crowds? Should a distinction be made between crowds at college games and at professional games?
4. Gallico admits that golf galleries know their sport, but he seems most amused by them. Does he make clear the source of this amusement?

5. With which crowd does Gallico show the most sympathetic understanding? Does he seem to identify with one crowd more than the others?
6. Does Gallico's generalization in the last sentence of paragraph 12 apply only to football and baseball fans, or to sports crowds generally?

STRUCTURE QUESTIONS

1. What bases of comparison does Gallico use to develop his contrasts? Why do you think these are more fully worked out in some cases than in others?
2. How effectively does Gallico use description to clarify his contrasts? Is the description generalized or specific? Concrete or abstract?
3. Note that Gallico adds to the humor in his treatment of golf galleries by describing the game as a complete outsider might see it ("to see a man push a little ball ... with a crooked iron stick"). Could Gallico achieve similar effects by using the same treatment with other sports? (One thinks of Khrushchev's dismissal of American football as senseless: "They all stand up; they all fall down.")
4. Compare Gallico's description of the fight crowd with that of football crowds to see how the connotations of words chosen affect the reader's attitude.

The American Nature of Football

John L. Finlay

John L. Finlay studied history at Jesus College, Cambridge, and received his Ph.D. at the University of Manitoba, Canada. He is thus familiar with both British soccer and American football. Professor Finlay now teaches history at the University of Manitoba. His article first appeared in the Queen's Quarterly, *and the following shortened version of it was reprinted in* Intellectual Digest.

In the last two decades North America has witnessed a startling rise in the popularity of football, so that this game and not baseball is now *the* American game. An explanation has been offered by Marshall McLuhan, who writes that "the TV image . . . spells for a while, at least, the doom of baseball. For baseball is a game of one-thing-at-a-time, fixed positions and visibly delegated specialist jobs such as belonged to the now passing mechanical age. . . . In contrast, American football is nonpositional, and any or all of the players can switch to any role during play. . . . It agrees very well with the new needs of decentralized team play in the electric age." 1

In order to isolate the elements of American football that are prized, it is not sufficient to compare it with baseball. Rather, it is necessary to examine not merely the American game, but other brands of football, too. These games are not independent; until about the middle of the nineteenth century there was but an ill-defined "ur-football." It was from this that the individual varieties crystallized, and in doing so they seized upon and developed aspects of the game that appealed to the host society. 2

Ur-football was weakly structured, but any game that is to become a professional mass spectacle must impose limits upon itself. Time is an aspect of limitation. In soccer and rugby the referee is the sole judge of time. Given his other duties, his timing must be rather hit-and-miss. The division of the games is similarly rudimentary; in order to equalize the advantage of sun, slope and so on, the game is simply divided into halves. In North America, not only is the measurement of time taken out of the hands of the referee and lodged in those of a specialist, but the element of "guessing" is removed. The game and the clock are stopped between actions, and time begins to elapse only when the referee whistles for play to resume. There is also a more sophisticated ordering of the game. Each half is divided into two, which helps 3

Excerpted from *Queen's Quarterly* (June, 1972) and reprinted by permission of the author.

to equalize opportunity more successfully. In soccer and rugby it is very easy to waste time, but in North America time is not only precise, it is precious.

The penalty for time wasting is the loss of territory. Here is another 4 limitation, the way in which space is conceived and handled. European games are most cavalier when it comes to fixing the playing area; in both soccer and rugby, maximum/minimum dimensions are given. These boundary lines serve to mark off a neutral, equal space. The only serious irruption into the emptiness of a soccer field is the penalty area around the goal, a magical exception designed to protect the goalkeeper, the one player permitted to handle the ball. Rugby is somewhat more space conscious. Although overall dimension is equally fluid, the dividing up of the field is more apparent.

Such thinking is foreign to the North American pattern. To begin with, 5 the dimensions of the playing area are rigidly prescribed. The game's characteristic — making ten yards' progress in a given number of attempts — calls for marking each yard on the field. No point of the field is of more value than any other. While soccer players know that the relatively small goal is all-important (an infraction inside the magic territory guarding it results in a penalty that is an almost automatic goal), the North American player refuses to acknowledge that any point is more important than another — forward movement at any point of the field is what counts.

At this point the deeper significance of space and its handling begins 6 to emerge, a significance that goes to the root of the various codes. Soccer sees its field, other than the goal area, as a neutral space within which the action is allowed to build up. The objective is the goal, and the field exists merely to allow the team to group itself, mount an attack, and move in on that goal. Rugby, while not so pure in this respect, is essentially very similar. On the other hand, for the North American player each piece of the field is, in a sense, the goal line. Whereas the soccer player scores explosively, the North American must score on the installment plan.

The basic divergence may be illustrated by a comparison of penalties. 7 In European games the method of compensating for infraction is a kick or "scrum" taken at the point of infraction, the ball being handed over to the team offended against. This amounts to little more than giving this team a chance of better position. In North America an infraction usually means the loss of a certain number of yards, so that the team offended against creeps another installment nearer.

The North American game is much more precise, standardized, indeed 8 efficient than the European. In short, it approaches the scientific criteria of control and replication as closely as any sport can without forfeiting that element of unpredictability that must always be there. The clinching point is the use of statistics. The American sports fan is avid for figures that will make possible "true" comparisons and facilitate that favorite pastime, the composition of "dream teams." While not totally unknown in Europe, such attitudes are exceptional. Nor is it enough to say that North American sports lend themselves to this approach whereas European ones do not; the development of North American games was governed precisely by this urge to quantify.

The next dimension is the way in which the participant is perceived. 9 Until recently European games have restricted a team to the actual number allowed by the rules to be in play at any one time. Should one player have to withdraw, no substitute was allowed. This situation has been modified of late, and limited substituting is now permitted. In North America, however, the practice of substitution has had a long history. Alongside this distinction is another akin to it. The North American coach never relinquishes control of his team, and he and his rooftop spotter are constantly analyzing the game and adjusting the team strategy accordingly: the captain on the field has but limited powers of shaping the game.

These two points taken together lead to the conclusion that in North 10 America the player is devalued — the players are not so much playing as being played. When unsatisfactory, the player is removed. The team, in a way, overshadows the individuals who compose it. This impression is confirmed by the American practice of specialization, and here McLuhan is quite wrong in his characterization. Rather than the game being one of interchanging players able "to switch to any role during play," football is a most restricted form. For a long time the game has been played by two squads, one for offense and one for defense, and a total changeover accompanies a change in ball possession. But specialization goes further than this: even on the offense, there are players who are held to be ineligible receivers, and clubs keep players on the roster whose sole function is to kick the ball! In European games the trend has been the other way. In older forms of soccer a distinction was made between the heavier backs and the lighter forwards. But the logic of the game, especially as developed by the Latins, destroyed this nascent specialization, and now all must be potential attackers, all possible defenders.

One must conclude that McLuhan was wrong in claiming that football 11 was not "a game of one-thing-at-a-time, fixed positions and visibly delegated specialist jobs." Far from football's belonging to the electronic age, it belongs to a way of life now superseded. If any sport is suited to the electronic age, that sport is soccer. . . .

SUBJECT QUESTIONS

1. What, according to Finlay, is wrong with McLuhan's explanation for the popularity of American football?
2. On what grounds does Finlay conclude that soccer is more suited to the electronic age than football?
3. Why do you suppose that Canada and the United States represent almost

the only segment of the world in which soccer is not the most popular sport? Does Finlay's analysis offer any clues?

4. In a portion of his article not reprinted here, Dr. Finlay argues that American football reflects a mature, conservative, cautious stage of capitalism. Would it follow that soccer is more "socialistic"?

5. Another difference that Finlay might have mentioned is the amount of scoring in each game. In British professional soccer, a typical score might be a 1-1 draw (the average number of scores by both sides is 2.4); in North American football, a typical score might be 35-28, with as many as fifteen or twenty scores (touchdowns, extra points, field goals). Should Finlay have developed this contrast? Would it have damaged his conclusion that football is more cautious and conservative?

STRUCTURE QUESTIONS

1. Finlay employs four bases of comparison and contrast; does he establish a real and significant difference in each case?

2. Does Finlay give enough information about soccer to make his contrasts clear? Should he have been more considerate of the fact that the average North American knows little about soccer?

3. What advantage does Finlay gain by going back to the source of both soccer and American football, the "ill-defined ur-football"? Would it matter if the two sports had developed from different sources?

4. This article was published in a "scholarly" rather than a "popular" journal. Do you think the level of language is too difficult for publication, say, in *Time?* Is it too difficult for college freshmen?

Football Red and
Baseball Green

Murray Ross

Murray Ross (b. 1912) is a native of Nova Scotia. He received his Ed.D. from Columbia University and is now president of York University, Toronto. A sociologist, Professor Ross is the author of books on community organization and the educational philosophies of new universities. In 1958, he was recipient of a UNESCO fellowship.

The Super Bowl, the final game of the professional football season, draws a 1
larger television audience than any of the moon walks or Tiny Tim's wedding.
This revelation is one way of indicating just how popular spectator sports
are in this country. Americans, or American men anyway, seem to care about
the games they watch as much as the Elizabethans cared about their plays,
and I suspect for some of the same reasons. There is, in sport, some of the
rudimentary drama found in popular theater: familiar plots, type characters,
heroic and comic action spiced with new and unpredictable variations. And
common to watching both activities is the sense of participation in a shared
tradition and in shared fantasies. If sport exploits these fantasies without significantly transcending them, it seems no less satisfying for all that.

It is my guess that sport spectating involves something more than the 2
vicarious pleasures of identifying with athletic prowess. I suspect that each
sport contains a fundamental myth which it elaborates for its fans, and that
our pleasure in watching such games derives in part from belonging briefly
to the mythical world which the game and its players bring to life. I am
especially interested in baseball and football because they are so popular and
so uniquely *American;* they began here and unlike basketball they have not
been widely exported. Thus whatever can be said, mythically, about these
games would seem to apply to our culture.

Baseball's myth may be the easier to identify since we have a greater 3
historical perspective on the game. It was an instant success during the Indus-
trialization, and most probably it was a reaction to the squalor, the faster
pace and the dreariness of the new conditions. Baseball was old-fashioned right
from the start; it seems conceived in nostalgia, in the resuscitation of the
Jeffersonian dream. It established an artificial rural environment, one removed
from the toil of an urban life, which spectators could be admitted to and

From *Chicago Review* (January-February, 1971), pp. 30–40. Copyright © 1971. Reprinted by permission of *Chicago Review*, Chicago, Illinois.

temporarily breathe in. Baseball is a *pastoral* sport, and I think the game can be best understood as this kind of art. For baseball does what all good pastoral does — it creates an atmosphere in which everything exists in harmony.

Consider, for instance, the spatial organization of the game. A kind of controlled openness is created by having everything fan out from home plate, and the crowd sees the game through an arranged perspective that is rarely violated. Visually this means that the game is always seen as a constant, rather calm whole, and that the players and the playing field are viewed in relationship to each other. Each player has a certain position, a special area to tend, and the game often seems to be as much a dialogue between the fielders and the field as it is a contest between players themselves: will that ball get through the hole? Can that outfielder run under that fly? As a moral genre, pastoral asserts the virtue of communion with nature. As a competitive game, baseball asserts that the team which best relates to the playing field (by hitting the ball in the right places) will win.

I suspect baseball's space has a subliminal function too, for topographically it is a sentimental mirror of older America. Most of the game is played between the pitcher and the hitter in the extreme corner of the playing area. This is the busiest, most sophisticated part of the ball park, where something is always happening, and from which all subsequent action originates. From this urban corner we move to a supporting infield, active but a little less crowded, and from there we come to the vast stretches of the outfield. As is traditional in American lore, danger increases with distance, and the outfield action is often the most spectacular in the game. The long throw, the double off the wall, the leaping catch — these plays take place in remote territory, and they belong, like most legendary feats, to the frontier.

Having established its landscape, pastoral art operates to eliminate any reference to that bigger, more disturbing, more real world it has left behind. All games are to some extent insulated from the outside by having their own rules, but baseball has a circular structure as well which furthers its comfortable feeling of self-sufficiency. By this I mean that every motion of extension is also one of return — a ball hit outside is a *home* run, a full circle. Home — familiar, peaceful, secure — it is the beginning and end. You must go out and come back; only the completed movement is registered.

Time is a serious threat to any form of pastoral. The genre poses a timeless world of perpetual spring, and it does its best to silence the ticking of clocks which remind us that in time the green world fades into winter. One's sense of time is directly related to what happens in it, and baseball is so structured as to stretch out and ritualize whatever action it contains. Dramatic moments are few, and they are almost always isolated by the routine texture of normal play. It is certainly a game of climax and drama, but it is perhaps more a game of repeated and predictable action: the foul balls, the walks, the pitcher fussing around on the mound, the lazy fly ball to centerfield. This is, I think, as it should be, for baseball exists as an alternative to a world of too much action, struggle and change. It is a merciful release from a more grinding and insistent tempo, and its time, as William Carlos Williams suggests, makes a virtue out of idleness simply by providing it:

The crowd at the ball game
is moved uniformly
by a spirit of uselessness
Which delights them. . . .

Within this expanded and idle time the baseball fan is at liberty to become a ceremonial participant and a lover of style. Because the action is normalized, how something is done becomes as important as the action itself. Thus baseball's most delicate and detailed aspects are often, to the spectator, the most interesting. The pitcher's windup, the anticipatory crouch of the infielders, the quick waggle of the bat as it poises for the pitch — these subtle miniature movements are as meaningful as the home runs and the strikeouts. It somehow matters in baseball that all the tiny rituals are observed: the shortstop must kick the dirt and the umpire must brush the plate with his pocket broom. In a sense baseball is largely a continuous series of small gestures, and I think it characteristic that the game's most treasured moment came when Babe Ruth pointed to where he subsequently hit a home run. 8

Baseball is a game where the little things mean a lot, and this, together with its clean serenity, its open space, and its ritualized action is enough to place it in a world of yesterday. Baseball evokes for us a past which may never have been ours, but which we believe was, and certainly that is enough. In the Second World War, supposedly, we fought for "Baseball, Mom and Apple Pie," and considering what baseball means that phrase is a good one. We fought then for the right to believe in a green world of tranquillity and uninterrupted contentment, where the little things would count. But now the possibilities of such a world are more remote, and it seems that while the entertainment of such a dream has an enduring appeal, it is no longer sufficient for our fantasies. I think this may be why baseball is no longer our preeminent national pastime, and why its myth is being replaced by another more appropriate to the new realities (and fantasies) of our time. 9

Football, especially professional football, is the embodiment of a newer myth, one which in many respects is opposed to baseball's. The fundamental difference is that football is not a pastoral game; it is a heroic one. One way of seeing the difference between the two is by the juxtaposition of Babe Ruth and Jim Brown, both legendary players in their separate genres. Ruth, baseball's most powerful hitter, was a hero maternalized (his name), an epic figure destined for a second immortality as a candy bar. His image was impressive but comfortable and altogether human: round, dressed in a baggy uniform, with a schoolboy's cap and a bat which looked tiny next to him. His spindly 10

legs supported a Santa-sized torso, and this comic disproportion would increase when he was in motion. He ran delicately, with quick, very short steps,
since he felt that stretching your stride slowed you down. This sort of super-
stition is typical of baseball players, and typical too is the way in which a
personal quirk or mannerism mitigates their awesome skill and makes them
poignant and vulnerable.

There was nothing funny about Jim Brown. His muscular and almost   11
perfect physique was emphasized further by the uniform which armored him.
Babe Ruth had a tough face, but boyish and innocent; Brown was an expres-
sionless mask under the helmet. In action he seemed invincible, the embodiment of speed and power in an inflated human shape. One can describe Brown
accurately only with superlatives, for as a player he was a kind of Superman,
undisguised.

Brown and Ruth are caricatures, yet they represent their games. Baseball   12
is part of a comic tradition which insists that its participants be humans, while
football, in the heroic mode, asks that its players be more than that. Football
converts men into gods, and suggests that magnificence and glory are as desirable as happiness. Football is designed, therefore, to impress its audience
rather differently than baseball.

As a pastoral game, baseball attempts to close the gap between the   13
players and the crowd. It creates the illusion, for instance, that with a lot
of hard work, a little luck, and possibly some extra talent, the average spectator might well be playing; not watching. For most of us can do a few of the
things the ball players do: catch a pop-up, field a ground ball, and maybe
get a hit once in a while. Chance is allotted a good deal of play in the game.
There is no guarantee, for instance, that a good pitch will not be looped over
the infield, or that a solidly batted ball will not turn into a double play. In
addition to all of this, almost every fan feels he can make the manager's
decision for him, and not entirely without reason. Baseball's statistics are easily
calculated and rather meaningful; and the game itself, though a subtle one,
is relatively lucid and comprehendible.

As a heroic game football is not concerned with a shared community   14
of near-equals. It seeks almost the opposite relationship between its spectators
and players, one which stresses the distance between them. We are not allowed to identify directly with Jim Brown any more than we are with Zeus,
because to do so would undercut his stature as something more than human.
The players do much of the distancing themselves by their own excesses of
speed, size and strength. When Bob Brown, the giant all-pro tackle says that
he could "block King Kong all day," we look at him and believe. But the
game itself contributes to the players' heroic isolation. As George Plimpton
has graphically illustrated in *Paper Lion*, it is almost impossible to imagine
yourself in a professional football game without also considering your imminent humiliation and possible injury. There is scarcely a single play that the

average spectator could hope to perform adequately, and there is even a difficulty in really understanding what is going on. In baseball what happens is what meets the eye, but in football each action is the result of eleven men acting simultaneously against eleven other men, and clearly this is too much for the eye to totally comprehend. Football has become a game of staggering complexity, and coaches are now wired in to several "spotters" during the games so they can find out what is happening.

If football is distanced from its fans by its intricacy and its "superhuman" play, it nonetheless remains an intense spectacle. Baseball, as I have implied, dissolves time and urgency in a green expanse, thereby creating a luxurious and peaceful sense of leisure. As is appropriate to a heroic enterprise, football reverses this procedure and converts space into time. The game is ideally played in an oval stadium, not in a "park," and the difference is the elimination of perspective. This makes football a perfect television game, because even at first hand it offers a flat, perpetually moving foreground (wherever the ball is). The eye in baseball viewing opens up; in football it zeroes in. There is no democratic vista in football, and spectators are not asked to relax, but to concentrate. You are encouraged to watch the drama, not a medley of ubiquitous gestures, and you are constantly reminded that this event is taking place in time. The third element in baseball is the field; in football this element is the clock. Traditionally heroes do reckon with time, and football players are no exceptions. Time in football is wound up inexorably until it reaches the breaking point in the last minutes of a close game. More often than not it is the clock which emerges as the real enemy, and it is the sense of time running out that regularly produces a pitch of tension uncommon in baseball.

A further reason for football's intensity is that the game is played like a war. The idea is to win by going through, around or over the opposing team and the battle lines, quite literally, are drawn on every play. Violence is somewhere at the heart of the game, and the combat quality is reflected in football's army language ("blitz," "trap," "zone," "bomb," "trenches," etc.). Coaches often sound like generals when they discuss their strategy. Woody Hayes of Ohio State, for instance, explains his quarterback option play as if it had been conceived in the Pentagon: "You know," he says, "the most effective kind of warfare is siege. You have to attack on broad fronts. And that's all the option is — attacking on a broad front. You know General Sherman ran an option through the south."

Football like war is an arena for action, and like war football leaves little room for personal style. It seems to be a game which projects "character" more than personality, and for the most part football heroes, publicly, are a rather similar lot. They tend to become personifications rather than individuals, and, with certain exceptions, they are easily read emblematically as embodiments of heroic qualities such as "strength," "confidence," "perfection," etc. — clichés really, but forceful enough when represented by the play of a Dick Butkus, a Johnny Unitas or a Bart Starr. Perhaps this simplification of personality results in part from the heroes' total identification with their mission, to the extent that they become more characterized by their work than by what they intrinsically "are." At any rate football does not make allowances for the idiosyncrasies that baseball actually seems to encourage, and as a result there have been few football players as uniquely crazy or human as, say, Casey Stengel or Dizzy Dean.

A further reason for the underdeveloped qualities of football person- [18] alities, and one which gets us to the heart of the game's modernity, is that football is very much a game of modern technology. Football's action is largely interaction, and the game's complexity requires that its players mold themselves into a perfectly coordinated unit. Jerry Kramer, the veteran guard and author of *Instant Replay*, writes how Lombardi would work to develop such integration:

He makes us execute the same plays over and over, a hundred times, two hundred times, until we do every little thing automatically. He works to make the kickoff-team perfect, the punt-return team perfect, the field-goal team perfect. He ignores nothing. Technique, technique, technique, over and over and over, until we feel like we're going crazy. But we win.

Mike Garrett, the halfback, gives the player's version:

After a while you train your mind like a computer — put the ideas in, and the body acts accordingly.

As the quotations imply, pro football is insatiably preoccupied with the [19] smoothness and precision of play execution, and most coaches believe that the team which makes the fewest mistakes will be the team that wins. Individual identity thus comes to be associated with the team or unit that one plays for to a much greater extent than in baseball. To use a reductive analogy, it is the difference between *Bonanza* and *Mission Impossible*. Ted Williams is mostly Ted Williams, but Bart Starr is mostly the Green Bay Packers. The latter metaphor is a precise one, since football heroes stand out not because of purely individual acts, but because they epitomize the action and style of the groups they are connected to. Kramer cites the obvious if somewhat self-glorifying historical precedent: "Perhaps," he writes, "we're living in Camelot." Ideally a football team should be what Camelot was supposed to have been, a group of men who function as equal parts of a larger whole, dependent on each other for total meaning.

The humanized machine as hero is something very new in sport, for [20] in baseball anything approaching a machine has always been suspect. The famous Yankee teams of the fifties were almost flawlessly perfect and never very popular. Their admirers took pains to romanticize their precision into something more natural than plain mechanics — Joe DiMaggio, for instance, was the "Yankee Clipper." Even so, most people hoped fervently the Brooklyn Dodgers (the "bums") would thrash them in every World Series. To take a more recent example, the victory of the Mets in 1969 was so compelling largely because it was at the expense of a superbly homogenized team, the Baltimore Orioles, and it was accomplished by a somewhat random collection of inspired leftovers. In baseball, machinery seems tantamount to villainy, whereas in football this smooth perfection is part of the expected integration a championship team must attain.

It is not surprising, really, that we should have a game which asserts   21 the heroic function of a mechanized group, since we have become a country where collective identity is a reality. Football as a game of groups is appealing to us as a people of groups, and for this reason football is very much an "establishment" game — since it is in the corporate business and governmental structures that group America is most developed. The game comments on the culture, and vice versa:

President Nixon, an ardent football fan, got a football team picture as an inaugural anniversary present from his cabinet. . . .
    Superimposed on the faces of real gridiron players were the faces of cabinet members. (A.P.)

This is not to say that football appeals only to a certain class, for group America is visible everywhere. A sign held high in the San Francisco Peace Moratorium . . . read: "49er Fans against War, Poverty and the Baltimore Colts."

Football's collective pattern is only one aspect of the way in which it   22 seems to echo our contemporary environment. The game, like our society, can be thought of as a cluster of people living under great tension in a state of perpetual flux. The potential for sudden disaster or triumph is as great in football as it is in our own age, and although there is something ludicrous in equating interceptions with assassinations and long passes with moonshots, there is also something valid and appealing in the analogies. It seems to me that football does successfully reflect those salient and common conditions which affect us all, and it does so with the end of making us feel better about them and our lot. For one thing, it makes us feel that something can be released and connected in all this chaos; out of the accumulated pile of bodies something can emerge — a runner breaks into the clear or a pass finds its way to a receiver. To the spectator plays such as these are human and dazzling. They suggest to the audience what it has hoped for (and been told) all along, that technology is still a tool and not a master. Fans get living proof of this every time a long pass is completed; they see at once that it is the result of careful planning, perfect integration and an effective "pattern," but they see too that it is human and that what counts as well is man, his desire, his natural skill and his "grace under pressure." Football metaphysically yokes heroic action and technology by violence to suggest that they are mutually supportive. It's a doubtful proposition, but given how we live it has its attractions.

Football, like the space program, is a game in the grand manner, yet 23 it is a rather sober sport and often seems to lack that positive, comic vision of which baseball's pastoral mannerisms are a part. It is a winter game, as those fans who saw the Minnesota Vikings play the Detroit Lions one Thanksgiving were graphically reminded. The two teams played in a blinding snowstorm, and except for the small flags in the corners of the end zones, and a patch of mud wherever the ball was downed, the field was totally obscured. Even through the magnified television lenses the players were difficult to identify; you saw only huge shapes come out of the gloom, thump against each other and fall in a heap. The movement was repeated endlessly and silently in a muffled stadium, interrupted once or twice by a shot of a barelegged girl who fluttered her pompons in the cold. The spectacle was by turns pathetic, compelling and absurd; a kind of theater of oblivion.

Games such as this are by no means unusual, and it is not difficult to 24 see why for many football is a gladiatorial sport of pointless bludgeoning played by armored monsters. However accurate this description may be, I still believe that even in the worst of circumstances football can be a liberating activity. In the game I have just described, for instance, there was one play, the turning point of the game, which more than compensated for the sluggishness of most of the action. Jim Marshall, the huge defensive end (who hunts on dogsleds during the off season), intercepted a pass deep in his own territory and rumbled upfield like a dinosaur through the mud, the snow, and the opposing team, lateraling at the last minute to another lineman who took the ball in for a touchdown. It was a supreme moment because Marshall's principal occupation is falling on quarterbacks, not catching the ball and running with it. His triumphant jaunt, something that went unequaled during the rest of that dark afternoon, was a hearty burlesque of the entire sport, an occasion for epic laughter in bars everywhere (though especially in Minnesota), and it was more than enough to rescue the game from the snowbound limbo it was in.

In the end I suppose both football and baseball could be seen as varieties 25 of decadence. In its preoccupation with mechanization, and in its open display of violence, football is the more obvious target for social moralists, but I wonder if this is finally more "corrupt" than the seductive picture of sanctuary and tranquillity that baseball has so artfully drawn for us. Almost all sport is vulnerable to such criticism because it is not strictly ethical in intent, and for this reason there will always be room for puritans like the Elizabethan John Stubbes who howled at the "wanton fruits which these cursed pastimes bring forth." As a long-time dedicated fan of almost anything athletic, I confess myself out of sympathy with most of this; which is to say, I guess, that I am vulnerable to those fantasies which these games support, and that I find happiness in the company of people who feel as I do.

A final note. It is interesting that the heroic and pastoral conventions which underlie our most popular sports are almost classically opposed. The contrasts are familiar: city versus country, aspirations versus contentment, activity versus peace and so on. Judging from the rise of professional football we seem to be slowly relinquishing that unfettered rural vision of ourselves that baseball so beautifully mirrors, and we have come to cast ourselves in a genre more reflective of a nation confronted by constant and unavoidable challenges. Right now, like the Elizabethans, we seem to share both heroic and pastoral yearnings, and we reach out to both. Perhaps these divided needs account in part for the enormous attention we as a nation now give to spectator sports. For sport provides one place where we can have our football and our baseball too.

26

SUBJECT QUESTIONS

1. Would you agree with the author's basic premise that the games which are most popular in a culture reflect the needs and fantasies of that culture? How does Ross reconcile this assumption with his belief that baseball and football are "almost classically opposed"?
2. On what bases does Ross call baseball a "pastoral" game? Do you think the adjectives "serene," "relaxed," "calm," and "tranquil" really apply to baseball (in comparison with football)?
3. If baseball is pastoral and football an heroic spectacle, into which category would you place other popular sports: golf, basketball, tennis, ice hockey, boxing?
4. Ross argues that football emphasizes machinelike perfection, and baseball individual performance. In which sport, then, would you expect a team of all-stars (who do not normally play together) to perform more satisfactorily? Is this expectation borne out by experience?
5. Ross says that football creates an image of superhuman activity; yet his example (paragraphs 23-24) of the Minnesota-Detroit game shows that the only thing interesting about it was the ludicrous run of Jim Marshall. Is Ross contradicting himself?

STRUCTURE QUESTIONS

1. Ross begins by comparing the American's love of sport with the Elizabethan's love of drama. As he does not develop this comparison beyond the first paragraph, do you find it a distraction from the main point, or a suitable way to get into his subject?
2. Would it have been just as simple for Ross to contrast baseball and football directly as to compare baseball to a pastoral tradition and football to heroic, and then to contrast these two traditions? Would he have achieved the same end?

3. Baseball and football being quite dissimilar games, one would expect Ross to have trouble finding adequate bases of contrast. What bases does he employ most effectively?
4. Ross seems to be wearing two hats when writing this article — sports fan and sociologist. Does this dual role cause any stylistic inconsistencies?
5. Does Ross assume too much knowledge of baseball and football on the part of his readers? Does he assume familiarity with the terms *pastoral* and *heroic*? If a reader did not know the meaning of either term, could he tell from the context what Ross means by them?

On Sex and Violence in the Movies

Peter Bogdanovitch

Peter Bogdanovitch, born in Kingston, N.Y. in 1939, began his career as a Shakespearean actor. He has since directed and produced movies and several off-Broadway plays, was editor of Showbill *for a time, and has been actively interested in American film. He has written a series of books on American directors for the Museum of Modern Art, among them* The Cinema of Orson Welles *(1961),* Howard Hawks *(1962), and* Alfred Hitchcock *(1963). He is also a frequent contributor of film criticism to* Film Quarterly *and to* Esquire, *where the following (abridged) review appeared.*

The courts are closing down *Deep Throat* across the country and I guess I'm supposed to be upset about it because I'm against censorship. The only trouble is I'm also against *Deep Throat,* which any idiot can see hasn't an ounce of "redeeming social value" (that Supreme Court fence under which all the hard-core fellows have been crawling); it's just a depressingly ugly piece of work that displays not a hint of talent in any department, isn't sexy and isn't funny (intentionally or not). . . . This lady, who calls herself Linda Lovelace, is among the three or four least attractive women I have seen in a pornographic film — hard-core or otherwise — though I have to admit that in the scenes illustrating the film's title, she does exhibit a certain flair. An almost touching awkwardness and passionate yearning to please come out in those couple of elongated sequences of fellatio, and what Linda Lovelace lacks in finesse or beauty she certainly attempts to compensate for with energy.

The irony is that these two or three numbers — the only salvageable parts of the hour-long movie — could have been spliced together into the usual short 8- or 16mm stag reel bought under the table for years for between twenty-five and fifty dollars and not raised even an eyebrow, much less become the N.Y. cocktail party hit of last season (since replaced by *Last Tango in Paris*) and made more money than any pornographic film in history (something like $6 million so far). Perhaps it's the very insipidness of the rest of the movie that gives Camp followers their thrill, because there certainly aren't any in the erotic department. In truth, the only memorably sexy pornographic film I've ever seen was the famous Candy Barr short, and part of the charm of that one was Candy's reluctance, her air of inaccessibility, not to mention her physical attractiveness. By the way, she would have nothing to do with

Miss Lovelace's specialty — in fact she got a little tough on her costar when he tried to assert his maleness into her face. The reel also looked remarkably candid, which added immeasurably to its voyeuristic impact and is perhaps the key to making screen pornography at all erotic.

What am I saying here? That Candy Barr was O.K. because she was [3] sexy and Linda Lovelace isn't because she's not? Well, that's part of it — sexiness in a woman is certainly a socially redeeming value — but I do also believe that a good deal of the effectiveness of pornography (to a degree like lovemaking itself) depends on its privacy and, more important, on its unspoken air of being forbidden. (Just for starters, it's simply more erotic to buy a dirty movie on the black market than to go to a theatre with a bunch of creeps.) Maybe what I'm getting at is the very reason I think the sexual freedom of the screen has led to so little art *or* eroticism. If the glory of a good movie is that it suspends one's sense of disbelief, that it makes you forget you're watching shadows on a wall and puts you instead into a world of illusion and magic, then the graphic portrayal of sexual intercourse on the screen will never work, since it is almost impossible to forget one is watching people doing something private publicly. I remember in a picture called *The Comedians* that when Richard Burton suddenly reached over and grabbed Elizabeth Taylor's breast, the audience I was with tittered. They were embarrassed, suddenly reminded that Taylor and Burton were married, that they must do things like that in private — whatever — it jarred them, took them out of the film. I felt the same way about most of the sex sequences in *Last Tango in Paris*. What was it like for Marlon Brando, the movie star, playing all those scenes with a naked woman? Any mood that may have been created went right out the window.

The only way I've ever really felt sex scenes work in a picture is when [4] they are treated for comedy, or when the sexuality is implied or veiled. That's one of the main reasons I actually think we've managed to become less erotic and less artistic the more of sex we've shown over the years. Way back in the heavily Code-supervised Forties, you never doubted for a moment that Bogart and Bacall had slept together in *To Have and Have Not* — I mean, it was clear in the movie when the event had taken place, and we didn't need to see it. In fact, we didn't want to. Of course, there were stupidities imposed on filmmakers then — no double beds, for instance, and the length of kisses was timed — but did it matter finally? There was a shorthand at work, and I don't mean panning over to the fireplace — it was more inventive than that. See Hitchcock's *Notorious* again sometime — it is quite apparent to anyone except a child (no ratings necessary) when Grant and Bergman have slept together and when she has gone off and slept with Claude Rains. Luckily, again, we didn't have to see it, as has become obligatory these days; the dramatic point was made with the action offscreen, since the fact, not the act, was important. Today, we're redundantly spelling everything out, leaving little to the imagination, and less to the human spirit.

The good directors also had something else beside the Code or ratings to guide them — they had taste. Not being shown what the child murderer (Peter Lorre) does to his poor victims in Fritz Lang's *M* is far more effective than the slow-motion pyrotechnics of Mr. Peckinpah's type of violence; so much more horrifying, too, since our imagination, with some skillful assistance, can conjure up unspeakable and unspecific terrors no camera can equal. The blood and gore of the Peckinpah school only manages to reaffirm the skills of the makeup and special-effects departments, forcing us either to look away from the screen in disgust or to wonder clinically how some particular bit of exploding flesh or decapitation was achieved. In either case, the spell is broken.

Arthur Penn was the first to use slow-motion violence — at the end of *Bonnie and Clyde* — but the reason it worked there, and hasn't since, is because Penn only slowed the movements enough to give us a sickening illusion of nightmare-come-true; you couldn't tell it was slow-motion — you weren't jarred into admiring technique and so remained involved. Peckinpah, however, is more interested in calling attention to what he is doing behind the camera than in telling a story. Now, Howard Hawks is a master of action and nobody has matched the vigor of the violence in *Scarface,* as one example, but it was terse, fast — before you had a chance to marvel, it was over. I asked him once what he thought of Peckinpah's *The Wild Bunch* and he said, "Oh, hell, I can kill ten guys in the time it takes him to kill one."

In Robert Altman's new film, *The Long Goodbye,* Mark Rydell (who used to be an actor, but is better known as a director) smashes a Coke bottle in the face of his girl friend. It's a horrifying moment, completely unexpected and brilliantly gratuitous (the character is trying to impress detective Elliott Gould that he means business), but Altman barely shows us any blood at all. (A good idea too since blood rarely looks real in movies, particularly in color). The whole incident is over before we've quite recovered from the initial shock, which seems to me the nature of most real violence — chillingly sudden, decisively final. . . .

Now, one would have hoped the past seventy years have proved that movies owe to literature or any other art only what they choose to owe, and if a director as good as Altman decides to make of [Raymond] Chandler what he has made, he should only be judged on the merits of his work, and I think this version of *The Long Goodbye* needs no apologies. It is its own vindication — just as every individual treatment of sex or violence (like Altman's Coke bottle scene which in other hands might easily have been awful) must be the very criterion by which to appraise it.

Finally, that's why any form of censorship can't really work, because who is to be the judge? There are too many cases in history where time has changed our values, and I personally don't like the idea of anyone telling me what I can or can't see. Inevitably that leads to artists being told what they can or cannot do and, like Mr. Altman, they should be free to go where their talent takes them. The intriguing thing is that *Deep Throat* is unwittingly a good example of the kind of moral decay Mr. Altman is talking about in *The Long Goodbye*. That grubby little porno film coupled with its incredible success could almost stand as evidence of the state of the country at this particular time of our lives. There is some deep self-revulsion at work that no amount of legislation is going to stop. Mr. Altman has given us a vivid glimpse of this in his new film, and a good work of art is a better cure for what ails us than any court decision.

SUBJECT QUESTIONS

1. On what basis does Bogdanovitch argue that the movie starring Candy Barr was more acceptable than that starring Linda Lovelace? What does he find wrong with *Last Tango in Paris*?
2. Why does the author avoid morality as a basis for judging pornographic films?
3. Which does Bogdanovitch find "sexier," the censored films of the 1940's or modern pornographic movies? Why? Do you think the average moviegoer would agree with him?
4. Do you agree that "every individual treatment of sex or violence . . . must be the very criterion by which to appraise it"? How could it be its own criterion? Is it possible under such a value system to say that one film is better than another?
5. Should artists "be free to go where their talent takes them"? Do you think that in art, as in politics, freedom entails responsibilities?

STRUCTURE QUESTIONS

1. When dealing with sex in film, Bogdanovitch contrasts modern movies with those of the Humphrey Bogart era; but when dealing with violence, his contrasts are not related to the date (both *M* and *The Long Goodbye* are examples of the proper use of violence). Does this change cause any confusion?
2. Does the chief basis of contrast change when Bogdanovitch changes his subject from sex to violence?
3. Bogdanovitch cannot expect every reader to have seen all the films he mentions. Does this situation interfere with the reader's understanding of the essay?
4. What kind of person is likely to read *Esquire,* where this article first appeared? Do the style and approach seem appropriate for such an audience?

Films, Television, and Tennis

Richard E. Peck

Richard E. Peck is a professor of English at Temple University. As a scholar, he has published a number of articles on American literature. He has also written numerous successful television scripts, and this experience gives him his competence to discuss the subject of the following essay – the difference between films for cinema and for television. Anyone who has watched a "movie of the week" on television has been irritated by the untimely commercial interruptions, which seem perfectly timely in television dramas. Here, Peck explains why the two media are – and should remain – separate.

... Television programming has come full circle, returning for its most char- 1
acteristic success to sports or variety shows, the fare of the 1939 pioneer telecasts. Sportscasts and an occasional special remain almost the only ex-amples of live television. An insatiable public appetite for entertainment became obvious early in the game, and television production moved toward film as the major vehicle. Even those few programs which may seem live, like NBC's *The Tonight Show*, are taped for delayed broadcast. The advantages of tape or film are clear: reruns help amortize initial production costs, bloopers can be edited out, and whole segments may be swapped between shows for better balance. It is finally cheaper to film, hiring extras ("atmosphere people," in TV jargon) for a single day's shooting, than to rehearse an entire cast for weeks before a live production.

The overwhelming majority of prime-time televised drama is now 2
filmed. The halcyon days of *Omnibus* or *Playhouse Ninety's* error-ridden live productions are long gone and longer lamented. Critics who bemoan the loss of live televised drama, whatever its quality, and the recent dominance of filmed drama do so out of noble motives. They see two theatrical genres distinctively different in conception drifting toward one another in disap-pointing ways.

The similarities are unmistakable. In the most general terms technical 3
production of a one-hour television drama differs little from that of a full-length feature film. Cameras and sound equipment, lighting techniques, pro-cessing methods in the lab, editing and scoring are identical. Even our home movies may get the same treatment. So the habit of discussing television and

From *Man and the Movies*, edited by W. R. Robinson. Reprinted by permission of Louisiana State University Press.

cinema in the same breath is understandable. Both offer a series of images which express a point of view or convey information. Actors move easily from one medium to the other. James Garner's success as Bret Maverick led to his work in motion pictures, and his apprenticeship in television gave him whatever acting skills he has. Richard Chamberlain moved from television to the Broadway stage. And Richard Burton's playing of Caliban in *The Tempest* some years back lacked nothing for its being performed before TV cameras rather than on "legitimate" boards. Directors more and more often break into cinematic work through television, a medium which demands of them precision and directness not so stringently required by the relatively leisurely pace of cinema direction. A filmed narrative does not change character because of the means of its distribution — wide screen or square box.

When one turns from the media's similarities to their differences, however, one finds that television influences cinema rather than being influenced. First, television is *not* minor league cinema. Granted, many of the same techniques apply; physical equipment and processing methods are similar, if not identical. The real distinction resembles that between free verse and the sonnet. Writing free verse is, in Robert Frost's famous phrase, like playing tennis with the net down. Like free verse, cinema is more nearly an open-ended form. The restrictions which control and limit the typical teleplay are stricter, more clearly prescribed, but not necessarily debilitating. A *Tom Jones*, perhaps even more a *Dear John*, reaches the screen as the director's creation, with the merits achieved by intricate cutting and editing, fine nuance of camera work, and a shuffling of constituent parts which is impossible in the short week available for the filming, editing, and scoring of an hour teleplay. But what arbiter decides that the enormous craft demanded in the creation of an hour teleplay should be demeaned in comparison? The contrast is ridiculous, rather like the question on an aptitude test that asks which one likes better, living in the country or in the summer. I opt for the craftsman, the man who stands facing a net raised high enough for volleyball and yet plays his tennis match without begging for a change in the rules.

To use the titles *Tom Jones* and *Dear John* as I have is to approach a new attitude toward an art only now fumbling its way into prominence. *Giles Goat-Boy* is characterized in several reviews as allegory, artifice, and even craft without content. The arrangement of the material figures in random discussions of that novel much more than the material itself: What is the allegory? How many levels of meaning obtrude? Such a concern with the artifice of art dominates *Tom Jones* as well. It is impossible not to notice the techniques: speeded-up film sequences, subtitles, ornate framing, shifts into and out of brilliant color. Albert Finney even reminds the audience forcefully that they are watching a filmed narrative by hanging his hat over the lens.

To oversimplify, one can generalize about the phenomenon by suggesting that we who compose today's audience don't require "realism" any longer;

we may not even respect it. Rather, we react to self-conscious art, to art forms which play with their own limitations and conventions. For that reason, television — that most stringently restricted of forms — sits perched securely atop what's happening. Perhaps by following a script from its birth as a vague idea in the writer's mind to the teleplay which results I can make my point, or at least suggest a new way of looking at a single hour of television drama.

The time necessary for revising, rewriting, editing, and correcting flaws — time which is afforded a team at work on a cinematic production — is denied the television producer. When he gets a script, he needs it ready to go. It may later be polished, or even rewritten, but at the cost of an expensive, ulcer-producing delay. Thus the whole process of shaping the final product for television falls more urgently into the writer's hands. He must follow a methodical plan. One of the best writers I know — "best" as opposed to "prolific" — employs the same series of steps for every script. He submits to the producer a five- or six-page "story treatment," a condensed plot. Given an OK for the idea, he moves on to a fifteen-page "step outline" in which he indicates breakdown into act and scene divisions, perhaps even a bit of dialogue for the flavor it will give his finished script. His work once more approved, he gets down to business. 7

Writing the finished teleplay, he finds himself entangled in the net I mentioned. There is no denying it — TV is formulaic; it has its own logic and rhetoric. Each show opens with a two- to five-minute "teaser," that capsule of drama which flashes on the screen to prevent our switching to Ed Sullivan or Lawrence Welk. In this brief span of time, the writer *must:* (1) Get our attention with a "hook" of unexplained action, striking character conflict, or a question important enough to make us eagerly await the answer; and (2) introduce the star or guest star for this particular episode. If he knows his business, he should also (1) introduce two or three other principal players, (2) distinguish the setting and historical period, (3) hint faintly at a secondary problem in the story to follow, and (4) conceal behind bright, forceful dialogue the fact that he is doing all this. If he is really good — and look to the all-too-rare scripts by names like Silliphant, Rose, McNeely, Mittleman, or the pseudonymous John Thomas James for examples — he will also make us laugh at, cry with, or hate a character on the screen. All this in the teaser, before the credits roll past and give permission for a quick trip to the pantry. A glassblower with hay fever has an easier job. 8

But the writer's problem has only begun. Ahead of him lies the creation of a four-act play whose acts average twelve to thirteen minutes. More, each act should ideally end as strongly as the teaser does, particularly the second, which coincides with the half-hour stroke of the clock and a viewer's recurrent impulse to catch at least the jugglers and the rock-and-roll band on the second half of Sullivan's spectacular. Once the viewer has switched channels he's gone to stay. He must be kept hooked, this time principally through effective 9 dialogue. Each line of dialogue gets tested: Does it: (1) Define character? (2) Advance the plot? (3) Evoke emotional reaction from the audience? If it does not, out it comes. In the best scripts each line will achieve at least two of these ends.

Assuming that his muse does not desert him, the writer finishes in a 10 matter of days — or weeks. But he has only a play, not a teleplay, and television differs even more from legitimate theater than from the cinema. The writer must now become director, sound technician, special effects man, even lighting and casting director. His completed script will contain comments unheard by any audience beyond the production staff. General camera directions are left to the director, but shots essential to creating a desired mood must be explicitly described in the script. The writer indicates essential sound cues, dramatically effective lighting, transitions between scenes — direct cut, slow dissolve, whatever paces his drama to best advantage. He includes with his script a summary description of sets and characters, perhaps even "typing" the characters according to what particular actor he might envision in each role.

And when he finally drops his pencil or leans back to let the typewriter 11 cool, he has a first draft, sixty typewritten pages. Then another test: Read it aloud. To his wife, or a friend, a tape recorder, his shaving mirror, someone critical yet sympathetic. Test it. Check it. Then rewrite. And rewrite. The final version handed the director offers a full blueprint of the entire hour, subject to whatever minor changes may occur to this harried man in his tight shooting schedule.

Even after the play is filmed, editing and scoring require more time. 12 Thus it becomes essential that a writer's ideas be explicit and readily translatable into action. Television is no medium for the improvisor who fondles and nurtures his creation to maturity; Bergman is a poor candidate for a job directing television drama. The time element assumes such major importance that a series may occasionally change because of it, shifting radically from the producer's original conception. I understand that the crew of *Maverick* found it impossible to complete episodes for that show in anything less than eight or ten days. Brother Bret, the Garner role, appeared in relief of Jack Kelly's Bart Maverick. With two production units at work on separate scripts it then became possible to meet weekly deadlines and to relieve pressure on the original company. And to many fans the show became Garner's, not Kelly's.

Given all these restrictions — time limits, formulaic act structure, eco- 13 nomic limitations (about $140,000 for a single episode as compared with about $3,000,000 for a feature film) — television is forced into a mold. The writer exercises his craft as well as he can; an intelligent audience watches him at work, fully aware of the rhetoric he employs.

Unfortunately, that mythical "intelligent audience" does not always in- 14 clude men in the *business* of television or cinema. No one in the audience seriously believes any longer that feature films come off well on TV. The necessity for commercial interruptions and station breaks destroys the original tempo and mood of the film. Yet some have tried to solve the problem by writing feature-length film-scripts specifically geared to the requirements of commercial television. They do both industries a disservice. *Fame Is the Name of the Game* recently fared well enough as a televised movie, but, transported into a theater as it will inevitably be, it must fail as cinema. An audience can hardly be expected to enjoy jolting through 100-plus minutes of plot in which a crisis leaps out at them every thirteen minutes to announce a commercial which never appears. And so the producers of that film define themselves as part of the group which persists in equating, and confusing, two distinct theatrical forms.

If cinema buffs complain that television turns leftover movies into Hollywood hash by mixing in liberal quantities of commercials and interruptions, how will they justify Hollywood's creating the same hash, to order? Which is now the dominant medium, cinema or television? More of these half-caste creations are promised. Perhaps their flaws will finally illustrate to all concerned that the media are essentially different. As cinema, television drama is poor stuff; just as certainly, cinema fails as television drama because it lacks the merits of conciseness, of direct and precise craftsmanship, where nothing else will serve. To consider each as *sui generis* is to recognize the merits, and shortcomings, of each. Even more, it is to admit that by confusing them one loses the virtues of both and is left with rubbish.

The formal differences between these genres begin to disappear as television extends its influence. A new sort of audience has been trained, a generation of viewers accustomed to certain technical devices and structural patterns which dominate television drama. More recently television's influence has begun to alter the rhetoric of cinema, either because producers and directors of cinema are themselves part of that great audience and succumb to a pressure they may not recognize, or because these same men *do* recognize and pander to the audience's new-found tastes. Everyone has noticed, perhaps without remarking on it, how audience reaction to a motion picture differs from that to a glowing television screen. The psychology of audience reaction is a study in itself, yet worth a brief comment here. Having paid his money and found a seat in a darkened theater, Mr. Average Cinemaddict is free to laugh or cry in general anonymity. People seated near him — all strangers — behave similarly; a great communion takes place. I laugh, you laugh, he laughs. But the same man ensconced in his favorite chair at home, in the glaring light of his living room and surrounded by his wife and kids, is reluctant to display his emotions; he feels foolish laughing alone. Understanding such a feeling, television moguls attempt to reproduce the conditions of the theater by providing accompaniment in the form of the comforting laugh track.

But this viewer's solitary reactions developed at home go with him on his next visit to a theater. He has been acclimated to technical devices and rhetorical traditions alien to cinema in its halcyon days of pre-television monopoly. To this man's mind slow dissolves from one scene to another no longer deepen mood so effectively; they presage a commercial. A transition through a gray or black screen may lose his attention completely. Witness the restless murmur that accompanies such a transition the next time you watch a feature film in a theater. Leisurely movement prevails no longer in any but the most consciously "arty" pieces.   17

The close-up, once reserved to give potent impact, has become such a common shot in many recent films that its virtues are lost. Within the brief span of an hour-long television drama a close-up allows the craftsman to say, "Look. This is important. Don't ignore it." He need underline a symbolic action or object only once, rather than repeating it as he might with more time available. But the fact that close-range camera work dominates TV seems little reason for its appearance in cinematic technique. *Genghis Khan* fairly screams at the viewer with close-ups of faces, spears, hands, swords, even maps and pointers: "Look. This is where we are now." I can stand a 21-inch screen full of face; thirty feet of forehead and mascaraed eyelashes overpowers unnecessarily. The influence seems clear.   18

Within the past half-dozen years cinema has adopted the teaser, a device essential to the peculiarities of television but worse than useless in the theater. It's not uncommon to find eight to ten minutes of plot preceding the credits on a wide screen, certainly to the detriment of the film's structural integrity. Nothing can account for such a mannerism except its accepted presence on the TV tube and the possibility of a television-trained director's having learned his lessons too well. In a theater the audience is already "hooked," has paid, and expects to be entertained. No one would consider leaving during the initial credits; no one can switch channels. A teaser under these circumstances satisfies expectations aroused in the audience not by the nature or traditions of cinema but by hours and hours of that other medium. Cinema, once blamed for too slavishly following a three-act structure inherited from the legitimate stage, deserves no less criticism for its currently frequent and illogical turn to the teaser-four-act structure of television.   19

"Don't give us a filmed stage play," critics once complained. And cinema moved outdoors to frolic in scenery, settings, and mobility unavailable onstage. But the public's insatiable demand for more and more televised drama forced TV producers back to the pattern of a small cast and few sets. Economics demands it; the audience accepts it, perhaps even considering it a new convention. But — once more — what law requires that cinema play follow-the-leader? *The Apartment* employs such a pattern. Only the opening sequence of a football game saves *The Fortune Cookie* from deserving the same criticism. The new traditions of television seem to sanction a return to theatrical patterns   20 once happily discarded. For cinema it's a step backward, but one that offers an out to film producers: an audience which accepts filmed stage plays is also obviously more willing to accept talky drama, the too-frequently exercised option of repeating a pattern from the Greek theater — action offstage discussed onstage. Second-rate cinema runs the risk of becoming third-rate television by falling back on dialogue in place of action.

Let each do what it can do best. If TV deserves any attack in this circular   21
mass of confusion, it is not because it too nearly approaches cinema but because it returns to formulas of the stage which film should long ago have overthrown. More, it leads cinema down the same garden path.

The influence of television, then, is pervasive, affecting certainly movies,   22
if not *the film* — that common distinction of the culturati. Let me suggest, finally, that even *the film* benefits from the fact of television's very existence. Hollywood's self-congratulation for cinema's new maturity is misdirected praise. "Adult films" of today would have given the censors apoplexy not too long ago. Honesty is rampant. Illicit love affairs in vivid detail, frank language, visible brutality — all mark the new maturity. But it takes no cynic to suggest that all this "honesty" is also profitable. Television, as the family medium, has staked its claim on subject matter long the staple of Hollywood's output. I can see on TV more situation comedy than a normal stomach will take; Andy Hardy will never come back in a wide-screen version. Westerns abound on television. Detectives chase criminals from network to network. Film producers who expect cash customers to pay for longer versions of the same scripts misunderstand the audience and soon become agents instead of producers. Only insofar as films surpass television drama in frankness, or brutality, or "honesty" can they attract a mass audience. Whatever credit cinema claims for its honesty should be laid instead at TV's door. This is the final influence: if movies are better than ever, television made them so.

It all has to do with that net. When one recognizes that *the film* and   23
television are different games, he can appreciate them both without resorting to comparisons which only cloud their differences. Let cinema play in its own backyard where television hasn't a chance to compete. And the next time you watch an hour teleplay pay attention to the net that gets in the TV playwright's way. It forces him to stretch a bit, to stay on his toes, a metaphorical exercise that might benefit all writers. A point harder won deserves more admiration. On its own court television serves up plenty of aces.

SUBJECT QUESTIONS

1. Does Peck seem to think that the taping of television drama is an improvement over live drama, or only a necessary evil?
2. What are the chief differences between the making of a TV drama and of a feature film? What are the differences in audience expectation?

3. Peck suggests that going to the cinema is a communal experience, like going to church or to a rock festival, while at home before a TV set each member of the audience retains his individuality. Would you agree? Do you think TV dramas make less embarrassing appeals to the emotions than films do?

4. What influences, according to Peck, has television had on cinema? Would it be fair to say that the good influences are those which emphasize the difference between the two media, and that the harmful influences are those which make cinema more like television?

5. Peck does not suggest ways in which cinema has influenced television. Do you think the tendency to expand half-hour shows into 60-minute dramas reflects such an influence? What happens when television shows are expanded? Is there twice as much action, or is the plot twice as involved?

6. Have you noticed that movies tend more and more to resemble television drama, as Peck complains? If so, do you find it objectionable?

7. In what direction *should* movies be going, according to Peck?

STRUCTURE QUESTIONS

1. In paragraph 4, Peck employs an analogy between cinema and free verse and between television drama and sonnet. Is the analogy a fair one? Does it help clarify the difference between the two media?

2. On what bases does Peck distinguish between the two media? Does he rely on these same bases when he discusses the influence of television on cinema?

3. As a television writer, Peck naturally has considerably more to say about the way TV dramas are made than about the making of feature films. Does this cause any difficulties in establishing the contrast?

4. Consider the appropriateness of the title to this essay. Is it misleading, or "catchy"? How does Peck use the tennis analogy as a unifying device?

Rock on the Rocks;
or, Bubblegum Anybody?

Irving Horowitz

Irving Louis Horowitz was born in New York City, in 1929. An educator and a sociologist, most of his work has been in political sociology and the sociology of development. Among his many books are The Rise and Fall of Project Camelot *(1967),* Radicalism and Revolt against Reason *(1968), and* The Struggle Is the Message *(1970). Here he turns his attention to a phenomenon that is not usually analyzed by professional sociologists.*

A year ago there were three AM radio stations in New York City that played only rock music. Now there is one. Four years ago dozens of discotheques and clubs featured rock music in New York. Now most of them are out of business. 1

Rock 'n' roll is dying. It is now going through the terminal symptoms that jazz went through in the forties and early fifties. And it will die the same way jazz did — by growing up, by being transformed. 2

Jazz picked up most of its fans during its dance stage. Post–World-War-II beboppers crowded into ballrooms across the country to hear the new music and dance the night away to toe-tapping rhythms. 3

It's got a good beat. You can dance to it. 4

Rapport. For many years there was a close mutual appreciation between performer and audience. but as the art form matured, so did the musicians. They came to know much more about jazz than their audiences did. The fans knew nothing of the notation system, complex rhythms, time signatures. They just wanted to hear *Caravan* or *One O'Clock Jump.* A professional distance began to develop between artist and listener — some musicians looked on their audiences with contempt and took few pains to conceal it. 5

Distance from the general audience was reinforced by the appearance in the late thirties of a new type of fan. In the slang of the day these jazz followers were known as alligators. Like the groupies of the late sixties, they didn't dance — they stood in front of the bandstand all night and listened. Alligators understood. They knew the music. They knew the instruments and the soloists and they appreciated what they heard. 6

In this context many musicians came to define their own worth not in   7
terms of the mass audience and the hit record, but in terms of peer approval.
If the guys in the band and a few sophisticated fans appreciated what one
was doing musically, then he was a success — and the rest of the audience
be damned. Before they would play, the Modern Jazz Quartet and the Charlie
Mingus Quartet often made outrageous demands for concert-hall levels of
silence in their audiences. The jazz musician came to expect a nonemotional
response to emotion. In some sense this is what the rock culture was originally
in rebellion against.

The transition from get-up-and-dance music to sit-down-and-listen   8
music took several years, but it was discernible in many later jazz bands — Cab
Calloway's and Duke Ellington's, for example — and in the swing orchestras
of Harry James and Benny Goodman.

Package.   Finally, jazz moved from the dance floor to the concert hall. Nor-   9
man Granz, the Bill Graham of his day, collected the biggest stars into one-
nighter packages — Jazz at the Philharmonic — that toured the largest audito-
riums in the country. These packaged performances stifled the creativity of
many brilliant musicians, but there was big money in them. As Granz's malignant concerts spread through the land, jazz began to die.

The big bands acknowledged their mass audiences and, when pressed,   10
they would play their familiar, danceable hits. But to maintain their self-esteem and professional integrity many artists sought other outlets. Small groups
began to develop within the larger bands. The big band was for mass appeal
— the small group was for displaying musical expertise and for building personal satisfaction. From Artie Shaw's orchestra came the Gramercy Five, and
from Benny Goodman's big outfit came the Benny Goodman Trio. Instead
of dancing, audiences were expected to sit and listen to Teddy Wilson's educated piano or to the cascading vibes of Lionel Hampton.

Thelonious Monk and Dizzy Gillespie achieved results similar to those   11
of Bartok and Stravinsky — by innovating and creatively extending their traditions. The soloist became king, and Charlie Parker and, later, John Coltrane
were canonized.

As the musicians grew older, so did their fans. Young, unsophisticated   12
ears didn't know enough about the music to appreciate a good tenor-sax solo
by Lester Young or Ben Webster. Artists became intraprofessional. Financial
success ceased to be a criterion for musical esteem. The musicians who did
reach mass audiences had by definition "sold out," and their sounds were
disdained — they were "commercial" and "Tin Pan Alley."

And then came rock 'n' roll.   13

It's got a good beat. You can dance to it.   14

The emphasis again was mass appeal. There were few intraprofessional 15 standards, so an artist's worth was defined in the simplest, most obvious way — in terms of how many records he could sell. The focus was on the 45 r.p.m. single, and the Top 40 list was updated every week.

Every music reflects the society in which it flourished. In the Renaissance 16 new needs for humanistic expression gave birth to tonal music which rejected the previous ecclesiastical doxology of the Medieval period. The ideals of freedom in the French Revolution gave rise to the chromatics and the gradual development from the sonata to the cyclical form of the Romantic Movement. Jazz itself, inherently an interracial music, represented a mixture of polyphonic African rhythms and modes with the tonal homophony of the European colonizers.

And rock music, a child of the technological age, reflects its parentage 17 in every aspect. Each year amplifiers and preamplifiers get more sophisticated and more powerful, speaker systems get larger and louder, and new electronic gimmicks alter the sound or become part of it (feedback, cross-phasing, fuzz tones, wah-wah).

The contemporary recording process is so complex that a new group 18 cannot make an album without sophisticated knowledge of electronics — mikeing, mixing and mastering. Since *Sergeant Pepper,* the multi-track tape recorder has taken over. Voices and instruments are cut onto separate tracks so that the producer can make the piano louder than the bass on one chorus, or add echo to one voice but not another. Six months later, if he feels like it, he can add a background of violins or cricket chirps.

Electronic experimentation has taken rock artists away from their roots 19 — the song and the beat. To hear the Beatles as a group one must return to *Revolver,* vintage 1966.

Today's young take all the gadgetry for granted — they are not alienated 20 by technological innovation, nor are they particularly impressed. Jazz musicians, on the other hand — especially followers of Gillespie and Monk — tend to resist technological innovation. Some, like Freddie Hubbard and Ornette Coleman, openly state their opposition to electronic music. They tend to think that any device not to be found in a nineteenth-century symphony orchestra is by definition not a musical instrument.

Hit. As rock has matured it has gone through many of the self-conscious 21 changes that marked the rise and fall of jazz. In the first place musicians have changed their definition of success. The hit single is no longer necessary. A group can have a successful album without the support of a Top 40 single (for example, Jefferson Airplane, Jimi Hendrix, Country Joe and the Fish). And if an artist is respected by his fellow musicians, finds approval from a devoted circle of sophisticated fans, and is certified by a semiprofessional publication like *Rolling Stone,* he can maintain high self-esteem even while remaining relatively unknown (for example, Van Dyke Parks, Randy Newman, Captain Beefheart). Some artists at their pinnacles — Bob Dylan, for example — have turned their backs on their audiences and retreated into seclusion. They may need to do this to preserve their sanity, but the effect is to increase the separation between artist and audience. The Beatles swore off personal appearances in 1966. Dylan retired to his Woodstock home after his motorcycle accident in 1966 and has made few public appearances since then; Elvis retreated from public appearances and holed up in his Tennessee mansion for nine years before his recent comeback at the International Hotel in Las Vegas.

Rock music has just entered the sit-and-listen stage. Even five years ago   22 one could see the young dancing wildly to the omnipresent beat at San Francisco's Fillmore Auditorium. Now the fans don't dance — they sit, they concentrate, they get close to the stage so they can watch the guitarist move his fingers. They know rock music; they know the electric guitar; and they can tell immediately whether their favorite soloist is in peak improvisational form.

Super-groups. Just as the stars of yesterday's big bands sought professional   23 recognition and creative opportunities by splitting off to form their own trios and quartets, the most talented musicians today look to each other for support in super-groups.

Many rock musicians have begun to look down on the mass audience.   24 The leader of a top English group said after a recent U.S. tour that American audiences are indiscriminately appreciative — they applaud and yell for more, whether the performance is inspired or inept. This instills in the rock artist the same disrespect and contempt for the audience that the jazz musician felt when he finally gave in to a half-dozen requests for *Tico Tico.* Frank Zappa, on the first dissolution of the Mothers of Invention, complained that most audiences "wouldn't know music if it came up and bit 'em on the ass."

Rock is dying because it has matured and its fans have become self-   25 selective. They sit intently and listen to complex guitar arrangements and improvisations. Eric Clapton, Mike Bloomfield and Frank Zappa are being hailed as the greatest guitarists and rock musicians of our age. Their fans are devoted, musically sophisticated, and old. Young teenagers find it very difficult to follow the improvisational music because they do not have background experience with rock. Their ears are not yet equipped to understand or appreciate complexity and innovation. Innovation is a break with tradition, and a thirteen-year-old has no tradition by which he can judge the improvisational forms being explored by many rock musicians.

Bubblegum.   Young teenagers don't like to sit and listen anyway. They want   26
to move. And so they turn to the simpler, more danceable music that has
come to be known as *bubblegum. It's got a good beat. You can dance to it.*

To the disbelief and dismay of rock fans, bubblegum music has scored   27
tremendous financial successes. *Sugar, Sugar* sold six million copies, making
it the fifth largest-selling record in history. It is the Archies, Tommy Roe and
Bobby Sherman who get the golden records — not Traffic, not Leon Russell,
and not Delaney and Bonnie.

Rock fans speak of bubblegum in a tone usually reserved for words like   28
excreta. They look down on the 1910 Fruitgum Company with the same
distaste that their parents reserved for Chuck Berry and Danny and the Juniors: *How can you listen to that garbage over and over? It's so simple, so
repetitious, so childish.* Is this observation any more true of *Sugar, Sugar* than
it was of *At the Hop?*

Different types of music appeal to different types of persons, yet there   29
are always artists at the interface who want to reconcile the generations. Thus,
in the mid-fifties white artists came out with cover versions of black rhythm-
and-blues songs. In the early sixties rock songs became legitimate when they
were set to the schmaltzy arrangements of Percy Faith, Ray Conniff, and the
Hollyridge Strings. These albums catered to the older audience. The younger
generation snickered as they would at a fifty-year-old housewife who wore
a miniskirt and headband. Staying young beyond one's chronology is a complex and often painful undertaking. As Jefferson Airplane explains: "One generation got old/One generation got soul."

Today there are fewer gap-bridging acts. This is partly because groups   30
are providing their own nostalgic ties with older musical styles. A Mantovani
version isn't needed any more — one can get lush, syrupy strings on the Beatles'
last album, *Let It Be;* and on *Self Portrait,* Bob Dylan provides his own under-
cover versions of *Blue Moon* and *I Forgot More Than You'll Ever Know About
Love.*

Voltage.   In the search for new identity and innovation it was inevitable that   31
rock would reiterate jazz. New bands don't feature just the electric guitar —
trumpets, flutes, violins and other traditional instruments are accepted in the
contemporary rock band, as long as they are electric. Many recent bands
(Blood, Sweat and Tears, Chicago, and Cold Blood, for example) are highly
reminiscent in their instrumentation of such earlier groups as Miles Davis'
Tentet in the late forties. And the loud, brassy arrangements are direct descendants of Count Basie. A promising new group, Ten Wheel Drive, provides
a mixture of Big Mama Thornton blues and a tenor sax reminiscent of Coltrane, all set to tight arrangements that remind one of The Jazz-Messengers
with Art Blakey and Horace Silver.

Other rock artists are reviving traditional jazz forms — on piano, Leon   32
Russell sounds like Jelly Roll Morton, and Janis Joplin was certainly the best
jazz singer since Ma Rainey and Bessie Smith.

With other artists — Miles Davis, Don Ellis and Gary Burton, for exam-   33
ple — the cross-fertilization between musical forms is so complete that classification becomes meaningless, or at least tedious.

Tracks. Other events in the evolution of jazz give hints of the future devel-   34
opment of rock. For a brief period jazz found acceptance as background music
in movies *(East of Eden, The Man With the Golden Arm)*, and later served
a similar function on action TV shows *(Peter Gunn, Richard Diamond)*. Similarly, rock has recently found its way onto the sound tracks of dramatic movies
(Easy Rider, Zabriskie Point), and we can expect that soon TV shows will
feature rock 'n' roll theme music. After the extended stay of The Who at
the Metropolitan Opera, anything can happen.

The musical statements that rock will make in its final years can only   35
be guessed at. Innovation in style and song is essential in recent rock music —
any group that fails to innovate does not attract a mass audience. No modern
artist becomes popular on someone else's songs, unless he has arranged unique
interpretations (e.g., Janis Joplin, Joe Cocker).

When any music reaches the sit-and-listen phase, it becomes a different   36
music — jazz becomes modern jazz, rock becomes *hard* or *acid* rock. The music
fails to pick up a new, young audience and it begins to die. Perhaps twenty
years from now we will look back on Woodstock as the beginning of the
end — similar to Benny Goodman's famous Paramount Theater and Carnegie
Hall engagements of 1938. It may have marked the crystallization of the
sit-and-listen phase, and therefore the imminent death of rock 'n' roll.

Perhaps fifteen years from now there will be a bubblegum revival, the   37
Archies will be likened to Bill Haley and the Comets, and Bobby Sherman
will be called the musical genius of his time who broke away from tradition
and forged the new music.

Sociological speculations are many and fascinating. But when some new   38
musical form sweeps the mass audience out from under the aging bubblegum
musicians, the young fans will have a clear and classic reason for liking the
new music: *It's got a good beat. You can dance to it.*

SUBJECT QUESTIONS

1. Horowitz believes that any form of popular music necessarily matures
   with its audience. Do you agree with this premise? Would it not be
   possible for the music to stay the same and for audiences to move on
   to more sophisticated forms of music? (Consider what Horowitz says
   about the musicians themselves.)

2. Do you think the same kinds of changes have taken place in other forms of popular music — country and western, "soul," and folk, for instance?

3. What similarity does Horowitz see between jazz at the Philharmonic and Woodstock? Are there important differences which he neglects?

4. This essay was written in 1971; do you see any evidence since then that bubblegum music is reaching a "sit-and-listen" stage? Has rock continued its aging process?

5. Horowitz does not mention that the dance styles which accompany the three kinds of music discussed have become progressively simpler — from the highly complex jitterbug to the twist to the unstructured movement associated with bubblegum music. Does this change affect the implication of the author's refrain line, "It's got a good beat. You can dance to it"?

STRUCTURE QUESTIONS

1. On what bases does Horowitz establish his comparison? Does his disregard of basic differences constitute a falsification of his thesis?

2. Horowitz is interested chiefly with similarities in historical development rather than with characteristics of the music itself. Does he give sufficient indication of what those characteristics are? Can he fairly assume that readers will not need to be told too much?

3. Horowitz mentions so many musicians and groups that few readers would be familiar with them all. Consider in what ways this essay would be changed had he discussed the similarities and differences in style and technique among these groups.

4. The author does not really say very much about bubblegum music. What justification is there for his giving it less space than jazz and rock?

5. The subtitles to various sections, like *Rapport* or *Hit,* were very likely added by the editors of *Psychology Today;* do you find them useful subdivisions?

A Patriotic Short

F. Scott Fitzgerald

F. Scott Fitzgerald (1896–1940) was a literary lion of the 1920's and early 30's. But because he wanted to live the image of the roaring twenties, he always spent money faster than he could earn it. His best books, The Great Gatsby *(1925) and* Tender Is the Night *(1934), could not sustain the kind of life he wanted. Finally he went to Hollywood as a scriptwriter in 1937, but his genius was channeled into comparatively mundane tasks, at which he was no better than many another lesser talent. Disillusioned, ill, with rapidly dwindling fortunes, he turned again to alcohol and drugs. Although Fitzgerald controlled this problem eventually, he was never again to enjoy the steady, high-salaried work which took him to Hollywood. During the last fifteen months of his life, Fitzgerald supported himself largely by writing for* Esquire *seventeen stories about Pat Hobby, a down-and-out Hollywood writer. Though Hobby can hardly be taken as a representation of the author, clearly Fitzgerald invested these stories with some of his own frustrations and disappointments. The story included here draws an interesting contrast between the Pat Hobby of the good old days and the indigent hack writer of 1939.*

Pat Hobby, the writer and the man, had his great success in Hollywood during what Irvin Cobb refers to as "the mosaic swimming-pool age — just before the era when they had to have a shinbone of St. Sebastian for a clutch lever." 1

Mr. Cobb no doubt exaggerates, for when Pat had his pool in those fat days of silent pictures, it was entirely cement, unless you should count the cracks where the water stubbornly sought its own level through the mud. 2

"But it *was* a pool," he assured himself one afternoon more than a decade later. Though he was now more than grateful for this small chore he had assigned him by producer Berners — one week at two-fifty — all the insolence of office could not take that memory away. 3

He had been called in to the studio to work upon an humble short. It was based on the career of General Fitzhugh Lee who fought for the Confederacy and later for the U.S.A. against Spain — so it would offend neither North nor South. And in the recent conference Pat had tried to co-operate. 4

"I was thinking —" he suggested to Jack Berners "— that it might be a good thing if we could give it a Jewish touch." 5

"What do you mean?" demanded Jack Berners quickly.   6

"Well I thought — the way things are and all, it would be a sort of good   7
thing to show that there were a number of Jews in it too."

"In what?"   8

"In the Civil War." Quickly he reviewed his meager history. "They   9
were, weren't they?"

"Naturally," said Berners, with some impatience, "I suppose everybody   10
was except the Quakers."

"Well, my idea was that we could have this Fitzhugh Lee in love with   11
a Jewish girl. He's going to be shot at curfew so she grabs a church bell —"

Jack Berners leaned forward earnestly.   12

"Say, Pat, you want this job, don't you? Well, I told you the story. You   13
got the first script. If you thought up this tripe to please me you're losing
your grip."

Was that a way to treat a man who had once owned a pool which had   14
been talked about by —

That was how he happened to be thinking about his long lost swimming   15
pool as he entered the shorts department. He was remembering a certain day
over a decade ago in all its details, how he had arrived at the studio in his
car driven by a Filipino in uniform; the deferential bow of the guard at the
gate which had admitted car and all to the lot, his ascent to that long lost
office which had a room for the secretary and was really a director's office . . .

His reverie was broken off by the voice of Ben Brown, head of the shorts   16
department, who walked him into his own chambers.

"Jack Berners just phoned me," he said. "We don't want any new angles,   17
Pat. We've got a good story. Fitzhugh Lee was a dashing cavalry commander.
He was a nephew of Robert E. Lee and we want to show him at Appomattox,
pretty bitter and all that. And then show how he became reconciled — we'll
have to be careful because Virginia is swarming with Lees — and how he
finally accepts a U.S. commission from President McKinley —"

Pat's mind darted back again into the past. The President — that was   18
the magic word that had gone around that morning many years ago. The
President of the United States was going to make a visit to the lot. Everyone
had been agog about it — it seemed to mark a new era in pictures because
a President of the United States had never visited a studio before. The executives of the company were all dressed up — from a window of his long lost
Beverly Hills house Pat had seen Mr. Maranda, whose mansion was next door
to him, bustle down his walk in a cutaway coat at nine o'clock, and had known
that something was up. He thought maybe it was clergy but when he reached
the lot he had found it was the President of the United States himself who
was coming . . .

"Clean up the stuff about Spain," Ben Brown was saying. "The guy that   19
wrote it was a Red and he's got all the Spanish officers with ants in their
pants. Fix up that."

In the office assigned him Pat looked at the script of *True to Two Flags*.   20
The first scene showed General Fitzhugh Lee at the head of his cavalry re-
ceiving word that Petersburg had been evacuated. In the script Lee took the
blow in pantomime, but Pat was getting two-fifty a week — so, casually and
without effort, he wrote in one of his favorite lines:

LEE: *(to his officers)*

Well, what are you standing here gawking for? DO *something! 6. Medium
Shot. Officers pepping up, slapping each other on back, etc.*

Dissolve to:

To what? Pat's mind dissolved once more into the glamorous past. On   21
that happy day in the twenties his phone had rung at about noon. It had been
Mr. Maranda.

"Pat, the President is lunching in the private dining room. Doug Fair-   22
banks can't come so there's a place empty and anyhow we think there ought
to be one writer there."

His memory of the luncheon was palpitant with glamor. The Great Man   23
had asked some questions about pictures and had told a joke and Pat had
laughed and laughed with the others — all of them solid men together — rich,
happy and successful.

Afterwards the President was to go on some sets and see some scenes   24
taken and still later he was going to Mr. Maranda's house to meet some of
the women stars at tea. Pat was not invited to that party but he went home
early anyhow and from his veranda saw the cortège drive up, with Mr.
Maranda beside the President in the back seat. Ah he was proud of pictures
then — of his position in them — of the President of the happy country where
he was born . . .

Returning to reality Pat looked down at the script of *True to Two Flags*   25
and wrote slowly and thoughtfully: *Insert: A calendar — with the years plainly
marked and the sheets blowing off in a cold wind, to show Fitzhugh Lee
growing older and older.*

His labors had made him thirsty — not for water, but he knew better   26
than to take anything else his first day on the job. He got up and went out
into the hall and along the corridor to the water-cooler.

As he walked he slipped back into his reverie.   27

That had been a lovely California afternoon so Mr. Maranda had taken   28
his exalted guest and the coterie of stars into his garden, which adjoined Pat's
garden. Pat had gone out his back door and followed a low privet hedge
keeping out of sight — and then accidentally come face to face with the Presidential party.

The President had smiled and nodded. Mr. Maranda smiled and nodded.   29

"You met Mr. Hobby at lunch," Mr. Maranda said to the President. "He's   30
one of our writers."

"Oh yes," said the President, "you write the pictures." 31

"Yes I do," said Pat. 32

The President glanced over into Pat's property. 33

"I suppose —" he said, "— that you get lots of inspiration sitting by the 34
side of that fine pool."

"Yes," said Pat, "yes, I do." 35

. . . Pat filled his cup at the cooler. Down the hall there was a group 36
approaching — Jack Berners, Ben Brown and several other executives and with
them a girl to whom they were very attentive and deferential. He recognized
her face — she was the girl of the year, the It girl, the Oomph girl, the Glamour
Girl, the girl for whose services every studio was in violent competition.

Pat lingered over his drink. He had seen many phonies break in and 37
break out again, but this girl was the real thing, someone to stir every pulse
in the nation. He felt his own heart beat faster. Finally, as the procession
drew near, he put down the cup, dabbed at his hair with his hand and took
a step out into the corridor.

The girl looked at him — he looked at the girl. Then she took one arm 38
of Jack Berners' and one of Ben Brown's and suddenly the party seemed to
walk right through him — so that he had to take a step back against the wall.

An instant later Jack Berners turned around and said back to him, "Hello, 39
Pat." And then some of the others threw half glances around but no one else
spoke, so interested were they in the girl.

In his office, Pat looked at the scene where President McKinley offers 40
a United States commission to Fitzhugh Lee. Suddenly he gritted his teeth
and bore down on his pencil as he wrote:

LEE

Mr. President, you can take your commission and go straight to hell.

Then he bent down over his desk, his shoulders shaking as he thought 41
of that happy day when he had had a swimming pool.

SUBJECT QUESTIONS

1. Why does Hobby attach so much importance to a cracked swimming
   pool?
2. What indications do you have that Hobby is not simply unlucky but that
   he no longer merits the high pay and steady work he once had? Does
   Hobby seem to recognize this?
3. Can you tell from the sketchy information about *True to Two Flags* under
   what kinds of restriction Hollywood writers were forced to work?
4. In 1939, Lee's directive "go straight to hell" would not have been allowed
   in a movie (*Gone With the Wind* was the first picture to get by with
   "damn"). Why does Hobby insert this line into the script he's working
   on?

STRUCTURE QUESTIONS

1. How is the incident of the "It" girl toward the end structurally related to the rest of the story?
2. Consider the role played by repetition (of words and themes) in the unity of this story.
3. The chief basis for comparison between the good old days and the present is not, as one might expect, money — or even swimming pools. What is it?
4. Examine the devices by which Fitzgerald gets Hobby into and back out of his reveries. Which ones work most smoothly? Could you suggest improvements for others? Do the successful ones operate by some formula not employed in the weaker ones?

To an Athlete Dying Young

A. E. Housman

Alfred Edward Housman (1859–1936) was an English poet and classical scholar. Although he failed his final examinations at St. John's College, Oxford, he continued to study Latin on his own and eventually became Professor of Latin at University College, London, and later at Trinity College, Cambridge. Housman's first book of poems, A Shropshire Lad *(1896), brought him instant fame. But his second volume,* Last Poems, *did not appear until twenty-six years later. Housman did, however, publish several important scholarly editions of the Latin poets. The poem that follows first appeared in* A Shropshire Lad.

The time you won your town the race
We chaired you through the market-place;
Man and boy stood cheering by,
And home we brought you shoulder-high.

To-day, the road all runners come,   5
Shoulder-high we bring you home,
And set you at your threshold down,
Townsman of a stiller town.

Smart lad, to slip betimes away
From fields where glory does not stay   10
And early though the laurel grows
It withers quicker than the rose.

Eyes the shady night has shut
Cannot see the record cut,
And silence sounds no worse than cheers   15
After earth has stopped the ears:

Now you will not swell the rout
Of lads that wore their honours out,
Runners whom renown outran
And the name died before the man.   20

So set, before its echoes fade,
The fleet foot on the sill of shade,
And hold to the low lintel up
The still-defended challenge-cup.

And round that early-laurelled head   25
Will flock to gaze the strengthless dead,
And find unwithered on its curls
The garland briefer than a girl's.

SUBJECT QUESTIONS

1. Housman's reassurances can hardly be consoling to the dead athlete;
   for whom *is* the poem intended? Does the poem's implication change
   if it is meant for the living rather than the dead?
2. If we grant that athletes who live long enough will only see their records
   broken and their glory fade, is that a "reason" for dying young? Is it
   a reason for not trying to break records?
3. What happens to athletes after their glory has been surpassed? Do they
   simply "fade away," like old soldiers? Or does their fame usually help
   them to more permanent jobs?
4. Think of some tasks in which the laurels usually go to the young, and
   others in which real success tends to come late in life. Which sort of
   task does youth seem more interested in pursuing? Can a valid generalization be made about such a question? Would you personally prefer
   to be a rock star or a supreme court judge?
5. In what sense is an athlete's garland "briefer than a girl's"? Why does
   Housman introduce this comparison at the end? Does it give the poem
   wider implications? Or is it only a sop to female readers who might be
   bored by a poem about an athlete?

STRUCTURE QUESTIONS

1. The contrast on which the poem is based is stated in the first two stanzas.
   There is a danger that such a contrast will become stickily sentimental;
   does Housman's word choice in these two stanzas help to combat that
   danger?

2. Housman twice uses a form of the verb "wither," in stanza 3 and in the closing lines. Is there a relationship between the images in which the word occurs?

3. In stanza 4, Housman creates for himself an awkward problem: the poet seems to comfort the dead athlete by telling him that he cannot see his record broken or hear the cheers of the crowd. But these statements remind us that the athlete cannot read or hear the poem, either. Do you think this is a deliberate tactic or an error on Housman's part? What adjustment does the reader have to make here?

4. The last two stanzas advise the athlete to hold up his victory cup to the admiration of the dead. Assuming that the advice is intended ironically, what is the effect of the irony?

5. To maintain his tight a-a-b-b rhyme scheme in the short, four-beat lines, Housman is forced to employ some unnatural word order (for example, "hold to the low lintel up"). Does the resulting pronounced artificiality seem appropriate to the theme and tone of the poem, or is it a distracting weakness?

4

THE COMPUTER-CARD CULTURE

Process

Probably ninety percent of scientific — and research paper — writing employs two methods of presentation: analysis of cause and effect and of process. The two can be distinguished quite easily: cause and effect analysis answers the question, *"Why* does something work or happen?" and process analysis answers the question, *"How* does it work or happen?" A study of the principles of physics which cause an internal combustion engine to operate would be analysis of cause and effect; an explanation of how an engine is constructed would be process analysis. The reason so much writing is of these two types is probably apparent. Although the first duty of a scientist is to observe accurately, the isolated facts he collects are meaningless until some relationships or applications are worked out. Cause and effect and process analysis show these relations and applications.

Process refers to the explanation, step by step, of the way in which something happens or operates. It does not, like cause and effect, have to tell *why* the phenomenon occurs, but only *how* it happens. Thus a recipe for devil's food cake is a simple process analysis. Such questions as "Why does yeast make dough rise?" do not need to be answered (although cause and effect analysis is frequently combined with process). If the process is followed correctly, the dough *will* rise, whether or not we understand why it does.

Generally speaking, there are two kinds of process analysis, mechanical and historical, though such a division overlaps to some degree.

Mechanical process explains the steps by which a thing is put together or operates. The instructions for setting up an experiment in chemistry lab are an example of mechanical process; so, in coded form, is the score for playing Mozart's "Jupiter" symphony. More complicated mechanical processes would be an analysis of how sea gulls fly and an explanation of how a linear accelerator is constructed.

Historical process analysis is the same sort of procedure, except that it represents a description of the steps by which an event or series of events took place historically. Of this type would be a logistical account of the Battle of Bull Run — the deployment of troops, position of artillery, steps in the attack procedure, and so on. A geological account of the formation of the Hawaiian Islands would also be an historical process, as would a description of the way in which Macbeth attained the throne.

Writing process papers is ordinarily somewhat easier than is analysis of cause and effect. Some processes, of course, are extremely complicated, but even so you do not have to worry about such problems as multiplicity of causes. If you understand the process clearly, then you have only to worry about writing carefully.

There are two important rules to keep in mind when writing a process paper. In the first place, the steps in any process must be kept in exact order. If you do not do this, a simple chemistry experiment can destroy both laboratory and experimenter. If you reverse the steps "add 2/3 cup milk" and "simmer 20 minutes," the result can be a plate of fudge best attacked with hammer and chisel.

This rule of exact order is obvious and hardly needs to be dwelled upon. More important for a writer to remember is the rule of clarity; if one step in a process involving fifty steps is not clearly explained, the whole process is useless to the reader. Forty-nine clear explanations out of fifty is a good average, but in process it will not do. Every girl who has made a dress probably knows the frustration of trying to decipher a step not clearly explained on the pattern, as does the builder of a foreign-made radio lab kit with directions written by an unskilled translator. Even the simplest process demands clarity in each step; the more complicated ones you will have to write as a college student — lab reports, research papers, case histories, and engineering reports — require even closer attention to clarity.

Many of these processes are of the least complicated variety, simple sets of directions. But the processes you will write in college frequently will not allow an explanation of steps in uninterrupted 1-2-3-4 order. One problem is that the subject is likely to demand descriptions and explanations which are not part of the process itself. Another is that in a complicated process several things may be happening simultaneously. Consequently, you may have to proceed by stages or subdivisions. Even in a purely mechanical process like the operation of an automobile engine, subdivisions would be necessary: the carburetion system; the ignition system, the piston, rod, and valve assembly and operation; and the transmission. (The steps in each subdivision, of course, must still be kept in order.) In such fields as biology and psychology, the processes may be even more complicated. Your problem then will be to find a way of organizing the material in such a way that the reader can understand all the factors involved and still see clearly the steps or stages of the process.

It is because of the absolute necessity for clarity that process writing is such useful practice for students in freshman composition. Process analysis can develop the habit of making certain that your reader will understand what you are trying to communicate. When you write a process paper, you should test your explanations by reading the first draft to someone who is not familiar with the process being explained. Any steps which he does not understand you can then rewrite and explain in greater detail. In extremely complicated processes, you may find diagrams useful in explaining some of the steps.

The Art of the Memorandum

Joseph Porter Clerk, Jr.

Joseph Porter Clerk, Jr. is a pseudonym. The author works for the federal government. This essay is one of a series on government red tape appearing in The Washington Monthly.

Armies move on their stomachs, governments on their memoranda. Memoranda are the devices by which bureaucrats communicate, make decisions, and record what has happened. You cannot succeed in government without mastering the art. Nor is it easy to come by. After seven years in government, I am just gaining a beginner's command over this indispensable tool of deceptively simple appearance. 1

When I entered government, I assumed a memorandum was an official document that bureaucrat A wrote to bureaucrat B when A wanted B to do something. This was naive. B's usual response is to do nothing. 2

This may be because B is too busy writing his own memoranda or, more likely, because B is one of those public servants whose impulses to action are thoroughly controlled by their awareness of the accompanying risks. 3

In either event, the primary rule of the memorandum is to expect no action from its recipient. 4

This rule, when first learned, tends to be dispiriting, but its advantages soon become apparent. Other men's inertia can be the secret of your power to act and to influence policy. 5

Consider a simple example. As a novice you would have written to your superior asking his permission to do such and such. You would have received no answer and therefore not had the authority to do what you had proposed doing. You now know that your memo should say, "Next Tuesday I plan to. . . ." No answer constitutes your authority to act. (The Navy has honored this tactic with the acronym UNODIR — "unless otherwise directed.") 6

This sort of thing won't work if there is the slightest hint of anything unusual about your proposal. The memorandum must imply, "I'm probably wasting your time to ask you to read what is obviously a matter of course, but I feel I should always lean over backwards to keep you fully informed." 7

You may, in fact, propose a revolutionary change in policy, but it should always be stated as an interpretation of present policy — an exegesis on scripture in the absence of new revelation. 8

New ideas are fragile in a bureaucracy. And their chances of survival   9
usually diminish when they are proclaimed as new ideas. Instead, say that
you are merely examining the assumptions underlying the status quo. While
your reputation for liveliness may suffer, your ideas may succeed.

Occasionally, however, you should advertise the novelty of your pro-   10
posal. There are some government officials who take great pride in being
"open to new approaches." The hazard in dealing with them is that some
mean it and some don't. Thus it is crucially important to know your readers.
Not only must you know the identity of those few lovers of new ideas for
whose benefit you can speak out boldly, but also of that other (not always
mutually exclusive) minority, the officials who actually do something when
they receive a memorandum.

But you can be assured that most of your readership will be the non-   11
responders. The key fact to realize about them is that everyone who reads
your memo and does nothing is to some degree implicated in the action you
propose or the policy interpretation you make.

Therefore you want to address the memo to (or at least note "copy to")   12
everyone whose assent you need. Since some of them are likely to be busy
and important people who might be able to claim they never read your
message in the event its result proves unpopular, you must make sure that
they do, in fact, read it.

One device that practically guarantees that B will read it is to add as   13
another addressee someone who is important to B — his superior, perhaps, or
the man who controls his budget or his personal allotment.

Mark the message "Secret" or "Confidential" or "For President's Eyes   14
Only." Security classifications were not devised for their value in catching
attention, but that only makes them more useful for the purpose.

Make your message stand out from the others. If blue paper is required   15
for memos, use pink. If most messages are in the form of official cables (as
is the case in U.S. embassies overseas), use a commercial cable or write a letter.
If messages are in letter form (as is generally true in domestic agencies), send
a telegram.

Another way to gain attention is to use concise English. However, there   16
is a risk here: you may be regarded as a dangerous eccentric. It should never
be tried by a new man, for he will be looked upon with pity as a novice
who simply lacks the appropriate vocabulary.

Sometimes you will want to make sure that a recipient does *not* read   17
your memorandum. He may be one of those unpredictable action-takers mentioned earlier, or he may be a man you know to be totally dedicated to
shooting down any idea of yours. Nevertheless, you need to have him implicated in this one. How do you manage it without having him read the memorandum? Make it long and dull. Make the subject sound highly technical. Send
a faint carbon or a bad Xerox. See that it is delivered late Friday afternoon.
It will join large piles of written material behind the executive's desk, where

it will testify to his good intentions until the day of his retirement. Or it will travel thousands of miles in the bottom of his briefcase waiting for a moment that will never come.

When I was working in the General Counsel's office at AID, I once 18 recommended that we send a complaint against a construction firm to the Department of Justice for suit. The firm had built a road in Southeast Asia which collapsed. It was important to get the case to the Department of Justice not so much because several million dollars of taxpayers' money was involved, but because once the problem was at Justice we could stop wasting our time answering inquiries from Congress and the General Accounting Office. We could simply reply that Justice was considering suit and that we had been asked not to comment.

My memorandum recommending suit had to do with the kind of decision 19 that the General Counsel would feel he should make himself but would never find time for. To get my memorandum through him I knew that I would have to persuade him at the outset that he would never study the matter. Assembling the relevant (and not so relevant) papers having to do with the case and labeling them exhibit 1, 2, 3, etc., I piled the whole mass in a shopping cart borrowed from the General Services Administration and wheeled it into his office, with my memo on top. I urged a personal study of the problem. I got his initials in three minutes.

Success with the memorandum can depend just as much on your fellow 20 senders as on the recipients. Mustering others to join in sending a memorandum accomplishes two things: it displays wider support for the message and, more important, it diffuses responsibility for it. The desirability of the latter becomes clear when the memorandum outrages a higher official.

Multiple authorship is ordinarily effected by a device known as "clear- 21 ance." This process consists of obtaining on the yellow copy of the memorandum the signatures or initials of persons other than the nominal sender of the memorandum. The most extraordinary thing about the process is that no one knows exactly what "clearance" means. Some degree of affirmation is presumed to be involved. The vagueness of that affirmation may make it easier to get B to clear a memorandum than to act upon it. He can mean "yes, in principle" without assuming an obligation to do anything. An additional advantage is that you can more easily pressure for a quick initialling, so as not to "hold up the memo."

Of course the reverse may also be a good tactic. Instead of asking such 22 known sympathizers as P and Q to clear the memorandum, put them down as addressees. This places them in the position of being able to initiate a favorable response. This device can even be extended to having someone else send to you the memorandum you would have liked to write (or maybe did in fact write) so that you can respond favorably. This is the only sure-fire method of assuring prompt action by the addressee.

Suppose all this art has been directed at you and there is now a memo-   23
randum on your desk from someone else proposing an action or supporting
a policy about which you are doubtful but don't wish to commit yourself,
even by implication.

Reply that the proposal is so interesting that it deserves to be the subject   24
of a large task force study. This will guarantee a six-month delay at the very
least.

SUBJECT QUESTIONS

1. The aim of this essay is clearly satiric; does that fact negate the validity
   of the process it describes?
2. Judging by this process, what would be the usual fate of a new idea?
3. If all bureaucrats actually used Clerk's technique, quite a bit might be
   accomplished. How can you know that they don't use it?
4. The author gives only one concrete example. Is it helpful? Should he
   have included more?

STRUCTURE QUESTIONS

1. Are the steps in the process clearly described?
2. Do you have any difficulty with the order of those steps? Are too many
   alternative procedures inserted?
3. Would it be possible for a reader to follow the directions given and get
   desired results without further information?
4. Does the counter-process offered in the final two paragraphs destroy
   the essay's unity, or does it form a suitable conclusion?

The Peter Principle

Raymond Hull

Raymond Hull is the collaborator with Dr. Laurence J. Peter on the book The Peter Principle *(1969).*

Bunglers are always with us and always have been. Winston Churchill tells   1
us, in his history of World War II, that in August, 1940, he had to take charge
personally of the Armed Forces' Joint Planning Committee because, after
almost twelve months of war, the Committee had not originated a single plan.

In the 1948 Presidential election, the advance public-opinion polls   2
awarded an easy victory to Thomas E. Dewey. In the Fifties, there was the
Edsel bungle. In 1965, Houston's domed baseball stadium opened and was
so ill-suited to baseball that, on sunny days, fielders could not see fly balls
against the blinding glare from the skylight.

We have come to expect incompetence as a necessary feature of civili-   3
zation. We may be irked, but we are no longer amazed, when our bosses make
idiotic decisions, when automobile makers take back thousands of new cars
for repairs, when store clerks are insolent, when law reforms fail to check
crime, when moon rockets can't get off the ground, when widely used medi-
cines are found to be poisons, when universities must teach freshmen to read,
or when a hundred-ton airliner is brought down by a duck.

We see these malpractices and mishaps as unconnected accidents, inevi-   4
table results of human fallibility.

But one man says, "These occurrences are not accidents; they are simply   5
the fruits of a system which, as I have shown, *develops, perpetuates and
rewards incompetence.*"

The Newton of incompetence theory is a burly, black-haired, slow-spo-   6
ken Canadian philosopher and iconoclast, Dr. Laurence J. Peter, who made
his living as Assistant Professor of Education at the University of British
Columbia until recently, when he moved down the coast to become a Professor of Education at the University of Southern California.

There is nothing incompetent about Dr. Peter. He is a successful author: 7
his *Prescriptive Teaching* is a widely used text on the education of problem
children. He built a house with his own hands, makes his own wine, is an

expert cook, a skilled woodcarver, and an inventor. (He created a new tool rack for school woodwork shops and perfected an apparatus for marking fifty exam papers at once.) Yet his chief claim to fame may be his founding of the science of hierarchiology.

Hierarchiology [he says,] is the study of hierarchies. "Hierarchy" originally meant "church government by clergy graded into ranks." The term now includes any organization whose members or employees are arranged by rank or grade.

Early in life, I faced the problem of occupational incompetence. As a young schoolteacher I was shocked, baffled, to see so many knotheads as principals, inspectors and superintendents.

I questioned older teachers. All I could find was that the knotheads, earlier in their career, had been capable, and that was why they had been promoted.

Eventually I realized that the same phenomenon occurs in all trades and professions, because the same basic rule governs the climb through every hierarchy. A competent employee is eligible for promotion, but incompetence is a bar to promotion. So an employee's final position must be one for which he is incompetent!

Suppose you own a drug-manufacturing firm, Perfect Pill Incorporated. Your foreman pill-roller dies of a perforated ulcer; you seek a replacement among the rank-and-file pill-rollers. Miss Cylinder, Mrs. Ellipse and Mr. Cube are variously incompetent and so don't qualify. You pick the best pill-roller, Mr. Sphere, and promote him to foreman.

Suppose Sphere proves highly competent in this new job: later, when deputy-works-manager Legree moves up one step, Sphere will take his place.

But if Sphere is incompetent as foreman, he won't be promoted again. He has reached what I call his *level of incompetence* and there he will stay till he retires.

An employee may, like Mr. Cube, reach his level of incompetence at the lowest rank: he is never promoted. It may take one promotion to place him at his level of incompetence; it may take a dozen. But, sooner or later, he does attain it.   8

Dr. Peter cites the case of the late General A. Jacks.° His hearty manner, informal dress, scorn for petty regulations and disregard for personal safety made him the idol of his men. He led them from victory to victory.   9

Had the war ended sooner, Jacks might have retired, covered in glory. But he was promoted to the rank of field marshal. Now he had to deal, not with fighting men, but with politicians of his own country, and with two punctilious Allied field marshals.

He quarreled with them all and took to spending whole days drunk, sulking in his trailer. The conduct of the war slipped out of his hands and into those of his subordinates.

The final promotion had brought him from doing what he *could* do, to attempting what he could not do. He had reached his level of incompetence.

° It is Dr. Peter's usual practice to employ fictitious names in his case histories.

The Jacks' case exemplifies the Peter Principle, the basic theorem of   10
hierarchiology. *In a hierarchy each employee tends to rise to his level of
incompetence: every post tends to be occupied by an employee incompetent
to execute its duties.*

How is it, then, that any work is done at all? Peter says, "Work is done   11
by people who have not yet attained final placement at their level of incompetence."

And how is it that we occasionally see a competent person at the very   12
top of the hierarchy? "Simply because there are not enough ranks for him
to have reached his level of incompetence: in other words, *in that hierarchy*
there is no task beyond his abilities."

As a rule, such a prodigy of competence eventually sidesteps into another hierarchy — say from the Armed Forces into industry, from law to politics, from business
to government — and there finds his level of incompetence. A well-known example
is Macbeth, a successful general, but an incompetent king.

In an unpublished monograph, *The Pathology of Success: Morbidity and*   13
Mortality at the Level of Incompetence, Peter expands his theory to take in
matters of health.

Certain physical conditions are associated with the final placement: peptic ulcers,
high blood pressure, nervous disorders, migraine headaches, alcoholism, insomnia,
obesity and cardiovascular complaints. Obviously such symptoms indicate the patient's constitutional incompetence for his level of responsibility.

Edgar Allan Poe, a highly competent writer, proved incompetent when raised
to the rank of editor. He became "nervous in a very unusual degree," took to drink
and then to drugs in a vain search for relief.

Such ailments, usually appearing two or more together, constitute the Final
Placement Syndrome.

Medication and surgery are often prescribed for F.P.S. patients, but they miss
the root cause of the condition. Psychoanalysis fails for the same reason. The analyst
is probing into the patient's subconscious for Oedipus complex, castration-complex,
penis-envy or whatnot, when the trouble really lies outside, in the patient's hierarchal
placement.

Is there no escape? Must every worker reach his level of incompetence,   14
suffer the miseries of Final Placement Syndrome and become a laughing stock
for his behavioral or temperamental symptoms?

Peter describes two escape routes. The first is for a man who realizes   15
that he has reached his level of incompetence, yet still wants to preserve
health, self-respect and sanity.

Many an employee adjusts to final placement by the process of Substitution. Instead
of executing his proper duties, he substitutes a set of irrelevant duties, and these
self-imposed tasks he carries out to perfection.

A. L. Tredwell, assistant principal of a secondary school, was intellectually competent and maintained good relationships with teachers, students, and parents. He was promoted to principal. Soon it became clear that he lacked the finesse to deal with newspaper reporters, school-board members, and the district superintendent. He fell out of favor with the officials, and his school lost community support. Realizing consciously or subconsciously — it doesn't matter which — that he was incompetent for the proper duties of a principal, Tredwell *Substituted*. He developed an obsessive concern with the movement of students and staff about the school.

He drew complex plans of traffic-flow, had white lines painted on floors and arrows on walls, spent hours prowling the building looking for violations of his rules, and bombarded professional journals with articles about his scheme.

Tredwell's Substitution is a great success. He is active and contented now, and shows no sign of the Final Placement Syndrome.

Peter's alternate escape route is for the employee who is capably and happily doing his work and who wants to avoid ever reaching his level of incompetence. 16

Merely to *refuse* promotion seldom leads to happiness. It annoys one's superiors, rouses suspicion among one's peers, and shames one's wife and children. Few people can endure all that. So one must contrive never to be offered promotion. 17

The first step is to avoid asking, or seeming to ask, for it. The oft-heard complaint, "My job lacks challenge," is usually understood as showing desire for promotion. So don't give voice to such complaints! 18

The second step is described by Peter in his lecture, Creative Incompetence: "I have found some employees who are contented in their work, and who seem to be using effective means of maintaining their position." 19

Adam Greenaway, a gardener, happily tends the landscaped grounds of the Ideal Trivet Company. He is competent in all aspects of his work but one: He keeps losing delivery slips for goods received. He gives vague explanations such as "I must have planted the papers with the shrubs." Most important, he concealed the fact that he wanted to avoid promotion.

Lack of delivery slips so upset the accounting department that, when a new maintenance foreman was needed, Greenaway was not considered for the post.

Thus he could stay indefinitely at a level of competence and enjoy the keen personal satisfaction of regularly accomplishing useful work. Surely this offers as great a challenge as the traditional drive for higher ranks!

By his Darwinian Extension Theorem, Peter applies his Principle to the whole human race. Man may go the way of the dinosaur and the sabre-tooth tiger. Those beasts were destroyed by excessive development of the qualities — bulk and fangs — that had originally favored their survival. Man's cleverness was originally a survival characteristic, but now he has become clever enough to destroy himself. If he takes that step, he will achieve his ultimate level of incompetence, in proving himself unfit to live. 20

"Man's one hope," says Peter, "lies in hierarchiology. I feel that it will   21
soon be recognized as the supreme science. Earlier sociological studies have
insufficiently recognized man's hierarchal nature."

A knowledge of the Peter Principle becomes more and more important as hierarchal
systems become stronger. Government and education are prime examples. Both already swollen, both expanding their demands for money and manpower, both extending their influence as more people stay longer in school, and as government
controls more functions of life. Even industry, once a stronghold of individualism,
is largely an aggregation of hierarchies. My point is that man ought to be using the
hierarchal system for his benefit. But he can't possibly use it unless he understands
it, and to do that he must understand the Peter Principle. Failing such understanding,
the system will destroy the individuals who comprise it.

Many people accept the Peter Principle on first hearing. It sounds so   22
obvious, so like common sense; it explains so aptly a group of hitherto mysti-
fying phenomena.

In academic circles, however, the Principle has made little impression.   23
A few of Peter's subordinates when he was at the University of British Columbia grasped it, but none of his superiors. Some of them saw it as a humorous
trifle, others as sociological heresy. Said Peter at the time: "I'm neither primarily funny or unfunny. I study society scientifically because I must live in
it. I present my findings to you because they describe the world you live in."

Anyway, I'm too busy to worry much about what others think of me. I teach future
schoolteachers how to work with handicapped and disturbed children. I'm pursuing
two fascinating lines of research: into autism, a profound emotional disorder in which
children have no sense of self, and no ability to learn by experience; and into developmental dyslexia, an inability to recognize printed words that often, tragically, pins
a "mentally retarded" label on a genuinely intelligent child. It's all deeply satisfying:
I'm about as happy in my work as anyone I know.

The thought then occurred that Peter's hierarchiology might, just might,   24
be *his* form of Creative Incompetence — a means of making himself slightly
suspect, and so avoiding an unwanted academic promotion.

"No, no! Of course not!" said the doctor. "But even if it were, of course   25
I wouldn't admit it!"

SUBJECT QUESTIONS

1. Test your understanding of the Peter Principle by applying it to a hierarchy not considered in detail in this essay.
2. Do you agree that the Peter Principle operates in every organization
   having a hierarchal structure? Can you think of any in which it does not
   apply?
3. If Peter believes that his principle applies to all organizations, why
   doesn't he advocate the abolition of hierarchies?

4. Criticize the following application of the Peter Principle: "The United Nations General Assembly accomplishes little because it is composed of formerly able statesmen who were promoted to their level of incompetence."
5. How, according to Peter, can a person avoid reaching his level of incompetence? How has Peter himself avoided it?
6. Can you suggest ways by which a hierarchy — say a school system or a business corporation — could avoid filling all its executive positions with incompetents?
7. Does the process which Peter calls "Substitution" strike you as a satisfactory way to avoid "Final Placement Syndrome"? Is it prevalent, judging from your own observation?

STRUCTURE QUESTIONS

1. Several separate processes are explained in this essay, including the historical process of how Peter arrived at his principle. Does including more than one process in the same article cause any confusion? Do they all belong here?
2. Professor Peter explains his principle with two illustrations, the cases of Mr. Sphere and General A. Jacks. Does this procedure give a clear idea of the process? Why must Peter resort to particular examples instead of outlining the steps in general?
3. Do you think Hull created a structural problem for himself by trying to tell his readers about Professor Peter and about the Peter Principle both in the same essay? Does one lead naturally into the other? How does Hull tie them together at the end?
4. Peter says that "man ought to be using the hierarchal system for his benefit." Does this essay make clear how man can do this, considering Peter's contention that his principle invariably operates at present? Should the essay have been expanded at this point? Or should the statement have been omitted?

Parkinson's Law

C. Northcote Parkinson

C. Northcote Parkinson (born in 1909), teacher and public lecturer, first devised his "law" when he was a professor of history at the University of Malaya. It occurred to him as a result of research into certain agencies of the British government. But his book, Parkinson's Law *(of which the selection here is the first chapter), argues that the law and its corollaries apply to all administrations, whether in government, education, or private enterprise.*

Work expands so as to fill the time available for its completion. General recognition of this fact is shown in the proverbial phrase "It is the busiest man who has time to spare." Thus, an elderly lady of leisure can spend the entire day in writing and dispatching a postcard to her niece at Bognor Regis. An hour will be spent in finding the postcard, another in hunting for spectacles, half an hour in a search for the address, an hour and a quarter in composition, and twenty minutes in deciding whether or not to take an umbrella when going to the mailbox in the next street. The total effort that would occupy a busy man for three minutes all told may in this fashion leave another person prostrate after a day of doubt, anxiety, and toil.

Granted that work (and especially paper work) is thus elastic in its demands on time, it is manifest that there need be little or no relationship between the work to be done and the size of the staff to which it may be assigned. A lack of real activity does not, of necessity, result in leisure. A lack of occupation is not necessarily revealed by a manifest idleness. The thing to be done swells in importance and complexity in a direct ratio with the time to be spent. This fact is widely recognized, but less attention has been paid to its wider implications, more especially in the field of public administration. Politicians and taxpayers have assumed (with occasional phases of doubt) that a rising total in the number of civil servants must reflect a growing volume of work to be done. Cynics, in questioning this belief, have imagined that the multiplication of officials must have left some of them idle or all of them able to work for shorter hours. But this is a matter in which faith and doubt seem equally misplaced. The fact is that the number of the officials and the quantity of work are not related to each other at all. The rise in the total of those employed is governed by Parkinson's Law and would be much the same whether the volume of the work were to increase, diminish, or even disappear. The importance of Parkinson's Law lies in the fact that it is a law of growth based upon an analysis of the factors by which that growth is controlled.

The validity of this recently discovered law must rest mainly on statisti-   3 cal proofs, which will follow. Of more interest to the general reader is the explanation of the factors underlying the general tendency to which this law gives definition. Omitting technicalities (which are numerous) we may distinguish at the outset two motive forces. They can be represented for the present purpose by two almost axiomatic statements, thus: (1) "An official wants to multiply subordinates, not rivals" and (2) "Officials make work for each other."

To comprehend Factor 1, we must picture a civil servant, called A, who   4 finds himself overworked. Whether this overwork is real or imaginary is immaterial, but we should observe, in passing, that A's sensation (or illusion) might easily result from his own decreasing energy: a normal symptom of middle-age. For this real or imagined overwork there are, broadly speaking, three possible remedies. He may resign; he may ask to halve the work with a colleague called B; he may demand the assistance of two subordinates, to be called C and D. There is probably no instance in history, however, of A choosing any but the third alternative. By resignation he would lose his pension rights. By having B appointed, on his own level in the hierarchy, he would merely bring in a rival for promotion to W's vacancy when W (at long last) retires. So A would rather have C and D, junior men, below him. They will add to his consequence and, by dividing the work into two categories, as between C and D, he will have the merit of being the only man who comprehends them both. It is essential to realize at this point that C and D are, as it were, inseparable. To appoint C alone would have been impossible. Why? Because C, if by himself, would divide the work with A and so assume almost the equal status that has been refused in the first instance to B; a status the more emphasized if C is A's only possible successor. Subordinates must thus number two or more, each being thus kept in order by fear of the other's promotion. When C complains in turn of being overworked (as he certainly will) A will, with the concurrence of C, advise the appointment of two assistants to help C. But he can then avert internal friction only by advising the appointment of two more assistants to help D, whose position is much the same. With this recruitment of E, F, G, and H the promotion of A is now practically certain.

Seven officials are now doing what one did before. This is where Factor   5 2 comes into operation. For these seven make so much work for each other that all are fully occupied and A is actually working harder than ever. An incoming document may well come before each of them in turn. Official E decides that it falls within the province of F, who places a draft reply before

C, who amends it drastically before consulting D, who asks G to deal with it. But G goes on leave at this point, handing the file over to H, who drafts a minute that is signed by D and returned to C, who revises his draft accordingly and lays the new version before A.

What does A do? He would have every excuse for signing the thing 6 unread, for he has many other matters on his mind. Knowing now that he is to succeed W next year, he has to decide whether C or D should succeed to his own office. He had to agree to G's going on leave even if not yet strictly entitled to it. He is worried whether H should not have gone instead, for reasons of health. He has looked pale recently — partly but not solely because of his domestic troubles. Then there is the business of F's special increment of salary for the period of the conference and E's application for transfer to the Ministry of Pensions. A has heard that D is in love with a married typist and that G and F are no longer on speaking terms — no one seems to know why. So A might be tempted to sign C's draft and have done with it. But A is a conscientious man. Beset as he is with problems created by his colleagues for themselves and for him — created by the mere fact of these officials' existence — he is not the man to shirk his duty. He reads through the draft with care, deletes the fussy paragraphs added by C and H, and restores the thing back to the form preferred in the first instance by the able (if quarrelsome) F. He corrects the English — none of these young men can write grammatically — and finally produces the same reply he would have written if officials C to H had never been born. Far more people have taken far longer to produce the same result. No one has been idle. All have done their best. And it is late in the evening before A finally quits his office and begins the return journey to Ealing. The last of the office lights are being turned off in the gathering dusk that marks the end of another day's administrative toil. Among the last to leave, A reflects with bowed shoulders and a wry smile that late hours, like gray hairs, are among the penalties of success.

From this description of the factors at work the student of political 7 science will recognize that administrators are more or less bound to multiply. Nothing has yet been said, however, about the period of time likely to elapse between the date of A's appointment and the date from which we can calculate the pensionable service of H. Vast masses of statistical evidence have been collected and it is from a study of this data that Parkinson's Law has been deduced. Space will not allow of detailed analysis but the reader will be interested to know that research began in the British Navy Estimates. These were chosen because the Admiralty's responsibilities are more easily measurable than those of, say, the Board of Trade. The question is merely one of numbers and tonnage. Here are some typical figures. The strength of the Navy in 1914 could be shown as 146,000 officers and men, 3249 dockyard officials and clerks, and 57,000 dockyard workmen. By 1928 there were only 100,000 officers and men and only 62,439 workmen, but the dockyard officials and clerks by then numbered 4558. As for warships, the strength in 1928 was a mere fraction of what it had been in 1914 — fewer than 20 capital ships in commission as compared with 62. Over the same period the Admiralty officials had increased in number from 2000 to 3569, providing (as was remarked) "a magnificent navy on land." These figures are more clearly set forth in tabular form.

Table 1
Admiralty Statistics

	Year		Increase or decrease
	1914	1928	
Capital ships in commission	62	20	−67.74%
Officers and men in R.N.	146,000	100,000	−31.5%
Dockyard workers	57,000	62,439	+9.54%
Dockyard officials and clerks	3249	4558	+40.28%
Admiralty officials	2000	3569	+78.45%

The criticism voiced at the time centered on the ratio between the numbers of those available for fighting and those available only for administration. But that comparison is not to the present purpose. What we have to note is that the 2000 officials of 1914 had become the 3569 of 1928; and that this growth was unrelated to any possible increase in their work. The Navy during that period had diminished, in point of fact, by a third in men and two-thirds in ships. Nor, from 1922 onward, was its strength even expected to increase; for its total of ships (unlike its total of officials) was limited by the Washington Naval Agreement of that year. Here we have then a 78 percent increase over a period of fourteen years; an average of 5.6 percent increase a year on the earlier total. In fact, as we shall see, the rate of increase was not as regular as that. All we have to consider, at this stage, is the percentage rise over a given period.

Can this rise in the total number of civil servants be accounted for except on the assumption that such a total must always rise by a law governing its growth? It might be urged at this point that the period under discussion was one of rapid development in naval technique. The use of the flying machine was no longer confined to the eccentric. Electrical devices were being multiplied and elaborated. Submarines were tolerated if not approved. Engineer officers were beginning to be regarded as almost human. In so revolutionary an age we might expect that storekeepers would have more elaborate inventories to compile. We might not wonder to see more draughtsmen on the payroll, more designers, more technicians and scientists. But these, the dockyard officials, increased only by 40 percent in number when the men of Whitehall increased their total by nearly 80 percent. For every new foreman or electrical engineer at Portsmouth there had to be two more clerks at Charing Cross. From this we might be tempted to conclude, provisionally, that the rate of increase in administrative staff is likely to be double that of the technical staff at a time when the actually useful strength (in this case, of seamen) is being reduced by 31.5 percent. It has been proved statistically, however, that this last percentage is irrelevant. The officials would have multiplied at the same rate had there been no actual seamen at all.

It would be interesting to follow the further progress by which the 8118   10
Admiralty staff of 1935 came to number 33,788 by 1954. But the staff of the Colonial Office affords a better field of study during a period of imperial decline. Admiralty statistics are complicated by factors (like the Fleet Air Arm) that make comparison difficult as between one year and the next. The Colonial Office growth is more significant in that it is more purely administrative. Here the relevant statistics are as follows:

1935	1939	1943	1947	1954
372	450	817	1139	1661

Before showing what the rate of increase is, we must observe that the   11
extent of this department's responsibilities was far from constant during these twenty years. The colonial territories were not much altered in area or population between 1935 and 1939. They were considerably diminished by 1943, certain areas being in enemy hands. They were increased again in 1947, but have since then shrunk steadily from year to year as successive colonies achieve self-government. It would be rational to suppose that these changes in the scope of Empire would be reflected in the size of its central administration. But a glance at the figures is enough to convince us that the staff totals represent nothing but so many stages in an inevitable increase. And this increase, although related to that observed in other departments, has nothing to do with the size — or even the existence — of the Empire. What are the percentages of increase? We must ignore, for this purpose, the rapid increase in staff which accompanied the diminution of responsibility during World War II. We should note rather, the peacetime rates of increase: over 5.24 percent between 1935 and 1939, and 6.55 percent between 1947 and 1954. This gives an average increase of 5.89 percent each year, a percentage markedly similar to that already found in the Admiralty staff increase between 1914 and 1928.

Further and detailed statistical analysis of departmental staffs would be   12
inappropriate in such a work as this. It is hoped, however, to reach a tentative
conclusion regarding the time likely to elapse between a given official's first
appointment and the later appointment of his two or more assistants.

Dealing with the problem of pure staff accumulation, all our researches   13
so far completed point to an average increase of 5.75 percent per year. This
fact established, it now becomes possible to state Parkinson's Law in mathematical form: In any public administrative department not actually at war,
the staff increase may be expected to follow this formula —

$$x = \frac{2k^m + l}{n}$$

k is the number of staff seeking promotion through the appointment of subordinates; l represents the difference between the ages of appointment and
retirement; m is the number of man-hours devoted to answering minutes
within the department; and n is the number of effective units being administered. x will be the number of new staff required each year. Mathematicians
will realize, of course, that to find the percentage increase they must multiply
x by 100 and divide by the total of the previous year, thus:

$$\frac{100\,(2k^m + l)}{yn}\,\%$$

where y represents the total original staff. This figure will invariably prove
to be between 5.17 percent and 6.56 percent, irrespective of any variation
in the amount of work (if any) to be done.

The discovery of this formula and of the general principles upon which   14
it is based has, of course, no political value. No attempt has been made to
inquire whether departments *ought* to grow in size. Those who hold that this
growth is essential to gain full employment are fully entitled to their opinion.
Those who doubt the stability of an economy based upon reading each other's
minutes are equally entitled to theirs. It would probably be premature to
attempt at this stage any inquiry into the quantitative ratio that should exist
between the administrators and the administered. Granted, however, that a
maximum ratio exists, it should soon be possible to ascertain by formula how
many years will elapse before that ratio, in any given community, will be
reached. The forecasting of such a result will again have no political value.
Nor can it be sufficiently emphasized that Parkinson's Law is a purely scientific discovery, inapplicable except in theory to the politics of the day. It is
not the business of the botanist to eradicate the weeds. Enough for him if
he can tell us just how fast they grow.

SUBJECT QUESTIONS

1. Since Parkinson is obviously interested in administration, why does he begin with the illustration of a lady sending a postcard?
2. Parkinson shows how the law works by giving specific examples of it in operation; although this is not a process of the "how to bake a pie" variety, is it possible to give an abstract outline of the steps involved?
3. Do you know of any local or national offices whose administrative staff has increased while that which it "administers" has decreased — as in Parkinson's examples of the British Navy and Colonial Offices? While the Congress of the United States has increased only slightly in size in the past twenty years, its staff has increased tremendously; would you say that this growth reflects added duties of Congress, or the operation of Parkinson's Law?
4. Why do you suppose Parkinson makes the disclaimer in the final paragraph? If the law does indeed operate, isn't it obvious that something should be done about it?

STRUCTURE QUESTIONS

1. Parkinson is clearly describing a process; yet it differs from other processes described in this section. In what ways?
2. If the aim of this passage is satire, why does Parkinson maintain such a deadpan tone?
3. The mathematical formulae at the end are of course useless; why does Parkinson include them?
4. Try to find the organizational scheme for this essay. Do the last two paragraphs fit into the scheme?

Bigness in Business:
Petrie's Law

Robert Townsend

Robert Townsend, the former chief executive of Avis, is the author of Up
the Organization. *Having spent many years in executive positions among
various corporations, he has firsthand knowledge about the operation of
Parkinson's Law. Here, he proposes a solution to it.*

True story: Once upon a time there was a small department in a large orga-   1
nization. It was a typical pyramid — a vice-president, below him a manager,
a secretary for the two of them, and below that five workers. To mesh with
the rest of the company, their work had to be errorless and finished by 7 P.M.
It wasn't.

Here's what was going on. The workers would finish and take the work   2
to the manager, who would make a few changes (otherwise what was he there
for?) He'd send it to the vice-president, who would make a few changes
(otherwise what was *he* there for?). The troops had learned that whatever
they did they'd have to do over, so they were giving it a lick and a promise.
Upshot: work finished at 11 P.M. full of errors.

For once, the traditional solution of adding more bodies was avoided.   3
Instead, the vice-president, the manager, and the secretary were de-hired. The
workers were called together and told how much was available for wages
and salaries. "Consider yourselves a partnership," they were told. "Hire
whomever you need, pay yourselves whatever the budget will stand, decide
who does what job — and see if you can get the work done without errors
by seven o'clock."

For a while work suffered, but one day it all began to come together.   4
It turned out the partners didn't need anybody else, so they were able to raise
salaries an average of 25 per cent (everybody got paid the same regardless
of seniority). They split up the responsibilities, named one partner to pick
up the odd problems, and discovered to their amazement that they could come
in at ten o'clock and still get the work done without errors by four. They're
all having a ball, the rest of the organization is jealous as hell, and the point
(five people in a partnership work a lot better than eight people in a pyramid)
is in danger of being missed.

The first time I noticed the fewer-the-better phenomenon was in 1952. I'd been working as a security analyst in American Express's investment department, a group of twenty-one men and women investing several billion dollars a year of traveler's cheque float. Our leader was a bright young man with the big picture and a good sense of humor who was in the running for the top job in the company; yet all was far from well. Two of the best people were underpaid, dissatisfied, and looking around; we needed an additional senior analyst and an economist. I knew about the unrest among the field hands because I was one of them. We put in the hours, went through the motions, but our hearts weren't in our work. We had jobs. We did what was required, didn't do what we didn't have to, and got our kicks on weekends, vacations, and after hours.

Unexpectedly our boss died, and the company, with that consistent irrationality I later grew to love, chose me to take his place. There must have been a shortage in the executive ranks of tall blond Princeton men who could hit the ball 280 yards off the tee, because that's about all I brought to the task.

Feeling not a little guilty, I called my first department meeting. Since we all knew each other well, it didn't take long to reach agreement on what needed doing. Where to get the money to do it was the stopper. American Express was a very rigid despotism, and amending the budget in midyear was unthinkable. The second meeting produced the answer: if we really wanted to be top-drawer, we'd have to give up our secretaries, typists, and file clerks in return for the new analyst, the economist, and fair pay for the rest.

The transition was accomplished gradually and without an increase in overall budget. What the twenty-one-man pyramid evolved into was a partnership of thirteen peers. My job as senior partner was to get us the tools we needed and keep the rest of American Express off our backs. The other partners' job was to run the best investment operation in town.

Having no secretaries, the analysts wrote briefer reports and depended more on oral presentations. The finance committee welcomed the relief from turgid essays. Having no file clerks, the analysts did their own filing. They threw out 90 per cent of the junk the clerks had put in there just to be on the safe side, and found they actually saved time by doing a little menial filing every day.

All of which led to my accidental discovery of Petrie's Law of detumescent organizations: "Fewer people paid more tends to produce excellence at no overall cost except to the people who get fired."

It should be noted that Petrie's Law (named after Donald A. Petrie, my fellow conspirator) is applicable to the public as well as the private sector. In *The Foreign Affairs Fudge Factory* the late John F. Campbell gave us an apt illustration:

Ellis Briggs when he was ambassador to Czechoslovakia shortly after the communist coup d'état of 1948 . . . had been pestering Washington, without success, to cut his staff of eighty personnel . . . by half, down to forty. One day the Czech government, unaware of this background, declared sixty-six of the American embassy's personnel *persona non grata* and gave them forty-eight hours to leave the country. . . . to Briggs it was a blessing in disguise. "The American embassy in Prague then consisted of thirteen people," Briggs remarked. "It was probably the most efficient embassy I ever headed."

It works in the professions, too. I know of a legal firm built on Petrie's 12
Law. There are no associates, no junior partners, no clerks. Nobody earns less than $100,000 a year. If the firm takes your case, it will be handled all the way by a partner. He does all the grundge work himself, so he knows what he's doing. If he needs specialists, he hires them. He's good. He enjoys his work. He doesn't waste time. Come to think of it, that's the basis of Ralph Nader's success. His projects are partnerships of eight to eleven people. Each project is housed in a different building to cut down on cross-fertilization, otherwise known as goofing off. It occurs to me that Nader may be the only man on earth profiting from the lesson Jesus Christ was at some pains to teach us: when you're starting an organization, twelve people is one too many.

Well, you may properly say, since it works so well, it must be just a 13
question of time until all our big public and private hierarchies discover Petrie's Law and start making themselves smaller and better. Right?

Wrong. As a matter of fact, they're all headed in the opposite direction 14
lickety-split. Everywhere you look the trend is toward more and more people paid just enough to get them out of bed in the morning — otherwise known as the Motor Vehicle Bureau Syndrome. Here is how you create that kind of organization.

Start with, say, ten thousand employees. Put them all in one building and 15
divide them into departments. When communication breaks down, develop inter- and intra-office memo forms, job descriptions, and a police manual. When expenses begin to get out of hand, develop rigid salary limits and layers of salary committees. Develop purchasing forms and procedures so that it takes six months to get a desk lamp. When the best people get frustrated and leave, the salary limits will ensure that each will be replaced by a warm body. At this point, Leo Rosten's Law (second-rate people hire third-rate people) will take over. Soon you'll have sixteen thousand sullen timeservers, each bitterly resentful of customer intrusions, and bent on getting even with the company any way they can.

This miserable kind of organization has become commonplace because 16
we've ignored Petrie's Law and fallen prey to its opposite — The Let-'em-eat-

cake Law: "More and more people getting a smaller and smaller share of the pie eventually produces total catastrophe for everybody involved."

Most of our big corporations and public institutions are dead or dying   17
pyramids. Like fish, they're rotting from the head down. Unlike fish, they can be revived by decapitation. The dead layer of top management must be removed and the remaining people encouraged to form an organism consisting of small partnerships — as few as possible, but enough to get the job done.

I can give you the key to organizational fun and excellence: it's Petrie's   18
Law. But I can't unlock the door for you. I don't know how you're going to lop the top off your pyramid; how you're going to take power away from the privileged presidents; how you're going to get power to people in partnerships. That's up to you.

So what's going to happen to all our overstuffed organizations?   19

Not a blessed thing is my guess. And I'm not at all persuaded that's   20
a mistake. American incompetence may be one of the best things the world has going for it. Suppose we had a widespread espousal of Petrie's Law. Productivity would go through the roof, and we'd bury the earth in automobiles, Princess telephones, frozen krinkle-kut potatoes, and peppermint vaginal sprays. Can you imagine, for example, how awful it would be if the Pentagon's weaponry really *worked?*

I think we should all relax and enjoy the twilight of our fading romance   21
with BIGNESS. Why fight it? Much easier to open another can of beer, switch on the boob tube, and get really serious about turning our brains into cornmeal mush. That way we can pass the time until the moment arrives when, to borrow Kurt Vonnegut's image, the noble American experiment, unable to sustain its giant organizations any longer, turns its swollen green belly up and goes pop in the noonday sun.

SUBJECT QUESTIONS

1. Does Townsend offer Petrie's Law as a serious, or only humorous, "cure" to Parkinson's Law? If Townsend is convinced his solution will work, why does he think it will not be used?
2. Other than increased profits to the company, what advantages are there to Townsend's suggestion?
3. If the proposal were applied nationwide, do you think one result would be widespread unemployment?
4. Is Townsend arguing against his own proposal in the last two paragraphs? Why does he include these remarks?
5. Does Townsend's proposal apply only to executive levels of business and government? Could it be used among factory workers, for instance?

STRUCTURE QUESTIONS

1. Allowing for the fact that different organizations work differently, has Townsend made clear the steps necessary in applying Petrie's Law? Could you apply it to an organization for which Townsend has given no example — say, a university administration?
2. Townsend's opening example is labeled "true story"; would it have carried more weight had he given such concrete details as the name of the company, the department involved, perhaps even dates?
3. Discuss the effectiveness of Townsend's decision to use four examples in limited detail rather than one example in complete detail.
4. How effectively do you think Townsend has employed irony, particularly in the last two paragraphs?
5. Townsend's style is less formal than that of most essays in this text. Should an essay on economics and business organization have had a more formal style? What ingredients in Townsend's style make for informality?

Upward Failure

William Zinsser

Since graduating from Princeton in 1944, William Zinsser (b. 1922) has been feature writer for the New York Herald Tribune (1946–1949), then its drama editor (1949–1954) and film critic (1954–1958). He was a columnist for Life Magazine until it collapsed in 1972. He has written eight books, including The City Dwellers (1962), The Haircurl Papers (1964), and Pop Goes America (1966). Zinsser first invented the National Refractory and Brake Company for an article in Life (Feb. 28, 1969), in which he reported on its attempts to deal with the ecology movement. Further reports followed the organizational entanglements of this imaginary corporation. Here, Zinsser summarizes the career of its most recent chairman.

To our stockholders: This special supplement to the annual report of the 1 American National United Allied General Corporation — formerly the National Refractory & Brake Company — is a salute to Chairman of the Board Harley G. Waller, whose resignation to accept a high-level government post was recently announced in the press. Truly it can be said of Mr. Waller: "He put us where we are today."

How does one begin to tell the story of so remarkable a captain, who 2 rose steadily upward from humble beginnings to steer a mighty corporation? Perhaps one should begin simply by saying that this was a man who kept his eye on "the big picture" and did not waste his energy on small details.

Harley Waller first felt the mantle of command descend on his rugged 3 shoulders when he was in India during World War II. The young pilot chafed under the incapacity of the C-47 to attain what he felt was optimal climbing speed in flying "over the Hump" to China. He went to Lieutenant General George Stratemeyer and begged for a chance to lead a squadron of still-experimental C-88s on a critical supply drop to Stilwell's beleaguered troops, pointing out that the aerodynamic properties of the C-88 were far better suited to the local altitude-mist factor.

This colorful mission continues to intrigue historians of World War II. 4 Of the 12 aircraft that roared off toward the skies of China, the sole returning plane was that of Lieutenant Waller, which he crashlanded near the base although three of its engines had dropped out. General Stratemeyer was so impressed by young Waller's feat and by his subsequent report appraising the C-88 as "not yet fully operational" that the boyish lieutenant was promoted to colonel and given command of the 92nd Bomber Brigade.

Inevitably, when the war was over his record caught the eye of highly placed officials, who brought him to Washington for the first of several tours of public service that have put him in that small circle of Americans who can only be described as businessmen-statesmen, ready to answer their country's call for top-quality brains. As Deputy Assistant Under Secretary of the Army in the late 1940s, Harley Waller tirelessly pressed his belief in the tank as the prime deterrent to Communist expansion in Asia. Members of congressional committees remember to this day the eloquent testimony of the engaging young man which resulted in a $200 million appropriation for development and production of the low-silhouette XM-42 "Grizzly Bear" battle tank at a time when advocates of air power were pleading for a buildup in fighter-plane strength.

Shortly after the outbreak of hostilities in Korea, in which the new enemy MIG jet proved to have greater maneuverability than the Grizzly Bear tank and a consequent advantage in destructive capability, Mr. Waller resigned to accept what he described as "an irresistible call" from private industry, namely, the executive vice-presidency of the troubled Bartlett Motor Company, which was fighting for its very life in the sharply competitive automotive field. Moving with characteristic vigor, he launched an all-out effort to produce a semi-compact convertible. "Your average driver," he said at a press conference announcing the ambitious program that would eventually cost $27 million, "is tired of being shut up in a steel box. He wants to get back in God's fresh air like his Dad did in the good old rumble seat."

Intense interest surrounded the choice of a name which would convey the speed and grace of the car that was rapidly taking shape on the drawing boards of Bartlett engineers. Mr. Waller himself proposed many — e.g., Puma and Gazelle — which brilliantly anticipated the industry's successful later use of names such as Mustang, Impala and Cougar. In the end, however, he chose to "go along with a hunch," as he put it, "that the consumer is at heart a pretty sentimental guy." Accordingly, he named the car for founder Karl E. Bartlett's son, Norbert, who was retiring that year as chairman of the board.

The first Norbert rolled off the assembly line on Jan. 3, 1954, a date that Mr. Waller hailed as "the veritable dawn of a new age for Mr. and Mrs. America." By an unanticipated coincidence, 1954 also saw the general introduction of air-conditioning in cars produced by rival automakers, a factor that markedly reduced consumer demand for the Norbert convertible. Sales of the Norbert came to 4,612 in 1954, to 1,889 in 1955, and ceased in 1956 with the dissolution of the Bartlett Motor Company. Harley Waller will always remember 1956; who could forget a year in which one is summoned to the telephone by a call from the White House? The Eisenhower administration was about to announce the creation of HMR — the Department of Human Mobility Resources — and it wanted Mr. Waller for the Cabinet-rank post of Secretary.

"The President told me," Mr. Waller subsequently recalled, "that   9 American ground transportation was in a whale of a mess, and he was bound and determined that HMR was going to make it possible for all Americans to exercise their inalienable right to get where they wanted to go whenever they wanted to go there. The President said he had 'kind of a feeling' about me because the grille on the Norbert put him in mind of the cowcatchers on the old trains back in Abilene. I guess it didn't hurt that I also happen to play a pretty good game of golf."

Harley Waller was sworn in as the nation's first Secretary of Human   10 Mobility Resources on Sept. 10, 1956 and pledged to "get the trains moving again." Washington quickly warmed to its newest Cabinet official, who, at only 34, was being spoken of as "someone to watch." Harley Waller and his attractive wife, Marjorie, were frequent guests at the White House, and it was Mr. Waller whom the President often tapped for a round of golf when the awesome burdens of the Oval Office became too heavy. "I can relax with Harley," the President said. "He knows just how far to go with that homespun humor of his." Veteran White House correspondents still chuckle over the time when Mr. Waller placed on Ike's tee a small cream pie that he had molded into the shape of a golf ball. The resulting consternation when the club connected for its "drive" brought tears of mirth to the President's eyes. "By golly," he is reported to have said, "I can almost face Foster Dulles again now."

At HMR, it did not take long for Harley Waller to analyze the problem   11 and to formulate a "grand design." As a boy he had enjoyed tinkering with machines; now he became fascinated by the emerging technology of computers as the answer to America's deteriorating human mobility apparatus.

"One of my options," he told the *New York Times*, "was to go along   12 with the top dozen men in the department who had years of experience in the surface transportation industry. But frankly, those old boys didn't throw anything onto the table that was much newer than the Iron Horse. I saw it was going to be up to me to dream up a sophisticated system of inputs that would bring ground transportation into the space age."

Mr. Waller felt that citizen dissatisfaction stemmed from the fact that   13 daily interstate passenger trains had dwindled from 20,000 in the late 1920s to 884. He blamed the downward trend on "skyrocketing" labor demands in the wage and featherbedding area. "Let's face it, there are a lot of guys just sitting on their butts getting a free ride around the country," he told a press breakfast, at which he announced his "Invisible Man" project. This, he said, would replace all but 217 of the nation's 1,058,000 railroad employees with an automated system of memory modules operated from the HMR Building in Washington. "At an average wage of $5,500 including benefits," he noted, "we can effectuate an annual savings of $5.8 billion, and if I can't get more trains running with that kind of dough, I'll be the most surprised guy in the world."

A feasibility study, launched in December of 1956, resulted in the 14 awarding of a contract to the Premier Electronics Corp. (PRELCO) for construction of a prototype memory module network. The prototype, which was completed early in 1958 and tested on a commuter run of the Long Island Rail Road between Jamaica and Patchogue, encouraged Mr. Waller to give the go-ahead for full-scale automation of America's railroads. Meanwhile, he initiated the graduated layoff plan whereby engineers, brakemen, switchmen, conductors and ticket clerks who died or retired would not be replaced. The personnel force had accordingly been pared by 28% when PRELCO finished construction and began installation of its $426 million TGX-32-0014A ("Dagwood") electronic nerve center in January of 1959. How impatiently Harley Waller waited for the day when the vast complex would be assembled and he could push a button that would commence the operation of all of America's trains from the HMR Building! That day finally arrived on July 16.

On July 17 the TGX-32-0014A was placed in standby condition pending 15 the outcome of further feasibility studies. Two weeks later President Eisenhower announced the appointment of Harley Waller as ambassador to Taiwan. "Believe me, I wouldn't give up a golf partner who shoots in the low 70s," Ike told reporters, "if I didn't think he was the only man with the sensitivity to human nature that is so important right now to our friendship with the peoples of the Far East."

Seasoned observers of Sino-American relations still mention the dogged 16 skill with which the new ambassador recovered from the "chink in the armor" speech that he delivered upon his arrival at Taipei, urging immediate reoccupation of the mainland. His persistent efforts to have Quemoy and Matsu admitted as full members of the United Nations are regarded as a bold diplomatic initiative to maintain a balance between "our guys" and "their guys," and Mr. Waller is known to have felt that these efforts fell short of fruition only because the Eisenhower administration was then in its waning months.

The time had come, he realized, to go back to the private sector, and 17 in August of 1960 he resigned to accept the presidency of the huge DeBuff Chemical Company. Once again he exhibited a sure instinct for the route where he could best serve humanity. Little could he know it, but his conception and leadership at DeBuff of the three-year, $62 million research program which developed the synthetic wool, Bufftron — "the suit that came out of a test tube" — was being watched by another chieftain of free enterprise. In his paneled office at the National Refractory & Brake Company, 82-year-old

Roger S. Bassinger was eager to turn over the reins to a man whose vision of the future would match the dreams that he himself had nurtured as an 18-year-old lad making bicycle brakes in a toolshed in Sandusky. Now, on a late December day in 1963, the old tycoon picked up the phone and invited Harley Waller to meet him for lunch.

Harley G. Waller became chairman and chief executive officer of National Refractory & Brake on March 1, 1964 at a salary of $211,000 plus stock options. He was just 42 and in the prime of health; nobody would guess from the ruddy and jovial face that his beloved Bufftron suit had just been put on the market and found to cause severe skin allergies. [18]

"This is one of those rare instances in the long march of American capitalism," declared Roger S. Bassinger at a company ceremony at which he handed over the key to his rolltop desk, "when the man and the job and the moment are ideally joined. He is a man who knows his way around Washington and, if I know Harley, that means one thing. It means that National Refractory is going to demand a much bigger slice of the defense-contract pie. With our nation poised on the eve of a bright sunrise in space and an expanding counter-deterrent presence in South Vietnam, Harley Waller is not, I assure you, a man to sit on the sidelines and watch some other team bring home the bacon." [19]

The new chairman lost no time translating into reality his personal dream of a vast industrial empire. DIVERSIFY OR PERISH was his credo, he said. Nevertheless, Wall Street was caught off-guard by his initial move — acquisition of Titan Films — not only because the motion picture firm had failed to produce a box-office hit since *Cleopatra Meets the Prodigal Son* but because the entertainment field was not one that the "smart money" expected N.R.&B. to enter. Wall Street soon learned, however, not to count on Harley Waller to do what was expected. His was a restless mind that despised the obvious. [20]

"Don't get me wrong, I love movies," he told financial reporters, "but very frankly Titan wasn't the apple I was after in that particular barrel. I acquired Titan in order to acquire the Smiley Rent-a-Car Corporation, which Titan had acquired in 1963, in order to acquire Full-o'-Pep Breakfast Cereals, which Smiley acquired in 1962, and of course Full-o'-Pep owns the Honolulu Mets. So what we have essentially done is to put National Refractory & Brake into a strong position virtually overnight in the consumer-interest areas of food and sport with their hoped-for high-profitability potential." [21]

The merger was but the first of many that soon brought under one umbrella a dazzling spectrum of companies which reflected Harley Waller's own wide-ranging intellect. It was inevitable, for example, that a man steeped in public service would feel impelled to take a leadership role in the education-and-opinion sector, and nobody who knew him was surprised by his 1966 acquisition of the KGB Communications Group, which comprised the *Macon Journal-Intelligencer*, station WGOB-TV in Lubbock, *Tee 'n' Green* magazine, [22] and Skool-Aid Learning Tools. Similarly, his purchase of Dalton Brothers, the venerable cough-drop concern, bespoke his passionate belief in a better life for Americans through cosmetic and pharmaceutical research. Indeed, that belief was attested by the lively public interest in two projects that he launched in the Dalton division: the attempt to develop a tangle-free hair curler and the quest for a "3-in-1" aspirin, nasal decongestant and birth-control pill.

But, pragmatist that he also was, Harley Waller knew that a corporation does   23
not live by peace alone. It was not enough for the humanist in him to broaden the firm's stake in a better America; the patriot in him served notice that the bread-and-butter task was to keep America strong, and he resolved to make N.R.&B. the largest producer of weaponry in the free world.

"You can count on it that somebody's always going to be doing a little   24
shooting somewhere," he said upon negotiation of a $270 million revolving credit loan with 18 banks in 1965, "and I pledge that wherever that shooting is going on — at sea, on land or in the skies — one of our products is going to be shooting back." The speech, so typical in its optimism, sent N.R.&B. stock up 11½ points, and Wall Street analysts sat back to see how even so shrewd a corporate architect as Harley Waller could put together an arsenal diverse enough to meet every contingency that a cunning enemy might devise.

They did not have long to wait. Moving with dramatic suddenness in   25
less than a month, N.R.&B. acquired Allied Affiliated Pomeroy, the conglomerate that had been formed only three weeks earlier by the merger of Allied Aircraft (manufacturer of the F-42 "Osprey"), Affiliated Aeronautics (manufacturer of the P-71 "Cormorant") and the Pomeroy Plane Company (maker of the Y-22 "Buzzard" helicopter).

"Here you've got a tragic situation," Mr. Waller noted, "of three great   26
companies making three great planes that are being sold to two-bit countries like Paraguay when they could be doing a job for our boys in the navy, the air force and the army in Vietnam and Laos. I'm going to Washington — and those planes are going to Vietnam and Laos!"

And go to Washington he did, returning from the Pentagon with $8.3   27
billion worth of contracts in his pocket for production and delivery of 7,395 planes of all three types over the next five years. It only remained for him to round out his "ideal team defense-wise" with the acquisition of General Fire & Bomb, the 102-year-old manufacturer of sporting and military explosives, which he converted to production of "atomic hardware," taking particular pride in being named contractor for the "hair-trigger" nuclear warhead for the multiple independently targeted reentry system of the "Night Watchman" ballistic missile.

Stage 1 was over. In only two years an edifice of staggering complexity   28 had been built. Now the job was to put it in smooth functioning order — and, incidentally, give it a new name. " 'National Refractory & Brake' doesn't really tell our story anymore," Harley Waller was quoted as saying in the *Time* cover article of Aug. 9, 1966 ("Modern Midas"). With his customary flair, he rechristened it the American National United Allied General Corporation.

A lesser man would have quailed at the challenge of running an industrial family that had mushroomed with incredible speed into 22 divisions and 113,-000 employees. But Harley Waller was "a clean-desk guy," and he streamlined top management into a decision-flow plan whereby 44 senior vice-presidents reported to 22 executive vice-presidents who reported to 11 group vice-presidents who reported to him. Democratic process, to Harley Waller, was the Holy Writ of business leadership. Yet in the final analysis he knew that command is a lonely burden, and he never shrank from using his veto to take the company on a course that might seem counter to the prevailing financial wisdom. {29}

No man, of course, is infallible, and no human institution exempt from the capricious winds of fortune. Harley Waller knew this as well as anyone, and he took a philosophical view of developments in several areas that markedly delayed product acceptability. In the Titan Films division, the revelation by Ralph Nader of a high phosphorus content in Full-o'-Pep Cereals, coupled with an "epidemic" of loose engine mounts in Smiley Rent-a-Car vehicles and of bone chips on the pitching staff of the Honolulu Mets, contributed to a reversal of anticipated upturn in these companies from 1966 to 1971. {30}

In the Skool-Aid Learning Tools line, the discovery of 127 misspellings in children's readers, with resultant adverse publicity, led to the cancellation of sizable textbook orders from the school systems of Chicago, Detroit and Los Angeles. One should also mention the negative impact on projected earnings in the Dalton Drug division, arising from lawsuits brought by "not 100% satisfied" users of the 3-in-1 aspirin, nasal decongestant and birth-control pill. Performance continued to be excellent, however, in the refractory and brake divisions, and as of December 1971 Mr. Waller announced that the shakedown phase was over in "all but one or two" of the consumer product companies. {31}

But what ultimately tested and proved the mettle of Harley G. Waller was the intricate task of arming the defenders of democracy in Southeast Asia. The Pentagon contracts called for delivery of 2,016 Osprey fighters by 1968 at a cost of $2.6 billion, 3,882 Cormorant jets by 1969 at $3.9 billion, and 1,497 Buzzard helicopters by 1970 at $1.8 billion. That these projections might prove unrealistic was sensed when the Osprey target date arrived in 1968 and 339 planes had been delivered at a cost of $3.5 billion. The 12,000% {32} overrun and write-off — 1,677 fewer planes for $900 million more — had the salubrious effect of enabling Harley Waller to "fully identify the areas where cost and time budgets were significantly below the upward inflationary spiral." He instigated a crash program to deliver both the Cormorant and the Buzzard substantially ahead of target date and below cost. What he could not have foreseen was the untimely "peace offensive" of 1968 and 1969 with its stretch-out in military procurement, resulting in the cancellation of Pentagon orders for the Cormorant and the Buzzard while both were in full production.

"It's a heck of an interesting situation," Harley Waller commented. "On 33 the Osprey I was over on cost and under on planes. On these two, I'm under on money and over on the planes. Well, I guess I can always sell them to Paraguay," he joked, with that resilience which so endeared him to his colleagues. Indeed, as 1971 drew to a close, he had successfully renegotiated the $270 million revolving credit loan, had concluded a $68 million long-term debt payment agreement with the Banque de Zurich, and had issued six million additional shares of common stock to raise $57 million for amortization of the Osprey write-off.

The only major item still unsettled was the $1.3 billion deficit for the 34 827 Cormorant and Buzzard aircraft which were in various stages of manufacture at the time of the Pentagon's canceling order and which Mr. Waller felt it was "only proper" to complete. "You can bet Uncle Sam will pick up that tab if they want the company to stay in business," he wrote in his Christmas letter to the employees, and nobody was more surprised than he when President Nixon entered the impasse on Feb. 16 and ruled that "the financial rescue of a corporation that finds itself in an overstockpiling situation would not only be an unhealthy precedent but, frankly, just too darn expensive."

"Happily, there is one other option," the Chief Executive stated, "and 35 I personally feel that it represents an eminently fair and forward-looking settlement in the best traditions of good sportsmanship."

So the moment came last month for Harley Waller to pack his bags 36 for Washington once again and to bid an emotional farewell in the company auditorium to his fellow voyagers on one of America's great adventures.

Goodbye, Harley. Our thoughts and prayers will go with you in your 37 new position as Secretary of Defense.

SUBJECT QUESTIONS

1. Because Harley Waller is fictitious, Zinsser's aim cannot be simply an exposition of Waller's career. What do you think his real purpose is?
2. What might be the purpose of the corporation's board of directors in publishing this "special supplement to the annual report"?

3. Can you recognize in Harley Waller's career any similarities to actual occurrences in the military-industrial complex with which you are familiar?

4. Do you think it is possible for a real-life executive to accomplish "upward failure"? What conditions make such an occurrence likely (or unlikely)? Are there times when it is more likely to happen than at other times?

5. The author has the problem of making this "report" both an exposé and an attempted cover-up of Waller's series of failures. How does he manage this? (Consider the statements following the conclusion of each failure.)

STRUCTURE QUESTIONS

1. What techniques does Zinsser use to give this fictionalized account an air of credibility?

2. Although fiction, the account is an example of "historical process." Has Zinsser explained the steps of that process in a logical and understandable order? What about the final step of Waller's becoming Secretary of Defense?

3. Find some instances where Zinsser has employed technical jargon, perhaps even double-talk. Do the instances have anything in common? Does his purpose justify his use of such jargon?

4. Find instances of cliché-ridden language. Where do these passages occur? Does Zinsser's purpose justify their use? What do they imply about the speakers?

Computers Don't Argue

Gordon R. Dickson

Gordon R. Dickson was born in Edmonton, Alberta, in 1923. He is best known as a mystery and science fiction writer. Dickson has published hundreds of short stories and novelettes, and a great many novels have followed his first science fiction book, Alien from Arcturus *(1956). Recently Dickson has been writing juvenile historical fiction as well as science fiction.*

Treasure Book Club   1
PLEASE DO NOT FOLD, SPINDLE OR MUTILATE THIS CARD
Mr: Walter A. Child Balance: $4.98
Dear Customer: Enclosed is your latest book selection. "Kidnapped,"
by Robert Louis Stevenson.

                                                        437 Woodlawn Drive   2
                                                        Panduk, Michigan
                                                        Nov. 16, 1965

Treasure Book Club
1823 Mandy Street
Chicago, Illinois

Dear Sirs:
I wrote you recently about the computer punch card you sent, billing me
for "Kim," by Rudyard Kipling. I did not open the package containing it
until I had already mailed you my check for the amount on the card. On
opening the package, I found the book missing half its pages. I sent it back
to you, requesting either another copy or my money back. Instead, you
have sent me a copy of "Kidnapped," by Robert Louis Stevenson. Will you
please straighten this out?
     I hereby return the copy of "Kidnapped."

                                                        Sincerely yours,
                                                        Walter A. Child

Reprinted by permission of the author and the author's agent, Robert P. Mills, Ltd.

Treasure Book Club 3
SECOND NOTICE
PLEASE DO NOT FOLD, SPINDLE OR MUTILATE THIS CARD
Mr: Walter A. Child Balance: $4.98
For "Kidnapped," by Robert Louis Stevenson
(If remittance has been made for the above, please disregard this notice)

437 Woodlawn Drive 4
Panduk, Michigan
Jan. 21, 1966

Treasure Book Club
1823 Mandy Street
Chicago, Illinois

Dear Sirs:
May I direct your attention to my letter of November 16, 1965? You are
still continuing to dun me with computer punch cards for a book I did not
order. Whereas, actually, it is your company that owes *me* money.

Sincerely yours,
Walter A. Child

Treasure Book Club 5
1823 Mandy Street
Chicago, Illinois
Feb. 1, 1966

Mr. Walter A. Child
437 Woodlawn Drive
Panduk, Michigan

Dear Mr. Child:
We have sent you a number of reminders concerning an amount owing to
us as a result of book purchases you have made from us. This amount,
which is $4.98 is now long overdue.

This situation is disappointing to us, particularly since there was no
hesitation on our part in extending you credit at the time original
arrangements for these purchases were made by you. If we do not receive
payment in full by return mail, we will be forced to turn the matter over to
a collection agency.

Very truly yours,
Samuel P. Grimes
Collection Mgr.

437 Woodlawn Drive 6
Panduk, Michigan
Feb. 5, 1966

Dear Mr. Grimes:
Will you stop sending me punch cards and form letters and make me some
kind of a direct answer from a human being?

I don't owe you money. *You* owe me money. Maybe I should turn your
company over to a collection agency.

Walter A. Child

FEDERAL COLLECTION OUTFIT 7

88 Prince Street
Chicago, Illinois
Feb. 28, 1966

Mr. Walter A. Child
437 Woodlawn Drive
Panduk, Michigan

Dear Mr. Child:
Your account with the Treasure Book Club, of $4.98 plus interest and
charges has been turned over to our agency for collection. The amount due
is now $6.83. Please send your check for this amount or we shall be forced
to take immediate action.

Jacob N. Harshe
Vice President

FEDERAL COLLECTION OUTFIT 8

88 Prince Street
Chicago, Illinois
April 8, 1966

Mr. Walter A. Child
437 Woodlawn Drive
Panduk, Michigan

Dear Mr. Child:
You have seen fit to ignore our courteous requests to settle your long
overdue account with Treasure Book Club, which is now, with accumulated
interest and charges, in the amount of $7.51.

If payment in full is not forthcoming by April 11, 1966 we will be
forced to turn the matter over to our attorneys for immediate court action.

Ezekiel B. Harshe
President

MALONEY, MAHONEY, MACNAMARA and PRUITT   9
  Attorneys

                                              89 Prince Street
                                              Chicago, Illinois
                                              April 29, 1966

Mr. Walter A. Child
437 Woodlawn Drive
Panduk, Michigan

Dear Mr. Child:
Your indebtedness to the Treasure Book Club has been referred to us for
legal action to collect.

  This indebtedness is now in the amount of $10.01. If you will send us
this amount so that we may receive it before May 5, 1966, the matter may
be satisfied. However, if we do not receive satisfaction in full by that date,
we will take steps to collect through the courts.

  I am sure you will see the advantage of avoiding a judgment against
you, which as a matter of record would do lasting harm to your credit
rating.

                                              Very truly yours,
                                              Hagthorpe M. Pruitt, Jr.
                                              Attorney at law

                                              437 Woodlawn Drive   10
                                              Panduk, Michigan
                                              May 4, 1966

Mr. Hagthorpe M. Pruitt, Jr.
Maloney, Mahoney, MacNamara and Pruitt
89 Prince Street
Chicago, Illinois

Dear Mr. Pruitt:
You don't know what a pleasure it is to me in this matter to get a letter
from a live human being to whom I can explain the situation.

  This whole matter is silly. I explained it fully in my letters to the
Treasure Book Company. But I might as well have been trying to explain to
the computer that puts out their punch cards, for all the good it seemed to
do. Briefly, what happened was I ordered a copy of "Kim," by Rudyard
Kipling, for $4.98. When I opened the package they sent me, I found the
book had only half its pages, but I'd previously mailed a check to pay them
for the book.

I sent the book back to them, asking either for a whole copy or my money back. Instead, they sent me a copy of "Kidnapped," by Robert Louis Stevenson — which I had not ordered; and for which they have been trying to collect from me.

Meanwhile, I am still waiting for the money back that they owe me for the copy of "Kim" that I didn't get. That's the whole story. Maybe you can help me straighten them out.

> Relievedly yours,
> Walter A. Child

P.S.: I also sent them back their copy of "Kidnapped," as soon as I got it, but it hasn't seemed to help. They have never even acknowledged getting it back.

MALONEY, MAHONEY, MACNAMARA and PRUITT   11
    Attorneys

> 89 Prince Street
> Chicago, Illinois
> May 9, 1966

Mr. Walter A. Child
437 Woodlawn Drive
Panduk, Michigan

Dear Mr. Child:
I am in possession of no information indicating that any item purchased by you from the Treasure Book Club has been returned.

I would hardly think that, if the case had been as you stated, the Treasure Book Club would have retained us to collect the amount owing from you.

If I do not receive your payment in full within three days, by May 12, 1966, we will be forced to take legal action.

> Very truly yours,
> Hagthorpe M. Pruitt, Jr.

COURT OF MINOR CLAIMS   12
    Chicago, Illinois

Mr. Walter A. Child
437 Woodlawn Drive
Panduk, Michigan

Be informed that a judgment was taken and entered against you in this court this day of May 26, 1966 in the amount of $15.66 including court costs.

Payment in satisfaction of this judgment may be made to this court or to the adjudged creditor. In the case of payment being made to the creditor, a release should be obtained from the creditor and filed with this court in order to free you of legal obligation in connection with this judgment.

Under the recent Reciprocal Claims Act, if you are a citizen of a different state, a duplicate claim may be automatically entered and judged against you in your own state so that collection may be made there as well as in the State of Illinois.

COURT OF MINOR CLAIMS   13
   Chicago, Illinois
PLEASE DO NOT FOLD, SPINDLE OR MUTILATE THIS CARD

Judgment was passed this day of May 27, 1966, under Statute $15.66
       Against: Child, Walter A. of 347 Woodlawn Drive, Panduk, Michigan.
Pray to enter a duplicate claim for judgment
       In: Picayune Court — Panduk, Michigan
       For amount: Statute 941

                                              437 Woodlawn Drive   14
                                              Panduk, Michigan
                                              May 31, 1966

Samuel P. Grimes
Vice President, Treasure Book Club
1823 Mandy Street
Chicago, Illinois

Grimes:
This business has gone far enough. I've got to come down to Chicago on business of my own tomorrow. I'll see you then and we'll get this straightened out once and for all, about who owes what to whom, and how much!

                                              Yours,
                                              Walter A. Child

From the desk of the Clerk   15
   Picayune Court

June 1, 1966

Harry:

The attached computer card from Chicago's Minor Claims Court against A.
Walter has a 1500-series Statute number on it. That puts it over in Criminal
with you, rather than Civil, with me. So I herewith submit it for your
computer instead of mine. How's business?

Joe

CRIMINAL RECORDS   16
   Panduk, Michigan
PLEASE DO NOT FOLD, SPINDLE OR MUTILATE THIS CARD

Convicted: (Child) A. Walter
On: May 26, 1966
Address: 437 Woodlawn Drive
Panduk, Mich.
Crim: Statute: 1566 (Corrected) 1567
Crime: Kidnap
Date: Nov. 16, 1965
Notes: At large. To be picked up at once.

POLICE DEPARTMENT, PANDUK, MICHIGAN. TO POLICE DEPARTMENT   17
CHICAGO ILLINOIS. CONVICTED SUBJECT A. (COMPLETE FIRST NAME UN-
KNOWN) WALTER, SOUGHT HERE IN CONNECTION REF. YOUR NOTIFICATION OF JUDG-
MENT FOR KIDNAP OF CHILD NAMED ROBERT LOUIS STEVENSON, ON NOV. 16,
1965. INFORMATION HERE INDICATES SUBJECT FLED HIS RESIDENCE, AT
437 WOODLAND DRIVE, PANDUK, AND MAY BE AGAIN IN YOUR AREA.
        POSSIBLE CONTACT IN YOUR AREA: THE TREASURE BOOK CLUB, 1823 MANDY
STREET, CHICAGO, ILLINOIS. SUBJECT NOT KNOWN TO BE DANGEROUS. PICK UP
AND HOLD, ADVISING US OF CAPTURE . . .

TO POLICE DEPARTMENT, PANDUK, MICHIGAN. REFERENCE YOUR REQUEST   18
TO PICK UP AND HOLD A. (COMPLETE FIRST NAME UNKNOWN) WALTER,
WANTED IN PANDUK ON STATUTE 1567, CRIME OF KIDNAPPING.
        SUBJECT ARRESTED AT OFFICES OF TREASURE BOOK CLUB, OPERATING
THERE UNDER ALIAS WALTER ANTHONY CHILD AND ATTEMPTING TO
COLLECT $4.98 FROM ONE SAMUEL P. GRIMES, EMPLOYEE OF THAT COMPANY.
        DISPOSAL: HOLDING FOR YOUR ADVICE.

POLICE DEPARTMENT PANDUK, MICHIGAN TO POLICE DEPARTMENT   19
CHICAGO, ILLINOIS
  REF. A. WALTER (ALIAS WALTER ANTHONY CHILD) SUBJECT WANTED FOR
CRIME OF KIDNAP, YOUR AREA, REF: YOUR COMPUTER PUNCH CARD
NOTIFICATION OF JUDGMENT, DATED MAY 27, 1966. COPY OUR CRIMINAL
RECORDS PUNCH CARD HEREWITH FORWARDED TO YOUR COMPUTER
SECTION.

CRIMINAL RECORDS   20
 Chicago, Illinois
PLEASE DO NOT FOLD, SPINDLE OR MUTILATE THIS CARD

SUBJECT (CORRECTION — OMITTED RECORD SUPPLIED)
APPLICABLE STATUTE NO. 1567
JUDGMENT NO. 456789
TRIAL RECORD: APPARENTLY MISFILED AND UNAVAILABLE
DIRECTION: TO APPEAR FOR SENTENCING BEFORE JUDGE JOHN ALEXANDER
MCDIVOT, COURTROOM A JUNE 9, 1966

From the Desk of   21
Judge Alexander J. McDivot

             June 2, 1966
Dear Tony:
I've got an adjudged criminal coming up before me for sentencing
Thursday morning — but the trial transcript is apparently misfiled.
  I need some kind of information (Ref: A. Walter — Judgment No.
456789, Criminal). For example, what about the victim of the kidnapping.
Was victim harmed?

             Jack McDivot

           June 3, 1966   22

Records Search Unit

Re: Ref: Judgment No. 456789 — was victim harmed?

           Tonio Malagasi
           Records Division

June 3, 1966   23

To: United States Statistics Office
Attn.: Information Section
Subject: Robert Louis Stevenson
Query: Information concerning

Records Search Unit
Criminal Records Division
Police Department
Chicago, Ill.

June 5, 1966   24

To: Records Search Unit
Criminal Records Division
Police Department
Chicago, Illinois

Subject: Your query re Robert Louis Stevenson (File no. 189623)

Action: Subject deceased. Age at death, 44 yrs. Further information requested?

A. K.
Information Section
U. S. Statistics Office

June 6, 1966   25

To: United States Statistics Office
Attn.: Information Division
Subject: RE: File no. 189623

No further information required.

Thank you.
Records Search Unit

Criminal Records Division   26
Police Department
Chicago, Illinois
June 7, 1966

To: Tonio Malagasi
Records Division
Re: Ref: judgment No. 456789 — victim is dead.

Records Search Unit

June 7, 1966

To: Judge Alexander J. McDivot's Chambers

Dear Jack:

Ref: Judgment No. 456789. The victim in this kidnap case was apparently slain.

From the strange lack of background information on the killer and his victim, as well as the victim's age, this smells to me like a gangland killing. This for your information. Don't quote me. It seems to me, though, that Stevenson — the victim — has a name that rings a faint bell with me. Possibly, one of the East Coast Mob, since the association comes back to me as something about pirates — possibly New York dockage hijackers — and something about buried loot.

As I say, above is only speculation for your private guidance.

Any time I can help . . .

> Best,
> Tony Malagasi
> Records Division

MICHAEL R. REYNOLDS
    Attorney-at-law

49 Water Street
Chicago, Illinois
June 8, 1966

Dear Tim:

Regrets: I can't make the fishing trip. I've been court-appointed here to represent a man about to be sentenced tomorrow on a kidnapping charge.

Ordinarily, I might have tried to beg off, and McDivot, who is doing the sentencing, would probably have turned me loose. But this is the damndest thing you ever heard of.

The man being sentenced has apparently been not only charged, but adjudged guilty as a result of a comedy of errors too long to go into here. He not only isn't guilty — he's got the best case I ever heard of for damages against one of the larger Book Clubs headquartered here in Chicago. And that's a case I wouldn't mind taking on.

It's inconceivable — but damnably possible, once you stop to think of it in this day and age of machine-made records — that a completely innocent man could be put in this position.

There shouldn't be much to it. I've asked to see McDivot tomorrow before the time for sentencing, and it'll just be a matter of explaining to him. Then I can discuss the damage suit with my freed client at his leisure.

Fishing next weekend?

Yours,
Mike

MICHAEL R. REYNOLDS
  Attorney-at-law

49 Water Street
Chicago, Illinois
June 10

Dear Tim:

In haste —

No fishing this coming week either. Sorry.

You won't believe it. My innocent-as-a-lamb-and-I'm-not-kidding client has just been sentenced to death for first-degree murder in connection with the death of his kidnap victim.

Yes, I explained the whole thing to McDivot. And when he explained his situation to me, I nearly fell out of my chair.

It wasn't a matter of my not convincing him. It took less than three minutes to show him that my client should never have been within the walls of the County Jail for a second. But — get this — McDivot couldn't do a thing about it.

The point is, my man had already been judged guilty according to the computerized records. In the absence of a trial record — of course there never was one (but that's something I'm not free to explain to you now) — the judge has to go by what records are available. And in the case of an adjudged prisoner, McDivot's only legal choice was whether to sentence to life imprisonment, or execution.

The death of the kidnap victim, according to the statute, made the death penalty mandatory. Under the new laws governing length of time for appeal, which has been shortened because of the new system of computerizing records, to force an elimination of unfair delay and mental anguish to those condemned, I have five days in which to file an appeal, and ten to have it acted on.

Needless to say, I am not going to monkey with an appeal. I'm going directly to the Governor for a pardon — after which we will get this farce reversed. McDivot has already written the governor, also, explaining that his sentence was ridiculous, but that he had no choice. Between the two of us, we ought to have a pardon in short order.

Then, I'll make the fur fly . . .

And we'll get in some fishing.

Best,
Mike

OFFICE OF THE GOVERNOR OF ILLINOIS   30

June 17, 1966

Mr. Michael R. Reynolds
49 Water Street
Chicago, Illinois

Dear Mr. Reynolds:
In reply to your query about the request for pardon for Walter A.
Child (A. Walter), may I inform you that the Governor is still on his trip
with the Midwest Governors Committee, examining the Wall in Berlin. He
should be back next Friday.

I will bring your request and letters to his attention the minute he
returns.

Very truly yours,
Clara B. Jilks
Secretary to the Governor

June 27, 1966   31

Michael R. Reynolds
49 Water Street
Chicago, Illinois

Dear Mike:
Where is that pardon?
My execution date is only five days from now!

Walt

June 29, 1966   32

Walter A. Child (A. Walter)
Cell Block E
Illinois State Penetentiary
Joliet, Illinois

Dear Walt:
The Governor returned, but was called away immediately to the White
House in Washington to give his views on interstate sewage.

I am camping on his doorstep and will be on him the moment he
arrives here.

Meanwhile, I agree with you about the seriousness of the situation.
The warden at the prison there, Mr. Allen Magruder will bring this letter to

you and have a private talk with you. I urge you to listen to what he has to say; and I enclose letters from your family also urging you to listen to Warden Magruder.

Yours,
Mike

June 30, 1966   33

Michael R. Reynolds
49 Water Street
Chicago, Illinois

Dear Mike: (This letter being smuggled out by Warden Magruder) As I was talking to Warden Magruder in my cell, here, news was brought to him that the Governor has at last returned for a while to Illinois, and will be in his office early tomorrow morning, Friday. So you will have time to get the pardon signed by him and delivered to the prison in time to stop my execution on Saturday.

Accordingly, I have turned down the Warden's kind offer of a chance to escape; since he told me he could by no means guarantee to have all the guards out of my way when I tried it; and there was a chance of my being killed escaping.

But now everything will straighten itself out. Actually, an experience as fantastic as this had to break down sometime under its own weight.

Best,
Walt

FOR THE SOVEREIGN STATE OF ILLINOIS   34

I, Hubert Daniel Willikens, Governor of the State of Illinois, and invested with the authority and powers appertaining thereto, including the power to pardon those in my judgment wrongfully convicted or otherwise deserving of executive mercy, do this day of July 1, 1966 announce and proclaim that Walter A. Child (A. Walter) now in custody as a consequence of erroneous conviction upon a crime of which he is entirely innocent, is fully and freely pardoned of said crime. And I do direct the necessary authorities having custody of the said Walter A. Child (A. Walter) in whatever place or places he may be held, to immediately free, release, and allow unhindered departure to him . . .

Interdepartmental Routing Service   35
PLEASE DO NOT FOLD, MUTILATE, OR SPINDLE THIS CARD
Failure to route Document properly.
To: Governor Hubert Daniel Willikens
Re: Pardon issued to Walter A. Child, July 1, 1966

Dear State Employee:
You have failed to attach your Routing Number.
PLEASE: Resubmit document with this card and form 876, explaining your
authority for placing a TOP RUSH category on this document. Form 876 must
be signed by your Departmental Superior
    RESUBMIT ON: Earliest possible date ROUTING SERVICE office is open.
In this case, Tuesday, July 5, 1966.
    WARNING: Failure to submit form 876 WITH THE SIGNATURE OF YOUR
SUPERIOR may make you liable to prosecution for misusing a Service of the
State Government. A warrant may be issued for your arrest.
    There are NO exceptions. YOU have been WARNED.

SUBJECT QUESTIONS

1. As a fiction writer, Dickson is less concerned with the *possible* than with
   the *probable,* to use Aristotle's terms. That is, even if we know that the
   events did not happen, we should be made to feel that they might have
   happened. Does Dickson succeed in giving his story this probability?
2. Despite his title, Dickson is not likely to be attacking computers themselves (computers merely handle the information given them by
   humans). What is the object of Dickson's attack?
3. Perhaps the major step in the process by which Walter Child was exe-
   cuted is the switch in the charge against him from civil to criminal (kidnapping). Examine the text carefully to see how this came about.
4. On whom should the blame for the miscarriage of justice described here
   finally rest?
5. What does the final memo to the governor imply about "who's in
   charge"?

STRUCTURE QUESTIONS

1. Because Dickson has invented this process, we should be able to assume
   that the steps are in correct and necessary order. Are there in fact any
   places where the steps could be rearranged and still give the same result?
2. Are there any steps in the process that are not clearly explained? (As
   this is process rather than cause-and-effect analysis, *why* they happened
   need not be explained.)

3. As this story is composed of various communications, the style is not, and should not be, consistent throughout the story. Does the style of each letter or memorandum seem appropriate to the type of person (or computer) who sent it?
4. "Computers Don't Argue" is obviously not constructed in the way most short stories are; did you find Dickson's approach confusing? Should he have begun with an introduction or explanation? Would the effect have been the same had he done so?

The Unknown Citizen

W. H. Auden

Wystan Hugh Auden (1907–1973) was born in England. He published some twenty-five volumes of poetry, five plays, five volumes of criticism, five translations, and edited twenty-seven other volumes. Auden won numerous awards for poetry, including Pulitzer and Bollingen prizes and the King's Gold Medal (1937). Although "The Unknown Citizen" should be judged primarily as a poem, it is also an interesting kind of double process analysis: it shows how the unknown citizen "got processed" by his society, and it is a recipe for cooking up a model citizen according to accepted standards. The poem was composed in 1940, but Auden might have written something not very different today.

(To JS/07/M/378
This Marble Monument
Is Erected by the State)

He was found by the Bureau of Statistics to be
One against whom there was no official complaint,
And all the reports on his conduct agree
That, in the modern sense of an old-fashioned word, he was a saint,
For in everything he did he served the Greater Community.   5
Except for the War till the day he retired
He worked in a factory and never got fired,
But satisfied his employers, Fudge Motors Inc.
Yet he wasn't a scab or odd in his views,
For his Union reports that he paid his dues,   10
(Our report on his Union shows it was sound)
And our Social Psychology workers found
That he was popular with his mates and liked a drink.
The Press are convinced that he bought a paper every day
And that his reactions to advertisements were normal in every way.   15
Policies taken out in his name prove that he was fully insured,
And his Health-card shows he was once in hospital but left it cured.
Both Producers Research and High-Grade Living declare

He was fully sensible to the advantages of the Instalment Plan
And had everything necessary to the Modern Man,   20
A phonograph, a radio, a car and a frigidaire.
Our researchers into Public Opinion are content
That he held the proper opinions for the time of year;
When there was peace, he was for peace; when there was war, he went.
He was married and added five children to the population,   25
Which our Eugenist says was the right number for a parent of his
    generation,
And our teachers report that he never interfered with their education.
Was he free? Was he happy? The question is absurd:
Had anything been wrong, we should certainly have heard.

SUBJECT QUESTIONS

1. Is there any way to tell whether the citizen acted from his own chosen values or because he had been perfectly programmed? (How does Auden make clear, in other words, that his intent is satire?)
2. In what sense can the citizen be called a "saint"? If he is a saint, why is he "unknown"?
3. "And our teachers report that he never interfered with their education"; what is implied by the choice of the pronoun "their"?
4. Do all the statistics on the unknown citizen add up to a coherent portrait? Is anything missing? (Note that his religion is not mentioned; should it be?)
5. Assuming that Auden's portrait is approximately what the establishment encourages — whether consciously or not — as a model, what would the result be if it succeeded in getting everyone to conform to that model? How would such a society differ from that pictured in Huxley's *Brave New World*?

STRUCTURE QUESTIONS

1. Try working out the rhyme scheme of the poem. Is there any regular rhythm (iambic pentameter, e.g.)? Do you think Auden was trying to write an "unpoetic poem"? Would there have been any advantage, given the subject, to making the meter and rhyme scheme monotonously regular?
2. The poem makes clear all the ingredients of the establishment's recipe for a model citizen; are they arranged in any logical order? Should they be?
3. Do you think the last two lines are really necessary to the poem? What effect do they have? Are they out of character with the rest of the inscription on the monument?

5

WORK IN AN ALIENATED SOCIETY

Cause and Effect

The immediate difficulty confronting the analyzer of cause and effect relations is the possibility of a "multiplicity of causes." Seldom in nature or in society does a one cause–one effect relationship occur; normally a number of factors contribute to any one result, and one cause such as the atom bomb can have any number of aftereffects. If a chemical reaction will not take place except under pressure, at a certain temperature, and in the presence of a catalyst, then pressure, temperature, and catalyst must be considered along with the chemicals actually involved in the reaction as "causes" of the reaction. In the social sciences the problems are even more complicated, and the observer who fails to expect many causes or effects is almost certain to distort his analysis. Gibbon in his great work, *The Decline and Fall of the Roman Empire,* failed to see the multiplicity of economic and political causes involved when he tried to show that the Roman Empire fell primarily because of the rise of Christianity.

Another danger in cause and effect analysis is the possible presence of incidental factors which are not really a part of the cause but which may appear to be so because of their very presence. "This must be a good theme — I spent six hours on it" or "I knew he'd fail that test: he went off on a pledge trip the previous week end" are common examples of too-hasty assumption of a cause and effect relationship. A less obvious example would be this: "No wonder I failed the test — I had a bad headache that day." The headache might, of course, have been a partial cause, but the student might also have done just as badly without the headache.

Certainly it would be a mistake to assume a one cause–one effect relationship here.

In spite of these difficulties of false cause and multiplicity of causes, analysis of cause and effect can be a profitable endeavor, even by the student untrained in the intricacies of logical analysis. Take the question, "Why did I come to college?" Perhaps the student has never really thought about an answer to this question, but if he considers it objectively he can probably discover the causes for his coming to college: a pure interest in learning, desire for a better job, parental pressure, desire to keep up with his friends, unreadiness to face the world on his own, and so on. Although he may miss a few causes his answer is likely to tell him something about himself which he hadn't realized before. Or take one more example: John asks himself, "Why do I love Jane?" Probably he will either invent a few likely sounding reasons (rationalize) or quickly put the question out of his head unanswered. But if he honestly and objectively tries to answer it, he may find that his love has a sounder basis than he suspected – or he may realize that he is being "taken."

At any rate, because students are constantly being called upon to analyze cause and effect relationships ("Why did Hamlet refuse to kill the king at prayers?" "Why does this painting seem to have more depth than that one?" "What factors influence juvenile delinquency rates?"), it is well to know some of the basic principles involved.

The primary requirement is an objective, unprejudiced approach. One must never make the mistake of assuming he knows the cause beforehand and then looking for supporting evidence. This is what happens when a tobacco company employs an "impartial" scientist to prove that there is no cause and effect relation between smoking and lung cancer. At best his chances of arriving at "truth" are cut in half before he even starts.

Another requirement, then, is that the analyzer gather all the facts available and consider all possible explanations, or causes, for an effect. If Joe asks Henrietta to go water skiing with him and she refuses, he cannot immediately conclude that Henrietta is either a snob or a fool. To arrive at the real cause or causes for this effect, Joe needs to collect as much pertinent evidence as he can, formulate various hypotheses from these facts, and then test each hypothesis to see if it might be the cause, or part of the cause, of Henrietta's refusal. Perhaps she doesn't like water skiing; she may have a cold; she may have several important tests coming up; she may be engaged to another man; or she may not like Joe. If Joe tests each of these possibilities and finds that Henrietta is healthy, loves water skiing, does not have another boy friend but does date, then Joe may suspect – but not yet definitely conclude – that Henrietta does not like him.

But how can he find out for certain? His next step would be a controlled experiment to check his remaining hypothesis. He might try asking Henrietta to a different social function, say a concert, on a different day. If she accepts gladly, Joe must go back and check on other possible causes of the water skiing fiasco. If on the other hand she still refuses, he has further corroborating evidence for his hypothesis that Henrietta doesn't like him. But it may be that she doesn't like concerts and refused the second date on that account. So Joe must test a bit further. He might induce his friend Jim to ask Henrietta to go water skiing at the same time and place Joe had suggested to her. If she accepts Joe can be fairly certain that *he* is at least partly the cause for Henrietta's refusal. As a final check, he could have a second friend ask Henrietta to the concert. If she accepts that date, too, Joe can start looking for greener pastures — or other girl friends.

But suppose Joe is interested only in Henrietta and wants to know *why* she doesn't like him. Then he must begin a whole new series of analyses. He must gather the facts about himself and Henrietta that might be pertinent to their relationship, and from these formulate hypotheses which could explain the effect. There may be a basic personality clash; she may be a foot taller than Joe; she may not like his taste in clothing; or perhaps he needs a better toothpaste. The point is that Joe must again employ the same principles of objective analysis and testing that he used in arriving at the first conclusion.

The same procedures apply for any analysis of cause and effect. Because the facts and circumstances will be different in different problems, no more specific advice than this can be given here. Tracking down cause and effect relations may sometimes seem frustrating, but it can be a fascinating search. It is what provides the excitement in almost any research project. If the student who attempts a cause and effect analysis will remember to be unprejudiced, to collect as many pertinent facts as possible, and to test each hypothesis, he should be able to make some significant contribution, at least to his own self-knowledge.

The Protest of Young Factory Workers

Herbert J. Gans

Herbert J. Gans is professor of sociology and planning at MIT and faculty associate of the MIT–Harvard Joint Center for Urban Studies. He is the author of The Urban Villagers *(1962),* The Levittowners' Ways of Life *(1967),* People and Plans *(1968), and* More Equality *(1973).*

When students at Berkeley and other elite campuses first began to demonstrate against the university — and against the Establishment — many observers explained their behavior as the consequences of being affluent and elite. Indeed, the myth of Middle America and its Silent Majority that emerged in response to student unrest postulates a basic difference between the "classes," suggesting that the former are satisfied with American society and only the snobs are unhappy. 1

It should be clear from the articles in this issue of *New Generation,* however, that this simple dichotomy is just not true; some blue-collar workers are at least as critical of the factory as students are of the multiversity. While they have not often resorted to media covered demonstrations and confrontations, they have probably been more effective in disrupting the assembly line than students, the university, through high rates of absenteeism and turnover, wildcat strikes, deliberately shoddy workmanship and occasional acts of sabotage. 2

From the limited journalistic and sociological research so far available, it would appear that a yet unknown number of blue-collar workers, particularly on the assembly line, complain, like the students, that their work is inauthentic and their workplace, dehumanizing. They do not use these terms, of course, but they find the work boring; they have no control over the job; they must obey arbitrary decisions by their foremen and they cannot take time off for personal business or even a phone call. In short, they are veritable prisoners of the assembly line and the people who run it. 3

Work: Old Feelings and New Expectations

Any explanation of the current blue-collar protest must begin with the fact that the feelings behind it are by no means new; indeed, discontent with working conditions is as old as the Industrial Revolution itself. Until fairly 4

From *New Generation* (Fall 1970). Copyright © 1970. Reprinted by permission of the National Committee on Employment of Youth.

recently, the discontent was voiced publicly mainly by middle class social critics, novelists and film-makers (remember Charlie Chaplin's classic critique of the assembly line, "Modern Times"), for the workers themselves could not easily protest about working conditions. Job insecurity was still rampant, and besides, their first priority was to achieve a living — and rising — wage. Still there is no doubt that the writers and film-makers expressed many of the workers' feelings. For example, Eli Chinoy's sociological study, *Automobile Workers and the American Dream*, published in 1955, concluded that the assembly line workers only endured the work to earn enough money for achieving their American dream: to buy a gas station or garage. When I studied a Boston working class neighborhood in the late 1950's, I heard many of the same complaints that workers are making today, but the West Enders, for whom even garage ownership was unachievable, had resigned themselves to the working conditions they could not change, and sought their satisfactions in family and peer group life.

Today, age-old feelings are being translated into action, mainly by some young workers, and especially the better educated among them. They are not saving up to buy a garage but are going to night school to become eligible for a white-collar job, and since they do not expect to spend the rest of their lives in the factory, they can express their discontent or quit when the work becomes unbearable.

Moreover, these young workers do not accept the traditional working class belief that the major purpose of the job is to finance the non-work parts of life. Whether or not they practice middle class life styles, many have embraced the expectation, common in the middle class, that the job itself should provide some satisfaction, and this is hard to find on the assembly line. But even for the men who are not looking forward to better jobs, the line no longer provides the same rewards it offered their fathers. When most blue-collar work was unskilled, the line was at least a gold-plated sweatship, as Walter Reuther put it. Today even the money is not that good anymore; there is less prestige than in skilled work, and opportunities for promotion are rare. Why else would blacks have been allowed on the line, and in such large numbers? (Today, over 60% of Detroit's assembly line workers are black.)

Still, the status of the assembly line has been declining for some time now; other reasons must explain why the protest has only surfaced in the last couple of years. First, younger men are an ever more important part of the work force; 40 percent of the current UAW members are under thirty. Second, some are increasingly unhappy with the union, which is more responsive to older workers — and *they* are naturally more interested in pensions than working conditions. Also, as B. J. Widick wrote recently in the *Nation*, "The old-timers think of the UAW as an organization that protects them from company abuse. Young workers think of the UAW as an outfit that had better get them what they think they deserve, and now. The young are not burdened with memories of the miseries of the past or the struggles of two decades ago." A third factor is the current recession. During more affluent years, dissatisfied assembly line workers could find better jobs outside the factory; now, these jobs are scarcer and the men feel trapped on the line.

Fourth, the blue-collar protest has erupted now because dissatisfied 8 workers, like other protesters, have learned from the civil rights and peace movements that demonstrations and confrontations are frequently more successful in bringing about change than traditional grievance procedures. To be sure, it has taken the workers some years to learn this, partly because such methods have only just become respectable in the politically conservative world of the working class, partly because the number of protesters had to reach a critical mass before they could act with impunity. But now that these conditions have been met, it is likely that the protest will spread.

Nevertheless, the prime reason for the protest comes from beyond the 9 factory, for the discontented workers are expressing a nation-wide upgrading of expectations about how life should be lived which is taking place in many levels and sectors of American society. Although what is happening is often described as a politico-cultural revolution or a youthful rebellion, the diverse new expectations also have in common a demand for more equality in America's principal institutions, and I prefer to label the change as the "equality revolution." As a result, one finds similar dissatisfactions and demands in many places: for example, among blacks who want equality with whites, and women, with men; among journalists who question the absolute power of editors, and enlisted men, that of officers; among professional athletes who resent being owners' chattel, clients who doubt the monopoly on wisdom of professionals, consumers who oppose the practices of manufacturers and merchants, adolescents who want the sexual privileges heretofore reserved for adults, and students who seek more power in their schools.

As in the factory, the feelings underlying the discontent are old; what 10 is new is the belief that the time has come to act on them, and all across the societal board. Young people are saying that age should be a lesser justification of authority than it has been; lower income groups, that income and status should not be the sole sources of rights and privileges; the less skilled, that expertise is not limited to experts; and citizens, that not all decisions should be made by politicians and bureaucrats. Seen in the light of the larger equality revolution, then, the blue-collar discontent is a demand for more of the satisfactions and rights of white-collar and even professional workers.

SUBJECT QUESTIONS

1. What historical causes does Gans suggest for the unrest of factory workers?
2. What new causes have brought this latent unrest to the surface?

3. One hears much less about worker disruption of assembly lines than about student disruption of universities. Does Gans suggest a reason for this?
4. Gans places the dissatisfaction of factory workers into a more general category, the "equality revolution." Would you agree that the aims of young factory workers are essentially the same as the aims of dissenting college students?
5. Although factory workers are of course not construction workers, would it be fair to say that the much-publicized "hard-hat" confrontations with college students weakens Gans's assessment of the extent of worker protest?

STRUCTURE QUESTIONS

1. This brief article represents more a summary of causes than a full cause and effect analysis. Given that limitation, does Gans succeed in showing a necessary relation between worker unrest and the causes he suggests for it?
2. Has Gans adequately considered the probability of a multiplicity of causes? Does his placing worker unrest into a more general movement, the "equality revolution," represent an oversimplification?
3. Does the explanation of why "the protest has only surfaced in the last couple of years" seem convincing? Can you think of other possible causes?
4. Compare the style of Gans's article with that of books and articles you have read by other sociologists. Would you say this essay is aimed at a general audience or at other sociologists? Does Gans ever lapse into sociological jargon?

Communes and the Work Crisis

Lewis M. Andrews

Lewis M. Andrews is a television producer and free-lance writer. He is the author of two books, Requiem for Democracy *(1971) and* Venice: A World Cultural Guide *(1971). The following article first appeared in* The Nation.

Until recently, work has enjoyed a good reputation. For most Americans who grew up during the depression, work and life were synonymous. Finding a job, any job, was the prime directive. Liberals and radicals criticized the capitalist economy, but their aim was to "humanize" work, to make it "fulfilling," not to eliminate it.

Now, however, work has fallen into disrepute, especially among young adults. Whereas it was once a solution to life's problems — were they as straightforward and fundamental as survival or as elusive as the need for self-expression — work is now in itself a problem. The question, "Plastics?," from the film *The Graduate* symbolizes an entire generation's disenchantment with the job options offered by the most diversified society in the world. The famous identity crisis, which is intimately bound up with occupational goals, is becoming a major problem for school guidance counselors. (Almost 65 percent of students who consult school psychologists and guidance counselors present themselves as vocationally confused.) A recent study of Stanford and Berkeley undergraduates found that vocational choice is seen by students as a threat instead of an opportunity.

Increasingly, the reaction of the young to the establishment work scene is to drop out. For some this means revolutionary political activism, for others it means "taking a few years off" to find themselves, and for still others it means an irrevocable break with "straight" society. Many bright college graduates become taxi drivers, waiters and supermarket checkers, in order to "keep themselves together" with a minimum of effort. Others go off to join one of the 300 known (and myriad unknown) hippie communes which have sprouted up across rural America during the past five years. [See "Living Together in California" by Maitland Zane, *The Nation*, October 19, 1970.] For obvious reasons, no one knows exactly how many are dropping out, but sociologists agree that the number is accelerating geometrically, with estimates ranging as high as 20,000 per year. More significant, however, is the fact that the dropouts are often among the most intelligent and best educated

Reprinted from *The Nation* (November 9, 1970) by permission of the publisher.

young people. Communes have been founded by renegades from Yale, Princeton, Stanford, Dartmouth and Berkeley.

This rebellion against the work ethic has potential dangers which even 4 the dropout recognizes. A completely work-free society is impossible to attain. Even if we could mechanize or eliminate all the menial, superficial and redundant jobs, society would still require doctors, programmers, teachers, technicians, firemen, maintenance men, supervisors and other skilled professionals. (I leave out lawyers and police on the premise that such a society would be free of conflict — a dubious assumption.) Unfortunately, the more leisure-oriented our society becomes, the more unevenly the work load is distributed. The burden of servicing an advanced technology falls upon its most intelligent and technically competent members — those very bright young people who are most ready to drop out! In short, the rebellion against the work ethic, if it continues, could lead to a bizarre economic situation: we may find ourselves dependent upon a complex technology that nobody can or will run. Dr. Stanley F. Yolles, former director of the National Institute of Mental Health, sees "serious dangers that large proportions of current and future generations will reach adulthood embittered towards the larger society, unequipped to take on parental, vocational and other citizen roles."

But even if society can successfully convince — that is, bribe — intelli- 5 gent young people to assume the burdens of technology management, as most economists believe it can, work alienation still presents a major social problem. Dissatisfaction with work is a growing source of emotional illness. Psychiatrist Salvatore Maddi finds that people who see themselves as mere players of social roles and who have an acute awareness of superficiality, two symptoms of work dissatisfaction, are highly susceptible to what he calls "existential neurosis"; that is, feelings of chronic meaninglessness, aimlessness and apathy, culminating in severe depression.

Why has work fallen into disrepute among the young? There are legitimate 6 reasons which by now have become clichés: work seems meaningless in a redundant economy that creates needless wants through advertising; work seems meaningless in a society that ignores real problems of poverty and pollution; the nine-to-five routine saps spontaneity and precludes the evolution of individual life styles, etc. But none of these reasons justifies the complete rejection of work. A doctor, lawyer, teacher, even a businessman, can always find work that is meaningful and flexible, *if he wants to find it*. To understand the work crisis, we must explore several illusions that have become axioms to many young Americans.

The first illusion is that work should be a continuous experience of 7 intellectual and emotional delight. Synonyms: self-actualizing and self-fulfilling. Television has undoubtedly played a major role in cultivating this particular illusion. Marcus Welby, M.D., performs at least one medical miracle each week, while over at NBC *The Bold Ones* are resolving crucial social issues at the same rate. And those TV characters who opt for a meaningful family life never have job problems. Did Jim Anderson *(Father Knows Best)* ever stay up late working on his client's insurance policies? Ever see Donna Reed's doctor husband lift as much as a tongue depressor? And who could figure out what Ozzie Nelson did for a living?

Educators also bear responsibility for supporting this particular illusion. 8 They spend so much time preparing students for future work that they forget to explain what the word *work* represents. Our neolithic ancestors were hardly concerned with "the quality of life." For them work — hunting, fishing, farming — was existence. Civilization offers three work advantages: it can make working conditions more pleasant, it can reduce the work load and, by dividing labor, it can offer individuals a choice among more or less satisfying jobs. But even the most rewarding work has its drawbacks. Doctors hate to read medical journals, psychologists dislike treating alcoholics, writers resent deadlines, and so on. Work does not promise Nirvana. That's why people are paid for their labor.

The illusion that work must be an orgasm leads to the corollary illusion that 9 people should be drawn to work by some calling, irrepressible commitment or mystical force. True, a few people know what they want to do at the age of 10, and follow this inspiration for the rest of their lives. Most of us, however, have to be introduced to a subject before we become interested in it. How many people who are happy in their present jobs have ever said, "I never thought I'd end up doing this!"?

The work ethic is further depreciated by two seemingly divergent 10 pseudo-philosophies gaining popularity among the nation's young. The first is a neo-Puritanism which holds that each man must justify his existence by forsaking personal gain and doing something socially constructive. This frequently means ghetto teaching, working in a free clinic, or community organizing. As Edward Banfield cogently observes in *The Unheavenly City*, self-justification has become a growth industry. Dedication to solving social ills is an admirable quality, but neo-Puritanism has had the effect of demeaning any form of work which is done for money, which includes about 99 percent of all existing jobs. As a result, many college graduates are ashamed to say they are working *just* for a living.

In opposition to neo-Puritanism among the young is a neo-Freudianism, 11 which also depreciates work but for different reasons. Popularized by Norman Brown *(Life Against Death)*, Herbert Marcuse *(Eros and Civilization)*, neo-Freudianism strives for the resurrection of what Freud called the Pleasure Principle. According to Brown, civilization represses the Pleasure Principle by instilling a sense of guilt which we literally work out in our respective jobs. The more guilty and repressed we are, the harder we work. The solution, writes Theodore Roszak, is the evolution of a "counter culture" that will turn our mundane work existence into a joyous festival, a spontaneous "celebration of life."

Neo-Freudianism has obvious merits. The fact that psychosomatic ill- 12 nesses are so prevalent among society's most "successful" members demonstrates a partial validity to Freud's theory of cultural repression. However, neo-Freudianism is grossly misinterpreted, especially by social malcontents who equate liberation with anarchy. Freud himself recognized that a certain degree of repression is necessary in order to buy freedom from a primitive existence. Furthermore, many modern psychologists disagree sharply with the premise of neo-Freudianism, arguing that discipline and acquisition of skills are highly satisfying activities. One psychologist has argued that the drive for competence, like the sex drive, is an innate motivation.

The young are not to be blamed for their susceptibility to illusion. They 13 have nothing else to trust. The young are, in a sense, the most victimized generation in history. "Manipulated for goals they cannot believe in," writes Paul Goodman, "the young are alienated." They have been exploited by status-conscious parents ("It's for your own good, my dear"), by businessmen eager to sap the youth market for dad's last penny, and by ambitious politicians, Left and Right. Even the most independent jobs demand a degree of trust that many members of the new paranoid generation are unwilling to give.

How is the work crisis to be resolved? In theory, the solution is simple; 14 a little realism would do the trick. The young must recognize that work is necessary for survival and, further, that any form of work necessarily involves discipline and sacrifice. At the same time, adult champions of the work ethic must learn what they already feel — that the good life is more than an impressive financial statement. Unfortunately, people would rather create illusions to justify their past actions than confront reality. Many dropouts support what youth psychologist Kenneth Keniston has called "the fallacy of romantic regression" — that is, an idealized vision of primitive living which never has and never will exist.

Similarly, "successful" businessmen and professionals extol ulcer- 15 producing work and competition as Christ-like virtues. These fantasies are supported and enriched by media that specialize in what their audiences want to hear. Underground papers such as the Berkeley *Barb*, the Los Angeles *Free Press*, and the New York *Rat* weekly herald the decline of the decadent establishment, while the respectable press gives us front-page stories about hippie teen-agers (especially girls from wealthy families) who come to a bad end as a result of drugs and shiftless commune living.

A few businesses have tried to solve the work crisis with token gestures. 16

Many law firms, for example, encourage young attorneys to spend part of their workday doing poverty law. People who work in television, advertising and other communications industries are allowed liberal dress, liberal hours and frequent leaves of absence for educational purposes. But tokenism wears thin. If the aspiring lawyer wants to stay with the firm, he works overtime to finish the firm's work. And the copywriter is still responsible for servicing the soap account.

A more successful approach to the work crisis is the rapidly growing phenom-   17
enon of the "work commune." Unlike the hippie commune which is organized around a simple life style, the work commune is organized around a professional skill or interest. Members strive for a secure income while, at the same time, advancing each person's independence and work satisfaction.

One such commune is the Farallones Institute, an architecture com-   18
mune, founded in Berkeley by two University of California graduate students. Members develop their own environmental design projects and then seek financial assistance to carry them off. The commune's first paycheck came from a government grant. (Work communes have few qualms about taking government money.) Assistance now comes from the Berkeley High School system, which is interested in the commune's ideas about new educational environments. In neighboring Sausalito is another architecture commune which calls itself the Ant Farm. Founded by two former architecture students, Chip Lord from Tulane and Doug Michaels from Yale, the Ant Farm currently specializes in building plastic "inflatables," balloon-type environments which are used at rock festivals and on children's playgrounds. The Berkeley area also includes numerous legal communes. Some specialize in reform projects; others simply seek a relaxed legal practice.

Work communes are not limited to professional skills. The Portola Insti-   19
tute of Menlo Park, Calif., is a thriving commune of full-time dilettantes. Billed as "a nonprofit co-operative to encourage, organize, and conduct innovative educational projects," it is actually a group of creative people, ranging in education from Ph.D. to high school dropout, whose common bond is the desire to play for a living. Current projects of the Portola Institute include maintaining a playroom for creative high school students, developing a teacher-training laboratory, exploring music theory, and publishing the *Whole Earth Catalog*, which provides the reader with information about books and tools and "enables him to shape his environment, internal and external." Because the *Catalog* has been so successful (circulation 140,000), the institute is under pressure to expand, but members prefer to keep it small. "When people come to us with new ideas," says member Sam Yanes, "we often tell them to start their own institute. We're happy staying about our present size." The institute has encouraged several projects which now function as independent work communes in other parts of California.

California, especially the San Francisco Bay area, has the largest con- 20
centration of work communes, but the phenomenon is spreading. The Communications Company, in Columbus, Ohio, publishes a handbook on alternative life styles. The Meeting, in Minneapolis, Minn., is an experimental school.
New York City's East Village houses numerous film communes and group-run
psychedelic shops. The growing number of free universities and underground
newspapers are also part of the work commune movement.

Work communes provide a promising model for a realistic balance be- 21
tween society's need for productive work in order to sustain itself, and the
individual's need for autonomy. Yanes, for example, has no illusions about
economics. "Frankly, I'm a capitalist," he admits. "I need the bread to live,
and working here at the [Portola] Institute is better than planting my own
garden." But given the necessity of working for a living, Yanes places paramount emphasis on the freedom to live as he chooses. "This is the best place
to work because I can do what I like. I couldn't work anywhere else for more
money or for anything."

However, not all dropouts are enthusiastic about the work commune 22
movement. Phil Trounstein, a Stanford radical, refers to the Portola Institute
as a "Fascist organization" in disguise. "No matter how they dress or act,
they still exploit people with their products." A lot of hippies are also critical,
but their reasons are more personal than political. "It's still work and routine,"
remarked one Berkeley nomad.

The fact that rebels from the traditional work ethic disagree among 23
themselves is probably more significant than any particular viewpoint. The
work crisis will not be resolved by black-white distinctions between glorified
Puritanism and unbridled hedonism. The young must feel free to experiment
with new life styles to find their own solutions to the problem of work.

SUBJECT QUESTIONS

1. Judging from your own observation, do you agree with Andrews that
   people least willing to join the work force are among the most intelligent
   and best educated of our youth?
2. Assuming that those who do not choose to work are the very ones most
   capable of finding work in a technological society, what "bizarre economic situation" does Andrews predict if the trend continues? Wouldn't
   this necessarily mean a return to a less complicated civilization?
3. In addition to the usual reasons given for the disrepute into which work
   has fallen, Andrews suggests three or four common "illusions" as contributing causes. Do you agree that these are illusions? What is the
   difference between an illusion and a delusion?
4. What hope does Andrews offer of a solution to the work crisis? How
   widespread would such a movement need to be in order to comprise
   a satisfactory solution? What factors work against such a solution?

5. Does the final paragraph strike you more as an appropriate summary or as a cop-out?
6. What is "the fallacy of romantic regression"?

STRUCTURE QUESTIONS

1. The average reader would probably think of "the work crisis" as high unemployment; does Andrews make clear the sense in which he is using the phrase? Does he offer convincing evidence that there *is* such a crisis?
2. In paragraph 6, Andrews mentions three commonly accepted causes for the current disillusionment with work. Although he says there are inadequate explanations, he does not reject them as partial causes; should he then have analyzed them to show that they are indeed partial causes?
3. How convincing a case does Andrews make for the common "illusions" as causes? Should he have explained the rather complicated neo-Freudian concept in greater detail? (That is, does Andrews assume more familiarity with the subject than the average reader is likely to have?)
4. Is Andrews trying to explain the work crisis to the young, to an older generation, or to both? What indications are there of any assumption by Andrews about the nature of his audience?
5. Andrews says that because attempts by business to solve the work crisis have failed, youth "must find their own solutions to the problem of work." What is the fallacy in his reasoning here?

The Ecology
of Unemployment
Edward Goldsmith

Edward Goldsmith attended schools in England, France, Switzerland, the West Indies, and Canada before majoring in politics and economics at Oxford. Since 1964 he has devoted most of his time to his chief interest, the development of a unified science. He has written a book and many articles on the necessity of bringing the sciences back together. Since 1970 he has been editor of The Ecologist, *a magazine that he founded.*

Economic growth is often justified on the grounds that it will reduce local unemployment; and industrial enterprises are then established — petrochemical, tin smelting, aluminum and oil refining works, for instance — which are evidently undesirable on environmental grounds. 1

As we all know, it is increasingly difficult to site such undertakings: people simply do not want them around, and there have been several instances (such as recently in the State of North Carolina) where plans for building plants of this sort have been turned down in spite of local unemployment. 2

Many such enterprises are unsatisfactory on another count: the work involved requires skills that are not necessarily available in the area where they are to be located. This means that very often a large number of people must be brought in from the outside. Thus, in Alsace, the car manufacturer, Peugeot, was induced to start a large car manufacturing plant in order to contribute to the solution of the local unemployment problem. 2,500 acres of a singularly beautiful forest were destroyed to provide a site. When at last the factory was built, the locals refused to work in it and thousands of Turks had to be imported and buildings put up to house them, causing still further environmental disruption. This is but a rather spectacular instance of a recurrent theme. Often too, the industrial enterprises are short-lived, as in the case of the mining industry. Take the case of the North Sea Oil Boom — massive installations are going to be built all along the North and East Scottish coast. Undoubtedly too, much skilled labour will have to be imported. The oil will probably last 20–30 years. What happens then? Local life will have been transformed, cultural patterns disrupted, and the population considerably increased in order to adapt to a freak situation. There will be nothing left to do but pray for a miracle to avert social chaos, and massive unemployment. 3

From *The Ecologist* (March, 1974) by permission of the publisher.

The problem is becoming more serious with the scale of modern eco- 4
nomic enterprises, whose establishment, as well as whose demise, can only
cause large-scale social changes. For instance, when such enterprises collapse
it is increasingly difficult to find somewhere for the workers to emigrate in
an increasingly overcrowded country and in a world in which constraints on
immigration are certain to increase.

The most obvious argument against economic growth as a cure for 5
unemployment is that in spite of the fact that everywhere economic growth
has been the fundamental aim of Government policy, unemployment has still
continued to rise, in the case of the Third World, to ever more dramatic levels.
(See Jimeh Omo Fadaka: *Poverty and Industrial Growth in the Third World.*)
This trend is partly the result of population growth, urbanisation and the
increased capital-intensiveness of industry, which inevitably accompanies the
spread of Western influence. As these trends occur, so more and more people
are brought within the compass of the cash economy. In the early stages of
industrialisation it is largely the men who take up employment, the women
tending to stay at home. As development proceeds however, and the material
requisites for survival in an urban setting correspondingly increase, so does
it become necessary for women to take up employment as well. The process
further increases the demand for jobs.

According to Mr. Wood, Minister of Overseas Development, the 6
"working" population in the developing countries is expected to increase by
25 per cent in the next 10 years. This means finding 170,000,000 jobs. How
does he suggest we do this? Needless to say — by further economic growth.

Let us look a little more closely at the reasons why economic growth 7
cannot in the long term, solve the unemployment problem.

One of its basic features is that for industry to be competitive, machines 8
must constantly be substituted for labour. This is "economic" because the
non-renewable resources and in particular the energy required by these machines are charged, or at least, have been up till now, at a ridiculously low
price, thereby increasing capital-intensiveness.

By doing this we are continually increasing the need for more capital- 9
investment. Work, by becoming more capital-intensive and hence more "productive" can be increasingly well remunerated. This is necessary to compensate people for the growing deterioration of their physical and social
environment and the increasing monotony of their work, also to increase their
purchasing capacity, as industrial society can only function if producers are
also consumers. In this way, effective demand continues to grow, thereby
stimulating further production. The inevitable concomitant of this process is
a reduction in the number of people employed for a given degree of capital-
investment and for a given level of economic activity.

The capital-intensiveness of industry, in the meantime, is increasing 10
faster than GNP, which means that every unit of GNP will provide an ever

smaller number of jobs. Consider the British chemical industry. It employed 407,000 in 1961 for a turnover of 4,875 million dollars. In 1967 it employed slightly less people, 406,000 people, for a turnover of 7,589 million dollars. Looked at slightly differently, sales were 55 per cent less efficient in providing jobs. If we presume an average reduction in efficiency of 7 per cent per annum, then, in this industry, turnover must double every seven years to ensure the same level of employment — which we know to be very unlikely indeed.

In the British textile industry, the number of people employed has fallen   11
from 719,000 to 584,900 between 1961 and 1968, and this in spite of a marginal increase in investment (from 257 million dollars to 271,300,000 dollars). Employment has thus fallen by 3 per cent per annum, while investment has risen by 0.5 per cent. (Sources: the Chemical Industry, the Textile Industry, OECD 1969–70 and 1968–69.) At this rate, by the year 2106, investment will have doubled while employment will have fallen as low as 18,000.

The capital-intensiveness of industry and the increasing cost of providing   12
a job are well illustrated by the present proposal to build an iron-ore terminal at Hunterton on the Clyde. This is to cost £26 million and is expected to provide a mere 200 jobs. This works out at £130,000 a job. At this rate, with a GNP of £40 billion, the country can afford to provide no more than 300,000 jobs. It should be quite obvious that if this trend were to continue much longer we would be faced with unemployment on a massive scale.

The Automation Race

This tendency is accentuated by competition between companies, and as the   13
scale of economic activity increases, between countries, a competition which is increasingly taking the form of an automation race which has much in common with the armaments race. Thus, even if it is undesirable to introduce containerisation into the Port of London, which means reducing very considerably the number of dockers employed, there is, under the present regime, very little choice, since the alternative is to give another port, such as Rotterdam, an advantage which would enable it to capture business which would otherwise have gone to London. This, of course, would have the effect of reducing employment still further. As in the case of the armaments race, the situation can only deteriorate, since whether we win the race or lose it, employment can only fall. It is very much a "heads you win, tails I lose" situation.

Dependence on the Technosphere

Of course the basic feature of economic growth is that it involves creating   14
a totally new organisation of matter, the technosphere, which is in competition with, and is systematically made to replace, the biosphere of which we are

an indisassociable part. This substitution has serious implications. For instance, it means that man is systematically isolated from the natural environment to which he has been adapted by millions of years of evolution, and which has always been capable of satisfying his basic biological and social needs.

Until the agricultural revolution, he probably never had any difficulty 15 in obtaining food and fresh water nor in finding the material with which to build a shelter, but now he is made to live in a vast built-up area and spend the better part of his day in a factory contributing in some way towards the manufacture of objects unrelated to his personal needs or to those of his family. He is in fact forced into the unenviable situation of having to purchase the necessities of life.

The same is true of social needs. Man previously lived as a member 16 of his family and community and these provided him with the optimum social environment, that which best satisfied basic social needs. In industrial society, however, everything conspires to destroy the family unit as well as the community. Thus, the state largely usurps the functions normally fulfilled by the father. It provides his children with free education for instance, and a free health service, reducing thereby the father's responsibilities. Large companies usurp the mother's functions, since most of the things that a woman would normally have to make for her family, clothes, pottery, bread and other staple foods, are now available at the supermarket, while functions that would normally be fulfilled by the children and possibly by some elderly relations, such as helping in the house, and washing up, have largely been taken over by domestic appliances. The family in industrial society has thus very much more reduced functions and becomes correspondingly more fragile. The community fares scarcely better. Mobility is normally such that people are rarely in the same place long enough for strong communal bonds to be established. They usually live in housing estates or residential areas, which are not real communities, since people work elsewhere, often at a considerable distance from their homes. To a large extent, the business enterprise a man works for, provides him with a surrogate communal environment. At his work he has an identity, which he lacks elsewhere. His work also provides him with a goal-structure, a sense of accomplishment and a corresponding measure of self-esteem. It is for this reason that unemployment is so intolerable. Even if the dole prevents an unemployed man from suffering serious material deprivation, he is nevertheless deprived of that essential, albeit surrogate, social environment which his job previously provided him. It is almost certainly the psychological effects of unemployment that render so many men in the ghettoes of the larger American conurbations incapable of fulfilling their family functions, establishing permanent relationships with their women, and looking after their children.

Employment in Primitive Societies

It is important to realise that this dependence on paid employment was un- 17
known among our paleolithic forbears, who, let us not forget, represent 99
per cent of all the people who have ever lived. The reason is simple. Contrary
to what is generally supposed, hunter-gatherers were not normally short of
food. On the contrary, it appears that they never actually consumed more
than about a third of available food supplies, very much as do insect popula-
tions. Also the amount of work required to satisfy their material requirements
was minimal, a few hours a day at the most; the rest of the day being spent
in such pursuits as gambling, gossiping and visiting friends. (Lee and Devore:
Man the Hunter.) It is not surprising that the very concept of work was
unknown to hunter-gatherer societies and that in their various languages one
finds no word for it. The gathering of roots and berries, the hunting of wild
animals, were simply part of a day's *routine*, not to be distinguished from
other ways of passing the time, such as gossiping and gambling, and almost
certainly equally enjoyable. Among tribal societies that have given up the
hunter-gatherer way of life in favour of pastoralism or subsistence agriculture,
very much the same is true. However by advancing this far along the road
to "progress," the amount of work they must do to keep alive increases correspondingly. Animals must be penned and fed, when previously they went free
and fed themselves. Fields must be tilled and their produce harvested, when
previously food plants grew profusely without human intervention. As Sahlins
suggests (Marshall Sahlins: *The Original Affluent Society*) the amount of leisure
decreases as society "advances."

Among such societies, trade was as much to reinforce social ties by 18
creating dependencies and obligations, as to satisfy material requirements.
People produced the essential for themselves and traded largely what was
to them superfluous. Economic activity took place at the level of the family — the basic economic unit, and occasionally families would co-operate to
undertake special projects at a communal level. Wage labour did not, and
could not exist. As Mungo Park, the famous traveller wrote towards the end
of the last century, "Paid service is unknown to the Negro, indeed African
languages ignore the word." (Burton, *A Mission to Gelele.*)

Under such conditions, there can be no unemployment in our sense of 19
the term. What can happen, however, is that a population can grow to that
point where it can no longer be usefully employed on the land, which would
cause surplus people to drift to the cities in search of work. This is in fact
what is happening today throughout Africa, but only because of Western
interference which has led to the introduction of labour-saving devices into
agriculture, and also to the suppression of those cultural controls which had
previously maintained a check on population growth. It is important to realise

that with the absorption of tribal peoples into the cash economy, they are now not only at the mercy of the vagaries of nature but also of those of the market economy, that our most learned economists are increasingly at a loss to predict, still more to prevent.

It is also interesting to consider that wage labour only appears in a   20 society where, in the words of Maine, "contract" has replaced "status" (Maine's *Primitive Law*) as the basis of economic obligations. Contract provides a very flimsy basis on which to build a lasting structure, status a very much stronger one.

Status depends on tradition and involves mutual obligations. Thus a man   21 could not be deprived of his means of livelihood unless he committed what was regarded as a sufficient crime against society to justify his being ostracised: the direst penalty imposed on tribal man, and this was only possible with the concurrence of the tribe as a whole. To break a contract with an anonymous member of a mass society is far easier. A skilful lawyer is the most that is needed.

The manorial system, though much maligned, was based on status rather   22 than contract. It was very much a system of mutual obligations. The serf could not leave his land, but neither in practice could the lord eject him. (Pirenne, *An Economic History of Mediaeval Europe.*) It is true that it was open to abuse since the lord was in a stronger position than the chief, let alone the council of elders, of a tribal society. It was undoubtedly less perfect a social system than the traditional tribe, far more perfect, however, than the type of society that replaced it. It was probably during the 13th century that the manorial system broke down in Western Europe. This was caused by increasing international trade and the development of markets, which in Pirenne's view had been impeded for a long time by the Arab stranglehold on the Mediterranean. The ecological advantage of the manorial system was that the manor produced for itself. It did not over-produce, and disrupt the environment as a result, as there was no market to which surplus produce could be sold. With the development of markets came over-production, deforestation, and slowly the manorial system broke down, the serf was freed and wage labour became the rule. Polanyi regards the switch from a subsistence to a market economy as one of the greatest calamities to have befallen western man (Karl Polanyi — *The Great Transformation*).

Resistance to Wage-Labour

As we have already noted, one of the principal pretexts for establishing indus-   23 trial enterprises in areas that have so far escaped their ravages is the provision of employment. It is ironic to note just how strongly has man, living in a traditional society, always resisted being transformed into a unit of wage-labour. In Assam, nothing would persuade the tribal Assami to work on the tea plantations, and labourers had to be imported from already over-populated Bihar. In Ceylon, British planters had to introduce Tamils from southern India to work on the plantations. In the West Indies the Spanish recruited for this purpose the indigenous Caribs. So little however, were they suited for this soul-destroying work, that it did not take long for the entire race to become extinct. As a result, Negroes were imported from Africa, as they were in North America. Akpapa provides a good illustration of this principle. He describes the difficulties encountered by the Enugu coalmining industry in Nigeria, in obtaining labour for its mines. (Akpapa: *Problems of initiating industrial labour in a pre-industrial community, Cahiers d'Etudes Africaines*, Spring 1973). Labourers, it appears, had to be press-ganged into working in the mines. Every day 700 of them disappeared never to be seen again, unless they had the misfortune to be "grabbed" again.

Eventually the chiefs were employed to force their subjects into working 24 for the mining company, and they were paid so much for each wage-labourer they provided. Those who refused to obey their chiefs were originally fined; eventually, however, it became necessary to sentence them to varying periods of hard labour.

This gives some idea of the difficulties involved in persuading people, 25 leading a perfectly satisfying, self-fulfilling life within their tribal units, to leave their family and community in order to indulge in monotonous, soul-destroying work in some large enterprise. Ironically, the setting up of such enterprises in areas lived in by tribal peoples has always been and still is justified on the grounds of relieving chronic unemployment.

Conclusion

As we have seen, people were perfectly well employed before there was a 26 market economy, before in fact wage labour was even thought of.

Economic growth is in fact, not the only means of providing employ- 27 ment but the only means of providing employment of a specific type — capital-intensive employment. Though it is probable that such employment is far less agreeable than any other type, it does permit, temporarily at least, a higher standard of consumption of manufactured goods. It is only in this way that producers can also be consumers and on a scale sufficient to maintain the industrial machine functioning at the required rate. On the other hand, the only reason why people require these jobs and the material goods which they enable them to procure, is that we have developed a particular type of society in which the requisites of life must be purchased, in which people are so far removed from their natural environment that they can no longer produce them themselves, and that their essential social environment has been so disrupted that people have become dependent on a surrogate one, that can only be maintained by working for some vast enterprise involved in activities totally divorced from the realities of their family and social life.

The argument that further economic growth is required to provide fur- 28 ther employment is only true if we insist on observing the rules of our industrial society, if we remain intent in further extending the technosphere at the cost of the biosphere, and in further increasing the capital-intensiveness of economic activities. It is not true if we reject these goals and opt out of the automation race. The choice is not as we are told between unemployment and economic growth but between unemployment, economic growth (with more unemployment at a later date) or the development of a labour-intensive economy in a sustainable decentralised society.

SUBJECT QUESTIONS

1. What, according to Goldsmith, are the major problems connected with establishing such new industrial sites as the North Sea or Alaska oil fields?
2. Why does unemployment rise even in areas of considerable economic growth?
3. If economic growth actually causes unemployment, why do you suppose most nations still seek such growth?
4. Do you think a major country like the United States could successfully "opt out" of the growth race if the other nations stayed in it? What might some of the results be?
5. If food-gathering societies consumed only one-third of their available food supply and had no word for work, why do you suppose there has been a continuous trend toward "capital-intensive systems"?

STRUCTURE QUESTIONS

1. Identify the main structural divisions of this essay. Was it good strategy for Goldsmith to begin with the present and work back to primitive societies?
2. Does Goldsmith successfully establish a cause-effect relationship between economic growth and unemployment? Does he consider other possible causes of rising unemployment?
3. Goldsmith argues for a return to a "decentralized society"; does he show that such a return would result in fuller and more meaningful employment, as he claims?
4. Should Goldsmith have been more careful to define such terms as "capital-intensive economy"? Is it possible to understand the essay without complete comprehension of such terms?
5. Goldsmith is writing for educated nonspecialists interested in ecology. Is the style about right for such readers? Can you suggest improvements?

Work in an Alienated Society

Erich Fromm

Dr. Erich Fromm was born in Germany in 1900. His training and his chief interest have been in social psychology. Since coming to the United States in 1934 to escape the Nazi persecution of Jews, Fromm has taught at Columbia, Bennington, Michigan State, NYU, and in Mexico, where he now lives. His books include the classic Escape from Freedom *(1941), which is still widely read in college classes,* Man for Himself *(1947),* The Art of Loving *(1956),* May Man Prevail? *(1961),* The Heart of Man *(1964), and* You Shall Be as Gods *(1966). The following passage is from* The Sane Society *(1955), one of the "sacred texts" of many who seek to avoid the alienation of living in a technological society by joining communes and other life style experiments. What Fromm argues for in this book is a "humanistic communitarian socialism."*

What becomes the meaning of *work* in an alienated society? 1

We have already made some brief comments about this question in the 2
general discussion of alienation. But since this problem is of utmost importance, not only for the understanding of present-day society, but also for any attempt to create a saner society, I want to deal with the nature of work separately and more extensively in the following pages.

Unless man exploits others, he has to work in order to live. However 3
primitive and simple his method of work may be, by the very fact of production, he has risen above the animal kingdom; rightly has he been defined as "the animal that produces." But work is not only an inescapable necessity for man. Work is also his liberator from nature, his creator as a social and independent being. *In the process of work, that is, the molding and changing of nature outside of himself, man molds and changes himself.* He emerges from nature by mastering her; he develops his powers of cooperation, of reason, his sense of beauty. He separates himself from nature, from the original unity with her, but at the same time unites himself with her again as her master and builder. The more his work develops, the more his individuality develops. In molding nature and re-creating her, he learns to make use of his powers, increasing his skill and creativeness. Whether we think of the beautiful paintings in the caves of Southern France, the ornaments on weapons among primitive people, the statues and temples of Greece, the cathedrals

of the Middle Ages, the chairs and tables made by skilled craftsmen, or the cultivation of flowers, trees or corn by peasants — all are expressions of the creative transformation of nature by man's reason and skill.

In Western history, craftsmanship, especially as it developed in the thirteenth and fourteenth centuries, constitutes one of the peaks in the evolution of creative work. Work was not only a useful activity, but one which carried with it a profound satisfaction. The main features of craftsmanship have been very lucidly expressed by C. W. Mills. "There is no ulterior motive in work other than the product being made and the processes of its creation. The details of daily work are meaningful because they are not detached in the worker's mind from the product of the work. The worker is free to control his own working action. The craftsman is thus able to learn from his work; and to use and develop his capacities and skills in its prosecution. There is no split of work and play, or work and culture. The craftsman's way of livelihood determines and infuses his entire mode of living."[1]

With the collapse of the medieval structure, and the beginning of the modern mode of production, the meaning and function of work changed fundamentally, especially in the Protestant countries. Man, being afraid of his newly won freedom, was obsessed by the need to subdue his doubts and fears by developing a feverish activity. The outcome of this activity, success or failure, decided his salvation, indicating whether he was among the saved or the lost souls. *Work, instead of being an activity satisfying in itself and pleasureable, became a duty and an obsession.* The more it was possible to gain riches by work, the more it became a pure means to the aim of wealth and success. Work became, in Max Weber's terms, the chief factor in a system of "inner-worldly asceticism," an answer to man's sense of aloneness and isolation.

However, work in this sense existed only for the upper and middle classes, those who could amass some capital and employ the work of others. For the vast majority of those who had only their physical energy to sell, work became nothing but forced labor. The worker in the eighteenth or nineteenth century who had to work sixteen hours if he did not want to starve was not doing it because he served the Lord in this way, nor because his success would show that he was among the "chosen" ones, but because he was forced to sell his energy to those who had the means of exploiting it. The first centuries of the modern era find the meaning of work divided into that of *duty* among the middle class, and that of *forced labor* among those without property.

The religious attitude toward work as a duty, which was still so prevalent in the nineteenth century, has been changing considerably in the last decades. Modern man does not know what to do with himself, how to spend his lifetime

---

[1] C. W. Mills, *White Collar*, Oxford University Press, New York, 1951, p. 220.

meaningfully, and he is driven to work in order to avoid an unbearable boredom. But work has ceased to be a moral and religious obligation in the sense
of the middle-class attitude of the eighteenth and nineteenth centuries. Something new has emerged. Ever-increasing production, the drive to make bigger
and better things, have become aims in themselves, new ideals. Work has
become alienated from the working person.

What happens to the industrial worker? He spends his best energy for   8
seven or eight hours a day in producing "something." He needs his work in
order to make a living, but his role is essentially a passive one. He fulfills
a small isolated function in a complicated and highly organized process of
production, and is never confronted with "his" product as a whole, at least
not as a producer, but only as a consumer, provided he has the money to
buy "his" product in a store. He is concerned neither with the whole product
in its physical aspects nor with its wider economic and social aspects. He is
put in a certain place, has to carry out a certain task, but does not participate
in the organization or management of the work. He is not interested, nor does
he know why one produces this, instead of another commodity — what relation it has to the needs of society as a whole. The shoes, the cars, the electric
bulbs, are produced by "the enterprise," using the machines. He is a part of
the machine, rather than its master as an active agent. The machine, instead
of being in his service to do work for him which once had to be performed
by sheer physical energy, has become his master. Instead of the machine being
the substitute for human energy, man has become a substitute for the machine.
*His work can be defined as the performance of acts which cannot yet be
performed by machines.*

Work is a means of getting money, not in itself a meaningful human   9
activity. P. Drucker, observing workers in the automobile industry, expresses
this idea very succinctly: "For the great majority of automobile workers, the
only meaning of the job is in the pay check, not in anything connected with
the work or the product. Work appears as something unnatural, a disagreeable, meaningless and stultifying condition of getting the pay check,
devoid of dignity as well as of importance. No wonder that this puts a premium
on slovenly work, on slow-downs, and on other tricks to get the same pay
check with less work. No wonder that this results in an unhappy and discontented worker — because a pay check is not enough to base one's self-respect
on."[2]

This relationship of the worker to his work is an outcome of the whole   10
social organization of which he is a part. Being "employed,"[3] he is not an
active agent, has no responsibility except the proper performance of the

---

[2] Cf. Peter F. Drucker, *Concept of the Corporation*, The John Day Company, New York,
1946, p. 179.
[3] The English "employed" like the German *angestellt* are terms which refer to things
rather than to human beings.

isolated piece of work he is doing, and has little interest except the one of bringing home enough money to support himself and his family. Nothing more is expected of him, or wanted from him. He is part of the equipment hired by capital, and his role and function are determined by this quality of being a piece of equipment. In recent decades, increasing attention has been paid to the psychology of the worker, and to his attitude toward his work, to the "human problem of industry"; but this very formulation is indicative of the underlying attitude; there is a human being spending most of his lifetime at work, and what should be discussed is the *"industrial problem of human beings," rather than "the human problem of industry."*

Most investigations in the field of industrial psychology are concerned 11 with the question of how the productivity of the individual worker can be increased, and how he can be made to work with less friction; psychology has lent its services to "human engineering," an attempt to treat the worker and employee like a machine which runs better when it is well oiled. While Taylor was primarily concerned with a better organization of the technical use of the worker's physical powers, most industrial psychologists are mainly concerned with the manipulation of the worker's psyche. The underlying idea can be formulated like this: if he works better when he is happy, then let us make him happy, secure, satisfied, or anything else, provided it raises his output and diminishes friction. In the name of "human relations," the worker is treated with all devices which suit a completely alienated person; even happiness and human values are recommended in the interest of better relations with the public. Thus, for instance, according to *Time* magazine, one of the best-known American psychiatrists said to a group of fifteen hundred Supermarket executives: "It's going to be an increased satisfaction to our customers if we are happy. . . . It is going to pay off in cold dollars and cents to management, if we could put some of these general principles of values, human relationships, really into practice." One speaks of "human relations" and one means the most in-human relations, those between alienated automatons; one speaks of happiness and means the perfect routinization which has driven out the last doubt and all spontaneity.

The alienated and profoundly unsatisfactory character of work results 12 in two reactions: one, the ideal of complete *laziness;* the other a deep-seated, though often unconscious *hostility* toward work and everything and everybody connected with it.

It is not difficult to recognize the widespread longing for the state of 13 complete laziness and passivity. Our advertising appeals to it even more than to sex. There are, of course, many useful and labor saving gadgets. But this usefulness often serves only as a rationalization for the appeal to complete passivity and receptivity. A package of breakfast cereal is being advertised as *"new — easier to eat."* An electric toaster is advertised with these words: ". . . the most distinctly different toaster in the world! Everything is done *for* you with this new toaster. You need not even bother to lower the bread. Power-action, through a unique electric motor, *gently takes the bread right out of your fingers!*" How many courses in languages, or other subjects are announced with the slogan "effortless learning, no more of the old drudgery." Everybody knows the picture of the elderly couple in the advertisement of a life insurance company, who have retired at the age of sixty, and spend their life in the complete bliss of having nothing to do except just travel.

Radio and television exhibit another element of this yearning for laziness: the idea of "push-button power"; by pushing a button, or turning a knob on my machine, I have the power to produce music, speeches, ball games, and on the television set, to command events of the world to appear before my eyes. The pleasure of driving cars certainly rests partly upon this same satisfaction of the wish for push-button power. By the effortless pushing of a button, a powerful machine is set in motion; little skill and effort are needed to make the driver feel that he is the ruler of space. 14

But there is far more serious and deep-seated reaction to the meaninglessness and boredom of work. It is a hostility toward work which is much less conscious than our craving for laziness and inactivity. Many a businessman feels himself the prisoner of his business and the commodities he sells; he has a feeling of fraudulency about his product and a secret contempt for it. He hates his customers, who force him to put up a show in order to sell. He hates his competitors because they are a threat; his employees as well as his superiors, because he is in a constant competitive fight with them. Most important of all, he hates himself, because he sees his life passing by, without making any sense beyond the momentary intoxication of success. Of course, this hate and contempt for others and for oneself, and for the very things one produces, is mainly unconscious, and only occasionally comes up to awareness in a fleeting thought, which is sufficiently disturbing to be set aside as quickly as possible. 15

SUBJECT QUESTIONS

1. Why, according to Fromm, has work changed from a basic and self-satisfying need to a loathsome task?
2. If craftsmanship provided happiness and security, why don't dissatisfied workers simply quit their jobs and become craftsmen once more?
3. Why would Renaissance man have been "afraid of his newly won freedom" (paragraph 5)?
4. When work becomes merely a "means of getting money," what are the effects (a) on production and (b) on attitudes toward work? Which of these does Fromm consider most serious?
5. Do you think modern man has become lazy, as Fromm suggests, or that he expends his energy in other directions (fishing, for instance)?

6. What basic mistake have industrial psychologists made in dealing with worker dissatisfaction? Have you any personal experience that would support Fromm's assessment of the problem?

STRUCTURE QUESTIONS

1. In his historical cause and effect analysis, Fromm says that "the meaning of work divided into that of *duty* among the middle class, and that of *forced labor* among those without property." From this point on, Fromm discusses effects on the laboring class — until the final paragraph, where without warning he changes his example to the resentment of a middle-class businessman. Does this shift constitute a flaw in his analysis?
2. In the closing paragraphs, Fromm discusses two results of unsatisfactory working conditions. One of these, laziness, is supported by numerous references to commercial advertising. Might there be other reasons for the advertising of labor saving gadgets?
3. Examine the analysis of "what happens to the industrial worker" in paragraph 8; would you class this as valid cause and effect analysis, a personal judgment, or the results of a cause and effect analysis without a full explanation?
4. Three complete sentences in this essay are cast in italic type; what is the relationship among them? Why are they in italics? Would their function be more clear if Fromm had not italicized words and phrases elsewhere in the essay?
5. Fromm clearly has tried to avoid the specialized jargon of social psychology. Specialists often point out that the danger in doing this is oversimplification — perhaps even unintentional falsification — of a scientifically defensible analysis. Do you think Fromm's essay might be faulted on this score?

Counterparts

James Joyce

James Joyce (1882–1941) was an Irish poet and novelist whose stream-of-consciousness novels, Ulysses *and* Finnegans Wake, *have had a strong influence on young writers of our own day. The story below was taken from his first book,* Dubliners *(1914).*

The bell rang furiously and, when Miss Parker went to the tube, a furious voice called out in a piercing North of Ireland accent:

"Send Farrington here!"

Miss Parker returned to her machine, saying to a man who was writing at a desk:

"Mr. Alleyne wants you upstairs."

The man muttered "*Blast* him!" under his breath and pushed back his chair to stand up. When he stood up he was tall and of great bulk. He had a hanging face, dark wine-coloured, with fair eyebrows and moustache: his eyes bulged forward slightly and the whites of them were dirty. He lifted up the counter and, passing by the clients, went out of the office with a heavy step.

He went heavily upstairs until he came to the second landing, where a door bore a brass plate with the inscription *Mr. Alleyne.* Here he halted, puffing with labour and vexation, and knocked. The shrill voice cried:

"Come in!"

The man entered Mr. Alleyne's room. Simultaneously Mr. Alleyne, a little man wearing gold-rimmed glasses on a clean-shaven face, shot his head up over a pile of documents. The head itself was so pink and hairless it seemed like a large egg reposing on the papers. Mr. Alleyne did not lose a moment:

"Farrington? What is the meaning of this? Why have I always to complain of you? May I ask you why you haven't made a copy of that contract between Bodley and Kirwan? I told you it must be ready by four o'clock."

"But Mr. Shelley said, sir —"

"*Mr. Shelley said, sir.* . . . Kindly attend to what I say and not to what *Mr. Shelley says, sir.* You have always some excuse or another for shirking work. Let me tell you that if the contract is not copied before this evening I'll lay the matter before Mr. Crosbie. . . . Do you hear me now?"

"Yes, sir."   12

"Do you hear me now? . . . Ay and another little matter! I might as well   13
be talking to the wall as talking to you. Understand once for all that you
get a half an hour for your lunch and not an hour and a half. How many
courses do you want, I'd like to know. . . . Do you mind me now?"

"Yes, sir."   14

Mr. Alleyne bent his head again upon his pile of papers. The man stared   15
fixedly at the polished skull which directed the affairs of Crosbie & Alleyne,
gauging its fragility. A spasm of rage gripped his throat for a few moments
and then passed, leaving after it a sharp sensation of thirst. The man recognised
the sensation and felt that he must have a good night's drinking. The middle
of the month was passed and, if he could get the copy done in time, Mr.
Alleyne might give him an order on the cashier. He stood still, gazing fixedly
at the head upon the pile of papers. Suddenly Mr. Alleyne began to upset
all the papers, searching for something. Then, as if he had been unaware of
the man's presence till that moment, he shot up his head again, saying:

"Eh? Are you going to stand there all day? Upon my word, Farrington,   16
you take things easy!"

"I was waiting to see . . ."   17

"Very good, you needn't wait to see. Go downstairs and do your work."   18

The man walked heavily towards the door and, as he went out of the   19
room, he heard Mr. Alleyne cry after him that if the contract was not copied
by evening Mr. Crosbie would hear of the matter.

He returned to his desk in the lower office and counted the sheets which   20
remained to be copied. He took up his pen and dipped it in the ink but he
continued to stare stupidly at the last words he had written: *In no case shall
the said Bernard Bodley be* . . . The evening was falling and in a few minutes
they would be lighting the gas: then he could write. He felt that he must
slake the thirst in his throat. He stood up from his desk and, lifting the counter
as before, passed out of the office. As he was passing out the chief clerk looked
at him inquiringly.

"It's all right, Mr. Shelley," said the man, pointing with his finger to   21
indicate the objective of his journey.

The chief clerk glanced at the hat-rack, but, seeing the row complete,   22
offered no remark. As soon as he was on the landing the man pulled a shep-
herd's plaid cap out of his pocket, put it on his head and ran quickly down
the rickety stairs. From the street door he walked on furtively on the inner
side of the path towards the corner and all at once dived into a doorway.
He was now safe in the dark snug of O'Neill's shop, and, filling up the little
window that looked into the bar with his inflamed face, the colour of dark
wine or dark meat, he called out:

"Here, Pat, give us a g.p., like a good fellow."   23

The curate brought him a glass of plain porter. The man drank it at   24 a gulp and asked for a caraway seed. He put his penny on the counter and, leaving the curate to grope for it in the gloom, retreated out of the snug as furtively as he had entered it.

Darkness, accompanied by a thick fog, was gaining upon the dusk of [25] February and the lamps in Eustace Street had been lit. The man went up by the houses until he reached the door of the office, wondering whether he could finish his copy in time. On the stairs a moist pungent odour of perfumes saluted his nose: evidently Miss Delacour had come while he was out in O'Neill's. He crammed his cap back again into his pocket and re-entered the office, assuming an air of absent-mindedness.

"Mr. Alleyne has been calling for you," said the chief clerk severely. [26] "Where were you?"

The man glanced at the two clients who were standing at the counter [27] as if to intimate that their presence prevented him from answering. As the clients were both male the chief clerk allowed himself a laugh.

"I know that game," he said. "Five times in one day is a little bit. . . . [28] Well, you better look sharp and get a copy of our correspondence in the Delacour case for Mr. Alleyne."

This address in the presence of the public, his run upstairs and the porter [29] he had gulped down so hastily confused the man and, as he sat down at his desk to get what was required, he realised how hopeless was the task of finishing his copy of the contract before half past five. The dark damp night was coming and he longed to spend it in the bars, drinking with his friends amid the glare of gas and the clatter of glasses. He got out the Delacour correspondence and passed out of the office. He hoped that Mr. Alleyne would not discover that the last two letters were missing.

The moist pungent perfume lay all the way up to Mr. Alleyne's room. [30] Miss Delacour was a middle-aged woman of Jewish appearance. Mr. Alleyne was said to be sweet on her or on her money. She came to the office often and stayed a long time when she came. She was sitting beside his desk now in an aroma of perfumes, smoothing the handle of her umbrella and nodding the great black feather in her hat. Mr. Alleyne had swivelled his chair round to face her and thrown his right foot jauntily upon his left knee. The man put the correspondence on the desk and bowed respectfully but neither Mr. Alleyne nor Miss Delacour took any notice of his bow. Mr. Alleyne tapped a finger on the correspondence and then flicked it towards him as if to say: *"That's all right: you can go."*

The man returned to the lower office and sat down again at his desk. [31] He stared intently at the incomplete phrase: *In no case shall the said Bernard Bodley be . . .* and thought how strange it was that the last three words began with the same letter. The chief clerk began to hurry Miss Parker, saying she would never have the letters typed in time for post. The man listened to the clicking of the machine for a few minutes and then set to work to finish his copy. But his head was not clear and his mind wandered away to the glare and rattle of the public-house. It was a night for hot punches. He struggled on with his copy, but when the clock struck five he had still fourteen pages to write. Blast it! He couldn't finish it in time. He longed to execrate aloud, to bring his fist down on something violently. He was so enraged that he wrote *Bernard Bernard* instead of *Bernard Bodley* and had to begin again on a clean sheet.

He felt strong enough to clear out the whole office single-handed. His body ached to do something, to rush out and revel in violence. All the indignities of his life enraged him.... Could he ask the cashier privately for an advance? No, the cashier was no good, no damn good: he wouldn't give an advance.... He knew where he would meet the boys: Leonard and O'Halloran and Nosey Flynn. The barometer of his emotional nature was set for a spell of riot.   32

His imagination had so abstracted him that his name was called twice before he answered. Mr. Alleyne and Miss Delacour were standing outside the counter and all the clerks had turned round in anticipation of something. The man got up from his desk. Mr. Alleyne began a tirade of abuse, saying that two letters were missing. The man answered that he knew nothing about them, that he had made a faithful copy. The tirade continued: it was so bitter and violent that the man could hardly restrain his fist from descending upon the head of the manikin before him.   33

"I know nothing about any other two letters," he said stupidly.   34

"*You — know — nothing.* Of course you know nothing," said Mr. Alleyne. "Tell me," he added, glancing first for approval to the lady beside him, "do you take me for a fool? Do you think me an utter fool?"   35

The man glanced from the lady's face to the little egg-shaped head and back again; and, almost before he was aware of it, his tongue had found a felicitous moment: 36

"I don't think, sir," he said, "that that's a fair question to put to me."   37

There was a pause in the very breathing of the clerks. Everyone was astounded (the author of the witticism no less than his neighbours) and Miss Delacour, who was a stout amiable person, began to smile broadly. Mr. Alleyne flushed to the hue of a wild rose and his mouth twitched with a dwarf's passion. He shook his fist in the man's face till it seemed to vibrate like the knob of some electric machine: 38

"You impertinent ruffian! You impertinent ruffian! I'll make short work of you! Wait till you see! You'll apologise to me for your impertinence or you'll quit the office instanter! You'll quit this, I'm telling you, or you'll apologise to me!"   39

He stood in a doorway opposite the office watching to see if the cashier would come out alone. All the clerks passed out and finally the cashier came out with the chief clerk. It was no use trying to say a word to him when   40 he was with the chief clerk. The man felt that his position was bad enough. He had been obliged to offer an abject apology to Mr. Alleyne for his impertinence but he knew what a hornets' nest the office would be for him. He could remember the way in which Mr. Alleyne had hounded little Peake out of the office in order to make room for his own nephew. He felt savage and thirsty and revengeful, annoyed with himself and with everyone else. Mr. Alleyne would never give him an hour's rest; his life would be a hell to him. He had made a proper fool of himself this time. Could he not keep his tongue in his cheek? But they had never pulled together from the first, he and Mr. Alleyne, ever since the day Mr. Alleyne had overheard him mimicking his North of Ireland accent to amuse Higgins and Miss Parker: that had been the beginning of it. He might have tried Higgins for the money, but sure Higgins never had anything for himself. A man with two establishments to keep up, of course he couldn't. . . .

He felt his great body again aching for the comfort of the public-house. 41 The fog had begun to chill him and he wondered could he touch Pat in O'Neill's. He could not touch him for more than a bob — and a bob was no use. Yet he must get money somewhere or other; he had spent his last penny for the g.p. and soon it would be too late for getting money anywhere. Suddenly, as he was fingering his watchchain, he thought of Terry Kelly's pawn-office in Fleet Street. That was the dart! Why didn't he think of it sooner?

He went through the narrow alley of Temple Bar quickly, muttering 42 to himself that they could all go to hell because he was going to have a good night of it. The clerk in Terry Kelly's said *A crown!* but the consignor held out for six shillings; and in the end the six shillings was allowed him literally. He came out of the pawn-office joyfully, making a little cylinder of the coins between his thumb and fingers. In Westmoreland Street the footpaths were crowded with young men and women returning from business and ragged urchins ran here and there yelling out the names of the evening editions. The man passed through the crowd, looking on the spectacle generally with proud satisfaction and staring masterfully at the office-girls. His head was full of the noises of tram-gongs and swishing trolleys and his nose already sniffed the curling fumes of punch. As he walked on he preconsidered the terms in which he would narrate the incident to the boys:

"So, I just looked at him — coolly, you know, and looked at her. Then 43 I looked back at him again — taking my time, you know. 'I don't think that that's a fair question to put to me,' says I."

Nosey Flynn was sitting up in his usual corner of Davy Byrne's and, 44 when he heard the story, he stood Farrington a half-one, saying it was as smart a thing as ever he heard. Farrington stood a drink in his turn. After a while O'Halloran and Paddy Leonard came in and the story was repeated to them. O'Halloran stood tailors of malt, hot, all round and told the story of the retort he had made to the chief clerk when he was in Callan's of Frownes's Street;

but, as the retort was after the manner of the liberal shepherds in the eclogues, he had to admit that it was not as clever as Farrington's retort. At this Farrington told the boys to polish off that and have another.

Just as they were naming their poisons who should come in but Higgins! Of course he had to join in with the others. The men asked him to give his version of it, and he did so with great vivacity for the sight of five small hot whiskies was very exhilarating. Everyone roared laughing when he showed the way in which Mr. Alleyne shook his fist in Farrington's face. Then he imitated Farrington, saying, *"And here was my nabs, as cool as you please,"* while Farrington looked at the company out of his heavy dirty eyes, smiling and at times drawing forth stray drops of liquor from his moustache with the aid of his lower lip.

When that round was over there was a pause. O'Halloran had money but neither of the other two seemed to have any; so the whole party left the shop somewhat regretfully. At the corner of Duke Street Higgins and Nosey Flynn bevelled off to the left while the other three turned back towards the city. Rain was drizzling down on the cold streets and, when they reached the Ballast Office, Farrington suggested the Scotch House. The bar was full of men and loud with the noise of tongues and glasses. The three men pushed past the whining match-sellers at the door and formed a little party at the corner of the counter. They began to exchange stories. Leonard introduced them to a young fellow named Weathers who was performing at the Tivoli as an acrobat and knockabout *artiste*. Farrington stood a drink all round. Weathers said he would take a small Irish and Apollinaris. Farrington, who had definite notions of what was what, asked the boys would they have an Apollinaris too; but the boys told Tim to make theirs hot. The talk became theatrical. O'Halloran stood a round and then Farrington stood another round, Weathers protesting that the hospitality was too Irish. He promised to get them in behind the scenes and introduce them to some nice girls. O'Halloran said that he and Leonard would go, but that Farrington wouldn't go because he was a married man; and Farrington's heavy dirty eyes leered at the company in token that he understood he was being chaffed. Weathers made them all have just one little tincture at his expense and promised to meet them later on at Mulligan's in Poolbeg Street.

When the Scotch House closed they went round to Mulligan's. They went into the parlour at the back and O'Halloran ordered small hot specials all around. They were all beginning to feel mellow. Farrington was just standing another round when Weathers came back. Much to Farrington's relief he drank a glass of bitter this time. Funds were getting low but they had enough to keep them going. Presently two young women with big hats and a young man in a check suit came in and sat at a table close by. Weathers saluted them and told the company that they were out of the Tivoli. Farrington's eyes wandered at every moment in the direction of one of the young

45

46

47

women. There was something striking in her appearance. An immense scarf of peacock-blue muslin was wound around her hat and knotted in a great bow under her chin; and she wore bright yellow gloves, reaching to the elbow. Farrington gazed admiringly at the plump arm which she moved very often and with much grace; and when, after a little time, she answered his gaze he admired still more her large dark brown eyes. The oblique staring expression in them fascinated him. She glanced at him once or twice and, when the party was leaving the room, she brushed against his chair and said "*O, pardon!* " in a London accent. He watched her leave the room in the hope that she would look back at him, but he was disappointed. He cursed his want of money and cursed all the rounds he had stood, particularly all the whiskies and Apollinaris which he had stood to Weathers. If there was one thing that he hated it was a sponge. He was so angry that he lost count of the conversation of his friends.

When Paddy Leonard called him he found that they were talking about 48 feats of strength. Weathers was showing his biceps muscle to the company and boasting so much that the other two had called on Farrington to uphold the national honour. Farrington pulled up his sleeve accordingly and showed his biceps muscle to the company. The two arms were examined and compared and finally it was agreed to have a trial of strength. The table was cleared and the two men rested their elbows on it, clasping hands. When Paddy Leonard said "*Go!* " each was to try to bring down the other's hand on to the table. Farrington looked very serious and determined.

The trial began. After about thirty seconds Weathers brought his oppo- 49 nent's hand slowly down to the table. Farrington's dark wine-coloured face flushed darker still with anger and humiliation at having been defeated by such a stripling.

"You're not to put the weight of your body behind it. Play fair," he 50 said.

"Who's not playing fair?" said the other. 51

"Come on again. The two best out of three." 52

The trial began again. The veins stood out on Farrington's forehead, 53 and the pallor of Weathers' complexion changed to peony. Their hands and arms trembled under the stress. After a long struggle Weathers again brought his opponent's hand slowly on to the table. There was a murmur of applause from the spectators. The curate, who was standing beside the table, nodded his red head towards the victor and said with stupid familiarity:

"Ah! that's the knack!" 54

"What the hell do you know about it?" said Farrington fiercely, turning 55 on the man. "What do you put in your gab for?"

"Sh, sh!" said O'Halloran, observing the violent expression of Farring- 56 ton's face. "Pony up, boys. We'll have just one little smahan more and then we'll be off."

A very sullen-faced man stood at the corner of O'Connell Bridge waiting for   57
the little Sandymount tram to take him home. He was full of smouldering
anger and revengefulness. He felt humiliated and discontented; he did not
even feel drunk; and he had only twopence in his pocket. He cursed everything. He had done for himself in the office, pawned his watch, spent all his
money; and he had not even got drunk. He began to feel thirsty again and
he longed to be back again in the hot reeking public-house. He had lost his
reputation as a strong man, having been defeated twice by a mere boy. His
heart swelled with fury and, when he thought of the woman in the big hat
who had brushed against him and said *Pardon!* his fury nearly choked him.

His tram let him down at Shelbourne Road and he steered his great   58
body along in the shadow of the wall of the barracks. He loathed returning
to his home. When he went in by the side-door he found the kitchen empty
and the kitchen fire nearly out. He bawled upstairs:

"Ada! Ada!"   59

His wife was a little sharp-faced woman who bullied her husband when   60
he was sober and was bullied by him when he was drunk. They had five
children. A little boy came running down the stairs.

"Who is that?" said the man peering through the darkness.   61

"Me, pa."   62

"Who are you? Charlie?"   63

"No, pa. Tom."   64

"Where's your mother?"   65

"She's out at the chapel."   66

"That's right.... Did she think of leaving any dinner for me?"   67

"Yes, pa. I —"   68

"Light the lamp. What do you mean by having the place in darkness?   69
Are the other children in bed?"

The man sat down heavily on one of the chairs while the little boy lit   70
the lamp. He began to mimic his son's flat accent, saying half to himself: *"At
the chapel. At the chapel, if you please!"* When the lamp was lit he banged
his fist on the table and shouted:

"What's for my dinner?"   71

"I'm going ... to cook it, pa," said the little boy.   72

The man jumped up furiously and pointed to the fire.   73

"On that fire! You let the fire out! By God, I'll teach you to do that   74
again!"

He took a step to the door and seized the walking-stick which was   75
standing behind it.

"I'll teach you to let the fire out!" he said, rolling up his sleeve in order   76
to give his arm free play.

The little boy cried *"O, pa!"* and ran whimpering round the table, but   77 the man followed him and caught him by the coat. The little boy looked about him wildly but, seeing no way of escape, fell upon his knees.

"Now, you'll let the fire out the next time!" said the man, striking at   78
him vigorously with the stick. "Take that, you little whelp!"

The boy uttered a squeal of pain as the stick cut his thigh. He clasped   79
his hands together in the air and his voice shook with fright.

"O, pa!" he cried. "Don't beat me, pa! And I'll . . . I'll say a *Hail Mary*   80
for you. . . . I'll say a *Hail Mary* for you, pa, if you don't beat me. . . . I'll
say a *Hail Mary*. . . ."

SUBJECT QUESTIONS

1. What is a counterpart? There is only one central figure in this story; is "Counterparts" an inappropriate title, then?
2. Each incident in the story causes the same mental reaction on Farrington's part; what is it? Does this day seem to be a rare "bad" one in Farrington's life, or a typical day? What clues does Joyce give?
3. What would you say is Farrington's basic problem? Consider his attitude toward his boss. Why does he do more daydreaming than work?
4. Why does Farrington beat his innocent son at the end? Trace the chain of cause and effect which results in this violence.
5. Do you think it is coincidence that Farrington's wife is at church when he comes home? Does she seem to be an innocent victim of Farrington's fury, or part of the cause of it?

STRUCTURE QUESTIONS

1. Because "Counterparts" is a narrative rather than expository prose, the principle of organization is naturally time sequence. Still, Joyce must select the incidents to put into that sequence. Do all the incidents contribute to a thematic unity without being redundant?
2. Joyce several times stops the narrative to include brief passages of exposition on the state of Farrington's mind. Examine some of these; are they an intrusion on the story? Are they necessary for a full understanding of the causes of Farrington's actions?
3. Does Joyce make clear and convincing the cause and effect relationships among the incidents narrated? Could he have been more explicit without damaging the story? Does he need to be more explicit?
4. How heavily does Joyce employ descriptive detail to bolster the effect of his narrative? Examine one of the incidents closely to see how much use is made of concrete detail.

Bloodstains

Joyce Carol Oates

Joyce Carol Oates was born in western New York in 1938. One of our most prolific young writers, she has already published three collections of short stories, By the North Gate (1963), Upon the Sweeping Flood (1965), and The Wheel of Love (1970); two volumes of poetry, Anonymous Sins (1969) and Love and Its Derangements (1970); two plays, and many novels, including With Shuddering Fall (1964), A Garden of Earthly Delights (1967), Expensive People (1968), and Them (1969). The latter, a kind of modern gothic novel, won the National Book Award for fiction in 1970. Miss Oates currently lives in Canada, where she is a professor of English at the University of Windsor. In her fiction, her chief interest seems to be in characters struggling in an environment they can neither understand nor control. As one critic, Alfred Kazin, puts it, "They are caught up in the social convulsion and move unheedingly, compulsively, blindly, through the paces assigned to them by the power god." "Bloodstains" first appeared in Harper's (August, 1971).

He sat. He turned to see that he was sharing the bench with a young mother 1 who did not glance around at him. The park they were in was a small noisy island around which traffic moved in a continual stream. Aged, listless men sat on other benches — a few women shoppers, pausing to rest, their eyes eagle-bright and their gloved fingers tugging at the straps of shoes or at hemlines — a few children, Negro and white, urchins from the tenement homes a few blocks off this wide main street. Great untidy flocks of pigeons rose and settled again and rose, startled, scattering. Lawrence Pryor looked at everything keenly. He knew that he was out of place here; he had come down from his office because his eleven o'clock appointment had canceled out; he was free for half an hour. The only place to sit had been beside this pretty young mother, who held her baby up to her face and took no interest at all in the pigeons or the chattering children or Lawrence himself. He was sitting in a patch of sunlight that fell upon him through the narrow channel between two tall buildings, as if singling him out for a blessing.

All these women shoppers! He watched them cross quickly to the island, 2 and quickly over to the other curb, for they rarely had the time to sit and

226

rest. They were in a hurry. Because of them, hurrying across the street, traffic was backed up waiting to make right-hand turns. Out of the crowd of shoppers he saw a blond woman appear, walking briskly and confidently. She hurried against a red light and a horn sounded. How American she was, how well-dressed and sure of herself! Lawrence found himself staring at her, imagining the face that might reveal itself to him if he were to approach her — startled and elegant and composed, seeing by his face that he was no danger to her, no danger.

She did not cross the little park but took the sidewalk that led around it. Avoiding the benchsitters and the pigeons. Lawrence was disappointed. And then, watching her, he saw that the woman was familiar — her brisk, impatient walk, her trim blue coat — and, indeed, he knew her well, the woman was his own wife! He tapped his jaw with the tips of his fingers in a gesture of amused surprise. Of course! Beverly! As if acting out embarrassment for an audience, he smiled up toward the sky . . . and when he looked back, his wife was already hurrying across the street, moving bravely against the light while buses and taxicabs pressed forward.

He got to his feet to follow her. But an extraordinarily tall man got in front of him, walking quickly, and then a small crowd of women shoppers, everyone hurrying now that the light had turned green. Something held Lawrence back. The tall man was hurrying as if to catch up with Beverly. He was strangely tall, freakishly tall, with silver-gray hair that was bunched around his head in tight little curls, like grapes. He wore a dark coat, and on the back of his neck there was a vivid red birthmark, a stain in the shape of a finger. The shoppers moved forward, in front of Lawrence, and the tall man and Lawrence's wife moved into the distance. All this motion made Lawrence feel slightly dizzy.

The legend about him was his fanaticism about work: Beverly complained of this, she worried about it, she was proud of it. He was a doctor and his patients were sacred to him. And so he had better not run after his wife, because she would be alarmed to see him out on the street at this time of day, and because it might be ten or fifteen minutes before he could get away again. She might want him to have lunch with her. She might want him to go into stores with her. Better to stay behind, to stay hidden. So he watched her disappear — his wife hurrying into the midst of the city — and he sat down again, feeling oddly pleased and excited. He felt as if something secret had been revealed to him.

Beside him the young woman was leaning her face to her child, whispering. She had a pale, angular face, illuminated by love, or by the child's reflecting face, or by the narrow patch of sunlight that was moving slowly from Lawrence and onto her. Women, seen like this, were gifts to men.

He considered smiling at her. But no, that might be a mistake — this was not a city in which people smiled freely at one another.

Herb Altman came into the office, striding forward with his head slightly   8
lowered. Bald, but only forty-five. He had a portly, arrogant body and his
clothes were always jaunty — today he wore a bright yellow necktie that
jumped in Lawrence's vision.

Shaking hands.   9

"How are you?"   10

"Not well. I can't sleep. I never sleep, you know that," Altman said.   11

He sat and began to talk. His voice was urgent and demanding. As he   12
spoke he shook his head so that his cheeks shivered. Altman's wife Connie
was a friend of Lawrence's wife. It seemed to Lawrence that the women in
their circle were all close friends; in a way they blended into one another.
The husbands, too, seemed to blend into one another. Many of them had
several lives, but the lives were somehow shared. They lived in one dimension
but turned up in other dimensions — downtown late in the afternoon, or in
downriver suburbs. Their expensive homes and automobiles and boats could
not quite contain them. Too much energy. Urgent, clicking, demanding words.
While Altman talked angrily about his insomnia and switched onto the complaints of his wife and then onto the complaints of his girl, Lawrence saw
again his own wife in the distance of his imagination, a dream he had dreamt
while awake, moving freely and happily along the sidewalk of this massive
city.

What mystery was in her, this woman he had lived with for so long?   13
They had one child, a daughter. They had known each other for two decades.
And yet, seeing her like that, Lawrence had been struck by the mystery of
her separateness, her being. . . .

Altman said in a furious whisper, "I'm going to have her followed!"   14

"Your wife?"   15

"Evie. *Evelyn*. Twenty-five years old, a baby, and she tells me the plans   16
she dreams up! She wants me to marry her next year!"

The numerals of Lawrence's watch were greenish-white, glowing up out   17
of a dark face. They were supposed to glow in the dark but they glowed in
the light as well.

"All right," Altman said, seeing Lawrence look at his watch, "so I'm   18
wasting your time with this. So. Check my heart, my blackened lungs, tap
me on the back to see if I have echoes inside, to see what's hollowed out — I'm
a sick man, we both know that. Here I am."

In the end Lawrence did as he always did: refilled Altman's prescription   19
for barbiturates. It was for six refills, and Altman would be back again in a
few weeks.

At the door Altman paused dramatically. His white shirt front bulged.   20

"Why do they keep after me?" he said. "Larry, what is it? Why are   21
they always after me? I can't sleep at night. I'm planning a trip in my mind
but when I get up I can't remember it — I don't sleep but I don't remember

what I think about. Why are they always after me, those women? What are they doing to me?"

Lawrence and his wife and daughter lived in a brick home that had been   22
painted white, a few blocks from the lake. The house glowed in the air of
twilight. It had the ghostly weightless look of something at the bottom of
a lake, made perfect. It was a place in which Lawrence might sleep soundly,
as he had never slept in his parents' oversized, combative home in Philadelphia. No more of that life! He had blocked out even the memory of that
life.

   Behind him in the city were his patients and the unhappy memories   23
of his patients. Ten, sometimes twelve hours of ailments — the shame of being
sick, of being weak, of uttering words better left unsaid. Office hours were
worse than hospital hours. During the day Lawrence's hand turned shaky and
reluctant, writing out so many prescriptions, smiling with his prescribed smile,
a forty-year-old face that was in danger of wearing out. His patients had too
many faces. They were blotched or sullen or impatient or, like Altman's,
familiar but eerily distant, demanding something Lawrence could not give
and could not understand.

   Many of the ailments were imaginary. They existed, yes, but they were   24
imaginary; how to cure them?

   The telephone was ringing as he entered his home. He had the idea   25
that it had been ringing for some time. When he went to answer it, in the
kitchen, it stopped ringing and he stood with his hand out, a few inches above
the receiver, listening to the silence of the house.

   His mother is coming to visit, due the next morning on the nine-thirty   26
flight from Philadelphia.

   Beverly and Edie are going out again; they get in each other's way by   27
the closet. Edie, fourteen years old and taller than her mother, sticks her arms
angrily into her coat. The coat is khaki-colored and lined with fake wool,
years old; Edie will not give it up in spite of her mother's pleas. Lawrence
stands with the evening newspaper, watching them. It is six-thirty. "Do you
have to go out now?" he says.

   "I forgot to get new towels. I wanted to get new towels for your mother,   28
I can't let her use those old ones," Beverly says.

   "New towels? You're going out now for new towels?"   29

   "Everything is sleazy. It isn't good enough for her."   30

   Beverly's jaws are hardening. Her eyes are bright, alert, restless. Edie   31
is shiny-faced and almost pretty, but always in a hurry, always bumping into
things. It is obvious to Lawrence that his wife and daughter have been arguing
about something. Edie knocks against a chair in the foyer and screws up her
face. "God!" she winces.

"Did you go shopping downtown today?" Lawrence asks his wife.   32

She is frowning into her purse, looking for something. "No."   33

"I thought I saw you."   34

"Saw me? When?"   35

"A little before noon."   36

She stares at him, closing her purse. There is a cold, bright look around   37
her eyes, a look Lawrence cannot understand. Then she smiles. "Oh, yes, I
was downtown ... I just drove down and back, looking for some things I
couldn't get out here. . . . I've been running around all day. I had to pick Edie
up at school and take her to the dentist and now ... now I have to go out
again."

"You're making too much out of it. My mother doesn't expect you to   38
fuss over her."

She shakes her head and avoids his eye. He thinks of the tall, silver-haired   39
man with the birthmark, hurrying along after her as if to catch up with her.

His mother. The airport. They have met his mother like this many times and   40
each time they say the same things; it seems that the same crowds are at
the airport. His mother begins at once to tell him about the news at home
and she will continue to tell him of funerals and weddings, births, illnesses,
surgery, surprises, all the way home, though she has written him about these
things in her weekly letters.

"Oh, look at this!" she says in disgust. She holds up her hands for them   41
to see her white gloves, which are soiled and even stained with something
that looks like rust or blood, a very faint red-brown color.

"I'll wash them out for you, Mother," Beverly says at once.   42

"Traveling is so dirty. Filthy," Lawrence's mother says.   43

He recalls her having said that before.   44

While his mother and his wife talk, Lawrence drives in silence. He's   45
happy that his mother is visiting them. She comes often, several times a year.
Lawrence has the idea that she blames him for having left Philadelphia and
coming to this city of strangers, where he has no relatives. The letters they
write to each other do not seem to express them. Beneath his neat, typed
lines, and beneath her slanted lines in their lavender ink, there seems to be
another dimension, a submerged feeling or memory, that the two of them
can only hint at but cannot express.

They are approaching Lawrence's home. "I like that house," his mother   46
says flatly, as she always does. This seems to settle something. Lawrence and
Beverly both feel relieved.

The old family home had been white also. Now Lawrence's mother lives   47
in an apartment favored by other widows, but for decades of her life she lived

in a house the size of a municipal building. In his dreams Lawrence sometimes climbs the stairway to the third floor, which had been closed off, to look through the stacks of his father's old medical journals, as he did when he was a child. There were bundles of journals. Small towers. He spent many hours looking through them, fascinated.

His mother's presence in his house, his own house, makes Lawrence *feel* *a little displaced.* It seems to him that time is confused. His own age is uncertain. But he is a good host to her, helping Beverly out; he is gallant to her. After dinner that night they look through snapshots, another ritual. The snapshots are passed around. Then, leaning toward him, in a sudden stiff motion that makes him realize how his mother is corseted — his wife, also, her body slim and deft but smoothly hard to the touch — she hands him a photograph that had been taken years ago. That photograph again! It is Lawrence, Larry Jr., sitting on a spotted pony at some forgotten fair, a rented pony, Lawrence's dark hair combed down onto his forehead in a way that makes him look like a moron, his stare startled and vacuous, his mouth too timid to smile. Lawrence stares at the photograph. Why does his mother treasure it so much? Why does she always bring it along with the more recent snapshots, as if she doesn't remember she has shown it to him on her last visit?   48

"Look at that, isn't that darling? A darling boy?" she says stubbornly.   49

Lawrence stares down at his own face, which is blank and stark in the photograph. It was a face that might have become anything. Any personality might have inhabited it. It *was so blank, that face — anything could inhabit it.*   50

He stands suddenly. His mother and his wife stare at him in alarm.   51

"Larry? What's wrong?" Beverly says.   52

He passes his hand over his eyes. He sits down again.   53

"Nothing."   54

"Did you hear something in the house?"   55

"No. Nothing."   56

Two evenings later he is driving home when a car veers out around him, passing him with its horn blaring. The car is filled with kids — boys and girls — and he thinks he sees Edie in with them. His heart jumps. But he cannot be sure.   57

When he gets home it is nearly dark. His mother kisses him on the side of the face. She is powdery and yet hard, a precise, stubborn little woman. What do they talk about all day, women? His mother and his wife? They are telling him now about what they have done today. Their chatter is like music, rising in snatches about them, airy and incomplete. It never quite completes itself; it has to continue.   58

"Is Edie home yet?" he says.   59

"No, not yet," says Beverly.   60

"Where is she?" 61

"She had something after school — choir practice —" 62

"All this time?" 63

"No, not all this time. She's probably at someone's house. She'll be home 64
in a few minutes."

"But you don't know where she is?" 65

"Not exactly. What's wrong? Why are you so angry?" 66

"I'm not angry." 67

When she comes in he will find out nothing from her. Nothing. She will 68
move her body jerkily through the kitchen and to the front closet, she will
take off her coat, she will sit slouching at dinner and stare down into her
plate or stare dutifully up at him, and he will find out nothing about her,
nothing. His heart pounds angrily. Once Beverly said of Edie, "She has all
that stuff on her face but you should see her neck — she never washes! I could
roll the dirt off her neck with my fingers!"

His mother asks him about his day. Did he work hard? Is he tired? 69

He answers her vaguely, listening for Edie to come in. But when she 70
does come in he will find out nothing from her. His mother switches to another
topic — complaints about one of his aunts — and he can't follow her. He is
thinking of Edie, then he is thinking of his wife. Then he finds himself thinking
of one of his patients, Connie Altman. She wept in his office that morning.
"I need something to help me sleep at night. I lie awake thinking. Then in
the morning I can't remember what I was thinking about. I'm so nervous,
my heart pounds, can you give me something stronger to help me sleep?
Everything is running out . . ."

This puzzled him. "What do you mean, everything is running out?" 71

"There isn't any point. I don't see it. We are all running out, people 72
our age, things are running out of us . . . draining out of us . . . I will have
to live out my life in this body . . ."

She is a woman of beauty, very small, with childish wrists and ankles. 73
But her face has begun to harden in the past few years.

"I need something to help me sleep. Please. I know that in the other 74
room *he* is awake, he can't sleep either, it drives me crazy! I prefer the nights
he stays out. At least he isn't in the house, lying awake like me, I don't care
who he's with . . . I need something to help me sleep, please. I can't stand
my thoughts all night long."

His daughter's room. Saturday afternoon. The house is empty for a few hours 75
and he may walk through it, anywhere, because it is his house and all the
rooms are his, his property.

Edie's room is piled with clothes, school books, shoes, junk. Two of the 76 three dresser drawers are pulled out. The top of the dresser is cluttered. Lawrence's reflection moves into the mirror and he looks at himself in surprise — is that really him, Dr. Pryor? He is disappointed. He is even a little angry. His soul is neat, neatly defined as the many cards he carries in his wallet, and as neat as the curve of his haircut against his neck; neat as his files at the office and as his car, which he takes pride in. But his body looks untidy — the shirt rumpled, though he has put it on fresh only that morning — his face sallow, edgy, his hands strangely empty. Is that really Dr. Pryor, that man? How has it happened that he must wake in the morning to this particular face and body, always, this particular human being?

He goes to the dresser, avoiding his own eyes in the mirror, and tugs   77
at the first drawer. A jumble of stockings, black tights, wool socks of various colors, filmy, gauzy things. A spool of white thread rolls harmlessly around. He starts to close the drawer and then remembers that it was partly open. Good. It is good he remembered that. He pulls out the second drawer — underclothes of various colors, pink and yellow and green, things jumbled together, releasing to him an air of fresh, clean laundry. He stares into this drawer. What if it falls out? What if the underclothes fall out and he can't put them back in order again? But they are not in any order, everything is a jumble. He smiles.

He has never come into this room alone in his memory. Never. But being   78
here this afternoon, so close to his daughter and yet safe from her fourteen-year-old's curious, sarcastic eye, he feels oddly pleased. She is very real to him at this moment: She might be standing close behind him, about to break into one of her greetings — "Hiya, buddy!" has been a commonplace remark of hers this past month — or about to hum into his ear one of her slangy, mysterious, banal little tunes.

He finds himself looking through the silky underclothes. Things stick   79
together; there is the crackle of minor electricity. He holds up a half-slip of mint green with tiny white bows on it. Pretty! It is very pretty. He wants to rub it against his face. And now a kind of despair rises in him as he thinks of his daughter and these clothes, his daughter out running around this afternoon at the shopping center with her girlfriends, and these clothes which are now in his possession, here in this room, safe. It is a mystery, his having a daughter. He cannot quite comprehend it. He looks through the drawer farther, this sense of despair rising strongly in him . . . Rolled up in a ball, stuck back in a corner of the drawer, are a pair of white underpants. He picks them up. They have several bloodstains on them, thick and stiff, almost caked. He stares. Why bloodstains? Why here? For a moment he feels nothing, he thinks nothing. He is not even surprised. Then it occurs to him that his daughter was ashamed to put these soiled underpants in the wash, that she had meant to wash them herself but had forgotten, and weeks, maybe months have gone

by . . . the blood grown old and hard, the stains impossible to get out . . . she has forgotten about them . . . balled up, rolled up, and stuck in the corner of the drawer, forgotten . . .

His mother is talking with some friends of theirs who have dropped in. An 80 ordinary Sunday afternoon. Beverly is handing drinks around. In the mirror above the fireplace his mother's bluish-white hair bobs weightlessly. Long white candlesticks in holders of silver, on the mantel; the wicks perfectly white, never burnt. What are they talking about so earnestly? Lawrence tries to listen. Beverly is chiding him gently for working so hard — it is a familiar pattern, almost a tune, the words of his mother to his father years ago — and he nods, smiles, he is Dr. Pryor, who works hard. The fact is that he has done nothing all day except sit in his study, at his desk, leafing through medical journals. He has not been able to concentrate on anything.

Ted Albrecht, a friend of many years, is talking in his usual fanciful 81 manner. He is a stockbroker but thinks of himself as a social critic. A short man, with glasses and lively eyebrows; he is considered a friend of Lawrence's, and yet the two men have never talked together, alone together. They always meet at parties, in someone's living room, with groups of other people around.

Ted says, "I guarantee you, a vehement hot time is coming for this 82 nation!"

Lawrence has not been able to concentrate on the conversation. He 83 thinks that he may not be able to endure this minute, this very minute.

Voices ring around him. It is a ring of concentric rings, a ring of voices 84 and breaths and bright glances, circling him. Like music, the voices do not come to rest. They pause shrilly; they pause in expectation. Lawrence accepts a drink from his wife, a woman whose face looks oddly brittle. The ice cubes in his glass make him think of the Arctic — pure crystal, pure colorless ice and air, where no germs survive. It is impossible, this minute. Impossible to stand with these people. He does not know what is wrong and yet he understands that it has become impossible, that his body is being pushed to the breaking point, that to contain himself — his physicalness, his being — would take the strength of a wrestler, a man not himself.

The minute expands slowly. Nothing happens. 85

Again, the airport. The reversal of the meeting last week: now she is going 86 home. The airliner will draw up into it a certain number of people, Lawrence's mother among them, and then it will be gone. Now there is a rush of words. Things to be said. His mother complains bitterly of one of his aunts — he nods in agreement, embarrassed that she should say these things in front of Beverly — he nods yes, yes; he will agree to anything. "What could she know?

She was never married!" Lawrence's mother says, twisting her mouth. Of Lawrence's father, who died in a boating accident when Lawrence was eighteen, she does not ever speak, exactly; she speaks around him, around that solitary mysterious event, alluding to it with petulant jerks of her stiff little body. Lawrence's father died on the lake, alone. He drowned, alone. The boat must have capsized and he drowned, alone, with no one to witness the death or to explain it.

Lawrence's mother begins to cry. She will back off from them, crying, 87 and then at a certain point she will stop crying, collecting herself, and she will promise to telephone them as soon as she lands in Philadelphia. The visit is concluded.

Though it was a weekday evening, they went to Dorothy Clair's art gallery, 88 where a young sculptor was having an opening. Dorothy Clair was a widow some years older than the Pryors, a wealthy woman on the periphery of their social group. It was a champagne opening. Lawrence and his wife were separated, drawn into different groups; Lawrence was not really taking part in the conversation, but he appeared enthusiastic. The champagne went to his head. His mother had stayed with them for nearly a week, the visit had gone well, everything was over. Good. It was a weekday evening but they had gone out as if to reward themselves.

Next to Lawrence there was a piece of sculpture — a single column of 89 metal, with sharp edges. It looked dangerous. A woman seemed about to back into it and Lawrence wondered if he should warn her. He could see his own reflection in its surface, blotchy and comic. All the pieces of sculpture were metallic. Some hung from the ceiling, heavily; others hung from the walls. Great massive hulks — not defined enough to be shapes — squatted on the floor. People drifted around the sculpture, sometimes bumping into it. A woman stooped to disentangle her skirt from some wire, a thick ball of wire that had been sprayed with white paint.

What were these strange forms? They were oppressive to Lawrence. 90 But no one else seemed to be uneasy. He went to examine the wire — it looked like chicken wire — and he could make no sense of it. Elsewhere in the crowded room there were balls of metal that were distorted, like planets wrenched out of shape. Their shiny surfaces reflected a galaxy of human faces, but the faces were not really human. They were cheerful and blatant and flat, as if there were no private depths to them. . . . How they were all chattering away, those faces! No privacy at all, nothing but the facial mask of flesh: no private depths of anguish or darkness or sweetness, nothing. The faces were all talking earnestly to one another.

Lawrence looked for his wife. He saw her across the room, talking to 91 a tall man with silvery hair. It was the man he had seen downtown! Astonished,

Lawrence could not move. He stood with his drink in his hand, as metallic and fixed as the pieces of sculpture. These columns punctuated the gallery, each reaching to the ceiling, with flat, shiny surfaces and edges that appeared razor-sharp. They made him think suddenly of the furniture in his parents' house that he had stood up on end, as a child — allowed by his mother to play with the furniture of certain rooms, upending tables and chairs so that he could crawl under them and pretend they were small houses, huts. He had crouched under them, peering out past the legs of tables and chairs. Sometimes his mother had given him a blanket to drape over the piece of furniture.

The man with the silver hair turned and Lawrence saw that it was not the stranger from downtown after all — it was someone he'd known for years. Yet he felt no relief. He was still paralyzed. Beverly, not seeing him, was looking around cautiously, nervously. The man was about to drift into another conversation and leave her. He had a big, heavy, handsome head, his silver-gray hair curly and bunched, his face florid and generous and a little too aggressive, too sure of itself. Lawrence felt a sudden dislike for him. And yet he was grateful that he had not become that man — grateful that, in the moment of paralysis and panic, his soul had not flown out of him and into that man, into that other body. It might have happened. Anything might happen!

He went out. He walked quickly out of his building and into the midday crowd, in a hurry, and once on the sidewalk he stayed near the curb so that he could walk fast. The day was cold and overcast. He walked several blocks to the end of the street and across the street to the riverfront. There were few people down here, only the most hardy of tourists. No shoppers bothered to come this far. There were no stores here, only concrete and walls and a ferry landing and the water, the grim cold water. He leaned over a railing. He stared down at the lapping water. It was not very clean; there were long streaks of foam in it, as long as six or eight feet, bobbing and curling and twisting like snakes.

The discontent of the past two weeks rose in his mind. What was wrong? What had happened? It had begun on that sunlit day when he'd seen his wife from a distance. His wife. His mother arrived the following morning; they picked her up at the airport as always. And his daughter — there had been something about his daughter as well — but he could not remember. In the dirty, bouncy water he saw Edie's face, grinning up at him. But she did not really see him. There was nothing there. He was alone. He thought in a panic of himself and the river: the fact of being alone like this, with the river a few yards beneath him.

There was a sensation of deadness around his eyes. His eyes had become hardened, crusted over, like crusts of blood; the wounds where eyes had once been. And now they might fall off . . . ? Another face was pushing its way through. He must scratch at the scabs of his eyes and scratch them off, to make way for the new face, digging the crusts of blood away with his nails. He must tear at himself. He must do it now, this minute . . . for at this minute his body could no longer contain itself, it was like a wrestler with superbly developed muscles bursting through his clothing, tearing his clothing with anger and joy!

The river beneath him was a river of souls: the murky, sour, rebellious   96
souls of all the children he had been meant to father, flowing out of him and helplessly, ferociously downstream. He stared at the water. All of these his children! Sons and daughters of his body! He had been meant to father these thousands, these thousands of millions of souls, and yet he was on the concrete walk, leaning against the guardrail, and the children of his body were flowing by him, bouncing, lapping noisily against the abutment, becoming lost.

For some time he stood in silence. His eyes did ache. He tried to think   97
of what he must do — had he planned something? Why had he come down here? If he were to drown, perhaps scenes of his past life would flash to him. He would see the upended furniture again — the clumsy gold-covered chair with its curved legs and its gauzy bottom, the springs visible through the dark gauze — he would crawl between the legs again, drawing his knees up to his chest, hiding there, sly and safe. He would see the big house, he would see the piles of magazines and he would smell the acrid, lovely odor of loneliness on the third floor of that house; he would pass into that room and live out his life there chastely and silently. But perhaps he would fall into the water screaming. He would thresh his arms and legs — he would sink at once, screaming — and no one could save him. People might come to gawk, but they could not save him. And perhaps he would see nothing at all, no visions, no memories, perhaps it was only a lie about a drowning man living his life again and he would see nothing, nothing, he would drown in agony and be washed downstream, lost.

He glanced at his watch. After one.   98

He hurried back to his office. The receptionist, a pretty Negro woman,   99
chided him for walking in the rain. She took his trench coat from him, shook it, hung it up. In the waiting room — he could see through two partly opened doors — a few people were sitting and had been sitting for a while. He went into his private office. In a few minutes the nurse showed in his first patient of the afternoon: Herb Altman.

"I'm back a little faster this time but everything is the usual. Diagnosis   100
the usual," Altman said flatly. He wore a stylish, wide green tie, mint green. There were tiny white streaks in it that bothered Lawrence's vision.

Shaking of hands.   101

"Maybe somebody should just shoot me. I should croak, eh?" Altman   102
laughed. "Anyway I still can't sleep, Larry. The same damn thing. Give me something strong to help me sleep, eh? And did you hear about that bastard,

that investigator, I got to follow Evie? He was a friend of hers! It turned out he was a friend of hers! He told her everything, he tipped her off. I fired him and I'm dumping her, believe you me, I think even she and my wife are comparing notes on me and laughing and it's no goddam wonder I can't sleep. Maybe I should just croak, eh? Make things easier for everybody? What's your opinion?"

"Let me do just a routine examination," Lawrence said. "You do look 103 a little agitated."

SUBJECT QUESTIONS

1. What seems to be bothering Lawrence Pryor? Does *he* know what is bothering him?
2. Would it be fair to say that this is a story in which nothing happens? Does inaction seem valid subject matter for a short story? How does Oates make it interesting?
3. How many of Lawrence's friends are mentioned in the story? How close is he to them? Is he close to his family?
4. How did Lawrence's father die? Does Oates seem to imply that the death was suicidal? Can you tell from the story whether the father's life was happier than the son's — or very different?
5. Read the final paragraph of Fromm's "Work in an Alienated Society"; does the description of an alienated man seem to apply to Lawrence? Is he alienated from society? from himself?
6. At the end, Lawrence seems to be carrying on his work very much as at the beginning; do you think he has made any adjustment?

STRUCTURE QUESTIONS

1. The incident of the bloodstains is a minor one in the story, one which Lawrence can't even remember at the end. Why do you suppose Oates chose this for the title?
2. The story is composed of half a dozen such minor incidents; how does Oates tie them all together?
3. What does the business about Herb Altman have to do with the story about Lawrence Pryor? Why does Oates bring it up again at the end?
4. Nothing ever comes of Lawrence's suspicions about his wife; what function does the incident play in the story? Does it matter whether or not the reader thinks she is unfaithful?
5. Although Lawrence is alone three times, Oates arranges the story so that most of his thoughts and daydreams occur in the presence of other people — when he ought, perhaps, to be carrying on a conversation. How does this arrangement strengthen the point of the story? (Note particularly Lawrence's detached observations about the people he is with.)

Bronzeville Woman in a Red Hat

Gwendolyn Brooks

Gwendolyn Brooks was born in Topeka, Kansas, in 1917 and now lives in Chicago. She has published many volumes of poetry since her first, A Street in Bronzeville *(1945). She has won the Pulitzer Prize (1950), two Guggenheim Fellowships, and awards from* Poetry *magazine,* Mademoiselle, *and the American Academy of Arts and Letters. Ms. Brooks is also a book reviewer and has lectured at many colleges and universities.*

HIRES OUT TO
MRS. MILES

I

They had never had one in the house before.
   The strangeness of it all. Like unleashing
A lion, really. Poised
To pounce. A puma. A panther. A black
Bear.   5
There it stood in the door,
Under a red hat that was rash, but refreshing —
In a tasteless way, of course — across the dull dare,
The semi-assault of that extraordinary blackness.
The slackness   10
Of that light pink mouth told little. The eyes told of heavy care. . . .
But that was neither here nor there,
And nothing to a wage-paying mistress as should
Be getting her due whether life had been good
For her slave, or bad.   15
There it stood
In the door. They had never had
One in the house before.

But the Irishwoman had left!
A message had come.   20

Something about a murder at home.
A daughter's husband — "berserk," that was the phrase:
The dear man had "gone berserk"
And short work —
With a hammer — had been made   25
Of this daughter and her nights and days.
The Irishwoman (underpaid,
Mrs. Miles remembered with smiles),
Who was a perfect jewel, a red-faced trump,
A good old sort, a baker   30
Of rum cake, a maker
Of Mustard, would never return.
Mrs. Miles had begged the bewitched woman
To finish, at least, the biscuit blending,
To tarry till the curry was done,   35
To show some concern
For the burning soup, to attend to the tending
Of the tossed salad. "Inhuman,"
Patsy Houlihan had called Mrs. Miles.
"Inhuman." And "a fool."   40
And "a cool
One."

The Alert Agency had leafed through its files —
On short notice could offer
Only this dusky duffer   45
That now made its way to her kitchen and sat on her kitchen stool.

II

Her creamy child kissed by the black maid! square on the mouth!
World yelled, world writhed, world turned to light and rolled
Into her kitchen, nearly knocked her down.

Quotations, of course, from baby books were great   50
Ready armor; (but her animal distress
Wore, too and under, a subtler metal dress,
Inheritance of approximately hate).
Say baby shrieked to see his finger bleed,
Wished human humoring — there was a kind   55
Of unintimate love, a love more of the mind
To order the nebulousness of that need.

— This was the way to put it, this the relief.
This sprayed a honey upon marvelous grime.
This told it possible to postpone the reef.   60
Fashioned a huggable darling out of crime.
Made monster personable in personal sight
By cracking mirrors down the personal night.
Disgust crawled through her as she chased the theme.
She, quite supposing purity despoiled,   65
Committed to sourness, disordered, soiled,
Went in to pry the ordure from the cream.
Cooing, "Come." (Come out of the cannibal wilderness,
Dirt, dark, into the sun and bloomful air.
Return to freshness of your right world, wear   70
Sweetness again. Be done with beast, duress.)

Child with continuing cling issued his No in final fire,
         Kissed back the colored maid,
         Not wise enough to freeze or be afraid.
         Conscious of kindness, easy creature bond.   75
         Love had been handy and rapid to respond.

Heat at the hairline, heat between the bowels,
Examining seeming coarse unnatural scene,
She saw all things except herself serene:
Child, big black woman, pretty kitchen towels.   80

SUBJECT QUESTIONS

1. Can you tell whether Mrs. Miles is excited or intimidated by having a black in her house for the first time?
2. What does the episode of the previous Irish maid tell you about Mrs. Miles?
3. Why does Mrs. Miles react as she does to the black maid's kissing the child?
4. What does she tell the maid?
5. What do the child and the maid have in common that Mrs. Miles lacks? Does Mrs. Miles understand when the child says "No"?
6. Do you think Mrs. Miles has learned a lesson? Can you tell what the outcome of this incident will be?

STRUCTURE QUESTIONS

1. Examine the nouns and adjectives applied to the new maid. Do they describe her, or Mrs. Miles's reaction to her? How can you tell?
2. Ms. Brooks suggests the causes for two effects here: the intimacy between child and maid, and Mrs. Miles's reaction to that intimacy. Are the causes made clear? Which is more carefully worked out?
3. How does the incident of the Irish maid fit into this causal analysis?
4. Does the ending of the poem imply what the result of this incident will be? Should Ms. Brooks have been more explicit? Does anything earlier in the poem give a clue?

6

LANGUAGE AND STYLE

Definition

Most students have been taught — and properly — to go to the dictionary if they cannot tell the meaning of a word from its context. And the development of the modern, carefully compiled dictionary within the last century has been invaluable in furthering communication. Unfortunately, however, the dictionary has its limitations. Consider for a moment how a dictionary goes about defining a word. Normally, it puts the word into a more general classification and then limits its description of that larger class until the definition can refer only to the one word being defined. Thus, "cocker spaniel: any of a breed of small spaniels having short legs, long floppy ears . . ." or "tamale: a native Mexican food having . . .". This procedure is useful if the general classification is more recognizable than the particular member of it being defined. If the reader has a fair idea of what the general class, "Mexican food" is like, he is enlightened by the definition of tamale as a "native Mexican food" having certain special characteristics.

But suppose the word to be defined is a very general or abstract concept like "love" or "bravery." The dictionary might classify such a concept as "an emotion" or "an attitude," but its doing so does not tell us much, even if we know what "an attitude" is. Adequate definitions of these broad concepts need much more space than a dictionary can devote to them.

Serious misunderstandings seldom occur from the use of specific or concrete terms like cocker spaniel. If a reader does not know what the word means, he can use his dictionary to find out. But an abstract term may cause two kinds of difficulty. First, if the reader does not know the term, he will get little help from his dictionary. And if he does know the term, his understanding of it may still be quite different from the meaning intended in any particular context. Settlement of the Vietnam crisis ran into a stalemate partly because of misunderstanding over the meaning of "aggressor." To the United States, the Viet Cong were the aggressors, for they were making war on an established government. But to the NLF and North Vietnam, "aggressor" was understood to mean "a foreigner who attacks"; when Vietnamese were fighting Vietnamese, there was civil war but not aggression, for no "foreigners" were involved until American forces arrived.

Most abstract terms have only a general *area* of meaning, not a particular meaning on which all can agree. This is because the concept has been abstracted from — drawn out of — a great many particular situations which are considerably varied in their details. Suppose, for instance, a South Pacific tribe witnesses, on three successive days, a tribesman killing a shark to save his friend, another rescuing some children from a burning hut, and a warrior killing seven enemies in one battle. To all of these acts they apply a word meaning "courage." Clearly, though, the deeds have little in common except this abstraction, courage. "Courage," then, does not mean "saving children from a burning hut"; the word has a much more general *area* of meaning.

Because no two people have identical sets of experiences, and because the meaning of an abstract concept is derived from experience, both firsthand and vicarious, it follows that an abstract term cannot mean exactly the same to any two people. The meanings of some terms may vary so slightly from person to person that we can use them without fear of serious misunderstanding. Other terms have such an infinite variety of meanings that no one really expects to know quite what someone else means by them. We make a kind of tacit agreement, for instance, that no one will inquire in too much detail what another person means by "love." We simply allow the word so much flexibility that it is possible for a person to express a "love" for mashed potatoes. In between these relatively harmless extremes, however, are a great many terms which are used as though they had a fairly specific and commonly accepted meaning. Not only do serious misunderstandings result from such careless use of abstract words and terms, but important differences in meaning are often obscured. One is likely to hear this type of argument, for example: "The Democratic and Republican parties both believe in the American Way of Life; so there isn't really any significant difference between them." The statement, of course, ignores the fact that "American Way of Life" does not mean the same for both parties — or even for various members of one party. Frequently such statements reflect a deliberate attempt to deceive, as when military leaders cover a disastrous defeat with the phrase "strategic withdrawal."

You should watch for careless use of abstractions in print and try to discover as nearly as possible from the context what the writer means by his terms. Perhaps more important, you should be aware of what *you* mean by terms when you use them, for such careless usage invariably leads to sloppy thinking. You should also make clear in your own writing your meaning of abstract concepts, either by the context in which you use them or, if necessary, by definition. This does not mean that every paper should be prefaced with the awkward and formal "definition of terms" paragraph so common in student themes. For the reader, remember, learns little by "According to Webster, courage means. . . ."

But if one cannot give an adequate dictionary definition, the reader may fairly ask, how does he go about making clear the meaning of his terms? The key is to keep in mind that the meaning of an abstract concept is the sum total of one's experiences which have that concept in common. The best way, then, to define the term is to put it back into specific context by giving typical and relevant examples from the writer's own experience. The easiest way to define "book" is to point to one and say, *"This* is a book." The same is true of abstract terms: to define "courage," point out examples of it. Enough instances, however, must be given so that the area of meaning is established.

If one cannot conveniently give sufficient illustrations from his own experience there are other methods of defining which can be employed. These are the same as the methods of presenting material which have been illustrated thus far in this book: comparison and contrast, classification and division, cause and effect, and process. Suppose, for instance, a writer needed to define "alcoholic." Certainly a description of a typical alcoholic would help – a personal acquaintance would be best. But it would also be helpful to discuss various theories concerning the *cause* of alcoholism, or its social consequences *(effects)*. The writer might want to show the *process* by which a person develops into an alcoholic. Or perhaps, through *comparison* and *contrast,* he would show the difference between a "drinker" and an "alcoholic." Finally, he could profitably *classify* alcoholics according to their various mental problems or *divide* them into subgroups. It would be possible for a writer to use all of these methods in a single extended definition. The important consideration is that the reader come to an understanding of the term as nearly as possible like that of the writer. The writer's definition may vary considerably from the reader's, but if the reader sees clearly this difference communication will be effected.

Extended definition is one of the most difficult types of writing; but it can be accomplished if the writer will remember to put the term into specific contexts. He needs only to watch out for two traps into which students frequently fall. (1) It is not necessary to establish a definition which will be valid for all men in all time. The writer's task is only to convey clearly what *he* means by the term. (2) You should beware of writing about the term as though it were already defined, that is, of assuming that the reader really knows from the beginning what the writer means by the term. He cannot possibly know exactly, and the slight differences are significant.

The Language of Soul

Claude Brown

Claude Brown was born in New York City in 1937 and educated at Harvard. A playwright and fiction writer, he is best known as the author of the autobiographical novel, Manchild in the Promised Land. *Mr. Brown lives in New York, where he is a member of the Harlem Improvement Project Group.*

Perhaps the most soulful word in the world is "nigger." Despite its very definite fundamental meaning (the Negro man), and disregarding the deprecatory connotation of the term, "nigger" has a multiplicity of nuances when used by soul people. Dictionaries define the term as being synonymous with Negro, and they generally point out that it is regarded as a vulgar expression. Nevertheless, to those of chitlins-and-neck-bones background the word nigger is neither a synonym for Negro nor an obscene expression. 1

"Nigger" has virtually as many shades of meaning in Colored English as the demonstrative pronoun "that," prior to application to a noun. To some Americans of African ancestry (I avoid using the term Negro whenever feasible, for fear of offending the Brothers X, a pressure group to be reckoned with), nigger seems preferable to Negro and has a unique kind of sentiment attached to it. This is exemplified in the frequent — and perhaps even excessive — usage of the term to denote either fondness or hostility. 2

It is probable that numerous transitional niggers and even established ex-soul brothers can — with pangs of nostalgia — reflect upon a day in the lollipop epoch of lives when an adorable lady named Mama bemoaned her spouse's fastidiousness with the strictly secular utterance: "Lord, how can one nigger be so hard to please?" Others are likely to recall a time when that drastically lovable colored woman, who was forever wiping our noses and darning our clothing, bellowed in a moment of exasperation: "Nigger, you gonna be the death o' me." And some of the brethren who have had the precarious fortune to be raised up, wised up, thrown up or simply left alone to get up as best they could, on one of the nation's South Streets or Lenox Avenues, might remember having affectionately referred to a best friend as "My nigger." 3

The vast majority of "back-door Americans" are apt to agree with 4

Copyright © 1968 by Claude Brown. Reprinted by permission of The Sterling Lord Agency.

247

Webster — a nigger is simply a Negro or black man. But the really profound contemporary thinkers of this distinguished ethnic group — Dick Gregory, Redd Foxx, Moms Mabley, Slappy White, etc. — are likely to differ with Mr. Webster and define nigger as "something else" — a soulful "something else." The major difference between the nigger and the Negro, who have many traits in common, is that the nigger is the more soulful.

Certain foods, customs and artistic expressions are associated almost   5
solely with the nigger: collard greens, neck bones, hog maws, black-eyed peas, pigs' feet, etc. A nigger has no desire to conceal or disavow any of these favorite dishes or restrain other behavioral practices such as bobbing his head, patting his feet to funky jazz, and shouting and jumping in church. This is not to be construed that all niggers eat chitlins and shout in church, nor that only niggers eat the aforementioned dishes and exhibit this type of behavior. It is to say, however, that the soulful usage of the term nigger implies all of the foregoing and considerably more.

The Language of Soul — or, as it might also be called, Spoken Soul or   6
Colored English — is simply an honest vocal portrayal of black America. The roots of it are more than three hundred years old.

Before the Civil War there were numerous restrictions placed on the   7
speech of slaves. The newly arrived Africans had the problem of learning to speak a new language, but also there were inhibitions placed on the topics of the slaves' conversation by slave masters and overseers. The slaves made up songs to inform one another of, say, the underground railroads' activity. When they sang *Steal Away* they were planning to steal away to the North, not to heaven. Slaves who dared to speak of rebellion or even freedom usually were severely punished. Consequently, Negro slaves were compelled to create a semi-clandestine vernacular in the way that the criminal underworld has historically created words to confound law-enforcement agents. It is said that numerous Negro spirituals were inspired by the hardships of slavery, and that what later became songs were initially moanings and coded cotton-field lyrics. To hear these songs sung today by a talented soul brother or sister or by a group is to be reminded of an historical spiritual bond that cannot be satis-factorily described by the mere spoken word.

The American Negro, for virtually all of his history, has constituted a   8
vastly disproportionate number of the country's illiterates. Illiteracy has a way of showing itself in all attempts at vocal expression by the uneducated. With the aid of colloquialisms, malapropisms, battered and fractured grammar, and a considerable amount of creativity, Colored English, the sound of soul, evolved.

The progress has been cyclical. Often terms that have been discarded   9
from the soul people's vocabulary for one reason or another are reaccepted years later, but usually with completely different meaning. In the Thirties

and Forties "stuff" was used to mean vagina. In the middle Fifties it was revived and used to refer to heroin. Why certain expressions are thus reactivated is practically an indeterminable question. But it is not difficult to see why certain terms are dropped from the soul language. Whenever a soul term becomes popular with whites it is common practice for the soul folks to relinquish it. The reasoning is that "if white people can use it, it isn't hip enough for me." To many soul brothers there is just no such creature as a genuinely hip white person. And there is nothing more detrimental to anything hip than to have it fall into the square hands of the hopelessly unhip.

White Americans wrecked the expression "something else." It was bad   10 enough that they couldn't say "sump'n else," but they weren't even able to get out "somethin' else." They had to go around saying *something else* with perfect or nearly perfect enunciation. The white folks invariably fail to perceive the soul sound in soulful terms. They get hung up in diction and grammar, and when they vocalize the expression it's no longer a soulful thing. In fact, it can be asserted that spoken soul is more of a sound than a language. It generally possesses a pronounced lyrical quality which is frequently incompatible to any music other than that ceaseless and relentlessly driving rhythm that flows from poignantly spent lives. Spoken soul has a way of coming out metered without the intention of the speaker to invoke it. There are specific phonetic traits. To the soulless ear the vast majority of these sounds are dismissed as incorrect usage of the English language and, not infrequently, as speech impediments. To those so blessed as to have had bestowed upon them at birth the lifetime gift of soul, these are the most communicative and meaningful sounds ever to fall upon human ears: the familiar "mah" instead of "my," "gonna" for "going to," "yo" for "your." "Ain't" is pronounced "ain' "; "bread" and "bed," "bray-ud" and "bay-ud"; "baby" is never "bay-bee" but "bay-buh"; Sammy Davis Jr. is not "Sammee" but a kind of "Sam-eh"; the same goes for "Eddeh" Jefferson. No matter how many "man's" you put into your talk, it isn't soulful unless the word has the proper plaintive, nasal "maee-yun."

Spoken soul is distinguished from slang primarily by the fact that the   11 former lends itself easily to conventional English, and the latter is diametrically opposed to adaptations within the realm of conventional English. Police (pronounced pō' lice) is a soul term, whereas "The Man" is merely slang for the same thing. Negroes seldom adopt slang terms from the white world and when they do the terms are usually given a different meaning. Such was the case with the term "bag." White racketeers used it in the Thirties to refer to the graft that was paid to the police. For the past five years soul people have used it when referring to a person's vocation, hobby, fancy, etc. And once the appropriate term is given the treatment (soul vocalization) it becomes soulful.

However, borrowings from spoken soul by white men's slang — particu- 12
larly teen-age slang — are plentiful. Perhaps because soul is probably the most
graphic language of modern times, everybody who is excluded from Soulville
wants to usurp it, ignoring the formidable fettering to the soul folks that has
brought the language about. Consider "uptight," "strung-out," "cop," "boss,"
"kill 'em," all now widely used outside Soulville. Soul people never question
the origin of a slang term; they either dig it and make it a part of their
vocabulary or don't and forget it. The expression "uptight," which meant
being in financial straits, appeared on the soul scene in the general vicinity
of 1953. Junkies were very fond of the word and used it literally to describe
what was a perpetual condition with them. The word was pictorial and
pointed; therefore it caught on quickly in Soulville across the country. In the
early Sixties when "uptight" was on the move, a younger generation of soul
people in the black urban communities along the Eastern Seaboard regener-
ated it with a new meaning; "everything is cool, under control, going my
way." At present the term has the former meaning for the older generation
and the latter construction for those under thirty years of age.

It is difficult to ascertain if the term "strung-out" was coined by junkies 13
or just applied to them and accepted without protest. Like the term "uptight"
in its initial interpretation, "strung-out" aptly described the constant plight
of the junkie. "Strung-out" had a connotation of hopeless finality about it.
"Uptight" implied a temporary situation and lacked the overwhelming despair
of "strung-out."

The term "cop" (meaning "to get") is an abbreviation of the word 14
"copulation." "Cop," as originally used by soulful teenagers in the early Fifties, was deciphered to mean sexual coition, nothing more. By 1955 "cop"
was being uttered throughout national Soulville as a synonym for the verb
"to get," especially in reference to illegal purchases, drugs, pot, hot goods,
pistols, etc. ("Man, where can I cop now?") But by 1955 the meaning was
all-encompassing. Anything that could be obtained could be "copped."

The word "boss," denoting something extraordinarily good or great, was 15
a redefined term that had been popular in Soulville during the Forties and
Fifties as a complimentary remark from one soul brother to another. Later
it was replaced by several terms such as "groovy," "tough," "beautiful" and,
most recently, "out of sight." This last expression is an outgrowth of the former
term "way out," the meaning of which was equivocal. "Way out" had an
ad hoc hickish ring to it which made it intolerably unsoulful and consequently
it was soon replaced by "out of sight," which is also likely to experience a
relatively brief period of popular usage. "Out of sight" is better than "way
out," but it has some of the same negative, childish taint of its predecessor.

The expression, "kill 'em," has neither a violent nor a malicious inter- 16
pretation. It means "good luck," "give 'em hell," or "I'm pulling for you,"
and originated in Harlem from six to nine years ago.

There are certain classic soul terms which, no matter how often borrowed, remain in the canon and are reactivated every so often, just as standard jazz tunes are continuously experiencing renaissances. Among the classical expressions are: "solid," "cool," "jive" (generally as a noun), "stuff," "thing," "swing" (or "swinging"), "pimp," "dirt," "freak," "heat," "larceny," "busted," "okee doke," "piece," "sheet" (a jail record), "squat," "square," "stash," "lay," "sting," "mire," "gone," "smooth," "joint," "blow," "play," "shot," and there are many more.

Soul language can be heard in practically all communities throughout the country, but for pure, undiluted spoken soul one must go to Soul Street. There are several. Soul is located at Seventh and "T" in Washington, D.C., on One Two Five Street in New York City; on Springfield Avenue in Newark; on South Street in Philadelphia; on Tremont Street in Boston; on Fortyseventh Street in Chicago, on Fillmore in San Francisco, and dozens of similar locations in dozens of other cities.

As increasingly more Negroes desert Soulville for honorary membership in the Establishment clique, they experience a metamorphosis, the repercussions of which have a marked influence on the young and impressionable citizens of Soulville. The expatriates of Soulville are often greatly admired by the youth of Soulville, who emulate the behavior of such expatriates as Nancy Wilson, Ella Fitzgerald, Eartha Kitt, Lena Horne, Diahann Carroll, Billy Daniels, or Leslie Uggams. The result — more often than not — is a trend away from spoken soul among the young soul folks. This abandonment of the soul language is facilitated by the fact that more Negro youngsters than ever are acquiring college educations (which, incidentally, is not the best treatment for the continued good health and growth of soul); integration and television, too, are contributing significantly to the gradual demise of spoken soul.

Perhaps colleges in America should commence to teach a course in spoken soul. It could be entitled the Vocal History of Black America, or simply Spoken Soul. Undoubtedly there would be no difficulty finding teachers. There are literally thousands of these experts throughout the country whose talents lie idle while they await the call to duty.

Meanwhile the picture looks dark for soul. The two extremities in the Negro spectrum — the conservative and the militant — are both trying diligently to relinquish and repudiate whatever vestige they may still possess of soul. The semi-Negro — the soul brother intent on gaining admission to the Establishment even on an honorary basis — is anxiously embracing and assuming conventional English. The other extremity, the Ultra-Blacks, are frantically adopting everything from a Western version of Islam that would shock the Caliph right out of his snugly fitting shintiyan to anything that vaguely hints of that big, beautiful, bountiful black bitch lying in the arms of the Indian and Atlantic Oceans and crowned by the majestic Mediterranean Sea. Whatever the Ultra-Black is after, it's anything but soulful.

SUBJECT QUESTIONS

1. Brown consistently refers to Soul as a spoken language; what prevents it from being also a written language?
2. Judging by Brown's discussion, would you say that Soul is characterized chiefly by its pronunciation, by the people who use it, or by its special shades of meaning?
3. What historical factors were involved in the development of a soul language?
4. Brown suggests that Soul might be taught as the Vocal History of Black America. Do you think it could be taught as a university course? What would the examinations be like?
5. If Soul is spoken primarily by illiterate blacks in city ghettoes, why does Brown regret the fact that "the picture looks dark for soul"?

STRUCTURE QUESTIONS

1. Consider Brown's choice of *nigger* as his opening example of soul language. What does it imply about the author's intentions? What is the effect on the reader? Was it a good choice?
2. How does Brown improve upon the dictionary definition of *nigger*? Does he make clear the contrast between *nigger* and *Negro*?
3. As he should do in definition, Brown relies largely on specific example. Most of his examples are single words or phrases rather than whole sentences. Do you see why he has avoided giving samples of dialogue?
4. How does Brown distinguish Soul from slang? Is it necessary that he do so?
5. Brown's own style in writing about Soul is rather stiff and formal. Why do you think he has chosen such a style? Should he have used a more "soulful" style?
6. How many different methods of development can you distinguish in this definition (example, comparison and contrast, etc.)?

The Language of Nowspeak

Valerie Carnes

Valerie Carnes teaches English at Roosevelt University, Chicago. The following essay originally appeared in The New Humanities: Culture, Crisis, Change *(1972) by Ralph L. Carnes and Valerie Carnes. Her term "Nowspeak," derived perhaps ironically from George Orwell's* 1984, *is here applied to the language of the youth culture. A lengthy glossary of Nowspeak terms has been omitted from the original essay.*

Now that much of the sound and fury over hippies, yippies, flower power, student power, Berkeley, Chicago, and Columbia has begun to die away, and pot, acid, and speed have become as much household words as the name of Spiro T. Agnew it is time at last for a long look at the language of the current youth movement. For at least one thing becomes increasingly clear as the underground begins to surface: the much-celebrated generation gap of the sixties was — and still *is* — largely a linguistic gap existing between standard English and Nowspeak, the language of the movement, the youth under thirty and their over-thirty sympathizers. 1

To accept even the mildest form of the linguistic relativity thesis entails the admission that one's world view is to some extent relative to his language system. Clearly the world view of a twenty-one-year-old radical whose universe is built around large categories labeled "pigs," "heads," "the System," and "the Revolution" will manifest itself quite differently from that of his Establishment counterpart who still operates in terms of more conventional classes: "liberals," "conservatives," "Commie rats," "anarchists," "Democrats," "Republicans." The very existence of the language that I have christened Nowspeak affirms the existence of a large and active youth Underground. It also institutionalizes the subculture of Beatles and Stones and Fugs and Ché Guevara-ism, of "Hair" and Tarot cards, witches and warlocks, acid and grass, and gives it in the public eye a local habitation and a name. Hippies, hipsters, beats, pushers, and heads have been part of the Scene for a very long time — since the 1920s, in fact; it is their group names that remind Peter Schrag's Forgotten Americans of these embarrassing Presences in a stolidly sentimental and conformist culture. 2

Thus for Movement and Establishment alike the language becomes   3
symbolic. It does not only "stand for" or "point to" the subculture: it *is* the
subculture. This fact should remind us of Paul Tillich's useful distinction
between a sign and a symbol: the sign, he says, points the way to the thing,
but the symbol participates in it. Nowspeak is a symbol of the life-style of
the emerging subculture and also serves as the System's plumber's-manual
guide to that life-style. It is symbolic in this sense both for those who use
it and those who do not. Users align themselves against non-users. Nowspeak-
ing youth draw a sense of solidarity and community from the language that
represents their chosen style while the Establishment feels itself to be the
nation's anointed people in part because it still speaks standard English.
Non-users, presenting their case in conventional pig-Americanese, argue that
Movement lingo is mindless, non-expressive, illiterate, obscene, and meaningless, while the other side argues with equal fervor that all the assertions
and experiences of youth are incapable of verbal expression. As one girl recently put it, "If you've been there, you'll know it, and you don't need to
talk about it." In the opening bars of *Their Satanic Majesties* the Stones urge
their listeners to "open your heads, let the pictures come." Indeed, one of
the hidden premises of Nowspeak is the assumption that there are many classes
of experience which cannot and should not be verbalized. The act of verbalization is itself a dodge, a corruption of the experience, a "sell-out" or "cop-
out" from the pure moment of sensation. I am well aware of the irony implicit
in this study. This is not an essay on the language of the youth culture but
instead on abstractions from that language as it is spoken, transposed onto the
printed page. The most important characteristic of the language is that it is
spoken, not written, and is therefore in a constant state of flux. Yet paradoxically the very nonverbal nature of the language is symbolic of the world view
it both influences and reflects — antirational, action-oriented, visual, tactile,
highly sensuous, primitive, ritualistic, colorful, emotive, solipsistic, and so
always the language of the present moment, the immediate Scene, the place
where the action is, or was — in short, the language of Now.

The primary source of Nowspeak is of course the language of other   4
American bohemian movements. Nineteen-twenties bohemianism — Parisian
expatriates, winos, Braque, Picasso, Hemingway, Stein and her beloved Alice
B. Toklas, the rash of "little" magazines, and Zelda and Scott, those lovely
lost children of Prohibition playing in the fountains at the Plaza — established
the standard bohemian style and attitude: a sadly romantic, fatalistic, cosmopolitan, nonconforming, and lost generation of street-cafe and attic subcul-
tures, writing poetry out of a golden alcoholic haze. Came the 1930s, and
hipsters, jazz musicians, and an authentic hard-core drug underground began
unwittingly to build the language that the young rebels of today's suburbia
still speak. Jazz usages yielded such important terms as *action* (a general term
for whatever is happening at the time), *bad* (for something very good, espe-

cially a woman), *blast* (get high), *bomb* (a failure), *bread* (money), *bug* (to annoy or disturb), *bust* (arrest), *cat* (any human being, especially a swinger), *chick* (a girl), *come down* (from a high), *cool* (ignore, snub, become less intense about a person or thing), *cut out* (leave), *dig* (understand or comprehend, in an emotional sense), *fag* (homosexual), *far out* (very advanced, ahead of its time), *funky* (basic, earthy, down-home), *groove* (a predilection or enjoyable thing), *head* (drug user), *lay* or *lay on* (to give or say), *make it* (have success), *put on* (to make fun of or ridicule without letting the victim know), *scene* (particular place or atmosphere), *stoned* (high or drunk), *turn on* (to get someone high on pot or to interest someone in a specific thing) and *wild* (remarkable). A high percentage of these terms still are in Nowspeak usage today.

Underworld language, which has found its way into Nowspeak, dates back to the time when the entire drug scene was largely confined to the fringes of society — the ghetto, the bohemian settlements, the underworld — and drug users were more or less forced by economic and social exigencies to live a life of petty crime. From this indigenous subculture come the standard slang terms referring to drug use: *cap* (drug capsule), *head* (user of drugs), *H, horse, shit, smack, duji* (heroin); *Mary Jane, MJ, pot, tea, grass, boo* (marijuana); *coke, snow, snowbird* (cocaine and its users). Most of these words are prepsychedelia and therefore refer to the more conventional drugs that were standard bohemian and ghetto fare from the twenties and thirties into the fifties and sixties — hashish, marijuana, heroin, cocaine, opium, benzedrine. Also from that nebulous area where underworld jargon coalesces with black ghetto talk come words dealing with the relations of the drug user and petty criminal with the police: *hit* (to be arrested), *bust* (to make an arrest, often for illegal drug use, as in "He got busted for possession last night"), *heat, fuzz,* or *the Man* (police), *uptight* and *strung out* (in desperate financial straits, usually as the result of intensive or prolonged drug use). One interesting term with underworld connotations is *straight*. A common word in homosexual and criminal society, it was first used to mean not with the particular "in" crowd in question (hence, heterosexual in one case, non-criminal in the other). Later the meaning became generalized so that the word now can refer to anyone who is not "with" a particular scene; hence, conventional, ordinary, not in the know, not "hip," generally "out of it." A more recent variant is more specific and less derogatory; it means "temporarily off drugs, clean for the moment," as in "Once I was straight for three days."

"Soultalk," the language of urban ghetto blacks, has become an increasingly important element in the vocabulary of the Nowspeaker, probably because of the heightened social consciousness of the Movement and its intense identification with minority groups of all kinds. Black "hip" and "soul" talk has added to Nowspeak such important words as *man* (generalized term of address, as in "Man, you're blowing my mind"), *ball* (to have sexual intercourse), *the Man* (the police; more generally, any Establishment figure, pre-

ferably white, in a position of power), *mother* (short for motherfucker, a term
of derision and often hatred), *cat* (any male human being, especially a hip one),
hip (with it, cool, in the know, under control), *hipster* (hip cat), *shit* (drugs
in general), *tell it* or *tell it, man, lis'en at him, nigger* (in a soulful affectionate
sense, not a condescending or derogatory one, as in "He's the baddest nigger
I ever saw"), *something else* (pronounced *sum'pn else*), *police* (pronounced
po-lice), *stuff* (heroin or the vagina), *bag* (originally, in the thirties, graft paid
to the po-lice; now, a person's vocation, hobby, fancy, whimsy, or caprice,
as in "that's your bag, man"), *strung out, uptight, cop* (originally an abbreviation for copulation, but by 1955 a synonym for the verb "to get," especially
in relation to pot, hard drugs, hot goods, pistols), *boss* (something extraordinarily good or great, later replaced by *groovy, tough, beautiful,* and *out
of sight*), *kill 'em* (for "give 'em hell," not as an expression of malice or
violence). Other classics that often overlap into underworld and "beat" diction
of the fifties and that have by now wandered into Nowspeak include *solid,
cool, jive* (as noun), *jive-ass, thing, swing,* and *swinging* (the sixties added
swinger), *pimp, dirt, freak, heat, right on* (term of approbation), *piece, sheet*
(a jail record), *squat, square, stash, lay, mire, gone, smooth, joint, blow, play,
shot, hassle, chick, junkie, bitch* (girl), *tight* (friendly), *O. D.* (overdose), *soul,
soulfood, gig.*

    Perhaps the single most important contribution of the black hipster is   7
the word *baby* (pronounced "bay-buh," *a la* Janis Joplin), used in address to
another, highly masculine, black male. Claude Brown offers this explanation
of the elusive term in *Manchild in the Promised Land:*

> The first time I heard the expression "baby" used by one cat to address another was
> up at Warwick in 1951. Gus Jackson used it. The term had a hip ring to it, a real
> colored ring. The first time I heard it I knew right away I had to start using it. It
> was like saying, "Man, look at me, I've got masculinity to spare." It was saying at
> the same time to the world, "I'm one of the hippest cats, one of the most uninhibited
> cats on the scene. I can say 'baby' to another cat, and he can say 'baby' to me, and
> we can say it with strength in our voices." If you could say it, this meant that you
> really had to be sure of yourself, sure of your masculinity.... The real hip thing
> about the "baby" term was it was something that only colored cats could say the
> way it was supposed to be said....

    Haight-Ashbury summer of 1967, with the subsequent growth of the   8
youth Underground and the more amorphous Movement, popularized and
brought to the surface dozens of terms like these that had once been indigenous black soultalk in the thirties, forties, fifties, and early sixties, then found
their way into the vocabularies of the children of affluent upper-middle-class
WASP society. That the drug culture itself followed precisely the same pattern, out of the ghetto and into suburbia, is significant, for it suggests that
the daily life-style of the Harlemite hipster and pusher was transformed into

a middle-class elitist cult tinged with mystical overtones largely by the use of a bona fide drug-and-underworld language.

The hipster who came into prominence in the thirties and forties and finally sprang full-blown from the media in the fifties and sixties was a young male, often black, who was "hip" (originally, "hep" to the beat), extraordinarily aware, in the know, especially about jazz, drugs, and the street scene. The word "hippie," which came into national prominence in 1967, was being used in Harlem in the early 1950s to describe the uptown white who played at being a black hipster. Robert George Reisner's *The Jazz Titans* (1960) defines a "hippie" as a young person who is trying to put on hip airs but doesn't quite make it — thus, one who may be overly hip. Malcolm X's *Autobiography* recalls a similar incident: "A few of the white men around Harlem, younger ones whom we called 'hippies,' acted more Negro than Negroes. This particular one talked more 'hip' talk than we did" (p. 94).   9

Beat language of the fifties drew on all these sources — soul-talk, jazz, drug, underworld and homosexual slang, hipster and hippie language. It incorporated all of these and yet, paradoxically, was unlike any of them. Norman Podhoretz in an early essay, "The Know-Nothing Bohemians," comments on the "urban, cosmopolitan bias" of twenties' bohemianism, whose ideals were "intelligence, cultivation, spiritual refinement." By contrast bohemianism in the thirties, with its abundance of card-carrying Communists and Marxists, was colored by political radicalism, intellectual seriousness, and social reform. Podhoretz succinctly sums up the difference between earlier and later bohemianisms. The 1950s "beat" ethos, he comments, was hostile to civilization, worshipped primitivism, instinct, energy, "blood," was "cool" but mystical, irrational, spontaneous, anti-language, anti-analytical, and fascinated perennially, like Ginsberg's "angel-headed hipsters" and Kerouac's Dharma bums, with violence, drugs, Dada, surrealism, wine, and madness. Interestingly enough, the word "beatnik" was media-created: its genesis coincided with the furor over the Russian satellite Sputnik, and thus were the beats subtly and erroneously identified with Communist tendencies. The word "beat" itself referred at least in part to the ubiquitous jazz beat that was so much a part of the fifties Scene; it also meant, according to Kerouac, "beatified" or "beatific," suggesting a kind of frantic hip holiness in the beat stance. For the uninitiated it also meant disgust with middle-class philistinism and provinciality, utter disgust and exhaustion with the straight scene.   10

Beat language, like the Nowspeak of the sixties, was relatively simple. Adjectives were pared down to an eloquent few: *great* (greatest), *tremendous, crazy, mad, wild, groovy.* Nouns and verbs were simple and expressive: *bread* (money), *crash* (to sleep, from an old Hell's Angels' term that means "to die"; may also be used to refer to a temporary residence or sleeping space, as in "He's running a crash pad for pot heads"), *joint* (a marijuana cigarette), *roach*   11 (the butt end of a joint), *pad* (place of residence, as in "Duke, they blowin' pot like mad up at Mildred's pad," from the R. Crumb cartoon, "The Adventures of Fritz"). Slang terms for drugs also were common beat usage, perhaps as a means of avoiding the fuzz: *MJ, pot, tea, grass, H, horse, shit, O, smack* and so on.

A merger between the beat culture and the folk song and the various 12 war–civil rights–free-speech protests of the early sixties brought the Movement as it then existed out of Greenwich Village and the Haight onto the college campuses and coffee shops and into the media. The Berkeley Free Speech Movement (FSM) institutionalized and sanctioned the use of four-letter words as an authentic gesture of protest; civil rights demonstrations publicized words like *sit-in, demonstration, nonviolence, passive resistance*, SNCC, CORE, NAACP, *civil disobedience* and *God is on our side* (both phrases from Thoreau's famous tract), *happening, love-in*, and *riot*. The folk-singing phase of the movement, centering around sad-eyed lady of the lowlands Joan Baez and early pre-electronic Dylan, was the aesthetic equivalent of social and political nonviolence. In it was the ageless lure of wild cold woods and wind and salty sea, snow-white doves and long black veils, cruel ladies and love-sick knights, and forlorn maidens haunted by restless ghosts. It was poignant, sad, archaic, funny, and full of a simple moral outrage at war and racism; yet it was also cruel with a kind of barbarous innocence, the savage tenderness of the most ruthless of the Scottish Child ballads. And of course since beauty hurts Mr. Vinyl it could not and did not last. Although folk singing added few new words as such to the growing lexicon of Nowspeak, it introduced a down-home earthy lowdown shackdown niggerbaby blues plainness of style that set the cultural stage for the earliest of hippie life-styles.

In the mid-sixties the long-standing feud of British Mods and Rockers 13 culminated in the cultural victory of Mod and so introduced a newly self-conscious element into the indigenous American youth cult. Magically the Scene shifted from Newport to Carnaby Street and Baez and Dylan were replaced overnight by Justin and Twiggy. Boutiques mushroomed in the most Establishment of department stores and funky sleazy minifashions, bell-bottoms, elephant pants, wide belts, boots, vinyl skirts, picture matches, fans, Tiffany paper lanterns, op, pop, the Liverpool sound. Victoriana, discothéques, light shows, go-go girls, vinyl hamburgers, and burgeoning Campbell soup cans spelled out the new message in dayglo colors: COME ALIVE, YOU'RE IN THE PEPSI GENERATION. Limp-haired and limpid-eyed Lolitas, chock full of vitamin pills and orange juice, put on granny glasses, French *yé-yé* knits, and little white vinyl boots. Boys adopted the Teddy Boy look and tried vainly to resemble John Lennon. The style of the hour was J. C. Penney transcendentalized by Quant and Courreges, and the media responded fittingly with a shiny new slickspeak: "where it's at," "the action generation," "the Now people," "the Pepsi generation," "the Beautiful People," "camp art," "happenings" (which included such questionable activities as smashing grand pianos with hammers while, in the background, thirteen radios blared *forte fortissimo* and painted go-go girls did action paintings on the side). Some of this jargonese was simulated British slang (girls were "birds" or "model girls," thanks to Twiggy and Mary Quant), and if they wore *minis* or *micro-minis*, they were *kooky*, *kinky*, and had "the knack" (after a British art film of that name). It was the heyday of the microcosm, the diminutive, a mod mod mod Lilliputian world for all the Little People. Everything from the poor-boy skinny-rib sweater to Vesuvius erupting was "fun," "crazy," "super," "marvellous," "fantastic" or "groovy." Clothes were fun things. Shoes were to fall in love with. Makeup was super stuff. Discothéques were fun places. Arnel was when. Yé-yé. Yeah. Yeah. Yeah.

Hippie summer of 1967, heralded by the Human Be-In in San Francisco [14] and by the haunting imperative issuing from every jukebox across the nation, instructing the new generation to wear a flower in its collective hair, saw the first full-scale surfacing of the new-style Underground of the sixties. By August of 1967 every major magazine from *Playboy* to the *Saturday Evening Post* was preparing its own lead article on the hippie phenomenon, complete with full-color photographs of lush paradisal landscapes where lank golden girls ran barefoot forever through the Kodachrome grass, their long manes tumbling in the wind, light shows and artlessly painted bodies gyrating in time to invisible acid rock bands, gaunt gurus wordlessly holy on acid, celluloid flowers, newspaper posters, head shops, Diggers, Hell's Angels, Leary and Ginsberg leading mantras, and bespectacled bearded boys with beads and bells and Digger hats and bloodshot eyes that seemed to see beyond the world they never made to some better secret cloud — cuckoo-land green with the sweet aroma of burning grass. The ceremony of innocence had begun, and from everywhere the summer hippies converged on the Haight. When they arrived they found a prefabricated culture waiting for them: buttons, a ready-made dress style, head shops full of groovy merchandise, records, drugs, crash pads, free stores, free food, free love, free rock and an instant name, "hippies." To go along with all this there was, not surprisingly, a language. With very minor variations it was 1920s bohemian, thirties hipster-drug-soultalk out of fifties beat by way of folk-protest-rock-yeah-yeah-mod-yé-yé, and all systematized and solidified by the ever-present media. The hippies' chief contribution to Nowspeak was in the area of drug euphemisms. Many of these were the old reliables of the twenties and thirties resurrected for the occasion: *pot, tea, boo, horse, O, joint, roach, grass, fix, connection, stash.* Others were relatively new, having sprung up like the holy mushrooms of Mexico in response to the new and popular psychedelics or "head" drugs: *hallucinogenic, buzz, flash, crash, LSD, acid, STP, speed, crystals, downer, bummer, freak-out, freaked out, freak* (as noun: acid freak, print freak, speed freak, motorcycle freak), *head, breakthrough* (also a military and scientific term), *trip, trip out, doing one's*

own thing, bag, groove. Many words used to describe the effects of the psychedelics were phrases taken over from descriptions of the state of alcoholic
inebriation: *high* (in a state of euphoria achieved by drugs or alcohol; as a
noun, the state itself, or more generally, an overall sense of joy or well-being,
as in "When I was on a high I thought I would found this groovy scene, see,
'Teen-age Evangelism' "), *stoned* (excessively high on drugs, "I want to save
that for later when we're stoned") and so on. *

Significantly, many "In" phrases at the time were implicit mechanical   15
metaphors like Timothy Leary's famous injunction to "tune in, turn on, drop
out" — figures of speech that are all drawn, implicitly or explicitly, from radio
or television. "Turned on," used as an adjective, meaning high or under the
influence of drugs or, more generally, receptive to drugs or to experience of
any kind, especially that of an unconventional nature, illustrates the tendency
of such words to broaden their range of possible meanings. (We already have
noted that early jazz usage limited the "turn-on" to drugs and Charlie Parker's
horn.) Another electronic-mechanical metaphor is the word *vibe*, short for
vibrations. Like *turned on* it also has a more generalized meaning than merely
the implicit mechanical metaphor: it may refer to the atmosphere or spirit
of a scene or person, or to the cosmic forces present in a particular setting.
Thus a person, scene, event, or general situation is said to send out *good vibes*
or *bad vibes*, depending on the speaker's reaction. Witches and warlocks were
much prized on the Haight-Ashbury scene in 1967 for their ability to psych
out good vibes. The term thus suggests a coalescence of electronic and cos-
mic-mystic metaphors of popular occultism. Mysticism and the occult also
added *guru, yoga, meditation* (one was said to be "on meditation" — an obvious transfer of the drug metaphor to a nondrug experience), *sadhana* (Hindu
equivalent of one's own thing), *karma* (destiny), *horoscope, zodiac, warlock,
witch, sitar, mantra, hare krishna, maharishi, swami, mandala, veda, Gita,
om,* and the elusive *vibe.*

It is difficult to overestimate the importance of the hippie subculture   16
that began in 1967. It gave disaffected American youth, disillusioned by an
ugly and senseless war and by a growing credibility gap, a rallying point and
a locus of their new self-image. It also gave rise to a whole horde of movements
that were and still are only tangentially related to hippiedom, but somehow
still acquire guilt or innocence by association: SDS, student power, antiwar
protest groups, YIPPIE (Youth International Party), the Chicago demonstrations of 1968, disturbances at Columbia, Harvard, Cornell, and San Francisco State, the Woodstock music festival, and the People's Park episode in
Berkeley, 1969. Out of each of these small movements has arisen a set of
chants, slogans, words, and phrases that for one reason or another caught on
and became part of the language system: "all power to the people," "up
against the wall, mofo," "into the streets," "down with pigs," "student power,"
"zap the world with love," "chicks up front," "give a flower to a cop," "Ho,

Ho, Ho Chi Minh," "Hey, hey, LBJ," "Right on!" Specific events have also added to this new idiom. Thus Abbie Hoffman in a passage from *Rights in Conflict* describes the origin of the two terms *pig* (cop) and *Yippie* (Youth International Party member), which became the semantic poles of the Chicago riots in the summer of 1968: "There we were, all stoned, rolling around the floor ... yippie! ... Somebody says oink and that's it, pig, it's a natural, man, we gotta win" (p. 29).

As the passage above illustrates, much of the language was an authentic   17
response to an immediate situation; some of it, however, was media-created or was given national prominence by the media: *name of the game, the generation gap, the credibility gap, where the action is, never trust anyone over thirty, the In Crowd, the Now Generation, the new morality, where it's at, the flower children, flower power* (this one attached to a photograph of a pig-hippie confrontation in San Francisco where the hippies zapped the barrels of the cops' guns with flowers), *charisma, tell it like it is* (possibly a corruption of the black "tell it" or "tell it, man"), *the Beautiful People* (originally a *Vogue-Bazaar* jet-set term transferred to the under-thirty crowd sometime during that eventful summer of 1967). Buttons contributed their share of slogans, too: "Save water, shower with a friend," "War is harmful to children and other living things," "Draft beer, not students," "Reality is a crutch," and "Frodo lives" and "Welcome to the Middle Earth," an in-signal for Tolkien lovers everywhere. Pop psychiatry and sociology contributed *confrontation, meaningful relationship* (*Newsweek*, 3 February 1969, calls this one a substitute for "campus sex"), *hang-up* (any psychological problem; also, any intense or consuming interest in anything), *strung out, relate, relevant, irrelevant* (said to be true of all academic pursuits), *therapy, shrink* (a psychiatrist, as in Arlo Guthrie's "Shrink, I wanna kill"), "group" (for group therapy), *group dynamics, T-group* (sensitivity-training session); *communicate, communication, nude therapy, body language, life-style, crisis, dialogue (or meaningful dialogue) and commitment....*

Like any language system, Nowspeak has its own value system built into   18
it. The language serves several purposes at once: it is a code to freak out the ever-present Establishment, it solidifies the feeling of community among this tenuously bound subculture and assures its members that the Underground, the Movement — even the Revolution — really do exist, even if it's only in your head, and finally, it polarizes present-day society into linguistic camps and thence into social and political camps that follow from these linguistic sets. It is no great revelation to anyone that the world looks quite different to a young man who thinks of everything from cutting his hair to negotiating with the college administration in terms of "selling out to the System" than it looks to his father, who is scarcely aware that there is a System, much less that he is himself a part of it. A common geographical space and roughly coincident chronology are practically all that the two share: their

politics, morality, aims, ideology, aesthetics — in short, their culture — are quite different, and the difference often starts and ends with the variance in languages. Ludwig Wittgenstein has hypothesized that the words that are used to describe aesthetic judgments play a very complicated but very definite role in the culture of a period. To describe their use or to describe what you mean by a cultured taste, you have to describe a whole culture. Since an entirely different cultural game with different rules is played in different ages, fully to describe a set of aesthetic rules means to describe the culture of a period. The fact that the Nowspeaker's highest accolades are "groovy," "wild," "beautiful!" "out of sight," and "naturally spaced" as opposed to his father's or professor's "very intelligent," "cultivated," "sensible," "successful" or "well-rounded" means something far more significant than merely the choice of one word over another: it means a totally new aesthetics and hence a whole new value system for the subculture.

Part of the point of the new aesthetic, of course, is that it is moving   19
toward a non-verbal orientation. Contentless courses, meditation, yoga, chanting, drugs, T-groups, nude therapy, action painting, onstage nudity, touch therapy, group gropes, guerilla theatre in the streets, seances, satanism, be-ins, body language, dancing, rock festivals, proclamations of the Age of Aquarius and everywhere action, action, action — all these signs of the times are indications that McLuhan's retribalized youth are trying desperately to develop ways of communicating with something other than words. It is not only the old politics, the old imperialism, the old morality, the old society that is under attack; it is rationality and language itself. To present the Now people with carefully-worded logical arguments against their world view is only to compound the irony. Words are a large part of what their revolt is about. If language is a tool of the Establishment, then to present a linguistic argument to the Now people is already to have sold out to the System.

But the wheel of civilization has not yet turned full circle, and we are   20
living literally in a transitional age between the old culture when intelligence was verbal almost by definition and the new nonverbal total-experience aesthetic. It is possible, then, to make one further step beyond our examination of the language and say that from an analysis of Nowspeak we can draw a number of valid inferences about the culture that it describes: its latent but intense romanticism, its folkishness and tribal qualities, its highly emotive nature, its solipsism, its "this-here-nowness" and orientation toward the present existential moment, its connotative and reductive aspects. Let us see how this is so.

Perhaps the most striking quality of Nowspeak is that it is a highly   21
romantic language, designed to mirror what all romanticisms ultimately mirror: the revolutionary transvaluation of all values. Thus the verbs of Nowspeak express action in onomatopoeic, slangy, quick and brittle phrases exploding like small balloons over the heads of some giant Superman or Phantom: *cop*

out, zap, zonk, sell out, bust, tune in, hit, flip, crash, groove. They are comic-book and cartoon-time verbs for a TV generation. Among the most-quoted quotes of the Movement is the saying of Mao Tse-Tung, "Act first, then think, then act, then think, then act." Nowspeak is an action language for an action generation naturally "spaced" on the power of the moment. Print is irrelevant, hopelessly linear and static; it doesn't move, doesn't swing, groove, jiggle, gyrate, rock, or roll. Worst of all, it can't keep up with the Scene, can't go where it's at or where it's just been. Only with pure spontaneous action can things not fall apart and the center hold just a little longer.

Nowspeak nouns express a world view that is divided, like the world of the ancient Manicheans, into the powers of light and the powers of darkness, the Beautiful People and the System. The powers of darkness are identified with authority, uptightness, non-grooving, stodginess, and age: *the Man, the Establishment, pigs, sell-outs, game-players, uncools, hang-ups, fascists.* The powers of light in Nowspeak become *the New Left, the Movement,* the "good people," the In Crowd, the Underground, the Scene, the Age of Aquarius. Adjectives express superlative approval ("Beautiful!" "Wild!" "Freaky!") or describe emotional excesses of disapproval ("fascist pigs!" "You're uptight, man, you're blowing my mind, don't hassle me," "That's a heavy scene, man," "Oh no, you don't want grim, man; you want grim, you go to Chicago"). The vast and amorphous movement that gave birth to Nowspeak shows the same characteristics as nineteenth-century English, French, and German romanticisms: energy, boldness of thought, emphasis on creativity, the adulation of the new, the cult of personalities and the hero of the surface, stress on spontaneity and freedom of expression, anti-mechanistic and anti-scientific tendencies, super-naturalism, strangeness, a glorification of all sensory experience, the exaltation of wild freaky individualism, nonconformity, social responsiblity, and the cult of sensibility. Nowspeak reflects to a greater or lesser degree all these romantic tendencies. The words as we have seen are highly emotive, intensional rather than extensional, connotative rather than denotative, expressive rather than emotionally neutral; and their impact is fully realized only by the "cool head" community of participants in this new cult of sensibility. Words furnish a kind of verbal shorthand to communicate to others who are also hip to the Scene: they know, for example, that *happening* refers to an event that's a trip of some kind for its participants and implies the excitement of something meaningful going on with a possibility of wonder and surprise; that you can get a *contact high,* or vicarious buzz, from interacting with someone who's up on drugs; that to *turn on* means to come alive and carries with it the implication that ordinary straight society creates people who are not alive and must be switched on to exist in any real sense. They also realize that *where it's at* refers to the whole physical or psychological locus of real and significant activity going on at some place and time, as opposed to the ritual and sham of the Establishment scene, and are hip to the implicit theatrical overtones of *Scene* itself: it suggests the whole of a setting and the action occurring with it — the physical setting plus mood (vibes) plus people (the theatrical analogue is set plus props plus staging plus actors plus script plus promoters *ad infinitum*). But there is no way that the straight world can know all these things unless it too switches on, psychs out the vibes, and goes.

All Western romanticisms are Edenic in impulse and origin, for all   23
presuppose the fact of the Fall, symbolically if not literally, and all affirm the necessity of returning to the primordial Garden before the intrusion of the serpent machine. There are accurate and often chilling parallels to be drawn between the present youth cult in the United States and similar nineteenth- and early twentieth-century European cults with their fierce Rousseauism, their revolutionary cries for liberty, fraternity, equality, their *Sturm und Drang,* Pantisocracies, lyrical ballads, Satanism, Gothicism, *Volkgeists* and *Wanderlust.* The life-style of the young in twentieth-century America is also romantic, tribalized, and folkish, comprised of one part beat-academic–plain-style–Susan-Sontag–bricks-and-boards–white-washed-walls–authentic-products of cottage-industry–Chianti-drinking–yogurt-growing ethos; one part light-show–Quant-by-quant–psychotic-acid-freak-rock-stoned media-bag; and two parts idealized peasant and tribal ethos — hence the long hair, the fierce tribal loyalties, the barefoot hippie girls drifting artlessly through endless meadows of the mind, beards, mustaches, sideburns, dashikis, tatty raccoon coats, caftans, beads, bells, buttons, sandals (always the sign of the bohemian in Weejun'd America), Afros, Digger hats, minis, maxis, boots, and Indian headbands. Marshall McLuhan in a recent *Playboy* interview (March 1969) comments perceptively on what he calls the retribalization of American youth: "Our teenage generation is already becoming part of a jungle clan.... Sexual freedom is as natural to newly tribalized youth as drugs.... LSD and related hallucinogenic drugs ... breed a highly tribal and communally oriented subculture, so it's understandable why the retribalized young take to drugs like a duck to water." The natural-man, tribal, folkish, Edenic aspect of the youth cult figures heavily in its language. There is a freer use of sexual, anal and other "taboo" terms and four-letter words: the language is simpler, the vocabulary is cut to a bare minimum, and there are many coined words, themselves authentic products of the Movement. Adjectives and nouns that denote approval are terms that express the ability to lose one's inhibitions, to move in a natural, uninhibited un-hung-up manner, to go where the action is and move with it, to put oneself in touch with cosmic rhythms — in short, to psych out the scene, feel its vibes, and then groove with it.

As we have seen, Nowspeak relies heavily on connotative power rather   24
than denotative meaning for its impact.... Nowspeak at its worst can be a slick, vague, repetitive, and frustrating Hipspeak that smacks of the hard sell

and fast deal quite as much as of the new morality and aesthetic. At its best, however, it is gutsy, emotive, colorful, and highly expressive of a whole range of thought and action that conventional English simply cannot express. Webster's offers us no exact equivalent for "pig" or "uptight" or "sell-out" or for the depth of ridicule and contempt that the terms convey, nor for the wildly enthusiastic approbation that lies behind "out of sight!" "spaced!" "freaky!" or "beautiful!" A friend of mine, recently turned twenty, spent a frustrating half-hour trying to describe to a gathering of cool heads the experiences of a recent acid trip and finally lapsed into "Oh, wow! If you only knew ... like wild! freaky scene, man, just this freaky scene.... Oh, wow ... spaced out ... like you know, stoned ... if you just knew, I mean, if you only knew." More intimate acquaintance with the dictionary would not have helped him communicate the incommunicable, for the experiences he was describing lie, for the moment at least, far beyond the pale of ordinary Sally-Dick-and-Jane reality. No wonder, then, that Nowspeak is against reason, against interpretation, against language itself: how else could it survive? Similarly for the use of taboo words, for it is a means of expressing utter disdain for ticky-tacky Establishment values to use obscenity in describing some of its more hallowed members and institutions.

If we think of the movement as McLuhan does in terms of a return 25 to a romanticized primitive tribal ethos, we must also recognize that this language serves as an in-group sign, the verbal equivalent of a secret handclasp, a password that simultaneously gives solidarity to the inner circle and freaks out and excludes non-users, the ubiquitous Establishment. This use of language reminds us of Kenneth Burke's theory of language as gesture, for Nowspeak is indeed a sort of symbolic nose-thumbing at the Establishment — a complex and fun way of saying "Screw you" in a linguistic set that only the initiates know. Nowspeak is the code that the System must break, and as such it unites the various branches of the nebulous movement with an often specious sense of community. Nowspeak appears deceptively simple; actually, it is quite complex and involves many subtleties of syntax and style. Since it is spoken, not written, it is transmitted and its conventions established by word-of-mouth communication. The only sure way to establish current usage is to be in constant contact with speakers, for the language changes daily and today's In phrase is liable to be tomorrow's tired-out cliché. A written version of the language is at best only an approximation of its spoken form. Youth-oriented magazines such as *Cavalier, Ramparts,* and *Evergreen* realize this and effect in their writing style a skillful synthesis between ordinary English and authentic Nowspeak by repeating key words in contexts that indicate the cultural sympathies of the editors. Dust jackets, theatre marquees, and record jackets also let the young audience know by verbal sleight-of-mouth that the designer or producer was "where it was at" when the artifact in question was produced. By succumbing to the hip sell and buying the product the young consumer is invited to join the cool community where he, too, can be Norman Mailer-ed, Maxwell Taylor-ed *ad nauseum.*

By nature Nowspeak is sensation-oriented rather than experi-   26 ence-oriented, solipsistic rather than chronological or historical. While typical standard English sentence structure is chronological ("It was raining," "They left with us on Tuesday," "He used to drop by for drinks on Wednesday nights"), Nowspeak is non-chronological, non-temporal, a language of, for, and about the present moment. It is a process language designed to express the shifts, the swift reversals, the kaleidoscopic flux, the insecurities and ephemera of an electric kool-aid acid world. Like the Hopi Indian's tongue, Nowspeak is designed to tell us only that "it is summering," not that "it is summer": witness the number of words that describe ongoing or continuing action *(happening, Scene, where it's at, swinging).* Thus the language is geared toward making what the American philosopher Charles Hartshorne has called "this-here-now" statements about immediate actions and present states of being. To listen to the Now people rapping or to read an underground news-paper is to live briefly in the historical present. Few if any of the verbs are in the past tense, and most of the sentences are short, simple declarative statements directed less toward imparting information than toward creating a mood or emotion. Most of the statements are action-directed imperatives ("screw in the streets," "kill the pigs," "stop the trial") or exclama-tory-declarative statements with a pithy, down-home epigrammatic brevity about them ("All power to the people," "This is a racist culture," "The streets belong to the people"). Daniel J. Boorstin, writing for the October 1968 *Esquire,* calls the Movement "the social expression of a movement from Expe-rience to Sensation" — the shift from cumulative and communicable observa-tion of or acquaintance with facts and events to simple awareness of percep-tion which by definition is personal, private, highly confined, and essentially incommunicable. "What history is to the person in quest of experience," he writes, "a 'happening' is to the person in quest of sensation. For a 'happening' is something totally discrete. It adds to our sensations without increasing our experience." Perhaps we can see in the sensation-orientation, the "this-here-now"-ness of Nowspeak and its speakers a popularization of pseudo-Whiteheadian process metaphysics. This new pop philosophy mirrors the shift in contemporary world view from traditional substance-attribute metaphysics to a *weltanschauung* where things fall apart, the center cannot hold, movies-within-films-within-metaflicks are cinematic commonplaces, and today's pop idol is tomorrow's Nowhere Man. Once-credible reality was shat-tered with the dreamy lyricism of early grass and acid rock ("Strawberry fields forever") and now like Humpty-Dumpty's egg, the pieces of this cosmic Chi-nese puzzle cannot be put back together. Nowspeak reflects all these things:

for a fragmented and incoherent time it offers us a pastiche-lingo whose silences and ellipses are more eloquent than its words.

Nowspeak, like most subculture languages, is more incantation than   27 analysis or definition and thus relies heavily on word connotation rather than denotation. We already have noted the proper names that have charisma and evocative power. Certain other words and phrases also have it: "The Revolution," "power (supply: black, student, flower)," "the System," "the Movement," "kill pigs," "do your own thing." Men have died for less clearly defined terms than these. Nat Hentoff in the April 1969 *Evergreen* tells the story of a recent meeting of young liberal teachers in New York that quickly degenerated into a name-calling contest on the word "racist." The fact that the word was left undefined during the meeting was irrelevant. The evocative power of the word was enough. The important thing about words like the Movement and the Establishment is not that anyone can point to referents for them, but that they are sufficient in emotional force to generate their own new myths as they gather the tribes about them. For the Nowspeaker, as for Lewis Carroll's Humpty Dumpty, the word can mean anything that pleases the speaker at the time: for example, the word *uptight*, which seems to change meanings with the seasons. Claude Brown in "The Language of Soul" (*Esquire*, April 1968) remarks that the word came into use about 1953 in Harlem and meant being in financial straits. In time, it came to be popular with junkies to describe their perpetual condition of needing money for the next fix. In the early sixties when "uptight" was first making its way into under-thirty jargon, a younger generation of people in black urban communities of the East revived the word with new meaning: "everything is cool, under control, going my way." For the Nowspeaker "uptight" may be either a term of approbation ("everything is proceeding according to plan," "I have it all psyched out," "I'm cool, I'm hip") or of derision (as an equivalent to "square," "uncool," "not with it"). Once again, it is not the denotative power of the word that counts (*uptight* may denote two completely antithetical states, depending on its usage); it is the connotation of the word, the manner of uttering it, the occasion, the context, and the emotive force that determine the word's meaning in a given situation.

Stanley Kripner's paper before the International Society of General   28 Semantics in August 1968 suggested that what the youthful user of "head drugs" learns from his earliest drug experiences is no very specific knowledge or information: instead he learns a new semantic set proper to the occasion ("spaced out," "groovy," "freak out," "high," "crash," "turned on"). To put the matter in good linguistic terminology, we might say that the Nowspeaker often mistakes the map for the territory; he speaks intensionally rather than extensionally, evocatively and incantatorially instead of analytically and rationally. Both in popular and a McLuhanesque sense of the word, Nowspeak is a "cool" language — indefinable, vague, often imprecise, requiring rigorous audience participation to fill in the holes in the content. Thus for the Nowspeaker the medium is quite literally the message.

Like George Orwell's famous Newspeak, Nowspeak is essentially a re- 29 ductive language intended to facilitate rather than stimulate thought by limiting the possible alternatives that can be articulated within the language set. Designed for instant speech, minimum thought, and instant replay, it is built around an implicit two-value logic that denies or disregards the possibility of compromise or alternative systems. It is easy for America's retribalized youth to think in terms of these neat polar opposites — pig and Yippie (the poles of the 1968 Chicago confrontation), New Left and Establishment, System and Revolution — for it provides a comfortable means of instantly categorizing all the possible experiences that one might have. For the Nowspeaker the world is all black or white with no redeeming shade of grey in between. Black is beautiful and white is a sell-out. The student is a nigger. All power to the people, death to pigs. Down with the System; up, up, and away with the Beautiful People. Reason is bad, feeling is good. Act, think, act, think, then act, act, act. Nietzsche's prophetic transvaluation of all values has at last come to pass. The lack of a middle ground, a middle term somewhere between the extremes of total conformity and total assault on the culture, makes it impossible for Nowspeak to reflect with accuracy any world other than one drawn in the starkest of blacks and whites. There is, for example, no such animal as "pig-hippie" for that would be an animal as anomalous and absurd as Suzanne Langer's "rabbit-dog." One must be one or the other, never both at once. Thus, for all its dayglo colors, its newspaper taxis and marshmallow people, plasticene ponies and insanity's horse adorning the skies, the world of Nowspeak is a strangely sinister, almost medieval world, a battlefield where the children of light and the sons of darkness, the Now Generation and the Oldthinkers, play out the psychedelic *psychomachia* to the finish. The lines were drawn long ago with deadly clarity, and it may be too late to turn back the clock. As Gore Vidal reminds us in the final essay of *Sex, Death and Money,* the wheel of civilization is once more beginning to turn and most of us can only watch in morbid fascination as the flower kids in this strangest of all Children's Crusades are pied-piped away by the idol of the hour.

Yet the case for language may not be totally lost. It may well be this 30 polarizing tendency of Nowspeak that will spell its end as the ruling subculture jargon. All philosophical systems have built into them certain basic assumptions that substantially limit the types of statements possible within each system. The same can be said of languages, for the verbal set of any culture (or subculture) determines to a great extent the limits of its possible assertions, its knowledge, its ideology, its perceptions, and hence its achievements. Like the heroine of Vilgot Sjöman's *I Am Curious (Yellow)* we all are feeling the need to smash our tidy op art cardboard archives with all the groovy letters and slogans and In words pasted all over the slick surface, and to find a new box with new labels for our collective files. Already hip young journalists, politicians, students, teachers, playwrights, poets, and critics are beginning to chafe at the restrictions of a language designed for incantation and slogans rather than for thoughtful analysis and action. Nat Hentoff's *Evergreen* article speaks of the New Left's "prison of words," and, after analysis of such phrases as Herbert Marcuse's "discriminative tolerance," Hentoff concludes that it is a polite euphemism for "elitist authoritarianism"; that "all power to all people" means not what it seems to say, but rather implies the implicitly snobbish view, "all power to me and everyone else who believes exactly as I do." For the first time perhaps in this decade we are beginning to look behind the words to the things and ideas, to search out hidden paradoxes ("All power to all people," and "America is a nation of fascist pigs," for example, are slogans as compatible as "Buddha is and is not" — and about equally meaning-ful).

Nowspeak has served its function and served it well and faithfully. 31 Despite obvious limitations of its own, it has freed standard Americanese from the impoverishment of Webster's, Madison Avenue, pop psychiatry, military-industrial jargon, academese, and koffee-klatch-and-pizza-late-late-show TV. It has introduced a colorful, freaky, rhythmic, whimsical, gutsy, outrageous, "sexy, childish, irreligious and mad" element into a language that was giving signs of languishing in its prime. It has elevated the jargon of the hipster, the black, the drug pusher, bohemian, beat, hippie, and general rebel with or without a cause to the status of legitimate usage and has infused instant glamour and expressiveness into the speech of millions (both the *New York Times* and David Brinkley have noted a special affinity for *uptight*). In a very real sense, Nowspeak is itself the pop poetry of the new age just as rock is its lyric voice. Yet in an equally real sense the greatest strength of Nowspeak lies in its power and need to be superseded. C. D. Burns put it this way in an essay called "The Sense of the Horizon" (1933):

The experience of any moment has its horizons. Today's experience, which is not tomorrow's, has in it some hints and implications which are tomorrow on the horizon of today. . . . However wide it may be, that common world also has its horizon; and on that horizon new experiences are always appearing.

That Nowspeak's horizon is Now is significant: that is at once its life- 32 blood and its death knell. Already the neon lights have burnt out on Carnaby Street, the Beatles have gone their separate ways, the Haight stands emptied of its brilliant frisking flower children, the orchard gone to ashes, and the dry leaves swirl like fallen Lucifer's host in the People's Park. Sergeant Pep-per's buried; he will not come out of his grave. The summer people have taken to the streets, and the old hippies have fled into the mountains, feeling some new wind brewing in them as they breathe. And which of us knows what rough beast of a newer Nowspeak, its hour come 'round at last, slouches toward San Francisco to be born?

SUBJECT QUESTIONS

1. Ms. Carnes says that the celebrated generation gap is "largely a linguistic gap." Does she mean to imply that if the older and younger generations talked alike they would think alike?
2. In what sense is Nowspeak "symbol" rather than "sign"? (See paragraph 3.) Could the same be said of "conventional pig-Americanese"?
3. If the subculture assumes that "the act of verbalization is itself a dodge," what is the point of having a new language? Could it be said that Nowspeak is a way of avoiding explicit communication? (Consider the most frequently used phrase in Nowspeak, "You know," which is often employed as many as six or eight times in a single statement.)
4. How much of the language of Nowspeak was invented by its users? What are its major sources, according to Ms. Carnes? What, if anything, do these sources have in common?
5. Does Carnes succeed in showing the relationship between world view and language system? (See paragraph 2.)

STRUCTURE QUESTIONS

1. What is the "irony implicit" in Ms. Carnes's attempt to define Nowspeak? How does she get around this difficulty?
2. Discuss the author's strategy in explicating the historical sources of Nowspeak; do these sources help to "define" Nowspeak?
3. Ms. Carnes has certainly given plenty of specific examples of Nowspeak; should she have been more selective? Why do you think she included so many?
4. Carnes's own style varies from "academic" to something close to "imitative form" (for example, "a down-home earthy lowdown shackdown niggerbaby blues plainness of style.") Do you see any advantage in this inconsistency, or is it a fault in her writing?

An Ethic of Clarity

Donald Hall

Donald Hall (b. 1916) is a poet and creative writing teacher. His poems have been published in many magazines as well as in separate volumes. He also has edited and written books on rhetoric and style and lectured on creative writing at conferences and workshops across the country. Mr. Hall is a professor of English at the University of Michigan. The following essay originally appeared as the introduction to The Modern Stylists *(1968).*

Ezra Pound, George Orwell, James Thurber, and Ernest Hemingway don't have much in common: a great poet who became a follower of Mussolini, a disillusioned left-wing satirist, a comic essayist and cartoonist, and a great novelist. If anything, they could represent the diversity of modern literature. Yet one thing unites them. They share a common idea of good style, an idea of the virtues of clarity and simplicity. This attitude toward style was not unknown to earlier writers, but never before has it been so pervasive and so exclusive. 1

Style is the manner of a sentence, not its matter. But the distinction between manner and matter is a slippery one, for manner affects matter. When *Time* used to tell us that President Truman slouched into one room, while General Eisenhower strode into another, their manner was trying to prejudice our feelings. The hotel that invites me to enjoy my favorite beverage at the Crown Room is trying not to sound crass: "Have a drink at the bar." One linguist, in discussing this problem, took Caesar's "I came; I saw; I conquered," and revised it as, "I arrived on the scene of the battle; I observed the situation; I won the victory." Here, the matter is the same, but Caesar's tone of arrogant dignity disappears in the pallid pedantry of the longer version. It is impossible to say that the matter is unaffected. But, let us say that this kind of difference, in the two versions of Caesar, is what we mean by style. 2

In the expression "good writing" or "good style," the word "good" has usually meant "beautiful" or "proficient" — like a good Rembrandt or a good kind of soap. In our time it has come to mean honest as opposed to fake. Bad writing happens when the writer lies to himself, to others, or to both. Probably, it is usually necessary to lie to oneself in order to lie to others; advertising men use the products they praise. Bad writing may be proficient; 3

it may persuade us to buy a poor car or vote for an imbecile, but it is bad because it is tricky, false in its enthusiasm, and falsely motivated. It appeals to a part of us that wants to deceive itself. I am encouraged to tell myself that I am enjoying my favorite beverage when, really, I am only getting sloshed.

"If a man writes clearly enough any one can see if he fakes," says   4
Hemingway. Orwell reverses the terms: "The great enemy of clear language is insincerity. . . . When there is a gap between one's real and one's declared aims, one turns as it were instinctively to long words and exhausted idioms, like a cuttlefish squirting out ink." Pound talks about the "gap between one's real and one's declared aims" as the distance between expression and meaning. In "The New Vocabularianism," Thurber speaks of the political use of clichés to hide a "menacing Alice in Wonderland meaninglessness."

As Robert Graves says, "The writing of good English is thus a moral   5
matter." And the morality is a morality of truth-telling. Herbert Read declares that "the only thing that is indispensable for the possession of a good style is personal sincerity." We can agree, but we must add that personal sincerity is not always an easy matter, nor is it always available to the will. Real aims, we must understand, are not necessarily conscious ones. The worst liars in the world may consider themselves sincere. Analysis of one's own style, in fact, can be a test of one's own feelings. And certainly, many habits of bad style are bad habits of thinking as well as of feeling.

There are examples of the modern attitude toward style in older writers.   6
Jonathan Swift, maybe the best prose writer of the language, sounds like George Orwell when he writes:

. . . Our English tongue is too little cultivated in this kingdom, yet the faults are nine in ten owing to affectation, not to want of understanding. When a man's thoughts are clear, the properest words will generally offer themselves first, and his own judgment will direct him in what order to place them, so as they may be best understood.

Here Swift appears tautological; clear thoughts only *exist* when they are embodied in clear words. But he goes on: "When men err against this method, it is usually on purpose," purposes, we may add, that we often disguise from ourselves.

Aristotle in his *Rhetoric* makes a case for plainness and truth-telling.   7
"The right thing in speaking really is that we should be satisfied not to annoy our hearers, without trying to delight them: we ought in fairness to fight our case with no help beyond the bare facts." And he anticipates the modern stylist's avoidance of unusual words: "Clearness is secured by using the words . . . that are current and ordinary." Cicero attacks the Sophists because they are "on the lookout for ideas that are neatly put rather than reasonable. . . ."

Yet, when we quote Cicero, the master rhetorician, on behalf of honest   8 clarity, we must remember that the ancients did not really think of style as we do. Style until recent times has been a division of rhetoric. To learn style, one learned the types of figures of speech and the appropriateness of each to different levels of discourse — high, middle, and low. The study of style was complex, but it was technical rather than moral. For some writers, Latin was high and the vernacular low, but in the Renaissance the vernacular took in all levels. It is only in modern times that style divorces itself from rhetoric — rhetoric belongs to the enemy, to the advertisers and the propagandists — and becomes a matter of ethics and introspection.

Ezra Pound, like some French writers before him, makes the writer's 9 function social. "Good writers are those who keep the language efficient. That is to say, keep it accurate, keep it clear." We must ask why this idea of the function of good style is so predominantly a modern phenomenon. Pound elsewhere speaks of the "assault," by which he means the attack upon our ears and eyes of words used dishonestly to persuade us, to convince us to buy or to believe. Never before have men been exposed to so many words — written words, from newspapers and billboards and paperbacks and flashing signs and the sides of buses, and spoken words, from radio and television and loudspeakers. Everyone who wishes to keep his mind clear and his feelings his own must make an effort to brush away these words like cobwebs from the face. The assault of the phoney is a result of technology combined with a morality that excuses any technique which is useful for persuasion. The persuasion is for purposes of making money, as in advertising, or winning power, as in war propaganda and the slogans of politicians. Politicians have always had slogans, but they never before had the means to spread their words so widely. The cold war of rhetoric between communism and capitalism has killed no soldiers, but the air is full of the small corpses of words that were once alive: "democracy," "freedom," "liberation."

It is because of this assault, primarily, that writers have become increas- 10 ingly concerned with the honesty of their style to the exclusion of other qualities. Concentration on honesty is the only way to exclude the sounds of the bad style that assault us all. These writers are concerned finally *to be honest about what they see, feel, and know.* For some of them, like William Carlos Williams, we can only trust the evidence of our eyes and ears, our real knowledge of our immediate environment.

Our reading of good writers and our attempt to write like them can 11 help to guard us against the dulling onslaught. But we can only do this if we are able to look into ourselves with some honesty. An ethic of clarity demands intelligence and self-knowledge. Really, the ethic is not only a defense against the assault (nothing good is ever merely defensive), but is a development of the same inwardness that is reflected in psychoanalysis. One cannot, after all, examine one's motives and feelings carefully if one takes a naïve view that the appearance of a feeling is the reality of that feeling.

Sometimes, the assault is merely pompous. Some people say "wealthy"   12
instead of "rich" in order to seem proper, or "home" instead of "house" in
order to seem genteel. George Orwell translates a portion of *Ecclesiastes* into
academic-pompous, for example; Quiller-Couch does something similar with
Hamlet's soliloquy. Years ago, James Russell Lowell ridiculed the newspapers
that translated "A great crowd came to see . . ." into "A vast concourse was
assembled to witness. . . ." None of these examples is so funny as a colonel's
statement on television that one of our astronauts "has established visual
contact" with a piece of his equipment. He meant that the astronaut had *seen*
it.

Comic as these pomposities are, they are signs that something has gone   13
wrong somewhere. (My father normally spoke a perfectly good plain English,
but, occasionally, when he was unhappy with himself, he would fall off dread-
fully; I remember him once admonishing me at dinner, "It is necessary to
masticate thoroughly.") The colonel must have been worried about the intellectual respectability of the space program when he resorted to phrases like
"visual contact." The lady who speaks of "luncheon" instead of "lunch" is
worried about her social status. She gives herself away. Something has gone
wrong, and it has gone wrong inside her mind and her emotions.

The style is the man. Again and again, the modern stylists repeat this   14
idea. By a man's metaphors you shall know him. When a commencement
orator advises students to enrich themselves culturally, chances are that he
is more interested in money than in poetry. When a university president says
that his institution turned out 1,432 B.A.s last year, he tells us that he thinks
he is running General Motors. The style is the man. Remy de Gourmont used
the analogy that the bird's song is conditioned by the shape of the beak. And
Paul Valery said, ". . . what makes the style is not merely the mind applied
to a particular action; it is the whole of a living system extended, imprinted
and recognizable in expression." These statements are fine, but they sound
too deterministic, as if one expresses an unalterable self and can no more
change the style of that self than a bird can change the shape of its beak.
Man is a kind of bird that can change his beak.

A writer of bad prose, to become a writer of good prose, must alter   15
his character. He does not have to become good in terms of conventional
morality, but he must become honest in the expression of himself, which means
that he must know himself. There must be no gap between expression and
meaning, between real and declared aims. For some people, some of the time,
this simply means *not* telling deliberate lies. For most people, it means learning when they are lying and when they are not. It means learning the real
names of their feelings. It means not saying or thinking, "I didn't *mean* to
hurt your feelings," when there really existed a desire to hurt. It means not
saying "luncheon" or "home" for the purpose of appearing upper-class or
well-educated. It means not using the passive mood to attribute to no one

in particular opinions that one is unwilling to call one's own. It means not disguising banal thinking by polysyllabic writing or the lack of feeling by clichés that purport to display feeling.

The style is the man, and the man can change himself by changing his 16 style. Prose style is the way you think and the way you understand what you feel. Frequently, we feel for one another a mixture of strong love and strong hate; if we call it love and disguise the hate to ourselves by sentimentalizing over love, we are thinking and feeling badly. Style is ethics and psychology; clarity is a psychological sort of ethic, since it involves not general moral laws, but truth to the individual self. The scrutiny of style is a moral and psychological study. By trying to scrutinize our own style, perhaps with the help of people like Orwell and Pound, Hemingway and Thurber, we try to understand ourselves. Editing our own writing, or going over in memory our own spoken words, or even inwardly examining our thought, we can ask *why* we resorted to the passive in this case or to clichés in that. When the smoke of bad prose fills the air, something is always on fire somewhere. If the style is really the man, the style becomes an instrument for discovering and changing the man. Language is expression of self, but language is also the instrument by which to know that self.

SUBJECT QUESTIONS

1. What change does Hall say has taken place in the attitude toward style among contemporary writers? How does he explain this change?
2. In what sense is good style "a moral matter"?
3. Consider the implications of the repeated sentence in paragraph 14, "the style is the man." Do you agree with the thesis? Does a pompous style indicate a pompous person? Does a tangled style imply a mixed-up writer?
4. How, according to Hall, can a poor prose writer become a good one?
5. Do you agree with Hall that a good way to know yourself better is to analyze your prose style? Or do you tend to think that a bad style is simply the result of bad training in composition?

STRUCTURE QUESTIONS

1. At the end of paragraph 2, Hall offers a one-sentence "definition" of style. Is it adequate? Does Hall think it is?
2. Do you find any correspondence between the methods of development Hall employs and logical subdivisions within the essay? What methods does he employ in this problem of definition?
3. Did you find the many quotations from other authors helpful or distracting? Some of the writers Hall cites will not be familiar to freshmen; does it matter that he does not identify them except by name?

4. The last part of the essay is an inducement to writers to improve their own styles. Is it separate from the definition, or is it actually part of the definition?
5. Hall writes much about honesty in style; does his own style seem to you honest? How do you test honesty in style?

Style and Good Style

Monroe Beardsley

Monroe C. Beardsley (b. 1915) is a professor of philosophy at Swarthmore College. He is active in various civil rights organizations, particularly the National Association for the Advancement of Colored People (NAACP) and the American Civil Liberties Union (ACLU), and has written several books on aesthetics and on logic, including Thinking Straight *(3rd ed., 1966). The essay printed here was originally a lecture given at the National Defense Education Act (NDEA) Institute on high school English in 1965.*

Recently I had occasion to look over a couple of manuscripts that had been pretty heavily copy-edited for the press. The copy-editors had very different suggestions for ideas about the ideal direction in which to mould the hapless works that had come their way, but one thing they did thoroughly agree upon: namely, that the authors did not know how to write, and would be helpless without an editor. The main trouble was apparently not grammar, or punctuation, or consistency of capitalization, but style. 1

Reading these manuscripts, comparing the harshly cancelled original sentences with the neatly written substitutes between the lines, led me to reflect again on the puzzling nature of style — a quality so evident to the sensitive reader, and yet so difficult to lay hold of and to talk sensibly about. It brought home to me the paradox of the situation in which one person undertakes to improve the style of something written by another. *A* writes his piece of discursive prose, say, and shows it to *B*. *B*, the style-improver, may be a copy-editor or a teacher correcting a composition by a student, or may even be *A* himself at some later time. How is it possible for *B* to improve *A's* work? It can't be that *A* has failed to say what he wanted to say, because if he hasn't said it, how does *B* know what it is? And if *A has* said what he wanted to say, what can be wrong with the style? 2

Whether or not this is a real paradox, and, if so, how deep it goes, is one of the questions that I shall be trying to answer. Evidently it calls for a careful consideration of the nature of style: what style is precisely, and what it means to change the style of a sentence. 3

It's just as well for us to recognize at the start that there are several 4

From *Reflections on High School English: NDEA Institute Lectures 1965*, ed. Gary Tate (Tulsa: University of Tulsa, 1966), pp. 91–105. Reprinted by permission of the author and Gary Tate.

very different concepts of style, or uses of the term. I will distinguish the three main ones briefly, so as to get my bearings.

First, there is the concept of *a* style (that is, the distinctive style of an author or a particular work). When we think of *a* style, in this sense, we have in mind, no doubt, certain recurrent features of the writing. A style is a set of stylistic features. To escape a futile circularity in this definition, we must go on to say what a stylistic feature is — that is, what features of a discourse count as elements of style, and which do not.

Second, there is the concept of a *good style*. The style-improver claims to make the style better, and presumably is guided by some criteria of evaluation. He must be able to say what is a fault of style, and why it is a fault, and how that fault can be eliminated — without creating some other fault.

Third, there is the concept of style itself — a part or aspect of the discourse, somehow distinguishable from what is called the substance or content.

The first concept will not concern us here; it is of aesthetic interest and importance, but we can set it aside. My chief attention will be on the second concept. My aim is to look at certain problems about style from the point of view of the style-improver — especially of the teacher who hopes not only to improve particular pieces of work by his students, but also to give them some guiding principles, or at least teach them a knack, so that they may become, as far as may be, their own style-critics.

Because of the special point of view I am adopting, I feel free to use the term "good style" in a modest way. When I speak of good style in this context I do not mean excellence or distinction — style that can claim special aesthetic merit. I mean only *not-bad style*, that is, style that is free of faults. It may seem over-generous to award this commendation to what may, at its best, pass unnoticed; but I think experienced teachers will agree with me that to achieve good style, even in the modest sense, is no mean feat. And it is no small ambition for a teacher or copy-editor to set himself the task of eliminating stylistic faults and helping others eliminate the faults in their own writing.

But in order to inquire what good style, or better style, is, I must lay the groundwork by giving, in summary, my answer to the third, and most fundamental question: what is style itself?[1] There are, then, three parts to my discourse: I shall consider what style is, and what good (or better) style is, and I shall discuss some of the practical consequences.

---

[1] The view sketched here has been formulated more precisely and fully in my *Aesthetics: Problems in the Philosophy of Criticism* (New York: Harcourt, Brace and World, 1958), pp. 221–27. How much I have learned from, and relied upon, William K. Wimsatt, Jr., will be evident to anyone who has read his essay on "Style as Meaning" in *The Prose Style of Samuel Johnson* (New Haven: Yale University, 1941; paperbound 1963).

I

Many charming, clever, and memorable things have been said about style — 11
most of which turn out to be highly misleading when subjected to analysis.
One of the best things was said by Pascal, in his twenty-third *Pensée,* and
I would like to take it as my text: "Words differently arranged have a different
meaning, and meanings differently arranged have different effects."[2] When
this double-barrelled aphorism is properly understood (that is, when I have
gotten through telling you how *I* want to construe it), it sums up concisely
the two theses I shall defend here, and it contains the two truths (the *only*
two really general and fundamental truths) about style. Anyone who grasps
their implications, and follows them out consistently in practice, will find that
the consequences are far-reaching.

The clearest way to say what style is, I think, is to say what a *difference* 12
in style is. Take two sentences or parts of sentences, S_1 and S_2. We say that
they differ in style when two things are true about them. First, they differ
to some extent in *meaning.* And second, the difference is not on the plane
of overt or explicit meaning, but on the plane of covert or implicit meaning.
The distinction between explicit and implicit meaning is one that requires
a certain amount of analysis to elucidate, but let me say in a general way
what sorts of things I have in mind, and leave it to the examples to clarify
the distinction. Implicit meaning includes what we would ascribe to the connotations rather than to the plain dictionary sense of a word, and it includes
what we would consider to be merely suggested, or hinted, or intimated by
a sentence rather than to what the sentence plainly states.

It is relatively easy to see what we are talking about when we compare 13
two similar English expressions with respect to their style. If they don't differ
at all in meaning, there is no difference in style (but this, as Pascal says, is
almost impossible, for if there are different words, or the same words in a
different order, there is almost certain to be some difference in meaning,
however small and subtle). If the meanings differ in some explicit way, there
is no difference in style. It follows from this analysis that the concept of style
is inherently comparative, and therefore variable with the context of concern.
To isolate a particular stylistic feature in any discourse is always to think of
a particular element of implicit meaning in terms of which that discourse
might differ from some other one. This is the first of my two theses, then:
that style is detail of implicit meaning.

To clarify and support this thesis I require a few examples. And I will 14
take them from a book on style that is regarded by many people with great
affection and respect — the E. B. White revision of William Strunk, Jr.'s *The*

---

[2] Trans. W. F. Trotter (New York: Modern Library, 1941), p. 11.

Elements of Style. I'm not choosing this as a bad example; when I speak critically of it, I do so more in sorrow than in anger. I can only say: what a pity that even so sound and sensible a book is so confused! In the final chapter, contributed by White, the view of style I have been sketching above is clearly stated and subscribed to: "Style has no such separate entity; it is non-detachable, unfilterable" (p. 55) — in other words, it is inseparable from meaning. But unfortunately the logical implications of this thesis are seldom kept in view.

Consider first the advice to use the active voice rather than the passive voice or constructions based on the verb "to be." "Many a tame sentence of description or exposition," say Strunk and White (p. 14), "can be made lively and emphatic by substituting a transitive in the active voice for some such perfunctory expression as *there is,* or *could be heard."* Here is a clearcut example of stylistic advice: how to make your sentence more lively and emphatic. Now take a look at some of their examples. The first one is this: Don't say "There were a great number of dead leaves lying on the ground;" but say "Dead leaves covered the ground." Granted there is a significant difference in style here. But isn't that a difference of meaning? For one thing, there are more leaves in the second sentence. The second one says that the ground was covered; the first one only speaks of a "great number." Stylistic advice is a rather odd sort of thing if it consists in telling students to pile up the leaves in their descriptions. Suppose the student brings the corrected paper back to his instructor and says, "Pardon me. You told me to say the leaves covered the ground, but actually they didn't; there was quite a bit of ground showing through. Still, there *were* a great many. Do I get a lower grade just for telling the truth?" What answer can the conscientious style-expert give to that? 15

Now, you may say, well it's not as if the student had used an exact number. Suppose he wrote, "There were 261 leaves on the ground," and his instructor commented in the margin: "Don't say there were 261; say there were 893 — that will be more effective." This would of course be telling the student to lie. Since this difference in meaning would be explicit, the change from 261 to 893 would not be a change in style. But isn't the change from "a great many leaves" to "covered the ground" a kind of lie, too — or at least a considerable exaggeration? Naturally it is more lively and emphatic, but is it honest? True, the deception will be partially concealed, because it is conveyed implicitly rather than explicitly, but that does not make it less reprehensible. 16

Take another example that Strunk and White use to illustrate the same rule about liveliness and emphasis. Don't say "The reason he left college was that his health became impaired;" say "Failing health compelled him to leave college." What's the difference here? Again, it is a difference in meaning — in the picture of the situation that is conjured up by the different words and different grammar. In the one case, the health grew worse, and finally after 17 some indecision, he left college — though health was not necessarily the sole consideration. The second sentence implies worse health: it left the student no choice. Naturally it is a more dramatic story. But is this what stylistic advice is all about? Are Strunk and White saying, "Never mind about the exact truth; always try to make things as dramatic as possible, provided you don't get caught in any explicit and easily detectable misstatements"?

The same sort of question can be raised about a great many of the   18
Strunk-White examples. "Put statements in a positive form," they urge — "Make definite assertions" (p. 14). For instance, don't say "He was not very often on time," but rather "He usually came late." Now it seems to me that if I were asked about so-and-so's punctuality I might very well reply, "He was not very often on time," if I wanted to be careful not to overstate the matter, or to suggest that so-and-so came *very* late, or that he was deliberate and inconsiderate in coming late, etc. I am saying precisely what I want to mean, and ought to mean. What right has anyone to tell me *not* to mean this?

One more example: "Use definite, specific, concrete language," say   19
Strunk and White (p. 15). If you take this seriously, it means, "Don't write philosophy, because that will require abstract language." But here is one of their examples: don't say "A period of unfavorable weather set in;" say "It rained every day for a week." But this is like the leaves example; the second sentence gives us a higher rainfall.

My immediate purpose is not to question the advice given, though I   20
suppose some of my skepticism has already emerged. I am coming to the question of good style shortly. My argument is that a difference of style is always a difference in meaning — though implicit — and an important and notable difference of style is always a sizeable difference in meaning. Some of the Strunk-White examples involve so considerable and obvious a change that it is questionable whether they are really stylistic changes. For example: don't say "He did not think that studying Latin was much use;" say "He thought the study of Latin useless" (p. 14). Now being useless (i.e., having no use at all), and not being of much use, are clearly different things. If anybody advised me to say the second after I had said the first, I would be rather annoyed — I would tell him not to go putting words in my mouth. I don't think that studying Latin is much use; but I would certainly not want to say that it is useless. I'm afraid our style-advisers got carried away on this one.

I can't resist one more example — this one not from Strunk and White   21
but from a religious publication via the filler-spaces in *The New Yorker*.

Words that sound happy put your reader in the right frame of mind to say "yes" to your request. Remember that a negative word or an unfriendly expression should never be used if there is a positive way to express the same thought. You might say: "We regret that we are unable to supply you with the item ordered. Is there another item which we may send you on the same subject?"

But your reader-reaction will be 100 per cent improved if you rephrase that sentence to read: "Fortunately for you, although the specific item you ordered is out of print, we have another which might serve your purpose."

Nothing could be plainer than that this change of style is a radical change in meaning. None of us would countenance such a bland invitation to write "words that sound happy" in order to con the subnormal reader into the appropriate "reader-reaction" — so that he gets the impression that you are practically doing him a favor by not sending him the item he ordered. But we encourage this sort of confusion when we speak of style as though it *were* detachable and manipulable independent of meaning — when we define style as the "how" of writing vs. the "what" — when, in short, we lose sight of the fact that style is nothing but meaning. That is what encourages people to entertain the absurd idea that, as this writer says, there is both a "positive" and a "negative . . . way to express the same thought."

II

Now, if we are agreed about what style is, we can go on to the second question: what is *good* (i.e., not-bad) style? I assume that there are such things as *faults* of style — or at least there are pieces of discourse that are faulty *in* style — and so the basic question is what such a fault may be. Then the absence of such faults will be goodness of style.   22

There is one sort of problem about good style that I want to make sure we set aside here. A person who accepted a dinner invitation at the White House in a long Faulknerian sentence, or who wrote a letter of condolence in early Hemingwayese, has no doubt committed some sort of error involving style. The error is not an error *of* style, I think, but an error in the choice of style; the result is not bad style, necessarily, but *inappropriate* style. It is a lack of decorum. In fact, it is just the sort of error that one might commit if he took some of the Strunk and White advice too earnestly. "The latter sentence [the one not recommended] is less direct, less bold, and less concise," they say at one point (p. 13). But what kind of reason is this? In effect, they are saying, "Always write so as to *appear* like a bold, decisive, forthright sort of person. Never mind how you actually feel, or what the occasion is; just act bold."   23

What I am concerned with, then, is stylistic fault, and again I take my cue from Pascal. "Meanings differently arranged have different effects" — or, as I should put it, when meanings are combined, some combinations are better than others. But there are different ways of being better. When explicit meanings are wrongly combined, you get a logical fault (this is oversimplifying somewhat, but take it as a first approximation). The trouble with a sentence like "He married his widow's younger sister" is that it describes a logical impossibility. There's nothing wrong with the style. Freedom from logical   24 error is good logic — though of course it may not be great cogency. But suppose the fault lies in the way explicit meanings are combined with *implicit* meanings. Then we have a fault of style. My second thesis is that such a fault is also a logical fault, though its locus is different from ordinary explicit logical error. In short, good style is logical congruity of explicit and implicit meaning. When what a sentence suggests or hints, and what its words connote, bear out the implications of the explicit meaning of the sentence, we have no fault of style; but when there is a clash, something must be remedied. And since we take the explicit meaning as primary, we think of the implicit meaning as what requires to be altered, so we say that the style is bad — just as we say that the hat is too small for the head, rather than that the head is too large for the hat.

As Wimsatt puts it (paperbound ed., p. 10), "Bad style is not a deviation   25
of words from meaning, but a deviation of meaning from meaning."

To prove this thesis would be more of a task than I could undertake   26
here — it is, in fact more of a task than anyone has ever undertaken. But a few examples will show how it can be supported, and you can test it further on your own favorite examples of horrible style.

My examples will come, again, from Strunk and White — and it is a   27
tribute to their slim volume that it yields so many provocative examples. "Place the emphatic words of a sentence at the end," they advise at one point, in boldface italics (p. 26). "The proper place in the sentence for the word or group of words that the writer desires to make most prominent is usually the end." This puts the cart before the horse. It is not correct to say that the emphatic words of a sentence should be placed at the end; it is correct to say that whatever words *are* placed at the end of an English sentence will thereby be given emphasis. In all practical discussions of style, it is essential to distinguish two kinds of things that can be said. They are related as the factual and the evaluative, the *is* and the *ought*.

The first kind of statement is what might be called a *stylistic fact*, or   28
a rhetorical fact. For example, "Whatever you place at the end of a sentence will tend to be emphasized." Or, "In general, the active voice carries with it a tone of greater assurance and decisiveness than the passive voice." Many inexperienced writers make mistakes because they do not grasp these facts about the very nature of English constructions. And the teacher can help a great deal merely by pointing these things out. "Look, by placing this at the end, you implicitly claim that it is more important than what you put earlier. Is this what you want to claim?" Or, "Look; here you use the passive voice; the active voice would make the sentence more direct and forthright. Which do you prefer?" In this way, a teacher sensitizes his students to stylistic facts so that they become more and more aware of exactly what they *are* saying, implicitly. But there is no call for the Strunk-White imperative here. The instruction is in the conditional form, like instruction in checkers, gardening,

golf, or winemaking: "If you do such-and-such, then such-and-such a meaning will result." Strunk and White's second sentence can be taken in this conditional form.

So there are stylistic facts; are there also *stylistic rules*, or recommendations? There may be, as I said, rules of appropriateness; such-and-such is the accepted style for a thank-you note. But what more can we say? What reason can we give for condemning style, quite apart from what the writer wished to do? Some of the Strunk-White examples of poor style break down at once if we suppose a different context. Take the first example under the sentences just quoted. They reject this sentence: "Humanity has hardly advanced in fortitude since that time, though it has advanced in many other ways." They substitute: "Humanity, since that time, has advanced in many other ways, but it has hardly advanced in fortitude." Suppose you wrote the first sentence, and your copy-editor substituted the second one. Couldn't you simply reply that the first one says exactly what you want to say? From this reply there is no appeal. The second sentence, but not the first one, suggests that what is important is the lack of advance in fortitude. As far as style is concerned, one sentence is no better than the other; they simply say (implicitly) different things, and the question is (or ought to be) which is true.

But when Strunk and White condemn one sentence and praise the other, it is clear that they are making a hidden assumption. They are thinking of the sentence in the context of a sort of Baconian essay on the subject of fortitude. It's not easy to illustrate this assumption very briefly. But imagine something like this foreshortened context:

Man is a miracle, or many miracles; but the most miraculous fact about him is his fortitude, his capacity to endure and to survive incredible hardships. Think of the conditions under which neolithic man kept going — the winters, the wild animals, the long distances of his migrations. Humanity has hardly advanced in fortitude since that time, though it has advanced in many other ways.

Here if we feel a slackness at the end, and a sort of betrayal of expectations, we can affirm a fault of style. For the end of the last sentence implicitly denies what the first sentence quite explicitly states: namely, that fortitude is the important topic under discussion. So there is a logical conflict after all, and this is the stylistic fault. Note that it is quite independent of the writer's intention and the reader's antecedent desires: it is internal to the discourse itself.

Compare another example that illustrates the same principle, though Strunk and White place it under the heading of active vs. passive voice. They cite: "I shall always remember my first visit to Boston," and continue "This is much better than 'My first visit to Boston will always be remembered by me'" (p. 13). But what's wrong with the latter sentence? If we look for the relevant stylistic fact, we find that it is the same one just considered. Putting the personal pronoun at the end rather than at the beginning of the sentence gives it an emphatic position, and the emphasis is increased by the unusual syntax. Compare these two analogous sentences:

(1) The police department will always remember my first visit to Boston.
(2) My first visit to Boston will always be remembered by the police department.

It would be silly to say that in this case the passive voice makes the second sentence "less direct, less bold, and less concise." I suppose it is less direct, but it is more dramatic and striking, because of its ominous overtones.

So it is not the active-passive difference that is important here. The difference is that the second sentence given by Strunk and White ("My first visit to Boston will always be remembered by me") implicitly claims that there is something noteworthy about *my* remembering it, as opposed to somebody else's remembering it. It says, in effect, "Others may forget it, but *I* certainly won't." Now this suggestion in itself can't make the sentence stylistically bad. One could invent a context in which it would be better than the sentence Strunk and White recommend. But they are tacitly thinking of it as in a context where the main topic under discussion has been, or is to be, the trip itself, its causes and consequences. And in *this* context, the implicit suggestion that there is something significant about *my* remembering it rather than somebody else introduces an irrelevant point. In effect, the sentence says, "It is important that *I* remember it," but the context shows that it is *not* important, because it has no logical bearing upon the other matters at hand. 32

At one point in their book, Strunk and White come close to making this point explicitly. They begin unpromisingly by giving advice that verges upon complete nullity. First they state their rule: "Use the active voice" (p. 13) — just like that, in so many words. But a little later they say, "This rule does not, of course, mean that the writer should entirely discard the passive voice, which is frequently convenient and sometimes necessary." All we need now is some explanation of how to tell when it is convenient and when necessary — but the much-praised conciseness of *The Elements of Style* naturally prevents them from pausing to give any such explanation. However, their example and comment are important. Compare "The dramatists of the Restoration are little esteemed today" with "Modern readers have little esteem for the dramatists of the Restoration." The authors add, "The first would be the preferred form in a paragraph on the dramatists of the Restoration; the second, in a paragraph on the tastes of modern readers." Excellent; right to the point. The difference in style is a difference in what is suggested about the focus of attention in the whole discourse. And the rightness or wrongness of the style depends on how that suggestion actually comports with the remainder of the discourse. 33

Some people may be puzzled by this sort of talk about style. In order 34 to show what style is, and what good style is, you have to work out the implicit meanings and state them baldly for examination. Then they are no longer implicit, of course, and the explication of them may seem forced and artificial. But implicit meanings can be understood and can be stated explicitly; and that is the only way to exhibit their connections or divergences. This is what I call style-analysis. And it is essential if our discussions of style are not to degenerate into murky rhapsody or painfully misleading aphorism.

Perhaps I am stacking the cards too much for my second thesis by choosing examples that have already been selected, or constructed, to illustrate particular stylistic faults. So let me venture out of the laboratory for a brief field trip in the outside world of prose. My first specimen is one that came to hand not long ago in a book review by Elizabeth Janeway. She referred to the author of this book[3] as "a mistress of nearly impenetrable prose," and offered the following sample:

> The tyranny of happiness forms the nucleus of the defense apparatus employed by the woman who does not quite dare to break out, though restless, but who must continually seek a validation for her way of life.

Now granted this would be much clearer if we had a context in which "the tyranny of happiness" was defined. But even with that explanation on hand, there would still be stylistic trouble. And that comes largely because the connotations of the words are constantly working against the basic logical pattern proposed by the very same words. They are also working against each other.

We are told that the woman does not "dare to break out" of something (I suppose, the frustrations of her second-class status as married woman); she is compelled to "seek a validation" for her way of life. So far, so good, though we could follow the logical order of relationships better if the sequence of phrases in the sentence reflected that order. The next step — which would be clearer if it followed rather than preceded the end of the sentence — is to note that in order to find that validation, the woman requires a "defense apparatus." But "defense" is hardly the *mot juste* here, since it suggests some sort of enemy or attack, and leads us to look around in the context for hints as to what it is — only to return empty-handed. Then the "defense apparatus" is said to have a "nucleus," and again we try to fit the connotations into the picture — if there is a nucleus it holds things together, or is the center, or is surrounded by other material, etc. No apparatus that is readily conceivable has, in the strict sense, a nucleus — though it may have a most important part. Finally (but this is put first), the nucleus is said to be formed by the tyranny of happiness. Is it the tyranny itself, or the acceptance of such tyranny, or

[3] Edith de Rham, *The Love Fraud* (New York: Clarkson N. Potter, 1965); see *The New York Times*, March 28, 1965.

some theory about such tyranny, or something else, that the woman relies on for her validation? The syntax, apparently elliptical, claims a causal connection that is unwarranted by the rest of the context, as far as we have it here. And that is the secret of its failure — as style.

It is always interesting, and often instructive, to see what reviewers pick out as objectionable in the style of the books they review. Recently Joseph Epstein, reviewing a book[4] in the *New Republic* (June 5, 1965), wrote: 37

Although every so often Coser will get off a cleanly barbaric sentence like "Geographical dispersion shades into or overlaps with functional differentiation," he occasionally achieves a graceful prose style and almost always commands a forceful one.

This example suggests many reflections — more than I will try to tease out now. It is just the sort of sentence of which Strunk and White would be likely to say: "Avoid abstract nouns. Be concrete. Be definite. Be forceful." But the trouble does not lie in the abstract nouns, I think, and they would not even obtrude on our attention if it weren't for the *active* and *concrete* verbs between them — namely "shades into" and "overlaps with." It is the connotations of these words that throw us off and leave us baffled when we try to figure out what is the exact relationship between geographical dispersion and functional differentiation that is being asserted.

Last week, in a hotel in Denver, I found a booklet containing information about restaurants and other tourist attractions.[5] One of the items read as follows: 38

LE PROFIL — 1560 Sherman St. (222–0758).
Richly adorned and unique of its kind, here dinner is an experience. French and Continental cuisine with an air of Paris sophistication is skillfully prepared and served with care. This is truly a swish dining emporium. The atmosphere is relaxed but polished.

I'm sure any composition teacher would itch to get at this piece of prose; it exhibits such a fascinating range of defects. But I pass by the dubiously attached modifier and the curious redundancy in the first sentence, and what philosophers would call a "category mistake" in the second sentence (I mean that it is not strictly the cuisine but the food that is served). These certainly introduce meanings that distract from the basic order of thought — they strew logical red herrings along the path of sense. But my favorite sentence is the third. "Truly a swish dining emporium!" It would be hard to find two words whose connotations — whose whole ambiences of meaning — are more at odds with one another.

---

[4] Lewis Coser, *Men of Ideas* (New York: Free Press, 1965).
[5] *Colorado Guestguide*, Vol. 7, 1965 summer edition, p. 8.

III

I promised some concluding remarks on practical applications, but as I look 39 back it seems to me that I have drawn the practical consequences pretty much as I went along. However, it may be well to summarize my argument concisely, and take one more look to see whether other useful points emerge.

The steps of my argument are these. (1) Different words or a different 40 order of words make different meanings — at least, they do if they make a difference in style, because style is detail of implicit meaning. (2) Therefore, if the teacher advises a change of words, or of word order, he is recommending a different meaning. And if he says one stylistic feature is better than another, he is saying that it is better to mean one thing rather than another. (3) No meaning as such is better than any other, considered solely from the stylistic point of view. (Of course there are moral and political and religious and other criteria in terms of which it is better to mean one thing rather than another.) (4) Therefore, if a change of meaning betters the style, that betterment must lie in the relationships of meanings. (5) The objective relationships that meanings have to each other are logical; meanings are compatible or incompatible, they are connected by causation, implication, coordination, subordination, etc. (6) Therefore, faults of style must be faults of logic; and good style must be compatibility of implicit and explicit meaning.

The practical problem for the writer is that of managing his implicit 41 meanings so that they do not impede or divert or conceal or obstruct his explicit meanings. It is a continuous tactical problem. The strategy of writing is large-scale organization of meanings — the main steps of the argument, explicit logical relationships. What is left is management of the small-scale, subtler, and under-the-surface meanings to make them carry the thought forward, adding details on the side (so to speak), but details that fit in and enrich the thought — and perhaps show how the writer looks upon his own argument: how confident or doubtful he is, how detached or involved, how serious or playful, and so on.

A teacher who fully realizes that to change style is always to change 42 meaning will never take his role as style-critic lightly, I think. He will shy away from simple absolute rules. He will not speculate about intentions, but focus on the discourse itself, and the way its parts work, or do not work, together. His main effort will be to help his pupils understand what I have called stylistic facts, so that they can become sensitive and discerning readers of their own work. And above all when he is faced with a hard writing-problem, he will insist that the sovereign remedy is to think out the logical connections clearly, and then make sure that the syntax and diction mirror those connections as clearly as possible.

I think I have time to play around with one final example from Strunk 43 and White — or rather from White's concluding chapter — and to draw another moral from it. The moral (to state it first) is that the doctrine of style as meaning and of good style as logical relevance has a liberating effect on the style-critic (the teacher or copy-editor); if he really accepts the doctrine, and all its consequences, he should become tolerant of very different styles and undictatorial about his own recommendations.

White has some fun with variations on Thomas Paine: "These are the 44 times that try men's souls." And the last and most outrageous variation is this: "Soulwise, these are trying times." White raises the question what is wrong with this — but he wisely makes no attempt to answer this question. Less wisely, no doubt, I rush in to fill the gap. Because it may seem that here, at any rate, is a stylistically bad sentence whose stylistic badness has nothing to do with logic, and therefore a sentence that can be rejected out of hand without taking into account relationships of meaning at all. Now of course, this sentence is a comedown from the original, and we can see how it differs and why it differs. "Trying times" and "times that try men's souls" are far from synonymous — a situation can be trying, in the modern sense, without constituting a real trial of one's whole self. And the "X-wise" construction has taken on foundation-board and executive-level overtones, besides its native vagueness and indeterminateness. "Soulwise, these are trying times" is flippant in tone, not deeply concerned. It reminds me of a crazy line from an S. J. Perelman television script: "A man in my position doesn't have as much freedom, choicewise."

But now suppose young Tom Paine were to bring you the first install- 45 ment of a political piece he is writing, called *The American Crisis*. You open it up and read the first sentence: "Soulwise, these are trying times." Somehow it won't do. But what can you tell him? First, you can help him see the relevant stylistic facts, so that he knows exactly what he has said, explicitly and implicitly. You cannot prove to him, I think, that his sentence in itself is bad style. It might make an excellent beginning of a piece by Perelman. But, second, you can ask what kind of book this sentence is to be the beginning of — you can read further into the context. If the next sentence says, explicitly, that these times are not for the summer soldier and the sunshine patriot, but call for deep commitment and solemn purpose, then you can tell him that, in this context, the first sentence is bad style. For it says, implicitly, that the situation is not serious and that the writer does not care deeply about what is happening.

Let us suppose that, armed with this new insight, Tom Paine goes away 46 to meditate. If you have helped him discern the logical jarring in his discourse, and have made him want to eliminate it, you have done your job. The rest is up to him. But of course if he returns the next day saying, 'I've got it! Listen to this: 'These are the times that try men's souls,' " then you can congratulate yourself, as well as him. Unfortunately, few of our students are likely to come up to this level. So we had better be content with the more limited purpose of showing what is wrong, and why. But — and this is my parting plea — when we give reasons to argue that the style is faulty, let us make sure that we give *good* reasons. For bad reasons are worse than none at all.

SUBJECT QUESTIONS

1. This essay is obviously addressed to English teachers; is it too difficult for college students? According to Beardsley's definition, could there be such a distinction as "difficult style" and "easy style"?

2. Explain Beardsley's statement in paragraph 13, "If the meanings differ in some explicit way, there is no difference in style." Does he mean that there is no difference in style between *Oedipus Rex* and a Batman comic book, because the meanings differ?

3. Beardsley says that all stylistic faults are really problems of meaning, or logic. And the examples he gives certainly support his contention. Try to find, or invent, examples which do "say what they mean" but which are still defective stylistically. What is the "fault" of the following sentence from a student theme? "Whenever I was out in the neighborhood I usually had some kids with me because they looked up to me because I seemed to be just one step ahead of them and so I was accepted as their leader because of my education."

4. In paragraph 22, Beardsley says that good style is the absence of faults. This statement would imply that the writing of this question for discussion is, provided it has no faults, as good as that of *Macbeth*. Would you agree? (Recall the latitude Beardsley earlier gave to his meaning of "good style.")

5. In paragraph 28, a "stylistic" fact is equated with a "rhetorical fact." Is there no difference between style and rhetoric?

STRUCTURE QUESTIONS

1. In paragraph 10, Beardsley gives a formal and rather old-fashioned "statement of intentions" for the rest of the essay. Is such a statement needed here?

2. Is the summary of what he has said (in paragraph 40) necessary? Is it helpful? (The numerous examples Beardsley uses throughout his essay may clarify meanings, but they may also obscure the general direction.)

3. Toward the beginning, Beardsley distinguishes three different meanings of "style"; how useful are these distinctions? Are they clear? (Since he is going to elaborate on the last two, it is really only necessary for us to understand at this point that "a style" is different from "style.")

4. What is Beardsley's chief method of defining "style" in the first section? What indication do you have that Beardsley himself does not consider his definition adequate, even though it extends for two paragraphs?

5. Once he has defined "style," how does Beardsley go about defining "good style"? Does his definition seem oversimplified? Can you think of anything other than the relationship between implicit and explicit meanings which might be considered an element of style?
6. Does the final illustration about Thomas Paine seem an effective way to end the essay? Explain.

Gobbledygook

Stuart Chase

Stuart Chase (b. 1888), a certified public accountant by training, has been a consultant for various branches of the federal government (1917–1941) and for UNESCO (1949). He is the author of some twenty-nine books, many of them on relations between business and government. But his best known works are The Proper Study of Mankind, and The Power of Words (1954), from which the following essay is taken.

Said Franklin Roosevelt, in one of his early presidential speeches: "I see 1
one-third of a nation ill-housed, ill-clad, ill-nourished." Translated into standard bureaucratic prose his statement would read:

It is evident that a substantial number of persons within the Continental boundaries of the United States have inadequate financial resources with which to purchase the products of agricultural communities and industrial establishments. It would appear that for a considerable segment of the population, possibly as much as 33.3333° percent of the total, there are inadequate housing facilities, and an equally significant proportion is deprived of the proper types of clothing and nutriment.

This rousing satire on gobbledygook — or talk among the bureau- 2
crats — is adapted from a report[1] prepared by the Federal Security Agency in an attempt to break out of the verbal squirrel cage. "Gobbledygook" was coined by an exasperated Congressman, Maury Maverick of Texas, and means using two, or three, or ten words in the place of one, or using a five-syllable word where a single syllable would suffice. Maverick was censuring the forbidding prose of executive departments in Washington, but the term has now spread to windy and pretentious language in general.

"Gobbledygook" itself is a good example of the way a language grows. 3
There was no word for the event before Maverick's invention; one had to say: "You know, that terrible, involved, polysyllabic language those government people use down in Washington." Now one word takes the place of a dozen.

From *The Power of Words*, copyright 1953, 1954, by Stuart Chase. Reprinted by permission of Harcourt Brace Jovanovich, Inc.
° Not carried beyond four places.
[1] This and succeeding quotations [except where otherwise noted] from F.S.A. report by special permission of the author, Milton Hall.

A British member of Parliament, A. P. Herbert, also exasperated with   4
bureaucratic jargon, translated Nelson's immortal phrase, "England expects
every man to do his duty":

England anticipates that, as regards the current emergency, personnel will face
up to the issues, and exercise appropriately the functions allocated to their respective
occupational groups.

A New Zealand official made the following report after surveying a plot   5
of ground for an athletic field:[2]

It is obvious from the difference in elevation with relation to the short depth
of the property that the contour is such as to preclude any reasonable developmental
potential for active recreation.

Seems the plot was too steep.

An office manager sent this memo to his chief: 6

Verbal contact with Mr. Blank regarding the attached notification of promotion
has elicited the attached representation intimating that he prefers to decline the
assignment.

Seems Mr. Blank didn't want the job.

A doctor testified at an English trial that one of the parties was suffering from
"circumorbital haematoma."

Seems the party had a black eye.

In August 1952 the U.S. Department of Agriculture put out a pamphlet entitled: "Cultural and Pathogenic Variability in Single-Condial and Hyphaltip Isolates
of Hemlin-Thosporium Turcicum Pass."

Seems it was about corn leaf disease.

On reaching the top of the Finsteraarhorn in 1845, M. Dollfus-Ausset,   7
when he got his breath, exclaimed:

The soul communes in the infinite with those icy peaks which seem to have
their roots in the bowels of eternity.

Seems he enjoyed the view.

A government department announced: 8

Voucherable expenditures necessary to provide adequate dental treatment
required as adjunct to medical treatment being rendered a pay patient in in-patient
status may be incurred as required at the expense of the Public Health Service.

Seems you can charge your dentist bill to the Public Health Service. Or can
you?

[2] This item and the next two are from the piece on gobbledygook by W. E. Farbstein,
New York Times, March 29, 1953.

Legal Talk

Gobbledygook not only flourishes in government bureaus but grows wild and   9
lush in the law, the universities, and sometimes among the literati. Mr. Mi-
cawber was a master of goggledygook, which he hoped would improve his
fortunes. It is almost always found in offices too big for face-to-face talk.
Gobbledygook can be defined as squandering words, packing a message with
excess baggage and so introducing semantic "noise." Or it can be scrambling
words in a message so that meaning does not come through. The directions
on cans, bottles, and packages for putting the contents to use are often a good
illustration. Gobbledygook must not be confused with double talk, however,
for the intentions of the sender are usually honest.

I offer you a round fruit and say, "Have an orange." Not so an expert   10
in legal phraseology, as parodied by editors of *Labor:*

> I hereby give and convey to you, all and singular, my estate and interests,
> right, title, claim and advantages of and in said orange, together with all rind, juice,
> pulp and pits, and all rights and advantages therein ... anything hereinbefore or
> hereinafter or in any other deed or deeds, instrument or instruments of whatever
> nature or kind whatsoever, to the contrary, in any wise, notwithstanding.

The state of Ohio, after five years of work, has redrafted its legal code   11
in modern English, eliminating 4,500 sections and doubtless a blizzard of
"whereases" and "hereinafters." Legal terms of necessity must be closely tied
to their referents, but the early solons tried to do this the hard way, by adding
synonyms. They hoped to trap the physical event in a net of words, but instead
they created a mumbo-jumbo beyond the power of the layman, and even many
a lawyer, to translate. Legal talk is studded with tautologies, such as "cease
and desist," "give and convey," "irrelevant, incompetent, and immaterial."
Furthermore, legal jargon is a dead language; it is not spoken and it is not
growing. An official of one of the big insurance companies calls their branch
of it "bafflegab." Here is a sample from his collection:[3]

> One-half to his mother, if living, if not to his father, and one-half to his
> mother-in-law, if living, if not to his mother, if living, if not to his father. Thereafter
> payment is to be made in a single sum to his brothers. On the one-half payable to
> his mother, if living, if not to his father, he does not bring in his mother-in-law as
> the next payee to receive, although on the one-half to his mother-in-law, he does
> bring in the mother or father.

You apply for an insurance policy, pass the tests, and instead of a   12
straightforward "here is your policy," you receive something like this:

---

[3] Interview with Clifford B. Reeves by Sylvia F. Porter, New York *Evening Post,* March
14, 1952.

This policy is issued in consideration of the application therefor, copy of which application is attached hereto and made part hereof, and of the payment for said insurance on the life of the above-named insured.

Academic Talk

The pedagogues may be less repetitious than the lawyers, but many use even   13
longer words. It is a symbol of their calling to prefer Greek and Latin deriva-
tives to Anglo-Saxon. Thus instead of saying: "I like short clear words," many
a professor would think it more seemly to say: "I prefer an abbreviated
phraseology, distinguished for its lucidity." Your professor is sometimes right,
the longer word may carry the meaning better — but not because it is long.
Allen Upward in his book *The New Word* warmly advocates Anglo-Saxon
English as against what he calls "Mediterranean" English, with its polysyllables built up like a skyscraper.

Professional pedagogy, still alternating between the Middle Ages and   14
modern science, can produce what Henshaw Ward once called the most
repellent prose known to man. It takes an iron will to read as much as a page
of it. Here is a sample of what is known in some quarters as "pedageese":

Realization has grown that the curriculum or the experiences of learners
change and improve only as those who are most directly involved examine their goals,
improve their understandings and increase their skill in performing the tasks necessary to reach newly defined goals. This places the focus upon teacher, lay citizen
and learner as partners in curricular improvement and as the individuals who must
change, if there is to be curriculum change.

I think there is an idea concealed here somewhere. I think it means: 15
"If we are going to change the curriculum, teacher, parent, and student must
all help." The reader is invited to get out his semantic decoder and check
on my translation. Observe there is no technical language in this gem of
pedageese, beyond possibly the word "curriculum." It is just a simple idea
heavily ververbalized.

In another kind of academic talk the author may display his learning   16
to conceal a lack of ideas. A bright instructor, for instance, in need of prestige
may select a common sense proposition for the subject of a learned monograph — say, "Modern cities are hard to live in" and adorn it with imposing
polysyllables: "Urban existence in the perpendicular declivities of meg-
alopolis . . ." et cetera. He coins some new terms to transfix the reader —
"mega-decibel" or "strato-cosmopolis" — and works them vigorously. He is
careful to add a page or two of differential equations to show the "scatter."
And then he publishes, with 147 footnotes and a bibliography to knock your
eye out. If the authorities are dozing, it can be worth an associate professor-
ship.

While we are on the campus, however, we must not forget that the   17
technical language of the natural sciences and some terms in the social
sciences, forbidding as they may sound to the layman, are quite necessary.
Without them, specialists could not communicate what they find. Trouble
arises when experts expect the uninitiated to understand the words; when they
tell the jury, for instance, that the defendant is suffering from "circumorbital
haematoma."

Here are two authentic quotations. Which was written by a distin-   18
guished modern author, and which by a patient in a mental hospital? You
will find the answer at the end of the chapter.

(1) Have just been to supper. Did not knowing what the woodchuck sent me
here. How when the blue blue blue on the said anyone can do it that tries. Such
is the presidential candidate.

(2) No history of a family to close with those and close. Never shall he be
alone to be alone to be alone to be alone to be alone to lend a hand and leave it
left and wasted.[4]

Reducing the Gobble

As government and business offices grow larger, the need for doing something   19
about gobbledygook increases. Fortunately the biggest office in the world is
working hard to reduce it. The Federal Security Agency in Washington,[5] with
nearly 100 million clients on its books, began analyzing its communication
lines some years ago, with gratifying results. Surveys find trouble in three main
areas: correspondence with clients about their social security problems, office
memos, official reports.

Clarity and brevity, as well as common humanity, are urgently needed   20
in this vast establishment which deals with disability, old age, and unemployment. The surveys found instead many cases of long-windedness, foggy meanings, clichés, and singsong phrases, and gross neglect of the reader's point of
view. Rather than talking to a real person, the writer was talking to himself.
"We often write like a man walking on stilts."

Here is a typical case of long-windedness: 21

Gobbledygook as found: "We are wondering if sufficient time has passed so
that you are in a position to indicate whether favorable action may now be taken
on our recommendation for the reclassification of Mrs. Blank, junior clerk-stenographer, CAF 2, to assistant clerk-stenographer, CAF 3?"

Suggested improvement: "Have you yet been able to act on our recommendation to reclassify Mrs. Blank?"

[4 This quotation comes from Gertrude Stein's *Lucy Church Amiably.*]
[5 Now the Department of Health, Education and Welfare.]

Another case: 22

Although the Central Efficiency Rating Committee recognizes that there are many desirable changes that could be made in the present efficiency rating system in order to make it more realistic and more workable than it now is, this committee is of the opinion that no further change should be made in the present system during the current year. Because of conditions prevailing throughout the country and the resultant turnover in personnel, and difficulty in administering the Federal programs, further mechanical improvement in the present rating system would require staff retraining and other administrative expense which would seem best withheld until the official termination of hostilities, and until restoration of regular operations.

The F.S.A. invites us to squeeze the gobbledygook out of this statement.   23
Here is my attempt:

The Central Efficiency Rating Committee recognizes that desirable changes could be made in the present system. We believe, however, that no change should be attempted until the war is over.

This cuts the statement from 111 to 30 words, about one-quarter of the   24
original, but perhaps the reader can do still better. What of importance have I left out?

Sometimes in a book which I am reading for information — not for   25
literary pleasure — I run a pencil through the surplus words. Often I can cut a section to half its length with an improvement in clarity. Magazines like *The Reader's Digest* have reduced this process to an art. Are long-windedness and obscurity a cultural lag from the days when writing was reserved for priests and cloistered scholars? The more words and the deeper the mystery, the greater their prestige and the firmer the hold on their jobs. And the better the candidate's chance today to have his doctoral thesis accepted.

The F.S.A. surveys found that a great deal of writing was obscure al-   26
though not necessarily prolix. Here is a letter sent to more than 100,000 inquirers, a classic example of murky prose. To clarify it, one needs to *add* words, not cut them:

In order to be fully insured, an individual must have earned $50 or more in covered employment for as many quarters of the coverage as half the calendar quarters elapsing between 1936 and the quarter in which he reaches age 65 or dies, whichever first occurs.

Probably no one without the technical jargon of the office could translate this; nevertheless, it was sent out to drive clients mad for seven years. One poor fellow wrote back: "I am no longer in covered employment. I have an outside job now."

Many words and phrases in officialese seem to come out automatically,   27
as if from lower centers of the brain. In this standardized prose people never

get jobs, they "secure employment"; *before* and *after* become "prior to" and "subsequent to"; one does not *do*, one "performs"; nobody *knows* a thing, he is "fully cognizant"; one never *says*, he "indicates." A great favorite at present is "implement."

Some charming boners occur in this talking-in-one's-sleep. For instance: 28

The problem of extending coverage to all employees, regardless of size, is not as simple as surface appearances indicate.

Though the proportions of all males and females in ages 16–45 are essentially the same . . .

Dairy cattle, usually and commonly embraced in dairying . . .

In its manual to employees, the F.S.A. suggests the following: 29

Instead of	Use
give consideration to	consider
make inquiry regarding	inquire
is of the opinion	believes
comes into conflict with	conflicts
information which is of a confidential nature	confidential information

Professional or office gobbledygook often arises from using the passive 30 rather than the active voice. Instead of looking you in the eye, as it were, and writing "This act requires . . ." the office worker looks out of the window and writes: "It is required by this statute that . . ." When the bureau chief says, "We expect Congress to cut your budget," the message is only too clear; but usually he says, "It is expected that the departmental budget estimates will be reduced by Congress."

Gobbled: "All letters prepared for the signature of the Administrator will be single spaced."

Ungobbled: "Single space all letters for the Administrator." (Thus cutting 13 words to 7.)

Only People Can Read

The F.S.A. surveys pick up the point . . . that human communication involves 31 a listener as well as a speaker. Only people can read, though a lot of writing seems to be addressed to beings in outer space. To whom are you talking? The sender of the officialese message often forgets the chap on the other end of the line.

A woman with two small children wrote the F.S.A. asking what she 32 should do about payments, as her husband had lost his memory. "If he never gets able to work," she said, "and stays in an institution would I be able to draw any benefits? . . . I don't know how I am going to live and raise my children since he is disable to work. Please give me some information. . . ."

To this human appeal, she received a shattering blast of goggledygook, 33
beginning, "State unemployment compensation laws do not provide any benefits for sick or disabled individuals . . . in order to qualify an individual must
have a certain number of quarters of coverage . . ." et cetera, et cetera. Certainly if the writer had been thinking about the poor woman he would not
have dragged in unessential material about old-age insurance. If he had pictured a mother without means to care for her children, he would have told
her where she might get help — from the local office which handles aid to
dependent children, for instance.

Gobbledygook of this kind would largely evaporate if we thought of 34
our messages as two way — in the above case, if we pictured ourselves talking
on the doorstep of a shabby house to a woman with two children tugging
at her skirts, who in her distress does not know which way to turn.

Results of the Survey

The F.S.A. survey showed that office documents could be cut 20 to 50 per 35
cent, with an improvement in clarity and a great saving to taxpayers in paper
and payrolls.

A handbook was prepared and distributed to key officials.[6] They read 36
it, thought about it, and presently began calling section meetings to discuss
gobbledygook. More booklets were ordered, and the local output of documents began to improve. A Correspondence Review Section was established
as a kind of laboratory to test murky messages. A supervisor could send up
samples for analysis and suggestions. The handbook is now used for training
new members, and many employees keep it on their desks along with the
dictionary. Outside the Bureau some 25,000 copies have been sold (at 20 cents
each) to individuals, governments, business firms, all over the world. It is now
used officially in the Veterans Administration and in the Department of Agriculture.

The handbook makes clear the enormous amount of gobbledygook 37
which automatically spreads in any large office, together with ways and means
to keep it under control. I would guess that at least half of all the words
circulating around the bureaus of the world are "irrelevant, incompetent, and
immaterial" — to use a favorite legalism; or are just plain "unnecessary" — to
ungobble it.

My favorite story of removing the gobble from gobbledygook concerns 38
the Bureau of Standards at Washington. I have told it before but perhaps
the reader will forgive the repetition. A New York plumber wrote the Bureau
that he had found hydrochloric acid fine for cleaning drains, and was it
harmless? Washington replied: "The efficacy of hydrochloric acid is indispu-

[6] By Milton Hall.

table, but the chlorine residue is incompatible with metallic permanence."

The plumber wrote back that he was mighty glad the Bureau agreed   39
with him. The Bureau replied with a note of alarm: "We cannot assume
responsibility for the production of toxic and noxious residues with hydrochloric acid, and suggest that you use an alternate procedure." The plumber
was happy to learn that the Bureau still agreed with him.

Whereupon Washington exploded: "Don't use hydrochloric acid; it eats   40
hell out of the pipes!"

SUBJECT QUESTIONS

1. How many different kinds of gobbledygook does Chase distinguish?
   What do they have in common? Wherein do they differ?
2. Judging from the examples Chase gives, what would you say are the chief
   weaknesses of gobbledygook as prose? Gobbledygook characteristically
   contains an inordinate number of prepositional phrases; examine the
   passage by the New Zealand official to discover what causes this heavy
   dependence on prepositional phrases.
3. See whether you can find in your textbooks (including this one) examples
   of "pedageese." (Textbook writers generally know their subjects well
   enough, but many have forgotten what they learned in composition
   classes.) Do you see any real justification for this pedageese?
4. Take one of the examples you have found and turn it into clear, informal
   English. How many words do you save? (Clarity is more important than
   word-saving, of course.)

STRUCTURE QUESTIONS

1. Chase gives three different "dictionary" definitions of "gobbledygook."
   Are they sufficiently characterizing? Does Chase assume that they are?
2. What method of definition does Chase use most frequently? How much
   attention does he give to the causes of gobbledygook?
3. How successfully does Chase avoid gobbledygook in his own writing?
   Does his style ever seem too informal?
4. Chase both begins and ends with specific examples rather than generalizations. Would he have done better had he added a "conclusion"? What
   makes the last example particularly appropriate?
5. What is the meaning of the curious subtitle, "Only people can read"?
   The section under that subtitle is not part of the definition of "gobbledygook"; does it belong in the essay?

Contexts

S. I. Hayakawa

S. I. Hayakawa (b. 1906), professor of language arts at San Francisco State College, has been a pioneer in the field of semantics. Most of his books have been in this area, including the one from which the following selection is taken, Language in Thought and Action *(rev. ed., 1963).*

[On being asked to define New Orleans jazz]: Man, when you got to ask what it is, you'll never get to know. . . . — Louis Armstrong

Dictionary definitions frequently offer verbal substitutes for an unknown term which only conceal a lack of real understanding. Thus a person might look up a foreign word and be quite satisfied with the meaning "bullfinch" without the slightest ability to identify or describe this bird. Understanding does not come through dealings with words alone, but rather with the things for which they stand. Dictionary definitions permit us to hide from ourselves and others the extent of our ignorance. — H. R. Huse°

How Dictionaries Are Made

It is widely believed that every word has a correct meaning, that we learn   1
these meanings principally from teachers and grammarians (except that most of the time we don't bother to, so that we ordinarily speak "sloppy English"), and that dictionaries and grammars are the supreme authority in matters of meaning and usage. Few people ask by what authority the writers of dictionaries and grammars say what they say. The writer once got into a dispute with an Englishwoman over the pronunciation of a word and offered to look it up in the dictionary. The Englishwoman said firmly, "What for? I am English. I was born and brought up in England. The way I speak *is* English." Such self-assurance about one's own language is not uncommon among the English. In the United States, however, anyone who is willing to quarrel with the dictionary is regarded as either eccentric or mad.

Let us see how dictionaries are made and how the editors arrive at   2
definitions. What follows applies, incidentally, only to those dictionary offices where first-hand, original research goes on — not those in which editors simply

From *Language in Thought and Action*, Second Edition, by S. I. Hayakawa, copyright 1941, 1949, © 1963, 1964, by Harcourt Brace Jovanovich, Inc., and reprinted with their permission.
° From *The Illiteracy of the Literate* by H. R. Huse, copyright 1933, by D. Appleton-Century Company, Inc.

copy existing dictionaries. The task of writing a dictionary begins with reading vast amounts of the literature of the period or subject that the dictionary is to cover. As the editors read, they copy on cards every interesting or rare word, every unusual or peculiar occurrence of a common word, a large number of common words in their ordinary uses, and also the sentences in which each of these words appears, thus:

> pail
> The dairy *pails* bring home increase of milk
> Keats, *Endymion*
> I, 44–45

That is to say, the context of each word is collected, along with the word itself. For a really big job of dictionary writing, such as the *Oxford English Dictionary* (usually bound in about twenty-five volumes), millions of such cards are collected, and the task of editing occupies decades. As the cards are collected, they are alphabetized and sorted. When the sorting is completed, there will be for each word anywhere from two or three to several hundred illustrative quotations, each on its card. 3

To define a word, then, the dictionary editor places before him the stack of cards illustrating that word; each of the cards represents an actual use of the word by a writer of some literary or historical importance. He reads the cards carefully, discards some, rereads the rest, and divides up the stack according to what he thinks are the several senses of the word. Finally, he writes his definitions, following the hard-and-fast rule that each definition *must* be based on what the quotations in front of him reveal about the meaning of the word. The editor cannot be influenced by what *he* thinks a given word *ought* to mean. He must work according to the cards or not at all. 4

The writing of a dictionary, therefore, is not a task of setting up authoritative statements about the "true meanings" of words, but a task of *recording*, to the best of one's ability, what various words *have meant* to authors in the distant or immediate past. *The writer of a dictionary is a historian, not a lawgiver.* If, for example, we had been writing a dictionary in 1890, or even as late as 1919, we could have said that the word "broadcast" means "to scatter" (seed and so on) but we could not have decreed that from 1921 on, the commonest meaning of the word should become "to disseminate audible messages, etc., by radio transmission." To regard the dictionary as an "authority," therefore, is to credit the dictionary writer with gifts of prophecy which neither he nor anyone else possesses. In choosing our words when we speak or write, we can be *guided* by the historical record afforded us by the dictionary, but we cannot be *bound* by it, because new situations, new experiences, 5 new inventions, new feelings, are always compelling us to give new uses to old words. Looking under a "hood," we should ordinarily have found, five hundred years ago, a monk; today, we find a motorcar engine.[1]

Verbal and Physical Contexts

The way in which the dictionary writer arrives at his definitions merely sys-   6
tematizes the way in which we all learn the meanings of words, beginning at infancy, and continuing for the rest of our lives. Let us say that we have never heard the word "oboe" before, and we overhear a conversation in which the following sentences occur:

He used to be the best *oboe* player in town.... Whenever they came to that *oboe* part in the third movement, he used to get very excited.... I saw him one day at the music shop, buying a new reed for his *oboe*.... He never liked to play the clarinet after he started playing the *oboe*.... He said it wasn't much fun, because it was too easy.

Although the word may be unfamiliar, its meaning becomes clear to   7
us as we listen. After hearing the first sentence, we know that an "oboe" is "played," so that it must be either a game or a musical instrument. With the second sentence the possibility of its being a game is eliminated. With each succeeding sentence the possibilities as to what an "oboe" may be are narrowed down until we get a fairly clear idea of what is meant. This is how we learn by *verbal context*.

But even independently of this, we learn by physical and social context.   8
Let us say that we are playing golf and that we have hit the ball in a certain way with certain unfortunate results, so that our companion says to us, "That's a bad *slice*." He repeats this remark every time our ball fails to go straight. If we are reasonably bright, we learn in a very short time to say, when it happens again, "That's a bad slice." On one occasion, however, our friend says to us, "That's not a *slice* this time; that's a *hook*." In this case we consider what has happened, and we wonder what is different about the last stroke from those previous. As soon as we make the distinction, we have added still another word to our vocabulary. The result is that after nine holes of golf, we can use both these words accurately — and perhaps several others as well, such as "divot," "number-five iron," "approach shot," *without ever having been told what they mean*. Indeed, we may play golf for years without ever being able to give a dictionary definition of "to slice": "To strike (the ball)

---

[1] *Webster's Third New International Dictionary* lists the word "hood" also as a shortened form of "hoodlum."

The time that elapsed between *Webster's Second Edition* (1934) and the *Third* (1961) indicates the enormous amount of reading and labor entailed in the preparation of a really thorough dictionary of a language as rapidly changing and as rich in vocabulary as English.

so that the face of the club draws inward across the face of the ball, causing it to curve toward the right in flight (with a right-handed player)" *(Webster's New International Dictionary, Second Edition)*. But even without being able to give such a definition, we should still be able to use the word accurately whenever the occasion demanded.

We learn the meanings of practically all our words (which are, it will   9
be remembered, merely complicated noises), not from dictionaries, not from definitions, but from hearing these noises as they accompany actual situations in life and then learning to associate certain noises with certain situations. Even as dogs learn to recognize "words," as for example by hearing "biscuit" at the same time as an actual biscuit is held before their noses, so do we all learn to interpret language by being aware of the happenings that accompany the noises people make at us — by being aware, in short, of contexts.

The definitions given by little children in school show clearly how they   10
associate words with situations; they almost always define in terms of physical and social contexts: "Punishment is when you have been bad and they put you in a closet and don't let you have any supper." "Newspapers are what the paper boy brings and you wrap up the garbage with it." These are good definitions. They cannot be used in dictionaries mainly because they are too specific; it would be impossible to list the myriads of situations in which every word has been used. For this reason, dictionaries give definitions on a high level of abstraction; that is, with particular references left out for the sake of conciseness. This is another reason why it is a great mistake to regard a dictionary definition as telling us all about a word.

Extensional and Intensional Meaning

Dictionaries deal with the world of intensional meanings, but there is another   11
world which a dictionary by its very nature ignores: the world of extensional meanings. *The extensional meaning of an utterance is that which it points to in the extensional (physical) world.* That is to say, the extensional meaning cannot be expressed in words, because it is that which words stand for. An easy way to remember this is *to put your hand over your mouth and point* whenever you are asked to give an extensional meaning.

Of course, we cannot always point to the extensional meanings of the   12
words we use. Therefore, so long as we are *discussing* meanings, we shall refer to that which is being talked about as the *denotation* of an utterance. For example, the denotation of the word "Winnipeg" is the prairie city of that name in southern Manitoba; the denotation of the word "dog" is a class of animals which includes dog_1 (Fido), dog_2 (Rex), dog_3 (Rover) ... dog_n.

The *intensional meaning* of a word or expression, on the other hand,   13
is that which is *suggested* (connoted) inside one's head. Roughly speaking,

whenever we express the meaning of words by uttering more words, we are giving intensional meaning, or connotations. To remember this, put your hand over your eyes and let the words spin around in your head.

Utterances may have, of course, both extensional and intensional mean-   14
ing. If they have no intensional meaning at all — that is, if they start no notions whatever spinning about in our heads — they are meaningless noises, like foreign languages that we do not understand. On the other hand, it is possible for utterances to have no extensional meaning at all, in spite of the fact that they may start many notions spinning about in our heads. The statement, "Angels watch over my bed at night," is one that has intensional but no extensional meaning. This does not mean that there are no angels watching over my bed at night. When we say that the statement has no extensional meaning, we are merely saying that we cannot see, touch, photograph, or in any scientific manner detect the presence of angels. The result is that, if an argument begins on the subject whether or not angels watch over my bed, *there is no way of ending the argument to the satisfaction of all disputants,* the Christians and the non-Christians, the pious and the agnostic, the mystical and the scientific. Therefore, whether we believe in angels or not, knowing in advance that any argument on the subject will be both endless and futile, we can avoid getting into fights about it.

When, on the other hand, statements have extensional content, as when   15
we say, "This room is fifteen feet long," arguments can come to a close. No matter how many guesses there are about the length of the room, all discussion ceases when someone produces a tape measure. This, then, is the important difference between extensional and intensional meanings: namely, when utterances have extensional meanings, discussion can be ended and agreement reached; when utterances have intensional meanings only and no extensional meanings, arguments may, and often do, go on indefinitely. Such arguments can result only in conflict. Among individuals, they may result in the breaking up of friendships; in society, they often split organizations into bitterly opposed groups; among nations, they may aggravate existing tensions so seriously as to become real obstacles to the peaceful settling of disputes.

Arguments of this kind may be termed "non-sense arguments," because   16
they are based on utterances about which no sense data can be collected. Needless to say, there are occasions when the hyphen may be omitted — that depends on one's feelings toward the particular argument under consideration. The reader is requested to provide his own examples of "non-sense arguments." Even the foregoing example of the angels may give offense to some people, despite the fact that no attempt is made to deny or affirm the existence of angels. Imagine, then, the uproar that might result from giving a number of examples from theology, politics, law, economics, literary criticism, and other fields in which it is not customary to distinguish clearly sense from non-sense.

The "One Word, One Meaning" Fallacy

Everyone, of course, who has ever given any thought to the meanings of words   17
has noticed that they are always shifting and changing in meaning. Usually,
people regard this as a misfortune, because it "leads to sloppy thinking" and
"mental confusion." To remedy this condition, they are likely to suggest that
we should all agree on "one meaning" for each word and use it only with
that meaning. Thereupon it will occur to them that we simply cannot make
people agree in this way, even if we could set up an ironclad dictatorship
under a committee of lexicographers who would place censors in every newspaper office and microphones in every home. The situation, therefore, appears
hopeless.

Such an impasse is avoided when we start with a new premise alto-   18
gether — one of the premises upon which modern linguistic thought is based:
namely, that *no word ever has exactly the same meaning twice.* The extent
to which this premise fits the facts can be demonstrated in a number of ways.
First, if we accept the proposition that the contexts of an utterance determine
its meaning, it becomes apparent that since no two contexts are ever *exactly*
the same, no two meanings can ever be exactly the same. How can we "fix
the meaning" even for so common an expression as "to believe in" when it
can be used in such sentences as the following:

I believe in you (I have confidence in you).
I believe in democracy (I accept the principles implied by the term democ-
racy).
I believe in Santa Claus (It is my opinion that Santa Claus exists).

Second, we can take, for example, a word of "simple" meaning, like   19
"kettle." But when John says "kettle," its intensional meanings to him are
the common characteristics of all the kettles John remembers. When Peter
says "kettle," however, its intensional meanings to him are the common characteristics of all the kettles he remembers. *No matter how small or how negligible the differences may be between John's "kettle" and Peter's "kettle," there
is some difference.*

Finally, let us examine utterances in terms of extensional meanings. If   20
John, Peter, Harold, and George each say "my typewriter," we would have
to point to four different typewriters to get the extensional meaning in each
case: John's new Olivetti, Peter's old Remington, Harold's Smith-Corona por-
table, and the undenotable intended "typewriter" that George plans some day
to buy: "My typewriter, when I buy it, will be an electric." Also, if John
says "my typewriter" today, and again "my typewriter" tomorrow, the extensional meaning is different in the two cases, because the typewriter is not
exactly the same from one day to the next (nor from one minute to the next):
slow processes of wear, change, and decay are going on constantly. Although

we can say, then, that the differences in the meanings of a word on one occasion, on another occasion a minute later, and on still another occasion another minute later, are negligible, we cannot say that the meanings are *exactly* the same.

To insist dogmatically that we know what a word means *in advance   21 of its utterance* is nonsense. All we can know in advance is *approximately* what it will mean. After the utterance, we interpret what has been said in the light of both verbal and physical contexts, and act according to our interpretation. An examination of the verbal context of an utterance, as well as the examination of the utterance itself, directs us to the intensional meanings; an examination of the physical context directs us to the extensional meanings. When John says to James, "Bring me that book, will you?" James looks in the direction of John's pointed finger (physical context) and sees a desk with several books on it (physical context); he thinks back over their previous conversation (verbal context) and knows which of those books is being referred to.

Interpretation *must* be based, therefore, on the totality of contexts. If   22 it were otherwise, we should not be able to account for the fact that even if we fail to use the right (customary) words in some situations, people can very frequently understand us. For example:

A: Gosh, look at that second baseman go!
B (looking): You mean the shortstop?
A: Yes, that's what I mean.

A: There must be something wrong with the oil line; the engine has started to balk.
B: Don't you mean "gas line"?
A: Yes — didn't I say "gas line"?

Contexts often indicate our meaning so clearly that we do not even have to say what we mean in order to be understood.

Ignoring Contexts

It is clear, then, that the ignoring of contexts in any act of interpretation is   23 at best a stupid practice. At its worst, it can be a vicious practice. A common example is the sensational newspaper story in which a few words by a public personage are torn out of their context and made the basis of a completely misleading account. There is the incident of a Veterans Day speaker, a university teacher, who declared before a high-school assembly that the Gettysburg Address was "a powerful piece of propaganda." The context clearly revealed that "propaganda" was being used, not according to its popular meaning, but rather, as the speaker himself stated, to mean "explaining the moral purposes of a war." The context also revealed that the speaker was a very great admirer of Lincoln. However, the local newspaper, ignoring the context, presented the account in such a way as to suggest that the speaker had called Lincoln a liar. On this basis, the newspaper began a campaign against the instructor. The speaker remonstrated with the editor of the newspaper, who replied, in effect, "I don't care what else you said. You said the Gettysburg Address was propaganda, didn't you?" This appeared to the editor complete proof that Lincoln had been maligned and that the speaker deserved to be discharged from his position at the university. Similar practices may be found in advertisements. A reviewer may be quoted on the jacket of a book as having said, "A brilliant work," while reading of the context may reveal that what he really said was, "It just falls short of being a brilliant work." There are some people who will always be able to find a defense for such a practice in saying, "But he did use the words, 'a brilliant work,' didn't he?"

People in the course of argument very frequently complain about words 24 meaning different things to different people. Instead of complaining, they should accept such differences as a matter of course. It would be startling indeed if the word "justice," for example, were to have the same meaning to each of the nine justices of the United States Supreme Court; we should get nothing but unanimous decisions. It would be even more startling if "justice" meant the same to President Kennedy as to Nikita Khrushchev. If we can get deeply into our consciousness the principle that no word ever has the same meaning twice, we will develop the habit of automatically examining contexts, and this will enable us to understand better what others are saying. As it is, however, we are all too likely, when a word sounds familiar, to assume that we understand it even when we don't. In this way we read into people's remarks meanings that were never intended. Then we waste energy in angrily accusing people of "intellectual dishonesty" or "abuse of words," when their only sin is that they use words in ways unlike our own, as they can hardly help doing, especially if their background has been widely different from ours. There are cases of intellectual dishonesty and the abuse of words, of course, but they do not always occur in the places where people think they do.

In the study of history or of cultures other than our own, contexts take 25 on special importance. To say, "There was no running water or electricity in the house," does not condemn an English house in 1570, but says a great deal against a house in Chicago in 1963. Again, if we wish to understand the Constitution of the United States, it is not enough, as our historians now tell us, merely to look up all the words in the dictionary and to read the interpretations written by Supreme Court justices. We must see the Constitution in its historical context: the conditions of life, the state of the arts and industries and transportation, the current ideas of the time — all of which helped to determine what words went into the Constitution and what those words meant to those who wrote them. After all, the words "United States of America" stood for quite a different-sized nation and a different culture in 1790 from what they stand for today. When it comes to very big subjects, the range of contexts to be examined — verbal, social, and historical — may become very large indeed.

In personal relations, furthermore, those who ignore psychological con-   26
texts often make the mistake of interpreting as insults remarks that are only intended in jest.

The Interaction of Words

All this is not to say, however, that the reader might just as well throw away   27
his dictionary, simply because contexts are so important. Any word in a sentence — any sentence in a paragraph, any paragraph in a larger unit — whose meaning is revealed by its context, is itself part of the context of the rest of the text. To look up a word in a dictionary, therefore, frequently explains not only the word itself, but the rest of the sentence, paragraph, conversation, or essay in which it is found. All words within a given context interact upon one another.

Realizing, then, that a dictionary is a historical work, we should under-   28
stand the dictionary thus: "The word *mother* has most frequently been used in the past among English-speaking people to indicate a female parent." From this we can safely infer, "If that is how it has been used, that is what it *probably* means in the sentence I am trying to understand." This is what we normally do, of course; after we look up a word in the dictionary, we reexamine the context to see if the definition fits. If the context reads, "Mother began to form in the bottle," one may have to look at the dictionary more carefully.

A dictionary definition, therefore, is an invaluable guide to interpreta-   29
tion. Words do not have a single "correct meaning"; they apply to *groups* of similar situations, which might be called *areas of meaning*. It is for defining these areas of meaning that a dictionary is useful. In each use of any word, we examine the particular context and the extensional events denoted (if possible) to discover the *point* intended within the area of meaning.

SUBJECT QUESTIONS

1. Much of this essay is devoted to showing that dictionary definitions are neither adequate nor authoritative; yet in the final paragraph Hayakawa says they are "invaluable." Has he changed his mind in the course of the essay? In what way does he consider dictionary definitions useful?
2. Do you agree with Hayakawa that no word ever has exactly the same meaning twice? Consider the case of the "constant lover"; does not his "I love Jane" on Monday mean the same as "I love Jane" on Tuesday? Shakespeare says that "Love is a babe." What does this mean in the light of Hayakawa's essay?

3. Would not certain scientific terms have constant meanings — sodium, 100 cc., 10° centigrade, for instance? What about such a word as the article "the"? (Does "the" have any meaning without an accompanying noun?)
4. Is it possible to examine a word or phrase free of any context? (In Question 3, for instance, you would consider the word "sodium" in the context of a question about its constant meaning. Does this context have any effect on the meaning of "sodium"?) Did the infuriated editor in Hayakawa's example really take the word "propaganda" out of context, or did he substitute his own context for the schoolteacher's original context?
5. Clarify Hayakawa's distinction between a "non-sense" argument and a "nonsense" one. Would any nonsense argument necessarily also be a non-sense one? Which of the following statements are arguable and which are non-sense?

   a. There is a God.
   b. Belief in God is necessary for a full life.
   c. My horse is faster than yours.
   d. Professor X is a better French teacher than Professor Y.
   e. You don't love me.
   f. A non-sense statement cannot be profitably argued.

STRUCTURE QUESTIONS

1. Hayakawa does not attempt to give a dictionary definition of the word "context." Does he make clear in the essay what he means by the term? What is his principal method of defining it?
2. Hayakawa does give dictionary definitions for the two key phrases "extensional meaning" and "intensional meaning." Examine these definitions. How clear and helpful are they? How does the author make their meaning clear? Because by his own argument these dictionary definitions cannot be adequate, why do you think he bothered to insert them?
3. How does Hayakawa go about defining the term "non-sense argument"? Should he have made a clearer distinction between "non-sense" and "nonsense"? How could he have done this?
4. Although Hayakawa's chief concern is contexts, the framework of the essay is the discussion of dictionary definitions. Does he manage to give the essay unity and coherence, or does it seem to squint in two directions?
5. The essay contains six subheadings. Does Hayakawa provide adequate transitions from one part to the next? Could the subheadings be dispensed with? If so, do they serve any useful purpose?

At the Fringe of Language

C. S. Lewis

C. S. Lewis (1898–1963), professor of medieval and renaissance literature at Cambridge, wrote numerous scholarly books, including one of the great works on medieval literature, Allegory of Love. *He is probably best known, however, for his writings on the place of Christianity in the modern world, particularly* Screwtape Letters. *The essay below is taken from* Studies in Words.

Language exists to communicate whatever it can communicate. Some things it communicates so badly that we never attempt to communicate them by words if any other medium is available. Those who think they are testing a boy's "elementary" command of English by asking him to describe in words how one ties one's tie or what a pair of scissors is like, are far astray. For precisely what language can hardly do at all, and never does well, is to inform us about complex physical shapes and movements. Hence descriptions of such things in the ancient writers are nearly always unintelligible. Hence we never in real life voluntarily use language for this purpose; we draw a diagram or go through pantomimic gestures. The exercises which such examiners set are no more a test of "elementary" linguistic competence than the most difficult bit of trick-riding from the circus ring is a test of elementary horsemanship. 1

    Another grave limitation of language is that it cannot, like music or gesture, do more than one thing at once. However the words in a great poet's phrase interanimate one other and strike the mind as a quasi-instantaneous chord, yet, strictly speaking, each word must be read or heard before the next. That way, language is as unilinear as time. Hence, in narrative, the great difficulty of presenting a very complicated change which happens suddenly. If we do justice to the complexity, the time the reader must take over the passage will destroy the feeling of suddenness. If we get in the suddenness we shall not be able to get in the complexity. I am not saying that genius will not find its own ways of palliating this defect in the instrument; only that the instrument is in this way defective. 2

    One of the most important and effective uses of language is the emotional. It is also, of course, wholly legitimate. We do not talk only in order to reason or to inform. We have to make love and quarrel, to propitiate and 3

From *Studies in Words* by C. S. Lewis. Reprinted by permission of the publisher, Cambridge University Press.

pardon, to rebuke, console, intercede, and arouse. "He that complains," said Johnson, "acts like a man, like a social being." The real objection lies not against the language of emotion as such, but against language which, being in reality emotional, masquerades — whether by plain hypocrisy or subtler self-deceit — as being something else.

All my generation are much indebted to Dr. I. A. Richards for having fully called our attention to the emotional functions of language. But I am hardly less indebted to Professor Empson for having pointed out that the conception of emotional language can be very easily extended too far.[1] It was time to call a halt.   4

We must obviously not call any utterance "emotional" language because it in fact arouses, even because it must arouse, emotion. "It is not cancer after all," "The Germans have surrendered," "I love you" — may all be true statements about matter of fact. And of course it is the facts, not the language, that arouse the emotion. In the last the fact communicated is itself the existence of an emotion but that makes no difference. Statements about crime are not criminal language; nor are statements about emotions necessarily emotional language. Nor, in my opinion, are value-judgements ("this is good," "this is bad") emotional language. Approval and disapproval do not seem to me to be emotions. If we felt at all times about the things we judge good the emotion which is appropriate, our lives would be easier. It would also be an error to treat "I am washed in the blood of the Lamb" as emotional language. It is of course metaphorical language. But by his metaphor the speaker is trying to communicate what he believes to be a fact. You may of course think the belief false in his particular case. You may think the real universe is such that no fact which corresponded to such a statement could possibly occur. You may say that the real cause which prompts a man to say things like that is a state of emotion. But if so, an emotion has produced erroneous belief about an impossible fact, and it is the fact erroneously believed in which the man is stating. A man's hasty belief that the Germans had surrendered (before they did) might well be caused by his emotions. That would not make "The Germans have surrendered" a specimen of emotional language. If you could find a man nowadays capable of believing, and saying, "The Russians have all been annihilated by magic," even this would not be emotional language, though his belief in magic might be a belief engendered by emotion.   5

All this is fairly plain sailing. We reach something harder in the things said by poets. For there the purpose of the utterance would be frustrated if no emotion were aroused. They do not merely, like the sentences cited above, arouse emotion in fact; it is their purpose — at any rate, part of their purpose — to do so. But we must be very careful here. Having observed that a poetical utterance in fact arouses emotion, and is intended to arouse emotion,   6

---

[1] *Seven Types of Ambiguity*, Ch. I.

and that if taken as a statement about reality — or even about the make-believe "realities" of a fictitious narrative — it would be nonsensical or at least false, can we conclude that it communicates nothing but emotion? I think not.

Nothing will convince me that "My soul is an enchanted boat"[2] is simply a better way — however much better — of doing what might be done by some exclamation like "Gee!" Asia has risen from the dark cave of Demogorgon. She is floating upwards. She is saluted as "Life of Life!" The reversed temporal process in II. 97–103 ("We have passed Age's icy caves" etc.), borrowed from Plato's *Politicus* (269^c sq.), marks the fact that at this moment the whole cycle is reversed and cosmos begins anew. She is undergoing apotheosis. What did it feel like? The poet says to us in effect "Think of going in a boat. But quite effortless" ("Like a sleeping swan" gliding with the current, he adds in the next line), "Like a boat without sail or oar; the motive power undiscoverable. Like a magic boat — you must have read or dreamed of such things — a boat drawn on, drawn swiftly on, irresistibly, smoothly, by enchantment." Exactly. I know now how it felt for Asia. The phrase has communicated emotion. But notice how. By addressing in the first instance my imagination. He makes me imagine a boat rushing over waves, which are also identified with sounds. After that he need do no more; my emotion will follow of itself. Poetry most often communicates emotions, not directly, but by creating imaginatively the grounds for those emotions. It therefore communicates something more than emotion; only by means of that something more does it communicate the emotion at all.

Burns compares his mistress to "a red, red rose"; Wordsworth his to "a violet by a mossy stone / Half hidden from the eye." These expressions do communicate to me the emotion each poet felt. But it seems to me that they do so solely by forcing me to imagine two (very different) women. I see the rose-like, overpowering, midsummer sweetness of the one; the reticent, elusive freshness, the beauty easily overlooked in the other. After that my emotions may be left to themselves. The poets have done their part.

This, which is eminently true of poetry, is true of all imaginative writing. One of the first things we have to say to a beginner who has brought us his MS. is, "Avoid all epithets which are merely emotional. It is no use *telling* us that something was 'mysterious' or 'loathsome' or 'awe-inspiring' or 'voluptuous.' Do you think your readers will believe you just because you say so? You must go quite a different way to work. By direct description, by metaphor and simile, by secretly evoking powerful associations, by offering the right stimuli to our nerves (in the right degree and the right order), and by the very beat and vowel-melody and length and brevity of your sentences, you must bring it about that we, we readers, not you, exclaim 'how mysterious!' or 'loathsome' or whatever it is. Let me taste for myself, and you'll have no need to *tell* me how I should react to the flavour."

7

8

9

---

[2] *Prometheus Unbound*, II, v, 72.

In Donne's couplet

10

> Your gown going off, such beautious state reveals
> As when from flowry meads th'hills shadow steales[3]

beautious is the only word of the whole seventeen which is doing no work.

There are exceptions to this principle. By very successful placing, a great [11] author may sometimes raise such words to poetic life. Wordsworth's lines are a specimen:

> Which, to the boundaries of space and time,
> Of melancholy space and doleful time,
> Superior — [4]

Here we have almost the reverse of the process I have been describing. The object (space and time) is in one way so familiar to our imaginations and in another so unimaginable — we have read so many tedious attempts to exalt or over-awe us with mere superlatives or even with simple arithmetic — that nothing can be made of it. This time, therefore, the poet withdraws the object (the ground for emotion) altogether and appeals directly to our emotions; and not to the quite obvious ones. Another exception is naturally to be found in drama or very dramatic lyric, where the poet — with discretion and a proper use of illusion — imitates the speech of people in some highly emotional situation — even, at need, their inarticulate cries. This in its purity, which purity a good poet never sustains for long, belongs to poetry not in so far as poetry is a special use of language but in so far as poety is *mimesis*. In themselves the "Ah! Ah!" or "Otototoi" or "Iou! Iou!" of characters in a Greek tragedy are not specimens of poetry any more than the "Bé, bé" of the lamb or the "Au! Au!" of the dog in Aristophanes.

In general, however, the poet's route to our emotions lies through our [12] imaginations.

We must also exclude from the category "emotional language" words [13] such as I have taken *supernatural* to be. The class of things which they refer to may be bound together chiefly by a common emotion; but the purpose of using the words is to assign something to that class, not merely to communicate the emotion which led to the classification.

Having thus narrowed the field, we can now make a new start. It will [14] be noticed that I have throughout used the word *emotional* rather than *emotive*. This is because I think the latter word applicable to only one aspect of emotional language. For an "emotive word" ought to mean one whose function is to arouse emotion. But surely we ought to distinguish utterances which arouse, from those which express, emotion? The first is directed towards producing some effect on a (real or imagined) hearer; the second discharges our own emotion, cleanses our stuffed bosom of some perilous stuff.

[3] *Elegy* xix, 13.
[4] *Prelude* vi, 134.

The distinction will seem straw-splitting if we have in mind the language [15] of love. For, as Samson says, "love seeks to have love," and it would be hard to say whether endearments serve more as expressions of love in the speaker or incitements to it in the beloved. But that tells us more about the nature of love than about the nature of language. One of my old headmasters once wisely said it was a pity that *amare* was the first Latin verb we all learn. He thought this led to an imperfect grasp of the difference between the active and the passive voice. It might be better to begin with *flagellare*. The difference between flogging and being flogged would come home to the business and bosoms of schoolboys far more effectively than that of loving and being loved. On the same principle, we can best see the distinction between the stimulant and the expressive function of emotional language in a quarrel; and best of all where the same word performs both. The man who calls me a low hound both expresses and (actually or intentionally) stimulates emotion. But not the same emotion. He expresses contempt; he stimulates, or hopes to stimulate, the almost opposite emotion of humiliation.

Again, in the language of complaint we often find the expressive without [16] the stimulant. When two people who have missed the last train stand on the silent platform saying "Damn" or "Bloody" or "Sickening," they neither intend nor need to stimulate each other's disappointment. They are just "getting it off their chests."

The vocabulary of endearment, complaint, and abuse, provides, I think, [17] almost the only specimens of words that are purely emotional, words from which all imaginative or conceptual content has vanished, so that they have no function at all but to express or stimulate emotion, or both. And an examination of them soon convinces us that in them we see language at its least linguistic. We have come to the frontier between language and inarticulate vocal sounds. And at that frontier we find a two-way traffic going on.

On the one hand we find inarticulate sounds becoming words with a [18] fixed spelling and a niche in the dictionary. Thus English *heigh-ho* and Latin *eheu* are clearly formalised imitations of the sigh; *ah*, of the gasp; *tut-tut*, of the tongue clicked against the hard palate. These are general. In particular situations the "verbification" of the inarticulate may occur *ad hoc*. A voluntary scream may become a cry for mercy. A voluntary groan, from a wounded man, uttered to attract the attention of the stretcher-bearers, may be the equivalent of a sentence ("There is a wounded man in this ditch").

But we also see the frontier being crossed in the opposite direction. In [19] the vocabulary of abuse and complaint we see things that once were words passing out of the realm of language (properly so called) and becoming the equivalents of inarticulate sounds or even of actions; of sighs, moans, whimperings, growls, or blows.

The "swear-words" — *damn* for complaint and *damn you* for abuse — [20] are a good example. Historically the whole Christian eschatology lies behind them. If no one had ever consigned his enemy to the eternal fires and believed that there were eternal fires to receive him, these ejaculations would never have existed. But inflation, the spontaneous hyperboles of ill temper, and the decay of religion, have long since emptied them of that lurid content. Those who have no belief in damnation — and some who have — now damn inanimate objects which would on any view be ineligible for it. The word is no longer an imprecation. It is hardly, in the full sense, a word at all when so used. Its popularity probably owes as much to its resounding phonetic virtues as to any, even fanciful, association with hell. It has ceased to be profane. It has also become very much less forceful. You may say the same of *sickening* in its popular, ejaculatory, use. There are alarms and disappointments which can actually produce nausea, or, at least, emotions which we feel to be somehow similar to it. But the man who says *sickening!* when he has missed the train is not thinking about that. The word is simply an alternative to *damn* or *bloody*. And of course far weaker than it would be if it still carried any suggestion of vomiting.

So with abusive terms. No one would now call his schoolfellow or next door neighbour a *swine* unless someone had once used this word to make a real comparison between his enemy and a pig. It is now a mere alternative to *beast* or *brute* or various popular unprintable words. They are all interchangeable. *Villain,* as we know, once really compared your enemy to a *villein*. Once, to call a man *cad* or *knave* assigned to him the status of a servant. And it did so because, earlier still, these words meant "boy" or "junior" (you address a slave as "boy" in Greek and a waiter as *garçon* in French).

Thus all these words have come down in the world. None of them started by being *merely* abusive, few of them by being abusive at all. They once stimulated emotion by suggesting an image. They made the enemy odious or contemptible by asserting he was like somebody or something we already disliked or looked down on. Their use was a sort of passionate parody of the syllogism: pigs (or servants or my juniors) are contemptible — John is like a pig (or servant or adolescent) — therefore John is contemptible. That was why they really hurt; because hurting was not the whole of what they did. They stimulated emotion because they also stimulated something else; imagination. They stimulated emotion in the particular case because they exploited emotions which already existed towards whole classes of things or persons. Now that they are nothing whatever but emotional stimulants, they are weak emotional stimulants. They make no particular accusation. They tell us nothing except that the speaker has lost his temper.

And even this they do not tell us linguistically, but symptomatically; as a red face, a loud voice, or a clenched fist, might do equally well. The fact of the other person's anger may hurt or frighten us; hurt us if we love him, or frighten us if he is larger and younger than ourselves and threatens violence. But his language as such has very little power to do the only thing it is intended to do. It would have been far more wounding to be called *swine* when the word still carried some whiff of the sty and some echo of a grunt;

far more wounding to be called a *villain* when this still conjured up an image of the unwashed, malodorous, ineducable, gross, belching, close-fisted, and surly boor. Now, who cares? Language meant solely to hurt hurts strangely little.

This can be seen clearly when we catch a word "just on the turn." *Bitch* 24 is one. Till recently — and still in the proper contexts — this accused a woman of one particular fault and appealed, with some success, to our contempt by calling up an image of the she-dog's comical and indecorous behaviour when she is in heat. But it is now increasingly used of any woman whom the speaker, for whatever reasons, is annoyed with — the female driver who is in front of him, or a female magistrate whom he thinks unjust. Clearly, the word is far more wounding in its narrower usage. If that usage is ever totally lost — as I think it will be — the word will sink to the level of *damn her*. Notice, too, how *cat* (of a woman) is still strong and useful because the image is still alive in it.

An important principle thus emerges. In general, emotional words, to 25 be effective, must not be solely emotional. What expresses or stimulates emotion directly, without the intervention of an image or concept, expresses or stimulates it feebly. And in particular, when words of abuse have hurting the enemy as their direct and only object, they do not hurt him much. In the field of language, however it may be in that of action, hatred cuts its own throat, and those who are too "willing to wound" become thereby impotent to strike. And all this is only another way of saying that as words become exclusively emotional they cease to be words and therefore of course cease to perform any strictly linguistic function. They operate as growls or barks or tears. "Exclusively" is an important adverb here. They die as words not because there is too much emotion in them but because there is too little — and finally nothing at all — of anything else.

In this there is not much to be lamented. If a mother with a baby, or 26 lovers in each other's arms, use language so emotional that it is really not language at all, I see no ground for shame or offence; and if men in an orgy of resentment, though (in the physical sense) they articulate, are really no more speaking — are saying no more — than a snarling animal, this is perhaps all for the best. The real corruption comes when men whose purpose in speaking is in fact purely emotional conceal this from others, and perhaps from themselves, by words that seem to be, but are not, charged with a conceptual content.

We have all heard *bolshevist, fascist, Jew,* and *capitalist,* used not to 27 describe but merely to insult. Rose Macaulay noticed a tendency to prefix "so called" to almost any adjective when it was used of those the speaker hated; the final absurdity being reached when people referred to the Germans as "these so-called Germans." *Bourgeois* and *middle class* often suffer the same fate.

A literary man of my acquaintance, on reading an unfavourable refer- 28 ence to his own works, called it *vulgar*. The charge brought against him was one that only highly educated people ever bring; the tone of the passage not otherwise offensive than by being unfavourable; the phrasing perfectly good English. If he had called it false, unintelligent, or malicious, I could have understood, though I might have disagreed. But why *vulgar?* Clearly, this word was selected solely because the speaker thought it was the one that the enemy, if he could hear it, would most dislike. It was the equivalent of an oath or a growl. But that was concealed from the speaker because "This is vulgar" sounds like a judgement.

When we write criticism we have to be continually on our guard against   29 this sort of thing. If we honestly believe a work to be very bad we cannot help hating it. The function of criticism, however, is "to get ourselves out of the way and let humanity decide"; not to discharge our hatred but to expose the grounds for it; not to vilify faults but to diagnose and exhibit them. Unfortunately to express our hatred and to revenge ourselves is easier and more agreeable. Hence there is a tendency to select our pejorative epithets with a view not to their accuracy but to their power of hurting. If writing which was intended to be comic has set our teeth on edge, how easily the adjectives *arch* or *facetious* trickle out of the pen! But if we do not know exactly what we mean by them, if we are not prepared to say how comic work which errs by *archness* and *facetiousness* differs from comic work which errs in any other way, it is to be feared that we are really using them not to inform the reader but to annoy the author — *arch* or *facetious* being among the most effective "smear-words" of our period. In the same way work which obviously aspires and claims to be mature, if the critic dislikes it, will be called *adolescent;* not because the critic has really seen that its faults are those of adolescence but because he has seen that adolescence is the last thing the author wishes or expects to be accused of.

The best protection against this is to remind ourselves again and again   30 what the proper function of pejorative words is. The ultimate, simplest and most abstract, is *bad* itself. The only good purpose for ever departing from that monosyllable when we condemn anything is to be more specific, to answer the question "Bad in what way?" Pejorative words are rightly used only when they do this. *Swine,* as a term of abuse is now a bad pejorative word, because it brings no one accusation rather than another against the person it vilifies; *coward* and *liar* are good ones because they charge a man with a particular fault — of which he might be proved guilty or innocent. As applied to literature, *dull, hackneyed, incoherent, monotonous, pornographic, cacophonous,* are good pejoratives; they tell people in what particular way we think a book faulty. *Adolescent* or *provincial* are not so good. For even when they are honestly used, to define, not merely to hurt, they really suggest a cause for the book's badness instead of describing the badness itself. We are saying in effect "He was led into his faults by being immature" or "by living in Lancashire." But would it not be more interesting to indicate the faults themselves and leave out our historical theory about their causes? If we find words like these — and *vulgar,* and others — indispensable to our criticism, if we find ourselves applying them to more and more different kinds of things, there is grave reason to suspect that — whether we know it or not — we are really using them not to diagnose but to hurt. If so, we are assisting in verbicide. For this is the downward path which leads to the graveyard of murdered words. First they are purely descriptive; *adolescent* tells us a man's age, *villain,* his status. Then they are specifically pejorative; *adolescent* tells us that a man's work displays "mawkishness and all the thousand bitters" confessed by Keats, and *villain* tells that a man has a churl's mind and manners. Then they become *mere* pejoratives, useless synonyms for *bad,* as *villain* did and as *adolescent* may do if we aren't careful. Finally they become terms of abuse and cease to be language in the full sense at all.

SUBJECT QUESTIONS

1. In defining "emotional" language, Lewis has limited the term almost out of existence. Is his procedure convincing, or has he created a *reductio ad absurdum* of his own argument?
2. What distinction does Lewis make between "emotive" and "emotional"? Does he not dismiss as "emotive" most of what we usually think of as emotional language? Is he arranging meanings to suit his own purposes?
3. "Nor, in my opinion, are value-judgements ('This is good,' 'this is bad') emotional language." "Good" and "bad" are fairly neutral words; if you substituted stronger ones, would you get emotional language?
4. How, according to Lewis, does a poet go about calling up emotions in his readers, if not with "emotional" language?
5. On what grounds does Lewis argue that abusive words cease to be language at all? Are grunts and groans language?

STRUCTURE QUESTIONS

1. The two opening paragraphs on the limitations of language are not properly a part of the definition of emotional language; do they serve any useful function in the essay?
2. Lewis arrives at his definition mainly by eliminating what is *not* emotional language. Given the narrow limits of his definition, was this the best way for him to proceed?
3. How effectively does Lewis use specific examples to clarify his definition? Is the writing too abstract in between the examples?

Sonnet 76, "Why Is My Verse So Barren of New Pride?"

William Shakespeare

William Shakespeare (1564–1616) joined a traveling acting company when he was about 23, and soon began writing plays to help increase the company's receipts. After six years, his reputation was sufficient for him to publish two long poems dedicated to the youthful Earl of Southampton. Although his sonnets, like his plays, were not intended or prepared for publication, Shakespeare did address most of them to the young earl. They circulated in manuscript form among the earl's friends for many years, until they were finally published in 1609. In Sonnet 76, Shakespeare offers a concise analysis (and illustration) of his own style — a style very different from the flamboyant overstatement of most sonnet writers in his time.

Why is my verse so barren of new pride?
So far from variation or quick change?
Why with the time do I not glance aside
To new-found methods and to compounds strange?
Why write I still all one, ever the same,   5
And keep invention in a noted weed,°
That every word doth almost tell my name,
Showing their birth and where they did proceed?
O know, sweet love, I always write of you,
And you and love are still my argument;   10
So all my best is dressing old words new,
Spending again what is already spent:
For as the sun is daily new and old,
So is my love still telling what is told.

SUBJECT QUESTIONS

1. Does Shakespeare seem to be blaming himself for not following new-fangled styles in poetry writing? Does he give any indication that he does not approve of these new styles?
2. What is his defense of his own style?
3. If his subject matter is always the same, does it follow that his style must also remain the same? Is there a flaw in Shakespeare's argument here?

° *in a noted weed:* in familiar clothing.

STRUCTURE QUESTIONS

1. Considering that the poem is nearly 400 years old, is there any expression other than "noted weed" that would be unfamiliar to a modern reader? Has Shakespeare sufficiently illustrated the simplicity of his own style?
2. Are there any words which might be called "pretentious," bigger than they need be to make the point? What are the four words of more than two syllables?
3. Despite the apparent plainness of the style, Shakespeare has used several implied and direct comparisons (metaphor and simile). Identify several of these; do they seem intended primarily for decoration, or to further the meaning?
4. What is Shakespeare's principal method of defining his style? Do you think comparison and contrast might have worked better?
5. Despite the poem's brevity, Shakespeare repeats himself several times; does this repetition detract from the force of the poem? Does it give any impression about the kind of man who is writing the poem?

7

FREEDOM AND RESPONSIBILITY

Argument

Argument as an essay form has little in common with the heated discussion which usually terminates a college bull session: it is not a technique for "outshouting" one's opponent in writing. By a devious route through Rome and Medieval Europe, its ancestor was the deliberative oration of ancient Athens. The deliberative oration, as taught by Aristotle and others, was a set form for speeches to be delivered before the Athenian Senate on matters of public policy and proposed legislation. Its chief feature was its carefully controlled, logical approach: it was intended to convince the senators of the reasonableness of the speaker's position – not, in our common use of the term "argument," to engage in a verbal free-for-all. Although the speaker might feel strongly about his subject, his aim was to stimulate a spirit of free and serious inquiry, not to overwhelm with rhetoric or to provoke anger.

This same honest, objective, and logical approach characterizes the argument as a literary form today. Although a week or two spent studying argument in a composition course is hardly a substitute for a class in logic, you can learn much by studying the various arguments presented in this section and by writing an argument yourself. You will want to watch for careless logic both in the essays and in your own thinking. You should recognize, for instance, that an opinion, no matter how forcefully presented, is still opinion, not fact. In your own argument you should support your opinions with typical and relevant evidence – facts, observations, and reasons. Rather than slinging mud at possible opponents of your

323

beliefs, you should remember that the purpose of argument is to invite free discussion in the hope of arriving at a workable solution to the problem under consideration. If the writer of an argument firmly believes that his solution is "right," he should by all means argue it forcefully; but he can still have the open-minded attitude which allows him to change his position in the light of new evidence. His job is to search for truth, not obscure it with dogmatism.

Although the original Greek deliberative oration contained some frosting with which we can dispense, a good written argument will contain the four basic ingredients of the old recipe. First, there should be a brief but penetrating introduction to, or analysis of, the problem which needs a solution. This analysis ought to be as objective and honest as the writer can make it; if he starts with a slanted interpretation, the aims of argument are defeated at the outset.

The second ingredient is a clear, concise statement of the author's proposed solution. Normally, this immediately follows the analysis of the problem, and it is sometimes repeated in summary at the end of the argument. Or the writer may prefer to save it for the end, as a logical conclusion to his arguments. If possible it should be concentrated into a sentence or two, so that the reader can readily grasp it in its entirety.

The other parts of a good argument are a refutation of an opponent's arguments, if there are any, and a confirmation of the writer's own position. The refutation may be placed before or after the confirmation, or the two may be intermixed. (The writer should remember, however, to save his strongest point for the last, whether it be proof or disproof.) In refuting an opponent's arguments, one ought to recognize that seldom is one side completely right and the other completely wrong; usually, taking sides should be a matter of weighing merits and demerits, and then deciding which side has more advantages. If the writer has honestly done this he need have no fear of admitting a few merits of the other side or the disadvantages of his own position. In no case should he resort to mere name-calling instead of disproof. ("Of course we don't want a government-operated medical plan — that's socialism!" or "As any fool can plainly see. . . .")

Because a good argument should be mainly positive, the writer will want to concentrate most heavily on his proof. He should be prepared to include as much evidence as his experience and the word limit of his paper will allow. The more specific the evidence, of course, the better. There are two major traps to watch for: insufficient evidence and atypical evidence. As one swallow doesn't make a summer, so one example, no matter how detailed, doesn't justify a generalization. ("Polio vaccine is worthless. I heard of a child who contracted polio after having three shots.") Although you may wish to concentrate on one piece of evidence, you ought at least to mention others briefly to show that more is available. Second, there is always the danger of selecting from a number of available facts certain ones which will only appear to prove the writer's point. Anyone who has watched political debates on television has probably noticed how both opponents cite numerous statistics to "prove" that they are right. Because the purpose of the argument as an essay form is not to win elections at all costs but to deal honestly with a problem, you will want to avoid either slanting your facts or selecting evidence which does not indicate the general trend of *all* the evidence. This is not always easy to do, but if the writer strives for integrity he will be much less likely to go wrong. Although he may not solve all the world's problems he will at least learn something about logical analysis and the objective search for truth.

Power

John Cogley

John Cogley has been contributing editor and religion editor for several national journals, including Commonweal. He has edited two collections of essays on religion, Religion in America (1958) and Natural Law and Modern Society (1963). He is currently editor of Center Magazine, the publication of the Center for the Study of Democratic Institutions. During 1971, the chief concern of Center Magazine was the subject of power — who has it, who ought to have it, the relationship of the individual to the state. In the following article, the editor inserted his own views on the subject. Despite its brevity, "Power" is a good example of the form for classic argument.

"All power to the people!" is a dangerous slogan. It is particularly dangerous   1
for the very persons who are most likely to be heard shouting it on the streets, for usually they represent unpopular minorities. If "the people" were taken in any numerical sense, they would have the most to lose from granting the fulness of power to the majority.

Even if "the people" means only the victims of injustice, there is no   2
indication they would rally in any significant number around the revolutionary banners. It is extremely doubtful that the black community en masse would join the revolutionaries, nor would the majority of students, and the so-called working class would be the last to fall in line. "All power" in any of these hands would be employed to sustain the very system the sloganeers despise, though certain reforms might be expected, different ones from different groups.

Just who are "the people"? If the word is used as it is in the basic   3
documents of the United States ("We the people . . ."), their power has already been claimed and is exercised through law. Not only is it exercised through law, it is modified and controlled by law.

"We the people," eschewing "all power," long ago bound ourselves by   4
solemn compact to tolerate dissent from the reigning opinion, for example; we bound ourselves to provide a fair trial for our enemies; we bound ourselves to accept the decisions of the majority after the votes were counted; we set up a number of safeguards to protect the individual against any government that rules in our name. We turned down "all power" for ourselves because we knew how easily it could be abused.

Reprinted with permission from the January/February, 1971, issue of *The Center Magazine*, a publication of the Center for the Study of Democratic Institutions, Santa Barbara, California.

At a time when "all power to the people!" has become a mindless slogan it may be a good idea to remind ourselves that no one, even the people, should have a claim on the plenitude of power. We are all aware of what omnipotent leaders have done; we are all familiar with the evils wrought by all-powerful elites. Totally empowering the people, supposing one could locate them, would be just as dangerous and perhaps even more so, since though there may be such things as benevolent dictators no one yet has ever discovered a benevolent mob — and a powerful populace uncontrolled by law is all too quickly turned into a mob.

Reinhold Niebuhr's most famous dictum is that "Man's capacity for justice makes democracy possible; but man's inclination to injustice makes democracy necessary." The statement incorporates both political and philosophical wisdom. These days one thinks of it again every time the demand for "all power to the people" rings in the air.

We know enough about men and societies to recognize the error in the slogan. We know, for example, that societies which have overemphasized human weakness have despaired of the ordinary citizen's capacity for self-government; we also know that those which have exaggerated human virtues have failed because they attributed to the "people" a mystical character, an innate nobility, and almost divine infallibility that the people do not have, no matter who is included in the phrase. In both cases the results have been tyrannical.

In the first instance, the tyranny was usually based on the notion that some few men — a hereditary sovereign, a chosen leader, a party, a race, a class, or a caste — have been ordained to rule over others. In the second, it was based on the idea that he who took it upon himself to speak for the mystic "people" had absolute power over the lonely individuals who stood out against popular opinion. We have learned from experience to beware of anyone who purports to be speaking for "the people" or who demands power in their name. In the first place, the people have not assigned any one or any group to speak for them. In the second, a grab for power, no matter how piously worded, remains just that, a grab for power.

All power, then, to no one.

SUBJECT QUESTIONS

1. How might advocates of the slogan "All power to the people" answer Cogley's objection that "no one yet has ever discovered a benevolent mob"?

2. Why, according to Cogley, is power for the people "particularly dangerous" to the very people who are demanding it?

3. What objection might there be to the argument that "we the people" "long ago bound ourselves by solemn compact"? Does one generation have a right to "bind" the next to anything — even freedom?

4. Why does Cogley quote Niebuhr in paragraph 6? Does he mean to imply that those who want "all power to the people" do not want democracy? What are the implications of Niebuhr's statement?

5. Advocates of "power to the people" argue (rightly, if public opinion polls are to be trusted) that the government does not always act according to the wishes of the majority — witness the "unpopular" war in Vietnam. *Should* an elected representative always do what the majority wants? If the government were abolished, how would the people execute their power?

6. Should a minority be free to ignore the will of the majority? What kind of system best guarantees the rights of minorities?

STRUCTURE QUESTIONS

1. In what order has Cogley placed the four traditional parts of argument? (See Introduction.)

2. In his final argument (paragraph 8), Cogley's supporting evidence is simply that "we have learned from experience"; should he have cited some specific examples, or do examples come readily to mind? (If so, there is little need for Cogley to waste time on examples.)

3. Does Cogley present his argument in the spirit of an open search for truth? (It is certainly allowable to dislike what one is arguing against, so long as that dislike is based on reason rather than prejudice.) Do you find any instances of "loaded" language?

4. To what group of people do you think this argument is addressed — revolutionaries, "the people," those who already dislike revolutionaries, those who are likely to be taken in by a phrase which sounds as equitable as "all power to the people"?

The Limits
of Law and Order

Robert M. Hutchins

Robert M. Hutchins (born in 1899) began his distinguished career as a lecturer at Yale Law School. He was later president, then chancellor, of the University of Chicago (1929–1951), where he fostered many radical educational innovations — guaranteeing that every graduate had a humanistic education in the Great Books, for instance, and granting advanced placement — ideas which have since become standard at most universities. Hutchins has been chairman of Encyclopaedia Britannica *since 1943, and presently is chairman of the Center for the Study of Democratic Institutions in Santa Barbara, California, where he resides. Hutchins has been awarded at least a dozen honorary degrees, and has published many books on experiments in university education and education in a democratic society. "The Limits of Law and Order" first appeared in* Center Magazine *(1971).*

During the campaign of 1968 Mr. Nixon told the country the big issue was 1
Law and Order. Though the figures, such as they are, were showing no important increase in serious crimes, Mr. Nixon thought it his duty to warn us that our lives and property were in the gravest danger. He strongly hinted that the principal reasons for this alarming condition were the weakness of the Attorney General, Ramsey Clark, and the leniency of the courts.

We now have a new Attorney General, who talks very tough, and we 2
are on the way to a new Supreme Court. The present Court has shown surprising liberality to some poor people in some respects. It has held Connecticut's fees in divorce cases unconstitutional for those who cannot pay them. It has invalidated laws requiring indigents to go to jail if they cannot pay their fines. This last decision suggests that the whole system of money bail is in contravention of due process and equal protection. If a poor man cannot be jailed after conviction because he is poor, how can he be held for that reason when he has not been tried and is presumed innocent?

Otherwise the new justices have confirmed Mr. Nixon's expectations. 3
They have been lax about the confrontation required by the Sixth Amendment, and they have sanctioned the use, for the purpose of impeaching the credibility of the defendant, of statements obtained from him in violation of the *Miranda* rules.[1]

Reprinted with permission from the May/June, 1971, issue of *The Center Magazine,* a publication of the Center for the Study of Democratic Institutions, Santa Barbara, California.
[1] The *Miranda* rules pertain to the rights of a suspect to remain silent and to have a lawyer present when being interrogated. See US Supreme Court decision, *Miranda v. Arizona* (384 US 436).

It is unlikely that Mr. Mitchell's speeches and press releases or recent   4
Court decisions will have much effect on Law and Order. For example, the
principal result of admitting statements obtained in violation of the *Miranda*
rules for purposes of impeachment will be to keep defendants off the stand.
If they take it, they may find remarks inadmissible in chief used to attack
their veracity. No matter what the instructions are, the jury is unlikely to
make the distinction between guilt and falsehood.

But Mr. Nixon did not rely on changes in the Department of Justice   5
and the courts alone. He also sponsored a large number of bills dealing with
crime, often referred to as his Law and Order "package." These bills have
now become law. Apart from major improvements in the judicial system of
the District of Columbia, these laws are intended to reduce crime by cracking
down harder, more frequently, and in more disagreeable ways on persons
suspected of it. They are designed to shift the balance in favor of the government and against the accused before and during prosecution and after conviction. In view of the tremendous imbalance that has always existed in favor
of the government against the accused, it seems likely that whatever reduction
in crime is brought about by this legislation will be purchased at the cost
of justice.

One thing is fairly certain and that is that any reduction in crime result-   6
ing from this legislation will be negligible. The reduction in civil liberties is
clear. "No-knock," preventive detention, wiretapping, etc., all restrict the
freedom of the citizen. If the constitutionality of these restrictions is upheld,
but crime is not reduced, the argument will be that these restrictions did not
go far enough and that we need additional restrictions on top of them. The
outcome of this process is likely to be unpleasant.

And what of the disillusionment that must ensue if the Administration's   7
program, which has been presented as a panacea, has little or no effect on
crime? Mr. Nixon must be hoping that voters have in fact the short memories
often attributed to them.

The most persuasive argument against the Administration's program is   8
that it is diversionary. It turns attention away from the real problems of crime
and criminal justice and leads citizens to suppose that a little tinkering here
and there involving some slight risk to their civil liberties, or rather to the
civil liberties of the poor and the black, will insure their safety. This means
that the intellectual and financial effort we must make if we are really going
to reduce crime will be still further postponed.

At the Center's Conference on Crime Control Legislation James V.   9
Bennett, former director of the United States Bureau of Prisons, estimated
the cost of modernizing the penal institutions of the country at eighteen billion
dollars. Nobody thought this figure was too high. Many of those present
thought it was too low. Whatever the correct figure is, it is a fraction of what
it would take to get a modern penal system, for Mr. Bennett was talking only
about modernizing buildings. The cost of a well-trained staff in numbers and

quality adequate to administer an enlightened program running from conviction through probation and parole would be many billions. More important, it would demand much intelligence, courage, and patience.

The same is true of every department of criminal justice. We need more and better judges, more and better prosecutors, more and better public defenders, more and better police, more and better probation officers and parole boards, and all these groups need more and better facilities. Of course, what they need most of all is more and better ideas.

The demand for more personnel and more facilities would diminish if the President, instead of ranting, would take up the one good idea he has in this field and educate the country to understand and accept it. This is the idea of "decriminalization," which became a sort of central theme of the conference at the Center and which the President referred to in a speech on March 11. As far as I can recall, it received unanimous support. Even Carl Rauh, of the Department of Justice, endorsed it. The reservations expressed about it had to do with details.

On the main point there was general agreement, and that was that offenses that did not damage the person or property of others, where there was no victim and no complainant, should as far as possible be taken out of the system of criminal justice.

This would remove from the scope of the criminal law people for whom that law can do nothing and who are now the principal burden upon it. Narcotics addicts and alcoholics cannot be helped by terms in the penitentiary. What they need is medical treatment. It was said at the Center's conference that sixty percent at least of all serious crime is drug-related and that alcoholics account for more than fifty percent of the arrests in the country. Although all statistics on crime are unreliable, these figures suggest what would happen if narcotics addicts and alcoholics were regarded as patients rather than criminals.

Some eight to ten million people in this country are said to be using marijuana in open violation of the law. In some states an enormous part of the apparatus of criminal justice is dedicated to detecting and convicting these people and to getting them locked up. If no convincing evidence can be offered that marijuana is more harmful than alcohol or tobacco, the possession and use of marijuana should be legalized. It should follow that the sale of marijuana would be legal as well.

The criminal law cannot stop the traffic in "hard" drugs. As Troy Duster pointed out at the Center's conference, the profits in the business are so large that dealers caught and jailed are immediately replaced. If criminal penalties were removed and the whole business were regulated or owned by government, if something like the British system were introduced, the resources now wasted in tracking down those involved in the drug business could be devoted to the invention of practical solutions to the problem.

Some form of gambling is legal everywhere. Some states have gone so far as to set up state owned gambling institutions. If all restrictions on gambling were removed, the strain it places on the system of criminal justice would be relieved. The hazards to civil liberties would be reduced. The only argument advanced for "no-knock" and wiretapping where "national security" is not involved is that in drug and gambling cases these procedures are necessary to obtain and preserve evidence. If there were no drug or gambling cases nobody would have the face to advocate these procedures.

Drugs turn out to be, too, an important argument for preventive detention: the addict out on bail must engage in crime in order to support his habit. Taking addicts out of the criminal system would minimize the demand to lock up people in order to protect the public from them.   17

Every reader can make his own list of those acts, now called criminal, which should be considered candidates for "decriminalization." Many readers may differ with some of the examples I have used. This is not material. The point is that the idea should be accepted and as many acts covered by it as possible as soon as possible.   18

Where there is a social problem with which the system of criminal justice is now vainly trying to deal, we do not solve the problem by removing it from the scope of the criminal law. We merely abandon a wasteful and futile attempt to cope with it. The problem remains. Attempts to take mentally ill persons out of the reach of the criminal law have been a dubious advantage to them. Most students of the subject agree that a mentally ill defendant in a criminal case is better off, in those jurisdictions which have civil commitment, if his illness is not referred to during his trial. If he is sent to the penitentiary, he has at least some idea when he will get out. If he is civilly committed he may be detained for years and in the meantime get little more or better treatment than he would have in prison.   19

Civil commitment was thought to be a great step forward when it was introduced. The reason that a noble, humanitarian effort has failed to produce better results is the same as that which must be given for the failure of the system of criminal justice. We as a people do not care to put the necessary intellectual and financial resources into the job. We are therefore an easy prey for snake-oil salesmen who tell us that if we will only stop "coddling criminals" we shall be secure.   20

Newsweek quotes Joe Olgiati, who runs a work-training program for probationers in New York, as saying, "If you were to eliminate all cops, judges, parole officers, and courts, it would have a highly negligible effect on crime in the streets. In fact, it might even be better. You wouldn't just be trying to repair what we have now."   21

The thought does cross one's mind as one listens to the horrors recited in a conference on crime control that it might be better if no criminal were ever caught. Everybody who is involved with the criminal law seems to be worse because of his contact with it. For example, the fifty-two percent of   22 the jail population who are being detained pending trial must be more dangerous to society as a result of this experience than they were before.

Yet we cannot dispense with the criminal law. Although we know very little about deterrence, it seems probable that the prospect of punishment does dissuade some people from the commission of some crimes. We should try to make the system of criminal justice work as swiftly, surely, and fairly as we can. As Ramsey Clark said at the Center's conference, safety and freedom are not incompatible; the thing to do is to enlarge both. Law and Order, in the modern interpretation of this slogan, will give us neither. 23

SUBJECT QUESTIONS

1. Why does Hutchins think the "law and order package" enacted under President Nixon will have little effect on law and order? Might there be political reasons for enacting such legislation even though it was known in advance that crime would not be reduced?
2. What adverse effects does Hutchins suggest will result from the legislation?
3. What advantages does Hutchins see in "decriminalization"? Does he give due recognition to the fact that ceasing to call an activity criminal does not eliminate that activity?
4. Would you agree that the examples cited are likely areas for decriminalization? Can you suggest others?
5. Do you agree with the statement by Joe Olgiati in paragraph 21? Does Hutchins? Is it possible that the system of law enforcement could cause more crime than it prevents?

STRUCTURE QUESTIONS

1. What kind of evidence does Hutchins provide to refute Nixon's solution to "crime in the streets"? How does he defend his own solution of decriminalization?
2. Hutchins several times cites outside authorities — James Bennett and Troy Duster, for instance — to support his position. Appeals to authority can be one form of avoiding logic (Vida Blue uses this brand of after-shave lotion). Is Hutchins's usage pertinent and reasonable?
3. Do you find any evidence of name-calling or ridicule as a way of refuting the opposition?
4. Does Hutchins's conclusion in the final paragraph follow logically from his argument? Should he have done more with "swiftness" of criminal justice?
5. Would you say that Hutchins reveals an open or a closed mind in his search for solutions to crime in the streets? What influence does his attitude have on the effectiveness of the argument?

Letter from Delano

César Chavez

César Chavez, born into a migrant farmworker's family, first went to work in the California grape fields when he was ten. After attending more than thirty different schools, he was finally forced to quit in the eighth grade to help support his family. In 1965, he attempted to organize a union for grape pickers in California; after five years of strikes and a national consumers' boycott, the union finally gained recognition. Chavez has since gone on to help organize other agricultural workers. Much is yet to be done: the average yearly earning of a migrant worker is still under $2,000, and some 800,000 children under 16 work in the fields without adequate legal protection.

The following argument was printed as an open letter on Good Friday, 1969, at the height of the struggle at Delano. It shows the strong influence on Chavez of Mahatma Gandhi's principle of nonviolent resistance. The letter is included here not so much because of its topical relevance as because it shows that in good argument strong feelings can be controlled without being disguised.

E. L. Barr, Jr., President   Good Friday 1969.
California Grape and Tree Fruit League
717 Market St.
San Francisco, California

Dear Mr. Barr:

I am sad to hear about your accusations in the press that our union movement and table grape boycott have been successful because we have used violence and terror tactics. If what you say is true, I have been a failure and should withdraw from the struggle; but you are left with the awesome moral responsibility, before God and man, to come forward with whatever information you have so that corrective action can begin at once. If for any reason you fail to come forth to substantiate your charges, then you must be held responsible for committing violence against us, albeit violence of the tongue. I am convinced that you as a human being did not mean what you said but rather acted hastily under pressure from the public relations firm that has been hired to try to counteract the tremendous moral force of our movement. How many times we ourselves have felt the need to lash out in anger and bitterness.

Today on Good Friday 1969 we remember the life and the sacrifice of Martin Luther King, Jr., who gave himself totally to the nonviolent struggle for peace and justice. In his "Letter from Birmingham Jail" Dr. King describes better than I could our hopes for the strike and boycott: "Injustice must be exposed, with all the tension its exposure creates, to the light of human conscience and the air of national opinion before it can be cured." For our part I admit that we have seized upon every tactic and strategy consistent with the morality of our cause to expose that injustice and thus to heighten the sensitivity of the American conscience so that farm workers will have without bloodshed their own union and the dignity of bargaining with their agribusiness employers. By lying about the nature of our movement, Mr. Barr, you are working against nonviolent social change. Unwittingly perhaps, you may unleash that other force which our union by discipline and deed, censure and education has sought to avoid, that panacean shortcut: that senseless violence which honors no color, class or neighborhood.

You must understand — I must make you understand — that our membership and the hopes and aspirations of the hundreds of thousands of the poor and dispossessed that have been raised on our account are, above all, human beings, no better and no worse than any other cross-section of human society; we are not saints because we are poor, but by the same measure neither are we immoral. We are men and women who have suffered and endured much, and not only because of our abject poverty but because we have been kept poor. The colors of our skins, the languages of our cultural and native origins, the lack of formal education, the exclusion from the democratic process, the numbers of our slain in recent wars — all these burdens generation after generation have sought to demoralize us, to break our human spirit. But God knows that we are not beasts of burden, agricultural implements or rented slaves; we are men. And mark this well, Mr. Barr, we are men locked in a death struggle against man's inhumanity to man in the industry that you represent. And this struggle itself gives meaning to our life and ennobles our dying.

As your industry has experienced, our strikers here in Delano and those who represent us throughout the world are well trained for this struggle. They have been under the gun, they have been kicked and beaten and herded by dogs, they have been cursed and ridiculed, they have been stripped and chained and jailed, they have been sprayed with the poisons used in vineyards; but they been taught not to lie down and die nor to flee in shame, but to resist with every ounce of human endurance and spirit. To resist not with retaliation in kind but to overcome with love and compassion, with ingenuity and creativity, with hard work and longer hours, with stamina and patient tenacity, with truth and public appeal, with friends and allies, with mobility and discipline, with politics and law, and with prayer and fasting. They were not trained in a month or even a year; after all, this new harvest season will mark our fourth full year of strike and even now we continue to plan and prepare for the years to come. Time accomplishes for the poor what money does for the rich.

This is not to pretend that we have everywhere been successful enough or that we have not made mistakes. And while we do not belittle or underestimate our adversaries — for they are the rich and the powerful and they possess the land — we are not afraid nor do we cringe from the confrontation. We welcome it! We have planned for it. We know that our cause is just, that history is a story of social revolution, and that the poor shall inherit the land.

Once again, I appeal to you as the representative of your industry and as a man. I ask you to recognize and bargain with our union before the economic pressure of the boycott and strike takes an irrevocable toll; but if not, I ask you to at least sit down with us to discuss the safeguards necessary to keep our historical struggle free of violence. I make this appeal because as one of the leaders of our nonviolent movement, I know and accept my responsibility for preventing, if possible, the destruction of human life and property. For these reasons and knowing of Gandhi's admonition that fasting is the last resort in place of the sword, during a most critical time in our movement last February 1968 I undertook a 25-day fast. I repeat to you the principle enunciated to the membership at the start of the fast: if to build our union required the deliberate taking of life, either the life of a grower or his child, or the life of a farm worker or his child, then I choose not to see the union built.

Mr. Barr, let me be painfully honest with you. You must understand these things. We advocate militant nonviolence as our means for social revolution and to achieve justice for our people, but we are not blind or deaf to the desperate and moody winds of human frustration, impatience and rage that blow among us. Gandhi himself admitted that if his only choice were cowardice or violence, he would choose violence. Men are not angels, and time and tide wait for no man. Precisely because of these powerful human emotions, we have tried to involve masses of people in their own struggle. Participation and self-determination remain the best experience of freedom, and free men instinctively prefer democratic change and even protect the rights guaranteed to seek it. Only the enslaved in despair have need of violent overthrow.

This letter does not express all that is in my heart, Mr. Barr. But if it says nothing else it says that we do not hate you or rejoice to see your industry destroyed; we hate the agribusiness system that seeks to keep us enslaved, and we shall overcome and change it not by retaliation or bloodshed but by a determined nonviolent struggle carried on by those masses of farm workers who intend to be free and human.

Sincerely yours,
CÉSAR E. CHAVEZ

United Farm Workers Organizing
Committee, A.F.L.-C.I.O.
Delano, California.

SUBJECT QUESTIONS

1. If this letter were intended only for grape growers, Mr. Chavez would have had no need to publish it in *The Christian Century*. What does he wish to accomplish by this open publication? To whom is the letter really addressed?
2. Would you say that his chief concern is to discredit the growers, to defend the workers' tactics, or to explain how workers feel about the strike?
3. Does anything in the letter prevent a possible charge that Mr. Chavez is really threatening violence if the growers refuse to negotiate peacefully?
4. The request (paragraph 6) that the growers sit down with the union to discuss ways of keeping the struggle free of violence seems fair and reasonable; why might the growers refuse to comply with this request, even if they did not want violence?

STRUCTURE QUESTIONS

1. The letter contains several old sayings and familiar quotations; identify some of them. Do they add to the writing's effectiveness or make it seem trite?
2. What is the "problem" that gives rise to this argument? Does Chavez offer a solution to the problem?
3. What refutation does Chavez offer to the opposing position? Are his tactics here fair and reasonable?
4. Does Chavez manage to keep the tone dispassionate? Do you think he maintains an open mind about solutions to the problem?
5. Conscious parallel construction in modern prose sometimes seems affected. Examine the parallel structure in paragraph 4. Is it pretentious or overdone? Is it effective?
6. At the beginning of paragraph 5, Chavez concedes certain setbacks and defeats; does this concession weaken the force of his argument?

Letter to the Fourth Congress
of Soviet Writers

Aleksandr Solzhenitsyn

Aleksandr Solzhenitsyn (b. 1918), novelist, poet, playwright, and short story writer, was a military hero during World War II, but was imprisoned in 1945 for criticizing Stalin in a letter to a friend. After eleven years he was released from concentration camp; assuming that the "thaw" following Stalin's death allowed him to be critical of the Russian establishment, he began work on a novel based on his experiences in concentration camp. One Day in the Life of Ivan Denisovitch *(1962) brought him worldwide acclaim and the distrust of Soviet authorities. Two later novels,* The First Circle *and* Cancer Ward, *were smuggled out of Russia and published abroad, but have still not been published in the Soviet Union. Most of his poems, plays, and short stories have also not been published.*

In 1967, Solzhenitsyn wrote the following "open" letter to the Soviet Writers' Congress, but he received no help from them. In 1969, he was thrown out of the writers' union and his name deleted from the Soviet version of Who's Who. *When he won the Nobel Prize for Literature in 1970, he did not dare go to Stockholm to receive the award. Finally, despairing of having his works published in his native land, he asked for permission to leave Russia. After much publicity and wrangling, Solzhenitsyn was escorted out of the country in 1974; shortly afterward, his family was allowed to join him.*

Since I am unable to speak from the platform, I would ask the congress to consider the following questions: 1

(1) The oppression, insupportable in the long run, to which our literature 2 has for decades and decades been subjected, on the part of the censorship, and which the Writers' Union can no longer tolerate.

The censorship, for which there is no provision in the Constitution and 3 which is therefore illegal, the censorship which never passes under its own name, has imposed its yoke on literature under the obscure name of "Glavlit." It gives to literary illiterates the possibility of taking arbitrary measures against writers. The censorship, this survival of the Middle Ages, has managed, like a kind of Methuselah, to live almost into the twenty-first century. In its refuge, it tries to assume the attributes of timelessness and to sort out the good books from the bad.

There is no suggestion, and no recognition of the right of our writers 4 to state publicly their opinions about the moral life of men and of society,

This letter is reproduced from *Survey*, no. 64 (July 1967), published by Oxford University Press.

to elucidate in their own way the social problems or the historical experiences which have so profoundly affected our country. Works which could have expressed the thoughts matured among the people, which might in time have exercised a valuable influence in the spiritual domain or on the evolution of the social conscience, are prohibited or distorted by the censorship as a result of calculations which, from the point of view of the people, are pettifogging, egotistic, and shortsighted.

Excellent manuscripts by young authors, still completely unknown, are today rejected by editors on the sole ground that they "will not pass" the censor. Many members of the Union, and even delegates to this congress, know how they themselves have had to bow to the pressures of the censorship, to capitulate on matters concerning the structure and orientation of their works. They have rewritten chapters, pages, paragraphs, phrases; they have sweetened them only because they wanted to have them published; and in so doing they have damaged them irreparably. If we bear in mind the special character of literary works, it is obvious that these mutilations are pernicious for works of talent, but quite imperceptible in others. What is best in our literature is mutilated when it appears.

At the same time the labels used by the censorship ("ideologically pernicious," "incorrect") are very ephemeral. They are changed and discarded before our eyes. Even Dostoevsky, the pride of world literature, could not at one time be published in our country (even today he is not published in full). He was excluded from educational curricula, he was made inaccessible to the reader, he was slandered. For how many years was Esenin considered a "counter-revolutionary" (and were not people imprisoned for possessing his books)? Was not Mayakovsky branded an "anarchist," a "political hooligan"? For decades the immortal poems of Akhmatova were considered to be "anti-Soviet." The first modest publication of the dazzling poetry of Tsvetaeva, which appeared about ten years ago, was declared a "crude political error." It was only after a delay of twenty or thirty years that we have been given the works of Bunin, Bulgakov, Platonov, Mandelshtam, Voloshin, Gumilev, Klyuev. "Recognition" of Zamyatin and Remizov could not be avoided. This is the decisive moment: after the death of an inconvenient writer, he is sooner or later given back to us "with the explanation of his errors." For a long time Pasternak's name could not be spoken aloud. Now he is dead: now his books are published and his poems are even quoted on ceremonial occasions.

Truly they bear witness to the truth of Pushkin's words: *"they are capable of loving only the dead."*

But the late publication or the "acceptance" of a name does not compensate at all for the social and artistic losses suffered by our people because of these monstrous delays, this stifling of the artistic conscience (in particular, there were the writers of the twenties, Pilnyak, Platonov, Mandelshtam, who at a very early stage denounced the birth of the personality cult and the characteristic traits of Stalin, but they were annihilated, they were stifled, instead of being listened to). Literature cannot develop between the categories "permitted" and "not permitted," you can write about this, you can't write about that. Literature which does not breathe the same air as contemporary society, which cannot communicate to it its pains and fears, which cannot give warning in time against moral and social dangers, does not deserve the name of literature. It deserves only the name of literary make-up. Such a literature loses the confidence of its people. Its books do not deserve to be read. They are nothing but printed paper.

Our literature has lost the leading position which it occupied in the   9 world at the end of the last century and the beginning of this; it has also lost the passion for experimentation which distinguished it during the twenties. The literature of our country appears today to all the world as infinitely poorer, more flat and worthless than it is in reality, than it would look if it were not being restricted, if it were not being prevented from developing. The loser is our country, as it is being judged by world opinion, and world literature is also the loser. If it had before it all the fruits of our literature, without restrictions, if it could gain a deeper insight as a result of our spiritual experience, the artistic evolution of the entire world would be different; it could find a new vigour and reach a new artistic level.

I propose that the congress should demand and obtain the abolition of   10 all censorship — open or concealed — of artistic works, that it should free the publishing houses of their obligation to obtain permission from the authorities before publishing any work.

(2) The obligations of the Union to its members. These obligations are   11 not clearly formulated in its statutes ("protection of rights of authorship" and "measures to protect the other rights of authors"). It is painful to have to state that for a third of a century the Union has not protected either these "other rights" or even the authorship rights of writers.

In their lifetime many writers have been exposed, in the press and from   12 the platform, to insults and slander without having any opportunity of replying. More, they have been exposed to violence and physical persecution (Bulgakov, Akhmatova, Tsvetaeva, Pasternak, Zoshchenko, Platonov, Alexander Grin, Vasily Grossman). Not only did the Union of Writers not offer them the columns of its journals for them to reply and defend themselves; not only did it not intervene on their behalf; the board of the Union always placed itself at the head of the persecutors. Those who are an ornament of our twentieth-century poetry have been excluded from the Union, assuming they were ever admitted. More still: the board of the Union in cowardly fashion abandoned to their misfortune those whom persecution finally condemned to exile, to the concentration camp, to death (Paul Vasiliev, Mandelshtam, Artem Vesely, Pilnyak, Babel, Tabidze, Zabolotsky and others). We have had to break off the list with "and others." After the twentieth party congress we learned that there were more than six hundred writers who were guilty of no crime and whom the Union obediently left to their fate in the prisons and the camps. But the list is still longer. Our eyes have not seen, and never will see, the end of the list, for it will never be fully unrolled. It contains the names of young writers and poets of whom we learnt only by chance, thanks to personal meetings, men whose talent withered in the camps before coming to flower, men whose writings have not been rescued from the offices of the security services since the days of Yagoda, Ezhov, Beria, Abakumov.

There is no reason in history for the board of the Union now elected to share with its predecessors responsibility for the past. 13

I propose that paragraph 22M of the statutes of the Union should formulate clearly all the guarantees of protection that the Union affords to those of its members who are exposed to slander and to unjustified persecution, in such a way as to make a repetition of the illegalities of the past impossible. 14

If the congress does not remain indifferent to what I have said, I ask it to pay attention to the prohibitions and persecutions to which I have myself been subjected: 15

(i) My novel *The First Circle* was taken from me nearly two years ago by the State Security Service, which has prevented me from submitting it to publishers. On the other hand, against my will and even without my being informed, this novel has been "published" in a "closed" edition, to be read by a selected but unnamed few. My novel has been made accessible to literary officials, but it has been concealed from the majority of writers. I am unable to get it openly discussed in the writers' sections of the Union, and I cannot prevent its being misused or plagiarised. 16

(ii) At the same time as the novel, my literary archives, collected over fifteen or twenty years, papers which were not intended for publication, were confiscated. Now tendentious extracts from these archives are being distributed in "closed editions" among the same selected circle. Some verses called "The Banquet of the Victors," which I wrote and learned by heart in the camp, and in which I appear under four different numbers (when we were abandoned to death, forgotten by society, and outside the camp nobody rose to our defence), these verses which I have long left far behind me, are now being described as my most recent piece of writing. 17

(iii) For the last three years an irresponsible campaign of slander has been waged against me, who spent the entire war as commander of a battery and received military decorations. It is now being said that I passed the war years as a common prisoner, or that I surrendered to the enemy (I was never a prisoner of war), that I "betrayed my country," "served the Germans." That is how they explain the eleven years which I spent in the camps and in exile, where I was sent for having criticised Stalin. This slander has been spread at meetings and at closed sessions by persons holding official positions. I have tried, but in vain, to stop the slander by appealing to the Russian Writers' 18

Union and to the press. I did not even get an answer from the Union, and no paper published my reply to the slanderers. On the contrary! Last year, the slander spread against me was reinforced, became sharper; they are using a distorted version of materials taken from my confiscated archives, and I am deprived of any possibility of replying.

(iv) My story, *The Cancer Ward* (25 folios), which was recommended 19 for publication (first part) by the prose-writers' section of the Moscow writers' organisation, cannot be published either in separate parts (five periodicals have rejected it), nor as a whole (rejected by *Novy Mir, Zvezda,* and *Prostor*).

(v) The Sovremennik Theatre, which accepted my play called "The Stag 20 and the Camp Prostitute" in 1962, has still not been given permission to present it.

(vi) The scenario of the film "The Tanks Know the Truth," the play 21 "The light within you," some short stories ("The true touch," and some other short pieces) have found neither a publisher nor producer.

(vii) Those of my stories which have been published in *Novy Mir* have 22 never appeared in book form. Everybody has refused (Soviet Writers Publishing House, State Literary Publishing House, the Ogonek Library). They remain, therefore, inaccessible to the public at large.

(viii) At the same time I have been forbidden to make any other contacts 23 with my readers, including public readings of my works (in November 1966 nine sessions out of eleven arranged were at the last moment cancelled), and radio broadcasts. Even the simple act of giving a manuscript for "reading and copying" is now something criminal in our country (the old Russian scribes could do it without hindrance five centuries ago).

In this way my work has been strangled, it has been slain and damned. 24

Will the fourth congress of the Writers' Union take it upon itself to 25 defend me against such a scurrilous attack on my rights as an author and my "other" rights? Yes or no? It seems to me that the choice to be made is not without importance for the literary future of many congress delegates.

I have a clear conscience, because I have fulfilled my duties as a writer 26 in all circumstances and because I will fulfill them even more successfully, more indisputably, when I am dead than I can while I am still alive. Nobody can bar the road to the truth. I am ready to accept death for the sake of the movement. But how many lessons do we need to teach us that the writer's pen should not be stopped while he still lives? Never once in our history have we been able to say this is so.

SUBJECT QUESTIONS

1. What does Solzhenitsyn believe the functions of literature are? Would he agree with Archibald MacLeish, who said that "A poem must not mean but be"?

2. Do you think Solzhenitsyn's concern for his country (and his protests of patriotism) are a pose to get more freedom from the writers' congress? Can a writer be patriotic and highly critical of his government at the same time?

3. On balance, do you think criticism is helpful or harmful in a country?

4. Solzhenitsyn says that censorship "mutilates" great literary works but is "imperceptible" in mediocre works. Why should this be so? Are great works like delicate flowers and mediocre works like crabgrass?

5. Solzhenitsyn complains, not that he is prevented from writing, but that he cannot get his works published. Is it necessary for a writer to publish to sustain his creative impulse? (Some of Melville's best stories, the poems of Emily Dickinson and Gerard Manley Hopkins, and half the plays of Shakespeare were not published in their lifetimes.) To what extent does the importance of publication depend on the author's notion of the function of literature?

STRUCTURE QUESTIONS

1. Solzhenitsyn offers two separate arguments in this letter; how does he manage to unite them at the end?

2. In the first argument, the solution to the problem of censorship is reserved until last; should it have been placed earlier?

3. Note that most of Solzhenitsyn's first argument is devoted to "refutation" rather than to confirmation of his own solution. Does this strategy constitute a weakness in the argument?

4. Locate and discuss instances of name-calling in the first argument. Is the tactic effective? Is it likely to win friends and influence the writers' union?

5. What is the "problem" that gives rise to the second argument? Where has Solzhenitsyn placed his solution this time?

6. Solzhenitsyn's evidence proceeds from the difficulties of writers in general to a detailed list of his own tribulations. Would his argument have had more, or less, force had he substituted a detailed list of some other writer's grievances?

7. Consider the suitability of the last two paragraphs as a conclusion to Solzhenitsyn's argument. (Is it calculated to stimulate constructive thought, to "expose" the writers' congress, or to force their hand?)

On the Duty of
Civil Disobedience

Henry David Thoreau

Henry David Thoreau (1817–1862) was an author and philosopher. Although he published only two books in his lifetime, his edited manuscripts run to twenty volumes. "On the Duty of Civil Disobedience" was published in 1849, just after Mexico had been forced to give up Texas and just before passage of the Second Fugitive Slave Law. Daniel Webster had spoken in favor of the measure, much to Thoreau's disappointment.

I heartily accept the motto —"That government is best which governs least"; and I should like to see it acted up to more rapidly and systematically. Carried out, it finally amounts to this, which also I believe, — "That government is best which governs not at all"; and when men are prepared for it, that will be the kind of government which they will have. Government is at best but an expedient; but most governments are usually, and all governments are sometimes, inexpedient. The objections which have been brought against a standing army, and they are many and weighty, and deserve to prevail, may also at last be brought against a standing government. The standing army is only an arm of the standing government. The government itself, which is only the mode which the people have chosen to execute their will, is equally liable to be abused and perverted before the people can act through it. Witness the present Mexican war, the work of comparatively a few individuals using the standing government as their tool; for, in the outset, the people would not have consented to this measure.

This American government — what is it but a tradition, though a recent one, endeavoring to transmit itself unimpaired to posterity, but each instant losing some of its integrity? It has not the vitality and force of a single living man; for a single man can bend it to his will. It is a sort of wooden gun to the people themselves. But it is not the less necessary for this; for the people must have some complicated machinery or other, and hear its din, to satisfy that idea of government which they have. Governments show us how successfully men can be imposed on, even impose on themselves, for their own advantage. It is excellent, we must all allow. Yet this government never of itself furthered any enterprise, but by the alacrity with which it got out of its way. *It* does not keep the country free. *It* does not settle the West. *It* does not educate. The character inherent in the American people has done all that has been accomplished; and it would have done somewhat more, if the gov-

ernment had not sometimes got in its way. For government is an expedient
by which men would fain succeed in letting one another alone; and, as has
been said, when it is most expedient, the governed are most let alone by it.
Trade and commerce, if they were not made of India-rubber, would never
manage to bounce over the obstacles which legislators are continually putting
in their way; and, if one were to judge these men wholly by the effects of
their actions and not partly by their intentions, they would deserve to be
classed and punished with those mischievous persons who put obstructions
on the railroads.

But, to speak practically and as a citizen, unlike those who call them- 3
selves no-government men, I ask for, not at once no government, but *at once*
a better government. Let every man make known what kind of government
would command his respect, and that will be one step toward obtaining it.

After all, the practical reason why, when the power is once in the hands 4
of the people, a majority are permitted, and for a long period continue, to
rule is not because they are most likely to be in the right, nor because this
seems fairest to the minority, but because they are physically the strongest.
But a government in which the majority rule in all cases cannot be based
on justice, even as far as men understand it. Can there not be a government
in which majorities do not virtually decide right and wrong, but conscience — in which majorities decide only those questions to which the rule
of expediency is applicable? Must the citizen ever for a moment, or in the
last degree, resign his conscience to the legislator? Why has every man a
conscience, then? I think that we should be men first, and subjects afterward.
It is not desirable to cultivate a respect for the law, so much as for the right.
The only obligation which I have a right to assume is to do at any time what
I think right. It is truly enough said, that a corporation has no conscience;
but a corporation of conscientious men is a corporation *with* a conscience.
Law never made men a whit more just; and, by means of their respect for
it, even the well-disposed are daily made the agents of injustice. A common
and natural result of an undue respect for law is, that you may see a file of
soldiers, colonel, captain, corporal, privates, powder-monkeys, and all,
marching in admirable order over hill and dale to the war, against their will,
ay, against their common sense and consciences, which makes it very steep
marching indeed, and produces a palpitation of the heart. They have no doubt
that it is a damnable business in which they are concerned; they are all
peaceably inclined. Now, what are they? Men at all? or small movable forts
and magazines, at the service of some unscrupulous man in power? Visit the
Navy-Yard, and behold a marine, such a man as an American government
can make, or such as it can make a man with its black arts — a mere shadow
and reminiscence of humanity, a man laid out alive and standing, and already,
as one may say, buried under arms with funeral accompaniments, though it
may be, —

> Not a drum was heard, not a funeral note,
>   As his corpse to the rampart we hurried;
> Not a soldier discharged his farewell shot
>   O'er the grave where our hero we buried.

The mass of men serve the state thus, not as men mainly, but as machines,   5
with their bodies. They are the standing army, and the militia, jailors, consta-
bles, posse comitatus, etc. In most cases there is no free exercise whatever
of the judgment or of the moral sense; but they put themselves on a level
with wood and earth and stones; and wooden men can perhaps be manufactured that will serve the purpose as well. Such command no more respect
than men of straw or a lump of dirt. They have the same sort of worth only
as horses and dogs. Yet such as these even are commonly esteemed good
citizens. Others — as most legislators, politicians, lawyers, ministers, and of-
fice-holders — serve the state chiefly with their heads: and, as they rarely make
any moral distinctions, they are as likely to serve the Devil, without *intending*
it, as God. A very few, as heroes, patriots, martyrs, reformers in the great
sense, and *men*, serve the state with their consciences also, and so necessarily
resist it for the most part; and they are commonly treated as enemies by it.
A wise man will only be useful as a man, and will not submit to be "clay,"
and "stop a hole to keep the wind away," but leave that office to his dust
at least: —

> I am too high-born to be propertied,
> To be a secondary at control,
> Or useful serving-man and instrument
> To any sovereign state throughout the world.

He who gives himself entirely to his fellow-men appears to them useless   6
and selfish; but he who gives himself partially to them is pronounced a bene-
factor and philanthropist.

How does it become a man to behave toward this American government   7
to-day? I answer, that he cannot without disgrace be associated with it. I
cannot for an instant recognize that political organization as *my* government
which is the *slave's* government also.

All men recognize the right of revolution; that is, the right to refuse   8
allegiance to, and to resist, the government, when its tyranny or its inefficiency
are great and unendurable. But almost all say that such is not the case now.
But such was the case, they think, in the Revolution of '75. If one were to
tell me that this was a bad government because it taxed certain foreign commodities brought to its ports, it is most probable that I should not make an
ado about it, for I can do without them. All machines have their friction;
and possibly this does enough good to counterbalance the evil. At any rate,
it is a great evil to make a stir about it. But when the friction comes to have
its machine, and oppression and robbery are organized, I say, let us not have
such a machine any longer. In other words, when a sixth of the population

of a nation which has undertaken to be the refuge of liberty are slaves, and a whole country is unjustly overrun and conquered by a foreign army, and subjected to military law, I think that it is not too soon for honest men to rebel and revolutionize. What makes this duty the more urgent is the fact that the country so overrun is not our own, but ours is the invading army.. . . .

> A drab of state, a cloth-o'-silver slut,
>   To have her train borne up, and her soul trail in the dirt

Practically speaking, the opponents to a reform in Massachusetts are not a hundred thousand politicians at the South, but a hundred thousand merchants and farmers here, who are more interested in commerce and agriculture than they are in humanity, and are not prepared to do justice to the slave and to Mexico, *cost what it may.* I quarrel not with far-off foes, but with those who, near at home, coöperate with, and do the bidding of, those far away, and without whom the latter would be harmless. We are accustomed to say, that the mass of men are unprepared; but improvement is slow, because the few are not materially wiser or better than the many. It is not so important that many should be as good as you, as that there be some absolute goodness somewhere; for that will leaven the whole lump. There are thousands who are *in opinion* opposed to slavery and to the war, who yet in effect do nothing to put an end to them; who, esteeming themselves children of Washington and Franklin, sit down with their hands in their pockets, and say that they know not what to do, and do nothing; who even postpone the question of freedom to the question of free-trade, and quietly read the prices-current along with the latest advices from Mexico, after dinner, and, it may be, fall asleep over them both. What is the price-current of an honest man and patriot to-day? They hesitate, and they regret, and sometimes they petition; but they do nothing in earnest and with effect. They will wait, well disposed, for others to remedy the evil, that they may no longer have it to regret. At most, they give only a cheap vote, and a feeble countenance and God-speed, to the right, as it goes by them. There are nine hundred and ninety-nine patrons of virtue to one virtuous man. But it is easier to deal with the real possessor of a thing than with the temporary guardian of it.

All voting is a sort of gaming, like checkers or backgammon, with a slight moral tinge to it, a playing with right and wrong, with moral questions; and betting naturally accompanies it. The character of the voters is not staked. I cast my vote, perchance, as I think right; but I am not vitally concerned that that right should prevail. I am willing to leave it to the majority. Its obligation, therefore, never exceeds that of expediency. Even voting *for the right* is *doing* nothing for it. It is only expressing to men feebly your desire that it should prevail. A wise man will not leave the right to the mercy of chance, nor wish it to prevail through the power of the majority. There is but little virtue in the action of masses of men. When the majority shall at length vote for the abolition of slavery, it will be because they are indifferent to slavery, or because there is but little slavery left to be abolished by their vote. *They* will then be the only slaves. Only *his* vote can hasten the abolition of slavery who asserts his own freedom by his vote.

I hear of a convention to be held at Baltimore, or elsewhere, for the selection of a candidate for the Presidency, made up chiefly of editors, and men who are politicians by profession; but I think, what is it to any independent, intelligent, and respectable man what decision they may come to? Shall we not have the advantage of his wisdom and honesty, nevertheless? Can we not count upon some independent votes? Are there not many individuals in the country who do not attend conventions? But no: I find that the respectable man, so called, has immediately drifted from his position, and despairs of his country, when his country has more reason to despair of him. He forthwith adopts one of the candidates thus selected as the only *available* one, thus proving that he is himself *available* for any purposes of the demagogue. His vote is of no more worth than that of any unprincipled foreigner or hireling native, who may have been bought. O for a man who is a *man*, and, as my neighbor says, has a bone in his back which you cannot pass your hand through! Our statistics are at fault: the population has been returned too large. How many *men* are there to a square thousand miles in this country? Hardly one. Does not America offer any inducement for men to settle here? The American has dwindled into an Odd Fellow, — one who may be known by the development of his organ of gregariousness, and a manifest lack of intellect and cheerful self-reliance; whose first and chief concern, on coming into the world, is to see that the Almshouses are in good repair; and, before yet he has lawfully donned the virile garb, to collect a fund for the support of the widows and orphans that may be; who, in short, ventures to live only by the aid of the Mutual Insurance Company, which has promised to bury him decently.

It is not a man's duty, as a matter of course, to devote himself to the eradication of any, even the most enormous wrong; he may still properly have other concerns to engage him; but it is his duty, at least, to wash his hands of it, and, if he gives it no thought longer, not to give it practically his support. If I devote myself to other pursuits and contemplations, I must first see, at least, that I do not pursue them sitting upon another man's shoulders. I must get off him first, that he may pursue his contemplations too. See what gross inconsistency is tolerated. I have heard some of my townsmen say, "I should like to have them order me out to help put down an insurrection of the slaves, or to march to Mexico; — see if I would go"; and yet these very men have each, directly by their allegiance, and so indirectly, at least, by their money, furnished a substitute. The soldier is applauded who refuses to serve in an unjust war by those who do not refuse to sustain the unjust government which makes the war; is applauded by those whose own act and authority he disregards and sets at naught; as if the state were penitent to that degree that it hired one to scourge it while it sinned, but not to that degree that it left off sinning for a moment. Thus, under the name of Order and Civil Government, we are all made at last to pay homage to and support our own meanness. After the first blush of sin comes its indifference; and from immoral it becomes, as it were, *un*moral, and not quite unnecessary to that life which we have made.

The broadest and most prevalent error requires the most disinterested 12 virtue to sustain it. The slight reproach to which the virtue of patriotism is commonly liable, the noble are most likely to incur. Those who, while they disapprove of the character and measures of a government, yield to it their allegiance and support are undoubtedly its most conscientious supporters, and so frequently the most serious obstacles to reform. Some are petitioning the state to dissolve the Union, to disregard the requisitions of the President. Why do they not dissolve it themselves — the union between themselves and the state, — and refuse to pay their quota into its treasury? Do not they stand in the same relation to the state that the state does to the Union? And have not the same reasons prevented the state from resisting the Union which have prevented them from resisting the state?

How can a man be satisfied to entertain an opinion merely, and enjoy 13 *it?* Is there any enjoyment in it, if his opinion is that he is aggrieved? If you are cheated out of a single dollar by your neighbor, you do not rest satisfied with knowing that you are cheated, or with saying that you are cheated, or even with petitioning him to pay you your due; but you take effectual steps at once to obtain the full amount, and see that you are never cheated again. Action from principle, the perception and the performance of right, changes things and relations; it is essentially revolutionary, and does not consist wholly with anything which was. It not only divides states and churches, it divides families; ay, it divides the *individual,* separating the diabolical in him from the divine.

Unjust laws exist: shall we be content to obey them, or shall we endeavor 14 to amend them, and obey them until we have succeeded, or shall we transgress them at once? Men generally, under such a government as this, think that they ought to wait until they have persuaded the majority to alter them. They think that, if they should resist, the remedy would be worse than the evil. But it is the fault of the government itself that the remedy *is* worse than the evil. *It* makes it worse. Why is it not more apt to anticipate and provide for reform? Why does it not cherish its wise minority? Why does it cry and resist before it is hurt? Why does it not encourage its citizens to be on the alert to point out its faults, and *do* better than it would have them? Why does it always crucify Christ, and excommunicate Copernicus and Luther, and pronounce Washington and Franklin rebels?

One would think, that a deliberate and practical denial of its authority 15 was the only offense never contemplated by government; else, why has it not assigned its definite, its suitable and proportionate penalty? If a man who has no property refuses but once to earn nine shillings for the state, he is put in prison for a period unlimited by any law that I know, and determined only by the discretion of those who placed him there; but if he should steal ninety times nine shillings from the state, he is soon permitted to go at large again.

If the justice is part of the necessary friction of the machine of government, let it go, let it go: perchance it will wear smooth, — certainly the machine will wear out. If the injustice has a spring, or a pulley, or a rope, or a crank, exclusively for itself, then perhaps you may consider whether the remedy will not be worse than the evil; but if it is of such a nature that it requires you to be the agent of injustice to another, then, I say, break the law. Let your life be a counter friction to stop the machine. What I have to do is to see, at any rate, that I do not lend myself to the wrong which I condemn.   16

As for adopting the ways which the state has provided for remedying the evil, I know not of such ways. They take too much time, and a man's life will be gone. I have other affairs to attend to. I came into this world, not chiefly to make this a good place to live in, but to live in it, be it good or bad. A man has not everything to do, but something; and because he cannot do *everything*, it is not necessary that he should do *something* wrong. It is not my business to be petitioning the Governor or the Legislature any more than it is theirs to petition me; and if they should not hear my petition, what should I do then? But in this case the state has provided no way: its very Constitution is the evil. This may seem to be harsh and stubborn and unconciliatory; but it is to treat with the utmost kindness and consideration the only spirit that can appreciate or deserves it. So is all change for the better, like birth and death, which convulse the body.   17

I do not hesitate to say, that those who call themselves Abolitionists should at once effectually withdraw their support, both in person and property, from the government of Massachusetts and not wait till they constitute a majority of one, before they suffer the right to prevail through them. I think that it is enough if they have God on their side, without waiting for that other one. Moreover, any man more right than his neighbors constitutes a majority of one already.   18

I meet this American government, or its representative, the state government, directly, and face to face, once a year — no more — in the person of its tax-gatherer; this is the only mode in which a man situated as I am necessarily meets it; and it then says distinctly, Recognize me; and the simplest, most effectual, and, in the present posture of affairs, the indispensablest mode of treating with it on this head, of expressing your little satisfaction with and love for it, is to deny it then. My civil neighbor, the tax-gatherer, is the very man I have to deal with, — for it is, after all, with men and not with parchment that I quarrel, — and he has voluntarily chosen to be an agent of the government. How shall he ever know well what he is and does as an officer of the government, or as a man, until he is obliged to consider whether he shall treat me, his neighbor, for whom he has respect, as a neighbor and   19

well-disposed man, or as a maniac and disturber of the peace, and see if he
can get over this obstruction to his neighborliness without a ruder and more
impetuous thought or speech corresponding with his action. I know this well,
that if one thousand, if one hundred, if ten men whom I could name, — if
ten *honest* men only, — ay, if *one* HONEST man, in this State of Massachusetts,
ceasing to hold slaves, were actually to withdraw from this copartnership,
and be locked up in the county jail therefor, it would be the abolition of slavery
in America. For it matters not how small the beginning may seem to be: what
is once well done is done forever. But we love better to talk about it: that
we say is our mission. Reform keeps many scores of newspapers in its service,
but not one man. If my esteemed neighbor, the State's ambassador, who will
devote his days to the settlement of the question of human rights in the Council
Chamber, instead of being threatened with the prisons of Carolina, were to
sit down the prisoner of Massachusetts, that State which is so anxious to foist
the sin of slavery upon her sister, — though at present she can discover only
an act of inhospitality to be the ground of a quarrel with her, — the Legislature
would not wholly waive the subject the following winter.

Under a government which imprisons any unjustly, the true place for
a just man is also a prison. The proper place to-day, the only place which
Massachusetts has provided for her freer and less desponding spirits, is in her
prisons, to be put out and locked out of the State by her own act, as they
have already put themselves out by their principles. It is there that the fugitive
slave, and the Mexican prisoner on parole, and the Indian come to plead the
wrongs of his race should find them; on that separate, but more free and
honorable ground, where the State places those who are not *with* her, but
against her, — the only house in a slave State in which a free man can abide
with honor. If any think that their influence would be lost there, and their
voices no longer afflict the ear of the State, that they would not be as an
enemy within its walls, they do not know by how much truth is stronger than
error, nor how much more eloquently and effectively he can combat injustice
who has experienced a little in his own person. Cast your whole vote, not
a strip of paper merely, but your whole influence. A minority is powerless
while it conforms to the majority; it is not even a minority then; but it is
irresistible when it clogs by its whole weight. If the alternative is to keep
all just men in prison, or give up war and slavery, the State will not hesitate
which to choose. If a thousand men were not to pay their tax-bills this year,
that would not be a violent and bloody measure, as it would be to pay them,
and enable the State to commit violence and shed innocent blood. This is,
in fact, the definition of a peaceable revolution, if any such is possible. If the
tax-gatherer, or any other public officer, asks me, as one has done, "But what
shall I do?" my answer is, "If you really wish to do anything, resign your
office." When the subject has refused allegiance, and the officer has resigned
his office, then the revolution is accomplished. But even suppose blood should
flow. Is there not a sort of blood shed when the conscience is wounded?

Through this wound a man's real manhood and immortality flow out, and he bleeds to an everlasting death. I see this blood flowing now.

I have contemplated the imprisonment of the offender, rather than the   21
seizure of his goods, — though both will serve the same purpose, — because they who assert the purest right, and consequently are most dangerous to a corrupt State, commonly have not spent much time in accumulating property. To such the State renders comparatively small service, and a slight tax is wont to appear exorbitant, particularly if they are obliged to earn it by special labor with their hands. If there were one who lived wholly without the use of money, the State itself would hesitate to demand it of him. But the rich man — not to make any invidious comparison — is always sold to the institution which makes him rich. Absolutely speaking, the more money, the less virtue; for money comes between a man and his objects, and obtains them for him; and it was certainly no great virtue to obtain it. It puts to rest many questions which he would otherwise be taxed to answer; while the only new question which it puts is the hard but superfluous one, how to spend it. Thus his moral ground is taken from under his feet. The opportunities of living are diminished in proportion as what are called the "means" are increased. The best thing a man can do for his culture when he is rich is to endeavor to carry out those schemes which he entertained when he was poor. Christ answered the Herodians according to their condition. "Show me the tribute-money," said he; — and one took a penny out of his pocket; — if you use money which has the image of Caesar on it and which he has made current and valuable, that is, *if you are men of the State,* and gladly enjoy the advantages of Caesar's government, then pay him back some of his own when he demands it. "Render therefore to Caesar that which is Caesar's, and to God those things which are God's," — leaving them no wiser than before as to which; for they did not wish to know. . . .

I have paid no poll-tax for six years. I was put into a jail once on this   22
account, for one night; and, as I stood considering the walls of solid stone, two or three feet thick, the door of wood and iron, a foot thick, and the iron grating which strained the light, I could not help being struck with the foolishness of that institution which treated me as if I were mere flesh and blood and bones, to be locked up. I wondered that it should have concluded at length that this was the best use it could put me to, and had never thought to avail itself of my services in some way. I saw that, if there was a wall of stone between me and my townsmen, there was a still more difficult one to climb or break through before they could get to be as free as I was. I did not for a moment feel confined, and the walls seemed a great waste of stone and mortar. I felt as if I alone of all my townsmen had paid my tax. They plainly did not know how to treat me, but behaved like persons who are underbred. In every threat and in every compliment there was a blunder; for they thought that my chief desire was to stand the other side of that stone wall. I could not but smile to see how industriously they locked the door on my meditations,

which followed them out again without let or hindrance, and *they* were really all that was dangerous. As they could not reach me, they had resolved to punish my body; just as boys, if they cannot come at some person against whom they have a spite, will abuse his dog. I saw that the State was half-witted, that it was timid as a lone woman with her silver spoons, and that it did not know its friends from its foes, and I lost all my remaining respect for it, and pitied it.

Thus the State never intentionally confronts a man's sense, intellectual   23 or moral, but only his body, his senses. It is not armed with superior wit or honesty, but with superior physical strength. I was not born to be forced. I will breathe after my own fashion. Let us see who is the strongest. What force has a multitude? They only can force me who obey a higher law than I. They force me to become like themselves. I do not hear of *men* being *forced* to live this way or that by masses of men. What sort of life were that to live? When I meet a government which says to me, "Your money or your life," why should I be in haste to give it my money? It may be in a great strait, and not know what to do: I cannot help that. It must help itself; do as I do. It is not worth the while to snivel about it. I am not responsible for the successful working of the machinery of society. I am not the son of the engineer. I perceive that, when an acorn and a chestnut fall side by side, the one does not remain inert to make way for the other, but both obey their own laws, and spring and grow and flourish as best they can, till one, perchance, over-shadows and destroys the other. If a plant cannot live according to its nature, it dies; and so a man. . . .

When I came out of prison, — for some one interfered, and paid that   24 tax, — I did not perceive that great changes had taken place on the common, such as he observed who went in a youth and emerged a tottering and gray-headed man; and yet a change had to my eyes come over the scene, — the town, and State, and country, — greater than any that mere time could effect. I saw yet more distinctly the State in which I lived. I saw to what extent the people among whom I lived could be trusted as good neighbors and friends; that their friendship was for summer weather only; that they did not greatly propose to do right; that they were a distinct race from me by their prejudices and superstitions, as the Chinamen and Malays are; that in their sacrifices to humanity they ran no risks, not even to their property; that after all they were not so noble but they treated the thief as he had treated them, and hoped, by a certain outward observance and a few prayers, and by walking in a particular straight though useless path from time to time, to save their souls. This may be to judge my neighbors harshly; for I believe that many of them are not aware that they have such an institution as the jail in their village.

It was formerly the custom in our village, when a poor debtor came   25 out of jail, for his acquaintances to salute him, looking through their fingers, which were crossed to represent the grating of a jail window. "How do ye do?" My neighbors did not thus salute me, but first looked at me, and then at one another, as if I had returned from a long journey. I was put into jail as I was going to the shoemaker's to get a shoe which was mended. When I was let out the next morning, I proceeded to finish my errand, and, having put on my mended shoe, joined a huckleberry party, who were impatient to put themselves under my conduct; and in half an hour, — for the horse was soon tackled, — was in the midst of a huckleberry field, on one of our highest hills, two miles off, and then the State was nowhere to be seen. . . .

I have never declined paying the highway tax, because I am as desirous   26
of being a good neighbor as I am of being a bad subject; and as for supporting schools, I am doing my part to educate my fellow-countrymen now. It is for no particular item in the tax-bill that I refused to pay it. I simply wish to refuse allegiance to the State, to withdraw and stand aloof from it effectually. I do not care to trace the course of my dollar, if I could, till it buys a man or a musket to shoot with, — the dollar is innocent, — but I am concerned to trace the effects of my allegiance. In fact, I quietly declare war with the State, after my fashion, though I will still make what use and get what advantage of her I can, as is usual in such cases.

If others pay the tax which is demanded of me, from a sympathy with   27
the State, they do but what they have already done in their own case, or rather they abet injustice to a greater extent than the State requires. If they pay the tax from a mistaken interest in the individual taxed, to save his property, or prevent his going to jail, it is because they have not considered wisely how far they let their private feelings interfere with the public good.

This, then, is my position at present. But one cannot be too much on   28
his guard in such a case, lest his action be biased by obstinacy or an undue regard for the opinions of men. Let him see that he does only what belongs to himself and to the hour.

I think sometimes, Why, these people mean well, they are only ignorant;   29
they would do better if they knew how: why give your neighbors this pain to treat you as they are not inclined to? But I think again, This is no reason why I should do as they do, or permit others to suffer much greater pain of a different kind. Again, I sometimes say to myself, When many millions of men, without heat, without ill will, without personal feeling of any kind, demand of you a few shillings only, without the possibility, such is their constitution, of retracting or altering their present demand, and without the possibility, on your side, of appeal to any other millions, why expose yourself to this overwhelming brute force? You do not resist cold and hunger, the winds and the waves, thus obstinately; you quietly submit to a thousand similar necessities. You do not put your head into the fire. But just in proportion as I regard this as not wholly a brute force, but partly a human force, and consider that I have relations to those millions as to many millions of men, and not of mere brute or inanimate things, I see that appeal is possible, first and instantaneously, from them to the Maker of them and, secondly, from

them to themselves. But if I put my head deliberately into the fire, there is no appeal to fire or to the Maker of fire, and I have only myself to blame. If I could convince myself that I have any right to be satisfied with men as they are, and to treat them accordingly, and not according, in some respects, to my requisitions and expectations of what they and I ought to be, then, like a good Mussulman and fatalist, I should endeavor to be satisfied with things as they are, and say it is the will of God. And, above all, there is this difference between resisting this and a purely brute or natural force, that I can resist this with some effect; but I cannot expect, like Orpheus, to change the nature of the rocks and trees and beasts.

I do not wish to quarrel with any man or nation. I do not wish to split   30
hairs, to make fine distinctions, or set myself up as better than my neighbors. I seek rather, I may say, even an excuse for conforming to the laws of the land. I am but too ready to conform to them. Indeed, I have reason to suspect myself on this head; and each year, as the tax-gatherer comes round, I find myself disposed to review the acts and position of the general and State governments, and the spirit of the people, to discover a pretext for conformity.

> We must affect our country as our parents,
> And if at any time we alienate
> Our love or industry from doing it honor,
> We must respect effects and teach the soul
> Matter of conscience and religion,
> And not desire of rule or benefit.

I believe that the State will soon be able to take all my work of this sort out of my hands, and then I shall be no better a patriot than my fellow-countrymen. Seen from a lower point of view, the Constitution, with all its faults, is very good; the law and the courts are very respectable; even this State and this American government are, in many respects, very admirable, and rare things, to be thankful for, such as a great many have described them; but seen from a point of view a little higher, they are what I have described them; seen from a higher still, and the highest, who shall say what they are, or that they are worth looking at or thinking of at all?

However, the government does not concern me much, and I shall bestow   31
the fewest possible thoughts on it. It is not many moments that I live under a government, even in this world. If a man is thought-free, fancy-free, imagination-free, that which *is not* never for a long time appearing *to be* to him, unwise rulers or reformers cannot fatally interrupt him.

I know that most men think differently from myself; but those whose   32
lives are by profession devoted to the study of these or kindred subjects content me as little as any. Statesmen and legislators, standing so completely within the institution, never distinctly and nakedly behold it. They speak of moving society, but have no resting-place without it. They may be men of a certain experience and discrimination, and have no doubt invented ingenious and even

useful systems, for which we sincerely thank them; but all their wit and usefulness lie within certain not very wide limits. They are wont to forget that the world is not governed by policy and expediency. Webster never goes behind government, and so cannot speak with authority about it. His words are wisdom to those legislators who contemplate no essential reform in the existing government; but for thinkers, and those who legislate for all time, he never once glances at the subject. I know of those whose serene and wise speculations on this theme would soon reveal the limits of his mind's range and hospitality. Yet, compared with the cheap professions of most reformers, and the still cheaper wisdom and eloquence of politicians in general, his are almost the only sensible and valuable words, and we thank Heaven for him. Comparatively, he is always strong, original, and, above all, practical. Still, his quality is not wisdom, but prudence. The lawyer's truth is not Truth, but consistency or a consistent expediency. Truth is always in harmony with herself, and is not concerned chiefly to reveal the justice that may consist with wrong-doing. He well deserves to be called, as he has been called, the Defender of the Constitution. There are really no blows to be given by him but defensive ones. He is not a leader, but a follower. His leaders are the men of '87. "I have never made an effort," he says, "and never propose to make an effort; I have never countenanced an effort, and never mean to countenance an effort, to disturb the arrangement as originally made, by which the various States came into the Union." Still thinking of the sanction which the Constitution gives to slavery, he says, "Because it was a part of the original compact, — let it stand." Notwithstanding his special acuteness and ability, he is unable to take a fact out of its merely political relations, and behold it as it lies absolutely to be disposed of by the intellect, — what, for instance, it behooves a man to do here in America to-day with regard to slavery, — but ventures, or is driven, to make some such desperate answer as the following while professing to speak absolutely, and as a private man, — from which what new and singular code of social duties might be inferred? "The manner," says he, "in which the governments of those States where slavery exists are to regulate it is for their own consideration, under their responsibility to their constituents, to the general laws of propriety, humanity, and justice, and to God. Associations formed elsewhere, springing from a feeling of humanity, or other cause, have nothing whatever to do with it. They have never received any encouragement from me, and they never will."

They who know of no purer sources of truth, who have traced up its 33 stream no higher, stand, and wisely stand, by the Bible and the Constitution, and drink at it there with reverence and humility; but they who behold where it comes trickling into this lake or that pool, gird up their loins once more, and continue their pilgrimage towards its fountainhead.

No man with a genius for legislation has appeared in America. They 34 are rare in the history of the world. There are orators, politicians, and eloquent men, by the thousand; but the speaker has not yet opened his mouth to speak who is capable of settling the much-vexed questions of the day. We love eloquence for its own sake, and not for any truth which it may utter, or any heroism it may inspire. Our legislators have not yet learned the comparative value of free-trade and of freedom, of union, and of rectitude, to a nation. They have no genius or talent for comparatively humble questions of taxation and finance, commerce and manufactures and agriculture. If we were left solely to the wordy wit of legislators in Congress for our guidance, uncorrected by the seasonable experience and the effectual complaints of the people, America would not long retain her rank among the nations. For eighteen hundred years, though perchance I have no right to say it, the New Testament has been written; yet where is the legislator who has wisdom and practical talent enough to avail himself of the light which it sheds on the science of legislation?

The authority of government, even such as I am willing to submit to, — 35 for I will cheerfully obey those who know and can do better than I, and in many things even those who neither know nor can do so well, — is still an impure one: to be strictly just, it must have the sanction and consent of the governed. It can have no pure right over my person and property but what I concede to it. The progress from an absolute to a limited monarchy, from a limited monarchy to a democracy, is a progress toward a true respect for the individual. Even the Chinese philosopher was wise enough to regard the individual as the basis of the empire. Is a democracy, such as we know it, the last improvement possible in government? Is it not possible to take a step further towards recognizing and organizing the rights of man? There will never be a really free and enlightened State until the State comes to recognize the individual as a higher and independent power, from which all its own power and authority are derived, and treats him accordingly. I please myself with imagining a State at last which can afford to be just to all men, and to treat the individual with respect as a neighbor; which even would not think it inconsistent with its own repose if a few were to live aloof from it, not meddling with it, nor embraced by it, who fulfilled all the duties of neighbors and fellow-men. A State which bore this kind of fruit, and suffered it to drop off as fast as it ripened, would prepare the way for a still more perfect and glorious State, which also I have imagined, but not yet anywhere seen.

SUBJECT QUESTIONS

1. What two situations prompted Thoreau to write this essay? Is he justified in refusing to cooperate with a government that condones slavery and indulges in armed aggression?

2. If one is confronted with a conflict between the law and his conscience, which should he obey? Would you be willing to disobey your government? A pacifist, even though he does not fight, must pay taxes to

support a war; is the government justified in thus forcing him to go against his conscience?

3. Does it logically follow that, if the best governments are those which govern least, the best possible government would govern not at all? Is Thoreau an anarchist?

4. Thoreau does not advocate violent revolution; what does he suggest the citizen should do if he disapproves of his government's activities? Would this solution be effective? How many people would be needed to make it work?

5. Thoreau does not seem to have much faith in the democratic principle of majority rule. Would he have more, or less, faith in an oligarchy? What would happen if every minority acted by Thoreau's principles?

6. Thoreau seems to make one fundamental error: he regards government as an enemy to individualism. But if we had no government at all, how much freedom would we have? Would you conclude that government necessarily requires compromising some freedoms to guarantee more important ones?

7. What would be Thoreau's reaction to modern government? Do you think the increased complexity of life today would force him to modify some of his views? If he were alive today, would he be more likely to vote Democratic or Republican? (The obvious answer to this question may have to be modified in view of what he says about Daniel Webster.)

STRUCTURE QUESTIONS

1. Summarize the position with which Thoreau wants his reader to agree. Does he try to sway the reader into accepting this position, or does he present arguments designed to encourage the reader to do some thinking on his own?

2. Occasionally Thoreau states his opinion without bothering to give supporting evidence. What are some of these assumptions? Why do you suppose Thoreau doesn't support them? Could he have done so?

3. Try outlining the essay. Could Thoreau have made it more effective by organizing it more carefully?

4. What would you say is Thoreau's strongest asset as a writer? What is his most obvious weakness?

5. Does Thoreau succeed in getting the reader to think objectively about the problem of government control? (He may strike some readers as an eccentric, but his purpose was not to be affable. It may be noted that Mahatma Gandhi successfully used Thoreau's idea of passive resistance in his battle for Indian independence.)

The Declaration of Independence

Thomas Jefferson

The Declaration of Independence was written between June 11 and June 28, 1776, mainly by Thomas Jefferson (1743–1826), but with considerable help from Benjamin Franklin and with suggestions from John Adams. After a few minor changes, it was passed by Congress on July 4, and the famous parchment copy of it signed on August 2. The text here is the version authorized by the State Department (1911).

In CONGRESS, July 4, 1776.

THE UNANIMOUS DECLARATION
OF THE THIRTEEN UNITED STATES OF AMERICA.

When in the Course of human events, it becomes necessary for one people 1
to dissolve the political bands which have connected them with another, and
to assume among the powers of the earth, the separate and equal station to
which the Laws of Nature and of Nature's God entitle them, a decent respect
to the opinions of mankind requires that they should declare the causes which
impel them to the separation.

We hold these truths to be self-evident, that all men are created equal, 2
that they are endowed by their Creator with certain unalienable Rights, that
among these are Life, Liberty and the pursuit of Happiness.

That to secure these rights, Governments are instituted among Men, 3
deriving their just powers from the consent of the governed.

That whenever any Form of Government becomes destructive of these 4
ends, it is the Right of the People to alter or to abolish it, and to institute
new Government, laying its foundation on such principles and organizing its
powers in such form, as to them shall seem most likely to effect their Safety
and Happiness. Prudence, indeed, will dictate that Governments long established should not be changed for light and transient causes; and accordingly
all experience hath shewn, that mankind are more disposed to suffer, while
evils are sufferable, than to right themselves by abolishing the forms to which
they are accustomed. But when a long train of abuses and usurpations, pursuing invariably the same Object evinces a design to reduce them under absolute
Despotism, it is their right, it is their duty, to throw off such Government,
and to provide new Guards for their future security.

Such has been the patient sufferance of these Colonies; and such is now 5
the necessity which constrains them to alter their former Systems of Govern-

ment. The history of the present King of Great Britain is a history of repeated injuries and usurpations, all having in direct object the establishment of an absolute Tyranny over these States. To prove this, let Facts be submitted to a candid world.

He has refused his Assent to Laws, the most wholesome and necessary   6
for the public good.

He has forbidden his Governors to pass Laws of immediate and pressing   7
importance, unless suspended in their operation till his Assent should be obtained; and when so suspended, he has utterly neglected to attend to them.

He has refused to pass other Laws for the accommodation of large   8
districts of people, unless those people would relinquish the right of Representation in the Legislature, a right inestimable to them and formidable to tyrants only.

He has called together legislative bodies at places unusual, uncom-   9
fortable, and distant from the depository of their public Records, for the sole purpose of fatiguing them into compliance with his measures.

He has dissolved Representative Houses repeatedly, for opposing with   10
manly firmness his invasions on the rights of the people.

He has refused for a long time, after such dissolutions, to cause others   11
to be elected; whereby the Legislative powers, incapable of Annihilation, have returned to the People at large for their exercise; the State remaining in the mean time exposed to all the dangers of invasion from without, and convulsions within.

He has endeavoured to prevent the population of these States; for that   12
purpose obstructing the Laws for Naturalization of Foreigners; refusing to pass others to encourage their migrations hither, and raising the conditions of new Appropriations of Lands.

He has obstructed the Administration of Justice, by refusing his Assent   13
to Laws for establishing Judiciary powers.

He has made Judges dependent on his Will alone, for the tenure of their   14
offices, and the amount and payment of their salaries.

He has erected a multitude of New Offices, and sent hither swarms of   15
Officers to harass our people, and eat out their substance.

He has kept among us, in times of peace, Standing Armies without the   16
Consent of our legislatures.

He has affected to render the Military independent of and superior to   17
the Civil power.

He has combined with others[1] to subject us to a jurisdiction foreign to   18
our constitution, and unacknowledged by our laws; giving his Assent to their Acts of pretended Legislation:

For Quartering large bodies of armed troops among us: 19

[1] The British Parliament.

For protecting them, by a mock Trial, from punishment for any Murders   20
which they should commit on the Inhabitants of these States:

For cutting off our Trade with all parts of the world: 21

For imposing Taxes on us without our Consent: 22

For depriving us in many cases, of the benefits of Trial by Jury: 23

For transporting us beyond Seas to be tried for pretended offenses: 24

For abolishing the free System of English Laws in a neighboring Pro-   25
vince[2] establishing therein an Arbitrary government, and enlarging its Boundaries so as to render it at once an example and fit instrument for introducing
the same absolute rule into these Colonies:

For taking away our Charters, abolishing our most valuable Laws, and   26
altering fundamentally the Forms of our Governments:

For suspending our own Legislatures, and declaring themselves invested   27
with power to legislate for us in all cases whatsoever.

He has abdicated Government here, by declaring us out of his Protection   28
and waging War against us:

He has plundered our seas, ravaged our Coasts, burnt our towns, and   29
destroyed the lives of our people.

He is at this time transporting large Armies of foreign Mercenaries[3] to   30
compleat the works of death, desolation and tyranny, already begun with
circumstances of Cruelty & perfidy scarcely paralleled in the most barbarous
ages, and totally unworthy the Head of a civilized nation.

He has constrained our fellow Citizens taken Captive on the high Seas   31
to bear Arms against their Country, to become the executioners of their friends
and Brethren, or to fall themselves by their Hands.

He has excited domestic insurrections amongst us, and has endeavoured   32
to bring on the inhabitants of our frontiers, the merciless Indian Savages,
whose known rule of warfare, is an undistinguished destruction of all ages,
sexes and conditions. In every stage of these Oppressions We have Petitioned
for Redress in the most humble terms: Our repeated Petitions have been
answered only by repeated injury. A Prince, whose character is thus marked
by every act which may define a Tyrant, is unfit to be the ruler of a free
people. Nor have We been wanting in attentions to our British brethren. We
have warned them from time to time of attempts by their legislature to extend
an unwarrantable jurisdiction over us. We have reminded them of the circumstances of our emigration and settlement here. We have appealed to their
native justice and magnanimity, and we have conjured them by the ties of
our common kindred to disavow these usurpations, which, would inevitably
interrupt our connections and correspondence. They too have been deaf to

---

[2] The Quebec Act (1774) promised concessions to the French Catholics, and restored the
French civil law, thus alienating the Province of Quebec from the seaboard colonies in the
growing controversy.

[3] German soldiers, principally Hessians, hired by the British for colonial service.

the voice of justice and of consanguinity. We must, therefore, acquiesce in the necessity, which denounces[4] our Separation, and hold them, as we hold the rest of mankind, Enemies in War, in Peace Friends.

WE, THEREFORE, the Representatives of the UNITED STATES OF AMERICA,   33 in General Congress Assembled, appealing to the Supreme Judge of the world for the rectitude of our intentions, do, in the Name and by Authority of the good People of these Colonies, solemnly publish and declare, That these United Colonies are, and of Right ought to be FREE AND INDEPENDENT STATES; that they are Absolved from all Allegiance to the British Crown, and that all political connection between them and the State of Great Britain, is and ought to be totally dissolved; and that as Free and Independent States, they have full Power to levy War, conclude Peace, contract Alliances, establish Commerce, and to do all other Acts and Things which Independent States may of right do.

And for the support of this Declaration, with a firm reliance on the   34 protection of divine Providence, we mutually pledge to each other our Lives, our Fortunes and our sacred Honor.

SUBJECT QUESTIONS

1. Under what circumstances do the authors claim revolution to be justified? Do you agree? Can you think of other circumstances which might justify rebellion? Can you see any consistency in the attitude of our State Department toward revolution in other countries in the past twenty or thirty years? (Consider, for instance, Red China, Dominican Republic, Cuba, Hungary, Czechoslovakia, and Viet Nam.)
2. Do the authors give the impression that they have exhausted every other recourse before turning to revolution?
3. Consider the long list of reasons given for turning to rebellion; do they strike you as adequate justification? Do you see any that might be interpreted differently?
4. Judging by the one remark about American Indians, do you suppose the new government intended to apply its belief that "all men are created equal" to them?

STRUCTURE QUESTIONS

1. How closely does the Declaration follow the traditional formula for argument? (See Introduction.)
2. This is a subject on which the Continental Congress clearly felt strongly; have the authors maintained objectivity in the presentation of their case? Is it possible for the *tone* to be objective while the handling of evidence is biased?

[4] Proclaims.

3. What reason do they give for making this public declaration? How is the Preamble calculated to affect the reader?
4. Because this argument is a justification for something that has already been decided, rather than an invitation to debate the merits of doing it, one might expect the authors to be less open-minded than in an ideal argument; does this seem to be the case? Can you tell by the wording whether or not there is any deliberate intention to deceive? Does there seem to be any unintentional self-deception?

The Declaration of Independence

Stan Freberg

Stan Freberg (b. 1926) is a comedian, musician, television personality, and advertising executive. He is best known for his musical satires of excesses and commercialism in our culture. Included here is part of the script from the album Stan Freberg Presents the United States of America *(1961), a satire on romanticized notions of American history. Three other volumes in a projected series were never released, and this album was banned from major radio networks.*

NARRATOR: The trouble continued to brew. It was a time for action — and a time for words. On a hot July night in 1776 Benjamin Franklin was aroused from his work by the Call of Destiny.

JEFFERSON [*knocking*]: Hey, ya in there, Ben?

FRANKLIN: Who's that, Sylvia? 5

MRS. FRANKLIN: It's the Call of Destiny.

FRANKLIN: Come on, take a look through the curtains, there.

MRS. FRANKLIN: It's Tom Jefferson.

FRANKLIN: What, again? [*More Knocking.*] Ah, it's no good, I'll have to let him in. I'm coming, I'm coming. 10

JEFFERSON: Hi, Ben.

FRANKLIN: Tom.

JEFFERSON: Ya got a minute?

FRANKLIN: Well, I'll tell you the truth, I was just going out of town for the week end. 15

JEFFERSON: But it's only Wednesday.

FRANKLIN: Yeh. Well, you know, "A penny saved is a penny earned."

JEFFERSON: Well, what has that got to do with anything, Franklin?

FRANKLIN: I don't know, just the first thing that came into my head. Just making conversation. "An idle brain is the Devil's playground," you 20 know.

JEFFERSON: Say, you're pretty good at that, aren't you?

FRANKLIN: Yeh, they're some new wise sayings I just made up.

JEFFERSON: "Wise sayings"?

FRANKLIN: Yeh, I call 'em "wise sayings." Well what can I do for you? 25

Stan Freberg's "The Declaration of Independence" and the lyrics to the accompanying song are reprinted by permission of the Freberg Music Corporation from the recording, *Stan Freberg Presents the United States of America*, Vol. I: "The Early Years." Words and music by Stan Freberg. Copyright 1961 by the Freberg Music Corporation.

JEFFERSON: Well, I got this petition here I've been circulating around the neighborhood. Kinda thought you'd like to sign it. It's called "The Declaration of Independence."

FRANKLIN: Yeh, I heard about that. Sounds a little suspect, if you ask me.

JEFFERSON: Whataya mean, "suspect"? 30

FRANKLIN: Well, you're advocating the overthrow of the British government by force and violence, aren't you?

JEFFERSON: Well, yeh, yeh. But we've had it with that royal jazz!

FRANKLIN: Who's we?

JEFFERSON: All the guys. 35

FRANKLIN: Who's all the guys?

JEFFERSON: Oh, George, Jim Madison, Alex Hamilton, Johnny Adams, you know, all the guys.

FRANKLIN: Heh! The lunatic fringe!

JEFFERSON: Oh, they are not. 40

FRANKLIN: Bunch of wild-eyed radicals, professional liberals. Don't kid me any.

JEFFERSON: Oh, you call George Washington a wild-eyed radical?

FRANKLIN: Washington? I don't see his name on here.

JEFFERSON: No, but he promised to sign. 45

FRANKLIN: Oh, yeh, that's George for ya. Talks up a storm with them wooden teeth — can't shut him off. But when it comes time to put the name on the old parchment-orooney, try and find him.

JEFFERSON: Hey, what are you so surly about today?

FRANKLIN: Surly to bed, surly to rise, makes a man . . . 50

JEFFERSON: All right, all right, let's knock off the one-line jokes and sign the petition, whataya say, huh, fella?

FRANKLIN: Well, let me skim down it here. "When in the course of human events, . . . and so and so and so and so . . . so and so and so and so . . . that among these are life, liberty, and — the purfuit of happineff"? 55

JEFFERSON: That's "pursuit of happiness."

FRANKLIN: Well, all your s's look like f's here.

JEFFERSON: It's stylish. It's in, it's very in.

FRANKLIN: Oh well, if it's in. Ahem: "We, therefore, the representatives of the United States of America . . . so and so and so and so . . . solemnly 60 publish and declare . . . so and so and so and so . . . that they are absolved of all allegiance . . . eh . . . to the British crown . . . and so on." Eh. Ahem . . . a . . . little overboard, isn't it?

JEFFERSON: Well, ah . . .

FRANKLIN: You write this? 65

JEFFERSON: Yeh, I knocked it out. It's just a first draft.

FRANKLIN: Well, I'll tell you, why don't you leave it with me and I'll mail it in.

JEFFERSON: Oh, come on.

FRANKLIN: No, I'll tell you, Tom, let me say this. I'm with you in spirit, I'm   70
sure you understand that. But I've got to play it conservative. I'm a
business man.

JEFFERSON: Yeh.

FRANKLIN: I've got the printing business going pretty good; *Almanac* made
Book of the Month; and then I've got the inventions, you know. Got   75
pretty good distribution on the stoves, now. And then of course every
Saturday evening I bring out the mag.

JEFFERSON: The what?

FRANKLIN: Magazine.

JEFFERSON: Oh. Oh, that reminds me, that artist I sent by — you look at his   80
stuff?

FRANKLIN: You mean the Rockwell boy? Skinny kid with the pipe?

JEFFERSON: Yeh, that's the kid.

FRANKLIN: Yeh, I glanced at it. He's too far out for me.

JEFFERSON: Oh, yeh. Well, I know you gotta play it safe. Uh, but getting back   85
to the signing of the petition — now, how about it, huh?

FRANKLIN: Well, I . . .

JEFFERSON: It's a harmless paper.

FRANKLIN: Oh, sure, harmless. I know how these things happen. You go to
a couple of "harmless" parties, sign a "harmless" petition, and forget   90
all about it. Ten years later you get hauled up before a committee. No
thank you, I'm not going to spend the rest of *my* life writing in Europe.

JEFFERSON: Aw, come on.

FRANKLIN: Come on, what?

Song

JEFFERSON: Come on and put your name on the dotted line.   95
FRANKLIN: I got to be particular what I sign!
JEFFERSON: It's just a piece of paper.
FRANKLIN: Just a piece of paper, that's what you say.
JEFFERSON: Come on and put your signature on the list.
FRANKLIN: It looks to have a very subversive twist.   100
JEFFERSON: How silly to assume it;
              Won't you *nom de plume* it, today?
              You're so skittish,
              Who possibly could care if you do?
FRANKLIN: The UnBritish   105
              Activities Committee, that's who!
JEFFERSON: Let's have a little drinko
              And fill the quill.
FRANKLIN: It sounds a little pinko
              To me, but still . . .   110

JEFFERSON: Knock off the timid manner:
                If you want a banner to raise
                You must take a stand
                For this brave new land;
                For who wants to live   115
                So conservative?
FRANKLIN: I don't disagree
                But a man can't be
                Too careful what he signs these days!

FRANKLIN: Well, if I sign it will you renew your subscription?   120

JEFFERSON: Yeh, if you promise not to keep throwing it on the roof.

FRANKLIN: Well, I . . .

JEFFERSON: If it isn't on the roof, it's in the rose bushes or the mud.

FRANKLIN: My eyesight isn't what it used to be, you know. Besides, it's hard
to hit the porch from a horse.   125

JEFFERSON: Now come on, all we want to do is hold a few truths to be
self-evident.

FRANKLIN: You're sure it's not gonna start a revolution or anything?

JEFFERSON: Trust me.

FRANKLIN: O.K., give it to me. You got a quill on you?   130

JEFFERSON: Yeh, here you are.

FRANKLIN: Heh! look at this show-off Hancock, will ya? Pretty flamboyant
signature for an insurance man! [*Signs.*]

JEFFERSON: Ah, ya did a good thing, Ben. You won't be sorry! Heh, heh, heh.
Now if I can just get another three or four more guys, we'll be all set.   135

FRANKLIN: Well, I'll tell ya one thing.

JEFFERSON: What's that?

FRANKLIN: Ya better get 'em to sign in the next couple of days, before they
all take off for the Fourth of July week end!

SUBJECT QUESTIONS

1. Would you say that Freberg's purpose was serious, or simply to ridicule
American history? Should a good American take such liberties with
American tradition? (The album from which this skit was taken was
banned by major radio networks.)

2. Did Freberg mean to imply that Jefferson was "wrong" and Franklin
"right"? Why does Freberg portray Jefferson as a "sneaky, subversive"
type?

3. Which attitude — Jefferson's or Franklin's — would be considered more
"correct" today? What would happen to a Jefferson today? What, then,
does Freberg imply has happened to the American character since the
days of the Revolution?

4. What inducements does Jefferson offer to cause Franklin to change his mind? Do they seem to be convincing? What do they tell about the type of person represented by Franklin?
5. Is there any reason other than entertainment for the insertion of the incidental humor (Franklin's proverbs, for instance)?

STRUCTURE QUESTIONS

1. This skit represents, of course, an imaginary conversation. As "extemporaneous conversation," it resembles much more closely in form a college bull session than the formal argument by John Cogley. What differences do you note between this conversation and written argument?
2. Freberg implies that the bulk of Jefferson's argument is contained in the Declaration of Independence. In this script, however, Franklin gives the major argument and Jefferson the counterargument. How much knowledge of Jefferson's position does Freberg assume that Franklin — and the listener — have?
3. Examine Franklin's arguments. Are they logical and objective? What are his implied but unstated basic assumptions?
4. Now look at Jefferson's arguments. Are they more, or less, logical than Franklin's?
5. Although the script deals ostensibly with the arguments of Franklin and Jefferson, one might say that Freberg includes by implication an argument of his own. Outline that argument.
6. Would the conversation have been more effective had it been correct grammatically? If your answer is no, would it furnish support for an argument that teachers should be more lenient in a composition course?

The Bear

William Faulkner

William Faulkner (1897–1962) was born and lived in Mississippi, and most of his fiction deals with southern social problems, from the Reconstruction period to the present. Faulkner received the Nobel Prize for Literature in 1950. The story reprinted here, The Bear, *has Faulkner's usual setting in Mississippi, but the careful reader will find its message to be universal and timeless.*

He was ten. But it had already begun, long before that day when at last he   1
wrote his age in two figures and he saw for the first time the camp where
his father and Major de Spain and old General Compson and the others spent
two weeks each November and two weeks again each June. He had already
inherited then, without ever having seen it, the tremendous bear with one
trap-ruined foot which, in an area almost a hundred miles deep, had earned
itself a name, a definite designation like a living man.

He had listened to it for years: the long legend of corncribs rifled, of   2
shotes and grown pigs and even calves carried bodily into the woods and
devoured, of traps and deadfalls overthrown and dogs mangled and slain, and
shotgun and even rifle charges delivered at point-blank range and with no
more effect than so many peas blown through a tube by a boy — a corridor
of wreckage and destruction beginning back before he was born, through
which sped, not fast but rather with the ruthless and irresistible deliberation
of a locomotive, the shaggy tremendous shape.

It ran in his knowledge before he ever saw it. It looked and towered   3
in his dreams before he even saw the unaxed woods where it left its crooked
print, shaggy, huge, red-eyed, not malevolent but just big — too big for the
dogs which tried to bay it, for the horses which tried to ride it down, for
the men and the bullets they fired into it, too big for the very country which was
its constricting scope. He seemed to see it entire with a child's complete
divination before he ever laid eyes on either — the doomed wilderness whose
edges were being constantly and punily gnawed at by men with axes and plows
who feared it because it was wilderness, men myriad and nameless even to
one another in the land where the old bear had earned a name, through which
ran not even a mortal animal but an anachronism, indomitable and invincible,

out of an old dead time, a phantom, epitome and apotheosis of the old wild life at which the puny humans swarmed and hacked in a fury of abhorrence and fear, like pygmies about the ankles of a drowsing elephant: the old bear solitary, indomitable and alone, widowered, childless, and absolved of mortality — old Priam reft of his old wife and having outlived all his sons.

Until he was ten, each November he would watch the wagon containing   4
the dogs and the bedding and food and guns and his father and Tennie's Jim, the Negro, and Sam Fathers, the Indian, son of a slave woman and a Chickasaw chief, depart on the road to town, to Jefferson, where Major de Spain and the others would join them. To the boy, at seven, eight, and nine, they were not going into the Big Bottom to hunt bear and deer, but to keep yearly rendezvous with the bear which they did not even intend to kill. Two weeks later they would return, with no trophy, no head and skin. He had not expected it. He had not even been afraid it would be in the wagon. He believed that even after he was ten and his father would let him go too, for those two weeks in November, he would merely make another one, along with his father and Major de Spain and General Compson and the others, the dogs which feared to bay at it and the rifles and shotguns which failed even to bleed it, in the yearly pageant of the old bear's furious immortality.

Then he heard the dogs. It was in the second week of his first time in   5
the camp. He stood with Sam Fathers against a big oak beside the faint crossing where they had stood each dawn for nine days now, hearing the dogs. He had heard them once before, one morning last week — a murmur, sourceless, echoing through the wet woods, swelling presently into separate voices which he could recognize and call by name. He had raised and cocked the gun as Sam told him and stood motionless again while the uproar, the invisible course, swept up and past and faded; it seemed to him that he could actually see the deer, the buck, blond, smoke-colored, elongated with speed, fleeing, vanishing, the woods, the gray solitude, still ringing even when the cries of the dogs had died away.

"Now let the hammers down," Sam said.   6

"You knew they were not coming here too," he said.   7

"Yes," Sam said. "I want you to learn how to do when you didn't shoot.   8
It's after the chance for the bear or the deer has done already come and gone that men and dogs get killed."

"Anyway," he said, "it was just a deer."   9

Then on the tenth morning he heard the dogs again. And he readied   10
the too-long, too-heavy gun as Sam had taught him, before Sam even spoke. But this time it was no deer, no ringing chorus of dogs running strong on a free scent, but a moiling yapping an octave too high, with something more than indecision and even abjectness in it, not even moving very fast, taking a long time to pass completely out of hearing, leaving then somewhere in the air that echo, thin, slightly hysterical, abject, almost grieving, with no

sense of a fleeting, unseen, smoke-colored, grass-eating shape ahead of it, and Sam, who had taught him first of all to cock the gun and take position where he could see everywhere and then never move again, had himself moved up beside him; he could hear Sam breathing at his shoulder, and he could see the arched curve of the old man's inhaling nostrils.

"Hah," Sam said. "Not even running. Walking." 11

"Old Ben!" the boy said. "But up here!" he cried. "Way up here!" 12

"He do it every year," Sam said. "Once. Maybe to see who in camp 13 this time, if he can shoot or not. Whether we got the dog yet that can bay and hold him. He'll take them to the river, then he'll send them back home. We may as well go back too; see how they look when they come back to camp."

When they reached the camp the hounds were already there, ten of 14 them crouching back under the kitchen, the boy and Sam squatting to peer back into the obscurity where they had huddled, quiet, the eyes luminous, glowing at them and vanishing, and no sound, only that effluvium of something more than dog, stronger than dog and not just animal, just beast, because still there had been nothing in front of that abject and almost painful yapping save the solitude, the wilderness, so that when the eleventh hound came in at noon and with all the others watching — even old Uncle Ash, who called himself first a cook — Sam daubed the tattered ear and the raked shoulder with turpentine and axle grease, to the boy it was still no living creature, but the wilderness which, leaning for the moment down, had patted lightly once the hound's temerity.

"Just like a man," Sam said. "Just like folks. Put off as long as she could 15 having to be brave, knowing all the time that sooner or later she would have to be brave to keep on living with herself, and knowing all the time beforehand what was going to happen to her when she done it."

That afternoon, himself on the one-eyed wagon mule which did not mind 16 the smell of blood nor, as they told him, of bear, and with Sam on the other one, they rode for more than three hours through the rapid, shortening winter day. They followed no path, no trail even that he could see; almost at once they were in a country which he had never seen before. Then he knew why Sam had made him ride the mule which would not spook. The sound one stopped short and tried to whirl and bolt even as Sam got down, blowing its breath, jerking and wrenching at the rein, while Sam held it, coaxing it forward with his voice, since he could not risk tying it, drawing it forward while the boy got down from the marred one.

Then, standing beside Sam in the gloom of the dying afternoon, he 17 looked down at the rotted over-turned log, gutted and scored with claw marks and, in the wet earth beside it, the print of the enormous warped two-toed foot. He knew now what he had smelled when he peered under the kitchen where the dogs huddled. He realized for the first time that the bear which had run in his listening and loomed in his dreams since before he could remember to the contrary, and which, therefore, must have existed in the listening and dreams of his father and Major de Spain and even old General Compson, too, before they began to remember in their turn, was a mortal animal, and that if they had departed for the camp each November without any actual hope of bringing its trophy back, it was not because it could not be slain, but because so far they had had no actual hope to.

"Tomorrow," he said.

"We'll try tomorrow," Sam said. "We ain't got the dog yet."

"We've got eleven. They ran him this morning."

"It won't need but one," Sam said. "He ain't here. Maybe he ain't nowhere. The only other way will be for him to run by accident over somebody that has a gun."

"That wouldn't be me," the boy said. "It will be Walter or Major or —"

"It might," Sam said. "You watch close in the morning. Because he's smart. That's how come he has lived this long. If he gets hemmed up and has to pick out somebody to run over, he will pick out you."

"How?" the boy said. "How will he know —" He ceased. "You mean he already knows me, that I ain't never been here before, ain't had time to find out yet whether I —" He ceased again, looking at Sam, the old man whose face revealed nothing until it smiled. He said humbly, not even amazed, "It was me he was watching. I don't reckon he did need to come but once."

The next morning they left the camp three hours before daylight. They rode this time because it was too far to walk, even the dogs in the wagon; again the first gray light found him in a place which he had never seen before, where Sam had placed him and told him to stay and then departed. With the gun which was too big for him, which did not even belong to him, but to Major de Spain, and which he had fired only once — at a stump on the first day, to learn the recoil and how to reload it — he stood against a gum tree beside a little bayou whose black still water crept without movement out of a canebrake and crossed a small clearing and into cane again, where, invisible, a bird — the big woodpecker called Lord-to-God by Negroes — clattered at a dead limb.

It was a stand like any other, dissimilar only in incidentals to the one where he had stood each morning for ten days: a territory new to him, yet no less familiar than that other one which, after almost two weeks, he had come to believe he knew a little — the same solitude, the same loneliness through which human beings had merely passed without altering it, leaving no mark, no scar, which looked exactly as it must have looked when the first ancestor of Sam Fathers' Chickasaw predecessors crept into it and looked about, club or stone ax or bone arrow drawn and poised; different only because, squatting at the edge of the kitchen, he smelled the hounds huddled and cringing beneath it and saw the raked ear and shoulder of the one who,

18

19

20

21

22

23

24

25

26

Sam said, had had to be brave once in order to live with herself, and saw yesterday in the earth beside the gutted log the print of the living foot.

He heard no dogs at all. He never did hear them. He only heard the 27 drumming of the woodpecker stop short off and knew that the bear was looking at him. He never saw it. He did not know whether it was in front of him or behind him. He did not move, holding the useless gun, which he had not even had warning to cock and which even now he did not cock, tasting in his saliva that taint as of brass which he knew now because he had smelled it when he peered under the kitchen at the huddled dogs.

Then it was gone. As abruptly as it had ceased, the woodpecker's dry, 28 monotonous clatter set up again, and after a while he even believed he could hear the dogs — a murmur, scarce a sound even, which he had probably been hearing for some time before he even remarked it, drifting into hearing and then out again, dying away. They came nowhere near him. If it was a bear they ran, it was another bear. It was Sam himself who came out of the cane and crossed the bayou, followed by the injured bitch of yesterday. She was almost at heel, like a bird dog, making no sound. She came and crouched against his leg, trembling, staring off into the cane.

"I didn't see him," he said. "I didn't, Sam!" 29

"I know it," Sam said. "He done the looking. You didn't hear him 30 neither, did you?"

"No," the boy said. "I —" 31

"He's smart," Sam said. "Too smart." He looked down at the hound, 32 trembling faintly and steadily against the boy's knee. From the raked shoulder a few drops of fresh blood oozed and clung. "Too big. We ain't got the dog yet. But maybe someday. Maybe not next time. But someday."

So I must see him, he thought. *I must look at him.* Otherwise, it seemed 33 to him that it would go on like this forever, as it had gone on with his father and Major de Spain, who was older than his father, and even with old General Compson, who had been old enough to be a brigade commander in 1865. Otherwise, it would go on so forever, next time and next time, after and after and after. It seemed to him that he could never see the two of them, himself and the bear, shadowy in the limbo from which time emerged, becoming time; the old bear absolved of mortality and himself partaking, sharing a little of it, enough of it. And he knew now what he had smelled in the huddled dogs and tasted in his saliva. He recognized fear. *So I will have to see him,* he thought, without dread or even hope. *I will have to look at him.*

It was in June of the next year. He was eleven. They were in camp 34 again, celebrating Major de Spain's and General Compson's birthdays. Although the one had been born in September and the other in the depth of winter and in another decade, they had met for two weeks to fish and shoot squirrels and turkey and run coons and wildcats with the dogs at night. That is, he and Boon Hoggenbeck and the Negroes fished and shot squirrels and ran the coons and cats, because the proved hunters, not only Major de Spain and old General Compson, who spent those two weeks sitting in a rocking chair before a tremendous iron pot of Brunswick stew, stirring and tasting, with old Ash to quarrel with about how he was making it and Tennie's Jim to pour whiskey from the demijohn into the tin dipper from which he drank it, but even the boy's father and Walter Ewell, who were still young enough, scorned such, other than shooting the wild gobblers with pistols for wagers on their marksmanship.

Or, that is, his father and the others believed he was hunting squirrels.   35
Until the third day, he thought that Sam Fathers believed that too. Each morning he would leave the camp right after breakfast. He had his own gun now, a Christmas present. He went back to the tree beside the bayou where he had stood that morning. Using the compass which old General Compson had given him, he ranged from that point; he was teaching himself to be a better-than-fair woodsman without knowing he was doing it. On the second day he even found the gutted log where he had first seen the crooked print. It was almost completely crumbled now, healing with unbelievable speed, a passionate and almost visible relinquishment, back into the earth from which the tree had grown.

He ranged the summer woods now, green with gloom; if anything,   36
actually dimmer than in November's gray dissolution, where, even at noon, the sun fell only in intermittent dappling upon the earth, which never completely dried out and which crawled with snakes — moccasins and water snakes and rattlers, themselves the color of the dappling gloom, so that he would not always see them until they moved, returning later and later, first day, second day, passing in the twilight of the third evening the little log pen enclosing the log stable where Sam was putting up the horses for the night.

"You ain't looked right yet," Sam said.   37

He stopped. For a moment he didn't answer. Then he said peacefully,   38
in a peaceful rushing burst as when a boy's miniature dam in a little brook gives way, "All right. But how? I went to the bayou. I even found that log again. I —"

"I reckon that was all right. Likely he's been watching you. You never   39
saw his foot?"

"I," the boy said — "I didn't — I never thought —"   40

"It's the gun," Sam said. He stood beside the fence motionless — the old   41
man, the Indian, in the battered faded overalls and the five-cent straw hat which in the Negro's race had been the badge of his enslavement and was now the regalia of his freedom. The camp — the clearing, the house, the barn and its tiny lot with which Major de Spain in his turn had scratched punily and evanescently at the wilderness — faded in the dusk, back into the immemorial darkness of the woods. *The gun*, the boy thought. *The gun.*

"Be scared," Sam said. "You can't help that. But don't be afraid. Ain't   42
nothing in the woods going to hurt you unless you corner it, or it smells that
you are afraid. A bear or a deer, too, has got to be scared of a coward the
same as a brave man has got to be."

The gun, the boy thought.   43

"You will have to choose," Sam said.   44

He left the camp before daylight, long before Uncle Ash would wake   45
in his quilts on the kitchen floor and start the fire for breakfast. He had only
the compass and a stick for snakes. He could go almost a mile before he would
begin to need the compass. He sat on a log, the invisible compass in his
invisible hand, while the secret night sounds, fallen still at his movements,
scurried again and then ceased for good, and the owls ceased and gave over
to the waking of day birds, and he could see the compass. Then he went fast
yet still quietly; he was becoming better and better as a woodsman, still
without having yet realized it.

He jumped a doe and a fawn at sunrise, walked them out of the bed,   46
close enough to see them — the crash of undergrowth, the white scut, the fawn
scudding behind her faster than he had believed it could run. He was hunting
right, upwind, as Sam had taught him; not that it mattered now. He had left
the gun; of his own will and relinquishment he had accepted not a gambit,
not a choice, but a condition in which not only the bear's heretofore inviolable
anonymity but all the old rules and balances of hunter and hunted had been
abrogated. He would not even be afraid, not even in the moment when the
fear would take him completely — blood, skin, bowels, bones, memory from
the long time before it became his memory — all save that thin, clear, immortal lucidity which alone differed him from this bear and from all the other
bear and deer he would ever kill in the humility and pride of his skill and
endurance, to which Sam had spoken when he leaned in the twilight on the
lot fence yesterday.

By noon he was far beyond the little bayou, farther into the new and   47
alien country than he had ever been. He was traveling now not only by the
old, heavy, biscuit-thick silver watch which had belonged to his grandfather.
When he stopped at last, it was for the first time since he had risen from
the log at dawn when he could see the compass. It was far enough. He had
left the camp nine hours ago; nine hours from now, dark would have already
been an hour old. But he didn't think that. He thought, *All right. Yes. But
what?* and stood for a moment, alien and small in the green and topless
solitude, answering his own question before it had formed and ceased. It was
the watch, the compass, the stick — the three lifeless mechanicals with which
for nine hours he had fended the wilderness off; he hung the watch and
compass carefully on a bush and leaned the stick beside them and relinquished
completely to it.

He had not been going very fast for the last two or three hours. He   48 went no faster now, since distance would not matter even if he could have gone fast. And he was trying to keep a bearing on the tree where he had left the compass, trying to complete a circle which would bring him back to it or at least intersect itself, since direction would not matter now either. But the tree was not there, and he did as Sam had schooled him — made the next circle in the opposite direction, so that the two patterns would bisect somewhere, but crossing no print of his own feet, finding the tree at last, but in the wrong place — no bush, no compass, no watch — and the tree not even the tree, because there was a down log beside it and he did what Sam Fathers had told him was the next thing and the last.

As he sat down on the log he saw the crooked print — the warped, 49 tremendous, two-toed indentation which, even as he watched it, filled with water. As he looked up, the wilderness coalesced, solidified — the glade, the tree he sought, the bush, the watch and the compass glinting where a ray of sunshine touched them. Then he saw the bear. It did not emerge, appear; it was just there, immobile, solid, fixed in the hot dappling of the green and windless noon, not as big as he had dreamed it, but as big as he had expected it, bigger, dimensionless, against the dappled obscurity, looking at him where he sat quietly on the log and looked back at it.

Then it moved. It made no sound. It did not hurry. It crossed the glade, 50 walking for an instant into the full glare of the sun; when it reached the other side it stopped again and looked back at him across one shoulder while his quiet breathing inhaled and exhaled three times.

Then it was gone. It didn't walk into the woods, the undergrowth. It 51 faded, sank back into the wilderness as he had watched a fish, a huge old bass, sink and vanish into the dark depths of its pool without even any movement of its fins.

He thought, *It will be next fall.* But it was not next fall, nor the next nor 52 the next. He was fourteen then. He had killed his buck, and Sam Fathers had marked his face with the hot blood, and in the next year he killed a bear. But even before that accolade he had become as competent in the woods as many grown men with the same experience; by his fourteenth year he was a better woodsman than most grown men with more. There was no territory within thirty miles of the camp that he did not know — bayou, ridge, brake, landmark, tree and path. He could have led anyone to any point in it without deviation, and brought them out again. He knew the game trails that even Sam Fathers did not know; in his thirteenth year he found a buck's bedding place, and unbeknown to his father he borrowed Walter Ewell's rifle and lay in wait at dawn and killed the buck when it walked back to the bed, as Sam had told him how the old Chickasaw fathers did.

But not the old bear, although by now he knew its footprints better 53 than he did his own, and not only the crooked one. He could see any one of three sound ones and distinguish it from any other, and not only by its size. There were other bears within these thirty miles which left tracks almost as large, but this was more than that. If Sam Fathers had been his mentor and the back-yard rabbits and squirrels at home his kindergarten, then the wilderness the old bear ran was his college, the old male bear itself, so long unwifed and childless as to have become its own ungendered progenitor, was his alma mater. But he never saw it.

He could find the crooked print now almost whenever he liked, fifteen   54 or ten or five miles, or sometimes nearer the camp than that. Twice while on stand during the three years he heard the dogs strike its trail by accident; on the second time they jumped it seemingly, the voices high, abject, almost human in hysteria, as on that first morning two years ago. But not the bear itself. He would remember than noon three years ago, the glade, himself and the bear fixed during that moment in the windless and dappled blaze, and it would seem to him that it had never happened, that he had dreamed that too. But it had happened. They had looked at each other, they had emerged from the wilderness old as earth, synchronized to the instant by something more than the blood that moved the flesh and bones which bore them, and touched, pledged something, affirmed something more lasting than the frail web of bones and flesh which any accident could obliterate.

Then he saw it again. Because of the very fact that he thought of nothing   55 else, he had forgotten to look for it. He was still hunting with Walter Ewell's rifle. He saw it cross the end of a long blow-down, a corridor where a tornado had swept, rushing through rather than over the tangle of trunks and branches as a locomotive would have, faster than he had ever believed it could move, almost as fast as a deer even, because a deer would have spent most of that time in the air, faster than he could bring the rifle sights up with it. And now he knew what had been wrong during all the three years. He sat on a log, shaking and trembling as if he had never seen the woods before nor anything that ran them, wondering with incredulous amazement how he could have forgotten the very thing which Sam Fathers had told him and which the bear itself had proved the next day and had now returned after three years to reaffirm.

And now he knew what Sam Fathers had meant about the right dog,   56 a dog in which size would mean less than nothing. So when he returned alone in April — school was out then, so that the sons of farmers could help with the land's planting, and at last his father had granted him permission, on his promise to be back in four days — he had the dog. It was his own, a mongrel of the sort called by Negroes a fyce, a ratter, itself not much bigger than a rat and possessing that bravery which had long since stopped being courage and had become foolhardiness.

It did not take four days. Alone again, he found the trail on the first   57 morning. It was not a stalk; it was an ambush. He timed the meeting almost as if it were an appointment with a human being. Himself holding the fyce muffled in a feed sack and Sam Fathers with two of the hounds on a piece of a plowline rope, they lay down wind of the trail at dawn of the second morning. They were so close that the bear turned without even running, as if in surprised amazement at the shrill and frantic uproar of the released fyce, turning at bay against the trunk of a tree, on its hind feet; it seemed to the boy that it would never stop rising, taller and taller, and even the two hounds seemed to take a desperate and despairing courage from the fyce, following it as it went in.

Then he realized that the fyce was actually not going to stop. He flung, threw the gun away, and ran; when he overtook and grasped the frantically pin-wheeling little dog, it seemed to him that he was directly under the bear. 58

He could smell it, strong and hot and rank. Sprawling, he looked up to where it loomed and towered over him like a cloudburst and colored like a thunderclap, quite familiar, peacefully and even lucidly familiar, until he remembered: This was the way he had used to dream about it. Then it was gone. He didn't see it go. He knelt, holding the frantic fyce with both hands, hearing the abashed wailing of the hounds drawing farther and farther away, until Sam came up. He carried the gun. He laid it down quietly beside the boy and stood looking down at him. 59

"You've done seed him twice now with a gun in your hands," he said. "This time you couldn't have missed him." 60

The boy rose. He still held the fyce. Even in his arms and clear of the ground, it yapped frantically, straining and surging after the fading uproar of the two hounds like a tangle of wire springs. He was panting a little, but he was neither shaking nor trembling now. 61

"Neither could you!" he said. "You had the gun! Neither did you!" 62

"And you didn't shoot," his father said. "How close were you?" 63

"I don't know, sir," he said. "There was a big wood tick inside his right hind leg. I saw that. But I didn't have the gun then." 64

"But you didn't shoot when you had the gun," his father said. "Why?" 65

But he didn't answer, and his father didn't wait for him to, rising and crossing the room, across the pelt of the bear which the boy had killed two years ago and the larger one which his father had killed before he was born, to the bookcase beneath the mounted head of the boy's first buck. It was the room which his father called the office, from which all the plantation business was transacted; in it for the fourteen years of his life he had heard the best of all talking. Major de Spain would be there and sometimes old General Compson, and Walter Ewell and Boon Hoggenbeck and Sam Fathers and Tennie's Jim, too, were hunters, knew the woods and what ran them. 66

He would hear it, not talking himself but listening — the wilderness, the 67
big woods, bigger and older than any recorded document of white man fatuous
enough to believe he had bought any fragment of it or Indian ruthless enough
to pretend that any fragment of it had been his to convey. It was of the men,
not white nor black nor red, but men, hunters with the will and hardihood
to endure and the humility and skill to survive, and the dogs and the bear
and deer juxtaposed and reliefed against it, ordered and compelled by and
within the wilderness in the ancient and unremitting contest by the ancient
and immitigable rules which voided all regrets and brooked no quarter, the
voices quiet and weighty and deliberate for retrospection and recollection
and exact remembering, while he squatted in the blazing firelight as Tennie's
Jim squatted, who stirred only to put more wood on the fire and to pass the
bottle from one glass to another. Because the bottle was always present, so
that after a while it seemed to him that those fierce instants of heart and
brain and courage and wiliness and speed were concentrated and distilled into
that brown liquor which not women, not boys and children, but only hunters
drank, drinking not of the blood they had spilled but some condensation of
the wild immortal spirit, drinking it moderately, humbly even, not with the
pagan's base hope of acquiring the virtues of cunning and strength and speed,
but in salute to them.

His father returned with the book and sat down again and opened it. 68
"Listen," he said. He read the five stanzas aloud, his voice quiet and deliberate
in the room where there was no fire now because it was already spring. Then
he looked up. The boy watched him. "All right," his father said. "Listen."
He read again, but only the second stanza this time, to the end of it, the last
two lines, and closed the book and put it on the table beside him. "She cannot
fade, though thou has not thy bliss, forever wilt thou love, and she be fair,"
he said.

"He's talking about a girl," the boy said. 69

"He had to talk about something," his father said. Then he said, "He 70
was talking about truth. Truth doesn't change. Truth is one thing. It covers
all things which touch the heart — honor and pride and pity and justice and
courage and love. Do you see now?"

He didn't know. Somehow it was simpler than that. There was an old 71
bear, fierce and ruthless, not merely just to stay alive, but with the fierce pride
of liberty and freedom, proud enough of the liberty and freedom to see it
threatened without fear or even alarm; nay, who at times even seemed deliberately to put that freedom and liberty in jeopardy in order to savor them,
to remind his old strong bones and flesh to keep supple and quick to defend
and preserve them. There was an old man, son of a Negro slave and an Indian
king, inheritor on the one side of the long chronicle of a people who had
learned humility through suffering, and pride through the endurance which
survived the suffering and injustice, and on the other side, the chronicle of

a people even longer in the land than the first, yet who no longer existed in the land at all save in the solitary brotherhood of an old Negro's alien blood and the wild and invincible spirit of an old bear. There was a boy who wished to learn humility and pride in order to become skillful and worthy in the woods, who suddenly found himself becoming so skillful so rapidly that he feared he would never become worthy because he had not learned humility and pride, although he had tried to, until one day and as suddenly he discovered that an old man who could not have defined either had led him, as though by the hand, to that point where an old bear and a little mongrel of a dog showed him that, by possessing one thing other, he would possess them both.

And a little dog, nameless and mongrel and many-fathered, grown, yet 72 weighing less than six pounds, saying as if to itself, "I can't be dangerous, because there's nothing much smaller than I am; I can't be fierce, because they would call it just a noise; I can't be humble, because I'm already too close to the ground to genuflect; I can't be proud, because I wouldn't be near enough to it for anyone to know who was casting the shadow, and I don't even know that I'm not going to heaven, because they have already decided that I don't possess an immortal soul. So all I can be is brave. But it's all right. I can be that, even if they still call it just noise."

That was all. It was simple, much simpler than somebody talking in 73 a book about youth and a girl he would never need to grieve over, because he could never approach any nearer her and would never have to get any farther away. He had heard about a bear, and finally got big enough to trail it, and he trailed it four years and at last met it with a gun in his hands and he didn't shoot. Because a little dog — But he could have shot long before the little dog covered the twenty yards to where the bear waited, and Sam Fathers could have shot at any time during that interminable minute while Old Ben stood on his hind feet over them. He stopped. His father was watching him gravely across the spring-rife twilight of the room; when he spoke, his words were as quiet as the twilight, too, not loud, because they did not need to be because they would last. "Courage, and honor, and pride," his father said, "and pity, and love of justice and of liberty. They all touch the heart, and what the heart holds to becomes truth, as far as we know the truth. Do you see now?"

Sam, and Old Ben, and Nip, he thought. And himself too. He had been 74 all right too. His father had said so. "Yes, sir," he said.

SUBJECT QUESTIONS

1. Faulkner makes clear from the beginning that Old Ben is more than just a bear; what does he represent?
2. Why do the hunters have no intention of killing Old Ben? If they don't mean to kill him, why do they hunt him every year?

3. Sam Fathers tells the boy that a bear — or a deer or a man — has more to fear from a coward than from a brave man. Do you agree?
4. If the boy must put himself in jeopardy in order to meet the bear, what does the bear mean to the boy? Why does Old Ben sometimes deliberately put *himself* in jeopardy?
5. What three things does the boy need in order to become skillful and worthy?
6. The boy's father explains to him why he didn't kill the bear by reading Keats's "Ode on a Grecian Urn," the point of which is that art, being a distillation of truth, is the only permanent beauty. What connection does that idea have with the boy's action? Does the father's final clarification help?
7. How does the boy explain to himself his refusal to kill Old Ben?

STRUCTURE QUESTIONS

1. This story has been placed in the section on argument, but it obviously does not have the structure of formal argument. In what sense, if any, is it an argument? (You might consider how the story would be changed if Faulkner had let Old Ben hide in a cave instead of exposing himself to danger.)
2. If a short story is to have symbolic meaning, it still ought to function on a literal level — that is, it ought to tell a consistent and comprehensible story. Is this one consistent on both levels?
3. When a writer uses symbols, one of his problems is to make clear what the symbols mean without being blatantly obvious. (The meaning of a symbol may be "felt" or "understood" in context even though it cannot be precisely stated in expository prose.) Did you have any trouble understanding, in the context, what the bear and the fyce stood for? Is the boy also a symbol?
4. Sam Fathers makes a distinction between two words usually considered synonymous, "scared" and "afraid." Should Faulkner have defined the terms to make the difference clear? Why doesn't he?

8

A MATTER OF FAITH

Persuasion

Just as the ancestor of argument was the deliberative oration of the Athenian Senate, so the forefather of persuasion was the forensic oration of Athenian law courts — or judicial assemblies. Its original purpose was to gain acquittal for the defendant. Because the lawyer delivering the oration was less interested in arriving at truth than in getting his client "off the hook," he did not feel obliged to limit his approach to the logical, objective one of the deliberative oration: an acquittal for illogical or emotional reasons was still an acquittal. Although the rather strict formula for the forensic oration is usually disregarded today, our trial lawyers still use many of the same tactics which Aristotle discussed in his *Rhetoric*. Defense attorneys are likely to distract attention from the specific charge by dragging in character witnesses, or by associating the client's cause with the patriotic or religious feelings of the jury by quoting Abe Lincoln and the Bible.

The ideal persuasion, certainly, would not be deliberately illogical, but it would be much less likely than argument to encourage free and impartial discussion of the problem at hand. The strong feelings about his subject that the writer of argument strives to control can actually be put to use in persuasion to sway the reader to the desired position. Normally, too, the writer of persuasion will not be anxious to discuss impartially his opponent's arguments. Although he wants the readers to have the impression that his arguments have been presented reasonably and fairly, he is more interested in their having a complete emotional conviction that he is right; hence, the writer does not want to distract them from this goal by allowing any implication of serious weakness in his own position.

The form of a persuasion is basically the same as that of written argument. Normally, it contains the same four parts: analysis of the problem; clear statement of the proposed solution; disproof of the opposition; and positive evidence. In addition persuasion ends with a "peroration," or a final strong emotional appeal. But the difference between persuasion and argument is almost entirely one of attitude: argument seeks to stimulate discussion, persuasion seeks to end it. The writer of persuasion can include anything which does not spoil his case by the obviousness of its intent — appeals to prejudice and sympathies, appeals to such respected authorities as prophets, movie stars, and baseball heroes, arguments against an opponent's character instead of his ideas, and so on. He does not have to take pains to ensure that his evidence is typical, relevant, impartial, and sufficient. He can even include brief digressions on related topics that, though they do not constitute proof, will sway the reader to his side by appealing to religious and political convictions, sense of justice and fair play, and so on. When Mark Antony delivered the famous funeral oration in Shakespeare's *Julius Caesar,* for instance, his aim was to convince the mob that Caesar was innocent of the charge of ambition. But Antony did not confine himself to relevant arguments alone. He aroused the people by displaying Caesar's corpse and pointing out the holes made by the daggers of the various assassins; he read Caesar's will; he made much of Brutus's having slain his best friend. In short, he used any argument which would either make the mob believe that his was the "reasonable" side or incense them against the conspirators.

Because the forensic oration was developed to incite the listeners to *do* something — that is, acquit the defendant — persuasion has traditionally been associated with this original aim. Argument can also be used to stimulate the reader to follow a desired course of action, but usually a reader is more likely to be stirred to action if he is given more motivation than cold logic. Persuasion, then, by combining logic with warmer appeals, is the ideal means of accomplishing such a purpose. (Persuasion can, however, be used simply to sway the reader to believe something without doing anything about it.) If the writer wishes his readers to take some action, he should be specific about the end he has in mind and should outline clearly the steps (process) by which that aim can be accomplished. As in any process, the steps should be in proper order and clearly explained. The P.T.A. speaker who convinces his audience that the town needs better schools may achieve nothing unless he explains a method of getting better schools. Mark Antony incited the mob to anger, but their anger and energy would gradually have dissipated had not Antony suggested specific action to them — to burn Brutus's house and drive the assassins from Rome. Although an audience or reader may be convinced that "something needs to be done," nothing will be done unless he is told how to do it. Even if the writer is not sure that the method he has in mind is the best way of achieving his goal, he should still offer it as a tentative plan: it will show the reader that something *can* be done and it may stimulate him to think of a better plan by giving him something specific to work with.

The greatest danger in writing persuasion is irresponsibility. The student who plans to write persuasion should remember that the aim of writing ought to be honest communication. The freedom to use emotional appeals in persuasion frequently misleads a student into thinking that he is free to use dishonest means to gain honest ends. Good persuasion, like good propaganda, does make use of motivations somewhat less respectable intellectually than those used in logical argument; still, the writer should believe in the rightness of what he wants the reader to do.

Writing persuasion can be an entertaining change of pace from the type of expository prose a student is usually called upon to write. It can also be a useful art: although few students are studying to become politicians or ministers, most of them do have to write home for money occasionally.

The selections illustrating persuasion were chosen from the general area of religion because that is a subject on which logical argument, in the truest sense, is virtually impossible. Many bull sessions on this topic go wrong because the participants fail to realize that it is an area for persuasion rather than argument. Matters of faith are seldom influenced by statistical evidence. You are urged to examine these writings as open-mindedly as possible. You should honestly expose your own ideas to comparison with those presented here, remembering that if a belief is worth having it ought to be able to withstand exposure to differing beliefs.

from The Apology of Socrates

Plato

Socrates was sentenced to death for "corrupting the youth of Athens." His method of teaching was to engage the supposedly wise in cross-examination and thereby prove them not to be wise. The passage which follows is part of his defense of himself at the trial as reported later by his student, Plato (427?–347 B.C.).

Someone will say: And are you not ashamed, Socrates, of a course of life which   1
is likely to bring you to an untimely end? To him I may fairly answer: There
you are mistaken: a man who is good for anything ought not to calculate
the chance of living or dying; he ought only to consider whether in doing
anything he is doing right or wrong — acting the part of a good man or of
a bad. . . .

Strange, indeed, would be my conduct, O men of Athens, if I, who when   2
I was ordered by the generals whom you chose to command me at Potidaea[1]
and Amphipolis and Delium, remained where they placed me, like any other
man, facing death — if now, when, as I conceive and imagine, God orders
me to fulfill the philosopher's mission of searching into myself and other men,
I were to desert my post through fear of death, or any other fear; that would
indeed be strange, and I might justly be arraigned in court for denying the
existence of the gods, if I disobeyed the oracle because I was afraid of death,
fancying that I was wise when I was not wise. For the fear of death is indeed
the pretense of wisdom, and not real wisdom, being a pretense of knowing
the unknown; and no one knows whether death, which men in their fear
apprehend to be the greatest evil, may not be the greatest good. Is not this
ignorance of a disgraceful sort, the ignorance which is the conceit that a man
knows what he does not know? And in this respect only I believe myself to
differ from men in general, and may perhaps claim to be wiser than they
are: that whereas I know but little of the world below, I do not suppose that
I know: but I do know that injustice and disobedience to a better, whether
God or man, is evil and dishonorable, and I will never fear or avoid a possible
good rather than a certain evil. And therefore if you let me go now, and are
not convinced by Anytus, who said that since I had been prosecuted I must
be put to death (or if not, that I ought never to have been prosecuted at

---

[1] Socrates had served in the Athenian infantry during some of the northern campaigns
of the Peloponnesian War.

all); and that if I escape now, your sons will all be utterly ruined by listening to my words — if you say to me, Socrates, this time we will not mind Anytus, and you shall be let off, but upon one condition, that you are not to inquire and speculate in this way any more, and that if you are caught doing so again you shall die; if this was the condition on which you let me go, I should reply: Men of Athens, I honor and love you; but I shall obey God rather than you, and while I have life and strength I shall never cease from the practice and teaching of philosophy, exhorting anyone whom I meet and saying to him after my manner: "You, my friend — a citizen of the great and mighty and wise city of Athens — are you not ashamed of heaping up the greatest amount of money and honor and reputation, and caring so little about wisdom and truth and the greatest improvement of the soul, which you never regard or heed at all?" And if the person with whom I am arguing, says: "Yes, but I do care"; then I do not leave him or let him go at once; but I proceed to interrogate and examine and cross-examine him, and if I think that he has no virtue in him, but only says that he has, I reproach him with undervaluing the greater and overvaluing the less. And I shall repeat the same words to everyone whom I meet, young and old, citizen and alien, but especially to the citizens, inasmuch as they are my brethren. For know that this is the command of God; and I believe that no greater good has ever happened in the state than my service to the God. For I do nothing but go about persuading you all, old and young alike, not to take thought for your persons or your properties, but first and chiefly to care about the greatest improvement of the soul. I tell you that virtue is not given by money, but that from virtue comes money and every other good of man, public as well as private. This is my teaching, and if this is the doctrine which corrupts the youth, I am a mischievous person. But if anyone says that this is not my teaching, he is speaking an untruth. Wherefore, O men of Athens, I say to you, do as Anytus bids or not as Anytus bids, and either acquit me or not; but whichever you do, understand that I shall never alter my ways, not even if I have to die many times.

Men of Athens, do not interrupt, but hear me; there was an understanding between us that you should hear me to the end; I have something more to say, at which you may be inclined to cry out; but I believe that to hear me will be good for you, and therefore I beg that you will not cry out. I would have you know that if you kill such an one as I am, you will injure yourselves more than you will injure me. Nothing will injure me, not Meletus nor yet Anytus — they cannot, for a bad man is not permitted to injure a better than himself. I do not deny that Anytus may, perhaps, kill him, or drive him into exile, or deprive him of civil rights; and he may imagine, and others may imagine, that he is inflicting a great injury upon him: but there I do not agree. For the evil of doing as he is doing — the evil of unjustly taking away the life of another — is greater far.

And now, Athenians, I am not going to argue for my own sake, as you   4
may think, but for yours, that you may not sin against the God by condemning
me, who am his gift to you. For if you kill me you will not easily find a
successor to me, who, if I may use such a ludicrous figure of speech, am a
sort of gadfly, given to the state by God; and the state is a great and noble
steed who is tardy in his motions owing to his very size, and requires to be
stirred into life. I am that gadfly which God has attached to the state, and
all day long and in all places am always fastening upon you, arousing and
persuading and reproaching you. You will not easily find another like me,
and therefore I would advise you to spare me. I dare say that you may feel
out of temper (like a person who is suddenly awakened from sleep), and you
think that you might easily strike me dead as Anytus advises, and then you
would sleep on for the remainder of your lives, unless God in his care of you
sent you another gadfly. When I say that I am given to you by God, the proof
of my mission is this: if I had been like other men, I should not have neglected
all my own concerns or patiently seen the neglect of them during all these
years, and have been doing yours, coming to you individually like a father
or elder brother, exhorting you to regard virtue; such conduct, I say, would
be unlike human nature. If I had gained anything, or if my exhortations had
been paid, there would have been some sense in my doing so; but now, as
you will perceive, not even the impudence of my accusers dares to say that
I have ever exacted or sought pay of anyone; of that they have no witness.
And I have a sufficient witness to the truth of what I say — my poverty.

Someone may wonder why I go about in private giving advice and   5
busying myself with the concerns of others, but do not venture to come
forward in public and advise the state. I will tell you why. You have heard
me speak at sundry times and in diverse places of an oracle or sign which
comes to me, and is the divinity which Meletus ridicules in the indictment.
This sign, which is a kind of voice, first began to come to me when I was
a child; it always forbids but never commands me to do anything which I
am going to do. This is what deters me from being a politician. And rightly,
as I think. For I am certain, O men of Athens, that if I had engaged in politics,
I should have perished long ago, and done no good either to you or to myself.
And do not be offended at my telling you the truth: for the truth is, that
no man who goes to war with you or any other multitude, honestly striving
against the many lawless and unrighteous deeds which are done in a state,
will save his life; he who will fight for the right, if he would live even for
a brief space, must have a private station and not a public one. . . .

SUBJECT QUESTIONS

1. Socrates' defense of himself, although it shows his honesty and apparent
   innocence, does not seem calculated to win his acquittal. Why not?
2. Do you think Socrates might deliberately have put his judges into a

position of having to convict him? What might he gain by doing so? What would the world think — or know — of Socrates had he asked for mercy and promised to quit teaching, and thereby been allowed to live?

3. Socrates says that the only way in which he is wiser than other men is that he knows his ignorance and they do not. Of what use, if any, would that sort of wisdom be? Does Socrates show through his speech that he is also wiser than his judges in other ways?

4. What is the rationale behind the concluding statement — "he who will fight for the right, if he would live even for a brief space, must have a private station and not a public one"? How can a reformer accomplish anything unless he secures some position of public power?

5. A reforming politician today, while in some danger of assassination, is in little danger of being put to death by the government. What is more likely to happen to him? Can you think of any politicians in recent years who have had to sacrifice their ideals in order to maintain an influential position in government? Can you think of any who, like Socrates, quit the government in order to maintain their integrity?

6. What is the gist of Socrates' argument that the government should acquit him for their own sakes rather than for his?

7. What parallels do you find between Socrates' trial and that of Jesus?

STRUCTURE QUESTIONS

1. Socrates' defense in its entirety follows the traditional formula for a forensic oration; how much of that formula can you detect in this extract?

2. To what extent, if any, does Socrates rely on emotional rather than rational appeal?

3. If Socrates' approach is primarily rational, what puts this speech in the category of persuasion rather than argument?

4. Examine Socrates' proof that he has been sent to the state by God (paragraph 4); does it constitute valid evidence? Is it "persuasive"?

The Way of Life

Laotzu

According to legend, Laotzu's father was a shooting star. After being carried in his mother's womb for sixty-two years, he was born in 604 B.C., white-haired and capable of philosophical discourse. He refused, throughout his long life of teaching, to write anything down for fear it would become scripture for some religious sect. But the legend says that when he finally rode off into the desert on a water buffalo, a border-guard persuaded him to write down a few of his thoughts for posterity. The result was the Tao Teh Ching, or The Way of Life. Ironically, the Tao did become the basis of religions far different in spirit from Laotzu's simple view of life: Taoism in China and Shin-tao (Shinto) in Japan. The aim of the Tao is described by Witter Bynner as "creative quietism." It does not emphasize transcendental meditation or inactivity, but it rejects all action based on greed, glory, or ego. Humility, patience, and fortitude are the key virtues. Laotzu felt that systems of religion, knowledge, and politics are likely to interfere with private virtue — unless one knows that "the way to do is to be." We offer here eight of the eighty-one sayings in the Tao Teh Ching. The translation is by Witter Bynner, a poet best known for the translation of The Jade Mountain.

17

A leader is best
When people barely know that he exists,
Not so good when people obey and acclaim him,
Worst when they despise him,
'Fail to honor people,   5
They fail to honor you;'
But of a good leader, who talks little,
When his work is done, his aim fulfilled,
They will all say, 'We did this ourselves.'

18

When people lost sight of the way to live   10
Came codes of love and honesty,
Learning came, charity came,

Hypocrisy took charge;
When differences weakened family ties
Came benevolent fathers and dutiful sons;   15
And when lands were disrupted and misgoverned
Came ministers commended as loyal.

19

Rid of formalized wisdom and learning
People would be a hundredfold happier,
Rid of conventionalized duty and honor   20
People would find their families dear,
Rid of legalized profiteering
People would have no thieves to fear.
These methods of life have failed, all three,
Here is the way, it seems to me: 25
Set people free,
As deep in their hearts they would like to be,
From private greeds
And wanton needs.

29

Those who would take over the earth   30
And shape it to their will
Never, I notice, succeed.
The earth is like a vessel so sacred
That at the mere approach of the profane
It is marred   35
And when they reach out their fingers it is gone.
For a time in the world some force themselves ahead
And some are left behind,
For a time in the world some make a great noise
And some are held silent,   40
For a time in the world some are puffed fat
And some are kept hungry,
For a time in the world some push aboard
And some are tipped out:
At no time in the world will a man who is sane   45
Over-reach himself,
Over-spend himself,
Over-rate himself.

30

One who would guide a leader of men in the uses of life
Will warn him against the use of arms for conquest. 50
Weapons often turn upon the wielder,
An army's harvest is a waste of thorns,
Conscription of a multitude of men
Drains the next year dry.
A good general, daring to march, dares also to halt, 55
Will never press his triumph beyond need.
What he must do he does but not for glory,
What he must do he does but not for show,
What he must do he does but not for self;
He has done it because it had to be done, 60
Not from a hot head.
Let life ripen and then fall,
Force is not the way at all:
Deny the way of life and you are dead.

31

Even the finest arms are an instrument of evil, 65
A spread of plague,
And the way for a vital man to go is not the way of a soldier.
But in time of war men civilized in peace
Turn from their higher to their lower nature.
Arms are an instrument of evil, 70
No measure for thoughtful men
Until there fail all other choice
But sad acceptance of it.
Triumph is not beautiful.
He who thinks triumph beautiful 75
Is one with a will to kill,
And one with a will to kill
Shall never prevail upon the world.
It is a good sign when man's higher nature comes forward,
A bad sign when his lower nature comes forward, 80
When retainers take charge
And the master stays back
As in the conduct of a funeral.
The death of a multitude is cause for mourning:
Conduct your triumph as a funeral. 85

32

Existence is infinite, not to be defined;
And, though it seem but a bit of wood in your hand, to carve as you please,
It is not to be lightly played with and laid down.
When rulers adhered to the way of life,
They were upheld by natural loyalty: 90
Heaven and earth were joined and made fertile,
Life was a freshness of rain,
Subject to none,
Free to all.
But men of culture came, with their grades and their distinctions;   95
And as soon as such differences had been devised
No one knew where to end them,
Though the one who does know the end of all such differences
Is the sound man;
Existence   100
Might be likened to the course
Of many rivers reaching the one sea.

33

Knowledge studies others,
Wisdom is self-known;
Muscle masters brothers,   105
Self-mastery is bone;
Content need never borrow,
Ambition wanders blind:
Vitality cleaves to the marrow
Leaving death behind.   110

SUBJECT QUESTIONS

1. Do you think that a good leader in the modern world could "barely be known to exist"? Does television even allow that possibility?
2. Laotzu suggests that people would be better without formal rules for good behavior. Do you agree? Would there be no thieves without laws against stealing?
3. Laotzu argues for freedom in Saying 19; what kind of freedom does he have in mind?
4. Laotzu believes that force solves nothing, yet he admits that its use may be necessary. Under what conditions? What should be the attitude of the military leader?

5. In Saying 32 occurs one of the key statements in the *Tao:* "Existence is infinite." Can you tell from the context what Laotzu means by this? Does Saying 33 help clarify the meaning?

STRUCTURE QUESTIONS

1. The *Tao Teh Ching* as a whole is only a loose collection of sayings; a sampling of these can hardly add to any sense of close organization. With this lack of structural coherence, is there any thematic unity in the selection?
2. Could the loose structure be related to the philosophical position? What would happen, for instance, to the statements of Saying 19 if they were developed in a tightly organized essay?
3. What is the "problem" for which Laotzu offers a solution? Does he make clear what that solution is? (If a solution is "negative" there may be a difficulty in developing it.)
4. What persuasive incentives does Laotzu offer to acceptance of his way of life? That is, does he threaten, does he paint a picture of a glorious new life, or what?
5. Note that the poetic form of each saying is different: some employ rhyme, others parallel structure, others repetition of key words (as in Saying 31). Which sayings seem most effective as poems? Analyze the structure of one of the better sayings.

A Letter to Street Christians

Two Brothers from Berkeley

Two anonymous Christians who wrote Letters to Street Christians *(1971) wanted to present a paraphrase (not a literal translation) of the New Testament Epistles. Although they worked from the original Greek and thirty different English versions of the New Testament, they wished their paraphrase to be a supplement, not a substitute. They felt that the original writers "wrote in a Greek called 'common' which was a language of the street. We wanted to get the New Testament down for right where kids are today. 'Cause of that, we had to get away from formal language and dusty religious rap." The letter reprinted here was based on 1 Thessalonians.*

To the brothers and sisters who know Jesus is coming back. Members of the Father's family everywhere are helped when they see how your trust in Jesus causes you to do His work. The way you serve other people with love and the way you look for Jesus' coming shows everybody that you belong to the Father. Remember, we didn't choose the Father, but He chose us and proved to us that His Good News was true by the power of His Spirit in our lives. Let's keep on copying Jesus and trusting His Spirit no matter what comes down. When we do that, we'll be examples for other brothers and sisters. And we won't have to go around telling people about how much we trust the Father because they'll be talking about what they see Him doing in our lives. They'll tell about how we turned away from the world system to trust the Father and wait for His Son Jesus to come back. And we should keep telling them that the Father raised Jesus from the dead to set us free from the punishment our rotten lives deserve. [1]

Sometimes when we go around telling the Good News, people are going to hate us for it and come down on us. We just have to keep trusting the Father to make us bold in talking about Jesus instead of copping out to the pressure. We also have to keep our heads straight about why we're sharing the Good News. People have to see that we're not out to burn them, not trying to jive them or just make them "see things our way." The Father wants us to spread the Good News in truth and love, not pleasing people but pleasing Him. Trusting His Spirit, we can act like Jesus and show people the very different life He has for them. [2]

A beautiful picture of the way the Father wants us to be spreading the   3
Good News is a mother breast-feeding her baby. It's a love so gentle and pure
that it wouldn't try to hurt or get anything for itself. That love only wants
to help and to give and make strong. When people feel secure in that love,
then we can feel free to beg, encourage, and even demand that they act like
children in the Father's forever family should.

When you really get behind serving the Father, you can expect a lot   4
of hassle because people get jealous of what they see in your life. A lot of
Jews in particular are gonna be burned when they see non-Jews getting to
know God. It was unbelieving Jews who killed their own prophets — and even
Jesus who was sent to free them. They've been against the Father's plan ever
since and the result is that they're going to do all they can to keep people
from trusting Him. All they're doing is building up their own punishment.
For us, though, the greatest happiness is seeing people trust the Father and
become members of His forever family. Think what it will be like to be
together with them and Jesus, our Liberator, when He comes back!

Now when the hassles come down, and they *are* gonna come down, keep   5
looking for ways to encourage each other. Don't let Satan get his claws into
any of the brothers and sisters. Let your trust in the Father be a shining light
for all the other members of the family who are really having it bad. When
you stand strong in your relationship with Jesus, all of us together experience
more of His life. There are no words that we can use to thank the Father
for the joy and happiness this togetherness brings. But we do know that He
makes our love for each other and everybody else keep on growing and
overflowing. He wants His family to be pure and clean when Jesus comes
back for us.

We know that a lot of you are really into your relationship with the Father.   6
We ask you not to stop and be satisfied where you are, but to keep on pushing
to know Him better. Be careful of the traps Satan wants to catch you in —
especially balling somebody you're not married to. There are some ways that
you can break your relationship with the Father and nobody knows it but
you and Him. But when you abuse His gift of sex, not only do you and the
one you're into it with get bummed up, but so do other brothers and sisters.
So the Father wants you to be pure about the way you handle your body
and do your part in making the family clean. He gave you His Spirit to teach
and lead you, and if you blow it, that's the One you're hurting.

God's love is the most important thing we can share with each other.   7
If you still have to learn that lesson, learn it good. If you've learned it, use
it. If you're using it, use it more. Learn to live a quiet life and enjoy simple

things. Don't be messin' with other people's business. Don't look for other people to support you, but work so that you'll be able to have what you need, be able to help others, and give people who don't know Jesus one less thing to bitch about.

One thing we all have to keep in our heads is what is happening to 8 all the brothers and sisters who die before Jesus comes back. People who don't know Jesus have a good excuse for being sad when someone they know dies. But us who know Jesus have all the reason in the world to be happy. And the Father proved what was going to happen to us when He brought Jesus out of that grave. We know that the spirits of those who have died trusting Him are with Him right now. When He comes back for us, the first thing that will happen will be their new bodies coming out of that old grave. Someday Jesus is going to come, and we'll hear an angel shout and a trumpet blow, and our dead brothers and sisters are going to fly right off this earth. And those of us who are still alive will fly right behind them to meet Jesus and be with Him *forever!* Keep reminding each other about this and dig it.

When is it going to happen? There's no need for us to get into that because 9 you know it's going to happen in a flash. People are going to be sitting around saying, "everything's cool, peace and love to all." And they're going to get smashed before they know where it's coming from. But that day that's going to bring death to so many is going to bring life to us. We won't be surprised if we've got our eyes on Jesus. If you can dig it, we are children of light and of the day and we don't belong to darkness and night. So let's keep our eyes open and our heads straight — not sleeping or loaded. Get wrapped up in trusting the Father and living in His love and protect your head with the thought of Jesus coming back. God's not going to vamp on us because Jesus has already taken our rap so that whether we're ready or not, He's going to take us to be with Himself. Groove on that, people.

To wrap it up, brothers and sisters, we want to remind you of a couple 10 of things. Respect your teachers and leaders and love them. Live in peace with each other. Warn those that don't behave themselves. Help out the weak ones. Pick up the hurt ones. Be patient with everybody. You don't heal hurt with more hurt so always do good. Stay happy. Talk with the Father all the time. Thank Him for *everything,* 'cause that's what He wants you to do. Don't put down spiritual gifts and abilities. Take a hard look at everything for what it is; hold on to what's good and turn loose what's bad.

We're trusting the Father to make you clean and pure, a healed and 11 whole human being waiting for Jesus to come for you. He asked you to be pure, so you can count on Him making you that way.

Remember us when you talk with the Father. 12

We love you all because of Jesus. 13

SUBJECT QUESTIONS

1. What would you say is the primary purpose of this letter? Is it calculated to win new converts?
2. The authors suggest (paragraph 3) that new converts should be treated as parents treat children: give them love first and discipline later. Considering that children often rebel against parental authority, does this seem like workable advice?
3. In paragraph 1, it is said that Christians have "turned away from the world system"; but later, advice is given to get a job, to respect and love teachers and leaders. Is there a contradiction here?
4. The authors warn that Christians can expect to be "hassled." Why would anyone hassle a brotherhood of love? Have you ever been irritated by Jesus freaks? If so, why?
5. Because this is a modernized paraphrase, would the writers have done better in paragraph 4 to substitute "the Establishment" for the "Jews" in the original? Who are the chief enemies of street Christians?

STRUCTURE QUESTIONS

1. It is often more difficult for religious leaders to prevent "backsliding" than it is to win new converts. What methods of persuasion do the writers use here to prevent backsliding?
2. The writers clearly have not tried to be too heavy-handed in their use of "street language"; do you think the compromise would achieve better rapport with street Christians than, say, the King James version?
3. Persuasion often employs language appealing much more to emotions than does argument. Do you find strong emotional appeals here? Is the degree of emotional appeal directly related to the convictions of the reader? (That is, might the emotional content seem stronger — or weaker — to a Christian than to an agnostic?)
4. What is the effect on tone of the rather loose organization of this letter? Would tighter organization have altered the implied relationship between writer and reader?
5. The writers "wrap it up" with a series of reminders about rules for good living. Should they have ended with some strong incentive to be good rather than a list of rules?

The Essence of OM
The Upanishads

The Upanishads, the formative portions of the Hindu scriptures (the Vedas), are not so much systematized theology as insights into the nature of religious experience. They are said to be divine revelations to saints and seers who lived hundreds of years before Christ. OM is the symbol of Brahman, or God. The word translated here as "Self" is Atman, or "God within." Ralph Waldo Emerson translated it as the "oversoul" in his transcendental philosophy. In Christianity the approximate equivalent is the Holy Ghost or Holy Spirit, the aspect of the Trinity that constitutes men's souls and is not mortal. You should remember that in Hinduism the aim is not to rise again from the dead but to avoid having to do so by becoming one with this holy spirit, or Atman. The translation is by Swami Prabhavananda and Frederick Manchester.

OM . . . peace — peace — peace. 1

This syllable is Brahman. This syllable is indeed supreme. He who knows it obtains his desire. 2

It is the strongest support. It is the highest symbol. He who knows it is reverenced as a knower of Brahman. 3

The Self, whose symbol is OM, is the omniscient Lord. He is not born. He does not die. He is neither cause nor effect. This Ancient One is unborn, imperishable, eternal: though the body be destroyed, he is not killed. 4

If the slayer think that he slays, if the slain think that he is slain, neither of them knows the truth. The Self slays not, nor is he slain. 5

Smaller than the smallest, greater than the greatest, this Self forever dwells within the hearts of all. When a man is free from desire, his mind and senses purified, he beholds the glory of the Self and is without sorrow. 6

Though seated, he travels far; though at rest, he moves all things. Who but the purest of the pure can realize this Effulgent Being, who is joy and who is beyond joy? 7

Formless is he, though inhabiting form. In the midst of the fleeting he abides forever. All-pervading and supreme is the Self. The wise man, knowing him in his true nature, transcends all grief. 8

The Self is not known through study of the scriptures, nor through subtlety of the intellect, nor through much learning; but by him who longs for him is he known. Verily unto him does the Self reveal his true being. 9

From *Upanishads*, translated by Swami Prabhavananda and Frederick Manchester. Published by The New American Library. Copyright The Vedanta Society of Southern California.

By learning, a man cannot know him, if he desist not from evil, if he ₁₀
control not his senses, if he quiet not his mind, and practice not meditation. . . .

When a man lacks discrimination and his mind is uncontrolled, his senses ₁₁
are unmanageable, like the restive horses of a charioteer. But when a man has
discrimination and his mind is controlled, his senses, like the well-broken horse
of a charioteer, lightly obey the rein.

He who lacks discrimination, whose mind is unsteady and whose heart ₁₂
is impure, never reaches the goal, but is born again and again. But he who
has discrimination, whose mind is steady and whose heart is pure, reaches
the goal, and having reached it is born no more.

The man who has a sound understanding for charioteer, a controlled ₁₃
mind for reins — he it is that reaches the end of the journey, the supreme
abode of Vishnu, the all-pervading.[1]

The senses derive from physical objects, physical objects from the mind, ₁₄
mind from intellect, intellect from ego, ego from the unmanifested seed, and
the unmanifested seed from Brahman — the Uncaused Cause.

Brahman is the end of the journey. Brahman is the supreme goal. ₁₅

This Brahman, this Self, deep-hidden in all beings, is not revealed to ₁₆
all; but to the seers, pure in heart, concentrated in mind — to them is he
revealed.

The senses of the wise man obey his mind, his mind obeys his intellect, ₁₇
his intellect obeys his ego, and his ego obeys the Self.

Arise! Awake! Approach the feet of the master and know THAT. Like ₁₈
the sharp edge of a razor, the sages say, is the path. Narrow it is, and difficult
to tread!

Soundless, formless, intangible, undying, tasteless, odorless, without be- ₁₉
ginning, without end, eternal, immutable, beyond nature, is the Self. Knowing
him as such, one is freed from death.

SUBJECT QUESTIONS

1. The notion that the slayer does not really kill may be comforting to those
   about to be slain; does it place too low a premium on human life?
2. Does the final statement about being "freed from death" seem to you
   compatible with what has been said earlier about death? What do you
   think the writer means here?
3. The writer says much about keeping a tight reign on the senses. Is he
   advocating elimination of physical pleasure? Does Christianity?
4. Like Jesus and Laotzu, the writer of this passage seems to have little
   respect for learning and scriptural study as a way to salvation. What
   prevents our labeling the passage "anti-intellectual"?

[1]Vishnu is here equivalent to Brahman.

STRUCTURE QUESTIONS

1. This passage does not have, of course, the tight logical organization that Plato and Aristotle bequeathed to Western prose. Does it have a unity and coherence of another kind?
2. Do you see any sequence or progression of thought in this passage, or is it a random collection of thoughts on the same subject? (Try rearranging some paragraphs to test your answer.)
3. Can you find in this brief passage the four traditional parts of a persuasive essay?
4. The author is faced with a problem inherent in his subject: he must "persuade" readers not to be influenced by emotion. How does he solve this problem?
5. Classical persuasion frequently ends with a peroration — a final exhortation of stronger force than the rest of the essay. Do the last two paragraphs here constitute such a peroration, or simply the logical conclusion of the passage?
6. Examine the long string of predicate adjectives describing the Self in the final paragraph. Is the author repeating himself and wasting words? Is there a cumulative effect that would not be accomplished by one or two representative adjectives? (Walt Whitman and Carl Sandburg, incidentally, frequently employed this device.)

A Free Man's Worship

Bertrand Russell

Bertrand Russell (1872–1970), mathematician and philosopher, also won the Nobel Prize for Literature (1950). Together with Alfred North Whitehead he published the great Principia Mathematica *(1910–13). Thereafter he published three dozen books, mostly on philosophy; his major interest is fairly summarized by the title of one of them:* New Hope for a Changing World *(1951). At the time of his death, Lord Russell was perhaps best known as a leader of pacifist movements — he was jailed several times for objecting to government policy and for leading protest demonstrations.* A Free Man's Worship *was written early in his career, when Russell was a young scientist forced to come to grips with the new world which post-Darwinian science had presented to him.*

To Dr. Faustus in his study Mephistopheles told the history of the Creation, saying:

The endless praises of the choirs of angels had begun to grow wearisome; for, after all, did he not deserve their praise? Had he not given them endless joy? Would it not be more amusing to obtain undeserved praise, to be worshipped by beings whom he tortured? He smiled inwardly, and resolved that the great drama should be performed.

For countless ages the hot nebula whirled aimlessly through space. At length it began to take shape, the central mass threw off planets, the planets cooled, boiling seas and burning mountains heaved and tossed, from black masses of cloud hot sheets of rain deluged the barely solid crust. And now the first germ of life grew in the depths of the ocean, and developed rapidly in the fructifying warmth into vast forest trees, huge ferns springing from the damp mould, sea monsters breeding, fighting, devouring, and passing away. And from the monsters, as the play unfolded itself, Man was born, with the power of thought, the knowledge of good and evil, and the cruel thirst for worship. And Man saw that all is passing in this mad, monstrous world, that all is struggling to snatch, at any cost, a few brief moments of life before Death's inexorable decree. And Man said: "There is a hidden purpose, could we but fathom it, and the purpose is good; for we must reverence something, and in the visible world there is nothing worthy of reverence." And Man stood aside from the struggle, resolving that God intended harmony to come out of chaos by human efforts. And when he followed the instincts which God had transmitted to him from his ancestry of beasts of prey, he called it Sin, and asked God to forgive him. But he doubted whether he could be justly forgiven, until he invented a divine Plan by which God's wrath was to have been appeased. And seeing the present was bad, he made it yet worse, that thereby the future might be better. And he gave God thanks for the strength that enabled him to forgo even the joys that were possible. And God smiled; and when he saw that Man had become perfect in renunciation and worship, he sent another sun through the sky, which crashed into Man's sun; and all returned again to nebula.

"Yes," he murmured, "it was a good play; I will have it performed again."

Such, in outline, but even more purposeless, more void of meaning, is the world which Science presents for our belief. Amid such a world, if anywhere, our ideals henceforward must find a home. That Man is the product of causes which had no prevision of the end they were achieving; that his origin, his growth, his hopes and fears, his loves and his beliefs, are but the outcome of accidental collocations of atoms; that no fire, no heroism, no intensity of thought and feeling, can preserve an individual life beyond the grave; that all the labours of the ages, all the devotion, all the inspiration, all the noonday brightness of human genius, are destined to extinction in the vast death of the solar system, and that the whole temple of Man's achievement must inevitably be buried beneath the débris of a universe in ruins — all these things, if not quite beyond dispute, are yet so nearly certain, that no philosophy which rejects them can hope to stand. Only within the scaffolding of these truths, only on the firm foundation of unyielding despair, can the soul's habitation henceforth be safely built. 2

How, in such an alien and inhuman world, can so powerless a creature as Man preserve his aspirations untarnished? A strange mystery it is that Nature, omnipotent but blind, in the revolutions of her secular hurryings through the abysses of space, has brought forth at last a child, subject still to her power, but gifted with sight, with knowledge of good and evil, with the capacity of judging all the works of his unthinking Mother. In spite of Death, the mark and seal of the parental control, Man is yet free, during his brief years, to examine, to criticise, to know, and in imagination to create. To him alone, in the world with which he is acquainted, this freedom belongs; and in this lies his superiority to the resistless forces that control his outward life. 3

The savage, like ourselves, feels the oppression of his impotence before the powers of Nature; but having in himself nothing that he respects more than Power, he is willing to prostrate himself before his gods, without inquiring whether they are worthy of his worship. Pathetic and very terrible is the long history of cruelty and torture, of degradation and human sacrifices endured in the hope of placating the jealous gods: surely, the trembling believer thinks, when what is most precious has been freely given, their lust for blood must be appeased, and more will not be required. The religion of Moloch — as such creeds may be generically called — is in essence the cringing submission of the slave, who dare not, even in his heart, allow the thought that his master 4

deserves no adulation. Since the independence of ideals is not yet acknowledged, Power may be freely worshipped, and receive an unlimited respect,
despite its wanton infliction of pain.

But gradually, as morality grows bolder, the claim of the ideal world   5
begins to be felt, and worship, if it is not to cease, must be given to gods
of another kind than those created by the savage. Some, though they feel the
demands of the ideal, will still consciously reject them, still urging that naked
Power is worthy of worship. Such is the attitude inculcated in God's answer
to Job out of the whirlwind: the divine power and knowledge are paraded,
but of the divine goodness there is no hint. Such also is the attitude of those
who, in our own day, base their morality upon the struggle for survival,
maintaining that the survivors are necessarily the fittest. But others, not content with an answer so repugnant to the moral sense, will adopt the position
which we have become accustomed to regard as specially religious, maintaining that, in some hidden manner, the world of fact is really harmonious with
the world of ideals. Thus Man creates God, all-powerful and all-good, the
mystic unity of what is and what should be.

But the world of fact, after all, is not good; and, in submitting our   6
judgment to it, there is an element of slavishness from which our thoughts
must be purged. For in all things it is well to exalt the dignity of Man, by
freeing him as far as possible from the tyranny of non-human Power. When
we have realised that Power is largely bad, that Man, with his knowledge
of good and evil, is but a helpless atom in a world which has no such knowledge, the choice is again presented to us: Shall we worship Force, or shall
we worship Goodness? Shall our God exist and be evil, or shall he be recognised as the creation of our own conscience?

The answer to this question is very momentous, and affects profoundly   7
our whole morality. The worship of Force, to which Carlyle and Nietzsche
and the creed of Militarism have accustomed us, is the result of failure to
maintain our own ideals against a hostile universe: it is itself a prostrate
submission to evil, a sacrifice of our best to Moloch. If strength indeed is to
be respected, let us respect rather the strength of those who refuse that false
"recognition of facts" which fails to recognise that facts are often bad. Let
us admit that, in the world we know, there are many things that would be
better otherwise, and that the ideals to which we do and must adhere are
not realised in the realm of matter. Let us preserve our respect for truth,
for beauty, for the ideal of perfection which life does not permit us to attain,
though none of these things meet with the approval of the unconscious universe. If Power is bad, as it seems to be, let us reject it from our hearts. In
this lies Man's true freedom: in determination to worship only the God created
by our own love of the good, to respect only the heaven which inspires the
insight of our best moments. In action, in desire, we must submit perpetually
to the tyranny of outside forces; but in thought, in aspiration, we are free,

free from our fellowmen, free from the petty planet on which our bodies impotently crawl, free even, while we live, from the tyranny of death. Let us learn, then, that energy of faith which enables us to live constantly in the vision of the good; and let us descend in action, into the world of fact, with that vision always before us.

When first the opposition of fact and ideal grows fully visible, a spirit of fiery revolt, of fierce hatred of the gods, seems necessary to the assertion of freedom. To defy with Promethean constancy a hostile universe, to keep its evil always in view, always actively hated, to refuse no pain that the malice of Power can invent, appears to be the duty of all who will not bow before the inevitable. But indignation is still a bondage, for it compels our thoughts to be occupied with an evil world; and in the fierceness of desire from which rebellion springs there is a kind of self-assertion which it is necessary for the wise to overcome. Indignation is a submission of our thoughts, but not of our desires; the Stoic freedom in which wisdom consists is found in the submission of our desires, but not of our thoughts. From the submission of our desires springs the virtue of resignation; from the freedom of our thoughts springs the whole world of art and philosophy, and the vision of beauty by which, at last, we half reconquer the reluctant world. But the vision of beauty is possible only to unfettered contemplation, to thoughts not weighted by the load of eager wishes; and thus Freedom comes only to those who no longer ask of life that it shall yield them any of those personal goods that are subject to the mutations of Time.

Although the necessity of renunciation is evidence of the existence of evil, yet Christianity, in preaching it, has shown a wisdom exceeding that of the Promethean philosophy of rebellion. It must be admitted that, of the things we desire, some, though they prove impossible, are yet real goods; others, however, as ardently longed for, do not form part of a fully purified ideal. The belief that what must be renounced is bad, though sometimes false, is far less often false than untamed passion supposes; and the creed of religion, by providing a reason for proving that it is never false, has been the means of purifying our hopes by the discovery of many austere truths.

But there is in resignation a further good element: even real goods, when they are unattainable, ought not to be fretfully desired. To every man comes, sooner or later, the great renunciation. For the young, there is nothing unattainable; a good thing desired with the whole force of a passionate will, and yet impossible, is to them not credible. Yet, by death, by illness, by poverty, or by the voice of duty, we must learn, each one of us, that the world was not made for us, and that, however beautiful may be the things we crave, Fate may nevertheless forbid them. It is the part of courage, when misfortune comes, to bear without repining the ruin of our hopes, to turn away our thoughts from vain regrets. This degree of submission to Power is not only just and right; it is the very gate of wisdom.

But passive renunciation is not the whole of wisdom; for not by renun-   11
ciation alone can we build a temple for the worship of our own ideals. Haunting foreshadowings of the temple appear in the realm of imagination, in music,
in architecture, in the untroubled kingdom of reason, and in the golden sunset
magic of lyrics, where beauty shines and glows, remote from the touch of
sorrow, remote from the fear of change, remote from the failures and disen-
chantments of the world of fact. In the contemplation of these things the vision
of heaven will shape itself in our hearts, giving at once a touchstone to judge
the world about us, and an inspiration by which to fashion to our needs
whatever is not incapable of serving as a stone in the sacred temple.

Except for those rare spirits that are born without sin, there is a cavern   12
of darkness to be traversed before that temple can be entered. The gate of
the cavern is despair, and its floor is paved with the gravestones of abandoned
hopes. There Self must die; there the eagerness, the greed of untamed desire
must be slain, for only so can the soul be freed from the empire of Fate. But
out of the cavern the Gate of Renunciation leads again to the daylight of
wisdom, by whose radiance a new insight, a new joy, a new tenderness, shine
forth to gladden the pilgrim's heart.

When, without the bitterness of impotent rebellion, we have learnt both   13
to resign ourselves to the outward rule of Fate and to recognise that the
nonhuman world is unworthy of our worship, it becomes possible at last so
to transform and refashion the unconscious universe, so to transmute it in the
crucible of the imagination, that a new image of shining gold replaces the
old idol of clay. In all the multiform facts of the world — in the visual shapes
of trees and mountains and clouds, in the events of the life of Man, even in
the very omnipotence of Death — the insight of creative idealism can find
the reflection of a beauty which its own thoughts first made. In this way mind
asserts its subtle mastery over the thoughtless forces of Nature. The more evil
the material with which it deals, the more thwarting to untrained desire, the
greater is its achievement in inducing the reluctant rock to yield up its hidden
treasures, the prouder its victory in compelling the opposing forces to swell
the pageant of its triumph. Of all the arts, Tragedy is the proudest, the most
triumphant; for it builds its shining citadel in the very centre of the enemy's
country, on the very summit of his highest mountain; from its impregnable
watch-towers, his camps and arsenals, his columns and forts, are all revealed;
within its walls the free life continues, while the legions of Death and Pain
and Despair, and all the servile captains of tyrant Fate, afford the burghers
of that dauntless city new spectacles of beauty. Happy those sacred ramparts,
thrice happy the dwellers on that all-seeing eminence. Honour to those brave
warriors who, through countless ages of warfare, have preserved for us the
priceless heritage of liberty, and have kept undefiled by sacrilegious invaders
the home of the unsubdued.

But the beauty of Tragedy does but make visible a quality which, in   14
more or less obvious shapes, is present always and everywhere in life. In the
spectacle of Death, in the endurance of intolerable pain, and in the irrevocableness of a vanished past, there is a sacredness, an overpowering awe, a
feeling of the vastness, the depth, the inexhaustible mystery of existence, in
which, as by some strange marriage of pain, the sufferer is bound to the world
by bonds of sorrow. In these moments of insight, we lose all eagerness of
temporary desire, all struggling and striving for petty ends, all care for the
little trivial things, that, to a superficial view, make up the common life of
day by day; we see, surrounding the narrow raft illumined by the flickering
light of human comradeship, the dark ocean on whose rolling waves we toss
for a brief hour; from the great night without, a chill blast breaks in upon
our refuge; all the loneliness of humanity amid hostile forces is concentrated
upon the individual soul, which must struggle alone, with what of courage
it can command, against the whole weight of a universe that cares nothing
for its hopes and fears. Victory, in this struggle with the powers of darkness,
is the true baptism into the glorious company of heroes, the true initiation
into the overmastering beauty of human existence. From that awful encounter
of the soul with the outer world, renunciation, wisdom, and charity are born;
and with their birth a new life begins. To take into the inmost shrine of the
soul the irresistible forces whose puppets we seem to be — Death and change,
the irrevocableness of the past, and the powerlessness of Man before the blind
hurry of the universe from vanity to vanity — to feel these things and know
them is to conquer them.

This is the reason why the Past has such magical power. The beauty   15
of its motionless and silent pictures is like the enchanted purity of late autumn,
when the leaves, though one breath would make them fall, still glow against
the sky in golden glory. The Past does not change or strive; like Duncan,
after life's fitful fever it sleeps well; what was eager and grasping, what was
petty and transitory, has faded away, the things that were beautiful and eternal
shine out of it like stars in the night. Its beauty, to a soul not worthy of it,
is unendurable; but to a soul which has conquered Fate it is the key of religion.

The life of Man, viewed outwardly, is but a small thing in comparison   16
with the forces of Nature. The slave is doomed to worship Time and Fate
and Death, because they are greater than anything he finds in himself, and
because all his thoughts are of things which they devour. But, great as they
are, to think of them greatly, to feel their passionless splendour, is greater
still. And such thought makes us free men; we no longer bow before the
inevitable in Oriental subjection, but we absorb it, and make it part of ourselves. To abandon the struggle for private happiness, to expel all eagerness
of temporary desire, to burn with passion for eternal things — this is
emancipation, and this is the free man's worship. And this liberation is effected

by a contemplation of Fate; for Fate itself is subdued by the mind which leaves nothing to be purged by the purifying fire of Time.

United with his fellow-men by the strongest of all ties, the tie of a   17 common doom, the free man finds that a new vision is with him always, shedding over every daily task the light of love. The life of Man is a long march through the night, surrounded by invisible foes, tortured by weariness and pain, towards a goal that few can hope to reach, and where none may tarry long. One by one, as they march, our comrades vanish from our sight, seized by the silent orders of omnipotent Death. Very brief is the time in which we can help them, in which their happiness or misery is decided. Be it ours to shed sunshine on their path, to lighten their sorrows by the balm of sympathy, to give them the pure joy of a never-tiring affection, to strengthen failing courage, to instill faith in hours of despair. Let us not weigh in grudging scales their merits and demerits, but let us think only of their need — of the sorrows, the difficulties, perhaps the blindnesses, that make the misery of their lives; let us remember that they are fellow-sufferers in the same darkness, actors in the same tragedy with ourselves. And so, when their day is over, when their good and their evil have become eternal by the immortality of the past, be it ours to feel that, where they suffered, where they failed, no deed of ours was the cause, but wherever a spark of the divine fire kindled in their hearts, we were ready with encouragement, with sympathy, with brave words in which high courage glowed.

Brief and powerless is Man's life; on him and all his race the slow, sure   18 doom falls pitiless and dark. Blind to good and evil, reckless of destruction, omnipotent matter rolls on its relentless way; for Man, condemned to-day to lose his dearest, to-morrow himself to pass through the gate of darkness, it remains only to cherish, ere yet the blow falls, the lofty thoughts that ennoble his little day; disdaining the coward terrors of the slave of Fate, to worship at the shrine that his own hands have built; undismayed by the empire of chance, to preserve a mind free from the wanton tyranny that rules his outward life; proudly defiant of the irresistible forces that tolerate, for a moment, his knowledge and his condemnation, to sustain alone, a weary but unyielding Atlas, the world that his own ideals have fashioned despite the trampling march of unconscious Power.

SUBJECT QUESTIONS

1. Why, when he does not believe in God except as a creation of man's mind, does Russell begin with the fable about God's creation of the world? What is the reader's reaction to it? Is the following a fair analysis of Russell's implication? If there is a god who created man, he must be capricious and arbitrary to have played such a dirty trick on man; hence, even if God exists, he is not worthy of worship.

2. If "Man is the product of causes which had no prevision of the end they were achieving," and if "resistless forces control his outward life," then in what sense can Russell claim that man is free? Is he overlooking the possibility that even man's thoughts may be determined by natural causes beyond his control? We know, for instance, that body temperature has considerable effect on man's thinking: If his normal body temperature were 105°, like that of birds, his "normal" thinking would resemble what we now call delirium.

3. Russell says that savages still make themselves slaves by worshiping gods which they believe to be omnipotent. Does he mean to imply that anyone who worships an omnipotent god is not quite civilized?

4. Russell assumes without offering proof that "in all things it is well to exalt the dignity of man." Most religions exalt humility and insignificance; some even stress innate depravity. Is Russell being unrealistic in thus placing man on a pedestal, particularly since he recognizes that man is doomed to extinction?

5. Another of Russell's basic assumptions is that "power is largely bad." From this premise he concludes that an all-powerful God would be evil and that "man's true freedom" lies in refusing to worship such a concept. Is there a fallacy in his reasoning here?

6. If man should not worship a god, what is "the free man's worship"?

7. In the last two paragraphs, Russell combines concepts of brotherly love and atheism. But if there is no God-given command to love our fellow men, why should we do it? Surely brotherly love is not natural or instinctive.

STRUCTURE QUESTIONS

1. Examine the language of this essay. Is it objectively denotative, or charged with connotations? Would you say, then, that the language is better suited to the purposes of argument, or of persuasion?

2. Does the essay as a whole invite an open search for truth, or does it assume the truth and try to persuade the reader to accept it?

3. What are some of the premises by which Russell arrives at his conclusions? Does he give evidence to substantiate these premises?

4. Examine the picture of the world which, according to Russell, science shows ours to be. Is it a fair summary? Does it need support?

The Efficacy of Prayer

C. S. Lewis

*C. S. Lewis (1898–1963) was professor of medieval and Renaissance litera-
ture at Cambridge. He is most famous for his numerous writings on the
place of Christianity in the modern world, particularly* Screwtape Letters.
"The Efficacy of Prayer" originally appeared in The Atlantic Monthly *(January 1959).*

Some years ago I got up one morning intending to have my hair cut in   1
preparation for a visit to London, and the first letter I opened made it clear
I need not go to London. So I decided to put the haircut off too. But then
there began the most unaccountable little nagging in my mind, almost like
a voice saying, "Get it cut all the same. Go and get it cut." In the end I
could stand it no longer. I went. Now my barber at that time was a fellow
Christian and a man of many troubles whom my brother and I had sometimes
been able to help. The moment I opened his shop door he said, "Oh, I was
praying you might come today." And in fact if I had come a day or so later
I should have been of no use to him.

It awed me; it awes me still. But of course one cannot rigorously prove   2
a causal connection between the barber's prayers and my visit. It might be
telepathy. It might be accident.

I have stood by the bedside of a woman whose thigh-bone was eaten   3
through with cancer and who had thriving colonies of the disease in many
other bones as well. It took three people to move her in bed. The doctors
predicted a few months of life; the nurses (who often know better), a few
weeks. A good man laid his hands on her and prayed. A year later the patient
was walking (uphill, too, through rough woodland) and the man who took
the last X-ray photos was saying, "These bones are as solid as rock. It's miraculous."

But once again there is no rigorous proof. Medicine, as all true doctors   4
admit, is not an exact science. We need not invoke the supernatural to explain
the falsification of its prophecies. You need not, unless you choose, believe
in a causal connection between the prayers and the recovery.

The question then arises, "What sort of evidence *would* prove the effi-   5 cacy of prayer?" The thing we pray for may happen, but how can you ever know it was not going to happen anyway? Even if the thing were indisputably miraculous it would not follow that the miracle had occurred because of your prayers. The answer surely is that a compulsive empirical proof such as we have in the sciences can never be attained.

Some things are proved by the unbroken uniformity of our experiences. 6 The law of gravitation is established by the fact that, in our experience, all bodies without exception obey it. Now even if all the things that people prayed for happened, which they do not, this would not prove what Christians mean by the efficacy of prayer. For prayer is request. The essence of request, as distinct from compulsion, is that it may or may not be granted. And if an infinitely wise Being listens to the requests of finite and foolish creatures, of course He will sometimes grant and sometimes refuse them. Invariable "success" in prayer would not prove the Christian doctrine at all. It would prove something much more like magic — a power in certain human beings to control, or compel, the course of nature.

There are, no doubt, passages in the New Testament which may seem 7 at first sight to promise an invariable granting of our prayers. But that cannot be what they really mean. For in the very heart of the story we meet a glaring instance to the contrary. In Gethsemane the holiest of all petitioners prayed three times that a certain cup might pass from Him. It did not. After that the idea that prayer is recommended to us as a sort of infallible gimmick may be dismissed.

Other things are proved not simply by experience but by those artifi- 8 cially contrived experiences which we call experiments. Could this be done about prayer? I will pass over the objection that no Christian could take part in such a project, because he has been forbidden it: "You must not try experiments on God, your Master." Forbidden or not, is the thing even possible?

I have seen it suggested that a team of people — the more the better — 9 should agree to pray as hard as they knew how, over a period of six weeks, for all the patients in Hospital A and none of those in Hospital B. Then you would tot up the results and see if A had more cures and fewer deaths. And I suppose you would repeat the experiment at various times and places so as to eliminate the influence of irrelevant factors.

The trouble is that I do not see how any real prayer could go on under 10 such conditions. "Words without thoughts never to heaven go," says the King in *Hamlet*. Simply to say prayers is not to pray; otherwise a team of properly trained parrots would serve as well as men for our experiment. You cannot pray for the recovery of the sick unless the end you have in view is their recovery. But you can have no motive for desiring the recovery of all the patients in one hospital and none of those in another. You are not doing it in order that suffering should be relieved; you are doing it to find out what happens. The real purpose and the nominal purpose of your prayers are at variance. In other words, whatever your tongue and teeth and knees may do, you are not praying. The experiment demands an impossibility.

Empirical proof and disproof are, then, unobtainable. But this conclusion will seem less depressing if we remember that prayer is request and compare it with other specimens of the same thing. 11

We make requests of our fellow creatures as well as of God: we ask for the salt, we ask for a raise in pay, we ask a friend to feed the cat while we are on our holidays, we ask a woman to marry us. Sometimes we get what we ask for and sometimes not. But when we do, it is not nearly so easy as one might suppose to prove with scientific certainty a causal connection between the asking and the getting. 12

Your neighbour may be a humane person who would not have let your cat starve even if you had forgotten to make any arrangement. Your employer is never so likely to grant your request for a raise as when he is aware that you could get better money from a rival firm and is quite possibly intending to secure you by a raise in any case. As for the lady who consents to marry you — are you sure she had not decided to do so already? Your proposal, you know, might have been the result, not the cause, of her decision. A certain important conversation might never have taken place unless she had intended that it should. 13

Thus in some measure the same doubt that hangs about the causal efficacy of our prayers to God hangs also about our prayers to man. Whatever we get we might have been going to get anyway. But only, as I say, in some measure. Our friend, boss, and wife may tell us that they acted because we asked; and we may know them so well as to feel sure, first that they are saying what they believe to be true, and secondly that they understand their own motives well enough to be right. But notice that when this happens our assurance has not been gained by the methods of science. We do not try the control experiment of refusing the raise or breaking off the engagement and then making our request again under fresh conditions. Our assurance is quite different in kind from scientific knowledge. It is born out of our personal relation to the other parties; not from knowing things about them but from knowing *them*. 14

Our assurance — if we reach an assurance — that God always hears and sometimes grants our prayers, and that apparent grantings are not merely fortuitous, can only come in the same sort of way. There can be no question of tabulating successes and failures and trying to decide whether the successes are too numerous to be accounted for by chance. Those who best know a man best know whether, when he did what they asked, he did it because they asked. I think those who best know God will best know whether He sent me to the barber's shop because the barber prayed. 15

For up till now we have been tackling the whole question in the wrong way and on the wrong level. The very question "Does prayer work?" puts 16 us in the wrong frame of mind from the outset. "Work": as if it were magic, or a machine — something that functions automatically. Prayer is either a sheer illusion or a personal contact between embryonic, incomplete persons (ourselves) and the utterly concrete Person. Prayer in the sense of petition, asking for things, is a small part of it; confession and penitence are its threshold, adoration its sanctuary, the presence and vision and enjoyment of God its bread and wine. In it God shows Himself to us. That He answers prayers is a corollary — not necessarily the most important one — from that revelation. What He does is learned from what He is.

Petitionary prayer is, nonetheless, both allowed and commanded to us: 17 "Give us our daily bread." And no doubt it raises a theoretical problem. Can we believe that God ever really modifies His action in response to the suggestions of men? For infinite wisdom does not need telling what is best, and infinite goodness needs no urging to do it. But neither does God need any of those things that are done by finite agents, whether living or inanimate. He could, if He chose, repair our bodies miraculously without food; or give us food without the aid of farmers, bakers, and butchers; or knowledge without the aid of learned men; or convert the heathen without missionaries. Instead, He allows soils and weather and animals and the muscles, minds, and wills of men to co-operate in the execution of His will. "God," said Pascal, "instituted prayer in order to lend to His creatures the dignity of causality." But not only prayer; whenever we act at all He lends us that dignity. It is not really stranger, nor less strange, that my prayers should affect the course of events than that my other actions should do so. They have not advised or changed God's mind — that is, His over-all purpose. But that purpose will be realized in different ways according to the actions, including the prayers, of His creatures.

For He seems to do nothing of Himself which He can possibly delegate 18 to His creatures. He commands us to do slowly and blunderingly what He could do perfectly and in the twinkling of an eye. He allows us to neglect what He would have us do, or to fail. Perhaps we do not fully realize the problem, so to call it, of enabling finite free wills to co-exist with Omnipotence. It seems to involve at every moment almost a sort of divine abdication. We are not mere recipients or spectators. We are either privileged to share in the game or compelled to collaborate in the work, "to wield our little tridents." Is this amazing process simply Creation going on before our eyes? This is how (no light matter) God makes something — indeed, makes gods — out of nothing.

So at least it seems to me. But what I have offered can be, at the very 19 best, only a mental model or symbol. All that we say on such subjects must be merely analogical and parabolic. The reality is doubtless not comprehensible by our faculties. But we can at any rate try to expel bad analogies and bad parables. Prayer is not a machine. It is not magic. It is not advice offered to God. Our act, when we pray, must not, any more than all our other acts, be separated from the continuous act of God Himself, in which alone all finite causes operate.

It would be even worse to think of those who get what they pray for　20 as a sort of court favorites, people who have influence with the throne. The refused prayer of Christ in Gethsemane is answer enough to that. And I dare not leave out the hard saying which I once heard from an experienced Christian: "I have seen many striking answers to prayer and more than one that I thought miraculous. But they usually come at the beginning: before conversion, or soon after it. As the Christian life proceeds, they tend to be rarer. The refusals, too, are not only more frequent; they become more unmistakable, more emphatic."

Does God then forsake just those who serve Him best? Well, He who　21 served Him best of all said, near His tortured death, "Why hast thou forsaken me?" When God becomes man, that Man, of all others, is least comforted by God, at His greatest need. There is a mystery here which, even if I had the power, I might not have the courage to explore. Meanwhile, little people like you and me, if our prayers are sometimes granted, beyond all hope and probability, had better not draw hasty conclusions to our own advantage. If we were stronger, we might be less tenderly treated. If we were braver, we might be sent, with far less help, to defend far more desperate posts in the great battle.

SUBJECT QUESTIONS

1. Lewis begins by citing two apparent examples of the efficacy of prayer, then he immediately denies that they constitute valid evidence. Does this denial seem to help or hurt Lewis's thesis? Is it in the nature of a "devastating concession"?
2. Lewis argues that the efficacy of prayer cannot be tested even by "scientific" experiment. Why not? Is his hypothetical controlled experiment merely a poor one, or would any other such experiment also fail?
3. If it cannot be proved that prayers are answered, on what grounds does Lewis believe that they are sometimes answered?
4. Because Lewis does not arrive at his conclusions by scientific induction, his argument must depend on certain undemonstrated assumptions. What are these?
5. If, as Lewis believes, his own answer is at best a "mental model," if "the reality is doubtless not comprehensible by our faculties," why does he try to give an answer at all? Or, to put the same question on a more general level, if religion is extralogical, why do so many people try to write logically about it?
6. Does Lewis mean to imply at the end that the more religious a person is the less likely he is to have his prayers answered?

STRUCTURE QUESTIONS

1. Note that, unlike most writers of persuasion, Lewis tries to avoid an emotional approach and maintain instead an objective, dispassionate tone. Is this tone appropriate to his purpose and subject? Would a different attitude be more effective?
2. What hints do you find that Lewis feels more strongly about his subject than the objective tone implies? Do these seem to be slips on Lewis's part, or deliberate devices? How do they influence the total impact of the essay?
3. At what point in the essay does Lewis abandon strict logic? Is there an accompanying change in language?
4. Examine the analogy between prayer to God and requests to fellow humans. Keeping in mind that an analogy is supposed to clarify but cannot prove a point, would you say that Lewis has used this analogy properly and to good purpose?
5. Does this essay follow the traditional organization of persuasion? Should Lewis have begun with an introductory paragraph instead of plunging immediately into a personal example of his theme?

Packed Dirt, Churchgoing,
a Dying Cat, a Traded Car
John Updike

Although John Updike (b. 1932) has written two bestselling novels, Couples *and* Rabbit, Run, *he is probably best known as a short story writer. His work is found in nearly every collection of contemporary short fiction. The story which follows originally appeared in* The New Yorker *and was included in* Pigeon Feathers, *a Book-of-the-Month Club selection in 1962.*

Different things move us. I, David Kern, am always affected — reassured, 1
nostalgically pleased, even, as a member of my animal species, made proud —
by the sight of bare earth that has been smoothed and packed firm by the
passage of human feet. Such spots abound in small towns: the furtive break
in the playground fence dignified into a thoroughfare, the trough of dust
underneath each swing, the blurred path worn across a wedge of grass, the
anonymous little mound or embankment polished by play and strewn with
pebbles like the confetti aftermath of a wedding. Such unconsciously humanized intervals of clay, too humble and common even to have a name, remind
me of my childhood, when one communes with dirt down among the legs,
as it were, of presiding fatherly presences. The earth is our playmate then,
and the call to supper has a piercingly sweet eschatological ring.

The corner where I now live was recently widened so that the cars going 2
back and forth to the summer colony on the Point would not be troubled
to slow down. My neighbor's house was sold to the town and wrecked and
picked clean by salvagers and finally burned in a great bonfire of old notched
beams and splintered clapboards that leaped tree-high throughout one whole
winter day's cold drizzle. Then bulldozers, huge and yellow and loud, appeared on the street and began to gnaw, it seemed, at the corner of our house.
My third child, a boy not yet two, came running from the window in tearful
panic. After I tried to soothe him with an explanation, he followed me through
the house sobbing and wailing "'Sheen 'Sheen!" while the machines made
our rooms shake with the curses of their labor. They mashed my neighbor's
foundation stones into the earth and trimmed the levelled lot just as my
grandmother used to trim the excess dough from the edge of the pieplate.
They brought the curve of the road right to the corner of my property, and
the beaten path that does for a sidewalk in front of my home was sheared
diagonally by a foot-high cliff.

Last night I was coming back from across the street, fresh from an 3
impromptu civic lamentation with a neighbor at how unsightly, now that the
snow was melted, the awkward-shaped vacant lot the bulldozers had left
looked, with its high raw enbankment gouged by rivulets and littered with
old chimney bricks. And soon, we concluded, now that spring was here, it
would be bristling with weeds. Crossing from this conversation, I noticed that
where my path had been lopped the cliff no longer existed; feet — children's
feet, mostly, for mostly children walk in our town — had worn the sharpness
away and molded a little ramp by which ascent was easier.

This small modification, this modest work of human erosion, seemed 4
precious to me not only because it recalled, in the slope and set of the dirt,
a part of the path that long ago had led down from my parents' back yard
to the high-school softball field. It seemed precious because it had been
achieved accidentally, and had about it that repose of grace that is beyond
willing. We in America have from the beginning been cleaving and baring
the earth, attacking, reforming the enormity of nature we were given, which
we took to be hostile. We have explored, on behalf of all mankind, this
paradox: the more matter is outwardly mastered, the more it overwhelms us
in our hearts. Evidence — gaping right-of-ways, acres mercilessly scraped,
bleeding mountains of muddy fill — surrounds us of a war that is incapable
of ceasing, and it is good to know that now there are enough of us to exert
a counter-force. If craters were to appear in our landscape tomorrow, the next
day there would be usable paths threading down the blasted sides. As our
sense of God's forested legacy to us dwindles, there grows, in these worn,
rubbed, and patted patches, a sense of human legacy — like those feet of
statues of saints which have lost their toes to centuries of kisses. One thinks
of John Dewey's definition of God as the union of the actual and the ideal.

There was a time when I wondered why more people did not go to church. 5
Taken purely as a human recreation, what could be more delightful, more
unexpected than to enter a venerable and lavishly scaled building kept warm
and clean for use one or two hours a week and to sit and stand in unison
and sing and recite creeds and petitions that are like paths worn smooth in
the raw terrain of our hearts? To listen, or not listen, as a poorly paid but
resplendently robed man strives to console us with scraps of ancient epistles
and halting accounts, hopelessly compromised by words, of those intimations
of divine joy that are like pain in that, their instant gone, the mind cannot
remember or believe them; to witness the windows donated by departed
patrons and the altar flowers arranged by withdrawn hands and the whole
considered spectacle lustrous beneath its patina of inheritance; to pay, for
all this, no more than we are moved to give — surely in all democracy there
is nothing like it. Indeed, it is the most available democratic experience. We
vote less than once a year. Only in church and at the polls are we actually

given our supposed value, the soul-unit of one, with its noumenal arithmetic of equality: one equals one equals one.

My preaching fouls the words and corrupts me. Belief builds itself un-   6
consciously and in consciousness is spent. Throughout my childhood I felt nothing in church but boredom and an oppressive futility. For reasons my father never explained, he was a dutiful churchman; my mother, who could use her senses, who had read Santayana and Wells, stayed home Sunday mornings, and I was all on her side, on the side of phenomena, in those years, though I went, with the other children, to Sunday school. It was not until we moved from the town and joined a country church that I, an adolescent of fifteen, my head a hotbed of girls and literature, felt a pleasant emotion in church. During Lent — that dull season, those forty suspended days during which Spring is gathering the mineral energy to make the resurrection that the church calendar seizes upon as conveniently emblematic — I ushered with my father at the Wednesday-night services. We would arrive in our old car — I think it was the Chevrolet then — on those raw March nights and it pleasantly surprised me to find the building warm, the stoked furnace already humming its devotions in the basement. The nave was dimly lit, the congregation small, the sermon short, and the wind howled a nihilistic counterpoint beyond the black windows blotted with garbled apostles; the empty pews, making the minister seem remote and small and emblematic, intensified our sensation of huddling. There was a strong sepia flavor of early Christianity: a minority flock furtively gathered within the hostile enormity of a dying, sobbing empire. From the rear, the broad back and baked neck of the occasional dutiful son loomed bullishly above the black straw hats of the mischievous-looking old ladies, gnarled by farmwork, who sat in their rows like withered apples on the shelves of a sweet-smelling cellar. My father would cross and uncross and recross his legs and stare at his thoughts, which seemed distant. It was pleasant to sit beside him in the rear pew. He was not much of a man for sitting still. When my parents and I went to the movies, he insisted on having the aisle seat, supposedly to give his legs room. After about twenty minutes he would leap up and spend the rest of the show walking around in the back of the theatre drinking water and talking to the manager while my mother and I, abandoned, consoled ourselves with the flickering giants of make-believe. He had nothing of the passive in him; a church always became, for him, something he helped run. It was pleasant, and even momentous, when the moment for action came, to walk by his side up the aisle, the thump of our feet the only sound in the church, and to take the wooden, felt-floored plates from a shy blur of white robes and to administer the submission of alms. Coins and envelopes sought to cover the felt. I condescended, stooping gallantly into each pew. The congregation seemed The Others, reaching, with quarters glittering in their crippled fingers, toward mysteries in which I was snugly involved. Even to usher at a church mixes us with the angels, and is a dangerous thing.

The churches of the Village had this Second Century quality. In Manhattan, Christianity is so feeble its future seems before it. One walks to church past clattering cafeterias and ravaged newsies in winter weather that is always a shade of Lent, on pavements spangled with last night's vomit. The expectantly hushed shelter of the church is like one of those spots worn bare by a softball game in a weed-filled vacant lot. The presence of the city beats like wind at the glowing windows. One hastens home afterward, head down, hurrying to assume the disguise — sweaters and suntans — of a nonchurchgoer. I tried not to go, but it was not in me not to go. I never attended the same church two Sundays in succession, for fear I would become known, and be expected. To be known by face and name and financial weight robs us of our unitary soul, enrolls us against those Others. Devil's work. We are the others. It is of the essence to be a stranger in church.

On the island the very color of my skin made me strange. This island had been abandoned to the descendants of its slaves. Their church was on a hill; it has since been demolished, I have learned from letters, by a hurricane. To reach it one climbed a steep path made treacherous by the loose rubble of coral rock, jagged gray clinkers that bore no visible relation to the pastel branches that could be plucked, still pliant, from the shallows by Maid's Beach. Dull-colored goats were tethered along the path; their forelegs were tangled in their ropes so tightly that whenever they nodded the bush anchoring them nodded in answer. For windows the church possessed tall arched apertures filled not with stained glass but with air and outward vision; one could see the goats stirring the low foliage and the brightly dressed little girls who had escaped the service playing on the packed dirt around the church. The service was fatiguingly long. There were exhaustive petitionary prayers (for the Queen, the Prime Minister, Parliament) and many eight-versed hymns sung with a penetrating, lingering joy and accompanied by a hand-pumped organ. The organ breathed in and out, loud and soft, and the congregation, largely female, followed its ebb and flow at a brief but noticeable distance; their lips moved behind the singing, so I seemed immersed in an imperfectly synchronized movie. Musical stress, the British accent, and Negro elision worked upon the words a triple harmony of distortion. "Lait eth's waadsa *cull* raio-ind . . ." Vainly seeking my place in the hymn — for without a visual key I was lost — I felt lifted within a sweet, soughing milk, an aspiring chant as patient as the nodding of the goats.

Throughout the service, restless deacons slipped in and out of the windows. Bored myself — for we grow sated even with consolation — I discovered that without moving from my pew I too could escape through those tall portals built to admit the breeze. I rested my eyes on earth's wide circle round. From this height the horizon of the sea was lifted halfway up the sky. The Caribbean seemed a steeply tilted blue plane to which the few fishing boats in the bay below had been attached like magnetized toys. God made the world, Aquinas says, in play.

Matter has its radiance and its darkness; it lifts and it buries. Things compete; a life demands a life. On another English island, in Oxford — it is a strange fact about Americans, that we tend to receive our supernatural mail on foreign soil — I helped a cat die. The incident had the signature: decisive but illegible. For six years I did not tell my wife about it, for fear it would frighten her. Some hours before, I had left her at the hospital in the early stages of labor. Wearing a sterilized gown and mask, I had visited her in a white-tiled room along whose walls gleaming gutters stood ready to drain torrents of blood. Her face, scrubbed and polished, was fervent like a child's, and she seemed, lying there swathed in white, ready for nothing so much as a graduation ceremony. She would break off talking, and listen as if to the distant voice of a schoolmistress, and her face would grow rapt, and when the contraction had passed she would sigh and say, "That was a good one," and chatter some more to me of how I would feed myself alone and who I would send the telegrams to.

Shooed from the room, stripped of my mask, I tried to wait, and was told, the comical husband of the American cartoons, to run on home; it would be a time. I went outside and took a bus home. It was the last day of March. I had been born in March, and I had looked forward to welcoming my child to the month; but she was late. We lived on Iffley Road, and around midnight, for some reason — I think to mail a letter, but what letter could have been that important? — I was out walking a few blocks from our flat. The night was cold enough for gloves. The sensations of turning into a father — or, rather, the lack of sensations; the failure of sympathetic pain, the hesitation of dread, the postponement of pride — made the street seem insubstantial. There was not that swishing company of headlights that along an American road throws us into repeated relief. The brick homes, save for an occasional introverted glow in an upstairs window, were dark in the vehement shadows of privacy behind the dry hedges and spiked walls. The streetlamps — wintry, reserved — drained color from everything. Myself a shadow, I noticed another in the center of the road. A puddle of black, as I watched, it curled on itself; its ends lifted from the macadam and seemed to stretch in a yawn. Then it became inert again. I was horrified; the shape was about the size of a baby. When it curled the second time, I went to it, my footsteps the only sound in the street.

It was a cat that had been struck by a car. Struck but not quite killed: a testament to the modest speed and sensible size of English automobiles. By the impersonal witness of the lamps burning in the trees I couldn't be sure what color its fur was — it seemed orange-yellow, tabbied with stripes of dark ginger. The cat was plump and wore a collar. Someone had loved it. Blackness from one ear obscured one side of its head and when I touched it it was like a cup. For the third time, the cat stretched, the tips of its hind feet quivering luxuriously in that way cats have. With a great spastic effort it flipped over onto its other side, but made no cry. The only sound between us was my crooning as I carried it to the side of the street and laid it behind the nearest hedge.

A sallow upstairs light in this home was glowing. I wondered if the cat   13 was theirs. Was it their love invested in my hands? Were they watching as I pushed, crouching, with my burden through their hedge? I wondered if I would be taken for a trespasser, a "poacher"; as an American, I was nervous of English tabus. In my own brutal country it was a not uncommon insult to kill a cat and throw the body into an enemy's yard, and I was afraid that this would be taken that way. I thought of writing a note to explain everything, but I had no paper and pen. I explained to the cat, how I was taking her (I felt it was female) out of the street so no more cars would hit her, how I would put her here in the nice safe dirt behind the hedge, where she could rest and get well. I did not believe she would get well; I think she was dead already. Her weight had felt dead in my hands and when I laid her down she did not stretch or twitch again.

Back in my flat, I discovered that one glove was smeared with blood.   14 Most of the palm and three of the fingers were dyed wine-brown. I hadn't realized there was so much blood. I took off my gloves and carefully wrote a note, explaining that I had found this cat in the middle of the street, still alive, and that I had put it behind this hedge to be safe. If, as I thought, the cat was dead, I hoped that the finders would bury it. After some deliberation, I signed my name and address. I walked back and tucked the note under the cat's body, which seemed at home behind the hedge; it suffered my intrusion a trifle stiffly. It suggested I was making too much fuss, and seemed to say to me, *Run on home.*

Back in my flat once more, I felt abruptly tired, though my heart was   15 pounding hugely. I went to bed and set the alarm for three and read a book. I remember the title, it was Chesterton's *The Everlasting Man.* I turned off the light and prayed for my wife and, though I did not believe myself capable of it, fell asleep. The alarm at three came crashing into some innocent walk of a dream and my frail head felt like a hollow cup. I dressed and went out to the public phone booth a block away and called the hospital. A chirping voice, after some rummaging in the records, told me that several hours ago, in the first hour of April (in the United States it was still March), a perfect female infant had been born. To me.

The next morning, after all the telegrams had been managed, I went   16 back to the hedge, and the cat and my note were gone. Though I had left my address, I never received a letter.

When we returned from England, we bought a car. We had ordered it   17 through my parents from folders they had sent us, and, though its shade of blue was more naïve, more like a robin's egg, than we had expected, this '55 Ford proved an excellent buy. Whether being shuffled from side to side of West Eighty-fifth Street every morning or being rammed in second gear up a washed-out mountain road in Vermont, it never complained. In New York, hot tar from a roof-patching job rained onto its innocent paint, and in Vermont its muffler was racked and rent on a shelf of rock, and in Massachusetts it wallowed, its hot clutch stinking, up from repeated graves of snow. Not only sand and candy wrappers accumulate in a car's interior, but heroisms and instants of communion. We in America make love in our cars, and listen to ball games, and plot out wooing of the dollar: small wonder the landscape is sacrificed to these dreaming vehicles of our ideal and onrushing manhood.

In the beginning, my wife and I would lovingly lave with soap and warm water the unflecked skin of the hood as if it were the thorax of a broad blue baby, and toward the end we let the gallant old heap rust where it would. Its eggshell finish grew grizzled with the stains of dropped maple seeds. Its doors balked at closing; its windows refused to roll down. But I somehow never believed we would ever trade it in, though the little girl born across the ocean in the ominous turning of April, now a vocal and status-conscious democrat of nearly six, applied more and more petulant pressure. The deal was consummated while my soul had its face turned, and Detroit the merciless mother contracted to devour her child. But before the new car arrived, there was a month's grace, and in this grace I enjoyed a final fling with my car, my first, my only — for all the others will be substitutes. It happened this way:

Dancing at a party with a woman not my wife, it seemed opportune to turn her hand in mine and kiss her palm. For some time her thighs had been slithering against mine, and, between dances, she developed a nervous clumsy trick of lurching against me, on tiptoe, and rubbing her breast against my forearm, which was braced across my chest as I held a cigarette. My first thought was that I might burn her; my second, that Nature in her gruff maternal way had arranged one of her opportunities — as my mother, when I was a child, would unpredictably determine to give me a birthday or Hallowe'en party. Obediently I bowed my head and kissed my friend's moist palm. As it withdrew from the advance, her fingertips caressed my chin in the absent-minded manner of one fingering the muzzle of an importunate dog. The exchange transposed us into a higher key; I could hardly hear my own voice, and our dancing lost all connection with the music, and my hand explored her spine from a great aerial distance. Her back seemed mysteriously taut and hard; the body of a strange woman retains more of its mineral content, not being transmuted, through familiarity, into pure emotion. In a sheltered corner of the room we stopped dancing altogether and talked, and what I distinctly remember is how her hands, beneath the steady and opaque appraisal of her eyes, in nervous slurred agitation blindly sought mine and seized and softly gripped, with infantile instinct, my thumbs. Just my thumbs she held, and as we talked she moved them this way and that as if she were steering me. When I closed my eyes, the red darkness inside my lids was trembling, and when I rejoined my wife, and held her to dance, she asked, "Why are you panting?"

After we got home, and surveyed our four children, and in bed read a few pages made unbearably brilliant by their patina of martinis, and turned out the light, she surprised me by not turning her back. Alcohol, with its loosening effect, touches women more deeply than men in this respect; or perhaps, like a matched pair of tuning forks, I had set her vibrating. Irritated by whatever illicit stimulations, we took it out on each other.

To my regret, I survived the natural bliss of satiety — when each muscle is like a petal snugly curved in a corolla of benediction — and was projected onto the wrinkled, azoic territory of insomnia. That feathery anxious embrace of my erect thumbs tormented me in twenty postures. My stomach turned in love of that woman; I feared I would be physically sick and lay on my back gingerly and tried to soothe myself with the caress of headlights as they evolved from bright slits on the wall into parabolically accelerating fans on the ceiling that then vanished: this phenomenon, with its intimations of a life beyond me, had comforted wakeful nights in my earliest childhood. In Sunday school I had been struck by the passage in which Jesus says that to lust after a woman in thought is the same as committing adultery. Now I found myself helplessly containing the conviction that souls, not deeds, are judged. To feel a sin was to commit it; to touch the brink was to be on the floor of the chasm. The universe that so easily permitted me to commit adultery became, by logical steps each one of which went more steeply down than the one above it, a universe that would easily permit me to die. The enormities of cosmic space, the maddening distension of time, history's forgotten slaughters, the child smothered in the dumped icebox, the recent breakdown of the molecular life-spiral, the proven physiological roots of the mind, the presence in our midst of idiots, Eichmanns, animals, and bacteria — all this evidence piled on, and I seemed already eternally forgotten. The dark vibrating air of my bedroom seemed the dust of my grave; the dust went up and up and I prayed upward into it, prayed, prayed for a sign, any glimmer at all, any microscopic loophole or chink in the chain of evidence, and saw none. I remembered a movie I had seen as a child in which a young criminal, moaning insanely, is dragged on rubber legs down the long corridor to the electric chair. I became that criminal. My brain in its calcium vault shouted about injustice, thundered accusations into the lustreless and tranquil homogeneity of the air. Each second my agony went unanswered justified it more certainly: the God who permitted me this fear was unworthy of existence. Each instant my horror was extended amplified God's non-existence, so, as the graph of certain equations fluctuates more and more widely as it moves along the lateral coordinate, or as the magnetic motive-power in atom-smashers accelerates itself, I was caught in a gathering vortex whose unbearably shrill pitch moved me at last to drop my weight on my wife's body and beg, "Wake up, Elaine. I'm so frightened."

I told her of the centuries coming when our names would be forgotten, of the millennia when our nation would be a myth and our continent an ocean, of the aeons when our earth would be vanished and the stars themselves diffused into a uniform and irreversible tepidity. As, an hour before, I had transferred my lust to her, so now I tried to pass my fear into her. It seemed to offend her sense of good taste that I was jealous of future aeons and frantic because I couldn't live through them; she asked me if I had never been so sick I gave up caring whether I lived or died. This contemptible answer — the decrepit Stoic response — required a curious corroboration; eventually, just as I had during the strenuous birth of my fatherhood, I fell asleep, and dreamt of innocent and charming scenes.

The next day, a Saturday, was my birthday. It passed like any day except that underneath the camouflage of furniture and voices and habitual actions I felt death like a wide army invisibly advancing. The newspaper told of nothing but atrocities. My children, wounded and appalled in their competition, came to me to be comforted and I was dismayed to see myself, a gutted shell, appearing to them as the embodiment and pledge of a safe universe. Friends visited, and for the first time truly in my life I realized that each face is suppressing knowledge of an immense catastrophe; our faces are dams that wrinkle under the strain. Around six the telephone rang. It was my mother calling from Pennsylvania; I assumed she had called because of my birthday, so I chattered humorously about the discomforts of growing old for a minute before she could tell me, her voice growing faint, the news. My father was in the hospital. He had been walking around with chest pains for two weeks and suffered shortness of breath at night. She had finally seduced him into a doctor's office; the doctor had taken a cardiogram and driven him to the hospital. He was a seriously sick man.

Instantly I was relieved. The weight of me rolled away. All day death had been advancing under cover and now it had struck, declared its position. My father had engaged the enemy and it would be defeated.

I was restored to crisp health in the play-world of action. That night we had a few friends in for my birthday party and the next day I took the two older children to Sunday school and went myself to church. The faintly lavender lozenge-panes of the white-mullioned windows glowed and dimmed fitfully. It was a spottily overcast day, spitting a little snow. While I was at church my wife had cooked a lamb dinner and as I drank the coffee it became clear that I must drive to Pennsylvania. My mother and I had agreed I would fly down and visit him in a few days; I would have to see about renting a car at the Philadelphia end. This was potentially awkward because, self-employed, I had no credit card. The awkwardness suddenly seemed easy to surmount. I would drive. The car would be traded in a few days, it had just been greased; I had a vision of escaping our foul New England spring by driving south. In half an hour my bag was packed and in my churchgoing suit I abandoned my family. *Run on home.*

Along Route 128 I picked up a young sailor who rode with me all the way to New York and, for two hours through Connecticut, drove my car. I trusted him. He had the full body, the frank and fleshy blue-eyed face of the docile Titans — guileless, competent, mildly earnest — that we have fattened, an ocean removed from the slimming Latin passions and Nordic anxieties of Europe, on our unprecedented abundance of milk and honey, vitamins and protein. He had that instinctive optimism of the young animal that in America is the only generatrix of hope we have allowed ourselves; until recently, it seemed enough. He was incongruously — and somehow reassuringly — tanned. He had got the tan in Key West, where he had spent twenty-four hours, hitching the rides to and from on Navy jets. He had spent the twenty-four hours sleeping on the beach and selecting souvenirs to send back to his parents and girl friend. His parents lived in Salem, his girl friend in Peabody. He wanted to marry her, but his parents had old-fashioned ideas, they thought he was too young. And a lot of these guys in the service say, Don't get married, don't ever get married. But she was a nice girl, not so pretty or anything, but really nice: he really wanted to marry her.

I asked him how old he was. He was twenty-two, and was being trained as an airplane mechanic. He wanted at the end of his hitch to come back to Salem and live. He figured an airplane mechanic could find some sort of job. I told him, with a paternal firmness that amazed my ears, to marry her; absolutely; his parents would get used to it. The thing about parents, I told him, was that secretly, no matter what you did, they liked you anyway. I told him I had married at the age of twenty-one and had never for a minute been sorry.

He asked me, "What do you do? Teach?"

This impressed me. My grandfather had been a teacher, and my father was a teacher, and from my childhood up it had been assumed by the people of our neighborhood that I in turn would become a teacher.

"No," I said. "I'm a writer."

He seemed less offended than puzzled. "What do you write?"

"Oh — whatever comes into my head."

"What's the point?"

"I don't know," I told him. "I wish I did."

We talked less freely after that. At his request I left him off in wet twilight at a Texaco station near the entrance of the New Jersey Turnpike. He hoped to get a ride from there all the way to Washington. Other sailors were clustered out of the rain in the doorways of the station. They hailed him as if they had been waiting for him, and as he went to them he became, from the back, just one more sailor, anonymous, at sea. He did not turn and wave goodbye. I felt I had frightened him, which I regretted, because he had driven for me very well and I wanted him to marry his girl. In the dark I drove down the pike alone. In the first years of my car, when we lived in Manhattan, it would ease up to seventy-five on this wide black stretch without our noticing; now the needle found its natural level at sixty. The windshield wipers beat, and the wonderland lights of the Newark refineries were swollen and broken like bubbles by the raindrops on the side windows. For a dozen seconds a solemn cross of colored stars was suspended stiffly in the upper part of the windshield: an airplane above me was coming in to land.

I did not eat until I was on Pennsylvania soil. The Howard Johnsons in Pennsylvania are cleaner, less crowded, more homelike in their furnishings. The decorative plants seem to be honestly growing, and the waitresses have just a day ago removed the Mennonite cap from their hair, which is still pulled into a smooth bun flattering to their pallid, sly faces. They served me with that swift grace that comes in a country where food is still one of the pleasures. The familiar and subtle irony of their smiles awakened in me that old sense, of Pennsylvania knowingness — of knowing, that is, that the truth is good. They were the innkeeper's daughters, God had given us crops, and my wagon was hitched outside.

When I returned to the car, the music on the radio had changed color. The ersatz hiccup and gravel of Atlantic Seaboard hillbilly had turned, inland, backwards into something younger. As I passed the Valley Forge intersection the radio relived a Benny Goodman quintet that used to make my scalp freeze in high school. The speedometer went up to seventy without effort.

I left the toll road for our local highway and, turning into our dirt road, I was nearly rammed from behind by a pair of headlights that had been pushing, Pennsylvania style, six feet behind me. I parked beside my father's car in front of the barn. My mother came unseen into the yard, and, two voices calling in the opaque drizzle, while the dogs yapped deliriously in their pen, we debated whether I should move my car further off the road. "Out of harm's way," my grandfather would have said. Complaining, I obeyed her. My mother turned as I carried my suitcase down the path of sandstone stepping-stones, and led me to the back door as if I would not know the way. So it was not until we were inside the house that I could kiss her in greeting. She poured us two glasses of wine. Wine had a ceremonial significance in our family; we drank it seldom. My mother seemed cheerful, even silly, and it took an hour for the willed impetus of gaiety to ebb away. She turned her head and looked delicately at the rug and the side of her neck blushed as she told me, "Daddy says he's lost all his faith."

Since I had also lost mine, I could find nothing to say. I remembered, in the silence, a conversation I had had with my father during a vacation from college. With the habitual simplicity of his eagerness to know, he had asked me, "Have you ever had any doubts of the existence of a Divine Being?"

"Sure," I had answered.   40

"I never have," he said. "It's beyond my ability to imagine it. The   41 divinity of Jesus, yes; but the existence of a Divine Being, never." He stated this not as an attempt to influence me, but as a moderately curious fact he had that moment discovered about himself.

"He never was much one for faith," my mother added, hurt by my failure   42 to speak. "He was strictly a works man."

I slept badly; I missed my wife's body, that weight of pure emotion,   43 beside me. I was enough of a father to feel lost out of my nest of little rustling souls. I kept looking out of the windows. The three red lights of the chimneys of the plant that had been built some miles away, to mine low-grade iron ore, seemed to be advancing over our neighbor's ridged field toward our farm. My mother had mistaken me for a stoic like my father and had not put enough blankets on the bed. I found an old overcoat of his and arranged it over me; its collar scratched my chin. I tipped into sleep and awoke. The morning was sharply sunny; sheep hustled, heads toppling, through the gauzy blue sky. It was authentic spring in Pennsylvania. Some of the grass in the lawn had already grown shiny and lank. A yellow crocus had popped up beside the BEWARE OF THE DOG sign my father had had a child at school make for him.

I insisted we drive to Alton in my car, and then was sorry, for it seemed   44 to insult their own. Just a few months ago my father had traded in on yet one more second-hand car: now he owned a '53 Plymouth. But while growing up I had been ambushed by so many mishaps in my father's cars that I insisted we take the car I could trust. Or perhaps it was that I did not wish to take my father's place behind the wheel of his car. My father's place was between me and Heaven; I was afraid of being placed adjacent to that far sky. First we visited his doctor. Our old doctor, a man who believed that people simply "wore out" and nothing could be done about it, had several years ago himself worn out and died. The new doctor's office, in the center of the city, was furnished with a certain raw sophistication. Rippling music leaked from the walls, which were hung with semi-professional oils. He himself was a wiry and firm-tongued young man not much older than myself but venerable with competence and witnessed pain. Such are the brisk shepherds who hop us over the final stile. He brought down from the top of a filing cabinet a plaster model of the human heart. "Your own heart," he told me, "is nice and thin like this; but your dad's heart is enlarged. We believe the obstruction is here, in one of these little vessels on the outside, luckily for your dad."

Outside, in the streets of Alton, my own heart felt enlarged. A white   45 sun warmed the neat façades of painted brick; chimneys like peony shoots thrust through budding treetops. Having grown accustomed to the cramped, improvised cities of New England, I was patriotically thrilled by Alton's straight broad streets and superb equipment of institutions. While my mother went off to buy my daughter a birthday present, I returned a book she had borrowed to the Alton Public Library. I had forgotten the deep aroma of that place, mixed of fust and cleaning fluid and binder's glue and sweet pastry baking in the shop next door. I revisited the shelf of P. G. Wodehouse that in one summer I had read straight through. I took down *Mulliner Nights* and looked in the back for the stamped date, in '47 or '48, that would be me. I never thought to look for the section of the shelves where my own few books would be placed. They were not me. They were my children, mysterious and self-willed.

In driving to the hospital on Alton's outskirts, we passed the museum grounds, where every tree and flower-bed wore a name-tag and black swans drifted through flotillas of crumbled bread. As a child I had believed literally that bread cast upon the waters came back doubled. I remembered that within the museum there were mummies with astonished shattered faces; a tiny gilt chair for a baby Pharaoh; an elephant tusk carved into thousands of tiny Chinamen and pagodas and squat leafy trees; miniature Eskimo villages that you lit up with a switch and peeped into like an Easter egg; cases of arrow-heads; rooms of stuffed birds; and, upstairs, wooden chests decorated with hearts and pelicans and tulips by the pious "plain people" and iridescent glassware from the kilns of Baron von Steigel and slashing paintings of Pennsylvania woodland by the Shearers and bronze statuettes of wrestling Indians that stirred my first erotic dreams and, in the round skylit room at the head of the marble stairs, a black-rimmed pool in whose center a naked green lady held to her pursed lips a shell whose lucent contents forever spilled from the other side, filling this whole vast upstairs — from whose Palladian windows the swans in their bready pond could be seen trailing fan-shaped wakes — with the music and chill romance of falling water. The world then seemed an intricate wonder displayed for my delight with no price asked. Above the trees across the pond one saw rose glints of the hospital, an orderly multitude of tall brick rectangles set among levelled and lovingly tended grounds, an ideal city of the ill.

I had forgotten how grand the Alton hospital was. I had not seen its stately entrance, approached down a grassy mall bright with the first flush of green, since, at the age of seven, I had left the hospital unburdened of my tonsils. Then, too, it had been spring, and my mother was with me. I recalled it to her, and she said, "I felt so guilty. You were so sick."

"Really? I remember it as so pleasant." They had put a cup of pink rubber over my nose and there had been a thunderous flood of the smell of cotton candy and I opened my eyes and my mother was reading a magazine beside my bed.

"You were such a hopeful boy," my mother said, and I did not look   49
at her face for fear of seeing her crying.

I wondered aloud if a certain girl in my high school class were still a   50
nurse here.

"Oh, dear," my mother said. "Here I thought you came all this way   51
to see your poor old father and all you care about is seeing —" And she used
the girl's maiden name, though the girl had been married as long as I had.

Within the hospital, she surprised me by knowing the way. Usually,   52
wherever we went, it was my father or I who knew the way. As I followed
her through the linoleum maze, my mother's shoulders seemed already to have
received the responsible shawl of widowhood. Like the halls of a palace, the
hospital corridors were lined with patient petitioners. Negro girls electrically
dramatic in their starched white uniforms folded bales of cotton sheets; gray
men pushed wrung mops. We went through an Exit sign, down a stairway,
into a realm where gaunt convalescents in bathrobes shuffled in and out of
doorways. I saw my father diagonally through a doorway before we entered
his room. He was sitting up in bed, supported sultanlike by a wealth of pillows
and clad in red-striped pajamas.

I had never seen him in pajamas before; a great man for the shortest   53
distance between two points, he slept in his underclothes. But, having been
at last captured in pajamas, like a big-hearted lion he did not try to miminize
his humiliation, but lay fully exposed, without a sheet covering even his feet.
Bare, they looked pale, gentle, and oddly unused.

Except for a sullen lymphatic glow under his cheeks, his face was totally   54
familiar. I had been afraid that his loss of faith would show, like the altered
shape of his mouth after he had had all his teeth pulled. With grins we
exchanged the shy handshake that my going off to college had forced upon
us. I sat on the window sill by his bed, my mother took the chair at the foot
of the bed, and my father's roommate, a tanned and fortyish man flat on his
back with a crushed vertebra, sighed and blew smoke toward the ceiling and
tried, I suppose, not to hear us. Our conversation, though things were radically
changed, followed old patterns. Quite quickly the talk shifted from him to
me. "I don't know how you do it, David," he said. "I couldn't do what you're
doing if you paid me a million dollars a day." Embarrassed and flattered, as
usual, I tried to shush him, and he disobediently turned to his roommate and
called loudly, "I don't know where the kid gets his ideas. Not from his old
man, I know that. I never gave that poor kid an idea in my life."

"Sure you did," I said softly, trying to take pressure off the man with   55
the painful back. "You taught me two things. Always butter bread toward
the edges because enough gets in the middle anyway, and No matter what
happens to you, it'll be a new experience."

To my dismay, this seemed to make him melancholy. "That's right,   56

David," he said. "No matter what happens to you, it'll be a new experience. The only thing that worries me is that *she*" — he pointed at my mother — "will crack up the car. I don't want anything to happen to your mother."

"The car, you mean," my mother said, and to me she added, "It's a sin, the way he worships that car." 57

My father didn't deny it. "Jesus I love that car," he said. "It's the first car I've ever owned that didn't go bad on me. Remember all those heaps we used to ride back and forth in?" 58

The old Chevy was always getting dirt in the fuel pump and refusing to start at awkward hours. Once, going down Fire Hill, the left front wheel had broken off the axle; my father wrestled with the steering wheel while the tires screamed and the white posts of the guard fence floated calmly toward my eyes. When the car slid sideways to a stop just short of the embankment my father's face was stunned and the corners of his mouth dribbled saliva. I was surprised; it had not occurred to me to be frightened. The '36 Buick had drunk oil, a quart every fifty miles, and loved to have flat tires after midnight, when I would be gliding home with a scrubbed brain and the smell of lipstick in my nose. Once, when we had both gone into town and I had dropped him off and taken the car, I had absent-mindedly driven home alone. I came in the door and my mother said, "Why, where's your father?" 59

My stomach sank. "My Lord," I said, "I forgot I had him!" 60

As, smiling, I took in breath and prepared to dip with him into reminiscence of these adventures, my father, staring stonily into the air above his pale and motionless toes, said, "I love this place. There are a lot of wonderful gentlemen in here. The only thing that worries me is that mother will crack up the car." 61

To my horror I saw that my mother, leaning forward red-faced in the chair at the foot of the bed, was silently crying. He glanced at her and said to me, "It's a funny feeling. The night before we went to see the doctor I woke up and couldn't get my breath and realized I wasn't ready to die. I had always thought I would be. It's a funny feeling." 62

"Luckily for your dad," "all his faith," "wonderful gentlemen": these phrases were borne in on me with a dreadful weight and my tongue seemed pressed flat on the floor of its grave. The pajama stripes under my eyes stirred and streamed, real blood. I wanted to speak, to say how I needed him and to beg him not to leave me, but there were no words, no form of words available in our tradition. A pillar of smoke poured upward from the sighing man in the other bed. 63

Into this pit hesitantly walked a plain, painfully clean girl with a pad and pencil. She had yellow hair, thick lips, and, behind pink-rimmed glasses, large eyes that looked as if they had been corrected from being crossed. They 64 flicked across our faces and focussed straight ahead in that tunnel-vision gaze of those who know perfectly well they are figures of fun. The Jehovah's Witnesses who come to the door wear that funnelled expression. She approached the bed where my father lay barefoot and, suppressing a stammer, explained that she was from Lutheran Home Missions and that they kept accounts of all hospitalized Lutherans and notified the appropriate pastors to make visitations. Clearly she had measured my father for a rebuff; perhaps her eyes, more practiced in this respect than mine, spotted the external sign of loss of faith that I had missed. At any rate my father was a Lutheran by adoption; he had been born and raised a Presbyterian and still looked like one.

"That's *aw*fully nice of you," he told the girl. "I don't see how you 65 people do it on the little money we give you."

Puzzled, she dimpled and moved ahead with her routine. "Your church 66 is — ?"

He told her, pronouncing every syllable meticulously and consulting my 67 mother and me as to whether the word "Evangelical" figured in the official title.

"That would make your pastor Reverend —" 68

"Yeah. He'll be in, don't worry about it. Wild horses couldn't keep him 69 away. Nothing he likes better than to get out of the sticks and drive into Alton. I didn't mean to confuse you a minute ago; what I meant was, just last week in church council we were talking about you people. We couldn't figure out how you do anything on the little money we give you. After we've got done feeding the furnace and converting the benighted Hindoo there isn't anything left over for you people that are trying to help the poor devils in our own back yard."

The grinning girl was lost in this onslaught of praise and clung to the 70 shreds of her routine. "In the meantime," she recited, "here is a pamphlet you might like to read."

My father took it from her with a swooping gesture so expansive I got 71 down from the window sill to restrain him physically, if necessary. That he must lie still was my one lever, my one certainty about his situation. "That's awfully nice of you," he told the girl. "I don't know where the hell you get the money to print these things."

"We hope your stay in the hospital is pleasant and would like to wish 72 you a speedy recovery to full health."

"Thank you; I know you're sincere when you say it. As I was telling 73 my son David here, if I can do what the doctors tell me I'll be all right. First time in my life I've ever tried to do what anybody ever told me to do. The kid was just telling me, 'No matter what happens to you, Pop, it'll be a new experience.' "

"Now if you will excuse me I have other calls to pay." 74

"Of course. You go right ahead, sick Lutherans are a dime a dozen. 75
You're a wonderful woman to be doing what you're doing."

And she left the room transformed into just that. As a star shines in our 76
heaven though it has vanished from the universe, so my father continued to
shed faith upon others. For the remainder of my visit with him his simple
presence so reassured me, filled me with such a buoyant humor, that my
mother surprised me, when we had left the hospital, by remarking that we
had tired him.

"I hadn't noticed," I said. 77

"And it worries me," she went on, "the way he talks about the movies 78
all the time. You know he never liked them." When I had offered to stay
another night so I could visit him again, he had said, "No, instead of that
why don't you take your mother to the movies?" Rather than do that, I said,
I would drive home. It took him a moment, it seemed, to realize that by my
home I meant a far place, where I had a wife and children; though at the
time I was impatient to have his consent, it has since occurred to me and
grieved me that during that instant his face was blank he was swallowing
the realization that he was no longer the center of even his son's universe.
Having swallowed, he told me how good I had been to come all this way
to see him. He told me I was a good son and a good father; he clasped my
hand. I felt I would ascend straight north from his touch.

I drove my mother back to her farm and got my bag and said goodbye 79
on the lawn. The little sandstone house was pink in the declining sunlight;
the lawn was a tinkling clutter of shy rivulets. Standing beside the BEWARE
OF THE DOG sign with its companion of a crocus, she smiled and said, "This
is like when you were born. Your father drove through a snowstorm all the
way from Wheeling in our old Ford." He had been working with the telephone
company then; the story of his all-night ride was the first myth in which I
was a character.

Darkness did not fall until New Jersey. The hour of countryside I saw 80
from the Pennsylvania Turnpike looked enchanted — the branches of the trees
underpainted with budding russet, the meadows nubbled like new carpets,
the bronze sun slanting on Valley Forge and Levittown alike. I do not know
what it is that is so welcome to me in the Pennsylvania landscape, but it is
the same quality — perhaps of reposing in the certainty that the truth is good
— that is in Pennsylvania faces. It seemed to me for this sunset hour that the
world is our bride, given to us to love, and the terror and joy of the marriage
is that we bring to it a nature not our bride's.

There was no sailor to help me drive the nine hours back. New Jersey 81
began in twilight and ended in darkness, and Manhattan made its gossamer
splash at its favorite hour, eight o'clock. The rest of the trip was more and
more steeply uphill. The Merritt Turnpike seemed meaninglessly coquettish,
the light-controlled stretch below Hartford maddeningly obstinate, and the

hour above that frighteningly empty. Distance grew thicker and thicker; the intricate and effortful mechanics of the engine, the stellar infinity of explosive sparks needed to drive it, passed into my body, and wearied me. Repeatedly I stopped for coffee and the hallucinatory comfort of human faces, and after every stop, my waiting car, companion and warm home and willing steed, responded to my pressure. It began to seem a miracle that the car could gather speed from my numb foot; the very music on the radio seemed a drag on our effort, and I turned it off, obliterating time. We climbed through a space fretted by scattered brilliance and bathed in a monotonous wind. I had been driving forever; furniture, earth, churches, women, were all things I had innocently dreamed. And through those aeons my car, beginning as a mechanical spiral of molecules, evolved into something soft and organic and consciously brave. I lost, first, heart, then head, and finally any sense of my body. In the last hour of the trip I ceased to care or feel or in any real sense see, but the car, though its soul the driver had died, maintained steady forward motion, and completed the endless journey safely. Above my back yard the stars were frozen in place, and the shapes of my neighbors' houses wore the wonder that children induced by whirling.

Any day now we will trade it in; we are just waiting for the phone to ring. I know how it will be. My father traded in many cars. It happens so cleanly, before you expect it. He would drive off in the old car up the dirt road exactly as usual and when he returned the car would be new, and the old was gone, gone, utterly dissolved back into the mineral world from which it was conjured, dismissed without a blessing, a kiss, a testament, or any ceremony of farewell. We in America need ceremonies, is I suppose, sailor, the point of what I have written. 82

SUBJECT QUESTIONS

1. The story concludes with the statement, "We in America need ceremonies, is I suppose, sailor, the point of what I have written." Who is the "sailor" to whom the statement is addressed? Why to him?
2. Can you see this concluding statement as the point of the four episodes? What does the story of the dead cat have to do with ceremonies?
3. The narrator, David, several times refers to his loss of faith. Why, then, does he feel the need for ceremonies? Why does he bother to go to church?
4. What connection does Updike make between "packed dirt" and a religious impulse? What does John Dewey's definition of God have to do with this? (See paragraph 4.)
5. Twice in the dying cat episode occurs the direction, "Run on home," which is repeated in the traded car episode; and at the end David leaves his dying father to "run on home." What special significance do you think Updike attaches to this command?

6. After a night of torment over his own insignificance in a dying universe, David is "relieved" to hear that his father is dying: "I was restored to crisp health in the play-world of action." Does the author intend for us to take David as a crass, uncaring son? What does he mean by the "play-world of action"? If action is the play-world, what is the real world?
7. Explain David's statement that churchgoing is "our most available democratic experience." Do you agree?

STRUCTURE QUESTIONS

1. Even the lengthy title implies that this story is about four separate episodes; what organizing principle, if any, justifies Updike's putting them together in one story?
2. Narrative poets frequently tie their poems, particularly ballads, together with refrains. Consider the effectiveness of Updike's use of this technique in fiction.
3. Until the fourth episode, we have only one indication that the narrator is "David" rather than the author, and the reader may feel that he is reading autobiography instead of fiction. What devices does Updike employ to give this impression? Why would he want to create such an impression?
4. Modern fiction writers seldom stop their narrative to comment on and interpret what happens (as in paragraph 4, for instance); are these commentaries necessary to understand the story? Do they interfere with emotional impact?
5. Because this is fiction, Updike does not use the traditional organization of persuasion. Does he manage to convey his beliefs effectively through fiction? Is Updike trying to "persuade" the reader, or only explain to him his own views? What advantages might fiction have as an instrument of persuasion?

Dover Beach

Matthew Arnold

Matthew Arnold (1822–1888), son of a headmaster at Rugby, was a social critic. The best-known of his many books is Culture and Anarchy, a criticism of the tastes and values of the middle class. "Dover Beach" is perhaps the best example of his meditative poetry, reflecting the nineteenth century's deep doubts about the purpose of the universe and man's place in it aroused by new scientific discoveries and particularly by the publication of Darwin's Origin of Species.

The sea is calm to-night,
The tide is full, the moon lies fair
Upon the Straits; — on the French coast, the light
Gleams, and is gone; the cliffs of England stand,
Glimmering and vast, out in the tranquil bay. 5
Come to the window, sweet is the night air!
Only, from the long line of spray
Where the sea meets the moon-blanched land,
Listen! you hear the grating roar
Of pebbles which the waves draw back, and fling, 10
At their return, up the high strand,
Begin, and cease, and then again begin,
With tremulous cadence slow, and bring
The eternal note of sadness in.

  Sophocles long ago 15
Heard it on the Ægean, and it brought
Into his mind the turbid ebb and flow
Of human misery; we
Find also in the sound a thought,
Hearing it by this distant northern sea. 20

The sea of faith
Was once, too, at the full, and round earth's shore
Lay like the folds of a bright girdle furled;
But now I only hear
Its melancholy, long, withdrawing roar, 25
Retreating to the breath
Of the night-wind, down the vast edges drear
And naked shingles of the world.

Ah, love, let us be true
To one another! for the world, which seems   30
To lie before us like a land of dreams,
So various, so beautiful, so new,
Hath really neither joy, nor love, nor light,
Nor certitude, nor peace, nor help for pain;
And we are here as on a darkling plain   35
Swept with confused alarms of struggle and flight,
Where ignorant armies clash by night.

SUBJECT QUESTIONS

1. What is it about the sea which reminds Arnold of human misery? Isn't the opening picture one of calm beauty rather than of misery?
2. What is the reasoning behind Arnold's conclusion that love is all he can have faith in? Is his "evidence" primarily logical, or emotional?
3. Arnold assumes that the universe is unconcerned with him; does he reciprocate with unconcern for the universe in his decision to trust only love? What is his attitude toward nature?
4. To what is Arnold referring in the concluding figure about ignorant armies in conflict?
5. Why does Arnold bring Sophocles into the poem? Does he represent something?

STRUCTURE QUESTIONS

1. The poem is divided into four stanzas; are these logical divisions or melodic divisions?
2. Analyze the rhyme schemes of the four stanzas. Do you find any correlation between the tightness of the rhyme and the idea expressed in each stanza?
3. Which lines seem to you to imitate most successfully the sound and rhythm of the sea? Do these imitations have any effect on the meaning of the poem, or are they exercises in poetic ingenuity?
4. Consider the way in which Arnold indicates transitions in thought with metrical variations. (Two good examples of this technique occur in the second stanza.)
5. The normal meter of this poem is iambic; why does Arnold vary this slightly in the last line? Consider other variations from iambic; do they serve any purpose? Are they weaknesses in the poem? Should Arnold have made the lines all the same length?
6. Evaluate the strengths and weaknesses of this poem as persuasion. Does poetry seem to have any particular advantage over prose as a medium of persuasion?
7. What is the effect of the repetitious structure in lines 33 and 34? Explain how these lines help tie the last stanza to the rest of the poem.

9

LESSONS FOR
THE FUTURE

Evaluation

The ability to evaluate, to judge, to decide that one way is better than another, is one of the great distinguishing characteristics of the human mind. It is what enables us to make use of our abilities to see likenesses and differences, to form generalizations from particulars, and to accumulate knowledge purposefully instead of indiscriminately as a pack rat saving objects. The discovery of scientific information, for instance, is not nearly so valuable to us as the ability to assess its importance — to see the significance of new facts in relation to known facts.

Evaluation is a practice in which learned minds are constantly indulging and of which everyone is more or less capable. Every time we make a decision we first evaluate the advantages and disadvantages of each possible course of action. We may not do this very carefully or logically, but we do it. Take a familiar example: When a student's alarm clock rings at 7:30 he finds himself faced with a decision. "Should I get up and go to my 8 o'clock class? Should I stay in bed and get some much-needed rest? Should I wander over to the student union for a leisurely and nourishing breakfast of black coffee and cigarette smoke?" The student may be handicapped by an inability to think clearly at this time of day, but he will still evaluate various factors: "I need sleep more than I need food. If I went to class, the professor would put me to sleep. But I sleep better in a prone position than sitting at a desk." A good evaluation, certainly, would be done much more carefully than that, but the basic process would be similar; consider all the pertinent facts and implications and pass judgment in the light of each possibility's relative merits.

Evaluation, whether it is simple or complex, always presupposes the existence of some standard of judgment. Standards may vary greatly with different people and may not be very explicitly formulated, but for any judgment there must be a standard. When a teacher evaluates a student theme, he compares it to certain standards of excellence: "The organization is fair, sentence structure good, clarity excellent, spelling and punctuation atrocious." Then he decides what its overall grade should be. A student does the same sort of thing when he decides "That was a good movie" or "He is a poor teacher." What makes a good movie? — photography, acting, directing, significance of plot, continuity, and so on. The evaluator may not have such explicit standards, however; perhaps he judges from a vague notion, accumulated by watching many movies, that a movie ought to evoke certain emotional responses. But almost no one is totally uncritical, that is, without any standards of judgment.

It will easily be seen from the preceding examples that the amount and diversity of one's experience have much to do with his ability to evaluate. The young child who has seen few movies will be tempted to boo the villain and shout warnings to the good guy; he will admire the good guy and detest the bad guy even if the latter is a much better actor. Similarly, a second grader is not nearly as capable of judging teaching effectiveness as is a college student. And the beginning teacher, lacking the experience which comes from reading thousands of papers of varying quality, may also lack that ability to know automatically what grade a paper should receive; he must make up in eagerness and carefulness what he lacks in experience. Of the two aspects of experience, variety is probably more important for good evaluation than mere quantity of experience, however. A person who has read much poetry but all of it comparatively easy (Service, Whitman, and Sandburg, for example) will still have trouble evaluating the more difficult poetry of Wallace Stevens or Dylan Thomas. His standards of judgment are simply too limited. A story is told of an African tribal chief who was taken to hear his first symphonic concert in an experiment to determine whether or not good music is naturally appealing to someone without prior training. The chief was quite pleased when the orchestra members were tuning their instruments, but the symphony itself left him coldly unappreciative.

In discussing standards of evaluation it is important to keep in mind that standards can be — and usually are — relative instead of absolute. We hold most standards tentatively, with an awareness that there may be specific instances to which a generally valid standard does not apply. Most people who endorse the principle, "Thou shalt not kill," do not hold it absolutely but mean "In *most cases* thou shalt not kill." If one man kills another and we are called upon to evaluate the criminality of his act, we make an exception to the principle if he was fighting in a war, acting in self-defense, or executing a convict. Our courts even distinguish "degrees" of murder: premeditated, unpremeditated, accidental, and justifiable. This same relativity of principles applies in most other areas as well. An English teacher may normally mark off heavily for errors in punctuation or sentence structure, but he is likely to be much more forgiving in these matters if a paper shows considerable insight and imagination. We say that the hero of a tragedy ought to have a recognizable "tragic flaw," but we readily admit that *Hamlet* is great even though its hero has no such flaw.

Evaluation as an essay form can be of three different types. One of these is *primary* evaluation: evaluation of a state of affairs or past action, such as a judgment of the accomplishments of Theodore Roosevelt's administration or of UNESCO's success in fostering mutual understanding among nations. Anther type is *secondary*, an evaluation of *someone else's* judgment. This includes book reviews and judgments of paintings, poems, movies — works which express the values of the artist. The process for this kind of evaluation is the same as for primary evaluation except that two sets of standards must be considered: those of the original author or artist and those of the reviewer or critic. Normally, such an evaluation is organized in three parts, answering the following questions: (1) What was the author trying to do? (2) How well did he accomplish his aims? (3) To what extent was the work worth doing? The answers to the first two questions should be in terms of the standards implied by the original author. If an artist was trying to produce an abstract painting it would hardly be fair to condemn his work for being insufficiently representational — that is, not "looking like" the scene which inspired it. The answer to the third question depends on the standards of the reviewer or critic. If he believes that abstract painting is foolish experimentation and that this particular painting cannot be great because it is abstract, such a judgment should come in the third rather than the second part. Thus a critic might conclude that the artist succeeded very well in what he was trying to do but that the attempt was not worth the effort.

You should remember that any evaluation, no matter how carefully worked out, is still opinion rather than fact. A viewer may be convinced that a certain movie was the "worst" of the year, and perhaps it was that bad if judged by a standard such as acting or plot. But perhaps its producer, his standard of judgment being monetary, might judge it to be "great" if a few suggestive scenes cause it to bring in considerable amounts of money. This is not to say, however, that all evaluations are equally valuable. Enlightened opinion can tell us much; snap judgments tell us little except something about the intellectual nature of the person making the judgment. The student who writes an evaluation should take pains to judge carefully and fairly, to consider as much relevant information as possible, to know and make clear what his standards of judgment are, and to recognize that they may not be the only applicable standards. Pursued properly, evaluation can be a rewarding experience and a valuable contribution to civilization. Done improperly, it can be a mere excuse for perpetrating one's prejudices.

Although *self-evaluation*, the third type, is on a subject obviously familiar to the writer, it is a very difficult kind of writing to handle competently. And it is the one type of writing which is generally more useful to the writer than to his reader. The great Dr. Samuel Johnson always kept a journal, and he urged his friend Boswell to do the same on the grounds that any person, no matter how successful or important he was, could profit by occasionally taking stock of himself. He found that a person, too easily losing sight of his personal values and goals, can drift through life discovering too late that he has not accomplished what he set out to do or anything else worthwhile.

Self-evaluation is especially valuable to a student, for he is in the process of committing himself to a set of standards and aims which will in large measure determine what the rest of his life will be like. The student who comes to school with an exalted and narrow-minded notion of his chosen career, whether it be in medicine, engineering, or creative writing, is likely to be making a tragic mistake if he staggers through a program for which he is not suited and refuses to consider other possible major fields. Again, unless he evaluates himself periodically a student may go through college thinking that a C-average and a house presidency are adequate recommendations for a job, and then suddenly discover too late that he wants to go on to graduate school.

In spite of the obvious benefit from occasional self-evaluation, the student is likely to encounter considerable difficulty in doing it. No one likes to admit that he is making a mistake or that his values are wrong; consequently, it is easier to avoid the possibility of having to make such an admission by dismissing self-evaluation as a "waste of time" or by substituting for honest analysis a few hasty rationalizations. Someone has said, however, that a student's greatest advantage is his right to be wrong: the student who is afraid of making a mistake never learns as much as the one who exposes his ideas to the criticism of his teachers and fellow students. Although a ten-year veteran of a specialized occupation can hardly afford to admit that he has chosen the wrong career, a student can admit it — and change — without too much inconvenience. If he can forget his fear of being wrong and make an honest effort to evaluate himself justly, he can learn a great deal about himself and at the same time gain a clearer view of where he is going and where he wants to go.

A complete self-evaluation contains the answers to two questions:

(1) Am I accomplishing my aims and living up to my standards? (2) Are my standards, basic assumptions, and goals the right ones for me? For most students, the first question is probably much easier to answer than the second, for the latter calls into question values which the student has been accumulating for years and about which he may have had no doubts before coming to college. Evaluating these values involves the same kind of difficulty faced by a person who takes a college biology course after having been taught at home or at church that the whole notion of evolution is atheistic nonsense. But because anyone's set of values is likely to include contradictions and unwarranted assumptions, it is particularly worthwhile to examine them before committing one's whole life to them. Most of our "cherished" goals are either handed to us or accumulated unconsciously, so that we have no real reason for being fiercely loyal to them. It would profit any student to take complete stock of himself at least as often as once every school year. The difficulty of the attempt ought to be compensated for by the knowledge that it is the student's own life which is at stake. It is because self-evaluation can be of such vital importance — and because backing off and examining one's self objectively is such a difficult task — that this subject has been reserved for the last part of the text.

Looking Back

Joyce Maynard

Joyce Maynard grew up in Durham, New Hampshire. Her mother, Fredelle Maynard, is a writer and authority on education and family relations; her father, Max Maynard, is a painter and professor of English. While she was still in high school, Joyce Maynard won several short story awards that led to publication in Seventeen *and* Woman's Day. *Since then, her pieces have been published in* Mademoiselle, McCall's, *and* The New York Sunday Times Magazine. *Her first book, of which the following is the last chapter, is called* Looking Back: A Chronicle of Growing Up Old in the Sixties. *It was published in 1973, when Ms. Maynard was 19 and a sophomore at Yale. After all that had been written about the "younger generation" by the older one, Ms. Maynard wanted to let her generation speak for itself.*

The words *ambitious, up-and-coming, go-getting* used to be the highest com-   1
pliment awarded to a bright young man just starting out on his career. Back
in those days, the label *businessman* held no unfortunate connotations, no
ring of war-mongering or conservatism or pollution. The future may have
been uncertain, but it was certainly considered, anyway, and the goals were
clear: a good marriage, a good job, a good income — that was a good life.

My generation's definition of The Good Life is harder to arrive at. Our   2
plans for the future are vague, because so many of us don't believe in planning,
because we don't quite believe in the future. Perhaps we make too much of
growing up with tension, from as far back as the Cuban Missile Crisis, but
the fact is that the tension of the sixties put us in a kind of suspension. There
were always fallout shelter signs, always secret servicemen and always, when
the words "we interrupt this program to bring you . . ." flashed on the screen,
the possibility of an assassination. When a plane flies low I wonder (just for
a second) — is it the Russians? The Chinese?

So we don't plan. We make a thing of spontaneity and informality.   3
(Parties just *happen;* couples hang around together — no more going on dates.)
Looking ahead to the future, planning, and pushing are seen as uncool ("take
it easy . . . no sweat"), aggressive.

It's impossible not to wonder where the young hip kids of today will   4
be twenty years from now. Their parents say they'll settle down ("We were
wild in our day too . . .") and some of them will — some will later join their
parents' establishment world just as, for now, they've joined a group that is

itself a kind of establishment. But there's another group, involved in much more than a fad, and their futures are less easy to predict. They've passed beyond faddishness, beyond the extreme activism of the late sixties and arrived at a calm isolationist position — free not just from the old establishment ambitions and the corporate tycoon style, but from the aggressiveness of the radical tycoon. The best thing to be, for them, isn't go-getting or up-and-coming, but cool. Broad social conscience has been replaced by personal responsibility, and if they plan at all, their plans will be to get away. The new movement is away from the old group forms of moratorium crowds and huge rock concerts and communes. Young doctors who once joined the Peace Corps are turning more and more to small-town private practices, Harvard scholars are dropping out to study auto mechanics or farming. Everybody wants to buy land in Oregon and Vermont. If we have any ambition at all now, it is not so much the drive to get ahead as it is the drive to get away.

When my friends and I were little, we had big plans. I would be a famous actress and singer, dancing on the side. I would paint my own sets and compose my own music, writing the script and the lyrics and reviewing the performance for the New York *Times*. I would marry and have three children (they don't allow us dreams like that any more) and we would live, rich and famous (donating lots to charity, of course, and periodically adopting orphans), in a house we designed ourselves. When I was older I had visions of good works. I saw myself in South American rain forests and African deserts, feeding the hungry and healing the sick with an obsessive selflessness, I see now, that was as selfish, in the end, as my first plans for stardom.

Now my goal is simpler. I want to be happy. And I want comfort — nice clothes, a nice house, good music and good food, and the feeling that I'm doing some little thing that matters. I'll vote and I'll give to charity, but I won't give myself. I feel a sudden desire to buy land — not a lot, not as a business investment, but just a small plot of earth so that whatever they do to the country I'll have a place where I can go — a kind of fallout shelter, I guess. As some people prepare for their old age, so I prepare for my twenties. A little house, a comfortable chair, peace and quiet — retirement sounds tempting.

I'm almost twenty now — two decades gone. I know now that I will never be a ballerina. That's not because of any conscious choice, because of anything I've done, but because of what's been neglected. It isn't that I ever longed to be one, but the knowledge scares me, that I can't — there's nothing, absolutely nothing I can do about it. I am too old to be a violin prodigy, or to learn championship chess; I'm closer to Ophelia now than Juliet. The word *woman* embarrasses me a little. (Why is that? Some leftover scrap of unliberation, that *boys* are *men*, while I remain, and will till I am fifty, always a *girl*.)

Once, I guess, youth was a handicap and coming of age an exciting, horizon-broadening time for long pants and freedom. For us, today, youth —

while it lasts — is a time we greedily hold onto, a fashionable, glorified age when, if we don't quite *swing*, at least we're told that's what we do, that these are the best years of our lives — it's all downhill from here.

But I'm basically an optimist. Somehow, no matter what the latest population figures say, I feel everything will work out — just like on TV. I may doubt man's fundamental goodness, but I believe in his power to survive. I say, sometimes, that I wonder if we'll be around in thirty years, but then I forget myself and speak of "when I'm fifty. . . ." Death has touched me now — from Vietnam and Biafra and a car accident that makes me buckle my seat belt — but like negative numbers and the sound of a dog whistle (too high-pitched for human ears), it's not a concept I can comprehend.

9

SUBJECT QUESTIONS

1. Do you think Ms. Maynard does, as she hints, "make too much of growing up with tension"? Did the preceding generation grow up with less "tension"?
2. Are there any signs of a change in attitude toward planning for the future since this essay was published in 1973?
3. Maynard's goal (paragraph 6) sounds curiously like the older generation's ultimate dream of buying a little place in the country and raising a few chickens. Is there any significant difference?
4. Is Maynard right in her judgment that today's young people, instead of looking forward to adult life, cling to youth in the belief that "it's all downhill from here"?
5. In the final paragraph, Ms. Maynard implies that her basic optimism springs from watching too much television. Writers have made much of television's increasing the awareness of youth. Do you think the endless doctor and lawyer and spy shows have also conditioned youth to demand a "happy ending" to all problems? Would such a possibility explain the choice to escape rather than to join an imperfect society where all endings are not happy?

STRUCTURE QUESTIONS

1. Discuss the devices — or comments — that give the impression that Maynard is making an honest attempt to evaluate herself justly.
2. Maynard's chief method of development here is comparison and contrast. Does it seem a natural choice? Does she use it to good effect?
3. What standards of judgment does Maynard use in this self-evaluation? When her aspirations changed, did her standards also change?
4. What purpose is served by paragraph 7, in which she lists some possibilities no longer open to her?
5. How would you characterize Maynard's style? If she is presenting herself as typical of the younger generation, should she have written in a style closer to "Nowspeak"?

A Very Easy Death

Simone de Beauvoir

*Renowned both for her fiction and for her autobiographical writings, Si-
mone de Beauvoir has the highest international reputation among contemporary women writers. In her twenties, she was the major force behind
the Existentialist movement in Paris, to which her close, lifelong friend
Jean-Paul Sartre later gave philosophical expression. In Europe, her prize-
winning novel,* The Mandarins, *is her bestselling book; in America, possibly
because of the women's liberation movement,* The Second Sex *is her best-
known work.* A Very Easy Death *(1964) was written shortly after her
mother's death. The final chapter, reprinted here, is an attempt to evaluate
the relationship between the mother, seventy-eight at death, and her
daughter, then fifty-seven. "Maman" had gone into the hospital with a
broken leg, cancer was discovered during routine tests, and four weeks
later she was dead. The book gives insight into the humiliation and loneliness of dying, as well as into the unavoidable hypocrisy of loved ones, who
want to give comfort — but from the other side of the awful gulf between
death and life.*

Why did my mother's death shake me so deeply? Since the time I left home 1
I had felt little in the way of emotional impulse towards her. When she lost
my father the intensity and the simplicity of her sorrow moved me, and so
did her care for others — "Think of yourself," she said to me, supposing that
I was holding back my tears so as not to make her suffering worse. A year
later her mother's dying was a painful reminder of her husband's: on the day
of the funeral a nervous breakdown compelled her to stay in bed. I spent
the night beside her: forgetting my disgust for this marriage-bed in which
I had been born and in which my father had died, I watched her sleeping;
at fifty-five, with her eyes closed and her face calm, she was still beautiful;
I wondered that the strength of her feelings should have overcome her will.
Generally speaking I thought of her with no particular feeling. Yet in my
sleep (although my father only made very rare and then insignificant appearances) she often played a most important part: she blended with Sartre, and
we were happy together. And then the dream would turn into a nightmare:
why was I living with her once more? How had I come to be in her power
again? So our former relationship lived on in me in its double aspect — a
subjection that I loved and hated. It revived with all its strength when

Maman's accident, her illness and her death shattered the routine that then governed our contacts. Time vanishes behind those who leave this world, and the older I get the more my past years draw together. The "Maman darling" of the days when I was ten can no longer be told from the inimical woman who oppressed my adolescence; I wept for them both when I wept for my old mother. I thought I had made up my mind about our failure and accepted it; but its sadness comes back to my heart. There are photographs of both of us, taken at about the same time: I am eighteen, she is nearly forty. Today I could almost be her mother and the grandmother of that sad-eyed girl. I am so sorry for them — for me because I am so young and I understand nothing; for her because her future is closed and she has never understood anything. But I would not know how to advise them. It was not in my power to wipe out the unhappiness in her childhood that condemned Maman to make me unhappy and to suffer in her turn from having done so. For if she embittered several years of my life, I certainly paid her back though I did not set out to do so. She was intensely anxious about my soul. As far as this world was concerned, she was pleased at my successes, but she was hurt by the scandal that I aroused among the people she knew. It was not pleasant for her to hear a cousin state, "Simone is the family's disgrace."

The changes in Maman during her illness made my sorrow all the greater. As I have already said, she was a woman of a strong and eager temperament, and because of her renunciations she had grown confused and difficult. Confined to her bed, she decided to live for herself; and yet at the same time she retained an unvarying care for others — from her conflicts there arose a harmony. My father and his social character coincided exactly: his class and he spoke through his mouth with one identical voice. His last words, "You began to earn your living very young, Simone: your sister cost me a great deal of money," were not of a kind to encourage tears. My mother was awkwardly laced into a spiritualistic ideology; but she had an animal passion for life which was the source of her courage and which, once she was conscious of the weight of her body, brought her towards truth. She got rid of the ready-made notions that hid her sincere and lovable side. It was then that I felt the warmth of an affection that had often been distorted by jealousy and that she expressed so badly. In her papers I have found touching evidence of it. She had put aside two letters, the one written by a Jesuit and the other by a friend; they both assured her that one day I should come back to God. She had copied out a passage from Chamson in which he says in effect "If, when I was twenty, I had met an older, highly-regarded man who had talked to me about Nietzsche and Gide and freedom, I should have broken with home." The file was completed by an article cut out of a paper — *Jean-Paul Sartre has saved a soul*. In this Rémy Roure said — quite untruthfully, by the way — that after *Bariona* had been acted at Stalag XII D an atheistical doctor was converted. I know very well what she wanted from these pieces — it was to be reassured about me; but she would never have felt the need if she had not been intensely anxious as to my salvation. "Of course I should like to go to Heaven: but not all alone, not without my daughters," she wrote to a young nun.

Sometimes, though very rarely, it happens that love, friendship or 3 comradely feeling overcomes the loneliness of death: in spite of appearances, even when I was holding Maman's hand, I was not with her — I was lying to her. Because she had always been deceived, gulled, I found this ultimate deception revolting. I was making myself an accomplice of that fate which was so misusing her. Yet at the same time in every cell of my body I joined in her refusal, in her rebellion: and it was also because of that that her defeat overwhelmed me. Although I was not with Maman when she died, and although I had been with three people when they were actually dying, it was when I was at her bedside that I saw Death, the Death of the dance of death, with its bantering grin, the Death of fireside tales that knocks on the door, a scythe in its hand, the Death that comes from elsewhere, strange and inhuman: it had the very face of Maman when she showed her gums in a wide smile of unknowingness.

"He is certainly of an age to die." The sadness of the old; their banish- 4 ment: most of them do not think that this age has yet come for them. I too made use of this cliché, and that when I was referring to my mother; I did not understand that one might sincerely weep for a relative, a grandfather aged seventy and more. If I met a woman of fifty overcome with sadness because she had just lost her mother, I thought her neurotic: we are all mortal; at eighty you are quite old enough to be one of the dead . . .

But it is not true. You do not die from being born, nor from having 5 lived, nor from old age. You die from *something*. The knowledge that because of her age my mother's life must soon come to an end did not lessen the horrible surprise: she had sarcoma. Cancer, thrombosis, penumonia: it is as violent and unforeseen as an engine stopping in the middle of the sky. My mother encouraged one to be optimistic when, crippled with arthritis and dying, she asserted the infinite value of each instant; but her vain tenaciousness also ripped and tore the reassuring curtain of everyday triviality. There is no such thing as a natural death: nothing that happens to a man is ever natural, since his presence calls the world into question. All men must die: but for every man his death is an accident and, even if he knows it and consents to it, an unjustifiable violation.

SUBJECT QUESTIONS

1. What is it that bothers Ms. de Beauvoir most about her mother's death? Probably most offspring feel guilt or regret more than loss when a parent dies. Is that the case here?

2. In the opening paragraph, de Beauvoir tells something of how her mother had reacted to family deaths; how does her own reaction differ from that of her mother?

3. Why do you think the mother's "spiritualistic ideology" has obscured her affection for her daughter? Is this generally the case with parents? Are parents most likely to exhibit disapproval of their children's behavior on principle, a naive faith in their children's good behavior, or a realistic acceptance of their children's attempts to find themselves?

4. What does de Beauvoir mean by "There is no such thing as a natural death"? Is not all death natural?

5. Of what is death "an unjustifiable violation"?

STRUCTURE QUESTIONS

1. Is the reader adequately prepared for the transition from a discussion of one person's death to the generalization of the last two paragraphs? How does de Beauvoir connect those paragraphs to what has gone before?

2. The death of a loved one is an area where rationalization and self-deception are not only possible but likely. How does de Beauvoir convince the reader that she is being honest about her reaction to her mother's death?

3. By what standard is de Beauvoir judging her relationship with her dying mother? It may help to decide first in what ways the relationship fell short of an ideal one.

4. By what standard does de Beauvoir judge death itself? Should she have given a fuller explanation of her attitudes expressed in the last two paragraphs?

5. This chapter was not, obviously, meant to stand alone. Does it in fact make sense by itself, or does it seem to you to depend too much on information that was probably given earlier in the book?

The Power
of the Presidency

Tom Wicker

Thomas Grey Wicker (b. 1926) has had a distinguished career as a newspaperman. After graduating from the University of North Carolina in 1948, he became a writer and editor for several newspapers in that state. Later he joined the staff of The New York Times, and from 1964 to 1966 was chief of the Washington Bureau of The Times. His column, "In the Nation," has appeared since 1966; and he has been Associate Editor of The Times since 1968. Wicker has also published half a dozen novels (three under the pseudonym of Paul Connolly), many articles in national magazines, and a political biography, Kennedy Without Tears (1964). The speech that follows was delivered at the University of Delaware in 1973, at a conference on the implications of the Watergate scandal. Despite subsequent events, it remains a valuable analysis of recent American political developments.

I am told that when George Washington's father said to him, "George did 1
you cut down that cherry tree?" what George actually said was, "Father,
I cannot tell a lie. I did not cut down that cherry tree — but I take full
responsibility." In that spirit, let us proceed to Watergate.

I want to state a thesis at the outset, if I may. I regard that complex 2
of events that we call Watergate, that has so shattered the Nixon presidency,
not as aberrational, not as an isolated occurrence due to the machinations
of evil men — though evil some of them may be. I regard those events as the
culmination of a long trend in our national life, particularly in our political
life. I think that had these things not occurred in the Nixon administration,
they or something like them would have occurred in some administration
sooner or later. I believe that we will delude ourselves if we believe that the
remedy for these events is merely to elect a whole new cast of characters
to hold office, Democrats or otherwise.

In my judgment, the essence of Watergate is that the government has 3
made a strong reach for a vast extension of its power over the rights of the
individual. If that is true, it should be the conservatives of America — whether
conservative Democrats or conservative Republicans — who are most outraged
by the reach of government for power over the rights of the individual.
But I think that most of the conservatives in our country — up until now — have
been too busy defending what they felt was a conservative administration —

defending the conservative position instead of the conservative principle — to have recognized what has happened.

On the other hand, liberal Democrats have been too busy calculating 4 how this can be turned into an advantage and liberal Democrats returned to power to see the fact that Watergate is a natural outgrowth of liberal Democratic policy: the development of a strong presidency relying on implied powers to get things done that might be politically awkward otherwise.

Starting from the point that this has been an attempt to extend the power 5 of government over the rights of the individual, but that neither conservatives — who should be most outraged — nor liberals — who had a great deal to do with producing the situation — have recognized the situation for what it is, I would like to examine how we got where we are and what we might do now to restore the balance.

At least since the 30's, since the administration of Franklin Roosevelt, 6 we have had a trend toward the expansion of the executive branch of government. In the New Deal, we saw the expansion of the powers and the staff and the responsibilities of the White House; the beginning, I think, through the personality of Roosevelt, of the glamorization of the presidency. That has not been the least important thing that has happened. The personality of Franklin Roosevelt had a great deal to do with the building of that sense on the part of the American people that the presidency was truly at the center of our national life.

My mother, for one (she is quite elderly now and lives down in North 7 Carolina), is the kind of Democrat who believes rather implicitly that there is a piece of paper somewhere with her name at the top of it and Franklin Roosevelt's at the bottom of it and that that piece of paper saved our house from being foreclosed by the bankers. Franklin Roosevelt had that kind of impact on people — through his personality, through the things he did during the Depression years, to be followed by Franklin Roosevelt as commander-in-chief. Never before had we really had a commander-in-chief on the global scale. Wilson during World War I had not been a very forward commander-in-chief. He left that pretty much to the commander of the expeditionary force, and did not take the role as strategist and general leader that Roosevelt did. We saw during World War II the newsreels of Roosevelt in his black cape at Casablanca and at Cairo meeting with Churchill, Stalin, and others; he became a very central character in the world — commander-in-chief. It was a role that no living Americans had seen before.

Then, as we emerged from World War II and the Depression, we 8 emerged as a great power in the world. Being a great power is not just a dramatic phrase; it requires some things. The first thing it requires is a substantial military force, and the resources to sustain it. And when you have a military force of that size, then the commander-in-chief's role continues to be important. Being a great power also demands continued diplomatic management by the president. So that after we emerged from World War II that role developed by which so many presidents in recent years have termed themselves — the leader of the free world. There again no Americans had ever seen a president in quite that way before.

Following the glamorous personality of Franklin Roosevelt we had the homely personality of Harry Truman, which added another kind of mystique to the presidency — an idea that somehow, succeeding into that office would transform even an ordinary American into the leader of the free world. So it became an office that had a certain exaltation about it; and precisely at that moment when this was happening, anyway, it dawned on people that the president of the United States, the leader of a free world, the commander-in-chief was the only man in history who had the power through atomic and nuclear weapons to destroy the human race. 9

All of this happening in a short period, just before, during, and after World War II, made the president an exalted being for the first time in our history. I believe it's true that before this period, with rare exceptions, Americans did not tend to exalt their politicians. Quite the opposite. Americans tended to be somewhat cynical and skeptical about politicians. Political figures were often objects of fun. We did not think of them as being superhuman, even when they were presidents, until this particular period that I am talking about. 10

That period then led into the long years of the 50's and the Cold War, when the president of the United States became a *permanent* commander-in-chief, with the constant build-up of his military might and the advertising of that military might which he commanded as being a force not for war, but for peace — so that another element of exaltation of this official into something beyond ordinary humanity took place. He was our peacemaker, not our warmaker. It was in that time, too, that we had the development of what I call the national security apparatus. The CIA was invented. The National Security Administration was invented. And so another myth was developed that because he had the CIA, because he could crack the codes, and because he had spies all over the world, and later on we had the satellites and so forth — for such reasons, we developed the myth that the president knows more than anybody else, the president has more information than anybody else. Hence, whether one is a senator, a newspaperman, or college professor, how dare he put his judgment against the president's? 11

In that same postwar era, following the New Deal and following World War II, it had become commonly accepted that the national economy had to be managed from the top to prevent things like the Depression of the thirties. Who was to manage the economy? Naturally, the president was to manage the economy. And as time went along, it became clear that the managed national economy needed to be fitted into the world economy in a more coherent way than in the past. And who was to take care of that? 12

The president was to take care of that, and so Congress abdicated many things to the president that they had controlled in the past. Senator Willis Robertson of Virginia told me once that when he was a boy the only difference between the two major parties was in their positions on the high protective tariff. Well, beginning in the thirties, Congress steadily abdicated most of the powers of tariff and trade matters to the executive. In fact, there was a progressive abdication by Congress throughout this time of powers that had been thought to be congressional to the presidency, to the point — for example — where foreign policy became almost the exclusive province of the president.

In 1958, when President Eisenhower sent troops to Lebanon, in that 13 now forgotten crisis of the Middle East, the next day in the House, Speaker Rayburn, of a different party, gavelled the House to order, immediately entertained a motion for adjournment, and put it through. When asked later why he had done this, he said, "Because I was not willing to let any member of the House stand up and criticize the president in a moment of crisis." Well, that is only fifteen years ago and how times have changed since then!

But we also saw Congress abdicating its trade powers, and much of its 14 power in the federal budget — after all, it is laughable to say that Congress has the power of the purse if the president sends up a $200 billion budget and then Congress, exercising the "power of purse" either cuts it to $198 or increases it to $202. Who really has the power of purse in such action as that?

In that same period, the "president's program," whatever it might hap- 15 pen to be, became almost the agreed-upon legislative agenda. So that, from 1946 to very recently, you can count on the fingers of your hand the major bills that went through Congress — major matters of national policy — which were not originally proposed by the president. I would say that two great labor bills and the Employment Act of 1946 are possibly the only ones you can mention in that whole period.

Finally, throughout this period that I have been talking about, perhaps 16 the most important factor in the glamorizing of the presidency, was the development of television, which made the president of the United States the central figure in our national life, which brought him into our living room and our dining room more than any local official, to the point that any American today is far more familiar with the president, with the way he talks, what he says, what his policies are, than he or she is with the mayor of the city or the governor of the state, or one's own congressman. The president, through the medium of television, is at the center of our national life.

Presidents know this, and that television tends to exaggerate the 17 mythology that already surrounds the president. On the night in 1968 when the Warsaw Pact invaded Czechoslovakia and snuffed out the brief experiment in something like democracy in that country — that night at the White House, President Johnson convened the National Security Council. Lights burned late and there were limousines coming and going and the reporters stood outside and filed breathless bulletins, the lead of which was that the National Security Council meeting continued. Then, later, Secretary Rusk left the National Security Council meeting looking grim. Breathless bulletins of that kind went on all night.

The next day, Senator Eugene McCarthy, who was running for presi-   18 dent, had a regularly scheduled news conference and someone got up and asked, "Senator McCarthy, what would you do about the Czechoslovakia crisis?" And he said, "Nothing." The reporter was taken aback and said, "Well, what do you mean, nothing?" Senator McCarthy said, "There's nothing that we *can* do." The reporter said, "That's not what President Johnson thinks. The National Security Council was meeting all last night." Senator McCarthy said, "I know, but there is nothing they can do either. That's just a show they are putting on over there."

In fact, it *was* just a show, but television and other news media conveyed   19 it with such impact that once again, even though there was really nothing they could do; even though it was a sham, once again the image was conveyed to the people of our "crisis manager," our man in the White House, thumb trembling above the button, dealing with world forces. That image has been conveyed to us steadily now for a quarter of a century, but it is only now that we are beginning to have some perspective on it.

In this period, without too much conscious usurpation by presidents of   20 powers that rightly belonged elsewhere, but through the process of natural change of circumstances, through the process of Congressional abdication, we have elevated the powers of the presidency far beyond the limits of these checks and balances that the Founding Fathers wisely designed in the Constitution nearly 200 years ago. Now if that is the case, it seems to me fallacious to suppose that we can reduce the presidency, that we can cut it down to size — to borrow Mr. Nixon's inelegant phrase, that we can cut the legs off the presidency. I do not think that we can do that. I do not think we should try. We cannot take the presidency back into the days of Herbert Hoover. The only alternative is to erect new forms of checks and balances that will cope with the new presidency so that we can return to some semblance of balanced and controlled and checked government in America.

I have some suggestions along that line which I would like to put forth.   21 It may be that there are others that would be more efficacious and more palatable, but these are some ideas that have occurred to me.

The first, and most vital, step in my judgment has been taken just re-   22 cently in the passage by Congress of a War Powers Bill. This particular War Powers Bill, I think, is not perfect. I have made the criticism myself, and others have echoed it, that it may, in fact, actually empower the president to do more than he actually could do before. But I think the legal language does not matter that much, although it might at some point in the future, and I hope that will be a matter of continuing study.

The legal language matters less for now than the fact that Congress on   23 behalf of the American people has made a firm declaration, after several years of study, that the American people will no longer tolerate war by the whim of one man, or continuing a war by the whim of one man. I think that is a powerfully important matter, for the reason that it is only through the power to make war that the president has the power to inculcate in the American people a wartime mentality. I define a wartime mentality as a view among the people that anything goes in the pursuit of victory. Now if anything goes in the pursuit of victory, that means that the American people, caught up in the wartime mentality, willing to crusade against Communism or whatever the enemy might be, are willing to see liberty suspended or liberties invaded or short cuts taken or other invasions of their rights in the name of whatever higher goal has been proclaimed. In the absence of an actual war, it is very difficult to inculcate such a wartime mentality; we are seeing that at this moment, because in my judgment neither President Nixon nor anyone else is going to be able, in this energy crisis, to galvanize the American people into a great period of sacrifice and patriotism merely on someone's say-so that there is an energy crisis. Without a war, without an overriding national purpose, people are not generally willing to get into that "anything goes" spirit. Passage of the War Powers Bill in my judgment was the first and most vital step in reestablishing a workable set of checks and balances against the modern presidency.

The second step that I would like to see taken, and which Congress 24 shows some signs of moving forward, is review and substantial revision of what I called above the national security apparatus. The existence of that national security apparatus gives the presidency the kind of dubious operating capability that we have seen at work in the Watergate matter.

For example, in 1966, when I was bureau chief for *The New York Times* 25 in Washington, we wrote a five-part series on the CIA, after many months of investigation. I believe it was probably the most definitive material on the CIA up to that point. And the point to which we addressed ourselves, the question we asked and tried to answer, was: "Is the CIA in control by the civilian government or is it out of control?"

Seven or eight years later we can see that perhaps the question we ought 26 to have been asking was: "Is the CIA too much under political direction? Is it too much the creature of the political directors?"

The CIA was set up in the early fifties for certain purposes. It was set 27 up with an operating division — the so-called dirty tricks division. Nearly twenty years later, when Lyndon Johnson became president, he discovered (according to one of his staff assistants in a recent issue of *Harper's Magazine*) that we were "operating a damned Murder Incorporated in the Caribbean." And I myself have heard President Johnson say — I have no other evidence of it, but I have heard him say directly — that the United States was responsible for the assassination of Rafael Leonidas Trujillo of the Dominican Republic.

There may have been, if we care to believe it, some justification in the 1950's for setting up an instrument of this kind with the capability of operating overseas not just to gather intelligence but to carry out projects — to overthrow governments, to assassinate people. There may have been some reason for that in the fifties, although in my judgment there is no justification whatsoever under the American Constitution for that kind of activity at any time. But there certainly can be no excuse for that now, in a time of so-called détente with the Soviet Union and rapprochement with Communist China.

So the time is ripe now for reevaluation of the CIA to see if we any longer need that kind of an operation in our country. Do not forget that it is precisely this kind of an operation that gives the presidency the ability to do many of the things that we have seen done in Watergate.

The same is true with the FBI. The FBI, if any institution ever was, is the lengthened shadow of one man. In the recent aftermath of his death, now is the right time to look at the FBI. It makes no sense simply to continue what J. Edgar Hoover built, merely because he built it, without having any idea as to whether or not this is precisely what a democratic country needs in the last third of the twentieth century.

For example, the FBI has the mandate to conduct counterespionage activities in this country. Now we know that there can be a very thin line between the paid agent, the paid spy of a foreign government, and a domestic political dissident who may share the general ideology of some foreign government but who is not necessarily, and could not be persuaded to be, a spy or a traitor. In carrying out counterespionage it is very hard to draw that line. You quickly find that the FBI, so far from neglecting its duty to try to ferret out spies, has expanded itself over into the surveillance of political dissidents who may or may not be spies, or who may have given agents some cause to think that they may be spies. That is one of the sources of the increasing surveillance of American citizens — increasing to the point where sound and knowledgeable critics of the FBI assert that today, or at least at the death of J. Edgar Hoover, political surveillance of Americans makes up the bulk of the FBI's work, not those exciting expeditions after bank robbings and kidnapings that you see on television. It is this whole area, the area of the national security apparatus, the FBI and the CIA — and the Secret Service I would add, too, because their powers have been vastly expanded since the assassination of President Kennedy — that needs to be reviewed and revised where necessary.

The third area in which I think it is vital to have some changes if we are going to reassert checks and balances on the presidency is that of civil liberties. We need throughout American life, and particularly in our political life, a reemphasis on individual liberty as against that mania for national security that has so occupied our minds in the past quarter of a century, in the Cold War period. How do we get that? I do not exactly know how we can get it.

28

29

30

31

32

I do not see an institutional reform of some kind that would work that out, although I am encouraged to see Lou Harris's poll that suggested for the first time in my memory that the American people are concerned about the Bill of Rights. Every other poll that I have seen on that subject suggested that they did not know what the Bill of Rights was. For the first time, in the wake of Watergate, the Lou Harris poll shows that the American people are beginning to be concerned that rights they have always taken for granted may be in danger.

I think there are two steps within the power of Congress which would have a good psychological effect on our feelings about individual liberties, and might have a practical effect against future dangers. The first is a thoroughgoing review of all the results so far, and a revision if necessary, of our national policy on the question of wiretapping. Wiretapping was not legal in this country until the Crime Act of 1968 was passed. That is, wiretapping was not legal, except there remained a question of the extent to which the president had the power to order wiretapping for foreign intelligence purposes.

Since 1968 we are beginning to have a body of evidence on the consequences of legitimated wiretapping. We find that the primary use of that weapon, the primary results that the police can claim for that weapon, is they put a lot of bookies in jail. Wiretapping is a good method against bookies, who tend to operate by telephone. It is not very good for prevention of other crimes: the wiretapping of all the people in the city of Wilmington is not going to keep a single person from being mugged tonight, because mugging does not yield to that tactic. The question I raise is whether the paucity of results from legitimated wiretapping really makes worthwhile the kind of risks that — as we see from Watergate — we run when we legalize it.

I say that eavesdropping is nothing more nor less than an invasion and an abridgment of the individual rights of American citizens, and before it is too late I think we ought to rise up and demand of our Congress that it be stopped.

Another area in which there is beginning to be some congressional movement, although it is almost too late, is computerized data banks linked by high-speed communication. The average American does not realize the extent to which almost every one of his transactions today is going into somebody's data bank and is being computerized. We do not know to what extent that is being transferred to other agencies, and interchanged, and so forth. We do know, for example, that the most obvious thing you might be concerned about is your arrest record. If you are an innocent citizen, you have never committed any crimes or anything of the sort, you still may have been arrested a couple of times, either on suspicion or for any other reason — it can happen. An arrest record can be very damaging. People can be denied jobs, students do not get admissions to colleges; there are many ways in which an arrest record can damage a perfectly innocent person. But the FBI keeps your arrest

33

34

35

36

37

record in a computer and while, so far as I know, they are pretty good about guarding those records against unauthorized use, nevertheless, when the police chief of Seattle, Washington, or somewhere, wires in to get somebody's record for whatever purpose, and it goes back out to him, how do we know what he does with it? Which computers *he* puts it in, and what credit agency in San Francisco then gets it, and who has access to that credit agency's data bank? When you apply for a passport and all your information goes into the State Department's data bank, does that mean that the Small Business Administration can get hold of it? And vice versa?

There is a great deal of danger here and considerable work needs to be done. We are in some danger of having every moment of our lives traced, all of our financial dealings and all of our personal relationships. This is an area in which we should demand that something be done to protect individual rights against the powers of the state, the powers of the corporation. 38

Also, in trying to reestablish checks and balances on the presidency, there are certain institutional reforms that we can make. For example, we have seen in President Nixon's administration the efficacy of the power of Senate confirmation of nominees to major jobs. After all, two Supreme Court nominees were turned down. The confirmation hearings on Mr. Gray to be director of the FBI led to the cracking open of the Watergate case. The confirmation hearings for Elliot Richardson to be attorney general led directly to the charter for the independent operations of the special prosecutor. And it was violation of that charter that caused Mr. Richardson and Mr. Ruckelshaus to resign and level probably the most powerful single blow at the President in all of this. The confirmation hearings on Gerald Ford, for example, have exacted from him certain pledges to conduct himself in certain ways. Confirmation of major appointments is a very powerful weapon if the Senate would use it that way. I think the Senate ought to assert that power of confirmation over all major positions that may be created by Presidential fiat. For instance, you may recall that John Erhlichman — I'm sure you all remember John Erhlichman — was chairman of the President's Domestic Council at the time of his resignation. The chairman of the Domestic Council not only had actual supervisory power over all of the domestic Cabinet posts, he was clearly, after the director of the Office of Management and Budget, the second most powerful domestic official. Yet neither he nor the director of the OMB had to be confirmed by the Senate because both of those jobs had been created by presidential fiat. Neither of those men had to be confirmed by the Senate even though most of the officials that each of them supervised, for instance, the secretary of the Interior, did have to be confirmed. The Senate ought to assert the constitutional power to confirm any nominee to a job that the president may create. If that job is of anything like Cabinet rank, Congress clearly has the right to do so. It has a duty to do so, in my judgment. 39

We need also a clearly understood and agreed-upon definition of execu- 40 tive privilege. Whether this is to come about through the courts or by statute, I do not know. Usually these things work themselves out by usage, but it seems quite clear to me now that we need a generally agreed-upon and understood definition of what the president has the power to withhold, under the doctrine of privilege. Certainly I think all Americans would agree that he does not have the power, or should not have the power, to withhold information about crime. On the other hand, quite clearly, he should have the power to withhold the most confidential discussions with his most confidential assistants on policy matters. Somewhere in between, there is a limit to executive privilege, and it is high time that we found and defined that limit.

Congress is not without its responsibilities. If we are to have a Congress   41
capable of exerting *any* form of checks and balances on the presidency, that Congress should move rapidly to establish some form of coherent budget-making machinery. It is almost forgotten now, the impoundment crisis of last winter before the Watergate scandal broke, but at that time President Nixon was asserting, and in my judgment quite rightly asserting, that Congress had neither the political will nor the administrative machinery to control itself on spending to the point where coherent budget-making was possible.

I did not agree with the president's remedy, which was the wholesale   42
impoundment of funds, even to the point of negating congressionally approved programs. I did not agree with that, but I thought his description of the problem was correct. At that time, the Congress was moving rather rapidly towards development of budgetary machinery; that was suspended as Watergate erupted. I think Congress has to go back to that because it cannot hope to be a practical partner in the governing process until it has more coherent budgetary machinery on Capitol Hill.

We have already seen Congress moving to reassert itself on the war   43
power. On several other fronts Congress needs to be able to speak with more authority than it has now. I call your attention to an instrument called the Joint Economic Committee of Congress, which is not a legislative committee. That is to say, it does not report out bills or develop legislation. It studies economic matters and makes reports and those reports, by and large, are widely respected by economists. But I raise the question why Congress does not build up that committee, and others like it, to the point where it can speak to the American public with the same authority and with as much prestige as the President's Council of Economic Advisers. Then Congress could have as much influence in national economic policy as the White House. Why should the Congress have to wait for the president to say what the economic situation is going to be before it acts?

The Joint Committee on Atomic Energy already is a far more powerful   44
agency than the Atomic Energy Commission. On the economic front and on several others, Congress needs to move in just that fashion to reassert itself as a major partner in government. Doing so is certainly within its power.

There are many other related problems which need solution — campaign   45 financing reform; corporate power in politics, and in corporate power I include labor union power; the maldistribution of income and wealth; the overburdening of our political system with social issues that politics has no ability to deal with — all of these are questions that we might well examine. But, in addition to those practical steps that I have suggested above, those steps that I think are within our political power to achieve, above and beyond all of that, we must have a change in public attitude — a change in public attitude arising precisely out of the reach for power that we have seen, first, in the Viet Nam War and, second, in the Watergate complex of events.

46   The next time that we have people putting themselves forward as presidential candidates, all the reforms that I suggest here will be to no avail if the American people continue to seek a two-gun ranch foreman to handle their affairs. If the American people continue to think that what they need in the White House is a crisis manager, a guy who is *really* a tough guy, who can handle anything, a guy to whom you can just turn over public affairs and say: "Let the president do it. He knows more about it than we do. I support the president. My president, right or wrong" — if the American people continue to look for such a president as that, if they continue to be impressed by a man who boasts that the people would rather have his hand on the button than somebody else's hand on the button, if they are going to continue to look for someone like that, then all the reforms that we might make are not going to save us from an overpowering presidency, from more Watergates and more Viet Nams.

47   On the other hand, as we examine those people who put themselves forward, if we can look — rather than for a crisis manager, rather than for a two-gun ranch foreman — if we can look for integrity, for openness with the people and with the other institutions of government, for humility in the exercise of power, if we can recognize that those qualities really go to a man's character much more directly than the mere words of a man who says "I can handle anything, I've got what it takes" — then there may be some chance that all of the reforms we have talked about can have some effect.

48   I think of Thomas Jefferson, who certainly was one of the strongest presidents this country ever had — Thomas Jefferson walking to his own inauguration. That night at the boarding house where he lived, waiting his turn for a place at the table, no one at the table stood up to give him a seat until the wife of a senator from Kentucky offered him her seat. Like any good Southern gentleman, he refused it. I think of that and I wonder why it is that we exalt presidents so much today. How much greater are they than Thomas Jefferson? And why should not our next president, whoever he might be, why should not he walk to his own inauguration? When asked why he did so, he could say, "I am walking to my own inauguration to dramatize the fact that public transportation in this country is a disgrace." And maybe we would get something done.

49   I think of President Johnson, for whom out of many years of personal

acquaintance I had great affection — I think of President Johnson at a dinner for his staff, a sort of Last Supper, as he was going out of office, President Johnson arising and saying to his staff that he hoped that they would all support President Nixon in coming years because President Nixon was going to need their support. After all he would be the only president they would have. And the president of the United States, he said, is like the pilot of an airplane and the American people are the passengers on that plane. If something happens to the pilot, it is going to happen to the people.

Well, I for one do not regard myself as a passenger on anybody's airplane. And I think the American people should get over that idea and begin to look for a president who will be one of them, who will run for that office in the spirit enunciated by Senator McCarthy in 1968 — in the early days of his campaign, he was generally derided for even seeking the office, and someone said to him, "Senator, what would you do if you win?" And he said, "I would take down the fence around the White House and let the people in."

If we look for someone who would run in that spirit, if indeed we will see to it that anyone who does not run in that spirit never again occupies the White House, then I think we can reestablish checks and balances. We can have a controlled and an open presidency.

I do not want to end on an apocalyptic note, but I must add to all this that I think it may be necessary, before we can get to any of the things that I am talking about, and I say this with great regret — it may be necessary to impeach and remove from office the present incumbent. I hope that is not received from me as a partisan statement; I do not intend it that way. I say it may become necessary for two reasons.

One is that there is in America today, to a greater extent than I have ever seen it, a cynicism, a lack of faith, a skepticism about the basic honesty of our politicians and of our political system, a feeling that the whole thing is a sham. It may be necessary, in order to restore any kind of faith in the integrity of the American political system, that we hold this president strictly to account and show that the system does exact penalties of those who try to distort it. It may also be necessary, beyond that, as due notice to the present incumbent's successors in office that Watergate, and all we mean by the word Watergate, is not going to be tolerated by a brave and democratic people. It is simply not going to be tolerated in the future.

Above all, it seems to me that in our disillusion of the moment, perhaps even our momentary despair, we Americans with those populist and democratic instincts which lie so nearly at our historical roots, however they may be temporarily suppressed — we Americans, it seems to me, must once again come to ask of every aspirant to power over our lives, of every political evangelist who preaches a higher cause than the individual, of every leader who proclaims a superior version of truth and demands submission to it — we must ask each of them relentlessly and irreverently, "Upon what meat doth this our Caesar feed, that he is grown so great?"

And if we will ask this relentlessly and irreverently, then I for one have   55
confidence that, across all the centuries, in that most imperishable voice of
the English language, will come the answer to our query, saying: "Oh it is
excellent to have a giant's strength, but it is tyrannous to use it like a giant."

SUBJECT QUESTIONS

1. Wicker says that what happened at Watergate was "a natural outgrowth
   of liberal Democratic policy." Is he blaming the liberals for what happened? Is he suggesting that Watergate would not have been possible
   without liberal policy?
2. Retrace the steps by which the presidency assumed, according to
   Wicker, too much power. How much of this accumulation of power
   looks like an accident of history and how much like a deliberate power
   grab? Could it have been prevented?
3. Wicker proposes some methods of dealing with presidential power;
   would these steps substantially reduce the power of the presidency, or
   merely keep it from expanding further?
4. In paragraph 37, Wicker recommends control over computerized data
   banks; how are data banks related to presidential power? Has Wicker
   momentarily got off his subject?
5. Wicker feels that Congress should take rapid steps to reestablish its own
   powers; why is it preferable to him to have strong congressional power
   rather than strong presidential power? Could not one be abused as easily
   as the other?
6. Is it unrealistic of Wicker to want a humble president instead of a "two-
   gun ranch foreman" in these days of international crisis when decisive
   action must be taken quickly? Could a president still "take down the
   fence around the White House and let the people in"?

STRUCTURE QUESTIONS

1. In this selection we have an evaluation of a situation: how it came about,
   what is wrong with it, and what can be done about it. Does the requirement that evaluation be based on explicit or implicit standards of judgment apply here?
2. Wicker at first seems to blame liberal policy for the power of the presidency, yet, near the end, his two exemplars are liberals, Thomas Jefferson
   and Eugene McCarthy. Is there an inconsistency in Wicker's standards
   of judgment?
3. This speech is organized, broadly, into three divisions. In which (if any)
   does Wicker explain why presidential power is dangerous? Should a
   separate section have been devoted to this question?
4. Did you notice any stylistic characteristics that mark this selection as a
   speech rather than a written essay? Does it make an effective speech?

5. How well does Wicker use specific examples to support his judgments? Are there places where a specific example might have been better than a theoretical or generalized one?
6. At the end, Wicker relies for emphasis upon two quotations from Shakespeare — an Englishman and a royalist. Would he have done better to select quotations from, say, Thomas Jefferson? Does it matter that the two quotations are from completely unrelated plays — *Julius Caesar* and *Measure for Measure*?

I Want a Wife

Judy Syfers

The following article appeared in the first issue of Ms., "the new magazine for women." Ms. bills itself as the voice of the women's movement; it is certainly the first quality magazine, published on a regular basis, to avoid the stereotyping and "preparation for housewifery" emphasis of most women's magazines. It is published by Elizabeth Harris and edited by Gloria Steinem. The author of "I Want a Wife," Judy Syfers, is not identified except by name.

I belong to that classification of people known as wives. I am A Wife. And, not altogether incidentally, I am a mother. 1

Not too long ago a male friend of mine appeared on the scene from the Midwest fresh from a recent divorce. He had one child, who is, of course, with his ex-wife. He is obviously looking for another wife. As I thought about him while I was ironing one evening, it suddenly occurred to me that I, too, would like to have a wife. Why do I want a wife? 2

I would like to go back to school so that I can become economically independent, support myself, and, if need be, support those dependent upon me. I want a wife who will work and send me to school. And while I am going to school I want a wife to take care of my children. I want a wife to keep track of the children's doctor and dentist appointments. And to keep track of mine, too. I want a wife to make sure my children eat properly and are kept clean. I want a wife who will wash the children's clothes and keep them mended. I want a wife who is a good nurturant attendant to my children, arranges for their schooling, makes sure that they have an adequate social life with their peers, takes them to the park, the zoo, etc. I want a wife who takes care of the children when they are sick, a wife who arranges to be around when the children need special care, because, of course, I cannot miss classes at school. My wife must arrange to lose time at work and not lose the job. It may mean a small cut in my wife's income from time to time, but I guess I can tolerate that. Needless to say, my wife will arrange and pay for the care of the children while my wife is working. 3

I want a wife who will take care of *my* physical needs. I want a wife who will keep my house clean. A wife who will pick up after my children, a wife who will pick up after me. I want a wife who will keep my clothes clean, ironed, mended, replaced when need be, and who will see to it that 4 my personal things are kept in their proper place so that I can find what I need the minute I need it. I want a wife who cooks the meals, a wife who is a *good* cook. I want a wife who will plan the menus, do the necessary grocery shopping, prepare the meals, serve them pleasantly, and then do the cleaning up while I do my studying. I want a wife who will care for me when I am sick and sympathize with my pain and loss of time from school. I want a wife to go along when our family takes a vacation so that someone can continue to care for me and my children when I need a rest and a change of scene.

I want a wife who will not bother me with rambling complaints about a wife's duties. But I want a wife who will listen to me when I feel the need to explain a rather difficult point I have come across in my course of studies. And I want a wife who will type my papers for me when I have written them.

I want a wife who will take care of the details of my social life. When my wife and I are invited out by my friends, I want a wife who will take care of the babysitting arrangements. When I meet people at school that I like and want to entertain, I want a wife who will have the house clean, will prepare a special meal, serve it to me and my friends, and not interrupt when I talk about the things that interest me and my friends. I want a wife who will have arranged that the children are fed and ready for bed before my guests arrive so that the children do not bother us. I want a wife who takes care of the needs of my guests so that they feel comfortable, who makes sure that they have an ashtray, that they are passed the hors d'oeuvres, that they are offered a second helping of the food, that their wine glasses are replenished when necessary, that their coffee is served to them as they like it. And I want a wife who knows that sometimes I need a night out by myself.

I want a wife who is sensitive to my sexual needs, a wife who makes love passionately and eagerly when I feel like it, a wife who makes sure that I am satisfied. And, of course, I want a wife who will not demand sexual attention when I am not in the mood for it. I want a wife who assumes the complete responsibility for birth control, because I do not want more children. I want a wife who will remain sexually faithful to me so that I do not have to clutter up my intellectual life with jealousies. And I want a wife who understands that *my* sexual needs may entail more than strict adherence to monogamy. I must, after all, be able to relate to people as fully as possible.

If, by chance, I find another person more suitable as a wife than the wife I already have, I want the liberty to replace my present wife with another one. Naturally, I will expect a fresh, new life; my wife will take the children and be solely responsible for them so that I am left free.

When I am through with school and have acquired a job, I want my wife to quit working and remain at home so that my wife can more fully and completely take care of a wife's duties.

My God, who *wouldn't* want a wife?

SUBJECT QUESTIONS

1. Note that Syfers never calls the wife she wants "he" or "she." Do you think she has a man in mind? Does it matter for the establishment of her point?
2. Do you think she has been fair in her assignment of tasks to the wife? Would most husbands expect so much of their wives?
3. The object of attack is obviously husbands, yet the article appeared in a magazine for women. Who is supposed to be persuaded by the essay, then, men or women?
4. What would you say is the aim of the essay?
5. If the wife in a typical marriage has this many responsibilities, doesn't the husband have a commensurate number?
6. How many of the wife's tasks seem to be the result of marriage itself? That is, how many are jobs that would not have to be done at all by bachelors? Does it follow that two people cannot live as efficiently together as separately?

STRUCTURE QUESTIONS

1. A single standard of judgment is implied though never stated in this brief essay; what is it? (Note that Syfers is simultaneously condemning a "double standard"!)
2. Do you see any progression or order in the list of services Syfers wants from a wife? What order would be most effective?
3. This evaluation of the wife's situation clearly ignores the fact that a working man's tasks, while different from the wife's, may be just as onerous (from being ordered about by an incompetent foreman to repairing the cesspool at home). Could Syfers have considered this fact and still made her point?
4. Would you say that the force of this essay derives primarily from the language or from the subject itself? Should she have made the tone less matter-of-fact?
5. The insistence on using "wife" instead of "he" or "she" results in some rather awkward and unnatural sentences ("... my wife will arrange to pay for the care of the children while my wife is working"). Do you think the advantage gained is worth this awkwardness?

The Weak Are
the Second Sex

Elizabeth Janeway

Elizabeth Hall Janeway (b. 1913) is a native of Brooklyn. She graduated from Barnard College in 1935, married, and published her first novel, The Walsh Girls, *in 1943. Since then she has published numerous novels, critical works, and short stories. She was one of the pioneers of women's liberation, and has contributed her share of articles on the question of women's rights. Her best known book is on this subject:* Man's World, Woman's Place: A Study in Social Mythology. *In the following article she evaluates, not just the movement itself, but also the objections that have been brought against it.*

The women's liberation movement — Am I boring you already? Do the words 1 turn you off? Then hang on for a minute, because that's what I want to talk about: the current state of mind which doesn't quite oppose "women's lib" but would really rather not hear any more about it at this point in time. It is very like the Silent Majority's reaction to Watergate-and-all-that: something has obviously been going on that should not have been, we admit that. But now we've admitted it (Yes, women should be paid equal wages for equal work. Yes, the President ought to give up the tapes), why don't you go away and stop bothering us?

This is a human and understandable response. The trouble with it is that 2 it doesn't seem to be working. The women's movement surfaced the better part of a decade ago (which is almost long enough, in our era, to make it a candidate for nostalgic revival), and it is still here, still large and lively. It is also still surrounded by confusion and mixed emotions, most signally a large-scale inability to see what all the fuss is about. Complaints about the movement are many: it hasn't defined its issues clearly, it differs within itself, its goals are either Utopian or minuscule and, above all, it traffics in emotion instead of logic. Yet it persists! In fact, its reach and its backing are steadily growing.

It appears to me that we have, in this illogical situation, a very fruitful 3 field for studying social dynamics and social mythology. If the women's movement cannot be easily contained within any set definition nor held to any stated program, perhaps that is because it is both larger and more novel than it has been thought to be. I believe that to be true. The movement seems to me to be a response to profound and irreversible historical forces involving economic, technological, and scientific shifts in our society. No wonder it hasn't yet found itself a satisfactory name or a coherent ideology! And no wonder that the psychological reactions of those who do not feel themselves involved in it are ones of bafflement and exasperation. But the disturbed emotions on one side and the unconscious drive on the other offer a rare opportunity to look at the process of human response to change while it is going on; and this I would like now to do.

Let us begin with the response, which is good clinical practice. What symptoms did the body politic display when invaded by the liberation virus? Demands for equal rights for women have produced, first, a flurry of joking and, next, some irritation and anger, but mainly and fundamentally a determination to pay no attention: a simple, almost animal, retreat into not listening. Not argument, hardly even refusal to argue, but something closer to an instinctive reflex — a refusal to *hear*.

"Playing possum" like this is a defensive mechanism which has often proved a useful tool for surviving. Women have been doing it for millennia as a defense against wanting to act when they are sure they can't, in a situation where raised consciousnesses are liabilities and ignorance is bliss. But if the external situation changes, blissful ignorance grows more perilous as well as more difficult. The peril is certainly not apparent as yet, but the difficulty is here. Most men still don't want to hear about the women's movement, but the buzzing goes on. A little is getting through, willy-nilly.

I think it is only natural that what is heard is largely misunderstood and what is passed on (by the men in whose hands lies the distribution of news) is mostly misrepresented because it is misunderstood. And a good deal of the time, too, the women's movement is still talking to itself. No doubt that's a necessary step in the formation of any movement: intercommunication helps to bond the group together and give it a cohesive identity, and since women are a group who have not, in recent history, had much to hold them together as a group (except outside pressure) they stand in need of a chance to learn sisterhood. Besides, talking to men who have made up their minds not to listen is a great waste of energy; and I speak as one who has addressed both listening male audiences, and retreating male backs. If we look at men's reactions to the women's movement, we find it described on the one hand as absurd, and on the other as threatening. It will undermine and destroy normal relationships of all kinds, and it will also disappear tomorrow morning by ten o'clock. Its adherents are sex-mad orgiasts who (contrariwise) want to castrate men. It's a hilarious joke with no sense of humor. Women are plotting to turn the tables on men and subject them to hideous indignities; but the whole fuss is really over who washes the dishes. Anyhow, most women don't believe in the "movement" at all; it's the plaything of a handful of highly publicized exhibitionists. Black women and working-class women aren't interested, all feminists are rich, white, and bored, and my secretary likes to make me coffee just as my wife wants to stay home. And if she didn't, I'd (a) fire her and (b) divorce her.

These contradictory descriptions don't attempt serious opposition to the feminist positions. They are, rather, justifications for ignoring the whole thing. I don't set them down to argue with them, for one can't, any more than one can argue with upholders of the Flat Earth theory, if they still exist. Such descriptions are of interest because of their origin. If women are going to respond intelligently, they will need to understand the psychic sources of these disorderly reactions. Where do they come from? Why are they verbalized in these forms? What do they tell us about the distress and uneasiness which women's apparently understandable desire for equality raises in the male breast? 7

I believe they tell us a great deal about the effect of demands on existing power relationships to alter these relationships, and thus about the fundamental sociopolitical structure of our society. When women ask for equality, this should be seen as an example of what happens when the weak challenge the powerful. I do not believe that one can (leave "should" aside) make a Case for Women and *only* for women, and I believe that until women see this they will waste time and energy fighting all men as if every issue that arises between them were political. In my view, the case for women is a paradigm, a brief in a class action for subordinated groups as a whole against a clumsy, inefficient, and stupidly solipsistic power center. But making a case for women is particularly useful because it is novel, and thus it brings to the surface hitherto undisturbed layers of mythic mental entanglements for our investigation. 8

The most rational opposition to women's desire to leave their place and move into man's world lies in the pejorative definition of that world as a rat race. This is the premise to quite a good argument, a kind of Catch-23, which goes like this: If women are daft enough to want to get out of the house and into the rat race, that in itself is a very good reason for protecting them from their folly. If they can't tell when they're well off — at home, protected, guaranteed a status, a role, and an identity (while men struggle for all three in the chaotic world of action) — then obviously their tiny minds can't be trusted to handle the work of this world. Leave us men alone in our rat race where we are sacrificing ourselves to keep you women happy. 9

Quite a few men find this a satisfying formula and it does have a sort of specious plausibility. But *is* the world really a rat race, for the great as well as the weak? If it is, men must be credited with selfless magnanimity. If man's world offers nothing but strain and unpleasure, it seems remarkable that more men wouldn't welcome help in coping with it. When women *do* get out of their place, they are almost universally assigned to the rattiest part of the race, the drudge work. Male magnanimity seems to end at home, and 10 the argument for keeping women there somehow comes to rest on womanly limitations per se, rather than on the unpleasantness of the world they wish to enter.

At once we are back in a contradictory muddle, for the limitations of   11
woman's nature, as usually presented, oppose each other. Women are defined on the one hand as too gentle and fine to do man's work, and on the other as too indecisive, slow, and self-centered. If the two objections are lumped together to say simply that women aren't fitted for man's world, we are still faced with a contradiction from another familiar argument, that their competition will be tough enough to take jobs away from deserving men. This tangle of contradictions suggests that rationalization has usurped the place of reason. When men say, "You don't belong here," they mean, "We don't want you here." I am not surprised that women get angry at that (though it is the first time in history that they *have* got angry at it, which is one reason men are surprised and discountenanced), and their anger will help to reinforce their desire for change. But no one can work effectively for change simply by looking at her own side of the question. If the opposition to equality for women is contradictory, that means its roots run deep, and straightforward argument won't change anything, by itself. If men would be better off listening to women, women would be better off seeing their cause in context.

And, of course, the concept of woman as mystery, woman as "other,"   12
is not the only justification in men's minds for their opposition to equality between the sexes. Certainly it's a primary obstacle, as Simone de Beauvoir saw and said long ago. But there's another catch which is less familiar and perhaps less obvious because it is contained within the very term "equality." What does reaching equality mean? For a woman, it is a *step up*, to a level where, like men, she will be in better control of her life and find her ambitions limited by fewer *a priori* barriers.

Unfortunately, and women don't often see this, a step up for women   13
will be seen by many men as a step *down* for men to an inferior level, woman's level. To these men, and they are a vast majority, equality doesn't mean, "A woman is as good as I am"; it means, "I'm no better than she is." Equality *for* women brings more competition, but for those who think of themselves as fair competitors, that isn't shattering. Equality *with* women, however, is something else. If you have been brought up to know that women are inferior — deservedly inferior — how can you accept that? It's shocking, it's insulting, it's UNFAIR.

Worse still — and here we come back to the hidden terror haunting   14
men — doesn't an acceptance of the equality of women cut men off (most men, nondominant men) from the alliance with the powerful which that handy old slogan, "It's a man's world," seems to validate? To divide the world by sex

is to bind males — both weak and powerful — together by means of the destiny of anatomy. Take that alliance away, and equate the men who stand outside the elite with women, and you are telling them that they can expect to be treated *like* women, objects, and "others," not doers but done to; and done to, yes, right down to sexual doing. Closing the male/female split means a drastic rearrangement of the barriers between the weak and the powerful. Then not women, but the weak, become the second sex, subordinate, submissive, subject to rape. . . .

If we try to sort out this visceral response to the women's movement, I think we can discern three stages of opposition. The first results from the fact that the movement raises the question of power. It is not simply, or even fundamentally, the demand that women be given a share in power that upsets men; it is that this demand forces upon men a review of their own position. If women are announcing themselves ready to storm the bastions of the Establishment, where does that leave the men who have failed to do so? who have settled down to live out their lives in submission and resignation? And that includes, one way or another, the great majority of men. Suddenly, past the doors of their cells, bursting out of the slave quarters, come women-the-inferiors, invading the corridors of power as if, by merely being human, they had a right to be there. But most men have given up that right in return for a quiet life and some sense of security, for government by law as an acceptable bargain between the weak and the powerful. The idea that women are now refusing to accept this bargain acts as a terrifying, a paralyzing, challenge to men. Either they too must revolt or they must acknowledge themselves lacking in the courage and ambition being shown by their traditionally inferior sisters.   15

Role-changing, I wrote in *Man's World, Woman's Place*, is hard on everyone but hardest on those members of a relationship who have not themselves initiated the changes in the role relations which they share. It's true that role changers have troubles. Today women who are attempting new roles still find it a daunting challenge to value themselves and their experience and ambitions as seriously as they do those of men. Doubting themselves, they can make unnerving mistakes, fall into negation and the mere reversal of old attitudes instead of working out creative new approaches to the demands of changed reality, and sometimes they despair. But men are worse handicapped by the fact that, in today's shifts in sex-roles, they are not the initiators. Women are motivated and often very strongly so. To the extent that they can contain and control the drive and anger they feel, it helps them. Men, however, would rather have had things left as they were; which means that in the present situation they are actually experiencing the unpleasant sensation of being done to instead of doing, and the anger they perceive among women is frightening.   16

They don't understand that it comes out of past frustration and assume, naturally enough, that it is an augury of future dominance. This observation seems still true, but when I wrote it I had not seen the further point I am making now: the changes women demand are compelling men to rethink their relationship not just to women but to the whole power structure of our society. It is a hard and unwelcome task.

Secondly, there is the very real problem that women's demands mean 17 different things to men from what they mean to women. We have seen how that works with the apparently fair demand for equality. The same difficulty dogs another seemingly uncomplicated statement made by women, of their similarity as human beings. We are not "others," say women, we are human beings like you in whom there exists merely a happenstantial sex difference. We acknowledge that difference, but why should it apply to more than sex? Why should it signify across-the-board differences of nature and capability? Anatomy is not destiny; it is simply anatomy. Let us be whole human beings together, accepting differences between us as individual excellences or defects, not determinants of character.

But the ability of women to see themselves as human beings first and 18 females only second is the product of a change in women's life-experience which has not yet, at any rate, been matched by a corresponding change in men's lives. The acceptance by women of a self-image totally different from the male's is diminishing as women's life-styles become more like those of men. In the last few months I have gone over a mass of newspaper clippings culled from the New York *Times* in the years from the 1890s to the present, relating to women and their activities. The long-term trend reveals a marked shift in the image of women that emerges: women are more and more seen as approaching the capable, active, involved human norm and leaving "otherness" behind. Their interests grow wider. They are assumed to arrive at their own decisions more frequently. They stop being adjuncts of parents or husbands. The jobs open to them shift from the most menial (salesgirls, domestics working for pittances, seamstresses, factory operatives, addressers of envelopes) toward the white-collar area, and then beyond it. Eighty years ago, marriage was not just the goal presented as proper to every young girl; marriage without parental consent might well involve elopement: which means that a marriageable girl was still something of an object of barter between father and husband. Fifty years ago, a daring middle-class girl could become a secretary without being immediately declassed. The advantage she gained, however, was not independence, but rather freedom from the absolute necessity of accepting the first man who asked her hand in marriage. Her job was not thought of as a career, but as a chance to build up a dowry for herself and gain her a better choice of marriage partner. Career women were things apart, and not expected to marry at all.

Today, middle-class women are very much somewhere else. I have 19 talked to enough of them in the last three years, in cities and small towns across the country, to bear witness to the transformation. If middle-class ideals are still influential, we must factor into American attitudes the idea that growing up and getting married to Mr. Right is now a very old-fashioned dream. It's a nice idea, but it isn't enough. The normal expectation now includes some kind of career-vocation-job which will continue to occupy and interest one throughout life, which is simply to say that women now, more than ever before, see their lives as being much more like the lives of men.

This shift of image is more than mere wishful thinking. The women's movement is a response to fundamental social and economic changes, changes that are long-term, continuing, and which affect women's lives both inside and outside the home. The number and proportion of women in the labor force grow every year. The proportion now stands at 40 percent and gives the push toward upper-level jobs a basis in logic and practice that didn't exist at the time of the first feminist wave. Young women are moving into the professions at a faster and faster clip. The increasing numbers of women law students who began their studies in 1970 are hitting the job market now and will become more obvious every year. Applications to medical school among women have also begun to rise. Young women in industry are less and less willing to be shunted off into lower management jobs, with top-level promotion going to a token few. In politics, women are increasingly active at neighborhood, county, and municipal levels, where they are able to command a power base that is not dependent on tactical appointment by male bosses. In time, they will move up.

This is the experience behind the questioning of happy-wife-and-motherdom as a total goal. Underlining the experience is the reason for it. Most of these women workers are not out in man's world primarily to find self-fulfillment. They are working because their families need the money. Very few men really grasp the fact that working women rarely have an option to work or not. Too many discussions of women at work assume they could all stay home if they wanted to. But six million women are heads of households, and at least sixteen million more bring in the wages that keep their families above the poverty line. With prices of food and fuel and housing and transport and education climbing steadily, more and more families are coming to depend on a second paycheck. Publicly rather than privately, the income of working wives has been a very important source of economic growth in America since the war, perhaps the most important. If a growth economy makes jobs, which is a fundamental tenet of our American creed, these working women are making jobs for men and other women, not cutting men out of the labor force.

It's true that most women at work are working in women's jobs, which are definable as routine, dead-end, and low-paid. But they are jobs in man's world, and that means that women's lives are coming closer and closer to approximate men's lives, particularly, of course, the lives of nondominant men who are also likely to hold the more routine and lower-paid jobs. The effect of this pattern on women is to reduce their sense of themselves as deserving that label of "other." In the workaday world, what distinguishes them from men is not their sex so much as their failure to hold and exercise power, a distinction that seems to bring them closer to the men who fall at the lower end of the power spectrum.

To many men, however, this identification of interests does not exist. 23 Some of the toughest opposition to the equal rights amendment has been mounted by unions, an interesting measure of the depth of repugnance within nondominant men toward the idea of equality with women. Union leaders who *prefer* a divided labor movement to giving women equality (and a shot at overtime pay) are clearly motivated by forces beyond the reach of logic. . . .

For what it's worth, my own feeling about the future of the sexes is hopeful. 24 Partly my optimism is based on as objective and historical-minded a judgment as I can come to. The fact that men's and women's lives are becoming more alike seems to me to open doors to understanding and affectionate friendship between them. In addition, the increased ability of women to look after themselves as independent beings suggests that when they give love, it will be real love, not a hypocritical sham exacted by their dependence and often hiding secret resentment. I don't at all believe, as Erich Fromm does, that polarization of the sexes is necessary for a sound relationship between them. At any rate, it doesn't guarantee it, or how explain the large amount of homosexuality present in two such polarized societies as Periclean Greece and Victorian England? No, it seems to me that getting rid of sexual stereotypes can only enlarge the variety of *petites différences* which add a spice to affection.

Beyond objectivity, I find myself unable to ignore my old novelist's sense 25 of mood. I have met an awful lot of liberated women in the last three years, and the constant impression they make is sheer enjoyment of life and good-feeling with each other. That is indeed a personal reaction, but it may be worth recording as an offset to the constant recurrence of sad tales about unhappy and lonesome women who have chosen feminism and therefore (!) left their mates, to their everlasting regret. The New York press seems rather to specialize in these cautionary fables; and while I don't agree with Spiro Agnew's view of effete Eastern journalism, it is only fair to say that things seemed different in Arkansas, Wisconsin, Louisiana, Oregon, and Iowa; in Missouri, Florida, Virginia, Michigan, Massachusetts, western Pennsylvania, upstate New York, and some way stations that I have overlooked. Most of the women I have run into and talked with are married, or see no reason why they may not be; lots of them have children, they are coping with jobs or with studies too, and they have been overwhelmingly energetic, cheerful, funny, and good-natured. They were also, those I met, of all ages, many backgrounds, and several colors. Discount my impression by all means, by whatever amount you desire, but it was everywhere the same, and everywhere positive.

Out of this experience and cogitation let me make two recommendations 26 for future discourse between the sexes. I think women would do well to widen the context in which they see their needs and present their demands. A change in sex roles is a challenge to personal dominance and to political power both; to men as individuals and to a male caste which has a stake in separating itself from women, or at least thinks it has. I believe also that women would profit by a study of power and its workings. They might even produce some effective new techniques just because they come fresh to macro-politics, but they also need to see how such political action differs from private tussles over domination in the personal sphere.

As for men, I suggest that more of them listen more to women, and 27 listen with the possibility in mind that some of what women say may not only be serious but even sensible. For the first time in history, perhaps, it is women's experience which is changing faster and more radically than that of men. In itself that bears witness to the profundity of the changes and it might alert men to the value of taking a look at them. Certainly it will not be easy to overcome men's fears of the effects of change in woman's role and image, but these fears are grounded in a mythology that is less and less in tune with social actuality. Mythologies do change as their support falls away, and perhaps we might find some cheer in the fact that men who habitually work with women, as equals in man's world, seem to be less disturbed by the ideas of equality for women than men who don't. In part, men's fear of equality is based on ignorance of how such a situation would work in practice. Our best evidence that the situation can work comes from the experience of those who have been living with it, and that seems to me realistically heartening.

SUBJECT QUESTIONS

1. What is the basis for the observation stated in the title, that "The weak are the second sex"? Do you think Ms. Janeway is seriously proposing a realignment of sexes on the basis of strength? Is this a trick to get male readers to think of themselves as among the strong?
2. Why, according to Janeway, has the women's movement persisted and grown in an era when most movements ten years old would be only candidates "for nostalgic revival"?
3. Do you think it true that most men still refuse either to listen or to argue about equal rights for women? Is it important that they listen, so long as the courts guarantee equal rights?

4. Does Janeway's description of the male objections that are voiced (paragraphs 6 and 9) seem fair and accurate? If contradictory statements are made about the movement, are they made by the same men? If they are, why does that mean the opposition's "roots run deep"?
5. In paragraph 21, Janeway argues that working women create more jobs for men rather than posing threats to men. But Edward Goldsmith ("The Ecology of Unemployment," Section 5) maintains that a growth economy actually increases unemployment. If that is true, does it negate Janeway's reassurance here?
6. What is the basis of Janeway's judgment that the arguments for women's rights are more in tune with reality than are the objections to them?
7. What gives Janeway cause for optimism "about the future of the sexes"? Does she weaken her case by admitting (paragraph 25) that her evidence is merely "a personal reaction"?

STRUCTURE QUESTIONS

1. Whether fairly or not, Janeway several times employs name-calling ("Silent Majority," "instinctive reflex," "playing possum," "upholders of the Flat Earth theory") in her judgment of objections to the women's movement. Such tactics could be expected to endear Janeway to women readers; how are men expected to react? By being jolted into paying attention, or by refusing to do so? Would the author have done better to omit such phrases?
2. Janeway is simultaneously judging the success of the movement and evaluating the criticism leveled against it. Are these two aims successfully integrated into one article? Does one ever get in the way of the other?
3. Against what standards does Janeway evaluate the objections to the movement? Obviously she cannot psychoanalyze each opponent; how does she handle the difficult task of assigning motives to these objections?
4. Do you think Janeway maintains a consistent level of language throughout this essay? Do "hard" words and slang expressions fit together without jarring?

The Suicide of the Sexes

George Gilder

*George Gilder was born in New York in 1939 and now lives in Massachu-
setts. He was editor and cofounder of* Advance *magazine as an under-
graduate at Harvard, and was later associate editor of the* New Leader. *He
has been a speechwriter for Nelson Rockefeller (1964), and in 1966 published a book on the 1964 election,* The Party That Lost Its Head. *Gilder
has also been a fellow at the Kennedy Institute of Politics. His latest book
is* Sexual Suicide (1973). *The following extract is an adaptation of that book
first published in* Harper's Magazine.

There's an extraordinary chorus in the land these days — all bouncing between   1
water beds and typewriters and talk shows — making sexual liberation ring
on the cash registers of revolution. They haven't much in common — these
happy hookers, Dr. Feelgoods, answer men, evangelical lesbians, sensuous
psychiatrists, pornographers, dolphins, swinging priests, polymorphous per-
verts, and playboy philosophers — but they are all at one in proclaiming the
advent of a new age of freedom between the sexes.

Nothing is free, however, least of all sex, which is bound to our deepest   2
sources of energy, identity, and emotion. Sex can be cheapened, of course,
but then it becomes extremely costly to the society as a whole. For sex is
the life force and cohesive impulse of a people, and their very character will
be deeply affected by how sexuality is sublimated and expressed, denied or
attained. When sex is devalued and deformed, as at present, the quality of
our lives declines and the social fabric unravels.

Even our attitude toward the concepts "sex" and "sexuality" illustrates   3
the problem. The words no longer evoke a broad pageant of relations and
differences between men and women, embracing every aspect of their lives.
Instead, "sex" and "sexuality" are assumed to refer chiefly to copulation, as
if our sexual lives were restricted to the male limits, as if the experiences
of motherhood were not paramount sexual events. In fact, sexual energy ani-
mates most of our activities and connects every individual to a family and
a community, and through these to a past and future. Sexuality is best examined not as sexology, physiology, or psychology, but as a study encompassing
all the deepest purposes of a society.

The differences between the sexes are perhaps the most important con-   4 dition of our lives. With the people we know best, in the moments most crucial in our lives together, sexual differences become all-absorbing. Intercourse, marriage, conception of a child, childbearing, breast-feeding are all events when our emotions are most intense, our lives most thoroughly changed, and society perpetuated in our own image. And they are all transactions of sexual differences reaching in symbol or consequence into the future.

These differences are embodied in a number of roles. The central ones are mother-father, husband-wife. They form neat and apparently balanced pairs. But in the most elemental sexual terms, there is little balance at all. In most of the key sexual events of our lives, the male role is trivial, easily dispensable. Although the man is needed in intercourse, artificial insemination can make his participation rudimentary indeed. Otherwise the man is completely unnecessary. It is the woman who conceives, bears, and suckles the child. Males are the sexual outsiders and inferiors. A far smaller portion of their bodies is directly erogenous. A far smaller portion of their lives is devoted to specifically sexual activity. Their own distinctively sexual experience is limited to erection and ejaculation; their primary sexual drive leads only toward copulation. Beside the socially indispensable and psychologically crucial experiences of motherhood, men are irredeemably subordinate.

The nominally equivalent role of father is in fact a product of marriage and other cultural contrivances. There is no biological need for the father to be around when the baby is born and nurtured, and in many societies the father has no special responsibility to support the children he sires; in some, paternity isn't even acknowledged. Without long-term commitments to and from women — without the institution of marriage — men are exiles from the procreative chain of nature.

One of the best ways to enrage a young feminist today is to accuse her of having a maternal instinct. In a claim contrary to the evidence of all human history and anthropology — and to an increasing body of hormonal research[1] — most of these women assert that females have no more innate disposition to nurture children than do men. The usual refrain is, "I know lots of men with far more interest in babies than I have." But whether instinctual or not, the maternal role originates in the fact that only the woman is necessarily present at birth and has an easily identifiable connection to the child — a tie on which society can depend. This maternal feeling is the root of human sexuality. If it is not deeply cultivated among the women, it does not emerge among the men. The idea that the father is inherently equal to the mother within the family, or that he will necessarily be inclined to remain with it, is nonsense. The man must be made equal by the culture; he must be given a way to make himself equal.

[1] The increasingly conclusive evidence that the two sex roles originate in profound biological differences is summarized and appraised in a brilliant new scholarly study by Steven Goldberg, *The Inevitability of Patriarchy* (Morrow).

A man's predicament begins in his earliest years. A male child is born, grows, and finds his being in relation to his own body and to the bodies of his parents, chiefly his mother. In trusting her he learns to trust himself, and trusting himself he learns to bear the slow dissolution of the primary tie. He moves away into a new world, into a sometimes frightening psychic space between his parents; and he must then attach his evolving identity to a man, his father. From almost the start, the boy's sexual identity is dependent on acts of exploration and initiative. Before he can return to a woman, he must assert his manhood in action. The Zulu warrior had to kill a man, the Irish peasant had to build a house, the American man must find a job. This is the classic myth and the mundane reality of masculinity, the low comedy and high tragedy of mankind.

Female histories are different. A girl's sexuality normally unfolds in an unbroken line, from a stage of utter dependency and identification with her mother through stages of gradual autonomy. Always, however, the focus of female identification is clear and stable. In a woman, moreover, sexual expression is not limited to a series of brief performances: her gender is affirmed and demonstrated monthly in menstruation, her breasts and womb further represent an extended sexual role. Even if a woman does not in fact bear a child, she is continually reminded that she can, that she is capable of performing the crucial act in the perpetuation of her family and the species. She alone can give sex an unquestionable meaning, an incarnate result.[2]

Regardless, then, of any other anxieties she may have in relation to her sexual role and how to perform it, she at least knows that she has a role. Her knowledge, indeed, is ontological: it is stamped in her very being — with the result that women rarely appreciate the significance of the absence of an extended sexual identity in men. Women take their sexuality for granted, when they are aware of it at all, and assume that were it not for some cultural peculiarity, some unfortunate wrinkle in the social fabric, men too might enjoy such deep-seated sexual authenticity.

Throughout the literature of feminism, in fact, there runs a puzzled complaint, "Why can't men be men, and just relax?" The reason is that, unlike femininity, relaxed masculinity is at bottom empty, a limp nullity. While the female body is full of internal potentiality, the male is internally barren (from the Old French bar, meaning man). Manhood at the most basic level can be validated and expressed only in action. For a man's body is full only of unde-

8

9

10

11

---

[2] Doris Lessing, a writer frequently praised and published in Ms., states the case with her usual vehemence. Speaking of feminist characters in her own work, she said in a recent interview, "We're very biological animals. We always tend to think that if one is in a violent state of emotional need, it is our unique emotional need or state, when in matter of fact it's probably just the emotions of a young woman whose body is demanding that she have children. . . . Anna and Molly [in The Golden Notebook] are women who are conditioned to be one way and are trying to be another. I know a lot of girls who don't want to get married or have children. And very vocal they are about it. Well, they're trying to cheat on their biology. . . . It will be interesting to see how they're thinking at thirty."

fined energies. And all these energies need the guidance of culture. He is therefore deeply dependent on the structure of the society to define his role in it.

Of all society's institutions that work this civilizing effect, marriage is 12 perhaps the most important. All the companionship, love, and inspiration that have come to be associated with marriage are secondary to its crucial social role. Marriage attaches men to families, the source of continuity, individuality, and order. As we should have long ago discovered from the frequent ineffectiveness of schools, prisons, mental hospitals, and psychiatric offices, the family is the only agency that can be depended upon to induce enduring changes in its members' character and commitment. It is, most importantly, the only uncoercive way to transform individuals, loose in social time and space, into voluntary participants in the social order.

Of course, families can exist without marriage. Almost always, they 13 consist of women and children. The problem is this leaves the men awash in what one set of marriage counselors approvingly terms the "nowness of self." And the problem with *that* is the willingness with which men grasp their "nowness." Throughout history, societies have recognized the great price to be paid in securing family commitments from men. The alternative male pattern of brief sexual exploits and predatory economics accords very nicely indeed with the many millions of years of male evolution as a hunter. Women have had to use all their ingenuity, all their powers of sexual attraction and discrimination to induce men to create and support families. And the culture has had to invest marriage with all the ceremonial sanctity of religion and law. This did not happen as a way to promote intimacy and companionship. It evolved and survived in the course of sustaining civilized societies, where love, intimacy, and companionship might flourish. . . .

What is happening in the United States today is a steady undermining 14 of the key conditions of male socialization. From the hospital, where the baby is abruptly taken from its mother; to early childhood, when he may be consigned to public care; to the home, where the father is frequently absent or ineffectual; to the school, where the boy is managed by female teachers and is often excelled by girls; possibly to a college, where once again his training is scarcely differentiated by sex; to a job, which, particularly at vital entry levels, is often sexually indistinct and which may not even be better paid than comparable female employment — through all these stages of development the boy's innately amorphous and insecure sexuality may be further subverted and confused.

In the end his opportunity to qualify for a family — to validate in society 15 his love and sex through becoming a husband and provider — may be jeopardized. The man discovers that manhood affords few wholly distinctive roles except in the military, which is less inviting than ever. The society prohibits, constricts, or feminizes his purely male activities. Most jobs reward obedience, regularity, and carefulness more than physical strength; and the amount of individual initiative and assertiveness that can be accommodated by the average enterprise is very small indeed. Thus the man will find few compensatory affirmations of masculinity to make possible his expected submission to female sexual and social rhythms; and without a confident manhood he feels a compulsive need to prove it sexually, which he will do in ways that feminists, like the respectable women they are, fear and despise.

SUBJECT QUESTIONS

1. Women's liberationists are not likely to appreciate the implication that they are working hand in hand with the Playboy philosophy. In what sense are they doing so, according to Gilder?
2. What does Gilder think will be the result of sexual liberation on men? What will be the eventual effect on society as a whole?
3. The chief tasks of males in primitive societies seem to be fighting and hunting. What substitutes does modern civilization offer for these methods of demonstrating physical prowess (or of justifying one's existence)?
4. If men are biologically as useless as drones in a beehive, why not let women dominate both the social structure and the economy, as the bees do? Why does Gilder think the more traditional system is preferable?
5. Because men cannot share in the fulfilling biological functions of women, Gilder seems to think it unfair that women should want to share in the less meaningful activities allowed to men. Do you agree? Does Gilder place too high a premium on the preservation of the human race?
6. Do you think Gilder is correct in his assertion that "men are almost completely dependent upon women for a civilized role in the society and for biological and sexual meaning"? Do you see why women's liberationists and Playboy philosophers would equally object to this notion?

STRUCTURE QUESTIONS

1. What are the values by which Gilder judges the movement toward sexual liberation? Does he make clear whether he holds these values for constructive, positive reasons, or merely from a commitment to the status quo?
2. Although he does employ comparison and contrast, much of Gilder's support for his evaluation is based upon cause and effect analysis. Does he seem adequately aware of the chief dangers in cause and effect analysis (false or apparent cause, and multiplicity of causes)?
3. Do you think Gilder tries to be fair in his assessment of opposing views about sexual liberation?
4. This evaluation is, perhaps understandably, couched in very generalized terms. Would the essay have been easier to grasp had Gilder used some specific examples? Could he conveniently have done so?

The Door

E. B. White

E. B. White (b. 1899) is an essayist and fiction writer. "The Door" (1939) is from The Second Tree from the Corner (1954); it was written after White had read accounts of (1) treatment of certain mental cases by performing prefrontal lobotomies and (2) laboratory experiments in which mice were frustrated into insanity.

Everything (he kept saying) is something it isn't. And everybody is always somewhere else. Maybe it was the city, being in the city, that made him feel how queer everything was and that it was something else. Maybe (he kept thinking) it was the names of the things. The names were tex and frequently koid. Or they were flex and oid or they were duroid (sani) or flexsan (duro), but everything was glass (but not quite glass) and the thing that you touched (the surface, washable, crease-resistant) was rubber, only it wasn't quite rubber and you didn't quite touch it but almost. The wall, which was glass but thrutex, turned out on being approached not to be a wall, it was something else, it was an opening or doorway — and the doorway (through which he saw himself approaching) turned out to be something else, it was a wall. And what he had eaten not having agreed with him.

He was in a washable house, but he wasn't sure. Now about those rats, he kept saying to himself. He meant the rats that the Professor had driven crazy by forcing them to deal with problems which were beyond the scope of rats, the insoluble problems. He meant the rats that had been trained to jump at the square card with the circle in the middle, and the card (because it was something it wasn't) would give way and let the rat into a place where the food was, but then one day it would be a trick played on the rat, and the card would be changed, and the rat would jump but the card wouldn't give way, and it was an impossible situation (for a rat) and the rat would go insane and into its eyes would come the unspeakably bright imploring look of the frustrated, and after the convulsions were over and the frantic racing around, then the passive stage would set in and the willingness to let anything be done to it, even if it was something else.

He didn't know which door (or wall) or opening in the house to jump at, to get through, because one was an opening that wasn't a door (it was a void, or koid) and the other was a wall that wasn't an opening, it was a sanitary cupboard of the same color. He caught a glimpse of his eyes staring into his eyes, in the thrutex, and in them was the expression he had seen in the picture of the rats — weary after convulsions and the frantic racing around, when they were willing and did not mind having anything done to them. More and more (he kept saying) I am confronted by a problem which is incapable of solution (for this time even if he chose the right door, there would be no food behind it) and that is what madness is, and things seeming different from what they are. He heard, in the house where he was, in the city to which he had gone (as toward a door which might, or might not, give way), a noise — not a loud noise but more of a low prefabricated humming. It came from a place in the base of the wall (or stat) where the flue carrying the filterable air was, and not far from the Minipiano, which was made of the same material nail-brushes are made of, and which was under the stairs. "This, too, has been tested," she said, pointing, but not at it, "and found viable." It wasn't a loud noise, he kept thinking, sorry that he had seen his eyes, even though it was through his own eyes that he had seen them.

First will come the convulsions (he said), then the exhaustion, then the   4
willingness to let anything be done. "And you better believe it *will* be."

All his life he had been confronted by situations which were incapable   5
of being solved, and there was a deliberateness behind all this, behind this changing of the card (or door), because they would always wait till you had learned to jump at the certain card (or door) — the one with the circle — and then they would change it on you. There have been so many doors changed on me, he said, in the last twenty years, but it is now becoming clear that it is an impossible situation, and the question is whether to jump again, even though they ruffle you in the rump with a blast of air — to make you jump. He wished he wasn't standing by the Minipiano. First they would teach you the prayers and the Psalms, and that would be the right door (the one with the circle) and the long sweet words with the holy sound, and that would be the one to jump at to get where the food was. Then one day you jumped and it didn't give way, so that all you got was the bump on the nose, and the first bewilderment, the first young bewilderment.

I don't know whether to tell her about the door they substituted or not,   6
he said, the one with the equation on it and the picture of the amoeba repro-ducing itself by division. Or the one with the photostatic copy of the check for thirty-two dollars and fifty cents. But the jumping was so long ago, although the bump is ... how those old wounds hurt! Being crazy this way wouldn't be so bad if only, if only. If only when you put your foot forward to take a step, the ground wouldn't come up to meet your foot the way it does. And the same way in the street (only I may never get back to the street unless I jump at the right door), the curb coming up to meet your foot, anticipating ever so delicately the weight of the body, which is somewhere else. "We could

take your name," she said, "and send it to you." And it wouldn't be so bad if only you could read a sentence all the way through without jumping (your eye) to something else on the same page; and then (he kept thinking) there was that man out in Jersey, the one who started to chop his trees down, one by one, the man who began talking about how he would take his house to pieces, brick by brick, because he faced a problem incapable of solution, probably, so he began to hack at the trees in the yard, began to pluck with trembling fingers at the bricks in the house. Even if a house is not washable, it is worth taking down. It is not till later that the exhaustion sets in.

But it is inevitable that they will keep changing the doors on you, he   7
said, because that is what they are for; and the thing is to get used to it and not let it unsettle the mind. But that would mean not jumping, and you can't. Nobody can not jump. There will be no not-jumping. Among rats, perhaps, but among people never. Everybody has to keep jumping at a door (the one with the circle on it) because that is the way everybody is, especially some people. You wouldn't want me, standing here, to tell you, would you, about my friend the poet (deceased) who said, "My heart has followed all my days something I cannot name"? (It had the circle on it.) And like many poets, although few so beloved, he is gone. It killed him, the jumping. First, of course, there were the preliminary bouts, the convulsions, and the calm and the willingness.

I remember the door with the picture of the girl on it (only it was spring),   8
her arms outstretched in loveliness, her dress (it was the one with the circle on it) uncaught, beginning the slow, clear, blinding cascade — and I guess we would all like to try that door again, for it seemed like the way and for a while it was the way, the door would open and you would go through winged and exalted (like any rat) and the food would be there, the way the Professor had it arranged, everything O.K., and you had chosen the right door for the world was young. The time they changed that door on me, my nose bled for a hundred hours — how do you like that, Madam? Or would you prefer to show me further through this so strange house, or you could take my name and send it to me, for although my heart has followed all my days something I cannot name, I am tired of the jumping and I do not know which way to go, Madam, and I am not even sure that I am not tired beyond the endurance of man (rat, if you will) and have taken leave of sanity. What are you following these days, old friend, after your recovery from the last bump? What is the name, or is it something you cannot name? The rats have a name for it by this time, perhaps, but I don't know what they call it. I call it plexikoid and it comes in sheets, something like insulating board, unattainable and ugliproof.

And there was the man out in Jersey, because I keep thinking about   9
his terrible necessity and the passion and trouble he had gone to all those years in the indescribable abundance of a householder's detail, building the

estate and the planting of the trees and in spring the lawn-dressing and in fall the bulbs for the spring burgeoning, and the watering of the grass on the long light evenings in summer and the gravel for the driveway (all had to be thought out, planned) and the decorative borders, probably, the perennials and the bug spray, and the building of the house from plans of the architect, first the sills, then the studs, then the full corn in the ear, the floors laid on the floor timbers, smoothed, and then the carpets upon the smooth floors and the curtains and the rods therefor. And then, almost without warning, he would be jumping at the same old door and it wouldn't give: they had changed it on him, making life no longer supportable under the elms in the elm shade, under the maples in the maple shade.

"Here you have the maximum of openness in a small room."   10

It was impossible to say (maybe it was the city) what made him feel   11
the way he did, and I am not the only one either, he kept thinking — ask any doctor if I am. The doctors, they know how many there are, they even know where the trouble is only they don't like to tell you about the prefrontal lobe because that means making a hole in your skull and removing the work of centuries. It took so long coming, this lobe, so many, many years. (Is it something you read in the paper, perhaps?) And now, the strain being so great, the door having been changed by the Professor once too often . . . but it only means a whiff of ether, a few deft strokes, and the higher animal becomes a little easier in his mind and more like the lower one. From now on, you see, that's the way it will be, the ones with the small prefrontal lobes will win because the other ones are hurt too much by this incessant bumping. They can stand just so much, eh, Doctor? (And what is that, pray, that you have in your hand?) Still, you never can tell, eh, Madam?

He crossed (carefully) the room, the thick carpet under him softly, and   12
went toward the door carefully, which was glass and he could see himself in it, and which, at his approach, opened to allow him to pass through; and beyond he half expected to find one of the old doors that he had known, perhaps the one with the circle, the one with the girl her arms outstretched in loveliness and beauty before him. But he saw instead a moving stairway, and descended in light (he kept thinking) to the street below and to the other people. As he stepped off, the ground came up slightly, to meet his foot.

SUBJECT QUESTIONS

1. What kind of a house is it that the man keeps talking about? To what do the strange names (thrutex, duroid, and so on) refer?
2. What does the frustrated man out in Jersey have to do with the narrator's problem? Why did he take his house apart brick by brick?
3. White suggests several times that living in the city may have aggravated the narrator's problem. What is it about the city to which White objects?

4. The man says that many doors have been changed on him, and he gives four examples. What does each door represent? What is the "food" he is prevented from obtaining? Why does White use symbols instead of stating directly what he means?
5. Does White mean to imply that someone is deliberately changing the doors in order to frustrate the average man? Who *is* changing the doors? What, according to White, will happen to man when he has become thoroughly frustrated?
6. What happens to the narrator at the end? What does the doctor have in his hand? If all those unable to adjust to changing conditions underwent a prefrontal lobotomy, frustration would be virtually eliminated; would that solve the problem about which White is writing?
7. How would White react to the General Electric slogan, "Progress is our most important product"? How would the makers of that slogan probably react to "The Door"?

STRUCTURE QUESTIONS

1. In this story White tried to make the style imitate the actual thinking of a frustrated man. If he has succeeded, he should be able to make the reader see things the way the character sees them. The danger in this method, however, is that the writing may become too incoherent for the reader to understand. The style is admittedly difficult, but you should give the story a second reading before you decide whether or not White succeeds.
2. Why might White have chosen this particular way of presenting his evaluation? Is it effective? Would it have been just as effective had he stated his points directly in expository prose?
3. Can you tell what White's standards of judgment are? Are they directly stated, or implied?

The Other Side
of the Hedge

E. M. Forster

E. M. Forster (1879–1969), a well-known British novelist, wrote compara-
tively few novels, but several of them have become standard classics. The
most famous is A Passage to India. *"The Other Side of the Hedge" appears*
in The Collected Tales of E. M. Forster *(1947).*

My pedometer told me that I was twenty-five; and, though it is a shocking   1
thing to stop walking, I was so tired that I sat down on a milestone to rest.
People outstripped me, jeering as they did so, but I was too apathetic to feel
resentful, and even when Miss Eliza Dimbleby, the great educationist, swept
past, exhorting me to persevere, I only smiled and raised my hat.

At first I thought I was going to be like my brother, whom I had had   2
to leave by the roadside a year or two round the corner. He had wasted his
breath on singing, and his strength on helping others. But I had travelled more
wisely, and now it was only the monotony of the highway that oppressed
me — dust under foot and brown crackling hedges on either side, ever since
I could remember.

And I had already dropped several things — indeed, the road behind was   3
strewn with the things we all had dropped; and the white dust was settling
down on them, so that already they looked no better than stones. My muscles
were so weary that I could not even bear the weight of those things I still
carried. I slid off the milestone into the road, and lay there prostrate, with
my face to the great parched hedge, praying that I might give up.

A little puff of air revived me. It seemed to come from the hedge; and,   4
when I opened my eyes, there was a glint of light through the tangle of boughs
and dead leaves. The hedge could not be as thick as usual. In my weak, morbid
state, I longed to force my way in, and see what was on the other side. No
one was in sight, or I should not have dared to try. For we of the road do
not admit in conversation that there is another side at all.

I yielded to the temptation, saying to myself that I would come back   5
in a minute. The thorns scratched my face, and I had to use my arms as a
shield, depending on my feet alone to push me forward. Halfway through
I would have gone back, for in the passage all the things I was carrying were
scraped off me, and my clothes were torn. But I was so wedged that return

was impossible, and I had to wriggle blindly forward, expecting every moment that my strength would fail me, and that I should perish in the undergrowth.

Suddenly cold water closed round my head, and I seemed sinking down 6 for ever. I had fallen out of the hedge into a deep pool. I rose to the surface at last, crying for help, and I heard someone on the opposite bank laugh and say: "Another!" And then I was twitched out and laid panting on the dry ground.

Even when the water was out of my eyes, I was still dazed, for I had 7 never been in so large a space, nor seen such grass and sunshine. The blue sky was no longer a strip, and beneath it the earth had risen gradually into hills — clean, bare buttresses, with beech trees in their folds, and meadows and clear pools at their feet. But the hills were not high, and there was in the landscape a sense of human occupation — so that one might have called it a park, or garden, if the words did not imply a certain triviality and constraint.

As soon as I got my breath, I turned to my rescuer and said: 8

"Where does this place lead to?" 9

"Nowhere, thank the Lord!" said he, and laughed. He was a man of 10 fifty or sixty — just the kind of age we mistrust on the road — but there was no anxiety in his manner, and his voice was that of a boy of eighteen.

"But it must lead somewhere!" I cried, too much surprised at his answer 11 to thank him for saving my life.

"He wants to know where it leads!" he shouted to some men on the 12 hillside, and they laughed back, and waved their caps.

I noticed then that the pool into which I had fallen was really a moat 13 which bent round to the left and to the right, and that the hedge followed it continually. The hedge was green on this side — its roots showed through the clear water, and fish swam about in them — and it was wreathed over with dog-roses and Traveller's Joy. But it was a barrier, and in a moment I lost all pleasure in the grass, the sky, the trees, the happy men and women, and realized that the place was but a prison, for all its beauty and extent.

We moved away from the boundary, and then followed a path almost 14 parallel to it, across the meadows. I found it difficult walking, for I was always trying to out-distance my companion, and there was no advantage in doing this if the place led nowhere. I had never kept step with anyone since I left my brother.

I amused him by stopping suddenly and saying disconsolately, "This is 15 perfectly terrible. One cannot advance: one cannot progress. Now we of the road —"

"Yes, I know." 16

"I was going to say, we advance continually." 17

"I know." 18

"We are always learning, expanding, developing. Why, even in my short 19

life I have seen a great deal of advance — the Transvaal War, the Fiscal
Question, Christian Science, Radium. Here for example —"

I took out my pedometer, but it still marked twenty-five, not a degree   20
more.

"Oh, it's stopped! I meant to show you. It should have registered all   21
the time I was walking with you. But it makes me only twenty-five."

"Many things don't work in here," he said. "One day a man brought   22
in a Lee-Metford, and that wouldn't work."

"The laws of science are universal in their application. It must be the   23
water in the moat that has injured the machinery. In normal conditions everything works. Science and the spirit of emulation — those are the forces that
have made us what we are."

I had to break off and acknowledge the pleasant greeting of people   24
whom we passed. Some of them were singing, some talking, some engaged
in gardening, hay-making, or other rudimentary industries. They all seemed
happy; and I might have been happy too, if I could have forgotten that the
place led nowhere.

I was startled by a young man who came sprinting across our path, took   25
a little fence in the fine style, and went tearing over a ploughed field till he
plunged into a lake, across which he began to swim. Here was true energy,
and I exclaimed: "A cross-country race! Where are the others?"

"There are no others," my companion replied; and, later on, when we   26
passed some long grass from which came the voice of a girl singing exquisitely
to herself, he said again: "There are no others." I was bewildered at the waste
in production, and murmured to myself, "What does it all mean?"

He said: "It means nothing but itself" — and he repeated the words   27
slowly, as if I were a child.

"I understand," I said quietly, "but I do not agree. Every achievement   28
is worthless unless it is a link in the chain of development. And I must not
trespass on your kindness any longer. I must get back somehow to the road,
and have my pedometer mended."

"First, you must see the gates," he replied, "for we have gates, though   29
we never use them."

I yielded politely, and before long we reached the moat again, at a point   30
where it was spanned by a bridge. Over the bridge was a big gate, as white
as ivory, which was fitted into a gap in the boundary hedge. The gate opened
outwards, and I exclaimed in amazement, for from it ran a road — just such
a road as I had left — dusty under foot, with brown crackling hedges on either
side as far as the eye could reach.

"That's my road!" I cried.   31

He shut the gate and said: "But not your part of the road. It is through   32
this gate that humanity went out countless ages ago, when it was first seized
with the desire to walk."

I denied this, observing that the part of the road I myself had left was 33
not more than two miles off. But with the obstinacy of his years he repeated:
"It is the same road. This is the beginning, and though it seems to run straight
away from us, it doubles so often, that it is never far from our boundary and
sometimes touches it." He stooped down by the moat, and traced on its moist
margin an absurd figure like a maze. As we walked back through the meadows,
I tried to convince him of his mistake.

"The road sometimes doubles, to be sure, but that is part of our disci- 34
pline. Who can doubt that its general tendency is onward? To what goal we
know not — it may be to some mountain where we shall touch the sky, it
may be over precipices into the sea. But that it goes forward — who can doubt
that? It is the thought of that that makes us strive to excel, each in his own
way, and gives us an impetus which is lacking with you. Now that man who
passed us — it's true that he ran well, and jumped well, and swam well; but
we have men who can run better, and men who can jump better, and who
can swim better. Specialization has produced results which would surprise
you. Similarly, that girl —"

Here I interrupted myself to exclaim: "Good gracious me! I could have 35
sworn it was Miss Eliza Dimbleby over there, with her feet in the fountain!"

He believed that it was. 36

"Impossible! I left her on the road, and she is due to lecture this evening 37
at Tunbridge Wells. Why, her train leaves Cannon Street in — of course my
watch has stopped like everything else. She is the last person to be here."

"People always are astonished at meeting each other. All kinds come 38
through the hedge, and come at all times — when they are drawing ahead
in the race, when they are lagging behind, when they are left for dead. I
often stand near the boundary listening to the sounds of the road — you know
what they are — and wonder if anyone will turn aside. It is my great happiness
to help someone out of the moat, as I helped you. For our country fills up
slowly, though it was meant for all mankind."

"Mankind have other aims," I said gently, for I thought him well-mean- 39
ing; "and I must join them." I bade him good evening, for the sun was declining, and I wished to be on the road by nightfall. To my alarm, he caught
hold of me, crying: "You are not to go yet!" I tried to shake him off, for
we had no interests in common, and his civility was becoming irksome to
me. But for all my struggles the tiresome old man would not let go; and, as
wrestling is not my speciality, I was obliged to follow him.

It was true that I could never have found alone the place where I came 40
in, and I hoped that, when I had seen the other sights about which he was
worrying, he would take me back to it. But I was determined not to sleep
in the country, for I mistrusted it, and the people too, for all their friendliness.
Hungry though I was, I would not join them in their evening meals of milk
and fruit, and, when they gave me flowers, I flung them away as soon as I

could do so unobserved. Already they were lying down for the night like cattle — some out on the bare hillside, others in groups under the beeches. In the light of an orange sunset I hurried on with my unwelcome guide, dead tired, faint for want of food, but murmuring indomitably: "Give me life, with its struggles and victories, with its failures and hatreds, with its deep moral meaning and its unknown goal!"

At last we came to a place where the encircling moat was spanned by   41
another bridge, and where another gate interrupted the line of the boundary hedge. It was different from the first gate; for it was half transparent like horn, and opened inwards. But through it, in the waning light, I saw again just such a road as I had left — monotonous, dusty, with brown crackling hedges on either side, as far as the eye could reach.

I was strangely disquieted at the sight, which seemed to deprive me   42
of all self-control. A man was passing us, returning for the night to the hills, with a scythe over his shoulder and a can of some liquid in his hand. I forgot the destiny of our race. I forgot the road that lay before my eyes, and I sprang at him, wrenched the can out of his hand, and began to drink.

It was nothing stronger than beer, but in my exhausted state it overcame   43
me in a moment. As in a dream, I saw the old man shut the gate, and heard him say: "This is where your road ends, and through this gate humanity — all that is left of it — will come in to us."

Though my senses were sinking into oblivion, they seemed to expand   44
ere they reached it. They perceived the magic song of nightingales, and the odour of invisible hay, and stars piercing the fading sky. The man whose beer I had stolen lowered me down gently to sleep off its effects, and, as he did so, I saw that he was my brother.

SUBJECT QUESTIONS

1. The road, of course, represents life in the modern world. What is Forster's judgment of it? Is he being fair? Most of us, after all, believe in
   progress of some sort.
2. What kind of life is on the other side of the hedge? Does it seem to
   you, as to the narrator, a meaningless existence? What about the traditional conception of life in heaven — does it seem meaningless?
3. If the road ultimately leads to this land, wouldn't it be foolish for a person
   to keep running on the road if he could take a shortcut through the
   hedge? What does the hedge represent? Why do people on the road
   refuse to admit that anything exists on the other side?
4. Why won't pedometers, watches, or automobiles work on the other side
   of the hedge? Would they be of any use if they did function?
5. Does Forster mean to imply that we should quit striving to get ahead
   and simply give up? If man went out of the ivory gate centuries ago,

mustn't he have been dissatisfied with simple happiness without worry? George Bernard Shaw suggests in *Man and Superman* that true happiness lies in facing and trying to solve problems, and that a life without problems would be hell, not heaven. Has Forster left this possibility out of consideration?

STRUCTURE QUESTIONS

1. This story is rather clearly allegorical. Is it allegorical in complete detail, or only in broad outlines? What, for instance, do the many things dropped in the road, the ivory gate, and the horn gate, stand for?
2. Why do you suppose Forster wrote his evaluation of modern life in the form of a story? Does the simple form — almost like that of a Biblical parable — emphasize, or weaken, his point?
3. What are Forster's standards of judgment? Does he have a spokesman in the story to make them clear? How else are they conveyed?
4. Forster uses concrete, vivid details throughout, but he simultaneously maintains a dreamlike atmosphere. How does he accomplish this? Was there anything in the story that should have been more clearly explained? Would he have lost the dreamlike quality if he had explained everything?

TO THE STUDENT:

As publishers, we realize that one way to improve education is to improve textbooks. We also realize that you, the student, largely determine the success or failure of textbooks. Although it is the instructor who assigns them, it is the student who buys and uses them. If enough of you don't like a particular book and make your feelings known, the chances are your instructor will not assign it again.

Usually only instructors are asked about the quality of a text; their opinion alone is considered as revisions are planned or as new books are developed. Now, Little, Brown would like to ask you about John Wasson's *Subject and Structure*, 5th Edition: how you liked or disliked it; why it was interesting or dull; if it taught you anything. Would you fill in this form and return it to us at: Little, Brown and Co., College Division, 34 Beacon Street, Boston, Mass. 02106. It is your chance to directly affect the publication of future textbooks.

School: _____

Course title: _____

Instructor's name: _____

Other texts required: _____

1. Did you like the book? _____

2. Was it too easy? _____

   Too difficult? _____

   Did you read it all? _____

   Which selections did you like most? _____

   _____

   _____

   Which selections did you like least? _____

   _____

   _____

3. Did you like the cover design? _____

(over)

4. Were the study questions useful? _____

   How might they be changed? _____

   _____

5. Did you find the headnotes to each selection helpful? _____

   How might they be improved? _____

   _____

6. Do you feel the instructor should continue to assign this book next

   year? _____

   _____

7. Will you keep *Subject and Structure* for your library? _____

8. Please add any general comments or suggestions. _____

   _____

   _____

   _____

   _____

   _____

   _____

9. May we quote you in our promotion efforts for this book?

   _____yes   _____no

   _____   _____
   date   signature

   _____
   address